# Principles of Macroeconomics

**Lee Coppock**
University of Virginia

**Dirk Mateer**
University of Kentucky

W·W·NORTON
NEW YORK · LONDON

W. W. Norton & Company has been independent since its founding in 1923, when William Warder Norton and Mary D. Herter Norton first published lectures delivered at the People's Institute, the adult education division of New York City's Cooper Union. The firm soon expanded its program beyond the Institute, publishing books by celebrated academics from America and abroad. By midcentury, the two major pillars of Norton's publishing program—trade books and college texts—were firmly established. In the 1950s, the Norton family transferred control of the company to its employees, and today—with a staff of four hundred and a comparable number of trade, college, and professional titles published each year—W. W. Norton & Company stands as the largest and oldest publishing house owned wholly by its employees.

Editor: Jack Repcheck

Developmental Editor: Rebecca Kohn

Manuscript Editor: Alice Vigliani

Project Editor: Jack Borrebach

Media Editor: Cassie del Pilar

Associate Media Editors: Nicole Sawa, Carson Russell

Assistant Editor: Hannah Bachman

Marketing Manager, Economics: John Kresse

Production Manager: Eric Pier-Hocking

Photo Editor: Nelson Colón

Photo Researcher: Dena Digilio Betz

Permissions Manager: Megan Jackson

Text Design: Lisa Buckley

Art Director: Rubina Yeh

Cover Design and "Snapshot" Infographics: Kiss Me I'm Polish

Composition: Jouve

Manufacturing: Courier Kendallville

A catalogue record for the full edition is available from the Library of Congress.
This edition: ISBN 978-0-393-93577-6 (pbk.)

W. W. Norton & Company, Inc., 500 Fifth Avenue, New York, NY 10110-0017
wwnorton.com

W. W. Norton & Company Ltd., Castle House, 75/76 Wells Street, London W1T 3QT

1 2 3 4 5 6 7 8 9 0

# Principles of Macroeconomics

To my father, who gave up a successful career in business and found his passion teaching finance. Thanks for encouraging me to become a teacher as well.

D.M.

To Krista: Many women do noble things, but you surpass them all.—Proverbs 31:29

L.C.

# BRIEF CONTENTS

# CONTENTS

# PART I  Introduction

## 1  The Five Foundations of Economics    4

# 4 Price Controls

# PART II  Macroeconomic Basics

## 7 Unemployment

## 10  Financial Markets and Securities   298

# PART III  The Long and Short of Macroeconomics

# 13 The Aggregate Demand–Aggregate Supply Model   392

# PART IV  Fiscal Policy

# PART V  Monetary Policy

# **18** Monetary Policy    546

# PART VI  International Economics

## Preface to the First Edition

We are teachers of principles of economics. That is what we do. We each teach principles of microeconomics and macroeconomics to over a thousand students a semester, every single semester, at the University of Kentucky and the University of Virginia.

We decided to write our own text for one big reason. We simply were not satisfied with the available texts and felt strongly that we could write an innovative book to which dedicated instructors like us would respond. It's not that the already available texts are bad or inaccurate—it's that they lack an understanding of what we, as teachers, have learned through fielding the thousands of questions that our students have asked us over the years. We do not advise policy makers, but we do advise students, and we know how their minds work.

For instance, there really is no text that shows an understanding for where students consistently trip up (for example, cost curves) and therefore provides an additional example, or better yet, a worked exercise. There really is no text that is careful to reinforce new terminology and difficult sticking points with explanations in everyday language. There really is no text that leverages the fact that today's students are key participants in the twenty-first-century economy, and that uses examples and cases from markets in which they interact all the time (for example, the markets for cell phones, social networking sites, computing devices, online book sellers, etc.).

What our years in the classroom have brought home to us is the importance of meeting students where they are. This means knowing their cultural touchstones and trying to tell the story of economics with those touchstones in mind. In our text we meet students where they are through resonance and reinforcement. In fact, these two words are our mantra—we strive to make each topic resonate and then make it stick through reinforcement.

Whenever possible, we use student-centered examples that resonate with students. For instance, many of our examples refer to jobs that students often hold and businesses that often employ them. If the examples resonate, students are much more likely to dig into the material wholeheartedly and internalize key concepts.

When we teach, we try to create a rhythm of reinforcement in our lectures that begins with the presentation of new material, followed by a concrete example, followed by a reinforcing device, and then closes with a "make it stick" moment. We do this over and over again. We have tried to bring that rhythm to the book. We believe strongly that this commitment to reinforcement works. To give just one example, in our chapter "Oligopoly and Strategic Behavior," while presenting the crucial-yet-difficult subject of game theory, we work through the concept of the prisoner's dilemma at least six different ways.

No educator is happy with the challenge we all face to motivate our students to read the assigned text. No matter how effective our lectures are, if our students are not reinforcing those lectures by reading the assigned text chapters, they are only partially absorbing the key takeaways that properly trained citizens need to thrive in today's world. A second key motivation for us to undertake this ambitious project was the desire to create a text that students would read, week in and week out, for the entire course. By following our commitment to resonance and reinforcement, we are confident that we have written a text that's a good read for today's students. So good, in fact, that we believe students will read entire chapters and actually enjoy them. Certainly the reports from our dozens of class testers indicate that this is the case.

What do we all want? We want our students to leave our courses having internalized fundamentals that they will remember for life. The fundamentals (understanding incentives, opportunity cost, thinking at the margin, etc.) will allow them to make better choices in the workplace, their personal investments, their long-term planning, their voting, and all their critical choices. The bottom line is that they will live more fulfilled and satisfying lives if we succeed. The purpose of this text is to help you succeed in your quest.

What does this classroom-inspired, student-centered text look like?

# A Simple Narrative

First and foremost, we keep the narrative simple. We always bear in mind all those office-hour conversations with students where we searched for some way to make sense of this foreign language—for them—that is economics. It is incredibly satisfying when you find the right expression, explanation, or example that creates the "Oh, now I get it . . ." moment with your student. We have filled the narrative with those successful "now I get it" passages.

The Ice Cream Float, a cool idea on a hot day at the lake.

stores often close by 9 p.m. because operating overnight would not generate enough revenue to cover the costs of remaining open. Or consider the Ice Cream Float, which crisscrosses Smith Mountain Lake in Virginia during the summer months. You can hear the music announcing its arrival at the public beach from over a mile away. By the time the float arrives, there is usually a long line of eager customers waiting for the float to dock. This is a very profitable business on hot and sunny summer days. However, during the late spring and early fall the float operates on weekends only. Eventually, colder weather forces the business to shut down until the crowds return the following season. This shutdown decision is a short-run calculation. If the float were to operate during the winter, it would need to pay for employees and fuel. Incurring these variable costs when there are so few customers would result in greater total costs than simply dry-docking the boat. When the float is dry-docked over the winter, only the fixed cost of storing the boat remains.

Fortunately, a firm can use a simple, intuitive rule to decide whether to operate or shut down in the short run: if the firm would lose less by shutting down than by staying open, it should shut down. Recall that costs are broken into two parts—fixed and variable. Fixed costs must be paid whether the business is open or not. Since variable costs are only incurred when the business is op... employee... will choo...

Prices act to ration scarce resources. When the demand for generators or other necessities is high, the price rises to ensure that the available units are distributed to those who value them the most. More important, the ability to charge a higher price provides sellers with an incentive to make more units available. If there is limited ability for the price to change when demand increases, there will be a shortage. Therefore, price gouging legislation means that devastated communities must rely exclusively on the goodwill of others and the slow-moving machinery of government relief efforts. This closes off a third avenue, entrepreneurial activity, as a means to alleviate poor conditions.

Figure 5.5 shows how price gouging laws work and the shortage they create. If the demand for gas generators increases immediately after a disaster ($D_{after}$), the market price rises from $530 to $900. But since $900 is considered excessive, sales at that price are illegal. This creates a binding price ceiling for as long as a state of emergency is in effect. Whenever a price ceiling is binding, it creates a shortage. You can see this in Figure 5.5 in the difference between quantity demanded and quantity supplied at the price ceiling level mandated by the law. In this case, the normal ability of supply and demand to ration the available generators is short-circuited. Since more people demand generators after the disaster than before it, those who do not get to the store soon enough are out of luck. When the emergency is lifted and the market returns to normal, the temporary shortage created by legislation against price gouging is eliminated.

**Incentives**

Large generator: $900 after Hurricane Wilma hit.

# Examples and Cases That Resonate and Therefore Stick

Nothing makes this material stick for students like good examples and cases that they relate to, and we have peppered our book with them. They are not in boxed inserts. They are part of the narrative, set off with an Economics in the Real World heading.

 **ECONOMICS IN THE REAL WORLD**

### The Wii Rollout and Changes in the Video Game Industry

When Nintendo launched the Wii console in late 2006, it fundamentally changed the gaming industry. The Wii uses motion-sensing technology. Despite relatively poor graphics, it provided a completely different gaming experience from its competitors, Playstation 3 (PS3) and the Xbox 360. Yet the PS3 and Xbox 360 had larger storage capacities and better graphics, in theory making them more attractive to gamers than the Wii.

During the 2006 holiday shopping season, the three systems had three distinct price points:

Wii = $249
Xbox = $399

The Wii rollout generated long waiting lines.

Wii and X
ply in stor
had hope
360 outso
ing, a mo
the deteri

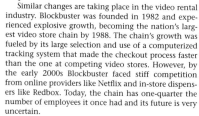 **ECONOMICS IN THE REAL WORLD**

### Blockbuster and the Dynamic Nature of Change

What happens if your customers do not return? What if you simply had a bad idea to begin with, and the customers never arrived in the first place?

When the long-run profit outlook is bleak, the firm is better off shutting down. This is a normal part of the ebb and flow of business. For example, once there were thousands of buggy whip companies. Today, as technology has improved and we no longer rely on horse-drawn carriages, few buggy whip makers remain. However, many companies now manufacture automobile parts.

Similarly, a succession of technological advances has transformed the music industry. Records were replaced by 8-track tapes, and then by cassettes. Already, the CD is on its way to being replaced by better technology as iPods, iPhones, and MP3 players make music more portable and as web sites such as Pandora and Spotify allow live streaming of almost any selection a listener wants to hear. However, there was a time when innovation meant playing music on the original Sony Walkman. What was cool in the early 1980s is antiquated today. Any business engaged in distributing music has had to adapt or close.

Similar changes are taking place in the video rental industry. Blockbuster was founded in 1982 and experienced explosive growth, becoming the nation's largest video store chain by 1988. The chain's growth was fueled by its large selection and use of a computerized tracking system that made the checkout process faster than the one at competing video stores. However, by the early 2000s Blockbuster faced stiff competition from online providers like Netflix and in-store dispensers like Redbox. Today, the chain has one-quarter the number of employees it once had and its future is very uncertain.

In addition to changes in technology, other factors such as downturns in the economy, changes in tastes, demographic factors, and migration can all force businesses to close. These examples remind us that the long-run decision to go out of business has nothing to do with the short-term profit outlook. ✳

Blockbuster's best days are long gone.

So far, we have examined the firm's decision-making process in the short run in the context of revenues versus costs. This has enabled us to determine the profits each firm makes. But now we pause to consider *sunk costs*, a special type of cost that all firms, in every industry, must consider when making decisions.

# Reinforcers

Practice What You Know boxes are in-chapter exercises that allow students to self-assess while reading and provide a bit more hand-holding than usual. While other books have in-chapter questions, no other book consistently frames these exercises within real-world situations that students relate to.

---

## PRACTICE WHAT YOU KNOW

### Income Elasticity

Question: A college student eats ramen noodles twice a week and earns $300/week working part-time. After graduating, the student earns $1,000/week and eats ramen noodles every other week. What is the student's income elasticity?

Yummy, or all you can afford?

Answer: The income elasticity of demand using the midpoint method is

$$\frac{(Q_2 - Q_1) \div [(Q_1 + Q_2) \div 2]}{(I_2 - I_1) \div [(I_1 + I_2) \div 2]}$$

$$\frac{(0.5 - 2.0) \div [(2.0 + 0.5) \div 2]}{(\$1000 - \$300) \div [(\$300 + \$1000) \div 2]}$$

$$E_I = \frac{-1.5 \div 1.25}{\$700 \div \$650}$$

demand is positive for normal goods and negative the negative coefficient indicates that ramen noo-the range of income—in this example, between should confirm your intuition. The higher post-student to substitute away from ramen noodles provide more nourishment and enjoyment.

---

## PRACTICE WHAT YOU KNOW

### Shift or Slide?

Cheap pizza or . . .

. . . cheap drinks?

Suppose that a local pizza place likes to run a "late-night special" after 11 p.m. The owners have contacted you for some advice. One of the owners tells you, "We want to increase the demand for our pizza." He proposes two marketing ideas to accomplish this:

1. Reduce the price of large pizzas.

2. Reduce the price of a complementary good—for example, offer two half-priced bottles or cans of soda with every large pizza ordered.

Question: What will you recommend?

Answer: First, consider why "late-night specials" exist in the first place. Since most people prefer to eat dinner early in the evening, the store has to encourage late-night patrons to buy pizzas by stimulating demand. "Specials" of all sorts are used during periods of low demand when regular prices would leave the establishment largely empty.

Next, look at what the question asks. The owners want to know which option would "increase demand" more. The question is very specific; it is looking for something that will increase (or shift) demand.

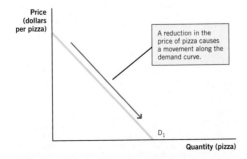

A reduction in the price of pizza causes a movement along the demand curve.

Price (dollars per pizza)

$D_1$

Quantity (pizza)

*(CONTINUED)*

# Additional Reinforcers

Another notable reinforcement device is the Snapshot that appears in each chapter. We have used the innovation of modern infographics to create a memorable story that reinforces a particularly important topic.

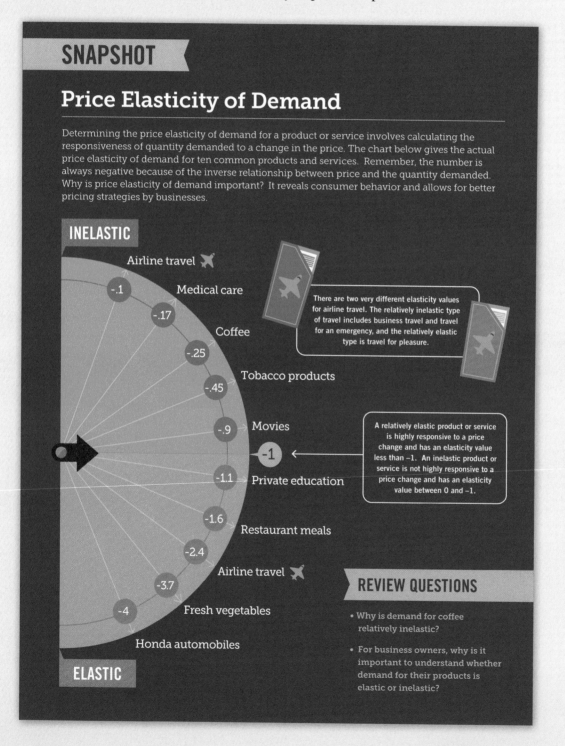

## SNAPSHOT

## Price Elasticity of Demand

Determining the price elasticity of demand for a product or service involves calculating the responsiveness of quantity demanded to a change in the price. The chart below gives the actual price elasticity of demand for ten common products and services. Remember, the number is always negative because of the inverse relationship between price and the quantity demanded. Why is price elasticity of demand important? It reveals consumer behavior and allows for better pricing strategies by businesses.

**INELASTIC**

Airline travel −.1
Medical care −.17
Coffee −.25
Tobacco products −.45
Movies −.9
−1
−1.1 Private education
−1.6
Restaurant meals −2.4
Airline travel −3.7
Fresh vegetables −4
Honda automobiles

**ELASTIC**

There are two very different elasticity values for airline travel. The relatively inelastic type of travel includes business travel and travel for an emergency, and the relatively elastic type is travel for pleasure.

A relatively elastic product or service is highly responsive to a price change and has an elasticity value less than −1. An inelastic product or service is not highly responsive to a price change and has an elasticity value between 0 and −1.

## REVIEW QUESTIONS

- Why is demand for coffee relatively inelastic?

- For business owners, why is it important to understand whether demand for their products is elastic or inelastic?

We have two additional elements that may seem trivial to you as a fellow instructor, but we are confident that they will help to reinforce the material with your students. The first appears near the end of each chapter, and is called Economics for Life. The goal of this insert is to apply economic reasoning to important decisions that your students will face early in their post-student lives, such as buying or leasing a car. And the second is Economics in the Media. These boxes refer to classic scenes from movies and TV shows that deal directly with economics. One of us has written the book (literally!) on economics in the movies, and and we have used these clips year after year to make economics stick with students.

## Costs in the Short Run

ECONOMICS IN THE MEDIA

### The Office

The popular TV series *The Office* had an amusing episode devoted to the discussion of costs. The character Michael Scott establishes his own paper company to compete with both Staples and his former company, Dunder Mifflin. He then outcompetes his rivals by keeping his fixed and variable costs low.

In one inspired scene, we see the Michael Scott Paper Company operating out of a single room and using an old church van to deliver paper. This means the company has very low *fixed costs*, which enables it to charge unusually low prices. In addition, Michael Scott keeps *variable costs* to a minimum by hiring only essential employees and not paying any benefits, such as health insurance. But this is a problem, since Michael Scott does not fully account for the cost of the paper he is selling. In fact, he is selling below unit cost!

As we will discover in upcoming chapters, firms with lower costs have many advantages in the market. Such firms can keep their prices lower to attract additional customers. Cost matters because price matters.

## Price Elasticity of Supply and Demand: Buying Your First Car

ECONOMICS FOR LIFE

When you buy a car, your knowledge of price elasticity can help you negotiate the best possible deal.

Recall that the three determinants of price elasticity of demand are (1) the share of the budget, (2) the number of available substitutes, and (3) the time you have to make a decision.

Let's start with your budget. You should have one in mind, but don't tell the salesperson what you are willing to spend; that is a vital piece of personal information you want to keep to yourself. If the salesperson suggests that you look at a model that is too expensive, just say that you are not interested. You might reply, "Buying a car is a stretch for me; I've got to stay within my budget." If the salesperson asks indirectly about your budget by inquiring whether you have a particular monthly payment in mind, reply that you want to negotiate over the invoice price once you decide on a vehicle. Never negotiate on the sticker price, which is the price you see in the car window, because it includes thousands of dollars in markup. You want to make it clear to the salesperson that the price you pay matters to you—that is, your demand is elastic.

Next, make it clear that you are gathering information and visiting other dealers. That is, reinforce that you have many available substitutes. Even if you really want a Honda, do not voice that desire to the Honda salesperson. Perhaps mention that you are also visiting the Toyota, Hyundai, and Ford showrooms. Compare what you've seen on one lot versus another. Each salesperson you meet should hear that you are seriously considering other options. This indicates to each dealership that your demand is elastic and that getting your business will require that they offer you a better price.

Taking your time to decide is also important. Never buy a car the first time you walk onto a lot. If you convey the message that you want a car immediately, you are saying that your demand is inelastic. If the dealership thinks that you have no flexibility, the staff will not give you their best offer. Instead, tell the salesperson that you appreciate their help and that you will be deciding over the next few weeks.

A good salesperson will know you are serious and will ask for your phone number or email address and contact you. The salesperson will sweeten the deal if you indicate you are narrowing down your choices and they are in the running. You wait. You win.

Also know that salespeople and dealerships have times when they want to move inventory. August is an especially good month to purchase. In other words, the price elasticity of supply is at work here as well. A good time to buy is when the dealer is trying to move inventory to make room for new models, because prices fall for end-of-the-model-year closeouts. Likewise, many sales promotions and sales bonuses are tied to the end of the month, so salespeople will be more eager to sell at that time.

Watch out for shady negotiation practices!

# Big-Picture Pedagogy

## Chapter-Opening Misconceptions

When we first started teaching we assumed that most of our students were taking economics for the first time and were therefore blank slates that we could draw on. Boy, were we wrong. We now realize that students come to our classes with a number of strongly held misconceptions about economics and the economy, so we begin each chapter recognizing that fact and then establishing what we will do to clarify that subject area.

## Big Questions

After the opening misconception, we present the learning goals for the chapter in the form of Big Questions. We come back to the Big Questions in the conclusion to the chapter with Answering the Big Questions.

> **CHAPTER 12**
>
> # Monopolistic Competition and Advertising
>
> Advertising increases the price of products without adding value for the consumer.
>
> **MIS CONCEPTION**
>
> If you drive down a busy street, you will find many competing businesses, often right next to one another. For example, in most places a consumer in search of a quick bite has many choices, and more fast-food restaurants appear all the time. These competing firms advertise heavily. The temptation is to see advertising as driving up the price of a product, without any benefit to the consumer. However, this misconception doesn't account for why firms advertise. In markets where competitors sell slightly differentiated products, advertising enables firms to inform their customers about new products and services; yes, costs rise, but consumers also gain information to help make purchase decisions.
>
> In this chapter, we look at *monopolistic competition*, a widespread market structure that has features of both competitive markets and monopoly. We also explore the benefits and disadvantages of advertising, which is prevalent in markets with monopolistic competition.

> # BIG QUESTIONS
>
> * What is monopolistic competition?
> * What are the differences among monopolistic competition, compe
>   and monopoly?
> * Why is advertising prevalent in monopolistic competition?

> ### ANSWERING THE BIG QUESTIONS
>
> **What is monopolistic competition?**
>
> * Monopolistic competition is a market characterized by free entry and many firms selling differentiated products.
> * Differentiation of products takes three forms: differentiation by style or type, location, and quality.
>
> **What are the differences among monopolistic competition, competitive markets, and monopoly?**
>
> * Monopolistic competitors, like monopolists, are price makers who have downward-sloping demand curves. Whenever the demand curve is downward sloping, the firm is able to mark up the price above marginal cost. This leads to excess capacity and an inefficient level of output.
> * In the long run, barriers to entry enable a monopoly to earn an economic profit. This is not the case for monopolistic competition or competitive markets.
>
> **Why is advertising prevalent in monopolistic competition?**
>
> * Advertising performs useful functions under monopolistic competition: it conveys information about the price of the goods offered for sale, the location of products, and new products. It also signals differences in quality. However, advertising also encourages brand loyalty, which makes it harder for other businesses to successfully enter the market. Advertising can be manipulative and misleading.

# Solved Problems

Last but certainly not least, we conclude each chapter with two fully solved problems that appear in the end-of-chapter material.

## SOLVED PROBLEMS

**5.**

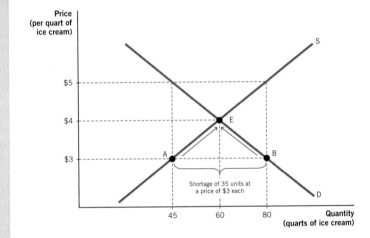

**a.** The equilibrium price is $4 and quantity is 60 units (quarts). The next step is to graph the curves. This is done above.

**b.** A shortage of 35 units of ice cream exists at $3; therefore, there is excess demand. Ice cream sellers will raise their price as long as excess demand exists. That is, as long as the price is below $4. It is not until $4 that the equilibrium point is reached and the shortage is resolved.

**8. a.** The first step is to set $Q_D = Q_S$. Doing so gives us $90 - 2P = P$. Solving for price, we find that $90 = 3P$, or $P = 30$. Once we know that $P = 30$, we can plug this value back into either of the original equations, $Q_D = 90 - 2P$ or $Q_S = P$. Beginning with $Q_D$, we get $90 - (30) = 90 - 60 = 30$, or we can plug it into $Q_S = P$, so $Q_S = 30$. Since we get a quantity of 30 for both $Q_D$ and $Q_S$, we know that the price of $30 is correct.

**b.** In this part, we plug $20 into $Q_D$. This yields $90 - 2(20) = 50$. Now we plug $20 into $Q_S$. This yields 20.

**c.** Since $Q_D = 50$ and $Q_S = 20$, there is a shortage of 30 units.

**d.** Whenever there is a shortage of a good, the price will rise in order to find the equilibrium point.

# Specifics about *Principles of Macroeconomics*

*Principles of Macroeconomics* follows the traditional structure found in most texts, but it contains several chapters on new topics that reflect the latest thinking and priorities in macroeconomics. First, at the end of the unit on macroeconomic basics, we have an entire chapter on financial markets, including coverage of securitization and mortgage-backed securities. The economic crisis of 2008–2009 made everyone aware of the importance of financial markets for the worldwide economy, and students want to know more about this fascinating subject.

Economic growth is presented before the short run, and we have two chapters devoted to the topic. The first focuses on the facts of economic growth. It discusses in largely qualitative terms how nations like South Korea and Singapore can be so wealthy, and nations like North Korea and Liberia can be so impoverished. The second chapter presents the Solow model in very simple terms. We've included this chapter to highlight the importance of growth and modeling. That said, it is optional and can be skipped by those instructors who have time for only one chapter on growth.

Coverage of the short run includes a fully developed chapter on the aggregate demand–aggregate supply model, and a second chapter that uses this key model to analyze—essentially side by side—the Great Depression and the Great Recession. We feel that this is a very effective way of presenting several of the key debates within economics.

Finally, we've written a unique chapter on the federal budget, which has allowed us to discuss at length the controversial topics of entitlements and the foreign ownership of U.S. national debt.

# Supplements and Media

## Norton Coursepack

Bring tutorial videos, assessment, and other online teaching resources directly into your new or existing online course with the Norton Coursepack. It's easily customizable and available for all major learning management systems including Blackboard, Desire2Learn, Angel, Moodle, and Canvas.

The Norton Coursepack for *Principles of Economics* includes:

* Concept Check quizzes
* A limited set of adapted Norton SmartWork questions
* Infographic quizzes
* Office Hours video tutorials
* Flashcards
* Links to the e-book
* Test bank

## The Ultimate Guide to Teaching Economics

*The Ultimate Guide to Teaching Economics* isn't just a guide to using *Principles of Economics,* it's a guide to becoming a better teacher. Combining more than 50 years of teaching experience, authors Dirk Mateer, Lee Coppock, Wayne Geerling (Penn State University), and Kim Holder (University of West Georgia) have compiled hundreds of teaching tips into one essential teaching resource. The *Ultimate Guide* is thoughtfully designed, making it easy for new instructors to incorporate best teaching practices into their courses and for veteran teachers to find new inspiration to enliven their lectures.

The hundreds of tips in *The Ultimate Guide to Teaching Microeconomics* and *The Ultimate Guide to Teaching Macroeconomics* include:

* Think-pair-share activities to promote small-group discussion and active learning
* "Recipes" for in-class activities and demonstrations that include descriptions of the activity, required materials, estimated length of time, estimated difficulty, recommended class size, and instructions. Ready-to-use worksheets are also available for select activities.
* Descriptions of movie clips, TV shows, commercials, and other videos that can be used in class to illustrate economic concepts
* Clicker questions
* Ideas for music examples that can be used as lecture starters
* Suggestions for additional real-world examples to engage students

In addition to the teaching tips, each chapter begins with an introduction by Dirk Mateer, highlighting important concepts to teach in the chapter and pointing out his favorite tips. Each chapter ends with solutions to the unsolved end-of-chapter problems in the textbook.

## Interactive Instructor's Guide

The Interactive Instructor's Guide brings all the great content from *The Ultimate Guide to Teaching Economics* into a searchable online database that can be filtered by topic and resource type. Subscribing instructors will be alerted by email as new resources are made available.

In order to make it quick and easy for instructors to incorporate the tips from *The Ultimate Guide to Teaching Economics,* the IIG will include:

* Links for video tips when an online video is available
* Links to news articles for real-world examples when an article is available
* Downloadable versions of student worksheets for activities and demonstrations
* Downloadable PowerPoint slides for clicker questions
* Additional teaching resources from dirkmateer.com and leecoppock.com

## Office Hours Video Tutorials

This collection of more than 45 videos brings the office-hour experience online. Each video explains a fundamental concept and was conceived by and filmed with authors Dirk Mateer and Lee Coppock.

Perfect for online courses, each Office Hours video tutorial is succinct (90 seconds to two minutes in length) and mimics the office-hour experience. The videos focus on topics that are typically difficult to explain just in writing (or over email), such as shifting supply and demand curves.

The Office Hours videos have been incorporated throughout the Norton SmartWork online homework system as video feedback for questions, integrated into the e-book, included in the Norton Coursepack, and available in the instructor resource folder.

## Test Bank

Every question in the *Principles of Economics* test bank has been author reviewed and approved. Each chapter (except Chapter 1) includes between 100 and 150 questions and incorporates graphs and images where appropriate.

The test bank has been developed using the Norton Assessment Guidelines. Each chapter of the test bank consists of three question types classified according to Bloom's taxonomy of knowledge types (Remembering, Understanding Applying, Analyzing Evaluating, and Creating). Questions are further classified by section and difficulty, making it easy to construct tests and quizzes that are meaningful and diagnostic.

## Presentation Tools

Norton offers a variety of presentation tools so new instructors and veteran instructors alike can find the resources that are best suited for their teaching style.

### Enhanced Lecture Powerpoint Slides

These comprehensive, "lecture-ready" slides are perfect for new instructors and instructors who have limited time to prepare for lecture. In addition to lecture slides, the slides also include images from the book, stepped-out versions of in-text graphs, additional examples not included in the chapter, and clicker questions.

### Art Slides and Art JPEGs

For instructors who simply want to incorporate in-text art into their existing slides, all art from the book (tables, graphs, photos, and Snapshot infographics) will be available in both PowerPoint and .jpeg formats. Stepped-out versions of in-text graphs and Snapshot infographics will also be provided and will be optimized for screen projection.

## Instructor Resource Folder

The Instructor Resource Folder includes the following resources in an all-in-one folder:

* The test bank in ExamView format on a CD
* Instructor's Resource Disc: PDFs of *The Ultimate Guide to Teaching Economics*, PowerPoints (enhanced lecture slides, active teaching slides, Snapshot slides, art slides, art .jpegs)
* Office Hours video tutorial DVD

## dirkmateer.com

Visit dirkmateer.com to find a library of over 100 recommended movie and TV clips, and links to online video sources to use in class.

## Coming for Fall 2014: Norton SmartWork for *Principles of Economics*

Norton SmartWork is a complete learning environment and online homework course designed to (1) support and encourage the development of problem-solving skills, and (2) deliver a suite of innovative tutorials, learning tools, and assessment woven together in a pedagogically effective way. Highlights include:

* Pre-created assignments to help instructors get started quickly and easily
* Guided learning tutorials to help students review each chapter objective
* Answer-specific feedback for every question to help students become better problem solvers
* An intuitive, easy-to-use graphing tool consistent with the coloration and notation of in-text graphs and art

# ACKNOWLEDGMENTS

We would like to thank the literally hundreds of fellow instructors who have helped us refine both our vision and the actual words on the page for this text. Without your help, we would never have gotten to the finish line. We hope that the result is the economics teacher's text that we set out to write.

Our class testers:

Jennifer Bailly, California State University, Long Beach
Mihajlo Balic, Harrisburg Community College
Erol Balkan, Hamilton College
Susan Bell, Seminole State College
Scott Benson, Idaho State University
Joe DaBoll-Lavoie, Nazareth College
Michael Dowell, California State University, Sacramento
Abdelaziz Farah, State University of New York, Orange
J. Brian O'Roark, Robert Morris University
Shelby Frost, Georgia State University
Karl Geisler, University of Nevada, Reno
Nancy Griffin, Tyler Junior College
Lauren Heller, Berry College
John Hilston, Brevard Community College
Kim Holder, University of West Georgia
Todd Knoop, Cornell College
Katharine W. Kontak, Bowling Green State University

Daniel Kuester, Kansas State University
Herman Li, University of Nevada, Las Vegas
Gary Lyn, University of Massachusetts, Lowell
Kyle Mangum, Georgia State University
Shah Mehrabi, Montgomery College
Sean Mulholland, Stonehill College
Vincent Odock, State University of New York, Orange
Michael Price, Georgia State University
Matthew Rousu, Susquehanna University
Tom Scales, Southside Virginia Community College
Tom Scheiding, University of Wisconsin, Stout
Clair Smith, St. John Fisher College
Tesa Stegner, Idaho State University
James Tierney, State University of New York, Plattsburgh
Nora Underwood, University of Central Florida
Michael Urbancic, University of Oregon
Marlon Williams, Lock Haven University

Our reviewers and advisors from focus groups:

Mark Abajian, California State University, San Marcos
Teshome Abebe, Eastern Illinois University
Rebecca Achee Thornton, University of Houston
Mehdi Afiat, College of Southern Nevada
Seemi Ahmad, State University of New York, Dutchess
Abdullah Al-Bahrani, Bloomsburg University
Frank Albritton, Seminole State College
Rashid Al-Hmoud, Texas Tech University
Tom Andrews, West Chester University

Becca Arnold, San Diego Mesa College
Lisa Augustyniak, Lake Michigan College
Dennis Avola, Bentley University
Roberto Ayala, California State University, Fullerton
Ron Baker, Millersville University
Kuntal Banerjee, Florida Atlantic University
Jude Bayham, Washington State University
Mary Beal-Hodges, University of North Florida
Stacie Beck, University of Delaware
Jodi Beggs, Northeastern University

Richard Beil, Auburn University
Doris Bennett, Jacksonville State University
Karen Bernhardt-Walther, The Ohio State University
Prasun Bhattacharjee, East Tennessee State University
Richard Bilas, College of Charleston
Kelly Blanchard, Purdue University
Inácio Bo, Boston College
Michael Bognanno, Temple University
Donald Boudreaux, George Mason University
Austin Boyle, Penn State
Elissa Braunstein, Colorado State University
Kristie Briggs, Creighton University
Stacey Brook, University of Iowa
Bruce Brown, California State Polytechnic University, Pomona
John Brown, Clark University
Vera Brusentsev, Swarthmore College
Laura Maria Bucila, Texas Christian University
Richard Burkhauser, Cornell University
W. Jennings Byrd, Troy University
Joseph Calhoun, Florida State University
Charles Callahan, State University of New York, Brockport
Douglas Campbell, University of Memphis
Giorgio Canarella, University of Nevada, Las Vegas
Semih Cekin, Texas Tech University
Sanjukta Chaudhuri, University of Wisconsin, Eau Claire
Shuo Chen, State University of New York, Geneseo
Monica Cherry, State University of New York, Buffalo
Larry Chisesi, University of San Diego
Steve Cobb, University of North Texas
Rhonda Collier, Portland Community College
Glynice Crow, Wallace State Community College
Chad D. Cotti, University of Wisconsin, Oshkosh
Damian Damianov, University of Texas, Pan American
Ribhi Daoud, Sinclair Community College
Kacey Douglas, Mississippi State University
William Dupor, The Ohio State University
Harold W. Elder, University of Alabama
Diantha Ellis, Abraham Baldwin Agricultural College
Tisha Emerson, Baylor University
Lucas Englehardt, Kent State University

Erwin Erhardt, University of Cincinnati
Molly Espey, Clemson University
Patricia Euzent, University of Central Florida
Brent Evans, Mississippi State University
Carolyn Fabian Stumph, Indiana University–Purdue University, Fort Wayne
Leila Farivar, The Ohio State University
Roger Frantz, San Diego State University
Gnel Gabrielyan, Washington State University
Craig Gallet, California State University, Sacramento
Wayne Geerling, Pennsylvania State University
Elisabetta Gentile, University of Houston
Menelik Geremew, Texas Tech University
Dipak Ghosh, Emporia State University
J. Robert Gillette, University of Kentucky
Rajeev Goel, Illinois State University
Bill Goffe, State University of New York, Oswego
Michael Gootzeit, University of Memphis
Paul Graf, Indiana University, Bloomington
Jeremy Groves, Northern Illinois University
Dan Hamermesh, University of Texas, Austin
Mehdi Haririan, Bloomsburg University
Oskar Harmon, University of Connecticut
David Harrington, The Ohio State University
Darcy Hartman, The Ohio State University
John Hayfron, Western Washington University
Jill Hayter, East Tennessee State University
Marc Hellman, Oregon State University
Wayne Hickenbottom, University of Texas, Austin
Mike Hilmer, San Diego State University
Lora Holcombe, Florida State University
Charles Holt, University of Virginia
James Hornsten, Northwestern University
Yu-Mong Hsiao, Campbell University
Alice Hsiaw, College of the Holy Cross
Yu Hsing, Southeastern Louisiana University
Paul Johnson, University of Alaska, Anchorage
David Kalist, Shippensburg University of Pennsylvania
Ara Khanjian, Ventura College
Frank Kim, University of San Diego
Colin Knapp, University of Florida
Mary Knudson, University of Iowa
Ermelinda Laho, LaGuardia Community College
Carsten Lange, California State Polytechnic University, Pomona
Tony Laramie, Merrimack College
Paul Larson, University of Delaware

Teresa Laughlin, Palomar College

Eric Levy, Florida Atlantic University

Charles Link, University of Delaware

Delores Linton, Tarrant County College

Xuepeng Liu, Kennesaw State University

Monika Lopez-Anuarbe, Connecticut College

Bruce Madariaga, Montgomery College

Brinda Mahalingam, University of California, Riverside

Chowdhury Mahmoud, Concordia University

Mark Maier, Glendale Community College

Daniel Marburger, Arkansas State University

Cara McDaniel, Arizona State University

Scott McGann, Grossmont College

Christopher McIntosh, University of Minnesota, Duluth

Evelina Mengova, California State University, Fullerton

William G. Mertens, University of Colorado, Boulder

Ida Mirzaie, The Ohio State University

Michael A. Mogavero, University of Notre Dame

Moon Moon Haque, University of Memphis

Mike Nelson, Oregon State University

Boris Nikolaev, University of South Florida

Caroline Noblet, University of Maine

Fola Odebunmi, Cypress College

Paul Okello, Tarrant County College

Stephanie Owings, Fort Lewis College

Caroline Padgett, Francis Marion University

Kerry Pannell, DePauw University

R. Scott Pearson, Charleston Southern University

Andrew Perumal, University of Massachusetts, Boston

Rinaldo Pietrantonio, West Virginia University

Irina Pritchett, North Carolina State University

Sarah Quintanar, University of Arkansas at Little Rock

Ranajoy Ray-Chaudhuri, The Ohio State University

Mitchell Redlo, Monroe Community College

Debasis Rooj, Northern Illinois University

Jason Rudbeck, University of Georgia

Naveen Sarna, Northern Virginia Community College

Noriaki Sasaki, McHenry County College

Jessica Schuring, Central College

Robert Schwab, University of Maryland

James Self, Indiana University, Bloomington

Gina Shamshak, Goucher College

Neil Sheflin, Rutgers University

Brandon Sheridan, North Central College

Joe Silverman, Mira Costa College

Brian Sloboda, University of Phoenix

Todd Sorensen, University of California, Riverside

Liliana Stern, Auburn University

Joshua Stillwagon, University of New Hampshire

Burak Sungu, Miami University

Vera Tabakova, East Carolina University

Yuan Emily Tang, University of California, San Diego

Anna Terzyan, Loyola Marymount University

Henry Thompson, Auburn University

Mehmet Tosun, University of Nevada, Reno

Robert Van Horn, University of Rhode Island

Adel Varghese, Texas A&M University

Marieta Velikova, Belmont University

Will Walsh, Samford University

Ken Woodward, Saddleback College

Jadrian Wooten, Washington State University

Anne York, Meredith College

Arindra Zainal, Oregon State University

Erik Zemljic, Kent State University

Kent Zirlott, University of Alabama

All of the individuals listed above helped us to improve the text and ancillaries, but a smaller group of them offered us extraordinary insight and support. They went above and beyond, and we would like them to know just how much we appreciate it. In particular, we want to recognize Alicia Baik (University of Virginia), Jodi Beggs (Northeastern University), Dave Brown (Penn State University), Jennings Byrd (Troy University), Douglas Campbell (University of Memphis), Shelby Frost (Georgia State University), Wayne Geerling (Penn State University), Paul Graf (Indiana University), Oskar Harmon (University of Connecticut), Jill Hayter (East Tennessee State University), John Hilston (Brevard Community College), Kim Holder (University of West Georgia), Todd Knoop (Cornell College), Katie Kontak (Bowling Green State

University), Brendan LaCerda (University of Virginia), Paul Larson (University of Delaware), Ida Mirzaie (Ohio State University), Charles Newton (Houston Community College), Boris Nikolaev (University of South Florida), J. Brian O'Roark (Robert Morris University), Andrew Perumal (University of Massachusetts, Boston), Irina Pritchett (North Carolina State University), Matt Rousu (Susquehanna College), Tom Scheiding (Cardinal Stritch University), Brandon Sheridan (North Central College), Clair Smith (Saint John Fisher College), James Tierney (SUNY Plattsburgh), Nora Underwood (University of Central Florida), Joseph Whitman (University of Florida), Erik Zemljic (Kent State University), and Zhou Zhang (University of Virginia).

We would also like to thank our partners at W. W. Norton & Company, who have been as committed to this text as we've been. They have been a pleasure to work with and we hope that we get to work together for many years. We like to call them Team Econ: Hannah Bachman, Jack Borrebach, Cassie del Pilar, Dan Jost, Lorraine Klimowich, John Kresse, Pete Lesser, Sasha Levitt, Jack Repcheck, Spencer Richardson-Jones, Carson Russell, and Nicole Sawa. Our development editor, Becky Kohn, was a big help, as was our copy editor, Alice Vigliani. The visual appeal of the book is the result of our photo researchers, Dena Digilio Betz and Nelson Colón, and the team at Kiss Me I'm Polish who created the front cover and the Snapshot infographics: Agnieszka Gasparska, Andrew Janik, and Annie Song. Thanks to all—it's been a wonderful adventure.

Finally, from Dirk: I'd like to thank my colleagues at Penn State—especially Dave Brown and Wayne Geerling—for their hard work on the supplements, my friends from around the country for the encouragement to write a textbook, and my family for their patience as the process unfolded. In addition, I want to thank the thousands of former students who provided comments, suggestions, and other insights that helped shape the book.

Finally, from Lee: First, I'd like to acknowledge Krista, my excellent wife, who consistently sacrificed to enable me to write this book. I'd also like to thank Jack Repcheck, who had the vision and the will to make this project a reality; we can't thank him enough. Finally, I'd also like to acknowledge Ken Elzinga, Charlie Holt, and Mike Shaub: three great professors who are my role models in the academy and beyond.

## Dirk Mateer

is Senior Lecturer at the University of Kentucky. He is the author of *Economics in the Movies*. He is also nationally recognized for his teaching. While at Penn State, he received the George W. Atherton Award, the university's highest teaching award (2011), and was voted the best overall teacher in the Smeal College of Business by the readers of *Critique* magazine (2010). He was profiled in the "Great Teachers in Economics" series of the Gus A. Stavros Center for the Advancement of Free Enterprise and Economic Education at Florida State University.

## Lee Coppock

is Associate Professor in the Economics Department at the University of Virginia. He has been teaching principles of economics for over twenty years, specializing in principles of macroeconomics. Before moving to UVA, he spent 9 years at Hillsdale College, where he learned how to reach college students. At UVA, Lee teaches two large sections (500+) of macro principles each spring. He has received teaching awards at both Hillsdale College and UVA. Lee lives in Charlottesville with his wife Krista and their four children: Bethany, Lee III, Kara, and Jackson.

# Principles of Macroeconomics

# PART 1

# INTRODUCTION

# The Five Foundations of Economics

**Economics is the dismal science.**

Perhaps you have heard of the "dismal science"? This derogatory term was first used by historian and essayist Thomas Carlyle in the nineteenth century. He called economics the dismal science after he read a prediction from economist Thomas Malthus stating that because our planet had limited resources, continued population growth would ultimately lead to widespread starvation.

Malthus was a respected thinker, but he was unduly pessimistic. The world population was one billion in 1800, and it is seven billion today. One of the things that Malthus did not take into account was increases in technology and productivity. Today, the efficiency of agricultural production enables seven billion people to live on this planet. Far from being the dismal science, economics in the twenty-first century is a vital social science that helps world leaders improve the lives of their citizens.

This textbook will provide the tools you need to be able to make your own assessments about the economy. What other discipline helps you discover how the world works, how to be an informed citizen, and how to live your life to the fullest? Economics can improve your understanding of the stock market and help you make better personal finance decisions. If you are concerned about Social Security, this textbook explains how it works. If you are interested in learning more about health care, the answers are here. Economics provides answers to all of these questions and much more.

In this chapter, you will learn about the five foundations of economics—incentives, trade-offs, opportunity cost, marginal thinking, and the principle that trade creates value. You will find that many of the more complex problems presented later in the text are derived from one of

Predicting the future is a tough business.

these foundations. Once you have mastered these five concepts, even the most complex processes can be reduced to combinations of these foundations. Think of this chapter as a road map that provides a broad overview of your journey into economics. Let's get started!

# BIG QUESTIONS

* **What is economics?**
* **What are the five foundations of economics?**

## What Is Economics?

Economists study how decisions are made. Examples of economic decisions include whether or not you should buy or lease a car, sublet your apartment, and buy that Gibson guitar you've been eyeing. And, just as individuals must choose what to buy within the limits of the income they possess, society as a whole must determine what to produce from its limited set of resources.

Of course, life would be a lot easier if we could have whatever we wanted whenever we wanted it. Unfortunately, life does not work that way. Our wants and needs are nearly unlimited, but the resources available to satisfy these wants and needs are always limited. The term used to describe the limited nature of society's resources is **scarcity**. Even the most abundant resources, like the water we drink and the air we breathe, are not always abundant enough everywhere to meet the wants and needs of every person. So, how do individuals and societies make decisions about scarce resources? This is the basic question economists seek to answer. **Economics** is the study of how people allocate their limited resources to satisfy their nearly unlimited wants.

**Scarcity**
refers to the limited nature of society's resources, given society's unlimited wants and needs.

**Economics**
is the study of how people allocate their limited resources to satisfy their nearly unlimited wants.

Water is scarce . . .

. . . and so are diamonds!

## Microeconomics and Macroeconomics

The study of economics is divided into two subfields: *microeconomics* and *macroeconomics*. **Microeconomics** is the study of the individual units that make up the economy. **Macroeconomics** is the study of the overall aspects and workings of an economy, such as inflation, growth, employment, interest rates, and the productivity of the economy as a whole. To see if you understand the difference, consider a worker who gets laid off and becomes unemployed. Is this an issue that would be addressed in microeconomics or macroeconomics? The question seems to fit parts of both definitions. The worker is an individual, which is micro, but employment is one of the broad areas of concern for economists, which is macro. Don't let this confuse you. Since only one worker is laid off, this is a micro issue. If many workers had been laid off and this led to a higher unemployment rate across the entire economy, it would be an issue broad enough to be studied by macroeconomists.

**Microeconomics** is the study of the individual units that make up the economy.

**Macroeconomics** is the study of the overall aspects and workings of an economy.

# What Are the Five Foundations of Economics?

The study of economics can be complicated, but we can make it very accessible by breaking down the specific economic process that you are exploring into a set of component parts. The five foundations that are presented here are the key component parts of economics. They are a bit like the natural laws of physics or chemistry. Almost every economic subject can be analyzed through the prism of one of these foundations. By mastering the five foundations, you will be on your way to succeeding in this course and thinking like an economist.

The five foundations of economics are: incentives; trade-offs; opportunity cost; marginal thinking; and the principle that trade creates value. Each of the five foundation concepts developed in this chapter will reappear throughout the book and enable you to solve complex problems.

Every time we encounter one of the five concepts, you will see an icon of a house to remind you of what you have learned. As you become more adept at economic analysis, it will not be uncommon to use two or more of these foundational ideas to explain the economic world around us.

Incentives
Trade-offs
Opportunity cost
Marginal thinking
Trade creates value

## Incentives

When you are faced with making a decision, you usually make the choice that you think will most improve your situation. In making your decision, you respond to **incentives**—factors that motivate you to act or to exert effort. For example, the choice to study for an exam you have tomorrow instead of spending the evening with your friends is based on the belief that doing well on the exam will provide a greater benefit. You are incentivized to study because you know that an A in the course will raise your grade-point average and make you a more attractive candidate on the job market when you are finished with school. We can further divide incentives into two paired categories: *positive and negative*, and *direct and indirect*.

Incentives

**Incentives** are factors that motivate a person to act or exert effort.

## Positive and Negative Incentives

Positive incentives are those that encourage action. For example, end-of-the-year bonuses motivate employees to work hard throughout the year, higher oil prices cause suppliers to extract more oil, and tax rebates encourage citizens to spend more money. Negative incentives also encourage action. For instance, the fear of receiving a speeding ticket keeps motorists from driving too fast, and the dread of a trip to the dentist motivates people to brush their teeth regularly. In each case, a potential negative consequence spurs individuals to action.

## PRACTICE WHAT YOU KNOW

This mosaic of the flag illustrates the difference between micro and macro.

### Microeconomics and Macroeconomics: The Big Picture

Identify whether each of the following statements identifies a microeconomic or a macroeconomic issue.

**The national savings rate is less than 2% of disposable income.**

Answer: The national savings rate is a statistic based on the average amount each household saves as a percentage of income. As such, this is a broad measure of savings and something that describes a macroeconomic issue.

**Jim was laid off from his last job and is currently unemployed.**

Answer: Jim's personal financial circumstances constitute a microeconomic issue.

**Apple decides to open up 100 new stores.**

Answer: Even though Apple is a very large corporation and 100 new stores will create many new jobs, Apple's decision is a microeconomic issue because the basis for its decision is best understood as part of the firm's competitive strategy.

**The government passes a jobs bill designed to stabilize the economy during a recession.**

Answer: You might be tempted to ask how many jobs are created before deciding, but that is not relevant to this question. The key part of the statement refers to "stabiliz[ing] the economy during a recession." This is an example of a *fiscal policy*, in which the government takes an active role in managing the economy. Therefore, it is a macroeconomic issue.

Conventional wisdom tells us that "learning is its own reward," but try telling that to most students. Teachers are aware that incentives, both positive and negative, create additional interest among their students to learn the course material. Positive incentives include bonus points, gold stars, public praise, and extra credit. Many students respond to these encouragements by studying more. However, positive incentives are not enough. Suppose that your instructor never gave any grade lower than an A. Your incentive to participate actively in the course, do assignments, or earn bonus points would be small. For positive incentives to work, they generally need to be coupled with negative incentives. This is why instructors require students to complete assignments, take exams, and write papers. Students know that if they do not complete these requirements they will get a lower grade, perhaps even fail the class.

## Direct and Indirect Incentives

In addition to being positive and negative, incentives can also be direct and indirect. For instance, if one gas station lowers its prices, it most likely will get business from customers who would not usually stop there. This is a direct incentive. Lower gasoline prices also work as an indirect incentive, since lower prices might encourage consumers to use more gas.

Direct incentives are easy to recognize. "Cut my grass and I'll pay you $30" is an example of a direct incentive. Indirect incentives are much harder to recognize. But learning to recognize them is one of the keys to mastering economics. For instance, consider the indirect incentives at work in welfare programs. Almost everyone agrees that societies should provide a safety net for those without employment or whose income isn't enough to meet basic needs. Thus, a society has a direct incentive to alleviate suffering caused by poverty. But how does a society provide this safety net without taking away the incentive to work? In other words, if the amount of welfare a person receives is higher than the amount that person can hope to make from a job, the welfare recipient might decide to stay on welfare rather than go to work. The indirect incentive to stay on welfare creates an *unintended consequence*—people who were supposed to use government assistance as a safety net until they can find a job use it instead as a permanent source of income.

Policymakers have the tough task of deciding how to balance such conflicting incentives. To decrease the likelihood that a person will stay on welfare, policymakers could cut benefits. But this might leave some people without enough to live on. For this reason, many government programs specify limits on the amount of time people can receive benefits. Ideally, this allows the welfare programs to continue to meet basic needs while creating incentives that encourage recipients to search for jobs and acquire skills that will enable them to do better in the workforce.

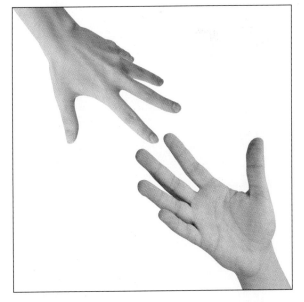

Public assistance: a hand in time of need or an incentive not to work?

**ECONOMICS IN THE REAL WORLD**

## How Incentives Create Unintended Consequences

Let's look at an example of how incentives operate in the real world and how they can lead to consequences no one envisioned when implementing them. Two Australian researchers noted a large spike in births on July 1, 2004, shown in Figure 1.1. The sudden spike was not an accident. Australia, like many other developed countries, has seen the fertility rate fall below replacement levels, which is the birthrate necessary to keep the population from declining. In response to falling birthrates, the Australian government decided to enact a "baby bonus" of $3,000 for all babies born on or after July 1, 2004. (One Australian dollar equals roughly one U.S. dollar.)

The policy was designed to provide a direct incentive for couples to have children and, in part, to compensate them for lost pay and the added costs of raising a newborn. However, this direct incentive had an indirect incentive attached to it, too—the couples found a way to delay the birth of their children until after July 1, perhaps jeopardizing the health of both the infants and the mothers. This was clearly an unintended consequence. Despite reassurances from the government that would-be parents would not put financial gain over the welfare of their newborns, over 1,000 births were switched from late June to early July through a combination of additional bed rest and push-

---

**FIGURE 1.1**

**Australian Births by Week in 2004**

The plunge and spike in births are evidence of an unintended consequence.

*Source*: See Joshua S. Gans and Andrew Leigh, "Born on the First of July: An (un)natural experiment in birth timing," *Journal of Public Economics* 93 (2009): 246–263.

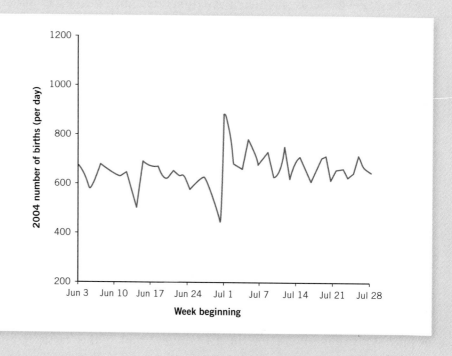

ing scheduled caesarian sections back a few days. This behavior is testament to the power of incentives.

On a much smaller scale, the same dynamic exists in the United States around January 1 each year. Parents can claim a tax credit for the entire year, whether the child is born in January or in December. This gives parents an incentive to ask for labor to be induced or for a caesarian section to be performed late in December so they can have their child before January 1 and thereby capitalize on the tax advantages. Ironically, hospitals and newspapers often celebrate the arrival of the first baby of the new year even though his or her parents might actually be financially worse off because of the infant's January 1 birthday. ✳

## Incentives and Innovation

Incentives also play a vital role in innovation, the engine of economic growth. There is no better example than Steve Jobs and Apple: between them, he and the company he founded held over 300 patents at the time of his death in 2011.

In the United States, the patent system and copyright laws guarantee inventors a specific period of time in which they can exclusively sell their work. This system encourages innovation by creating a powerful financial reward for creativity. Without patents and copyright laws, inventors would bear all the costs, and almost none of the rewards, for their efforts. Why would firms invest in research and development or artists create new music if others could immediately copy and sell their work? To reward the perspiration and inspiration required for innovation, society needs patents and copyrights to create the right incentives for economic growth.

In recent years, new forms of technology have made the illegal sharing of copyrighted material quite easy. As a result, illegal downloads of music and movies are widespread. When musicians, actors, and studios cannot effectively protect what they have created, they earn less. So illegal downloads reduce the incentive to produce new content. Will the next John Lennon or Jay-Z work so hard? Will the next Dan Brown or J. K. Rowling hone their writing craft so diligently if there is so much less financial reward for success? Is the "I want it for free" culture causing the truly gifted to be less committed to their craft, thus depriving society of excellence? Maintaining the right rewards, or incentives, for hard work and innovation is essential for advancing our society.

## Incentives Are Everywhere

There are many sides to incentives. However, financial gain almost always plays a prominent role. In the film *All the President's Men*, the story of the Watergate scandal that led to the unraveling of the Nixon administration in the early 1970s, a secret source called "Deep Throat" tells Bob Woodward, an investigative reporter at the *Washington Post*, to "follow the money." Woodward responds, "What do you mean? Where?" Deep Throat responds, "Just . . . follow the money." That is exactly what Woodward did. He eventually pieced everything together and followed the "money" trail all the way to President Nixon.

## Incentives

### *Ferris Bueller's Day Off*

Many people believe that the study of economics is boring. In *Ferris Bueller's Day Off* (1986), Ben Stein plays a high school economics teacher who sedates his class with a monotone voice while referring to many abstract economic theories and uttering the unforgettable "Anyone, anyone?" while trying to engage his students. The scene is iconic because it is a boring economics lecture that inspires Ferris and his friends to skip school, which leads to his wild adventures. In fact, the movie is really about incentives and trade-offs.

Was this your first impression of economics?

Understanding the incentives that caused the participants in the Watergate scandal to do what they did led Bob Woodward to the truth. Economists use the same process to explain how people make decisions, how firms operate, and how the economy functions. In fact, understanding incentives, from positive to negative and direct to indirect, is the key to understanding economics. If you remember only one concept from this course, it should be that incentives matter!

Trade-offs

## Trade-offs

In a world of scarcity, each and every decision incurs a cost. Even time is a scarce resource; after all, there are only 24 hours in a day. So deciding to read one of the Harry Potter books now means that you won't be able to read one of the Twilight books until later. More generally, doing one thing often means that you will not have the time, resources, or energy to do something else. Similarly, paying for a college education can require spending tens of thousands of dollars that might be used elsewhere instead.

Trade-offs are an important part of policy decisions. For instance, one decision that some governments face is the trade-off between a clean environment and a higher level of income for its citizens. Transportation and industry cause air pollution. Developed nations can afford expensive technology that reduces pollution-causing emissions. But developing nations, like China, generally have to focus their resources elsewhere. In the months leading up to the 2008 Olympics, China temporarily shut down many factories and discouraged the use of automobiles in order to reduce smog in Beijing. The air improved, and the Olympics showcased China's remarkable growth into a global economic powerhouse. However, the cost of keeping the air clean—shutting down factories and restricting transportation—was not a trade-off China is willing to make for longer than a few weeks. The Chinese people, like the rest of us, want clean air *and* a high standard of living, but for the time being most Chinese seem willing to accept increased pollution if it means the potential for a higher level of income. In more developed countries, higher standards of living already exist, and the cost of pollution control will not cause the economy's growth to slow down to unacceptable levels. People in these countries are much less likely to accept more pollution in order to raise the level of income even further.

Would you choose clean air or economic prosperity?

## Opportunity Cost

The existence of trade-offs requires making hard decisions. Choosing one thing means giving up something else. Suppose that you receive two invitations—the first to spend the day hiking, and the second to go to a concert—and both events occur at the same time. No matter which event you choose, you will have to sacrifice the other option. In this example, you can think of the cost of going to the concert as the lost opportunity to be on the hike. Likewise, the cost of going hiking is the lost opportunity to go to the concert. No matter what choice you make, there is an *opportunity cost*, or next-best alternative, that must be sacrificed. **Opportunity cost** is the highest-valued alternative that must be sacrificed in order to get something else.

Opportunity cost

Every time we make a choice, we experience an opportunity cost. The key to making the best possible decision is to minimize your opportunity cost by selecting the option that gives you the largest benefit. If you prefer going to a concert, you should go to the concert. What you give up, the hike, has less value to you than the concert; so it has a lower opportunity cost.

**Opportunity cost** is the highest-valued alternative that must be sacrificed in order to get something else.

The hiking/concert choice is a simple and clear example of opportunity cost. Usually, it takes deliberate effort to see the world through the opportunity-cost prism. But it is a worthwhile practice because it will help you make better decisions. For example, imagine you are a small-business owner. Your financial officer informs you that you have had a successful year and made a sizable profit. So everything is good, right? Not so fast. An economist will tell you to ask yourself, "Could I have made *more* profit doing something differently?" Good economic thinkers ask this question of themselves all the time. "Could I be using my time, talents, or energy on another activity that would be even more profitable for me?"

Do you have the moves like Jagger?

Profits on an income statement are only part of the story, because they only measure how well a business does relative to the bottom line. Accountants cannot measure what *might* have been better. For example, suppose that your business had decided against an opportunity to open a new store. A few months later, a rival opened a very successful store in the same location you had considered. Your profits were good for the year, but if you had made the investment in the new store, your profits could have been even better. So when economists mention opportunity cost, they are assessing whether the alternatives are better than what you are currently doing, which considers a larger set of possible outcomes.

Mick Jagger did just that. Before joining the Rolling Stones, he had been attending the London School of Economics. For Mick, the opportunity cost of becoming a musician was forgoing a degree in economics. Given the success of the Rolling Stones, it is hard to fault his decision!

## PRACTICE WHAT YOU KNOW

### The Opportunity Cost of Attending College

**Question: What is the opportunity cost of attending college?**

**Answer:** When people think about the cost of attending college, they usually think of tuition, room and board, textbooks, and travel-related expenses. While those expenses are indeed a part of going to college, they are not its full opportunity cost. The opportunity cost is the next-best alternative that is sacrificed. This means that the opportunity cost—or what you potentially could have done if you were not in college—includes the lost income you could have earned working a full-time job. If you take the cost of attending college plus the forgone income lost while in college, it is a very expensive proposition. Setting aside the question of how much more you might have to pay for room and board at college rather than elsewhere, consider the costs of tuition and books. Those fees can be $40,000 or more at many of the nation's most expensive colleges. Add those out-of-

Spending thousands on college expenses? You could be working instead!

pocket expenses to the forgone income from a full-time job that might pay $40,000, and your four years in college can easily cost over a quarter of a million dollars.

## ECONOMICS IN THE REAL WORLD

### Breaking the Curse of the Bambino: How Opportunity Cost Causes a Drop in Hospital Visits While the Red Sox Play

If you are injured or severely ill, you head straight to the emergency room, right? Not so fast! A 2005 study published in the *Annals of Emergency Medicine* found that visits to the ER in the Boston area fell by as much as 15% when the Red Sox were playing games in the 2004 playoffs. Part of the decline is attributable to more people sitting inside at home—presumably watching the ballgame—instead of engaging in activities that might get them hurt. But the study was able to determine that this did not explain the entire decline in emergency room visits. It turns out that a surprising number of people are willing to put off seeking medical attention for a few hours. Apparently, for some people the opportunity cost of seeking medical attention is high enough to postpone care until after the Red Sox game. ✳

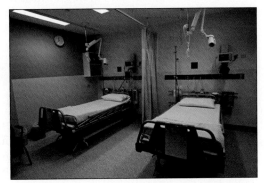

Emergency room beds are empty. Are the Sox playing?

## Marginal Thinking

Marginal
thinking

The process of systematically evaluating a course of action is referred to as *economic thinking*. **Economic thinking** involves a purposeful evaluation of the available opportunities to make the best decision possible. In this context, economic thinkers use a process called *marginal analysis* to break down decisions into smaller parts. Often, the choice is not between doing and not doing something, but between doing more or less of something. For instance, if you take on a part-time job while in school, you probably wrestle with the question of how many hours to work. If you work a little more, you can earn additional income. If you work a little less, you have more time to study. Working more has a tangible benefit (more money) and a tangible cost (poor grades). All of this should sound familiar from our earlier discussion about trade-offs. The work-study trade-off affects how much money you have and what kind of grades you make.

**Economic thinking**
requires a purposeful
evaluation of the available
opportunities to make the
best decision possible.

An economist would say that your decision—weighing how much money you want against the grades you want—is a decision at the *margin*. What exactly does the word "margin" mean? There are many different definitions. To a reader, the margin is the blank space bordering a page. A "margin" can also be thought of as the size of a victory. In economics, **marginal thinking** requires decision-makers to evaluate whether the benefit of one more unit of something is greater than its cost. This can be quite challenging, but understanding how to analyze decisions at the margin is essential to becoming a good economist.

**Marginal thinking**
requires decision-makers to
evaluate whether the benefit
of one more unit of some-
thing is greater than its cost.

For example, have you ever wondered why people straighten their places, vacuum, dust, scrub the bathrooms, clean out their garages, and wash their windows, but leave the dust bunnies under the refrigerator? The answer lies in thinking at the margin. Moving the refrigerator out from the wall to clean requires a significant effort for a small benefit. Guests who enter the kitchen can't see under the refrigerator. So most of us ignore the dust bunnies and just clean the visible areas of our homes. In other words, when economists say that you should think at the margin, what they really mean is that people weigh the costs and benefits of their actions and choose to do the things with the greatest payoff. For most of us, that means being willing to live with dust bunnies. The *marginal cost* of cleaning under the refrigerator (or on top of the cabinets, or even behind the sofa cushions) is too high and the added value of making the effort, or the *marginal benefit*, is too low to justify the additional cleaning.

### ECONOMICS IN THE REAL WORLD

### Why Buying and Selling Your Textbooks Benefits You at the Margin

New textbooks are expensive. The typical textbook purchasing pattern works as follows: you buy a textbook at the start of the term, often at full price, and sell it back at the end of the term for half the price you paid. Ouch. Nobody likes to make a bad investment, and textbooks depreciate the moment that students buy them. Even non-economists know not to buy high and sell low—but that is the textbook cycle for most students.

One solution would be to avoid buying textbooks in the first place. But that is not practical, nor is it a good decision. To understand why, let's use marginal analysis to break the decision into two separate components: the decision to buy and the decision to resell.

Let's start with the decision to buy. A rational buyer will only purchase a textbook if the expected value of the information included in the book is greater than the cost. For instance, say the book contains mandatory assignments or information that is useful for your major and you decide that it is worth $200 to you. If you are able to purchase the book for $100, the gain from buying the textbook would be $100. But what if the book is supplemental reading and you think it is worth only $50? If you value the book at $50 and it costs $100, purchasing the book would entail a $50 loss. If students only buy the books from which they receive gains, every textbook bought will increase the welfare of someone.

A similar logic applies to the resale of textbooks. At the end of the course, once you have learned the information inside the book, the value of hanging on to it is low. You might think it is worth $20 to keep the textbook for future reference, but if you can sell it for $50, the difference represents a gain of $30. In this case, you would decide to sell.

We have seen that buying and selling are two separate decisions made at the margin. If you combine these two decisions and argue that the purchase price ($100) and resale price ($50) are related, as most students typi-

Why do students buy and sell textbooks?

cally think they are, you will arrive at a faulty conclusion that you have made a poor decision. That is simply not true.

Textbooks may not be cheap, but they create value twice—once when bought and again when sold. This is a win-win outcome. Since we assume that decision-makers will not make choices that leave them worse off, the only way to explain why students buy textbooks and sell them again later is because the students benefit at the margin from both sides of the transaction. ✳

## Trade

Imagine trying to find food in a world without grocery stores. The task of getting what you need to eat each day would require visiting many separate locations. Traditionally, this need to bring buyers and sellers together was met by weekly markets, or bazaars, in central locations like town squares. **Markets** bring buyers and sellers together to exchange goods and services. As commerce spread throughout the ancient world, trade routes developed. Markets grew from infrequent gatherings, where exchange involved trading goods and services for other goods and services, into more sophisticated systems that use cash, credit, and other financial instruments. Today, when we think of markets we often think of eBay or Craigslist, where goods can be transferred from one person to another with the click of a mouse. For instance, if you want to find a rare DVD of season 1 of *Entourage*, there is no better place to look than eBay, which allows users to search for just about any product, bid on it, and then have it sent directly to their homes.

**Trade** is the voluntary exchange of goods and services between two or more parties. Voluntary trade among rational individuals creates value for everyone involved. Imagine you are on your way home from class and you want to pick up a gallon of milk. You know that milk will be more expensive at a convenience store than it will be at the grocery store five miles away, but you are in a hurry to study for your economics exam and are willing to pay up to $5.00 for the convenience of getting it quickly. At the store, you find that the price is $4.00 and you happily purchase the milk. This ability to buy for less than the price you are willing to pay provides a positive incentive to make the purchase. But what about the seller? If the store owner paid $3.00 to buy the milk from a supplier, and you are willing to pay the $4.00 price that he has set in order to make a profit, the store owner has an incentive to sell. This simple voluntary transaction has made both sides better off.

By fostering the exchange of goods, trade helps to create additional growth through specialization. **Comparative advantage** refers to the situation in which an individual, business, or country can produce at a lower opportunity cost than a competitor can. Comparative advantage harnesses the power of specialization. As a result, it is possible to be a physician, teacher, or plumber and not worry about how to do everything yourself. The physician becomes proficient at dispensing medical advice, the teacher at helping students, and the plumber at fixing leaks. The physician and the teacher call the plumber when they need work on their plumbing. The teacher and the plumber see the doctor when they are sick. The physician and the plumber send their children to school to learn from the teacher. On a broader scale, this type of trading of services increases the welfare of everyone in society. Trade creates gains for everyone involved.

**Trade creates value**

**Markets**
bring buyers and sellers together to exchange goods and services.

**Trade**
is the voluntary exchange of goods and services between two or more parties.

**Comparative advantage**
refers to the situation where an individual, business, or country can produce at a lower opportunity cost than a competitor can.

Our economy depends on specialization.

The same process is at work among businesses. For instance, Starbucks specializes in making coffee and Honda makes automobiles. You would not want to get your morning cup of joe at Honda any more than you would want to buy a car from Starbucks!

Specialization exists at the country level as well. Some countries have highly developed workforces capable of managing and solving complex processes. Other countries have large pools of relatively unskilled labor. As a result, businesses that need skilled labor gravitate to countries where they can easily find the workers they need. Likewise, firms with production processes that rely on unskilled labor look for employees in less-developed countries. By harnessing the power of increased specialization, global companies and economies create value through increased production and growth.

However, globalized trade is not without controversy. When goods and jobs are free to move across borders, not everyone benefits equally. Consider the case of an American worker who loses her job when her position is outsourced to a call center in India. The jobless worker now has to find new employment—a process that will require significant time and energy. In contrast, the new position in the call center in India provides a job and an income that improve the life of another worker. Also, the American firm enjoys the advantage of being able to hire lower-cost labor elsewhere. The firm's lower costs often translate into lower prices for domestic consumers. None of those advantages make the outsourcing of jobs any less painful for affected workers, but it is an important component of economic growth in the long run.

## Conclusion

Is economics the dismal science?

We began this chapter by discussing this misconception. Now that you have begun your exploration of economics, you know that this is not true. Economists ask, and answer, big questions about life. This is what makes the study of economics so fascinating. Understanding how an entire economy operates and functions may seem like a daunting task, but it is not nearly as hard as it sounds. If you remember the first time you drove a car, the process is similar. When you are learning to drive, everything seems difficult and unfamiliar. Learning economics is the same way. However, once you learn a few key principles, and practice them, you can become a good driver quite quickly. In the next chapter, we will use the ideas developed here to explore the issue of trade in greater depth.

# The Foundations of Economics

There are five foundations of economics—incentives, trade-offs, opportunity cost, marginal thinking, and the principle that trade creates value. Once you have mastered these five concepts, even complex economic processes can be reduced to smaller, more easily understood parts. If you keep these foundations in mind, you'll find that understanding economics is rewarding and fun.

**OPPORTUNITY COST**

**INCENTIVES**

In making a decision, you respond to incentives—factors that motivate you to act or to exert effort. Incentives also play a vital role in innovation, the engine of economic growth.

**TRADE-OFFS**

**TRADE CREATES VALUE**

**MARGINAL THINKING**

Marginal thinking is the hallmark of economic analysis. It requires forward thinking that compares the extra benefits of each activity with the extra costs.

## REVIEW QUESTIONS

- Which of the five foundations explains what you give up when you choose to buy a new pair of shoes instead of attending a concert?

- What are four types of incentives discussed in the chapter? Why do incentives sometimes create unintended consequences?

ECONOMICS FOR LIFE

# Midcareer Earnings by Selected Majors

A 2012 study by PayScale surveyed full-time employees across the United States who possessed a bachelor's degree but no advanced degree. Twenty popular subjects are listed in the graph below.

Not all majors are created equal. However, the majors that produce more income initially do not necessarily keep their advantage a decade or two later. That means that today's newly minted economics majors, with a median starting salary of $48,500, will likely surpass those who majored in civil engineering in earnings by the time they reach midcareer. The same holds true for political science majors, who have a lower starting salary than business majors but eventually surpass them. In the long run, pay growth matters to income level as much as, if not more than, starting salary. In terms of salary, any decision about what to major in that only looks at starting pay is misleading. How much you make over your whole career is what matters!

Will you make more by majoring in economics or finance?

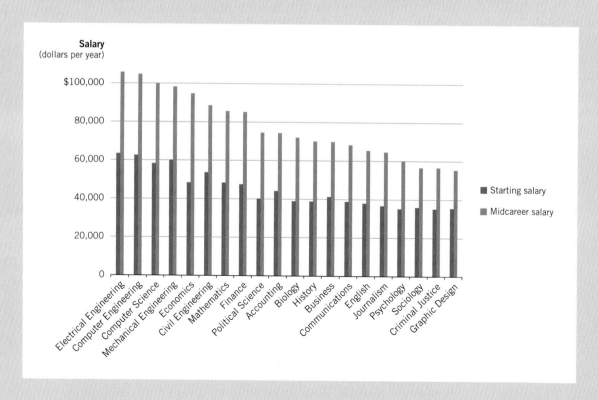

**Salary**
(dollars per year)

■ Starting salary
■ Midcareer salary

# ANSWERING THE BIG QUESTIONS

## What is economics?

* Economics is the study of how people allocate their limited resources to satisfy their nearly unlimited wants. Because of the limited nature of society's resources, even the most abundant resources are not always plentiful enough everywhere to meet the wants and needs of every person. So how do individuals and societies make decisions about how to use the scarce resources at our disposal? This is the basic question economists seek to answer.

## What are the five foundations of economics?

The five foundations of economics are: incentives; trade-offs; opportunity cost; marginal thinking; and the principle that trade creates value.

* Incentives matter because they help economists explain how decisions are made.
* Trade-offs exist when a decision-maker has to choose a course of action.
* Each time we make a choice, we experience an opportunity cost, or a lost chance to do something else.
* Marginal thinking requires a decision-maker to weigh the extra benefits against the extra costs.
* Trade creates value because participants in markets are able to specialize in the production of goods and services that they have a comparative advantage in making.

## CONCEPTS YOU SHOULD KNOW

comparative advantage (p. 17)
economics (p. 6)
economic thinking (p. 15)
incentives (p. 7)

macroeconomics (p. 7)
marginal thinking (p. 15)
markets (p. 17)
microeconomics (p. 7)

opportunity cost (p. 13)
scarcity (p. 6)
trade (p. 17)

## QUESTIONS FOR REVIEW

1. How would you respond if your instructor gave daily quizzes on the course readings? Is this a positive or a negative incentive?

2. Explain why many seniors often earn lower grades in their last semester before graduation. Hint: this is an incentive problem.

3. What is the opportunity cost of reading this textbook?

4. Evaluate the following statement: "Trade is like football: one team wins and the other loses."

5. Give a personal example of how pursuing your self-interest has made society better off.

## STUDY PROBLEMS (*solved at the end of the section)

* 1. What role do incentives play in each of the following situations?
    a. You learn that you can resell a ticket to next week's homecoming game for twice what you paid.
    b. A state government announces a "sales tax holiday" for back-to-school shopping during one week each August.

2. Compare your standard of living with that of your parents when they were the same age as you are now. Ask them or somebody you know around their age to recall where they were living and what they owned. What has happened to the average standard of living over the last 25 years? Explain your answer.

3. By referencing events in the news or something from your personal experiences, describe one example of each of the five foundations of economics.

* 4. Suppose that Colombia is good at growing coffee but not very good at making computer software, and that Canada is good at making computer software but not very good at growing coffee. If Colombia decided to grow only coffee and Canada only made computer software, would both countries be better or worse off? Can you think of a similar example from your life?

5. After some consideration, you decide to hire someone to help you move. Wouldn't it be cheaper to move yourself? Do you think this is a rational choice? Explain your response.

* 6. The website ultrinsic.com has developed an "*ult*erior motive that causes the person to have an int*rinsic* love of knowledge." At Ultrinsic, students pay a small entry fee to compete in grades-based contests for cash prizes. Suppose that 20 students from your economics class each pay $20 to enter a grades-based contest. This would create a $400 prize pool. An equal share of the $400 pot is awarded at the end of the term to each contestant who earns an A in the course. If four students earn A's, they each receive $100. If only one student earns an A, that person gets the entire $400 pot. What economic concept is Ultrinsic harnessing in order to encourage participants to learn more?

# SOLVED PROBLEMS

**1.a.** Since your tickets are worth more than you paid for them, you have a direct positive incentive to resell them.

**b.** The "sales tax holiday" is a direct positive incentive to buy more clothes during the back-to-school period. An unintended consequence of this policy is that fewer purchases are likely to be made both before and after the tax holiday.

**4.** If Colombia decided to specialize in the production of coffee, it could trade coffee to Canada in exchange for computer software. This process illustrates gains from specialization and trade. Both countries have a comparative advantage in producing one particular good. Colombia has ideal coffee-growing conditions, and Canada has a workforce that is more adept at writing software. Since each country specializes in what it does best, they are able to produce more value than what they could produce by trying to make both products on their own.

**6.** Ultrinsic is using the power of incentives to motivate learning. Earning a letter grade is a positive motivation to do well, or a penalty—or negative incentive—when you do poorly. Ultrinsic takes this one step further, as the student who earns an A also receives a small cash payment—a positive incentive. This provides extra motivation to study hard and achieve an A, since it pays, as opposed to earning a B or lower.

# Model Building and Gains from Trade

**Trade always results in winners and losers.**

When most people think of trade, they think of it as a zero-sum game. For instance, suppose that you and your friends are playing Magic. Players collect cards with special powers in order to assemble decks to play the game. Magic players love to trade their cards, and it is often the case that novice players do not know which cards are the most powerful or rare. When someone swaps one of the desirable cards, the other player is probably getting a much better deal. In other words, there is a winner and a loser. Now think of international trade. Many people believe that rich countries exploit the natural resources of poor countries and even steal their most talented workers. In this view, the rich countries are winners and the poor countries are losers. Still others think of trade as the redistribution of goods. If you trade your kayak for a friend's bicycle, no new goods are created; so how can this possibly create value? After all, someone must have come out ahead in the trade.

In this chapter, we will see that trade is not an imbalanced equation of winners and losers. To help us understand trade, the discussion will make a number of simplifying assumptions. We will also consider how economists use the scientific method to help explain the world we live in. These foundations will serve as the tools we need to explore the more nuanced reasons why trade creates value.

**Jace, Memory Adept** — 3⬡⬡

Planeswalker — Jace — M13

+1: Draw a card. Target player puts the top card of his or her library into his or her graveyard.

0: Target player puts the top ten cards of his or her library into his or her graveyard.

−7: Any number of target players each draw twenty cards.

*D. Alexander Gregory*
™ & © 1993–2012 Wizards of the Coast LLC 56/249

4

**Chandra, the Firebrand** — 3🔥

Planeswalker — Chandra — M13

+1: Chandra, the Firebrand deals 1 damage to target creature or player.

−2: When you cast your next instant or sorcery spell this turn, copy that spell. You may choose new targets for the copy.

−6: Chandra, the Firebrand deals 6 damage to each of up to six target creatures and/or players.

*D. Alexander Gregory*
™ & © 1993–2012 Wizards of the Coast LLC 123/249

3

**Garruk, Primal Hunter** — 2🌿🌿🌿

Planeswalker — Garruk — M13

+1: Put a 3/3 green Beast creature token onto the battlefield.

−3: Draw cards equal to the greatest power among creatures you control.

−6: Put a 6/6 green Wurm creature token onto the battlefield for each land you control.

*D. Alexander Gregory*
™ & © 1993–2012 Wizards of the Coast LLC 174/249

3

**Ajani, Caller of the Pride** — 1☀☀

Planeswalker — Ajani — M13

+1: Put a +1/+1 counter on up to one target creature.

−3: Target creature gains flying and double strike until end of turn.

−8: Put X 2/2 white Cat creature tokens onto the battlefield, where X is your life total.

*D. Alexander Gregory*
™ & © 1993–2012 Wizards of the Coast LLC 1/249

4

Trade is vital to Magic players, and vital to the economy.

# BIG QUESTIONS

* How do economists study the economy?
* What is a production possibilities frontier?
* What are the benefits of specialization and trade?
* What is the trade-off between having more now and having more later?

# How Do Economists Study the Economy?

Economics is a social science that uses the scientific method. This is accomplished by the use of economic models that focus on specific relationships in the economy. In order to create these models, economists make many simplifying assumptions. This approach helps identify the key relationships that drive the economic decisions that we are interested in exploring. In this section, you will begin to learn about how economists approach their discipline and the tools they use.

## The Scientific Method in Economics

On the television show *MythBusters*, popular myths are put to the test by Jamie Hyneman and Adam Savage. In Savage's words, "We replicate the circumstances, then duplicate the results." The entire show is dedicated to scientifically testing the myths. At the end of each episode, the myth is confirmed, labeled plausible, or busted. For instance, during a memorable episode Hyneman and Savage explored the reasons behind the *Hindenburg* disaster. The *Hindenburg* was a German passenger airship, or zeppelin, that caught fire and was destroyed as it attempted to dock in New Jersey on May 6, 1937. Thirty-six people died during the disaster.

Some people have hypothesized that the painted fabric used to wrap the zeppelin sparked the fire. Others have claimed that the hydrogen used to give the airship lift was the primary cause of the disaster. To test the hypothesis that the potentially incendiary paint used on the fabric was to blame, Hyneman and Savage built two small-scale models. The first model was filled with hydrogen and had a nonflammable skin; the second model used a replica of the original fabric for the skin but did not contain any hydrogen. Hyneman and Savage then compared the burn times of their models with the original footage of the disaster.

After examining the results, they determined that the myth of the incendiary paint was "busted"; the model containing the hydrogen burned twice as fast as the one with just the painted fabric skin.

Economists work in much the same way: they use the scientific method to answer questions about observable phenomena and to explain how the world works. The scientific method consists of several steps. First, researchers observe a phenomenon that interests them. Based on these observations, they develop a hypothesis, which is an explanation for the phenomenon. Then, they construct a model to test the hypothesis. Finally, they design experiments to test how well the model (which is based on the hypothesis) works. After collecting the data from the experiments, they can verify, revise, or refute the hypothesis. After many tests, they may agree that the hypothesis is well supported enough to qualify as a theory. Or, they may determine that it is not supported by the evidence and that they must continue searching for a theory to explain the phenomenon.

The scientific method was used to discover why the *Hindenburg* caught fire.

The economist's laboratory is the world around us, and it ranges from the economy as a whole to the decisions made by firms and individuals. As a result, economists cannot always design experiments to test their hypotheses. Often, they must gather historical data or wait for real-world events to take place—for example, the Great Recession of 2008–2009—in order to better understand the economy.

## Positive and Normative Analysis

As scientists, economists strive to approach their subject with objectivity. This means that they rigorously avoid letting personal beliefs and values influence the outcome of their analysis. In order to be as objective as possible, economists deploy positive analysis. A **positive statement** can be tested and validated. Each positive statement can be thought of as a description of "what is." For instance, the statement "the unemployment rate is 7.0%" is a positive statement because it can be tested by gathering data. In contrast, a **normative statement** cannot be tested or validated; it is about "what ought to be." For instance, the statement "an unemployed worker should receive financial assistance to help make ends meet" is a matter of opinion. One can reasonably argue that financial assistance to the unemployed is beneficial for society as a whole because it helps eliminate poverty. However, many would argue that financial assistance to the unemployed provides the wrong incentives. If the financial assistance provides enough to meet basic needs, workers may end up spending more time remaining unemployed than they otherwise would. Neither opinion is right or wrong; they are differing viewpoints based on values, beliefs, and opinions.

A **positive statement** can be tested and validated; it describes "what is."

A **normative statement** is an opinion that cannot be tested or validated; it describes "what ought to be."

Economists are concerned with positive analysis. In contrast, normative statements are the realm of policy-makers, voters, and philosophers. For example, if the unemployment rate rises, economists try to understand the conditions that created the situation. Economics does not attempt to determine who should receive unemployment assistance, which involves normative analysis. Economics, done properly, is confined to positive analysis.

# Economic Models

Thinking like an economist means learning how to analyze complex issues and problems. Many economic topics, such as international trade, Social Security, job loss, and inflation, are complicated. To analyze these phenomena and to determine the effect of various policy options related to them, economists use models, or simplified versions of reality. Models help us analyze the component parts of the economy.

The Wright brothers' wind tunnel

A good model should be simple to understand, flexible in design, and able to make powerful predictions. Let's consider one of the most famous models in history, designed by Wilbur and Orville Wright. Before the Wright brothers made their famous first flight in 1903, they built a small wind tunnel out of a six-foot-long wooden box. Inside the box they placed an aerodynamic measuring device, and at one end they attached a small fan to supply the wind. The brothers then tested over 200 different wing configurations to determine the lifting properties of each design. Using the data on aerodynamics they collected, the Wright brothers were able to determine the best type of wing to use on their aircraft.

Similarly, economic models provide frameworks that enable us to predict the effect that changes in prices, production processes, and government policies have on real-life behavior.

## Ceteris Paribus

**Ceteris paribus**
is the concept under which economists examine a change in one variable while holding everything else constant.

Using a controlled setting that held many other variables constant enabled the Wright brothers to experiment with different wing designs. By altering only a single element—for example, the angle of the wing—they could test whether the change in design was advantageous. The process of examining a change in one variable while holding everything else constant involves a concept known as **ceteris paribus**, from the Latin meaning "other things being equal." This idea is central to model building. If the Wright brothers had changed many variables simultaneously and found that the wing worked better, they would have had no way of knowing which change was responsible for the improved performance. For this reason, engineers generally modify only one element at a time and test only that one element before moving on to test additional elements.

Like the Wright brothers, economists start with a simplified version of reality. Economists build models, change one variable at a time, and ask whether the change in the variable had a positive or negative impact on performance. Perhaps the best-known economic model is supply and demand, which economists use to explain how markets function. We'll get to supply and demand in Chapter 3.

## Endogenous versus Exogenous Factors

Models must account for factors that we can control and factors that we can't. The Wright brothers' wind tunnel was critical to their success because it enabled them to control for as many *endogenous factors* as possible before attempting to fly. Factors that we know about and can control are **endogenous factors**. For example, the wind tunnel enabled the Wright brothers to see how well each wing design—an important part of the model—performed under controlled conditions.

Once the Wright brothers had determined the best wing design, they built the full-scale airplane that took flight at Kitty Hawk, North Carolina. At that point the plane, known as the "Flyer," was no longer in a controlled environment. It was subject to the gusting wind and other *exogenous factors* that made the first flight so challenging. Factors beyond our control—outside the model—are known as **exogenous factors**.

Building an economic model is very similar to the process Wilbur and Orville used. We need to be mindful of three factors: (1) what we include in the model, (2) the assumptions we make when choosing what to include in the model, and (3) the outside conditions that can affect our model's performance. In the case of the first airplane, the design was an endogenous factor because it was within the Wright brothers' control. In contrast, the weather (wind, air pressure, and other atmospheric conditions) was an exogenous factor because it was something that the Wright brothers could not control. Because the world is a complex place, an airplane model that flies perfectly in a wind tunnel may not fly reliably once it is exposed to the elements. Therefore, if we add more exogenous variables, or factors we cannot control—for example, wind and rain—to test our model's performance, the test becomes more realistic.

**Endogenous factors** are the variables that can be controlled for in a model.

**Exogenous factors** are the variables that cannot be controlled for in a model.

## The Danger of Faulty Assumptions

In every model, we make certain choices about which variables to include and how to model them. Ideally, we would like to include all the important variables inside the model and exclude all the variables that should be ignored.

However, no matter what we include, using a model that contains faulty assumptions can lead to spectacular policy failures. There is no better example than the financial crisis and Great Recession that began in December 2007.

In the years leading up to the crisis, banks sold and repackaged mortgage-backed securities under the faulty assumption that real estate prices would always rise. (Mortgage-backed securities are investments that are backed by the underlying value of a bundle of mortgages.) In fact, the computer models used by many of the banks did not even have a variable for declining real estate prices. Investors around the globe bought these securities because they thought they were safe. This sounded perfectly reasonable in a world where real estate prices were rising on an annual basis. Unfortunately, that assumption turned out to be false. From 2006 to 2008, real estate prices fell. Because of one faulty assumption, the entire financial market teetered on the edge of collapse. This vividly illustrates the danger of poor modeling.

Models can be useful, but as the financial crisis shows, they are also potentially dangerous. Because a model is always a simplification, decision-makers must be careful about assuming that a model can present a solution for complex problems.

In the late 1990s and early 2000s, some investors believed that real estate prices could only rise.

# PRACTICE WHAT YOU KNOW

## Positive versus Normative Statements

Question: Which of the following statements are positive and which ones are normative?

1. Winters in Arkansas are too cold.
2. Everyone should work at a bank to see the true value of money.
3. The current exchange rate is 0.7 British pounds per U.S. dollar.
4. On average, people save 15% when they switch to Geico.
5. Everyone ought to have a life insurance policy.
6. University of Virginia graduates earn more than Duke University graduates.
7. Harvard University is the top education institution in the country.
8. The average temperature in Fargo, North Dakota, in January is 56 degrees Fahrenheit.

You should eat five servings of fruit or vegetables each day. Is that a positive or a normative statement?

Answers

1. The word "too" is a matter of opinion. This is a normative statement.
2. While working at a bank might give someone an appreciation for the value of money, the word "should" is an opinion. This is a normative statement.
3. You can look up the current exchange rate and verify if this statement is true or false. This is a positive statement.
4. This was a claim made by the insurance company Geico in one of its commercials. Don't let that fool you. It is still a testable claim. If you had the data from Geico, you could see if the statement is correct or not. This is a positive statement.
5. It sounds like a true statement, or at least a very sensible one. However, the word "ought" makes it an opinion. This is a normative statement.
6. You can look up the data and see which university's graduates earn more. This is a positive statement.
7. Many national rankings indicate that this is true, but others do not. Since different rankings are based on different assumptions, it is not possible to identify a definitive "top" school. This is a normative statement.
8. The statement is wrong. North Dakota is much colder than that in January. However, the statement can be verified by looking at climatological data. This is a positive statement.

# What Is a Production Possibilities Frontier?

Now it's time for our first economic model. However, before you go on, you might want to review the appendix on graphing at the end of this chapter. It covers graph-reading skills that are used in this section. Graphs are one of the key tools in economics because they provide a visual display of the relationship between two variables over time. Your ability to read a graph and understand the model it represents is crucial to learning economics.

In Chapter 1, we learned that economics is about the trade-offs individuals and societies face every day. For instance, you may frequently have to decide between spending more time studying to get better grades or going to a party with your friends. The more time you study, the less time you have for your friends. Similarly, a society has to determine how to allocate its resources. The decision to build new roads will mean there is less money available for new schools, and vice versa.

Trade-offs

A **production possibilities frontier** is a model that illustrates the combinations of outputs that a society can produce if all of its resources are being used efficiently. In order to preserve *ceteris paribus*, we assume that the technology available for production and the quantity of resources remain constant. These assumptions allow us to model trade-offs more clearly.

A **production possibilities frontier** is a model that illustrates the combinations of outputs that a society can produce if all of its resources are being used efficiently.

Let's begin by imagining a society that produces only two goods—pizzas and chicken wings. This may not seem very realistic, since a real economy comprises millions of different goods and services, but the benefit of this approach is that it enables us to understand the trade-offs in the production process without making the analysis too complicated.

Figure 2.1 shows the production possibilities frontier for our two-product society. Remember that the number of people and the total resources in this two-product society are fixed. Later, we will relax these assumptions and make our model more realistic. If the economy uses all of its resources to produce pizzas, it can produce 100 pizzas and 0 wings. If it uses all of its resources to produce wings, it can make 300 wings and 0 pizzas. These outcomes are represented by points A and B on the production possibilities frontier. It is unlikely that the society will choose either of these extreme outcomes because it is human nature to enjoy variety.

If our theoretical society decides to spend some of its resources producing pizzas and some of its resources making wings, its economy will end up with a combination of pizzas and wings that can be placed somewhere along the production possibilities frontier (PPF) between points A and B. At point C, for example, the society would deploy its resources to produce 70 pizzas and 90 wings. At point D, the combination would be 50 pizzas and 150 wings. Each point along the production possibilities frontier represents a possible set of outcomes that the society can choose if it uses all of its resources efficiently.

Notice that some combinations of pizza and wings cannot be produced. This is because resources within the society are scarce. Our theoretical society would enjoy point E, but given the available resources, it cannot produce at that output level. Points beyond the production possibilities frontier are desirable but not feasible, given the resources and technology that the society has available.

FIGURE 2.1

**The Production Possibilities Frontier for Pizza and Wings**

The production possibilities frontier shows the trade-off between producing pizzas and producing wings. Any combination of pizzas and wings is possible along, or inside, the line. Combinations of pizza and wings beyond the production possibilities frontier—for example, at point E—are not possible with the current set of resources. Point F and any other points located in the shaded region are inefficient.

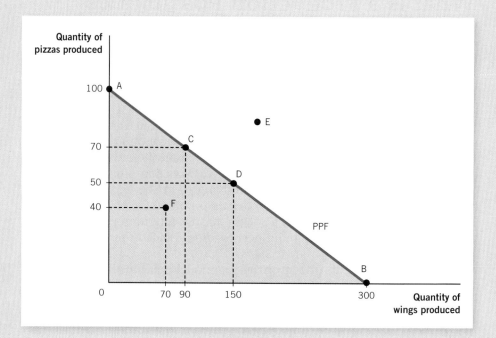

At any combination of wings and pizzas along the production possibilities frontier, the society is using all of its resources in the most productive way possible. But what about point F and any other points that might be located in the shaded region? These points represent outcomes inside the production possibilities frontier, which indicate an inefficient use of the society's resources. Consider, for example, the resource of labor. If employees spend many hours at work surfing the Web instead of doing their jobs, the output of pizzas and wings will drop and will no longer be efficient. As long as the workers use all of their time efficiently, they will produce the maximum amount of pizza and wings.

Whenever society is producing on the production possibilities frontier, the only way to get more of one good is to accept less of another. Since an economy operating along the frontier will be efficient at any point, economists do not favor one point over another. But a society may favor one particular point over another because it prefers that combination of goods. For example, in our theoretical two-good society, if wings suddenly become more popular, the movement from point C to point D will represent a desirable trade-off. The society will have 20 fewer pizzas (from 70 to 50) but 60 additional wings (from 90 to 150).

## The Production Possibilities Frontier and Opportunity Cost

**Trade-offs**

Since our two-good society produces only pizzas and wings, the trade-offs that occur along the production possibilities frontier represent the opportunity cost of producing one good instead of the other. As we noted in Chapter 1, an opportunity cost is the highest-valued alternative given up to pursue another course of action. As Figure 2.1 shows, when society moves from point C to point D, it gives up 20 pizzas; this is the opportunity cost of producing more wings. The movement from D to C has an opportunity cost of 60 wings.

Opportunity cost

Until now, we have assumed that there would be a constant trade-off between the number of pizzas and the number of wings produced. However, that is not typically the case. Not all resources in our theoretical society are perfectly adaptable for use in making pizzas and wings. Some workers are good at making pizzas, and others are not so good. When the society tries to make as many pizzas as possible, it will be using both types of workers. That is, to get more pizzas, the society will have to use workers who are increasingly less skilled at making them. This means that pizza production will not expand at a constant rate. You can see this in the new production possibilities frontier in Figure 2.2; it is bowed outward rather than a straight line.

Since resources are not perfectly adaptable, production does not expand at a constant rate. For example, in order to produce 20 extra pizzas, the society can move from point D (30 pizzas) to point C (50 pizzas). But moving from

## FIGURE 2.2

### The Law of Increasing Relative Cost

To make more pizzas, the society will have to use workers who are increasingly less skilled at making them. As a result, as we move up along the PPF, the opportunity cost of producing an extra 20 pizzas rises from 30 wings between points D and C to 80 wings between points B and A.

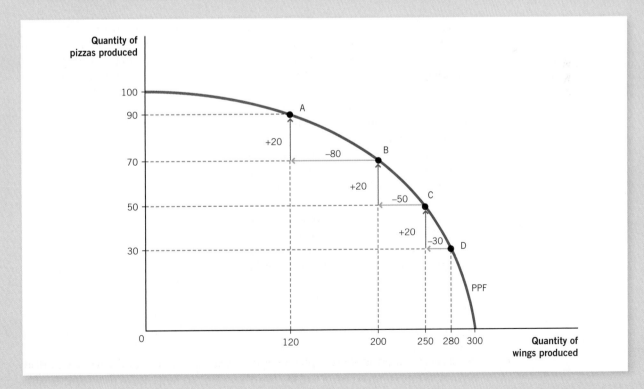

point D (280 wings) to point C (250 wings) means giving up 30 wings. So moving from D to C has an opportunity cost of 30 wings. Suppose that the society decides it wants even more pizza and moves from point C (50 pizzas) to point B (70 pizzas). Now the opportunity cost of more pizza is 50 wings, since wing production declines from 250 to 200. If the society decides that 70 pizzas are not enough, it can expand pizza production from point B (70 pizzas) to point A (90 pizzas). Now the society gives up 80 wings. Notice that as we move up along the PPF, the opportunity cost of producing an extra 20 pizzas rises from 30 wings to 80 wings. This reflects the increased trade-off necessary to produce more pizzas.

A bowed-out production possibilities frontier reflects the increasing opportunity cost of production. This is described by the **law of increasing relative cost**, which states that the opportunity cost of producing a good rises as a society produces more of it. Changes in relative cost mean that a society faces a significant trade-off if it tries to produce an extremely large amount of a single good.

> The **law of increasing relative cost** states that the opportunity cost of producing a good rises as a society produces more of it.

## The Production Possibilities Frontier and Economic Growth

So far, we have modeled the location of the production possibilities frontier as a function of the resources available to society at a particular moment in time. However, most societies hope to create economic growth. Economic growth is the process that enables a society to produce more output in the future.

We can use the production possibilities frontier to explore economic growth. For example, we can ask what would happen to the PPF if our two-good society developed a new technology that increases efficiency and, therefore, productivity. Suppose that a new pizza assembly line improves the pizza production process and that the development of the new assembly line does not require the use of more of the society's resources—it is simply a redeployment of the resources that already exist. This development would allow the society to make more pizza with the same number of workers. Or it would allow the same amount of pizza to be made with fewer workers than previously. Either way, the society has expanded its resource base. The change is shown in Figure 2.3.

With the new technology, it becomes possible to produce 120 pizzas using the same number of workers and in the same amount of time that it previously took to produce 100 pizzas. Although the ability to produce wings has not changed, the new pizza-making technology causes the production possibilities frontier to expand outward from $PPF_1$ to $PPF_2$. It is now possible for the society to move from point A to point B, where it can produce more of both (80 pizzas and 220 wings). Why can the society produce more of both? Because the improvement in pizza-making technology—the assembly line—allows a redeployment of the labor force that also increases the production of wings. Improvements in technology make point B possible.

The production possibilities frontier will also expand if the population grows. A larger population means more workers to help make pizza and wings. Figure 2.4 illustrates what happens when the society adds a worker to help

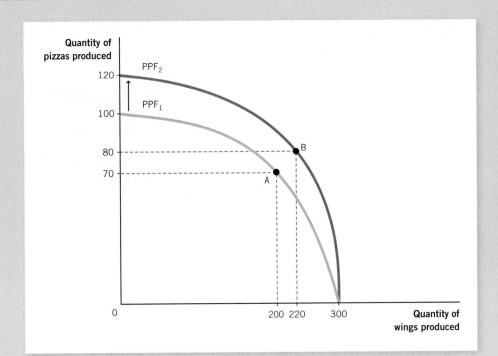

FIGURE 2.3

**A Shift in the Production Possibilities Frontier**

A new pizza assembly line that improves the productive capacity of pizza-makers shifts the PPF upward from PPF$_1$ to PPF$_2$. Not surprisingly, more pizzas can be produced. Comparing points A and B, you can see that the enhanced pizza-making capacity also makes it possible to produce more wings at the same time.

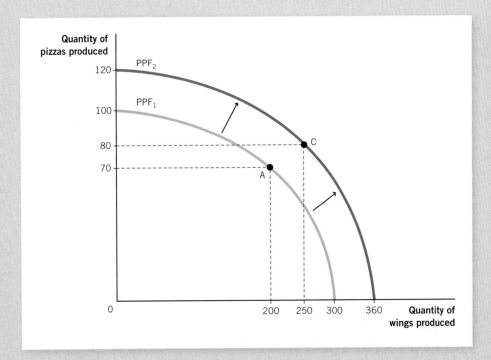

FIGURE 2.4

**More Resources and the Production Possibilities Frontier**

When more resources are available for the production of either pizza or wings, the entire PPF shifts upward and outward. This makes a point like C, along PPF$_2$, possible.

# PRACTICE WHAT YOU KNOW

## The Production Possibilities Frontier: Bicycles and Cars

Question: Are the following statements true or false? Base your answers on the PPF shown below.

There is a trade-off between making bicycles and cars.

1. Point A represents a possible amount of cars and bicycles that can be sold.
2. The movement along the curve from point A to point B shows the opportunity cost of producing more bicycles.
3. If we have high unemployment, the PPF shifts inward.
4. If an improved process for manufacturing cars is introduced, the *entire* PPF will shift outward.

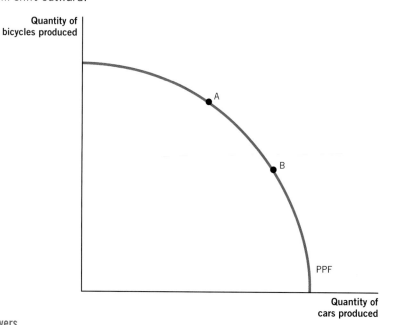

Answers

1. False. Point A represents a number of cars and bicycles that can be *produced*, not sold.
2. False. Moving from point A to point B shows the opportunity cost of producing more cars, not more bicycles.
3. False. Unemployment does not shift the curve inward, since the PPF is the maximum that can be produced when all resources are being used. More unemployment would locate society at a point inside the PPF, since some people who could help produce more cars or bicycles would not be working.
4. False. The PPF will shift outward along the car axis, but it will not shift upward along the bicycle axis.

produce pizza and wings. With more workers, the society is able to produce more pizzas and wings than before. This causes the curve to shift from $PPF_1$ to $PPF_2$, expanding up along the $y$ axis and out along the $x$ axis. Like improvements in technology, additional resources expand the frontier and enable the society to reach a point—in this case, C—that was not possible before. The extra workers have pushed the entire frontier out, not just one end, as the pizza assembly line did.

# What Are the Benefits of Specialization and Trade?

We have seen that improving technology and adding resources make an economy more productive. A third way to create gains for society is through specialization and trade. Determining what to specialize in is an important part of this process. Every worker, business, or country is relatively good at producing certain products or services. Suppose that you decide to learn about information technology. You earn a certificate or degree and find an employer who hires you for your specialized skills. Your information technology skills determine your salary. As a result, you can use your salary to purchase other goods and services that you desire and that you are not so skilled at making yourself.

In the next section, we will explore why specializing and exchanging your skilled expertise with others makes gains from trade possible.

## Gains from Trade

Let's return to our two-good economy. Now we'll make the further assumption that this economy has only two people. One person is better at making pizzas, and the other is better at making wings. When this is the case, the potential gains from trade are clear. Each person will specialize in what he or she is better at producing and then will trade in order to acquire some of the good that the other person produces.

Trade creates value

Figure 2.5 shows the production potential of the two people in our economy, Debra Winger and Mike Piazza. From the table, we see that if Debra Winger devotes all of her work time to making pizzas, she can produce 60 pizzas. If she does not spend any time on pizzas, she can make 120 wings. In contrast, Mike Piazza can spend all his time on pizzas and produce 24 pizzas, or all his time on wings and produce 72 wings.

The graphs show an illustration of the amount of pizza and wings that each person produces daily. Wing production is plotted on the $x$ axis, and pizza production is on the $y$ axis. Each of the production possibilities frontiers is drawn from data in the table at the top of the figure.

Debra and Mike each face a constant trade-off between producing pizza and producing wings. Debra produces 60 pizzas for every 120 wings; this means her trade-off between producing pizza and wings is fixed at 1:2. Mike produces 24 pizzas for every 72 wings. His trade-off between producing pizzas and wings is fixed at 1:3. Since Debra and Mike can choose to produce at

FIGURE 2.5

**The Production Possibilities Frontier with No Trade**

Debra Winger (a) can produce more pizza and more wings than Mike Piazza (b). Since Debra is more productive in general, she produces more of each food. If Debra and Mike each want to produce an equal number of pizzas and wings on their own, Debra makes 40 units of each and Mike makes 18 units of each.

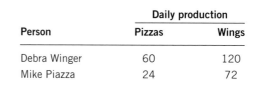

| | Daily production | |
|---|---|---|
| Person | Pizzas | Wings |
| Debra Winger | 60 | 120 |
| Mike Piazza | 24 | 72 |

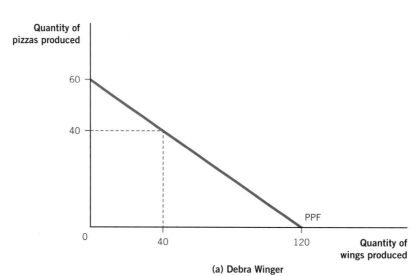

(a) Debra Winger

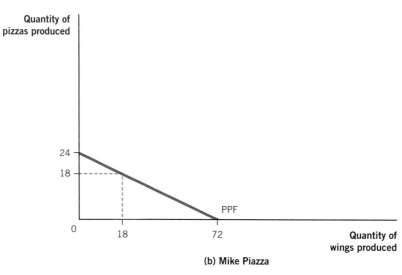

(b) Mike Piazza

any point along their production possibilities frontiers, let's assume that they each want to produce an equal number of pizzas and wings. When this is the case, Debra produces 40 pizzas and 40 wings, while Mike produces 18 pizzas and 18 wings. Since Debra is more productive in general, she produces more of each food. We say that Debra has an **absolute advantage**, meaning that she has the ability to produce more with the same quantity of resources than Mike can produce.

**Absolute advantage** refers to the ability of one producer to make more than another producer with the same quantity of resources.

At first glance, it would appear that Debra should continue to work alone. But consider what happens if they each specialize and then trade. Table 2.1 compares production with and without specialization and trade. Without trade, Debra and Mike have a combined production of 58 units of pizza and wings (Debra's 40 + Mike's 18). But when Debra specializes and produces only pizza, her production is 60 units. In this case, her individual pizza output is greater than the combined output of 58 pizzas (Debra's 40 + Mike's 18). Similarly, if Mike specializes in wings, he is able to make 72 units. His individual wing output is greater than their combined output of 58 wings (Debra's 40 + Mike's 18). Specialization has resulted in the production of 2 additional pizzas and 14 additional wings.

Trade creates value

Specialization leads to greater productivity. But Debra and Mike would like to eat both pizza and wings. So if they specialize and then trade with each other, they will benefit. If Debra gives Mike 19 pizzas in exchange for 47 wings, they are each better off by 1 pizza and 7 wings. This result is evident in the final column of Table 2.1 and in Figure 2.6.

In Figure 2.6a, we see that at point A Debra produces 60 pizzas and 0 wings. If she does not specialize, she produces 40 pizzas and 40 wings, represented at B. If she specializes and then trades with Mike, she can have 41 pizzas and 47 wings, shown at C. Her value gained from trade is 1 pizza and 7 wings. In Figure 2.6b, we see a similar benefit for Mike. If he produces only wings, he will have 72 wings, shown at A. If he does not specialize, he produces 18 pizzas and 18 wings. If he specializes and trades with Debra, he can have 19 pizzas and 25 wings, shown at C. His value gained from trade is 1 pizza and 7 wings. In spite of Debra's absolute advantage in making both pizzas and wings, she is still better off trading with Mike. This amazing result occurs because of specialization. When they spend their time on what they do best, they are able to produce more collectively and then divide the gain.

## TABLE 2.1

### The Gains from Trade

| Person | Good | Without trade | | With specialization and trade | | Gains from trade |
| | | Production | Consumption | Production | Consumption | |
|---|---|---|---|---|---|---|
| Debra | Pizza | 40 | 40 | 60 | 41 (keeps) | + 1 |
| | Wings | 40 | 40 | 0 | 47 (from Mike) | + 7 |
| Mike | Pizza | 18 | 18 | 0 | 19 (from Debra) | + 1 |
| | Wings | 18 | 18 | 72 | 25 (keeps) | + 7 |

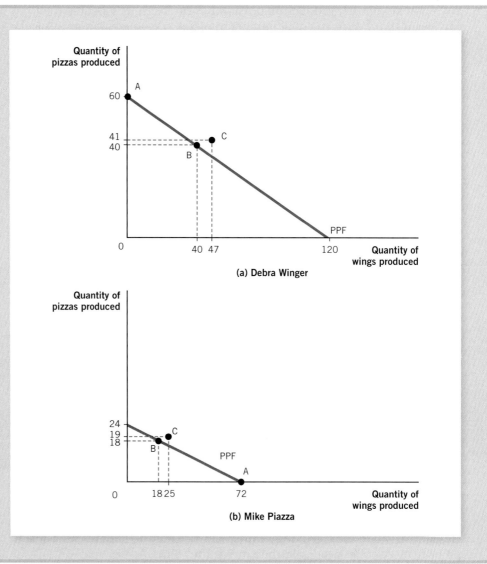

**FIGURE 2.6**

**The Production Possibilities Frontier with Trade**

(a) If Debra produces only pizza, she will have 60 pizzas, shown at point A. If she does not specialize, she will produce 40 pizzas and 40 wings (B). If she specializes and trades with Mike, she will have 41 pizzas and 47 wings (C).

(b) If Mike produces only wings, he will have 72 wings (A). If he does not specialize, he will produce 18 pizzas and 18 wings (B). If he specializes and trades with Debra, he can have 19 pizzas and 25 wings (C).

(a) Debra Winger

(b) Mike Piazza

## Comparative Advantage

We have seen that specialization enables workers to enjoy gains from trade. The concept of opportunity cost provides us with a second way of validating the principle that trade creates value. Recall that opportunity cost is the highest-valued alternative that is sacrificed to pursue something else. Looking at Table 2.2, you can see that in order to produce 1 more pizza Debra must give up producing 2 wings. We can say that the opportunity cost of 1 pizza is 2 wings. We can also reverse the observation and say that the opportunity cost of one wing is $\frac{1}{2}$ pizza. In Mike's case, each pizza he produces means giving up the production of 3 wings. In other words, the opportunity cost for him to produce 1 pizza is 3 wings. In reverse, we can say that when he produces 1 wing, he gives up $\frac{1}{3}$ pizza.

Recall from Chapter 1 that comparative advantage is the ability to make a good at a lower cost than another producer. Looking at Table 2.2, you can see

| TABLE 2.2 | | |
|---|---|---|
| **The Opportunity Cost of Pizza and Wings** | | |
| | Opportunity cost | |
| **Person** | **1 Pizza** | **1 Wing** |
| Debra Winger | 2 wings | $\frac{1}{2}$ pizza |
| Mike Piazza | 3 wings | $\frac{1}{3}$ pizza |

that Debra has a lower opportunity cost of producing pizzas than Mike—she gives up 2 wings for each pizza she produces, while he gives up 3 wings for each pizza he produces. In other words, Debra has a comparative advantage in producing pizzas. However, Debra does not have a comparative advantage in producing wings. For Debra to produce 1 wing, she would have to give up production of $\frac{1}{2}$ pizza. Mike, in contrast, gives up $\frac{1}{3}$ pizza each time he produces 1 wing. So Debra's opportunity cost for producing wings is higher than Mike's. Because Mike is the low-opportunity-cost producer of wings, he has a comparative advantage in producing them. Recall that Debra has an absolute advantage in the production of both pizzas and wings; she is better at making both. However, from this example we see that she cannot have a comparative advantage in making both goods.

Opportunity cost

Applying the concept of opportunity cost helps us to see why specialization enables people to produce more. Debra's opportunity cost of producing pizzas (she gives up making 2 wings for every pizza) is less than Mike's opportunity cost of producing pizzas (he gives up 3 wings for every pizza). Therefore, Debra should specialize in producing pizzas. If you want to double-check this result, consider who should produce wings. Debra's opportunity cost of producing wings (she gives up $\frac{1}{2}$ pizza for every wing she makes) is more than Mike's opportunity cost of producing wings (he gives up $\frac{1}{3}$ pizza for every wing he makes). Therefore, Mike should specialize in producing wings. When Debra produces only pizzas and Mike produces only wings, their combined output is 60 pizzas and 72 wings.

## Finding the Right Price to Facilitate Trade

We have seen that Debra and Mike will do better if they specialize and then trade. But how many wings should it cost to buy a pizza? How many pizzas for a wing? In other words, what trading price will benefit both parties? To answer this question, we need to return to opportunity cost. This process is similar to the trading of lunch food that you might recall from grade school. Perhaps you wanted a friend's apple and he wanted a few of your Oreos. If you agreed to trade three Oreos for the apple, the exchange benefited both parties because you valued your three cookies less than your friend's apple and your friend valued your three cookies more than his apple.

In our example, Debra and Mike will benefit from exchanging a good at a price that is lower than the opportunity cost of producing it. Recall that Debra's opportunity cost is 1 pizza per 2 wings. We can express this as a ratio of 1:2. This means that any exchange with a value lower than 1:2 (0.50) will be beneficial to her since she ends up with more pizza and wings than she

Opportunity cost

## TABLE 2.3

### Gaining from Trade

| Person | Opportunity cost | Ratio |
| --- | --- | --- |
| Debra Winger | 1 pizza equals 2 wings | 1:2 = 0.50 |
| Terms of trade | 19 pizzas for 47 wings | 19:47 = 0.40 |
| Mike Piazza | 1 pizza equals 3 wings | 1:3 = 0.33 |

had without trade. Mike's opportunity cost is 1 pizza per 3 wings, or a ratio of 1:3 (0.33). For trade to be mutually beneficial, the ratio of the amount exchanged must fall between the ratio of Debra's opportunity cost of 1:2 and the ratio of Mike's opportunity cost of 1:3. If the ratio falls outside of that range, Debra and Mike will be better off without trade, since the price of trading, which is the ratio in this case, will not be attractive to both parties. In the example shown in Table 2.3, Debra trades 19 pizzas for 47 wings. The ratio of 19:47 (0.40) falls between Debra's and Mike's opportunity costs.

**Trade creates value**

As long as the terms of trade fall between the opportunity costs of the trading partners, the trade benefits both sides. But if Mike insists on a trading ratio of 1 wing for 1 pizza, which would be a good deal for him, Debra will refuse to trade because she will be better off producing both goods on her own. Likewise, if Debra insists on receiving 4 wings for every pizza she gives to Mike, he will refuse to trade with her because he will be better off producing both goods on his own.

## ECONOMICS IN THE REAL WORLD

### Why Shaquille O'Neal Has Someone Else Help Him Move

Shaquille O'Neal is a mountain of a man—7'1" tall and over 300 pounds. At times during his Hall of Fame basketball career, he was traded from one team to another. Whenever he was traded, he had to relocate to a new city. Given his size and strength, you might think that Shaquille would have moved his household himself. But despite the fact that he could replace two or more ordinary movers, he kept playing basketball and hired movers. Let's examine the situation to see if this was a wise decision.

During his career, Shaquille had an absolute advantage in both playing basketball and moving furniture. But, as we have seen, an absolute advantage doesn't mean that Shaquille should do both tasks himself. When he was traded to a new team, he could have asked for a few days to pack up and move, but each day spent moving would have been one less day he was able to work with his new team. When you are paid millions of dollars to play a game, the time spent moving is time lost practicing or playing basketball, which incurs a substantial opportunity cost. The movers, with a much lower opportunity cost of their time, have a comparative advantage in moving—so Shaq made a smart decision to hire them!

However, since Shaquille is now retired, the value of his time is lower. If the opportunity cost of his time becomes low enough, it is conceivable that next time he will move himself rather than pay movers. ✳

# Shaq and Comparative Advantage

If you ever saw Shaquille O'Neal use his size and strength on the basketball court, you might wonder how someone could have any kind of advantage over him. But when it comes to comparative advantage, opportunity costs tell the tale. Let's take a look at the numbers.

Shaq was a basketball star, but he also would have been a star mover. Experienced movers can earn $20 an hour. With Shaq's strength, he might have been worth $40 an hour. He had an absolute advantage in basketball AND moving.

But Shaq made an average of $15 million a year playing basketball! That's over $40,000 a day. Giving up basketball for moving would have meant a huge opportunity cost. When it comes to moving, the movers had a comparative advantage. It was a no-brainer for Shaq to hire them and devote his time to hoops!

## REVIEW QUESTIONS

- If you are better than your roommate at both cooking dinner and cleaning the apartment, does that mean you should be responsible for both tasks? Use comparative advantage to explain.

- If you have a comparative advantage in doing something, do you experience a high or low opportunity cost?

# PRACTICE WHAT YOU KNOW

## Opportunity Cost

**Question:** Imagine that you are traveling to visit your family in Chicago. You can take a train or a plane. The plane ticket costs $300, and it takes 2 hours each way. The train ticket costs $200, and it takes 12 hours each way. Which form of transportation should you choose?

**Answer:** The key to answering the question is learning to value time. The simplest way to do this is to calculate the financial cost savings of taking the train and compare that to the value of the time you would save if you took the plane.

Will you travel by plane or train?

| Cost savings with train | Round-trip time saved with plane |
|:---:|:---:|
| $300 − $200 = $100 | 24 hours − 4 hours = 20 hours |
| (plane) − (train) | (train) − (plane) |

A person who takes the train can save $100, but it will cost 20 hours to do so. At an hourly rate, the savings would be $100/20 hours = $5/hour. If you value your time at exactly $5 an hour, you will be indifferent between plane and train travel. If your time is worth more than $5 an hour, you should take the plane, and if your time is worth less than $5 an hour, you should take the train.

It is important to note that this approach gives us a more realistic answer than simply observing ticket prices. The train has a lower ticket price, but very few people ride the train instead of flying because the opportunity cost of their time is worth more to them than the difference in the ticket prices. This is why most business travelers fly—it saves valuable time. Good economists learn to examine the full opportunity cost of their decisions, which must include both the financials and the cost of time.

We have examined this question by holding everything else constant, or applying the principle of *ceteris paribus*. In other words, at no point did we discuss possible side issues such as the fear of flying, sleeping arrangements on the train, or anything else that might be relevant to someone making the decision.

Opportunity
cost

## Opportunity Cost

### Saving Private Ryan

In most war movies, the calculus of battle is quite apparent. One side wins if it loses fewer airplanes, tanks, or soldiers during the course of the conflict or attains a strategic objective worth the cost. These casualties of war are the trade-off that is necessary to achieve victory. The movie *Saving Private Ryan* (1998) is different because in its plot the calculus of war does not add up: the mission is to save a single man. Private Ryan is one of four brothers who are all fighting on D-Day—June 6, 1944—the day the Allies landed in Normandy, France, to liberate Europe from Nazi occupation. In a twist of fate, all three of Ryan's brothers are killed. As a result, the general in charge believes that the family has sacrificed enough and sends orders to find Ryan and return him home.

The catch is that in order to save Private Ryan the army needs to send a small group of soldiers to find him. A patrol led by Captain Miller loses many good men in the process, and those who remain begin to doubt the mission. Captain Miller says to the sergeant, "This Ryan better be worth it. He better go

Saving one life means sacrificing another.

home and cure a disease, or invent a longer-lasting light bulb." Captain Miller hopes that saving Private Ryan will be worth the sacrifices they are making. That is how he rationalizes the decision to try to save him.

The opportunity cost of saving Private Ryan ends up being the lives that the patrol loses—lives that otherwise could have been pursuing a strategic military objective. In that sense, the entire film is about opportunity cost.

# What Is the Trade-off between Having More Now and Having More Later?

So far, we have examined short-run trade-offs. In looking at our wings-pizza trade-off, we were essentially living in the moment. But both individuals and society as a whole must weigh the benefits available today with those available tomorrow.

Many of life's important decisions are about the long run. We must decide where to live, whether and whom to marry, whether and where to go to college, and what type of career to pursue. Getting these decisions right is far more important than simply deciding how many wings and pizzas to produce. For instance, the decision to save money requires giving up something you want to buy today for the benefit of having more money available in the future. Similarly, if you decide to go to a party tonight, you benefit today, while staying home to study creates a larger benefit at exam time. We are constantly making decisions that reflect this tension between today and

Study now . . .

. . . enjoy life later.

**Trade-offs**

tomorrow—eating a large piece of cake or a healthy snack, taking a nap or exercising at the gym, buying a jet ski or investing in the stock market. Each of these decisions is a trade-off between the present and the future.

## Consumer Goods, Capital Goods, and Investment

**Consumer goods** are produced for present consumption.

**Capital goods** help produce other valuable goods and services in the future.

**Investment** is the process of using resources to create or buy new capital.

**Opportunity cost**

We have seen that the trade-off between the present and the future is evident in the tension between what we consume now and what we plan to consume later. Any good that is produced for present consumption is a **consumer good**. These goods help to satisfy our wants now. Food, entertainment, and clothing are all examples of consumer goods. **Capital goods** help in the production of other valuable goods and services in the future. Capital goods are everywhere. Roads, factories, trucks, and computers are all capital goods.

For households, education is also a form of capital. The time you spend earning a college degree makes you more attractive to future employers. Even though education is not a durable good, like a house, it can be utilized in the future to earn more income. When you decide to go to college instead of working, you are making an *investment* in your human capital. **Investment** is the process of using resources to create or buy new capital.

Since we live in a world with scarce resources, every investment in capital goods has an opportunity cost of forgone consumer goods. For example, if you decide to buy a new laptop to take notes in class, you cannot use the money you spent to travel over spring break. Similarly, a firm that decides to invest in a new factory to expand future production is unable to use that money to hire more workers now.

The decision between whether to consume or to invest has a significant impact on economic growth in the future, or the long run. What happens when society makes a choice to produce many more consumer goods than capital goods? Figure 2.7a shows the result. When relatively few resources

# FIGURE 2.7

**Investing in Capital Goods and Promoting Growth**

(a) When a society chooses point A in the short run, very few capital goods are created. Since capital goods are needed to enhance future growth, the long-run PPF$_2$ expands, but only slightly.

(b) When a society chooses point B in the short run, many capital goods are created, and the long-run PPF$_2$ expands significantly.

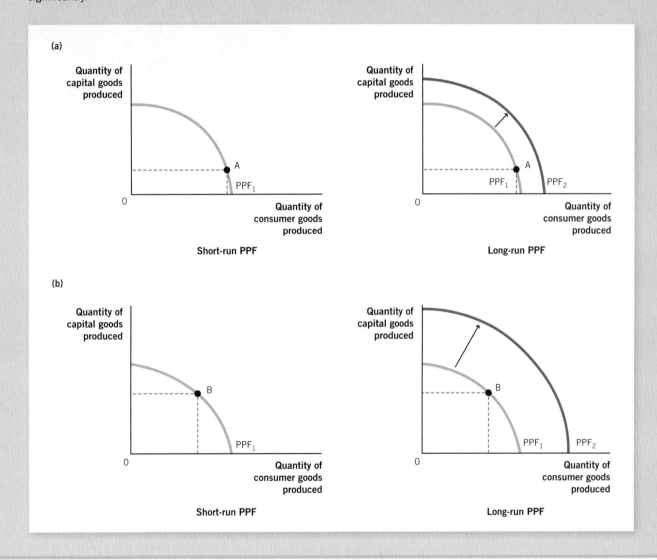

are invested in producing capital goods in the short run, not very much new capital is created. Since new capital is a necessary ingredient for economic growth in the future, the long-run production possibilities curve only expands a small amount.

What happens when society makes a choice to plan for the future by producing more capital goods than consumer goods? Figure 2.7b shows the

# The Trade-off between the Present and the Future

## A Knight's Tale

Before the late Heath Ledger starred in *Brokeback Mountain*, or played the Joker in *The Dark Knight*, he played an entrepreneurial peasant in *A Knight's Tale* (2001).

In the movie, three peasants unexpectedly win a jousting tournament and earn 15 silver coins. Then they face a choice about what to do next. Two of the three want to return to England and live the high life for a while, but the third (played by Ledger) suggests that they take 13 of the coins and reinvest them in training for the next tournament. He offers to put in all 5 of his coins and asks the other two for 4 coins each. His partners are skeptical about the plan because Ledger's character is good with the sword and not very good with the lance. For them to win additional tournaments, they will have to invest considerable resources in training and preparation.

The movie illustrates the trade-off between enjoying consumer goods in the short run and investing in capital goods in the long run. The peasants' choice to forgo spending their winnings

Learning to joust is a long-term skill.

to enjoy themselves now in order to prepare for the next tournament is not easy. None of the three has ever had any money. Five silver coins represent an opportunity, at least for a few days, to live the good life. However, the plan will elevate the three out of poverty in the long term if they can learn to compete at the highest level. Therefore, investing the 13 coins is like choosing point B in Figure 2.8b. Investing now will allow their production possibilities frontier to grow over time, affording each of them a better life in the long run.

result. With investment in new capital, the long-run production possibilities curve expands outward much more.

All societies face the trade-off between spending today and investing for tomorrow. Emerging global economic powers like China and India are good examples of the benefit of investing in the future. Over the last 20 years, the citizens of these countries have invested significantly more on the formation of capital goods than have the citizens in wealthier nations in North America and Europe. Not surprisingly, economic growth rates in China and India are much higher than in more developed countries. Part of the difference in these investment rates can be explained by the fact that the United States and Europe already have larger capital stocks per capita and have less to gain than developing countries from operating at point B in Figure 2.7b. China clearly prefers point B at this stage of its economic development, but point B is not necessarily better than point A. Developing nations, like China, are sacrificing the present for a better future, while many developed countries, like the United States, take a more balanced approach to weighing current needs against future growth. For Chinese workers, this trade-off typically means longer work hours and higher savings rates than their American counterparts

**Trade-offs**

## PRACTICE WHAT YOU KNOW

### Trade-offs

**Question:** Your friend is fond of saying he will study later. He eventually does study, but he often doesn't get quite the grades he had hoped for because he doesn't study enough. Every time this happens, he says, "It's only one exam." What advice would you give?

**Answer:** Your friend doesn't understand long-term trade-offs. You could start by reminding him that each decision has a consequence at the margin and also later in life. The marginal cost of not studying enough is a lower exam grade. To some extent, your friend's reasoning is correct. How well he does on one exam over four years of college is almost irrelevant. The problem is that many poor exam scores have a cumulative effect over the semesters. If your friend graduates with a 2.5 GPA instead of a 3.5 GPA because he did not study enough, his employment prospects will be significantly diminished.

No pain, no gain.

Marginal
thinking

can claim, despite far lower average salaries. In contrast, American workers have much more leisure time and more disposable income, a combination that leads to far greater rates of consumption.

# Conclusion

Does trade create winners and losers? After reading this chapter, you should know the answer: trade creates value. We have dispelled the misconception that many first-time learners of economics begin with—that every trade results in a winner and a loser. The simple, yet powerful, idea that trade creates value has far-reaching consequences for how we should organize our society. Voluntary trades will maximize society's wealth by redistributing goods and services to people who value them the most.

Trade
creates
value

We have also developed our first model, the production possibilities frontier. This model illustrates the benefits of trade and also enables us to describe ways to grow the economy. Trade and growth rest on a more fundamental idea—specialization. When producers specialize, they focus their efforts on those goods and services for which they have the lowest opportunity cost and trade with others who are good at making something else. In order to have something valuable to trade, each producer, in effect, must find its comparative advantage. As a result, trade creates value and contributes to an improved standard of living in society.

In the next chapter, we examine the supply-and-demand model to illustrate how markets work. While the model is different, the fundamental result we learned here—that trade creates value—still holds.

ECONOMICS FOR LIFE

## Failing to Account for Exogenous Factors When Making Predictions

Predictions are often based on past experiences and current observations. Many of the least accurate predictions fail to take into account how much technological change influences the economy. Here, we repeat a few predictions as a cautionary reminder that technology doesn't remain constant.

**PREDICTION:** "There is no reason anyone would want a computer in their home." Said in 1977 by Ken Olson, founder of Digital Equipment Corp. (DEC), a maker of mainframe computers.

**FAIL:** Over 80% of all American households have a computer today.

**PREDICTION:** "There will never be a bigger plane built." Said in 1933 by a Boeing engineer referring to the 247, a twin-engine plane that holds 10 people.

**FAIL:** Today, the Airbus A380 can hold more than 800 people.

**PREDICTION:** "The wireless music box has no imaginable commercial value. Who would pay for a message sent to no one in particular?" Said by people in the communications industry when David Sarnoff (founder of NBC) wanted to invest in the radio.

**FAIL:** Radio programs quickly captured the public's imagination.

**PREDICTION:** "The world potential market for copying machines is five thousand at most." Said in 1959 by executives of IBM to the people who founded Xerox.

**FAIL:** Today, a combination printer, fax machine, and copier costs less than $100. There are tens of millions of copiers in use throughout the United States.

**PREDICTION:** "The Americans have need of the telephone, but we do not. We have plenty of messenger boys." Said in 1878 by Sir William Preece, chief engineer, British Post Office.

**FAIL:** Today, almost everyone in Britain has a telephone.

These predictions may seem funny to us today, but note the common feature: they did not account for how the new technology would affect consumer demand and behavior. Nor do these predictions anticipate how improvements in technology through time make future versions of new products substantially better. The lesson: don't count on the status quo. Adapt with the times to take advantage of opportunities.

*Source:* Listverse.com, "Top 30 Failed Technology Predictions"

Epic fail: planes have continued to get larger despite predictions to the contrary.

## ANSWERING THE BIG QUESTIONS

### How do economists study the economy?

* Economists design theories and then test them by collecting real data. The economist's laboratory is the world around us; it ranges from the economy as a whole to the decisions that firms and individuals make. A good model should be simple to understand, flexible in design, and able to make powerful predictions. A model is both more realistic and harder to understand when it involves many variables. Maintaining a positive framework is crucial for economic analysis because it allows decision-makers to observe the facts objectively.

### What is a production possibilities frontier?

* A production possibilities frontier is a model that illustrates the combinations of outputs that a society can produce if all of its resources are being used efficiently. Economists use this model to illustrate trade-offs and to explain opportunity costs and the role of additional resources and technology in creating economic growth.

### What are the benefits of specialization and trade?

* Society is better off if individuals and firms specialize and trade on the basis of the principle of comparative advantage.
* Parties that are better at producing goods and services than their potential trading partners, or hold an absolute advantage, still benefit from trade because this allows them to specialize and trade what they produce for other goods and services that they are not as skilled at making.
* As long as the terms of trade fall between the opportunity costs of the trading partners, the trade benefits both sides.

### What is the trade-off between having more now and having more later?

* All societies face a crucial trade-off between consumption in the short run and greater productivity in the long run. Investments in capital goods today help to spur economic growth in the future. However, since capital goods are not consumed in the short run, this means that society must be willing to sacrifice how well it lives today in order to have more later.

## CONCEPTS YOU SHOULD KNOW

absolute advantage (p. 39)
capital goods (p. 46)
*ceteris paribus* (p. 28)
consumer goods (p. 46)
endogenous factors (p. 29)

exogenous factors (p. 29)
investment (p. 46)
law of increasing relative
   cost (p. 34)
normative statement (p. 27)

positive statement (p. 27)
production possibilities
   frontier (p. 31)

## QUESTIONS FOR REVIEW

1. What is a positive economic statement? What is a normative economic statement? Provide an example of each.

2. Is it important to build completely realistic economic models? Explain your response.

3. Draw a production possibilities frontier curve. Illustrate the set of points that is feasible, the set of points that is efficient, and the set of points that is infeasible.

4. Why does the production possibilities frontier bow out? Give an example of two goods for which this would be the case.

5. Does having an absolute advantage mean that you should undertake everything on your own? Why or why not?

6. What criteria would you use to determine which of two workers has a comparative advantage in performing a task?

7. Why does comparative advantage matter more than absolute advantage for trade?

8. What factors are most important for economic growth?

## STUDY PROBLEMS (✳ *solved at the end of the section*)

✳ 1. Michael and Angelo live in a small town in Italy. They work as artists. Michael is the more productive artist. He can produce 10 small sculptures each day but only 5 paintings. Angelo can produce 6 sculptures each day but only 2 paintings.

| | Output per day | |
|---|---|---|
| | Sculptures | Paintings |
| Michael | 10 | 5 |
| Angelo | 6 | 2 |

  a. What is the opportunity cost of a painting for each artist?
  b. Based on your answer in part a, who has a comparative advantage in producing paintings?
  c. If the two men decide to specialize, who should produce the sculptures and who should produce the paintings?

✳ 2. The following table shows scores that a student can earn on two upcoming exams according to the amount of time devoted to study:

| Hours spent studying for economics | Economics score | Hours spent studying for history | History score |
|---|---|---|---|
| 10 | 100 | 0 | 40 |
| 8 | 96 | 2 | 60 |
| 6 | 88 | 4 | 76 |
| 4 | 76 | 6 | 88 |
| 2 | 60 | 8 | 96 |
| 0 | 40 | 10 | 100 |

  a. Plot the production possibilities frontier.
  b. Does the production possibilities frontier exhibit the law of increasing relative cost?
  c. If the student wishes to move from a grade of 60 to a grade of 88 in economics, what is the opportunity cost?

3. Think about comparative advantage when answering this question: Should your professor, who has highly specialized training in economics, take time out of his teaching schedule to mow his lawn? Defend your answer.

✳ 4. Are the following statements positive or normative?
   a. My dog weighs 75 pounds.
   b. Dogs are required by law to have rabies shots.
   c. You should take your dog to the veterinarian once a year for a check-up.
   d. Chihuahuas are cuter than bulldogs.
   e. Leash laws for dogs are a good idea because they reduce injuries.

5. How does your decision to invest in a college degree add to your capital stock? Show this on your projected production possibilities frontier for 10 years from now compared to your production possibilities frontier without a degree.

✳ 6. Suppose that an amazing new fertilizer doubles the production of potatoes. How would this discovery affect the production possibilities frontier between potatoes and carrots? Would it now be possible to produce more potatoes *and* more carrots, or only more potatoes?

7. Suppose that a politician tells you about a plan to create two expensive but necessary programs to build more production facilities for solar power and wind power. At the same time, the politician is unwilling to cut any other programs. Use the production possibilities frontier graph below to explain if this is possible.

✳ 8. Two friends, Rachel and Joey, enjoy baking bread and making apple pies. Rachel takes 2 hours to bake a loaf of bread and 1 hour to make a pie. Joey takes 4 hours to bake a loaf and 4 hours to make a pie.
   a. What are Joey's and Rachel's opportunity costs of baking bread?
   b. Who has the absolute advantage in making bread?
   c. Who has a comparative advantage in making bread?
   d. If Joey and Rachel each decides to specialize in order to increase their joint production, what should Joey produce? What should Rachel produce?
   e. The price of a loaf of bread can be expressed in terms of an apple pie. If Joey and Rachel are specializing in production and decide to trade with each other, what range of ratios of bread and apple pie would allow both parties to benefit from trade?

9. Where would you plot unemployment on a production possibilities frontier? Where would you plot full employment on a production possibilities frontier? Now suppose that in a time of crisis everyone pitches in and works much harder than usual. What happens to the production possibilities frontier?

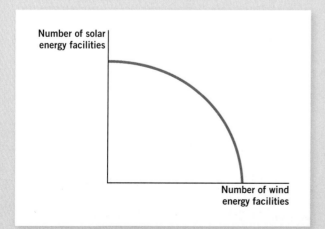

## SOLVED PROBLEMS

**1.a.** Michael's opportunity cost is 2 sculptures for each painting he produces. How do we know this? If he devotes all of his time to sculptures, he can produce 10. If he devotes all of his time to paintings, he can produce 5. The ratio 10:5 is the same as 2:1. Michael is therefore twice as fast at producing sculptures as he is at producing paintings. Angelo's opportunity cost is 3 sculptures for each painting he produces. If he devotes all of his time to sculptures, he can produce 6. If he devotes all of his time to paintings, he can produce 2. The ratio 6:2 is the same as 3:1.

**b.** For this question, we need to compare Michael's and Angelo's relative strengths. Michael produces 2 sculptures for every painting, and Angelo produces 3 sculptures for every painting. Since Michael is only twice as good at producing sculptures, his opportunity cost of producing each painting is 2 sculptures instead 3. Therefore, Michael is the low-opportunity-cost producer of paintings.

**c.** If they specialize, Michael should paint and Angelo should do the sculptures. You might be tempted to argue that Michael should just work alone, but if Angelo does the sculptures, it frees up Michael to concentrate on the paintings. This is what comparative advantage is all about.

**b.** Yes, since it is not a straight line.

**c.** The opportunity cost is that the student's grade falls from 96 to 76 in history.

**4.a.** Positive.

**b.** Positive.

**c.** Normative.

**d.** Normative.

**e.** Normative.

**6.** A new fertilizer that doubles potato production will shift the entire PPF out along the potato axis but not along the carrot axis. Nevertheless, the added ability to produce more potatoes means that less acreage will have to be planted in potatoes and more land can be used to produce carrots. This makes it possible to produce more potatoes and carrots at many points along the production possibilities frontier. Figure 2.3 has a nice illustration if you are unsure how this works.

**8.a.** Rachel gives up 2 pies for every loaf she makes. Joey gives up 1 pie for every loaf he makes.

**b.** Rachel.

**c.** Joey.

**d.** Joey should make the bread and Rachel the pies.

**e.** Rachel makes 2 pies per loaf and Joey makes 1 pie per loaf. So any trade between 2:1 and 1:1 would benefit them both.

**2.a.**

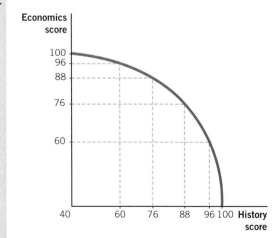

# Graphs in Economics

Many beginning students try to understand economics without taking the time to learn the meaning and importance of graphs. This is shortsighted. You can "think" your way to a correct answer in a few cases, but the models we build and illustrate with graphs are designed to help analyze the tough questions, where your intuition can lead you astray.

Economics is fundamentally a quantitative science. That is, in many cases economists solve problems by finding a numerical answer. For instance, economists determine the unemployment rate, the rate of inflation, the growth rate of the economy, prices, costs, and much more. Economists also like to compare present-day numbers to numbers from the immediate past and historical data. Throughout your study of economics, you will find that many data-driven topics—for example, financial trends, transactions, the stock market, and other business-related variables—naturally lend themselves to graphic display. You will also find that many theoretical concepts are easier to understand when depicted visually in graphs and charts.

Economists also find that graphing can be a powerful tool when attempting to find relationships between different sets of observations. For example, the production possibilities frontier model we presented earlier in this chapter involved the relationship between the production of pizzas and wings. The graphical presentations made this relationship, the trade-off between pizzas and wings, much more vivid.

In this appendix, we begin with simple graphs, or visuals, involving a single variable and then move to graphs that consist of two variables. Taking a few moments to read this material will help you learn economics with less effort and with greater understanding.

## Graphs That Consist of One Variable

There are two common ways to display data with one variable: bar graphs and pie charts. A **variable** is a quantity that can take on more than one value. Let's look at the market share of the largest carbonated beverage companies. Figure 2A.1 shows the data in a bar graph. On the vertical axis is the market share held by each firm. On the horizontal axis are the three largest firms (Coca-Cola, Pepsi, and Dr. Pepper Snapple) and the separate category for the remaining firms, called "Others." Coca-Cola Co. has the largest market share at 42%, followed by PepsiCo Inc. at 30% and Dr. Pepper Snapple at 16%. The height of each firm's bar represents its market share percentage. The combined market share of the other firms in the market is 12%.

A **variable** is a quantity that can take on more than one value.

We illustrate the same data from the beverage industry on a pie chart in Figure 2A.2. Now the market share is expressed as the size of the pie slice for each firm.

The information in a bar graph and a pie chart is the same, so does it matter which visualization you use? Bar graphs are particularly good for comparing sizes or quantities, while pie charts are generally better for illustrating proportions. But it doesn't really matter which visualization you use; what matters is how the audience sees your graph or chart.

## FIGURE 2A.1

**Bar Graphs**

Each firm's market share in the beverage industry is represented by the height of the bar.

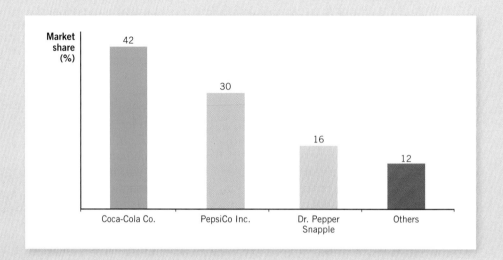

## FIGURE 2A.2

**Pie Chart**

Each firm's market share in the beverage industry is represented by the size of the pie slice.

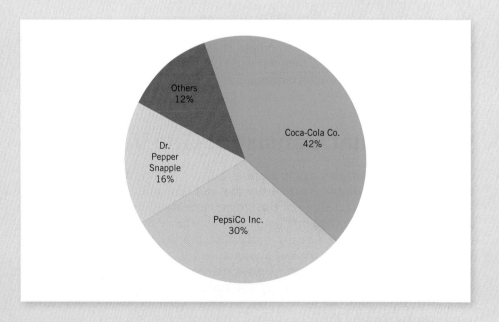

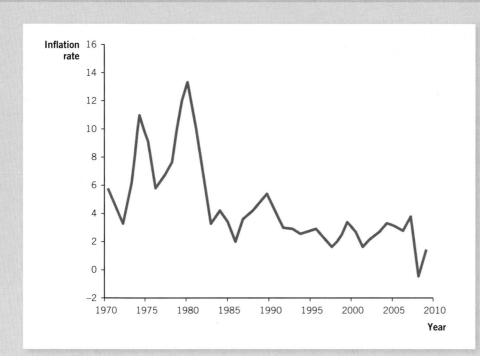

**FIGURE 2A.3**

**Time-Series Graph**
In a time-series graph, you immediately get a sense of when the inflation rate was highest and lowest, the trend through time, and the amount of volatility in the data.

## Time-Series Graphs

A time-series graph displays information about a single variable across time. For instance, if you want to show how the rate of inflation has varied over a certain period of time, you could list the annual inflation rates in a lengthy table, or you could illustrate each point as part of a time series in a graph. Graphing the points makes it possible to quickly determine when inflation was at its highest and lowest without having to scan through the entire table. Figure 2A.3 illustrates this point.

# Graphs That Consist of Two Variables

Sometimes, understanding graphs requires you to visualize relationships between two economic variables. Each variable is plotted on a coordinate system, or two-dimensional grid. The coordinate system allows us to map a series of ordered pairs that show how the two variables relate to each other. For instance, suppose that we examine the relationship between the amount of lemonade sold and the air temperature, as shown in Figure 2A.4.

The air temperature is graphed on the $x$ axis (horizontal) and cups of lemonade sold on the $y$ axis (vertical). Within each ordered pair $(x,y)$, the first value, $x$, represents the value along the $x$ axis and the second value, $y$, represents the value along the $y$ axis. For example, at point A, the value of $x$, or the

## FIGURE 2A.4

**Plotting Points in a Coordinate System**

Within each ordered pair (*x,y*), the first value, *x*, represents the value along the *x* axis and the second value, *y*, represents the value along the *y* axis. The combination of all the (*x,y*) pairs is known as a scatterplot.

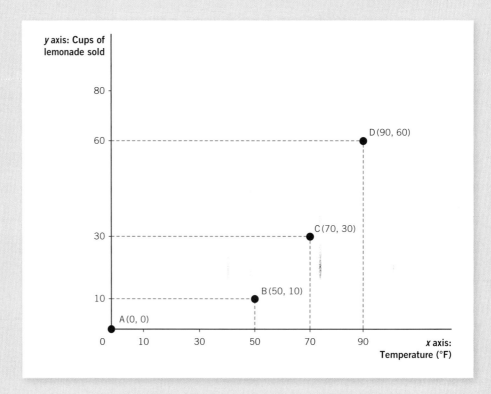

A scatterplot is a graph that shows individual (x,y) points.

**Positive correlation** occurs when two variables move in the same direction.

**Negative correlation** occurs when two variables move in the opposite direction.

temperature, is 0 and the value of *y*, or the amount of lemonade sold, is also 0. No one would want to buy lemonade when the temperature is that low. At point B, the value of *x*, the air temperature, is 50 degrees and *y*, the number of cups of lemonade sold, is 10. By the time we reach point C, the temperature is 70 degrees and the amount of lemonade sold is 30 cups. Finally, at point D, the temperature has reached 90 degrees and 60 cups of lemonade are sold.

The type of graph you see in Figure 2A.4 is known as a **scatterplot**; it shows the individual (*x,y*) points in a coordinate system. Note that in this example the amount of lemonade sold rises as the temperature increases. When the two variables move together in the same direction, we say that there is a **positive correlation** between them. Conversely, if we graph the relationship between hot chocolate sales and temperature, we find that they move in opposite directions; as the temperature rises, hot chocolate consumption goes down (see Figure 2A.5). This data reveals a **negative correlation**; it occurs when two variables, such as hot chocolate and temperature, move in opposite directions. Since economists are ultimately interested in using models and graphs to make predictions and test theories, the coordinate system makes both positive and negative correlations easy to observe.

Figure 2A.5 illustrates the difference between a positive correlation and a negative correlation. Figure 2A.5a uses the same information as Figure 2A.4. When the temperature increases, the quantity of lemonade sold increases as well. However, in 2A.5b we have a very different set of ordered pairs. Now, as the temperature increases, the quantity of hot chocolate sold falls. This

## FIGURE 2A.5

**Positive and Negative Correlations**
Panel (a) displays the positive relationship, or correlation, between lemonade consumption and higher temperatures.
Panel (b) displays the negative relationship, or correlation, between hot chocolate consumption and higher temperatures.

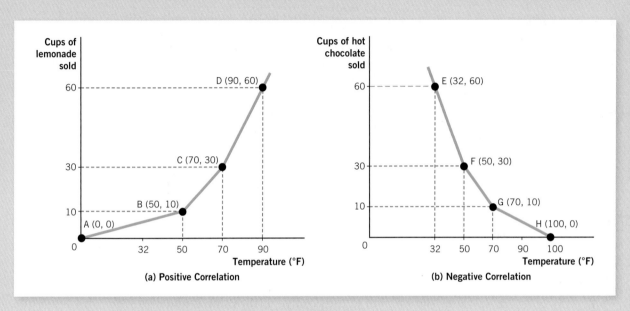

**(a) Positive Correlation**

**(b) Negative Correlation**

can be seen by starting with point E, where the temperature is 32 degrees and hot chocolate consumption is 60 cups. At point F, the temperature rises to 50 degrees, but hot chocolate consumption falls to 30 cups. Finally, at point G the temperature is 70 degrees and hot chocolate consumption is down to 10 cups. The green line connecting points E–G illustrates the negative correlation between hot chocolate consumption and temperature, since the line is downward sloping. This contrasts with the positive correlation in Figure 2A.5a, where lemonade consumption rises from point B to point D and the line is upward sloping.

## The Slope of a Curve

A key element in any graph is the **slope**, or the rise along the $y$ axis (vertical) divided by the run along the $x$ axis (horizontal). The *rise* is the amount that the vertical distance changes. The *run* is the amount that the horizontal distance changes.

$$\text{slope} = \frac{\text{change in } y}{\text{change in } x}$$

A slope can take on a positive, negative, or zero value. A slope of zero—a straight horizontal line—indicates that there is no change in $y$ for a given change in $x$. However, that result is not very interesting. The slope can be

**Slope**
refers to the change in the rise along the $y$ axis (vertical) divided by the change in the run along the $x$ axis (horizontal).

positive, as it is in Figure 2A.5a, or negative, as it is in 2A.5b. Figure 2A.6 high-lights the changes in *x* and *y* between the points on Figure 2A.5. (The change in a variable is often notated with a Greek delta symbol, Δ.)

In Figure 2A.6a, the slope from point B to point C is

$$\text{slope} = \frac{\text{change in } y}{\text{change in } x} = \frac{(30 - 10) \text{ or } 20}{(70 - 50) \text{ or } 20} = 1$$

All of the slopes in Figure 2A.6 are tabulated in Table 2A.1.

Each of the slopes in Figure 2A.6a is positive, and the values slowly increase from 0.2 to 1.5 as you move along the curve from point A to point D. How-ever, in Figure 2A.6b, the slopes are negative as you move along the curve from E to H. An upward, or positive, slope indicates a positive correlation, while a downward, or negative, slope indicates a negative correlation.

Notice that in both panels of Figure 2A.6 the slope changes values from point to point. Because of this, we say that the relationships are *nonlinear*. The slope tells us something about how responsive consumers are to changes in temperature. Consider the movement from point A to point B in Figure 2A.6a. The change in *y* is 10, while the change in *x* is 50 and the slope (10/50) is 0.2. Since zero indicates no change and 0.2 is close to zero, we can say that lem-onade customers are not very responsive as the temperature rises from 0 to 50 degrees. However, they are much more responsive from point C to point D, when the temperature rises from 70 to 90 degrees. At this point, lemonade consumption—the change in *y*—rises from 30 to 60 cups and the slope is now 1.5. The strength of the positive relationship is much stronger, and as a result the curve is much steeper, or more vertical. This contrasts with the movement from point A to point B, where the curve is flatter, or more horizontal.

The same analysis can be applied to Figure 2A.6b. Consider the movement from point E to point F. The change in *y* is −30, the change in *x* is 18, and the slope is −1.7. This value represents a strong negative relationship, so we would say that hot chocolate customers were quite responsive; as the tempera-ture rose from 32 to 50 degrees, they cut their consumption of hot chocolate by 30 cups. However, hot chocolate customers are not very responsive from point G to point H, where the temperature rises from 70 to 100 degrees. In this case, consumption falls from 10 to 0 cups and the slope is −0.3. The strength of the negative relationship is much weaker (closer to zero) and, as a result, the line is much flatter, or more horizontal. This contrasts with the movement from point E to point F, where the curve was steeper, or more vertical.

| TABLE 2A.1 | | | | |
|---|---|---|---|---|
| **Positive and Negative Slopes** | | | | |
| | **(a)** | | **(b)** | |
| Points | Slope | Points | Slope | |
| A to B | 0.2 | E to F | −1.7 | |
| B to C | 1.0 | F to G | −1.0 | |
| C to D | 1.5 | G to H | −0.3 | |

## Positive and Negative Slopes

Notice that in both panels the slope changes value from point to point. Because of this we say that the relationships are non-linear. In (a), as you move along the curve from point A to point D, the slopes are positive. However, in (b) the slopes are negative as you move along the curve from E to H. An upward, or positive, slope indicates a positive correlation, while a negative slope indicates a negative correlation.

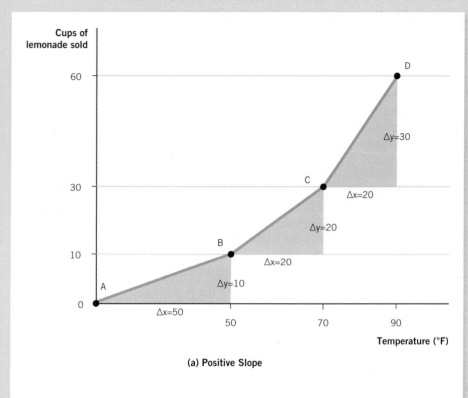

**(a) Positive Slope**

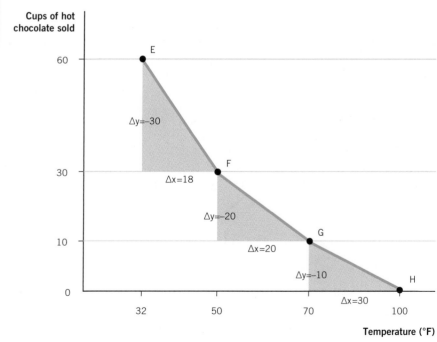

**(b) Negative Slope**

# Formulas for the Area of a Rectangle and a Triangle

Sometimes, economists interpret graphs by examining the area of different sections below a curve. Consider the demand for Bruegger's bagels shown in Figure 2A.7. The demand curve has a downward slope, which tells us that when the price of bagels falls, consumers will buy more bagels. But this curve also can tell us about the revenue the seller receives—one of the most important considerations for the firm. In this case, the sale price of each bagel is $0.60 and Bruegger's sells 4,000 bagels each week. We can illustrate the total amount Bruegger's takes in by shading the area bounded by the number of sales and the price—the green rectangle in the figure. In addition, we can identify the benefit consumers receive from purchasing bagels. This is shown by the blue triangle. Since many buyers are willing to pay more than $0.60 per bagel, we can visualize the "surplus" that consumers get from Bruegger's Bagels by highlighting the blue triangular area under the blue line and above $0.60.

To calculate the area of a rectangle, we use the formula:

$$\text{Area of a rectangle} = \text{height} \times \text{base}$$

In Figure 2A.7, the green rectangle is the amount of revenue that Bruegger's Bagels receives when it charges $0.60. The total revenue is $0.60 × 4,000, or $2,400.

To calculate the area of a triangle, we use the formula:

$$\text{Area of a triangle} = \tfrac{1}{2} \times \text{height} \times \text{base}$$

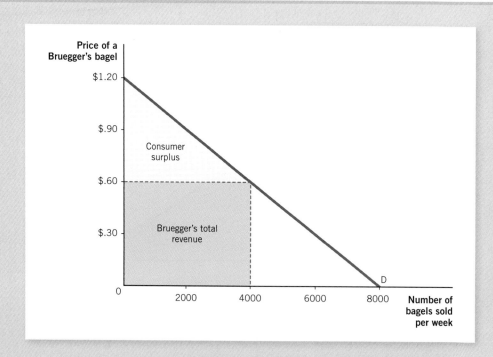

**FIGURE 2A.7**

**Working with Rectangles and Triangles**

We can determine the area of the green rectangle by multiplying the height by the base. This gives us $0.60 × 4,000, or $2,400 for the total revenue earned by Bruegger's Bagels. We can determine the area of a triangle by using the formula $\frac{1}{2}$ × height × base. This gives us $\frac{1}{2}$ × $0.60 × 4,000, or $1,200 for the area of consumer surplus.

In Figure 2A.7, the blue triangle represents the amount of surplus consumers get from buying bagels. The amount of consumer surplus is $\frac{1}{2} \times \$0.60 \times \$4,000$, or $1,200.

# Cautions in Interpreting Numerical Graphs

In Chapter 2, we utilized *ceteris paribus*, or the condition of holding everything else around us constant while analyzing a specific relationship. Suppose that you omitted an important part of the relationship. What effect would this have on your ability to use graphs as an illustrative tool? Consider the relationship between lemonade consumption and bottles of suntan lotion. The graph of the two variables would look something like Figure 2A.8.

Looking at Figure 2A.8, you would not necessarily know that something is misleading. However, when you stop to think about the relationship, you quickly recognize that the result is deceptive. Since the slope is positive, the graph indicates that there is a positive correlation between the number of bottles of suntan lotion used and the amount of lemonade people drink. At first glance this seems reasonable, since we associate suntan lotion and lemonade with summer activities. But the association is not **causal**, occurring when one variable influences the other. Using more suntan lotion does not cause people to drink more lemonade. It just so happens that when it is hot outside, more suntan lotion is used and more lemonade is consumed. In

**Causality**
occurs when one variable influences the other.

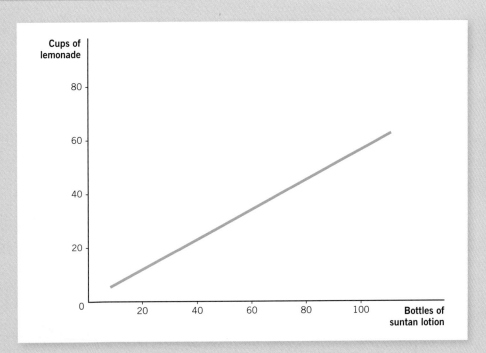

**FIGURE 2A.8**

**Graph with an Omitted Variable**

What looks like a strongly positive correlation is misleading. The demand for both lemonade and suntan lotion rises because the temperature rises, so the correlation between lemonade and suntan lotion use is deceptive, not informative.

this case, the causal factor is heat! The graph makes it look like the number of people using suntan lotion affects the amount of lemonade being consumed, when in fact they are not directly related.

Another possible mistake is known as **reverse causation**, which occurs when causation is incorrectly assigned among associated events. Suppose that in an effort to fight the AIDS epidemic in Africa, a research organization notes the correlation shown in Figure 2A.9.

After looking at the data, it is clear that as the number of doctors per 1,000 people goes up, so do rates of death from AIDS. The research organization puts out a press release claiming that doctors are responsible for increasing AIDS deaths, and the media hypes the discovery. But hold on! Maybe there happen to be more doctors in areas with high incidences of AIDS because that's where they are most needed. Coming to the correct conclusion about the data requires that we do more than simply look at the correlation.

**Reverse causation**
occurs when causation is incorrectly assigned among associated events.

## FIGURE 2A.9

**Reverse Causation and an Omitted Variable**

At a quick glance, this figure should strike you as odd. AIDS deaths are associated with having more doctors in the area. But the doctors are there to help and treat people, not harm them. This is an example of reverse causation.

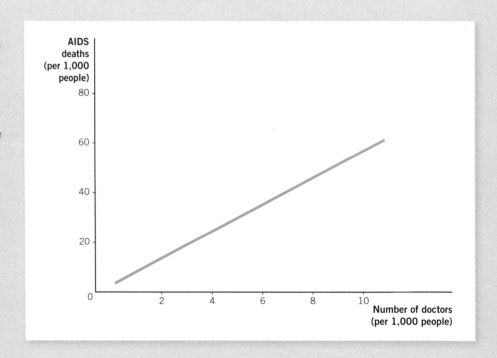

## CONCEPTS YOU SHOULD KNOW

causality (p. 63)                   reverse causation (p. 64)          variable (p. 55)
negative correlation (p. 58)        scatterplot (p. 58)
positive correlation (p. 58)        slope (p. 59)

## STUDY PROBLEMS

1.  The following table provides the price and the ✳ 2. In the following graph, calculate the value of
    quantity demanded of apples (per week).          the slope if the price rises from $20 to $40.

    | Price per Apple | Quantity Demanded |
    |:---------------:|:-----------------:|
    | $0.25           | 10                |
    | $0.50           | 7                 |
    | $0.75           | 4                 |
    | $1.00           | 2                 |
    | $1.25           | 1                 |
    | $1.50           | 0                 |

    a. Plot the data provided in the table into a
       graph.
    b. Is the relationship between the price of
       apples and the quantity demanded negative
       or positive?

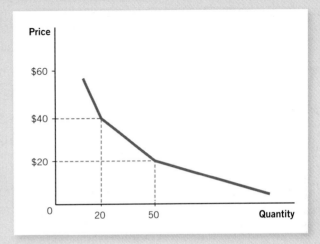

3.  Explain the logical error in the following sen-
    tence: "As ice cream sales increase, the number
    of people who drown increases sharply. There-
    fore, ice cream causes drowning."

## SOLVED PROBLEMS

2.  The slope is calculated by using the formula:

$$\text{slope} = \frac{\text{change in } y}{\text{change in } x} = \frac{\$40 - \$20}{20 - 50} = \frac{\$20}{-30} = -0.6667$$

# The Market at Work
## Supply and Demand

**Demand matters more than supply.**

What do Starbucks, Nordstrom, and Microsoft have in common? If you guessed that they all have headquarters in Seattle, that's true. But even

more interesting is that each company supplies a product much in demand by consumers. Starbucks supplies coffee from coast to coast and seems to be everywhere someone

wants a cup of coffee. Nordstrom, a giant retailer with hundreds of department stores, supplies fashion apparel to meet a broad spectrum of individual demand, from the basics to designer collections. Microsoft supplies software for customers all over the world. Demand for Microsoft products has made large fortunes for founder Bill Gates and the other investors in the company.

Notice the two recurring words in the previous paragraph: "supply" and "demand." These words are consistently used by economists when describing how an economy functions. Many people think that demand matters more than supply. This occurs because most people have much more experience as buyers than as sellers. Often our first instinct is to wonder how much something costs to buy rather than how much it costs to produce. This one-sided impression of the market undermines our ability to fully appreciate how prices are determined. To help correct this misconception, this chapter describes how markets work and the nature of competition. To shed light on the process, we will introduce the formal model of demand and supply. We will begin by looking at demand and supply separately. Then we will combine them to see how they interact to establish the market price and determine how much is produced.

Black Friday crush at Target.

# BIG QUESTIONS

* What are the fundamentals of markets?
* What determines demand?
* What determines supply?
* How do supply and demand shifts affect a market?

## What Are the Fundamentals of Markets?

In a **market economy**, resources are allocated among households and firms with little or no government interference.

Markets bring trading partners together to create order out of chaos. Companies supply goods and services, and customers want to obtain the goods and services that companies supply. In a **market economy**, resources are allocated among households and firms with little or no government interference. Adam Smith, the founder of modern economics, described the dynamic best: "It is not from the benevolence of the butcher, the brewer, or the baker, that we expect our dinner, but from their regard to their own interest." In other words, producers earn a living by selling the products that consumers want. Consumers are also motivated by self-interest; they must decide how to use their money to select the goods that they need or want the most. This process, which Adam Smith called the *invisible hand*, guides resources to their highest-valued use.

The exchange of goods and services in a market economy happens through prices that are established in markets. Those prices change according to the level of demand for a product and how much is supplied. For instance, hotel rates near Disney World are reduced in the fall when demand is low, and they peak in March near the week of Easter when spring break occurs. If spring break takes you to a ski resort instead, you will find lots of company and high prices. But if you are looking for an outdoor adventure during the summer, ski resorts have plenty of lodging available at great rates.

Similarly, many parents know how hard it is to find a reasonably priced

Peak season is expensive . . .

hotel room in a college town on graduation weekend. Likewise, a pipeline break or unsettled political conditions in the Middle East can disrupt the supply of oil and cause the price of gasoline to spike overnight. When higher gas prices continue over a period of time, consumers respond by changing their driving habits or buying more fuel-efficient cars.

Why does all of this happen? Supply and demand tell the story. We will begin our exploration of supply and demand by looking at where they interact—in markets. The degree of control over the market price is the distinguishing feature between *competitive markets* and *imperfect markets*.

## Competitive Markets

Buyers and sellers of a specific good or service come together to form a market. Formally, a market is a collection of buyers and sellers of a particular product or service. The buyers create the demand for the product, while the sellers produce the supply. It is the interaction of

. . . but off-season is a bargain.

the buyers and sellers in a market that establishes the price and the quantity produced of a particular good or the amount of a service offered.

Markets exist whenever goods and services are exchanged. Some markets are online, and others operate in traditional "brick and mortar" stores. Pike Place Market in Seattle is a collection of markets spread across nine acres. For over a hundred years, it has brought together buyers and sellers of fresh, organic, and specialty foods. Since there are a number of buyers and sellers for each type of product, we say that the markets at Pike Place are *competitive*. A **competitive market** is one in which there are so many buyers and sellers that each has only a small impact on the market price and output. In fact, the impact is so small that it is negligible.

> A **competitive market** exists when there are so many buyers and sellers that each has only a small impact on the market price and output.

At Pike Place Market, like other local produce markets, the goods sold are similar from vendor to vendor. Because each buyer and seller is small relative to the whole market, no single buyer or seller has any influence over the market price. These two characteristics—similar goods and many participants—create a highly competitive market in which the price and quantity sold are determined by the market rather than by any one person or business.

To understand how this works, let's take a look at sales of salmon at Pike Place Market. On any given day, dozens of vendors sell salmon at this market. So, if a single vendor is absent or runs out of salmon, the quantity supplied that day will not be significantly altered—the remaining sellers will have no trouble filling the void. The same is true for those buying salmon—customers will have no trouble finding

One of many vendors at Pike Place Market

salmon at the remaining vendors. Whether a particular salmon buyer decides to show up on a given day makes little difference when hundreds of buyers visit the market each day. No single buyer or seller has any appreciable influence over the price that prevails in the salmon market. As a result, the market for salmon at Pike Place Market is a competitive one.

An **imperfect market** is one in which either the buyer or the seller has an influence on the market price.

A **monopoly** exists when a single company supplies the entire market for a particular good or service.

The **quantity demanded** is the amount of a good or service that buyers are willing and able to purchase at the current price.

The Empire State Building has the best view in New York City.

## Imperfect Markets

Markets are not always competitive, though. An **imperfect market** is one in which either the buyer or the seller has an influence on the market price. For example, the Empire State Building affords a unique view of Manhattan. Not surprisingly, the cost of taking the elevator to the top of the building is not cheap. But many customers buy the tickets anyway because they have decided that the view is worth the price. The managers of the Empire State Building can set a high price for tickets because there is no other place in New York City with such a great view. From this, we see that when sellers produce goods and services that are different from their competitors', they gain some control, or leverage, over the price that they charge. The more unusual the product being sold, the more control the seller has over the price. When a seller has some control over the price, we say that the market is imperfect. Specialized products, such as popular video games, front-row concert tickets, or dinner reservations at a trendy restaurant, give the seller substantial pricing power.

In between the highly competitive environment at the Pike Place Market and markets characterized by a lack of competition, such as the Empire State Building with its iconic view, there are many other varieties of markets. Some, like the market for fast-food restaurants, are highly competitive but sell products that are not identical. Other businesses—for example, Comcast cable—function like *monopolies*. A **monopoly** exists when a single company supplies the entire market for a particular good or service. Different market structures such as monopoly need their own kind of analysis, but even in imperfect markets, the forces of supply and demand have a significant influence on producer and consumer behavior. For the time being, we'll keep our analysis focused on supply and demand in competitive markets.

# What Determines Demand?

Demand exists when an individual or a group wants something badly enough to pay or trade for it. How much an individual or a group actually buys will depend on the price. In economics, the amount of a good or service purchased at the current price is known as the **quantity demanded**.

# The Invisible Hand

Why is the fish you want for dinner available in the store? It is because at each point in the economy's supply chain, the participants are concerned with their own profit. The process starts with the boat that catches the fish, then moves to the processing facility, to the truck, and finally to the store where the clerk sells the fish to you and me. At each step, the participant works to deliver the fish because they are acting in their own self-interest—matching supply to demand as if guided by an invisible hand.

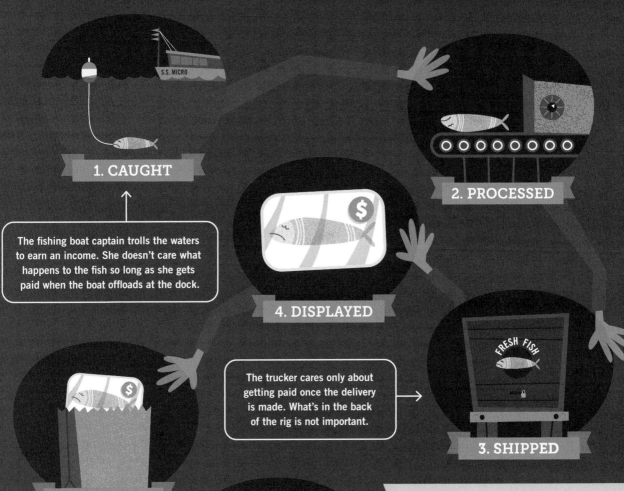

**1. CAUGHT**

**2. PROCESSED**

**4. DISPLAYED**

**3. SHIPPED**

**5. PURCHASED**

**6. EATEN**

The fishing boat captain trolls the waters to earn an income. She doesn't care what happens to the fish so long as she gets paid when the boat offloads at the dock.

The trucker cares only about getting paid once the delivery is made. What's in the back of the rig is not important.

The consumers care about freshness and price. They don't care to know the name of the fishing captain or trucker that brought the fish to the store for them to enjoy.

## REVIEW QUESTIONS

- What if someone in the supply chain is not allowed to earn a profit? How will this affect their actions and the supply chain as a whole?

- If fewer Alaskan salmon are caught, what will happen the price of salmon?

# PRACTICE WHAT YOU KNOW

## Markets and the Nature of Competition

Question: Which of the following are competitive markets?

1. Gas stations at a busy interstate exit
2. A furniture store in an isolated small town
3. A fresh produce stand at a farmer's market

Is this a competitive market?

**Answers**

1. Because each gas station sells the same product and competes for the same customers, they often charge the same price. This is a competitive market. However, gas stations also differentiate themselves by offering many conveniences such as fast food, clean restrooms, ATM machines, and so forth. The result is that individual stations have some market power.

2. Residents would have to travel a significant distance to find another store. This allows the small-town store to charge more than other furniture stores. The furniture store has some monopoly power. This is not a competitive market.

3. Since consumers can buy fresh produce in season from many stands at a farmer's market, individual vendors have very little market pricing power. They must charge the same price as other vendors in order to attract customers. This is a competitive market.

When the price of a good increases, consumers often respond by purchasing less of the good or buying something else. For instance, many consumers who would buy salmon at $5.00 per pound would likely buy something else if the price rose to $20.00 per pound. Therefore, as price goes up, quantity demanded goes down. Similarly, as price goes down, quantity demanded goes up. This inverse relationship between the price and the quantity demanded is referred to as the *law of demand*. The **law of demand** states that, all other things being equal, the quantity demanded falls when the price rises, and the quantity demanded rises when the price falls. This holds true over a wide range of goods and settings.

The **law of demand** states that, all other things being equal, quantity demanded falls when prices rise, and rises when prices fall.

## The Demand Curve

A table that shows the relationship between the price of a good and the quantity demanded is known as a **demand schedule**. Table 3.1 shows Meredith Grey's hypothetical demand schedule for salmon. When the price is $20.00 or more per pound, Meredith will not purchase any salmon. However, below $20.00 the amount that Meredith purchases is inversely related to the price. For instance, at a price of $10.00, Meredith's quantity demanded is 4 pounds per month. If the price rises to $12.50 per pound, she demands 3 pounds. Every time the price increases, Meredith buys less salmon. In contrast, every time the price falls, she buys more. If the price falls to zero, Meredith would demand 8 pounds. That is, even if the salmon is free, there is a limit to her demand because she would grow tired of eating the same thing.

A **demand schedule** is a table that shows the relationship between the price of a good and the quantity demanded.

The numbers in Meredith's demand schedule from Table 3.1 are plotted on a graph in Figure 3.1, known as a *demand curve*. A **demand curve** is a graph of the relationship between the prices in the demand schedule and the quantity demanded at those prices. For simplicity, the demand "curve" is often drawn as a straight line. Economists always place the independent variable, which is the price, on the *y* axis, and the dependent variable, which is the quantity demanded, on the *x* axis. The relationship between the price and the quantity demanded produces a downward-sloping curve. In Figure 3.1, we see that as the price rises from $0.00 to $20.00 along the *y* axis, the quantity demanded decreases from 8 to 0 pounds along the *x* axis.

A **demand curve** is a graph of the relationship between the prices in the demand schedule and the quantity demanded at those prices.

## Market Demand

So far, we have studied individual demand, but markets comprise many different buyers. In this section, we will examine the collective demand of all of the buyers in a given market.

### TABLE 3.1

**Meredith's Demand Schedule for Salmon**

| Price of salmon (per pound) | Pounds of salmon demanded (per month) |
|---|---|
| $20.00 | 0 |
| $17.50 | 1 |
| $15.00 | 2 |
| $12.50 | 3 |
| $10.00 | 4 |
| $ 7.50 | 5 |
| $ 5.00 | 6 |
| $ 2.50 | 7 |
| $ 0.00 | 8 |

FIGURE 3.1

**Meredith's Demand Curve for Salmon**

Meredith's demand curve for salmon plots the data from Table 3.1. When the price of salmon is $10.00 per pound, she buys 4 pounds. If the price rises to $12.50 per pound, Meredith reduces the quantity that she buys to 3 pounds. The figure illustrates the law of demand by showing a negative relationship between price and the quantity demanded.

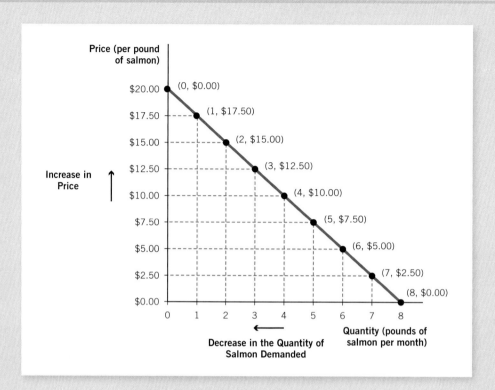

Price (per pound of salmon)

Increase in Price

Decrease in the Quantity of Salmon Demanded

Quantity (pounds of salmon per month)

**Market demand**
is the sum of all the individual quantities demanded by each buyer in the market at each price.

The **market demand** is the sum of all the individual quantities demanded by each buyer in a market at each price. During a typical day at Pike Place Market, over 100 individuals buy salmon. However, to make our analysis simpler, let's assume that our market consists of only two buyers, Derek and Meredith, each of whom enjoys eating salmon. Figure 3.2 shows individual demand schedules for the two people in this market, a combined market demand schedule, and the corresponding graphs. At a price of $10.00 per pound, Derek buys 2 pounds a month, while Meredith buys 4 pounds. To determine the market demand curve, we add Derek's 2 pounds to Meredith's 4 for a total of 6. As you can see in the table within Figure 3.2, by adding Derek and Meredith's demand we arrive at the total (that is, combined) market demand. The law of demand is shown on any demand curve with movements up or down the curve that reflect the effect of a change in price on the quantity demanded for the good or service. Only a change in price can cause a movement along a demand curve.

## Shifts in the Demand Curve

We have examined the relationship between price and quantity demanded. This relationship, described by the law of demand, shows us that when price changes, consumers respond by altering the amount they purchase. But in addition to price, many other variables influence how much of a good or service is purchased. For instance, news about the possible risks or benefits associated with the consumption of a good or service can change overall demand.

## FIGURE 3.2

**Calculating Market Demand**

To calculate the market demand for salmon, we add Derek's demand and Meredith's demand.

| Price of salmon (per pound) | Derek's demand (per month) | Meredith's demand (per month) | Combined market demand |
|---|---|---|---|
| $20.00 | 0 | 0 | 0 |
| $17.50 | 0 | 1 | 1 |
| $15.00 | 1 | 2 | 3 |
| $12.50 | 1 | 3 | 4 |
| $10.00 | 2 | 4 | 6 |
| $ 7.50 | 2 | 5 | 7 |
| $ 5.00 | 3 | 6 | 9 |
| $ 2.50 | 3 | 7 | 10 |
| $ 0.00 | 4 | 8 | 12 |

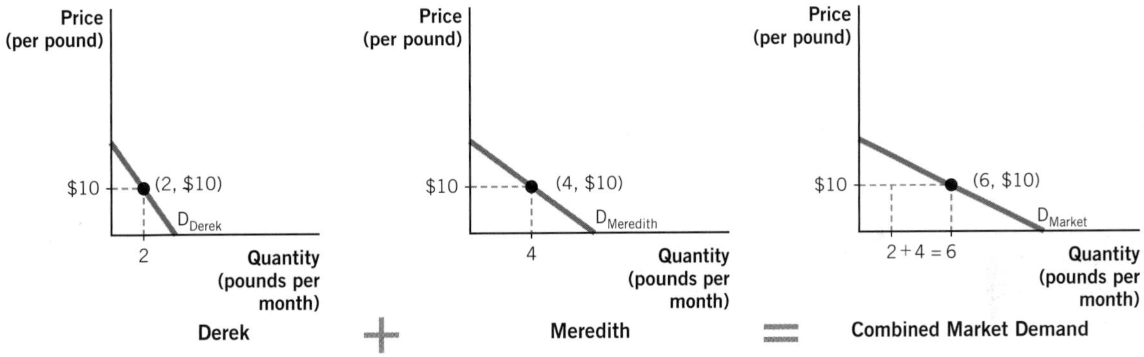

Suppose that the government issues a nationwide safety warning that cautions against eating cantaloupe because of a recent discovery of the *Listeria* bacteria in some melons. The government warning would cause consumers to buy fewer cantaloupes at any given price, and overall demand would decline. Looking at Figure 3.3, we see that an overall decline in demand will cause the entire demand curve to shift to the left of the original curve (which represents 6 cantaloupes), from $D_1$ to $D_2$. Note that though the price remains at $5 per cantaloupe, demand has moved from 6 melons to 3. Figure 3.3 also shows what does *not* cause a shift in demand curve: the price. The orange arrow along $D_1$ indicates that the quantity demanded will rise or fall in response to a price change. *A price change causes a movement along a given demand curve, but it cannot cause a shift in the demand curve.*

A decrease in overall demand causes the demand curve to shift to the left. What about when a variable causes overall demand to increase? Suppose that the press has just announced the results of a medical study indicating that cantaloupe contains a natural substance that lowers cholesterol. Because of the newly discovered health benefits of cantaloupe, overall demand for it would increase. This increase in demand would shift the demand curve to the right, from $D_1$ to $D_3$, as Figure 3.3 shows.

In the example above, we saw that demand shifted because of changes in consumers' tastes and preferences. However, there are many different variables that can shift demand. These include changes in buyers' income, the price of related goods, changes in buyers' taste and preferences, expectations regarding the future price, and the number of buyers.

*If a new medical study indicates that eating more cantaloupe lowers cholesterol, would this finding cause a shift in demand or a slide along the demand curve?*

Figure 3.4 provides an overview of the variables or factors that can shift demand. The easiest way to keep all of these elements straight is to ask yourself a simple question: *Would this change cause me to buy more or less of the good?* If the change lowers your demand for the good, you shift the demand curve to the left. If the change increases your demand for the good, you shift the curve to the right.

## FIGURE 3.3

### A Shift in the Demand Curve

When the price changes, the quantity demanded changes along the existing demand curve in the direction of the orange arrow. A shift in the demand curve, indicated by the black arrows, occurs when something other than price changes.

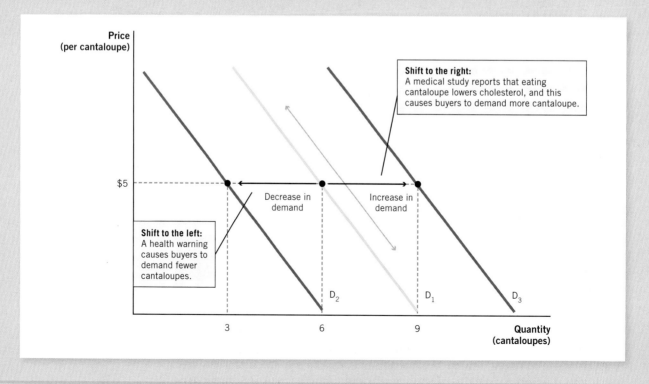

## FIGURE 3.4

**Factors That Shift the Demand Curve**

The demand curve shifts to the left when a factor adversely affects—decreases—demand. The demand curve shifts to the right when a factor positively affects—increases—demand. (*Note*: a change in price does not cause a shift. Price changes cause slides along the demand curve.)

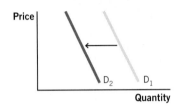

**Factors That Shift Demand to the Left (Decrease Demand)**

- Income falls (demand for a normal good).
- Income rises (demand for an inferior good).
- The price of a substitute good falls.
- The price of a complementary good rises.
- The good falls out of style.
- There is a belief that the future price of the good will decline.
- The number of buyers in the market falls.

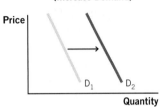

**Factors That Shift Demand to the Right (Increase Demand)**

- Income rises (demand for a normal good).
- Income falls (demand for an inferior good).
- The price of a substitute good rises.
- The price of a complementary good falls.
- The good is currently in style.
- There is a belief that the future price of the good will rise.
- The number of buyers in the market increases.

## Changes in Income

When your income goes up, you have more to spend. Assuming that prices don't change, individuals with higher incomes are able to buy more of what they want. Similarly, when your income declines, your purchasing power, or how much you can afford, falls. In either case, the amount of income you make affects your overall demand.

When economists look at how consumers spend, they often differentiate between two types of goods: *normal* and *inferior*. A consumer will buy more of a **normal good** as his or her income goes up (assuming all other factors remain constant). An example of a normal good is a meal at a restaurant. When income goes up, the demand for restaurant meals increases and the demand curve shifts to the right. Similarly, if income falls and the demand for restaurant meals goes down, the demand curve shifts to the left.

While a consumer with an increase in income may purchase more of some things, the additional purchasing power will mean that he or she purchases less of other things, such as *inferior goods*. An **inferior good** is purchased out of necessity rather than choice. Examples include used cars as opposed to new cars, rooms in boarding houses as opposed to one's own apartment or house, and hamburger as opposed to filet mignon. As income goes up, consumers

Consumers buy more of a **normal good** as income rises, holding other things constant.

An **inferior good** is purchased out of necessity rather than choice.

buy less of an inferior good because they can afford something better. Within a specific product market, you can often find examples of inferior and normal goods in the form of different brands.

## The Price of Related Goods

Another factor that can shift the demand curve is the price of related goods. Certain goods directly influence the demand for other goods. These goods are known as *complements* and *substitutes*. **Complements** are two goods that are used together. **Substitutes** are two goods that are used in place of each other.

**Complements**
are two goods that are used together. When the price of a complementary good rises, the demand for the related good goes down.

**Substitutes**
are two goods that are used in place of each other. When the price of a substitute good rises, the quantity demanded falls and the demand for the related good goes up.

Consider this pair of complements: color ink cartridges and photo paper. You need both to print a photo in color. What happens when the price of one—say, color ink cartridges—rises? As you would expect, the quantity demanded of ink cartridges goes down. But demand for its complement, photo paper, also goes down. This is because people are not likely to use one without the other.

Substitute goods work the opposite way. When the price of a substitute good increases, the quantity demanded declines and the demand for the alternative good increases. For example, if the price of the Nintendo Wii goes up and the price of Microsoft's Xbox remains unchanged, the demand for Xbox will increase while the quantity demanded of the Wii will decline.

## Changes in Tastes and Preferences

In fashion, types of apparel go in and out of style quickly. Walk into Nordstrom or another clothing retailer, and you will see that fashion changes from season to season and year to year. For instance, what do you think of Madras shorts? They were popular 20 years ago and they may be popular again now, but it is safe to assume that in a few years Madras shorts will once again go out of style. While something is popular, demand increases. As soon as it falls out of favor, you can expect demand for it to return to its former level. Tastes and preferences can change quickly, and this fluctuation alters the demand for a particular good.

Though changes in fashion trends are usually purely subjective, other changes in preferences are often the result of new information about the goods and services that we buy. Recall our example of shifting demand for cantaloupe as the result of either the *Listeria* infection or new positive medical findings. This is one example of how information can influence consumers' preferences. Contamination would cause a decrease in demand because people would no longer care to eat cantaloupe. In contrast, if people learn that eating cantaloupe lowers cholesterol, their demand for the melon will go up.

## Expectations Regarding the Future Price

Have you ever waited to purchase a sweater because warm weather was right around the corner and you expected the price to come down? Conversely, have you ever purchased an airline ticket well in advance because you figured that the price would rise as the flight filled up? In both cases, expectations about the future influenced your current demand. If we expect a price to be higher tomorrow, we are likely to buy more today to beat the price increase. This leads to an increase in current demand. Likewise, if you expect a price to decline soon, you might delay your purchases to try to capitalize on a lower price in the future. An expectation of a lower price in the future will therefore decrease current demand.

Fashion faux pas, or *c'est magnifique?*

# PRACTICE WHAT YOU KNOW

## Shift or Slide?

Cheap pizza or . . .

. . . cheap drinks?

Suppose that a local pizza place likes to run a "late-night special" after 11 p.m. The owners have contacted you for some advice. One of the owners tells you, "We want to increase the demand for our pizza." He proposes two marketing ideas to accomplish this:

**1.** Reduce the price of large pizzas.

**2.** Reduce the price of a complementary good—for example, offer two half-priced bottles or cans of soda with every large pizza ordered.

**Question: What will you recommend?**

**Answer:** First, consider why "late-night specials" exist in the first place. Since most people prefer to eat dinner early in the evening, the store has to encourage late-night patrons to buy pizzas by stimulating demand. "Specials" of all sorts are used during periods of low demand when regular prices would leave the establishment largely empty.

Next, look at what the question asks. The owners want to know which option would "increase demand" more. The question is very specific; it is looking for something that will increase (or shift) demand.

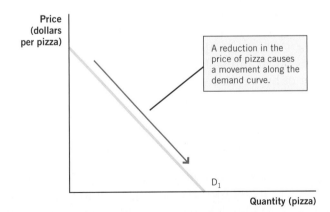

*A reduction in the price of pizza causes a movement along the demand curve.*

*(CONTINUED)*

*(CONTINUED)*

Consider the first option, a reduction in the price of pizzas. Let's look at this graphically (see above). A reduction in the price of a large pizza causes a movement along the demand curve, or a change in the quantity demanded.

Now consider the second option, a reduction in the price of a complementary good. Let's look at this graphically (see below). A reduction in the price of a complementary good (like soda) causes the entire demand curve to shift. This is the correct answer, since the question asks which marketing idea would increase (or shift) demand more.

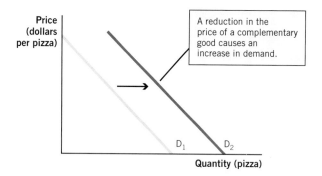

Recall that a reduction in the price of a complementary good shifts the demand curve to the right. This is the correct answer by definition! The other answer, cutting the price of pizzas, will cause an increase in the quantity demanded, or a movement along the existing demand curve.

If you move along a curve instead of shifting it, you will analyze the problem incorrectly.

## The Number of Buyers

Recall that the market demand curve is the sum of all individual demand curves. Therefore, another way for the market demand to increase is for more individual buyers to enter the market. In the United States, we add 3 million people each year to our population through immigration and births. All those new people have needs and wants like the 300 million of us who are already here. Collectively, they add about 1% to the overall size of many existing markets on an annual basis.

The number of buyers also varies by age. Consider two markets—one for baby equipment, such as diapers, high chairs, and strollers, and the other for health care, including medicine, cancer treatments, hip replacement surgery, and nursing facilities. In countries with aging populations—for example, in Italy, where the birthrate has plummeted over several generations—the demand for baby equipment will decline and the demand for health care will expand. Therefore, demographic changes in society are another source of shifts in demand. In many markets, ranging from movie theater attendance to home ownership, population trends play an important role in determining whether the market is expanding or contracting.

# Shifting the Demand Curve

### *The Hudsucker Proxy*

This 1994 film chronicles the introduction of the hula hoop, a toy that set off one of the greatest fads in U.S. history. According to Wham-O, the manufacturer of the hoop, when the toy was first introduced in the late 1950s over 25 million were sold in four months.

One scene from the movie clearly illustrates the difference between movements along the demand curve and a shift of the entire demand curve.

The Hudsucker Corporation has decided to sell the hula hoop for $1.79. We see the toy-store owner leaning next to the front door waiting for customers to enter. But business is slow. The movie cuts to the president of the company, played by Tim Robbins, sitting behind a big desk waiting to hear about sales of the new toy. It is not doing well. So the store lowers the price, first to $1.59, then to $1.49, and so on, until finally the hula hoop is "free with any purchase." But even this is not enough to attract consumers, so the toy-store owner throws the unwanted hula hoops into the alley behind the store.

One of the unwanted toys rolls across the street and around the block before landing at the foot of a boy who is skipping school. He picks up the hula hoop and tries it out. He is a natural. When school lets out, a throng of students rounds the corner and sees him playing with the hula hoop. Suddenly, everyone wants a hula hoop and there is a run on the toy store. Now preferences have changed, and the overall demand has increased. The hula hoop craze is born. In economic terms, we can say that the increased demand has shifted the entire demand curve to the right. The toy store responds by ordering new hula hoops and raising the price to $3.99—the new market price after the increase, or shift, in demand.

This scene reminds us that changes in price cannot shift

How did the hula hoop craze start?

the demand curve. Shifts in demand can only happen when an outside event influences human behavior. The graph below uses demand curves to show us the effect.

**First part of the scene:** The price drops from $1.79 to "free with any purchase." Demand does not change—we only slide downward along the demand curve ($D_1$), resulting in a negligible increase in the quantity demanded.

**Second part of the scene:** The hula hoop craze begins and kids run to the toy store. The sudden change in behavior is evidence of a change in tastes, which shifts the demand curve to the right ($D_2$).

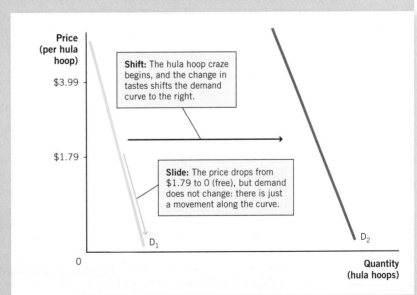

Price (per hula hoop)

$3.99

$1.79

**Shift:** The hula hoop craze begins, and the change in tastes shifts the demand curve to the right.

**Slide:** The price drops from $1.79 to 0 (free), but demand does not change: there is just a movement along the curve.

$D_1$

$D_2$

0

Quantity (hula hoops)

# What Determines Supply?

Even though we have learned a great deal about demand, our understanding of markets is incomplete without also analyzing supply. Let's start by focusing on the behavior of producers interested in selling fresh salmon at Pike Place Market.

We have seen that with demand, price and output are negatively related. With supply, however, the price level and quantity supplied are positively related. For instance, few producers would sell salmon if the market price was $2.50 per pound, but many would sell it if the price was $20.00. (At $20.00, producers earn more profit than when the price they receive is $2.50.) The **quantity supplied** is the amount of a good or service that producers are willing and able to sell at the current price. Higher prices cause the quantity supplied to increase. Conversely, lower prices cause the quantity supplied to decrease.

When price increases, producers often respond by offering more for sale. As price goes down, quantity supplied also goes down. This direct relationship between price and quantity supplied is referred to as the *law of supply*. The **law of supply** states that, all other things being equal, the quantity supplied increases when the price rises, and the quantity supplied falls when the price falls. This law holds true over a wide range of goods and settings.

The **quantity supplied** is the amount of a good or service that producers are willing and able to sell at the current price.

The **law of supply** states that, all other things being equal, the quantity supplied of a good rises when the price of the good rises, and falls when the price of the good falls.

## The Supply Curve

A **supply schedule** is a table that shows the relationship between the price of a good and the quantity supplied. The supply schedule for salmon in Table 3.2 shows how many pounds of salmon Sol Amon, owner of Pure Food Fish, would sell each month at different prices (Pure Food Fish is a fish stand that sells all kinds of freshly caught seafood). When the market price is $20.00 per pound, Sol is willing to sell 800 pounds. At $12.50, Sol's quantity offered is 500 pounds. If the price falls to $10.00, he offers 100 fewer pounds, or 400. Every time the price falls, Sol offers less salmon. This means he is constantly adjusting the amount he offers. As the price of salmon falls, so does Sol's profit from selling it. Since Sol's livelihood depends on selling seafood, he has to find a way to compensate for the lost income. So he might offer more cod instead.

A **supply schedule** is a table that shows the relationship between the price of a good and the quantity supplied.

Sol and the other seafood vendors must respond to price changes by adjusting what they offer for sale in the market. This is why Sol offers more salmon when the price rises, and less salmon when the price declines.

When we plot the supply schedule in Table 3.2, we get the *supply curve* shown in Figure 3.5. A **supply curve** is a graph of the relationship between the prices in the supply schedule and the quantity supplied at those prices. As you can see in Figure 3.5, this relationship produces an upward-sloping curve. Sellers are more willing to supply the market when prices are high, since this generates more profits for the business. The upward-sloping curve means that the slope of the supply curve is positive, which illustrates a direct relationship between the price and the quantity offered for sale. For instance, when the price of salmon increases from $10.00 to $12.50 per pound, Pure Food Fish will increase the quantity it supplies to the market from 400 to 500 pounds.

A **supply curve** is a graph of the relationship between the prices in the supply schedule and the quantity supplied at those prices.

| TABLE 3.2 |
| --- |

**Pure Food Fish's Supply Schedule for Salmon**

| Price of salmon (per pound) | Pounds of salmon supplied (per month) |
| --- | --- |
| $20.00 | 800 |
| $17.50 | 700 |
| $15.00 | 600 |
| $12.50 | 500 |
| $10.00 | 400 |
| $ 7.50 | 300 |
| $ 5.00 | 200 |
| $ 2.50 | 100 |
| $ 0.00 | 0 |

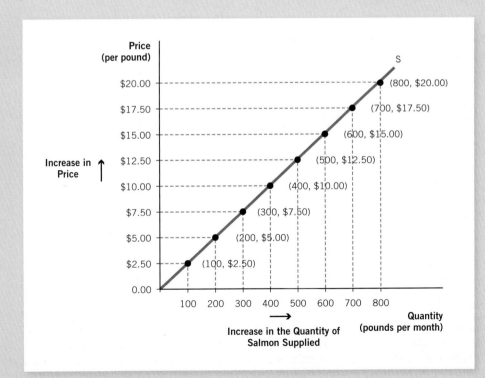

## FIGURE 3.5

**Pure Food Fish's Supply Curve for Salmon**

Pure Food Fish's supply curve for salmon plots the data from Table 3.2. When the price of salmon is $10.00 per pound, Pure Food Fish supplies 400 pounds. If the price rises to $12.50 per pound, Pure Food Fish increases the quantity that it supplies to 500 pounds. The figure illustrates the law of supply by showing a positive relationship between price and the quantity supplied.

## Market Supply

**Market supply**
is the sum of the quantities
supplied by each seller in
the market at each price.

Sol Amon is not the only vendor selling fish at the Pike Place Market. The **market supply** is the sum of the quantities supplied by each seller in the market at each price. However, to make our analysis simpler, let's assume that our market consists of just two sellers, City Fish and Pure Food Fish, each of which sells salmon. Figure 3.6 shows supply schedules for those two fish sellers and the combined, total-market supply schedule and the corresponding graphs.

Looking at the supply schedule (the table within the figure), you can see that at a price of $10.00 per pound, City Fish supplies 100 pounds of salmon, while Pure Food Fish supplies 400. To determine the total market supply, we add City Fish's 100 pounds to Pure Food Fish's 400 for a total market supply of 500.

## FIGURE 3.6

### Calculating Market Supply

Market supply is calculated by adding together the amount supplied by individual vendors. Each vendor's supply, listed in the second and third columns of the table, is illustrated graphically below. The total supply, shown in the last column of the table, is illustrated in the Combined Market Supply graph below.

| Price of salmon (per pound) | City Fish's supply (per month) | Pure Food Fish's supply (per month) | Combined Market supply (pounds of salmon) |
|---|---|---|---|
| $20.00 | 200 | 800 | 1000 |
| $17.50 | 175 | 700 | 875 |
| $15.00 | 150 | 600 | 750 |
| $12.50 | 125 | 500 | 625 |
| $10.00 | 100 | 400 | 500 |
| $ 7.50 | 75 | 300 | 375 |
| $ 5.00 | 50 | 200 | 250 |
| $ 2.50 | 25 | 100 | 125 |
| $ 0.00 | 0 | 0 | 0 |

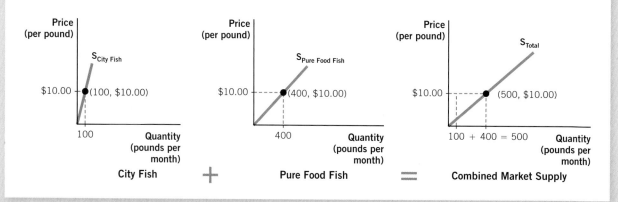

## Shifts in the Supply Curve

When a variable other than the price changes, the entire supply curve shifts. For instance, suppose that beverage scientists at Starbucks discover a new way to brew a richer coffee at half the cost. The new process would increase the company's profits because its costs of supplying a cup of coffee would go down. The increased profits as a result of lower costs motivate Starbucks to sell more coffee and open new stores. Therefore, overall supply increases. Looking at Figure 3.7, we see that the supply curve shifts to the right of the original curve, from $S_1$ to $S_2$. Note that the retail price of coffee ($3 per cup) has not changed.

The first Starbucks opened in 1971 in Pike Place Market.

When we shift the curve, we assume that price is constant and that something else has changed. In this case, the new brewing process, which has reduced the cost of producing coffee, has stimulated additional supply.

### FIGURE 3.7

**A Shift in the Supply Curve**

When price changes, the quantity supplied changes along the existing supply curve, illustrated here by the orange arrow. A shift in supply occurs when something other than price changes, illustrated by the black arrows.

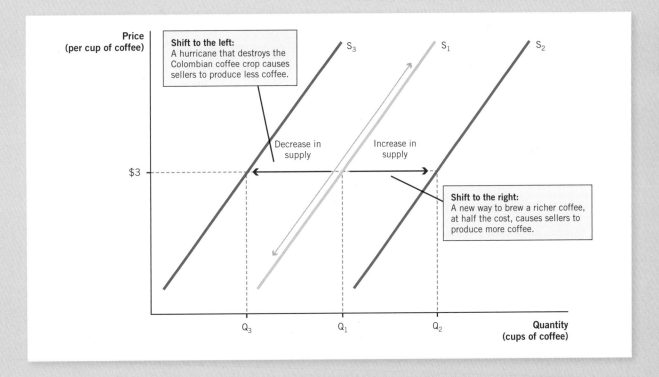

We have just seen that an increase in supply causes the supply curve to shift to the right. But what happens when a variable causes supply to decrease? Suppose that a hurricane devastates the coffee crop in Colombia and reduces world supply by 10% for that year. There is no way to make up for the destroyed coffee crop, and for the rest of the year at least, the quantity of coffee supplied will be less than the previous year. This decrease in supply shifts the supply curve in Figure 3.7 to the left, from $S_1$ to $S_3$.

Many variables can shift supply, but Figure 3.7 also reminds us of what does *not* cause a shift in supply: the price. Recall that price is the variable that causes the supply curve to slope upward. The orange arrow along $S_1$ indicates that the quantity supplied will rise or fall in response to a price change. *A price change causes a movement along the supply curve, not a shift in the curve.*

Factors that shift the supply curve include the cost of inputs, changes in technology and the production process, taxes and subsidies, the number of firms in the industry, and price expectations. Figure 3.8 provides an overview of these variables that shift the supply curve. The easiest way to keep them all straight is to ask yourself a simple question: *Would the change cause a*

## FIGURE 3.8

### Factors That Shift the Supply Curve

The supply curve shifts to the left when a factor negatively affects—decreases—supply. The supply curve shifts to the right when a factor positively affects—increases—supply. (*Note*: a change in price does not cause a shift. Price changes cause slides along the supply curve.)

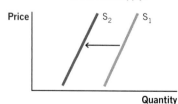

**Factors That Shift Supply to the Left**
**(Decrease Supply)**

- The cost of an input rises.
- Business taxes increase or subsidies decrease.
- The number of sellers decreases.
- The price of the product is anticipated to rise in the future.

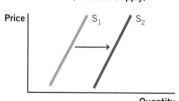

**Factors That Shift Supply to the Right**
**(Increase Supply)**

- The cost of an input falls.
- Business taxes decrease or subsidies increase.
- The number of sellers increases.
- The price of the product is expected to fall in the future.
- The business deploys more efficient technology.

*business to produce more or less of the good?* If the change would lower the business's willingness to supply the good or service, the supply curve shifts to the left. If the change would increase the business's willingness to supply the good or service, the supply curve shifts to the right.

## The Cost of Inputs

**Inputs** are resources used in the production process. Inputs can take a number of forms and may include workers, equipment, raw materials, buildings, and capital. Each of these resources is critical to the production process. When the prices of inputs change, so does the seller's profit margin. If the cost of inputs declines, profit margins improve. Improved profit margins make the firm more willing to supply the good. So, for example, if Starbucks is able to purchase coffee beans at a significantly reduced price, it will want to supply more coffee. Conversely, higher input costs reduce profits. For instance, at Starbucks, the salaries of store employees, or baristas as they are commonly

**Inputs**
are resources used in the production process.

called, are a large part of the production cost. An increase in the minimum wage would require Starbucks to pay its workers more. This would raise the cost of making coffee, cut into Starbucks' profits, and make Starbucks less willing to supply coffee at the same price.

## Changes in Technology or the Production Process

Technology encompasses knowledge that producers use to make their products. An improvement in technology enables a producer to increase output with the same resources or to produce a given level of output with fewer resources. For example, if a new espresso machine works twice as fast as the old technology, Starbucks could serve its customers more quickly, reduce long lines, and increase the number of sales it makes. As a result, Starbucks would be willing to produce and sell more espressos at each price in its established menu. In other words, if the producers of a good discover a new and improved technology or a better production process, there will be an increase in supply; the supply curve for the good will shift to the right.

Baristas' wages make up a large share of the cost of selling coffee.

## Taxes and Subsidies

Taxes placed on suppliers are an added cost of doing business. For example, if property taxes are increased, this raises the cost of doing business. A firm may attempt to pass along the tax to consumers through higher prices, but this will discourage sales. In other cases, the firm will simply have to accept the taxes as an added cost of doing business. Either way, a tax makes the firm less profitable. Lower profits make the firm less willing to supply the product and, thus, shift the supply curve to the left. As a result, the overall supply declines.

The reverse is true for a subsidy, which is a payment made by the government to encourage the consumption or production of a good or service. Consider a hypothetical example where the government wants to promote flu shots for high-risk cohorts like the young and elderly. One approach would be to offer large subsidies to producers such as clinics and hospitals, offsetting the production costs of immunizing the targeted groups. The supply curve of immunizations greatly shifts to the right under the subsidy, so the price falls. As a result, vaccination rates increase over what they would be in a market where the price was determined solely by the intersection of the market demand and supply curves.

### The Number of Firms in the Industry

We saw that when there were more total buyers, the demand curve shifted to the right. A similar dynamic happens with an increase in the number of sellers in an industry. Each additional firm that enters the market increases the available supply of a good. In graphic form, the supply curve shifts to the right to reflect the increased production. By the same reasoning, if the number of firms in the industry decreases, the supply curve will shift to the left.

Changes in the number of firms in a market are a regular part of business. For example, if a new pizza joint opens up nearby, more pizzas can be produced and supply expands. Conversely, if a pizza shop closes, the number of pizzas produced falls and supply contracts.

### Price Expectations

A seller who expects a higher price for a product in the future may wish to delay sales until a time when it will bring a higher price. For instance, florists know that the demand for roses spikes on Valentine's Day and Mother's Day. Because of higher demand, they can charge higher prices. In order to be able to sell more flowers during the times of peak demand, many florists work longer hours and hire temporary employees. This allows them to make more deliveries and therefore increase their ability to supply flowers while the price is high.

Likewise, the expectation of lower prices in the future will cause sellers to offer more while prices are still relatively high. This is particularly noticeable in the electronics sector where newer—and much better—products are constantly being developed and released. Sellers know that their current offerings will soon be replaced by something better and that consumer demand for the existing technology will then plummet. This means that prices typically fall when a product has been on the market for a time. Since producers know that the price will fall, they supply as many of the new models as possible before the next wave of innovation cuts the price that they can charge.

## ECONOMICS IN THE REAL WORLD

### Why Do the Prices of New Electronics Always Drop?

The first personal computers released in the 1980s cost as much as $10,000. Today, a laptop computer can be purchased for less than $500. When a new technology emerges, prices are initially very high and then tend to fall rapidly. The first PCs created a profound change in the way people could work with information. Prior to the advent of the PC, complex programming could be done only on large mainframe computers that often took up as much space as a whole room. But at first only a few people could afford a PC. What makes emerging technology so expensive when it is first introduced and so inexpensive later in its life cycle? Supply and demand tell the story.

In the case of PCs and other recent technologies, both demand and supply increase through time. Demand increases as consumers find more uses for the new technology. An increase in demand, by itself, would ordinarily drive the price up. However, producers are eager to supply this new market and ramp up production quickly. Since the supply expands more rapidly than the demand, there is both an increase in the quantity sold and a lower price.

Differences in expectations account for some of the difference between the increase in supply and demand. Both parties expect the price to fall, and they react accordingly. Suppliers try to get their new products to market as quickly as possible—before the price starts to fall appreciably. Therefore, the willingness to supply the product expands quickly. Consumer demand is slower to pick up because consumers expect the price to fall. This expectation tempers their desire to buy the new technology immediately. The longer they wait, the lower the price will be. Therefore, demand does not increase as fast as the supply. ✳

Why did consumers pay $5,000 for this?

## PRACTICE WHAT YOU KNOW

### The Supply and Demand of Ice Cream

Question: Which of the following will increase the demand for ice cream?

a. A decrease in the price of the butterfat used to make ice cream

b. A decrease in the price of ice cream

c. An increase in the price of the milk used to make ice cream

d. An increase in the price of frozen yogurt, a substitute for ice cream

I scream, you scream, we all scream for ice cream.

Answer: If you answered b, you made a common mistake. A change in the price of a good cannot change overall market demand; it can only cause a movement along an existing curve. So, as important as price changes are, they are not the right answer. First, you need to look for an event that shifts the entire curve.

Answers a and c refer to the prices of butterfat and milk. Since these are the inputs of production for ice cream, a change in prices will shift the supply curve. That leaves answer d as the only possibility. Answer d is correct since the increase in the price of frozen yogurt will cause the consumer to look elsewhere. Consumers will substitute away from frozen yogurt and toward ice cream. This shift in consumer behavior will result in an increase in the demand for ice cream even though its price remains the same.

Question: Which of the following will decrease the supply of chocolate ice cream?

a. A medical report finding that consuming chocolate prevents cancer

b. A decrease in the price of chocolate ice cream

c. An increase in the price of chocolate, an ingredient used to make ice cream

d. An increase in the price of whipped cream, a complementary good

Answer: We have already seen that b cannot be the answer because a change in the price of the good cannot change supply; it can only cause a movement along an existing curve. Answers a and d would both cause a change in demand without affecting the supply curve. That leaves answer c as the only possibility. Chocolate is a necessary ingredient used in the production process. Whenever the price of an input rises, it squeezes profit margins, and this results in a decrease in supply at the existing price.

# How Do Supply and Demand Shifts Affect a Market?

We have examined supply and demand separately. Now it is time to see how the two interact. The real power and potential of supply and demand analysis is in how well it predicts prices and output in the entire market.

## Supply, Demand, and Equilibrium

Let's consider the market for salmon again. This example meets the conditions for a competitive market because the salmon sold by one vendor is essentially the same as the salmon sold by another, and there are many individual buyers.

In Figure 3.9, we see that when the price of salmon fillets is $10 per pound, consumers demand 500 pounds and producers supply 500. This is represented graphically at point E, known as the point of **equilibrium**, where the demand curve and the supply curve intersect. At this point, the two opposing forces of supply and demand are perfectly balanced.

Notice that at $10.00 per fillet, the quantity demanded equals the quantity supplied. At this price, and only this price, the entire supply of salmon in the market is sold. Moreover, every buyer who wants salmon is able to find some and every producer is able to sell his or her entire stock. We say that $10.00 is the **equilibrium price** because the quantity supplied equals the quantity demanded. The equilibrium price is also called the *market-clearing*

**Equilibrium** occurs at the point where the demand curve and the supply curve intersect.

The **equilibrium price** is the price at which the quantity supplied is equal to the quantity demanded. This is also known as the *market-clearing price.*

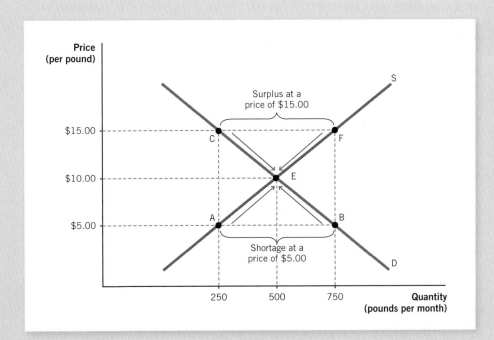

**The Salmon Market**
At the equilibrium point, E, supply and demand are perfectly balanced. At prices above the equilibrium price, a surplus of goods exists, while at prices below the equilibrium price, a shortage of goods exists.

The **equilibrium quantity** is the amount at which the quantity supplied is equal to the quantity demanded.

The **law of supply and demand** states that the market price of any good will adjust to bring the quantity supplied and the quantity demanded into balance.

*price,* since this is the only price at which no surplus or shortage of the good exists. Similarly, there is also an **equilibrium quantity**, of 500 pounds, at which the quantity supplied equals the quantity demanded. When the market is in equilibrium, we sometimes say that *the market clears* or that *the price clears the market.* The equilibrium point has a special place in economics because movements away from that point throw the market out of balance. The equilibrium process is so powerful that it is often referred to as the *law of supply and demand.* According to the **law of supply and demand**, market prices adjust to bring the quantity supplied and the quantity demanded into balance.

## Shortages and Surpluses

How does the market respond when it is not in equilibrium? Let's look at two other prices for salmon shown on the *y* axis in Figure 3.9: $5.00 and $15.00 per pound.

At a price of $5.00 per pound, salmon is quite attractive to buyers but not very profitable to sellers—the quantity demanded is 750 pounds, represented by point B on the demand curve (D). However, the quantity supplied, which is represented by point A on the supply curve (S), is only 250. So at $5.00 per pound there is an excess quantity of 500 pounds demanded. This excess demand creates disequilibrium in the market.

A **shortage** occurs whenever the quantity supplied is less than the quantity demanded.

When there is more demand for a product than sellers are willing or able to supply, we say there is a *shortage.* A **shortage** occurs whenever the quantity supplied is less than the quantity demanded. In our case, at a price of $5.00 there are three buyers for each pound of salmon. New shipments of salmon fly out the door. This is a strong signal for sellers to raise the price. As the market price increases in response to the shortage, sellers continue to increase the quantity that they offer. You can see this on the graph in Figure 3.9 by following the upward-sloping arrow from point A to point E. At the same time, as the price rises, buyers will demand an increasingly smaller quantity, represented by the upward-sloping arrow from point B to point E along the demand curve. Eventually, when the price reaches $10.00, the quantity supplied and the quantity demanded will be equal. The market will be in equilibrium.

What happens when the price is set above the equilibrium point—say, at $15.00 per pound? At this price, salmon is quite profitable for sellers but not very attractive to buyers. The quantity demanded, represented by point C on the demand curve, is 250 pounds. However, the quantity supplied, represented by point F on the supply curve, is 750. In other words, sellers provide 500 pounds more than buyers wish to purchase. This excess supply creates disequilibrium in the market. Any buyer who is willing to pay $15.00 for a pound of salmon can find some since there are three pounds available for every customer. This situation is known as a *surplus.* A **surplus**, or excess supply, occurs whenever the quantity supplied is greater than the quantity demanded.

A **surplus** occurs whenever the quantity supplied is greater than the quantity demanded.

When there is a surplus, sellers realize that salmon has been oversupplied. This is a strong signal to lower the price. As the market price decreases in response to the surplus, more buyers enter the market and purchase salmon. This is represented on the graph in Figure 3.9 by the downward-sloping arrow moving from point C to point E along the demand curve. At the same time, sellers reduce output, represented by the downward-sloping arrow moving

from point F to point E on the supply curve. As long as the surplus persists, the price will continue to fall. Eventually, the price will reach $10.00 per pound. At this point, the quantity supplied and the quantity demanded will be equal and the market will be in equilibrium again.

In competitive markets, surpluses and shortages are resolved through the process of price adjustment. Buyers who are unable to find enough salmon at $5.00 per pound compete to find the available stocks; this drives the price up. Likewise, businesses that cannot sell their product at $15.00 per pound must lower their prices to reduce inventories; this drives the price down.

Every seller and buyer has a vital role to play in the market. Venues like the Pike Place Market bring buyers and sellers together. Amazingly, all of this happens spontaneously, without the need for government planning to ensure an adequate supply of the goods that consumers need. You might think that a decentralized system would create chaos, but nothing could be further from the truth. Markets work because buyers and sellers can rapidly adjust to changes in prices. These adjustments bring balance. When markets were suppressed in communist command economies during the twentieth century, shortages were commonplace, in part because there was no market price system to signal that additional production was needed. (A command economy is one in which supply and price are regulated by the government rather than by market forces.) This led to the creation of many black markets (see Chapter 4).

How do markets respond to additional demand? In the case of the bowling cartoon shown above, the increase in demand comes from an unseen customer who wants to use a bowling lane already favored by another patron. An increase in the number of buyers causes an increase in demand. The lane is valued by two buyers, instead of just one, so the owner is contemplating a price increase! This is how markets work. Price is a mechanism to determine which buyer wants the good or service the most.

In summary, Figure 3.10 provides four examples of what happens when either the supply or the demand curve shifts. As you study these, you should develop a sense for how price and quantity are affected by changes in supply and demand. When one curve shifts, we can make a definitive statement about how price and quantity will change. In the chapter appendix that follows, we consider what happens when supply and demand change at the same time. There you will discover the challenges in simultaneously determining price and quantity when more than one variable changes.

## FIGURE 3.10

**Price and Quantity When Either Supply or Demand Changes**

| Change | Illustration | Impact on price and quantity |
|---|---|---|
| **1. Demand increases; supply does not change.** | | The demand curve shifts to the right. As a result, the equilibrium price and the equilibrium quantity increase. |
| **2. Supply increases; demand does not change.** | | The supply curve shifts to the right. As a result, the equilibrium price decreases and the equilibrium quantity increases. |
| **3. Demand decreases; supply does not change.** | | The demand curve shifts to the left. As a result, the equilibrium price and the equilibrium quantity decrease. |
| **4. Supply decreases; demand does not change.** | | The supply curve shifts to the left. As a result, the equilibrium price increases and the equilibrium quantity decreases. |

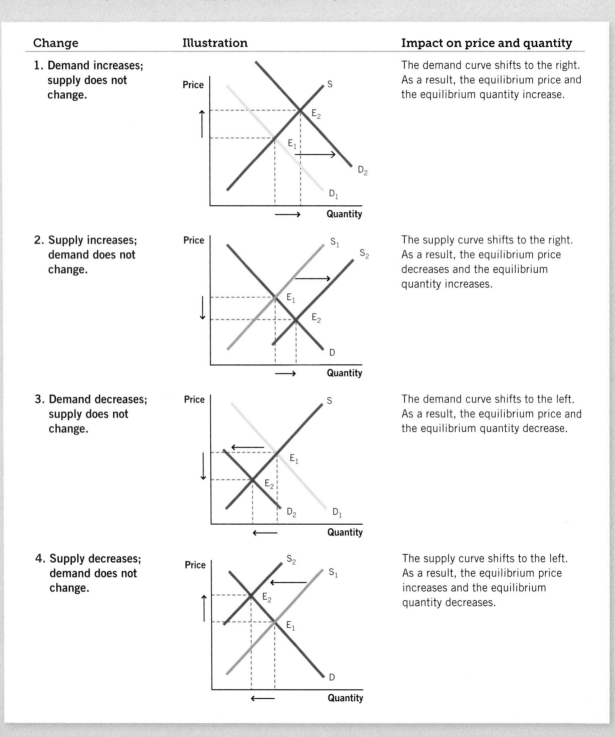

# Bringing Supply and Demand Together: Advice for Buying Your First Place

There is an old adage in real estate, "location, location, location." Why does location matter so much? Simple. Supply and demand. There are only so many places to live in any given location—that is the supply. The most desirable locations have many buyers who'd like to purchase in that area—that is the demand.

Consider for a moment all of the variables that can influence where you want to live. As you're shopping for your new home, you may want to consider proximity to where you work, your favorite restaurants, public transportation, and the best schools. You'll also want to pay attention to the crime rate, differences in local tax rates, traffic concerns, noise issues, and nearby zoning restrictions. In addition, many communities have restrictive covenants that limit how owners can use their property. Smart buyers determine how the covenants work and whether they would be happy to give up some freedom in order to maintain an attractive neighborhood. Finally, it is always a good idea to visit the neighborhood in the evening or on the weekend to meet your future neighbors before you buy. All of these variables determine the demand for any given property.

Once you've done your homework and settled on a neighborhood, you will find that property values can vary tremendously across very short distances. A home along a busy street may sell for half the price of a similar property that backs up to a quiet park a few blocks away. Properties near a subway line command a premium, as do properties with views or close access to major employers and amenities (such as parks, shopping centers, and places to eat). Here is the main point to remember, even if some of these things aren't important to you: when it comes time to sell, the location of the home will always matter. The number of potential buyers depends on the characteristics of your neighborhood and the size and condition of your property. If you want to be able to sell your place easily, you'll have to consider not only where you want to live now but who might want to live there later.

All of this discussion brings us back to supply and demand. The best locations are in short supply and high demand. The combination of low supply and high demand causes property values in those areas to rise. Likewise, less desirable locations have lower property values because demand is relatively low and the supply is relatively high. Since first-time buyers often have wish lists that far exceed their budgets, considering the costs and benefits will help you find the best available property.

There is a popular HGTV show called *Property Virgins* that follows first-time buyers through the process of buying their first home. If you have never seen the show, watching an episode is one of the best lessons in economics you'll ever get. Check it out, and remember that even though you may be new to buying property, you still can get a good deal if you use some basic economics to guide your decision.

*Where* you buy is more important than *what* you buy.

# Conclusion

Does demand matter more than supply? As you have learned in this chapter, the answer is no. Demand and supply contribute equally to the functioning of markets. Five years from now, if someone asks you what you remember about your first course in economics, you will probably respond with two words, "supply" and "demand." These two opposing forces enable economists to model market behavior through prices. Prices help establish the market equilibrium, or the price at which supply and demand are in balance. At the equilibrium point, every good and service produced has a corresponding buyer who wants to purchase it. When the market is out of equilibrium, it causes a shortage or surplus. These conditions persist until buyers and sellers have a chance to adjust the quantity they demand and the quantity they supply, respectively. This refutes the misconception we noted at the beginning of the chapter.

In the next chapter, we will apply our understanding of supply and demand to the topic of government price controls. This will give us insight into the unintended consequences of interfering in markets.

## ANSWERING THE BIG QUESTIONS

### What are the fundamentals of markets?

* A market consists of a group of buyers and sellers for a particular product or service.
* When competition is present, markets produce low prices.
* Not all markets are competitive. When suppliers have market power, markets are imperfect and prices are higher.

### What determines demand?

* The law of demand states that there is an inverse relationship between the price and the amount that the consumer wishes to purchase.
* As a result of the law of demand, the demand curve is downward sloping.
* A price change causes a movement along the demand curve, not a shift in the curve.
* Changes in something other than price cause the demand curve to shift.

## What determines supply?

* The law of supply states that there is a direct relationship between the price and the amount that is offered for sale.
* The supply curve is upward sloping.
* A price change causes a movement along the supply curve, not a shift in the curve.
* Changes in the prices of inputs, new technologies, taxes, subsidies, the number of sellers, and expectations about the future price all influence the location of the new supply curve and cause the original supply curve to shift.

## How do supply and demand shifts affect a market?

* Supply and demand interact through the process of market coordination.
* Together, supply and demand create a process that leads to equilibrium, the balancing point between the two opposing forces. The market-clearing price and output are determined at the equilibrium point.
* When the price is above the equilibrium point, a surplus exists and inventories build up. This will cause suppliers to lower their price in an effort to sell the unwanted goods. The process continues until the equilibrium price is reached.
* When the price is below the equilibrium point, a shortage exists and inventories are depleted. This will cause suppliers to raise their price in order to ration the good. The price rises until the equilibrium point is reached.

## CONCEPTS YOU SHOULD KNOW

competitive market (p. 69)
complements (p. 78)
demand curve (p. 73)
demand schedule (p. 73)
equilibrium (p. 91)
equilibrium price (p. 91)
equilibrium quantity (p. 92)
imperfect market (p. 70)
inferior good (p. 77)

inputs (p. 87)
law of demand (p. 72)
law of supply (p. 82)
law of supply and demand (p. 92)
market demand (p. 74)
market economy (p. 68)
market supply (p. 84)
monopoly (p. 70)
normal good (p. 77)

quantity demanded (p. 70)
quantity supplied (p. 82)
shortage (p. 92)
substitutes (p. 78)
supply curve (p. 82)
supply schedule (p. 82)
surplus (p. 92)

## QUESTIONS FOR REVIEW

1. What is a competitive market, and how does it depend on the existence of many buyers and sellers?

2. Why does the demand curve slope downward?

3. Does a price change cause a movement along a demand curve or a shift of the entire curve? What factors cause the entire demand curve to shift?

4. Describe the difference between inferior and normal goods.

5. Why does the supply curve slope upward?

6. Does a price change cause a movement along a supply curve or a shift of the entire curve? What factors cause the entire supply curve to shift?

7. Describe the process that leads the market toward equilibrium.

8. What happens in a competitive market when the price is above or below the equilibrium price?

9. What roles do shortages and surpluses play in the market?

## STUDY PROBLEMS (* solved at the end of the section)

1. In the song "Money, Money, Money" by ABBA, the lead singer, Anni-Frid Lyngstad, is tired of the hard work life requires and plans to marry a wealthy man. If she is successful, how would this marriage change the artist's demand for goods? How would it change her supply of labor? Illustrate both changes with supply and demand curves. Be sure to explain what is happening in the diagrams. (Note: the full lyrics for the song can be found by Googling the song title and ABBA. For inspiration, try listening to the song while you solve the problem!)

2. For each of the following scenarios, determine if there is an increase or a decrease in demand for the good in *italics*.

   a. The price of *oranges* increases.
   b. The cost of producing *tires* increases.

c. Samantha Brown, who is crazy about *air travel*, gets fired from her job.

d. A local community has an unusually wet spring and a subsequent problem with mosquitos, which can be deterred with *citronella*.

e. Many motorcycle enthusiasts enjoy riding without *helmets* (in states where this is permitted by law). The price of new motorcycles rises.

3. For each of the following scenarios, determine if there is an increase or a decrease in supply for the good in *italics*.

   a. The price of *silver* increases.
   b. Growers of *tomatoes* experience an unusually good growing season.

c. New medical evidence reports that consumption of *organic products* reduces the incidence of cancer.

d. The wages of low-skill workers, a resource used to help produce *clothing*, increase.

e. The price of movie tickets, a substitute for *video rentals*, goes up.

4. Are laser pointers and cats complements or substitutes? (Not sure? Search for videos of cats and laser pointers online.) Discuss.

✴ 5. The market for ice cream has the following demand and supply schedules:

| Price (per quart) | Quantity demanded (quarts) | Quantity supplied (quarts) |
|---|---|---|
| $2 | 100 | 30 |
| $3 | 80 | 45 |
| $4 | 60 | 60 |
| $5 | 40 | 75 |
| $6 | 20 | 90 |

a. What are the equilibrium price and equilibrium quantity in the ice cream market? Confirm your answer by graphing the demand and supply curves.

b. If the actual price was $3 per quart, what would drive the market toward equilibrium?

6. Starbucks Entertainment announced in a 2007 news release that Dave Matthews Band's *Live Trax* CD was available only at the company's coffee shops in the United States and Canada. The compilation features recordings of the band's performances dating back to 1995. Why would Starbucks and Dave Matthews have agreed to partner in this way? To come up with an answer, think about the nature of complementary goods and how both sides can benefit from this arrangement.

7. The Seattle Mariners wish to determine the equilibrium price for seats for each of the next two seasons. The supply of seats at the ballpark is fixed at 45,000.

| Price (per seat) | Quantity demanded in year 1 | Quantity demanded in year 2 | Quantity supplied |
|---|---|---|---|
| $25 | 75,000 | 60,000 | 45,000 |
| $30 | 60,000 | 55,000 | 45,000 |
| $35 | 45,000 | 50,000 | 45,000 |
| $40 | 30,000 | 45,000 | 45,000 |
| $45 | 15,000 | 40,000 | 45,000 |

Draw the supply curve and each of the demand curves for years 1 and 2.

✴ 8. Demand and supply curves can also be represented with equations. Suppose that the quantity demanded, $Q_D$, is represented by the following equation:

$$Q_D = 90 - 2P$$

The quantity supplied, $Q_S$, is represented by the equation:

$$Q_S = P$$

a. Find the equilibrium price and quantity. **Hint:** Set $Q_D = Q_S$ and solve for the price, $P$, and then plug your result back into either of the original equations to find Q.

b. Suppose that the price is $20. Determine $Q_D$ and $Q_S$.

c. At a price of $20, is there a surplus or a shortage in the market?

d. Given your answer in part c, will the price rise or fall in order to find the equilibrium point?

## SOLVED PROBLEMS

**5.**

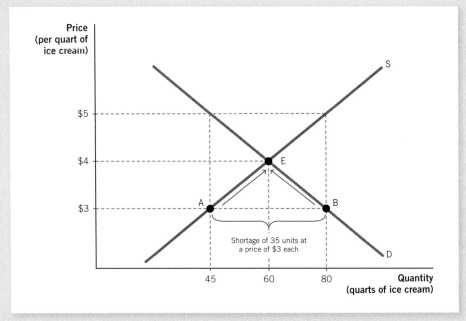

**a.** The equilibrium price is $4 and quantity is 60 units (quarts). The next step is to graph the curves. This is done above.

**b.** A shortage of 35 units of ice cream exists at $3; therefore, there is excess demand. Ice cream sellers will raise their price as long as excess demand exists. That is, as long as the price is below $4. It is not until $4 that the equilibrium point is reached and the shortage is resolved.

**8. a.** The first step is to set $Q_D = Q_S$. Doing so gives us $90 - 2P = P$. Solving for price, we find that $90 = 3P$, or $P = 30$. Once we know that $P = 30$, we can plug this value back into either of the original equations, $Q_D = 90 - 2P$ or $Q_S = P$. Beginning with $Q_D$, we get $90 - (30) = 90 - 60 = 30$, or we can plug it into $Q_S = P$, so $Q_S = 30$. Since we get a quantity of 30 for both $Q_D$ and $Q_S$, we know that the price of $30 is correct.

**b.** In this part, we plug $20 into $Q_D$. This yields $90 - 2(20) = 50$. Now we plug $20 into $Q_S$. This yields 20.

**c.** Since $Q_D = 50$ and $Q_S = 20$, there is a shortage of 30 units.

**d.** Whenever there is a shortage of a good, the price will rise in order to find the equilibrium point.

# Changes in Both Demand and Supply

We have considered what would happen if supply *or* demand changed. But life is often more complex than that. To provide a more realistic analysis, we need to examine what happens when supply and demand both shift at the same time. Doing this adds considerable uncertainty to the analysis.

Suppose that a major drought hits the northwest United States. The water shortage reduces both the amount of farmed salmon and the ability of wild salmon to spawn in streams and rivers. Figure 3A.1a shows the ensuing decline in the salmon supply, from point S progressively leftward, represented by the dotted supply curves. At the same time, a medical journal reports that people who consume at least four pounds of salmon a month live five years longer than those who consume an equal amount of cod. Figure 3A.1b shows the ensuing rise in the demand for salmon, from point D progressively rightward, represented by the dotted demand curves. This scenario leads to a two-fold change. Because of the water shortage, the supply of salmon shrinks. At the same time, new information about the health benefits of eating salmon causes demand for salmon to increase.

It is impossible to predict exactly what happens to the equilibrium point when both supply and demand are shifting. We can, however, determine a region where the resulting equilibrium point must reside.

In this situation, we have a simultaneous decrease in supply and increase in demand. Since we do not know the magnitude of the supply reduction or the demand increase, the overall effect on the equilibrium quantity cannot be determined. This result is evident in Figure 3A.1c, as illustrated by the purple region. The points where supply and demand cross within this area represent the set of possible new market equilibriums. Since each of the possible points of intersection in the purple region occurs at prices greater than $10.00 per pound, we know that the price must rise. However, the left half of the purple region produces equilibrium quantities less than 500 pounds of salmon, while the right half of the purple region results in equilibrium quantities greater than 500. Therefore, the equilibrium quantity may rise or fall.

The world we live in is complex, and often more than one variable will change simultaneously. When this occurs, it is not possible to be as definitive as when only one variable—supply or demand—changes. You should think of the new equilibrium, $E_2$, not as a single point but as a range of outcomes represented by the shaded purple area in Figure 3A.1c. Therefore, we cannot be exactly sure at what point the new price *and* quantity will settle. For a closer look at four possibilities, see Figure 3A.2.

### A Shift in Supply and Demand

When supply and demand both shift, the resulting equilibrium can no longer be identified as an exact point. This is seen in (c), which combines the supply shift in (a) with the demand shift in (b). When supply decreases and demand increases, the result is that the price must rise, but the equilibrium quantity can either rise or fall.

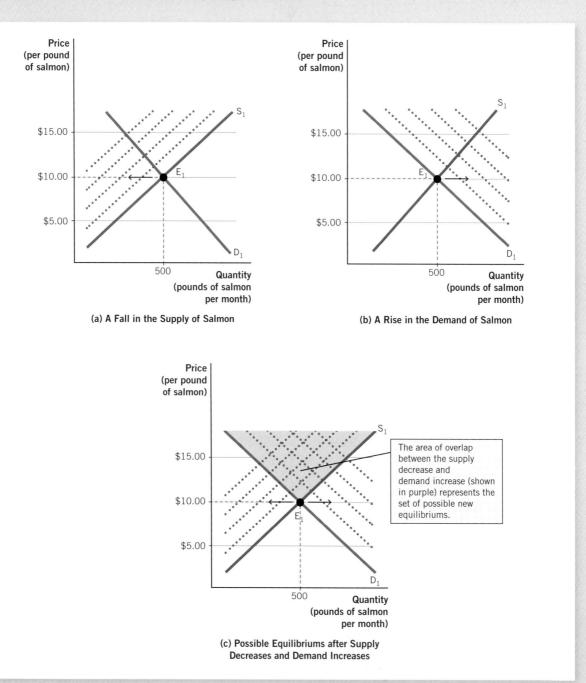

(a) A Fall in the Supply of Salmon

(b) A Rise in the Demand of Salmon

The area of overlap between the supply decrease and demand increase (shown in purple) represents the set of possible new equilibriums.

(c) Possible Equilibriums after Supply Decreases and Demand Increases

**Price and Quantity When Demand and Supply Both Change**

| Change | Illustration | Impact on price and quantity |
|---|---|---|
| **1. Demand and supply both increase.** | | The demand and supply curves shift to the right. The shifts reinforce each other with respect to quantity, which increases, but they act as countervailing forces along the Price axis. Price could be either higher or lower. |
| **2. Demand and supply both decrease.** | | The demand and supply curves shift to the left. The shifts reinforce each other with respect to quantity, which decreases, but they act as countervailing forces along the Price axis. Price could be either higher or lower. |
| **3. Demand increases and supply decreases.** | | The demand curve shifts to the right and the supply curve shifts to the left. The shifts reinforce each other with respect to price, which increases, but they act as countervailing forces along the Quantity axis. Quantity could be either higher or lower. |
| **4. Demand decreases and supply increases.** | | The demand curve shifts to the left and the supply curve shifts to the right. The shifts reinforce each other with respect to price, which decreases, but they act as countervailing forces along the Quantity axis. Quantity could be either higher or lower. |

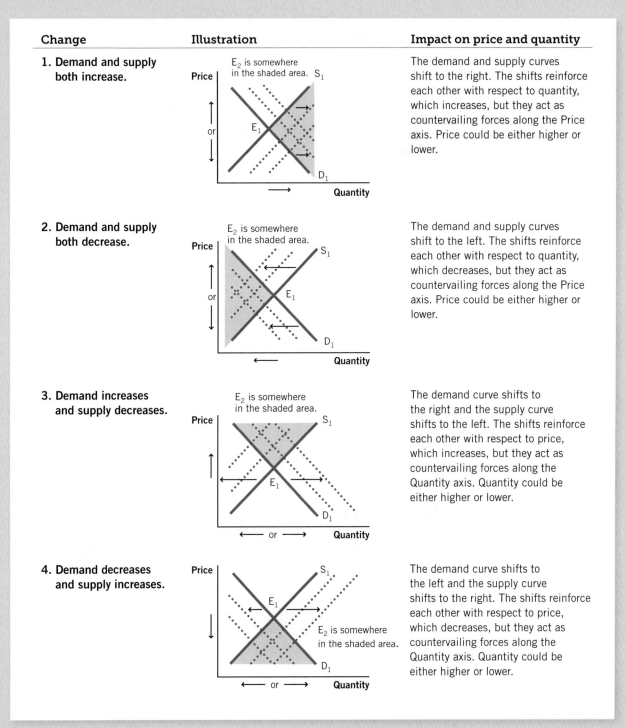

# PRACTICE WHAT YOU KNOW

## When Supply and Demand Both Change: Hybrid Cars

**Question:** At lunch, two friends are engaged in a heated argument. Their exchange goes like this:

The first friend begins, "The supply of hybrid cars and the demand for hybrid cars will both increase, I'm sure of it. I'm also sure the price of hybrids will go down."

The second friend interrupts, "I agree with the first part of your statement, but I'm not sure about the price. In fact, I'm pretty sure that hybrid prices will rise."

They go back and forth endlessly, each unable to convince the other, so they turn to you for advice. What do you say to them?

**Answer:** Either of your friends could be correct. In this case, supply and demand both shift out to the right, so we know the quantity bought and sold will increase. However, an increase in supply would normally lower the price and an increase in demand would typically raise the price. Without knowing which of these two effects on price is stronger, you can't predict how it will change. The overall price will rise if the increase in demand is larger than the increase in supply. However, if the increase in supply is larger than the increase in demand, prices will fall. But your two friends don't know which condition will be true—so they're locked in an argument that no one can win!

Hybrid cars are becoming increasingly common.

## QUESTIONS FOR REVIEW

1. What happens to price and quantity when supply and demand change at the same time?

2. Is there more than one potential equilibrium point when supply and demand change at the same time?

## STUDY PROBLEM

1. Check out the short video at forbes .com called "Behind Rising Oil Prices," from 2008. (Search online for "behind rising oil prices forbes video.") Using your understanding of the market forces of supply and demand, explain how the market works. In your explanation, be sure to illustrate how increasing global demand for oil has impacted the equilibrium price.

**The minimum wage helps everyone earn a living wage.**

You are probably familiar with the minimum wage, which is an example of a *price control*. If you have ever worked for the minimum wage, you

probably think that raising it sounds like a great idea. You may support minimum wage legislation because you believe it will help struggling workers to make ends meet. After all,

it seems reasonable that firms should pay workers at least enough to cover the necessities of life, or what is referred to as a living wage.

Price controls are not a new idea. The first recorded attempt to control prices was four thousand years ago in ancient Babylon, when King Hammurabi decreed how much corn a farmer could pay for a cow. Similar attempts to control prices occurred in ancient Egypt, Greece, and Rome. Each attempt ended badly. In Egypt, farmers revolted against tight price controls and intrusive inspections, eventually causing the economy to collapse. In Greece, the Athenian government set the price of grain at a very low level. Predictably, the quantity of grain supplied dried up. In 301 CE, the Roman government under Emperor Diocletian prescribed the maximum price of beef, grains, clothing, and many other articles. Almost immediately, markets for these goods disappeared.

History has shown us that price controls generally do not work. Why? Because they disrupt the normal functioning of the market. By the end of this chapter, we hope that you will understand why price controls such as minimum wage laws are rarely the win-win propositions that legislators often claim. To help you understand why price controls lead to disequilibrium in markets, this chapter focuses on the two most common types of price controls: *price ceilings* and *price floors*.

The Code of Hammurabi established the first known price controls.

# BIG QUESTIONS

* When do price ceilings matter?
* What effects do price ceilings have on economic activity?
* When do price floors matter?
* What effects do price floors have on economic activity?

## When Do Price Ceilings Matter?

**Price controls**
are an attempt to set prices through government involvement in the market.

**Price ceilings**
are legally established maximum prices for goods or services.

**Price controls** are an attempt to set prices through government involvement in the market. In most cases, and certainly in the United States, price controls are enacted to ease perceived burdens on society. A **price ceiling** creates a legally established maximum price for a good or service. In the next section, we will consider what happens when a price ceiling is in place. Price ceilings create many unintended effects that policymakers rarely acknowledge.

## Understanding Price Ceilings

To understand how price ceilings work, let's try a simple thought experiment. Suppose that prices are rising because of inflation. The government is concerned that people with low incomes will not be able to afford enough to eat. To help the disadvantaged, legislators pass a law stating that no one can charge more than $0.50 for a loaf of bread. (Note that this price ceiling is about one-third the typical price of generic white bread.) Does the new law accomplish its goal? What happens?

The law of supply and demand tells us that if the price drops, the quantity that consumers demand will increase. At the same time, the quantity supplied will fall because producers will be receiving lower profits for their efforts. This twin dynamic of increased quantity demanded and reduced quantity supplied will cause a shortage of bread.

On the demand side, consumers will want more bread than is available at the legal price. There will be long lines for bread, and many people will not be able to get the bread they want. On the supply side, producers will look for ways to maintain their profits. They can reduce the size of each loaf they produce. They can also use cheaper ingredients, thereby lowering

Empty shelves signal a shortage of products.

the quality of their product, and they can stop making fancier varieties. In addition, *black markets* will develop to help supply meet demand.

**Black markets** are illegal markets that arise when price controls are in place. For instance, in the former Soviet Union price controls on bread and other essentials led to very long lines. In our bread example, many people who do not want to wait in line for bread, or who do not obtain it despite waiting in line, will resort to illegal means to obtain it. This means that sellers will go underground and charge higher prices to deliver customers the bread they want.

Table 4.1 summarizes the likely outcome of price controls on bread.

**Black markets**
are illegal markets that arise when price controls are in place.

Incentives

## TABLE 4.1

### A Price Ceiling on Bread

| Question | Answer / Explanation | | Result |
|----------|---------------------|---|--------|
| **Will there be more or less bread for sale?** | Consumers will want to buy more since the price is lower (the law of demand), but producers will manufacture less (the law of supply). The net result will be a shortage of bread. | | Empty shelves. |
| **Will the size of a typical loaf change?** | Since the price is capped at $0.50 per loaf, manufacturers will try to maintain profits by reducing the size of each loaf. | | No more giant loaves. |
| **Will the quality change?** | Since the price is capped, producers will use cheaper ingredients, and many expensive brands and varieties will no longer be profitable to produce. Thus the quality of available bread will decline. | | Focaccia bread will disappear. |
| **Will the opportunity cost of finding bread change?** | The opportunity cost of finding bread will rise. This means that consumers will spend significant resources going from store to store to see if a bread shipment has arrived and waiting in line for a chance to get some. | | Bread lines will become the norm. |
| **Will people have to break the law to buy bread?** | Since bread will be hard to find and people will still need it, a black market will develop. Those selling and buying on the black market will be breaking the law. | | Black-market bread dealers will help reduce the shortage. |

If you can touch the ceiling, you can't go any higher. A binding price ceiling stops prices from rising.

# The Effect of Price Ceilings

Now that we have some understanding of how a price ceiling works, we can transfer that knowledge into the supply and demand model for a deeper analysis of how price ceilings affect the market. To explain when price ceilings matter in the short run, we will examine the outcomes of two types of price ceilings: nonbinding and binding.

## Nonbinding Price Ceilings

The effect of a price ceiling depends on the level at which it is set. When a price ceiling is above the equilibrium price, we say it is *nonbinding*. Figure 4.1 shows a price ceiling of $2.00 per loaf in a market where $2.00 is above the equilibrium price ($P_E$). All prices at or below $2.00 (the green area) are legal. Prices above the price ceiling (the red area) are illegal. But since the market equilibrium (E) occurs in the green area, the price ceiling does not influence the market; it is nonbinding. As long as the equilibrium price remains below the price ceiling, price will continue to be regulated by supply and demand. Since there is rarely a compelling political reason to set a price ceiling above the equilibrium price, nonbinding price ceilings are unusual.

## Binding Price Ceilings

When a price ceiling is below the market price, it creates a binding constraint that prevents supply and demand from clearing the market. In Figure 4.2,

---

FIGURE 4.1

**A Nonbinding Price Ceiling**

The price ceiling ($2.00) is set above the equilibrium price ($1.00). Since market prices are set by the intersection of supply (S) and demand (D), as long as the equilibrium price is below the price ceiling, the price ceiling is nonbinding and has no effect.

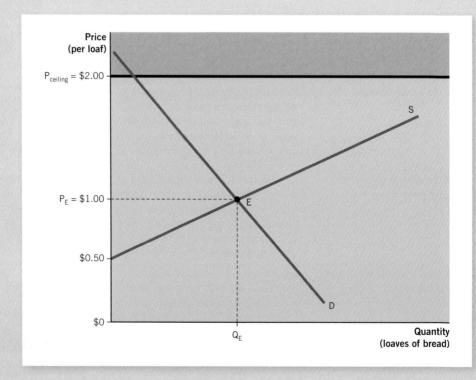

the price ceiling for bread is set at $0.50 per loaf. Since $0.50 is well below the equilibrium price of $1.00, this creates a binding price ceiling. Notice that at a price of $0.50, the quantity demanded ($Q_D$) is greater than the quantity supplied ($Q_S$)—in other words, a shortage exists. Shortages typically cause prices to rise, but the imposed price ceiling prevents that from happening. A price ceiling of $0.50 allows only the prices in the green area. The market cannot reach the equilibrium point E at $1.00 per loaf because it is located above the price ceiling, in the red area.

The black-market price is also set by supply and demand. Since prices above $0.50 are illegal, sellers are unwilling to produce more than $Q_S$. Once the price ceiling is in place, sellers cannot legally charge prices above the ceiling, so the incentive to produce along the original supply curve vanishes. Since a shortage still exists, an illegal market will form to resolve the shortage. At that point, purchasers can illegally resell what they have just bought at $0.50 for far more than what they just paid. Since the supply of legally produced bread is $Q_S$, the intersection of the vertical dashed line that reflects $Q_S$ and the demand curve at point $E_{black\ market}$ establishes a black-market price $P_{black\ market}$, at $2.00 per loaf for illegally sold bread. Since the black-market price is substantially more than the market equilibrium price ($P_E$) of $1.00, illegal suppliers (underground bakers) will also enter the market in order to satisfy demand. As a result, the black-market price eliminates the shortage caused by the price ceiling. However, the price ceiling has created two unintended consequences: a smaller quantity of bread supplied ($Q_S$ is less than $Q_E$), and a higher price for those who are forced to purchase it on the black market.

Incentives

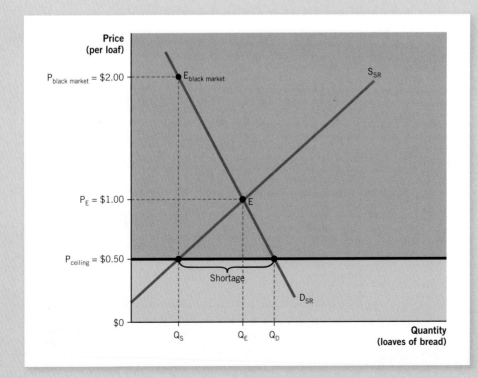

**A Binding Price Ceiling**

A binding price ceiling prevents sellers from increasing the price and causes them to reduce the quantity they offer for sale. As a consequence, prices no longer signal relative scarcity. Consumers desire to purchase the product at the price-ceiling level, and this creates a shortage in the short run; many will be unable to obtain the good. As a result, those who are shut out of the market will turn to other means to acquire the good. This establishes an illegal market for the good at the black market price.

# Price Ceilings in the Long Run

In the long run, supply and demand become more elastic, or flatter. When consumers have additional time to make choices, they find more ways to avoid high-priced goods and more ways to take advantage of low prices. Additional time also gives producers the opportunity to produce more when prices are high and less when prices are low. In this section, we consider what will happen if a binding price ceiling on bread remains in effect for a long time. We have already observed that when binding price ceilings are in effect in the short run, shortages and black markets develop. Are the long-run implications of price ceilings more or less problematic than the short-run implications? Let's find out by looking at what happens to both supply and demand.

Figure 4.3 shows the result of a price ceiling that remains in place for a long time. Here the supply curve is more elastic than its short-run counterpart in Figure 4.2. The supply curve is flatter because in the long run producers respond by producing less bread and converting their facilities to make similar products that are not subject to price controls—for example, bagels and rolls—that will bring them a reasonable return on their investments. Therefore, in the long run the quantity supplied ($Q_S$) grows even smaller.

The demand curve is also more elastic in the long run. In the long run, more people will attempt to take advantage of the low price ceiling by changing their eating habits to consume more bread. Even though consumers will

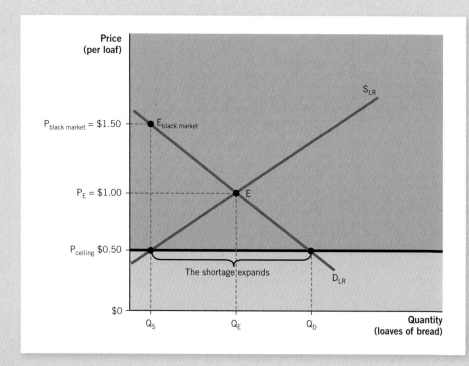

## FIGURE 4.3

**The Effect of a Binding Price Ceiling in the Long Run**

In the long run, increased elasticity on the part of both producers and consumers makes the shortage larger than it was in the short run. Consumers adjust their demand to the lower price and want more bread. Producers adjust their supply and make less of the unprofitable product. As a result, products become progressively harder to find.

# Price Ceilings

### *Moscow on the Hudson*

This 1984 film starring Robin Williams chronicles the differences between living in the United States and the former Soviet Union. In Moscow, we see hundreds of people waiting in line to receive essentials like bread, milk, and shoes. In the Soviet Union, production was controlled and prices were not allowed to equalize supply and demand. As a result, shortages were common. Waiting in line served as a rationing mechanism in the absence of price adjustments.

This film is memorable because of the reactions that Robin Williams's character has once he immi-

Soviet-era food-rationing coupon

Soviet-era bread line

grates to the United States. In one inspired scene, he walks into a supermarket to buy coffee. He asks the manager where the coffee aisle is located, and when he sees that the aisle is not crowded, he asks the manager where the coffee line is located. The manager responds that there is no coffee line, so Williams walks down the coffee aisle slowly, naming each variety. We see his joy at being able to buy coffee without waiting and at having so many options to choose from. This scene nicely showcases the differences between the market system of the United States and the controlled economy of the former Soviet Union.

often find empty shelves in the long run, the quantity demanded of cheap bread will increase. At this point, a flatter demand curve means that consumers are more flexible. As a result, the quantity demanded ($Q_D$) expands and bread is hard to find at $0.50 per loaf. The shortage will become so acute that consumers will turn to bread substitutes, like bagels and rolls, that are more plentiful because they are not price controlled.

Increased elasticity on the part of both producers and consumers magnifies the unintended consequences we observed in the short run. Therefore, products subject to a price ceiling become progressively harder to find in the long run. A black market will develop. However, in the long run our bread consumers will choose substitutes for expensive black-market bread. This will cause somewhat lower black-market prices in the long run.

## PRACTICE WHAT YOU KNOW

### Price Ceilings: Concert Tickets

Question: Suppose that fans of Avicii persuade Congress to impose a price ceiling of $25 for every Avicii concert ticket. Would this policy affect the number of people who attend his concerts?

You've got a good feeling about this concert.

Answer: The price ceiling prevents supply and demand from reaching the equilibrium price. As a result, at $25 there is a shortage of tickets. Since Avicii controls when and where he tours, he will choose to tour less in the United States and more in countries that do not regulate the ticket prices he can charge. This will make it more difficult for his U.S. fans to see him perform live, so the answer to the question is yes: the policy will influence the number of people who attend Avicii concerts (fewer in the United States, and more abroad).

# What Effects Do Price Ceilings Have on Economic Activity?

We have seen the logical repercussions of a hypothetical price ceiling on bread and the incentives it creates. Now let's use supply and demand analysis to examine two real-world price ceilings: *rent control* and *price gouging laws*.

## Rent Control

**Rent control**
is a price ceiling that applies to the housing market.

Under **rent control**, a local government caps the price of apartment rentals to keep housing affordable. While this may be a laudable goal, rent control doesn't work. In fact, it doesn't help poor residents of a city to find affordable housing or gain access to housing at all. In addition, these policies contribute to dangerous living conditions.

Mumbai, India, provides a chilling example of what can happen when rent controls are applied over an extended period. In Mumbai, many rent-controlled buildings have become dilapidated. Every monsoon season, several of these buildings fall—often with tragic consequences. Since the rent that property owners are permitted to charge is so low, they have less income to use for maintenance. Therefore, they cannot afford to maintain the buildings properly and make a reasonable profit. As a result, rent-control policies have led to the decay of many apartment buildings. Similar controls have caused the same problem in cities worldwide.

To understand how a policy can backfire so greatly, let's look at the history of rent control in New York City. In 1943, in the midst of World War II, the federal government established the Emergency Price Control Act. The act was designed to keep inflation in check during the war, when many essential commodities were scarce. After the war, the federal government ended price controls, but the city of New York continued rent control. Today, there are approximately one million rent-controlled units in New York City. Rent controls limit the price a landlord can charge a tenant for rent. They also require that the landlord provide certain basic services; but not surprisingly, landlords keep maintenance to a minimum.

Many apartment buildings in Mumbai, India, are dilapidated as a result of rent-control laws.

Does the presence of so many rent-controlled apartments mean that less affluent households can easily find a cheap place to rent? Hardly. When a rent-controlled unit is vacated, the property is generally no longer subject to rent control. Since most rent-controlled apartments are passed by tenants from generation to generation to remain in the program, rent control no longer even remotely serves its original purpose of helping low-income households. Clearly, the law was never intended to subsidize fancy vacation homes, but that's what it does! This has happened, in part, because some tenants who can afford to live elsewhere choose not to. Their subsidized rent enables them to save enough money to have a second or third home in places such as upstate New York, Florida, or Europe.

Incentives

The attempt to make housing more affordable in New York City has, ironically, made housing harder to obtain. It has encouraged the building of upscale properties rather than low-income units, and it has created a set of behaviors among landlords that is inconsistent with the ideals of justice and affordability that rent control was designed to address. Figure 4.4 shows why rent control fails. As with any price ceiling, rent control causes a shortage since the quantity demanded in the short run ($Q_{D_{SR}}$) is greater than the quantity supplied in the short run ($Q_{S_{SR}}$). Because rent-controlled apartments are vacated slowly, the supply of rent-controlled units contracts in the long run, which causes the supply curve to become more elastic ($S_{LR}$). Demand also becomes more elastic in the long run ($D_{LR}$), which causes the quantity demanded for rent-controlled units to rise ($Q_{D_{LR}}$). The combination of fewer available units and more consumers looking for rent-controlled units leads to a larger shortage in the long run.

## Price Gouging

Another kind of price control, **price gouging laws**, places a temporary ceiling on the prices that sellers can charge during times of national emergency until markets function normally again. Over 30 states in the United States

**Price gouging laws** place a temporary ceiling on the prices that sellers can charge during times of emergency.

have laws against price gouging. Like all price controls, price gouging laws have unintended consequences. This became very apparent in the southern United States in 2005.

The hurricane season of 2005 was arguably the worst in U.S. history. Katrina and Rita plowed through the Gulf of Mexico with devastating effects, especially in Louisiana and Texas. Later that year, Wilma grew into the most powerful hurricane ever recorded in the Atlantic basin. When Wilma hit Fort Myers, Florida, in November, it ended a season for the record books. Florida has one of the strictest price gouging laws in the country. The statute makes it illegal to charge an "excessive" price immediately following a natural disaster. The law is designed to prevent the victims of natural disasters from being exploited in a time of need. But does it work?

Consider David Medina of Miami Beach. Immediately after Wilma hit, he drove to North Carolina, purchased 35 gas-powered generators, and returned to Florida, where he sold them from the back of his truck. He charged $900 for large generators, which he had purchased for $529.99, and $600 for small generators, which had cost him $279.99. After selling most of the units, Medina was arrested for price gouging. Under Florida law, his remaining generators were confiscated, and he was fined $1,000 for each sale. In addition, he was charged with selling without a business license. While there is no doubt that Medina intended to capitalize on the misfortune of others, it is hard to prove that he did any harm. The people who bought from him did so voluntarily, each believing that the value of the generator was greater than the price Medina was charging.

## FIGURE 4.4

**Rent Control in the Short Run and Long Run**

Because rent-controlled apartments are vacated slowly, the supply of units contracts in the long run and the supply curve becomes more elastic. Demand also becomes more elastic in the long run, causing the quantity demanded to rise. The combination of fewer units available to rent and more consumers looking to find rent-controlled units leads to a larger shortage in the long run.

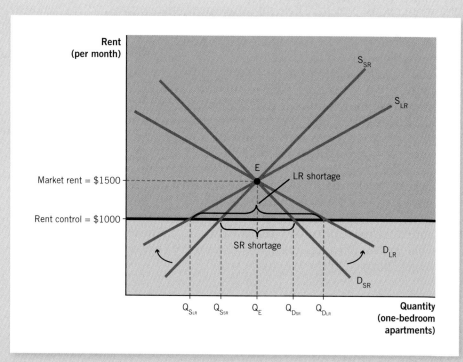

Prices act to ration scarce resources. When the demand for generators or other necessities is high, the price rises to ensure that the available units are distributed to those who value them the most. More important, the ability to charge a higher price provides sellers with an incentive to make more units available. If there is limited ability for the price to change when demand increases, there will be a shortage. Therefore, price gouging legislation means that devastated communities must rely exclusively on the goodwill of others and the slow-moving machinery of government relief efforts. This closes off a third avenue, entrepreneurial activity, as a means to alleviate poor conditions.

**Incentives**

Large generator: $900 after Hurricane Wilma hit.

Figure 4.5 shows how price gouging laws work and the shortage they create. If the demand for gas generators increases immediately after a disaster ($D_{after}$), the market price rises from $530 to $900. But since $900 is considered excessive, sales at that price are illegal. This creates a binding price ceiling for as long as a state of emergency is in effect. Whenever a price ceiling is binding, it creates a shortage. You can see this in Figure 4.5 in the difference between quantity demanded and quantity supplied at the price ceiling level mandated by the law. In this case, the normal ability of supply and demand to ration the available generators is short-circuited. Since more people demand generators after the disaster than before it, those who do not get to the store soon enough are out of luck. When the emergency is lifted and the market returns to normal, the temporary shortage created by legislation against price gouging is eliminated.

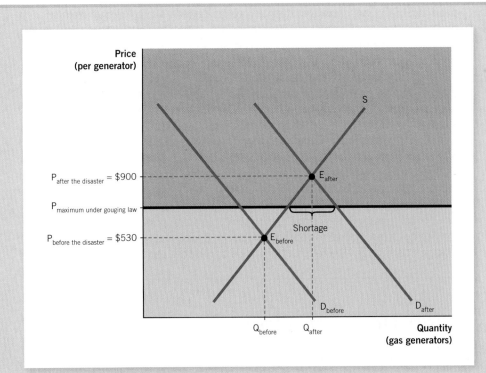

## FIGURE 4.5

### Price Gouging

Price gouging laws serve as a nonbinding price ceiling during normal times. However, when a natural disaster strikes, price gouging laws go into effect. In our example, this shifts the demand curve for generators to the right and causes the new equilibrium price ($E_{after}$) to rise above the legal limit. This creates a shortage. When the emergency is lifted, the market demand returns to normal, and the temporary shortage created by price gouging legislation is eliminated.

**PRACTICE WHAT YOU KNOW**

### Price Ceilings: Student Rental Apartments

Here is a question that often confuses students.

Question: Imagine that a city council decides that the market price for renting student apartments is too high and passes a law that establishes a rental price ceiling of $600 per month. The result of the price ceiling is a shortage. Which of the following caused the shortage of apartments?

a. Both suppliers and demanders. Landlords will cut the supply of apartments, and the demand from renters will increase.

b. A spike in demand from many students who want to rent cheap apartments

c. The drop in supply caused by apartment owners pulling their units off the rental market and converting them into condos for sale

d. The price ceiling set by the city council

Answer: Many students think that markets are to blame when shortages (or surpluses) exist. The first reaction is to find the culpable party—either the supplier or the demander, or both.

Answer (a) is a typical response. But be careful. Supply and demand have not changed—they are exactly the same as they were before the price ceiling was implemented. What *has* changed is the quantity of apartments supplied at $600. This change in quantity would be represented by a movement along the existing supply curve. The same is true for renters. The quantity demanded at $600 is much larger than it was when the price was not controlled. Once again, there will be a movement along the demand curve.

The same logic applies to answers (b) and (c). Answer (b) argues that there is a spike in student demand caused by the lower price. But price cannot cause a shift in the demand curve; it can only cause a movement along a curve. Likewise, (c) argues that apartment owners supply fewer units for rent. Landlords cannot charge more than $600 per unit, so they convert some apartments into private residences and offer them for sale in order to make more profit. Since fewer apartments are available at $600, this would be represented by a movement along the apartment supply curve.

This brings us to (d). There is only one change in market conditions: the city council passed a new price ceiling law. A binding price ceiling disrupts the ability of the market to reach equilibrium. Therefore, we can say that the change in the price as a result of the price ceiling caused the shortage.

# When Do Price Floors Matter?

In this section, we examine price floors. Like price ceilings, price floors create many unintended effects that policymakers rarely acknowledge. However, unlike price ceilings, price floors result from the political pressure of suppliers to keep prices high. Most consumers prefer lower prices when they shop, so the idea of a law that keeps prices high may sound like a bad one to you. However, if you are selling a product or service, you might think that legislation to keep prices high is a very good idea. For instance, many states establish minimum prices for milk. As a result, milk prices are higher than they would be if supply and demand set the price. **Price floors** create legally established minimum prices for goods or services. The minimum wage law is another example of a price floor. In this section, we will follow the same progression that we did with price ceilings. We begin with a simple thought experiment. Once we understand how price floors work, we will use supply and demand analysis to examine the short- and long-term implications for economic activity.

## Understanding Price Floors

To understand how price floors affect the market, let's try a thought experiment. Suppose that a politician suggests we should encourage dairy farmers to produce more milk so that supplies will be plentiful and everyone will get enough calcium. In order to accomplish this, a price floor of $6 per gallon—about twice the price of a typical gallon of fat-free milk—is enacted to make production more attractive to producers. What repercussions should we expect?

First, more milk will be available for sale. We know this because the higher price will cause dairies to increase the quantity that they supply. At the same time, because consumers must pay more, the quantity demanded will fall. The result will be a surplus of milk. Since every gallon of milk that is produced but not sold hurts the dairies' bottom line, sellers will want to lower their prices enough to get as many sales as possible before the milk goes bad. But the price floor will not allow the market to respond, and sellers will be stuck with milk that goes to waste. They will be tempted to offer illegal discounts in order to recoup some of their costs.

If you're doing a handstand, you need the floor for support. A binding price floor keeps prices from falling.

**Price floors**
are legally established minimum prices for goods or services.

What happens next? Since the surplus cannot be resolved through lower prices, the government will try to help equalize supply and demand through other means. This can be accomplished in one of two ways: by restricting the supply of the good or by stimulating additional demand. Both solutions are problematic. If production is restricted, dairy farmers will not be able to generate a profitable amount of milk. Likewise, stimulating additional demand is not as simple as it sounds. Let's consider how this works with other crops.

In many cases, the government purchases surplus agricultural production. This occurs most notably with corn, soybeans, cotton, and rice. Once the government buys the surplus production, it often sells the surplus below cost to developing countries to avoid having the crop go to waste. This strategy has the unintended consequence of making it cheaper for consumers in these developing nations to buy excess agricultural output from developed nations like the United States than to have local farmers grow the crop. International treaties ban the practice of dumping surplus production, but it continues under the guise of humanitarian aid. This practice makes little economic sense. Table 4.2 summarizes the result of our price-floor thought experiment using milk.

## The Effect of Price Floors

We have seen that price floors create unintended consequences. Now we will use the supply and demand model to analyze how price floors affect the market. We'll take a look at the short run first.

Got milk? Maybe not, if there's a price floor.

| TABLE 4.2 | | |
|---|---|---|
| **A Price Floor on Milk** | | |
| **Question** | **Answer / Explanation** | **Result** |
| Will the quantity of milk for sale change? | Consumers will purchase less since the price is higher (the law of demand), but producers will manufacture more (the law of supply). The net result will be a surplus of milk. | There will be a surplus of milk. |
| Would producers sell below the price floor? | Yes. A surplus of milk would give sellers a strong incentive to undercut the price floor in order to avoid having to discard leftover milk. | Illegal discounts will help to reduce the milk surplus. |
| Will dairy farmers be better off? | Not if they have trouble selling what they produce. | There might be a lot of spoiled milk. |

## Nonbinding Price Floors

Like price ceilings, price floors can be binding or nonbinding. Figure 4.6 illustrates a nonbinding price floor of $2 per gallon on milk. As you can see, at $2 the price floor is below the equilibrium price ($P_E$), so the price floor is nonbinding. Since the actual market price is above the legally established minimum price ($P_{floor}$), the price floor does not prevent the market from reaching equilibrium at point E. Consequently, the price floor has no impact on the market. As long as the equilibrium price remains above the price floor, price is regulated by supply and demand.

Full shelves signal a market at equilibrium.

## Binding Price Floors

For a price floor to have an impact on the market, it must be set above the market equilibrium price. In that case, it is known as a binding price floor. And with a binding price floor, the quantity supplied will exceed the quantity demanded. Figure 4.7 illustrates a binding price floor in the short run. Continuing our example of milk prices, at $6 per gallon the price floor is above the equilibrium price of $3. Market forces always attempt to restore the equilibrium between supply and demand at point E. So we know that there is downward pressure on the price. At a price floor

FIGURE 4.6

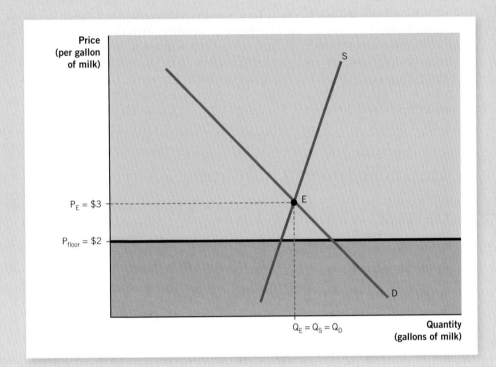

**A Nonbinding Price Floor**

Under a nonbinding price floor, price is regulated by supply and demand. Since the price floor ($2) is below the equilibrium price ($3), the market will voluntarily charge more than the legal minimum. Therefore, this price floor will have no effect on sales and purchases of milk.

FIGURE 4.7

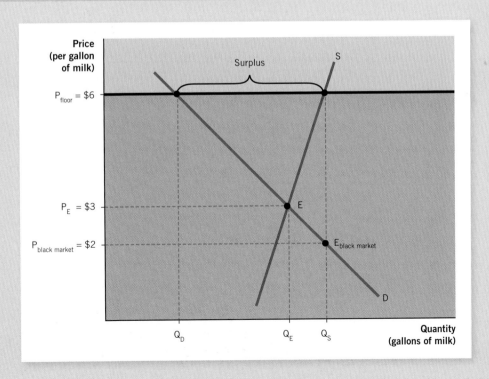

**A Binding Price Floor in the Short Run**

A binding price floor creates a surplus. This has two unintended consequences: a smaller demand than the equilibrium quantity ($Q_D < Q_E$), and a lower black-market price to eliminate the glut of the product.

Incentives

of $6, we see that $Q_S > Q_D$. The difference between the quantity supplied and the quantity demanded results in a surplus. Since the price mechanism is no longer effective, sellers find themselves holding unwanted inventories of milk. In order to eliminate the surplus, which will spoil unless it is sold, a black market may develop with prices substantially below the legislated price. At a price ($P_{black\ market}$) of $1, the black market eliminates the surplus that the price floor caused. However, the price floor has created two unintended consequences: a smaller demand for milk ($Q_D < Q_E$), and a black market to eliminate the glut.

## Price Floors in the Long Run

Once price-floor legislation is passed, it can be politically difficult to repeal. What happens if a binding price floor on milk stays in effect for a long time? To help answer that question, we need to consider elasticity. We have already observed that in the short run binding price ceilings cause shortages and that black markets follow.

Figure 4.8 shows a price floor for milk that remains in place well past the short run. The long run gives consumers a chance to find milk substitutes—for example, products made from soy, rice, or almond that are not subject to the price floor—at lower prices. This added flexibility on the part of consumers makes the long-run demand for milk more elastic in an unregulated market. As a result, the demand curve depicted in Figure 4.8 is more elastic

## FIGURE 4.8

**The Effect of a Binding Price Floor in the Long Run**

When a price floor is left in place over time, supply and demand each become more elastic. This leads to a larger surplus ($Q_S > Q_D$) in the long run. Since sellers are unable to sell all that they produce at $6 per gallon, a black market develops in order to eliminate the glut of milk.

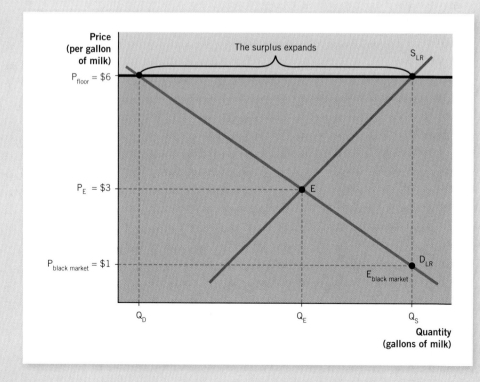

than its short-run counterpart in Figure 4.7. The supply curve also becomes flatter since firms (dairy farms) are able to produce more milk by acquiring additional land and production facilities. Therefore, a price floor ($6) that remains in place over time causes the supply and demand curves to become more elastic. This magnifies the shortage.

What happens to supply? In the long run, producers are more flexible and therefore supply is more elastic. The pool of potential milk producers rises as other closely related businesses retool their operations to supply more milk. The flatter supply curve in Figure 4.8 reflects this flexibility. As a result, $Q_S$ expands and becomes much larger than it was in Figure 4.7. The increased elasticity on the part of both producers and consumers (1) makes the surplus larger in the long run and (2) magnifies the unintended consequences we observed in the short run.

## PRACTICE WHAT YOU KNOW

### Price Floors: Fair-Trade Coffee

Fair-trade coffee is sold through organizations that purchase directly from growers. The coffee is usually sold for a higher price than standard coffee. The goal is to promote more humane working conditions for the coffee pickers and growers. Fair-trade coffee has become more popular but still accounts for a small portion of all coffee sales, in large part because it is substantially more expensive to produce.

**Question:** Suppose that a one-pound bag of standard coffee costs $8 and that a one-pound bag of fair-trade coffee costs $12. Congress decides to impose a price floor of $10 per pound. Will this policy cause more or fewer people to buy fair-trade coffee?

**Answer:** Fair-trade producers typically sell their product at a higher price than mass-produced coffee brands. Therefore, a $10 price floor is binding for inexpensive brands like Folgers but nonbinding for premium coffees, which include fair-trade sellers. The price floor will reduce the price disparity between fair-trade coffee and mass-produced coffee.

Would fair-trade coffee producers benefit from a price floor?

To see how this works, consider a fair-trade coffee producer who charges $12 per pound and a mass-produced brand that sells for $8 per pound. A price floor of $10 reduces the difference between the price of fair-trade coffee and the inexpensive coffee brands, which now must sell for $10 instead of $8. This lowers the consumer's opportunity cost of choosing fair-trade coffee. Therefore, some consumers of the inexpensive brands will opt for fair-trade instead. As a result, fair-trade producers will benefit indirectly from the price floor. Thus the answer to the question at the top is that *more* people will buy fair-trade coffee as a result of this price-floor policy.

Opportunity cost

# What Effects Do Price Floors Have on Economic Activity?

We have seen the logical repercussions of a hypothetical price floor on milk and the incentives it creates. Now let's use supply and demand analysis to examine two real-world price floors: *minimum wage laws* and *agricultural price supports*.

## The Minimum Wage

The **minimum wage** is the lowest hourly wage rate that firms may legally pay their workers. Minimum wage workers can be skilled or unskilled and experienced or inexperienced. The common thread is that these workers, for a variety of reasons, lack better prospects. A minimum wage functions as a price floor. Figure 4.9 shows the effect of a binding minimum wage. Note that the wage, or the cost of labor, on the *y* axis ($10 per hour) is the price that must be paid. However, the market equilibrium wage ($7), or $W_E$, is below the minimum wage. The minimum wage prevents the market from reaching $W_E$ at E (the equilibrium point) because only the wages in the green shaded area are legal. Since the demand for labor depends on how much it costs, the minimum wage raises the cost of hiring workers. Therefore, a higher minimum wage will lower the quantity of labor demanded. However, since

The **minimum wage** is the lowest hourly wage rate that firms may legally pay their workers.

---

**FIGURE 4.9**

**Price Floors and a Binding Minimum Wage Market in the Short and Long Run**

A binding minimum wage is a price floor above the current equilibrium wage, $W_E$. At $10 per hour, the number of workers willing to supply their labor ($S_{SR}$) is greater than the demand for workers ($D_{SR}$). The result is a surplus of workers (which we recognize as unemployment). Since the supply of workers and demand for workers both become more elastic in the long run, unemployment expands ($S_{LR} > D_{LR}$).

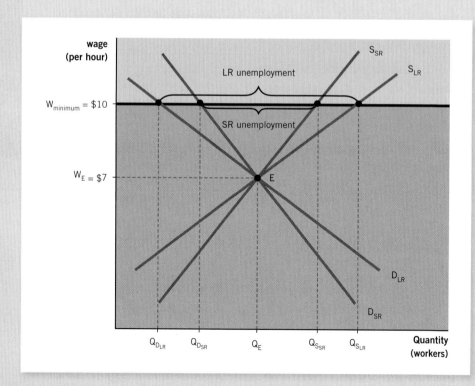

businesses still need to serve their customers, this means that labor expenses for the firm ordinarily rise in the short run. At the same time, firms will look for ways to substitute additional capital for workers. As a result, a binding minimum wage results in unemployment in the short run since $Q_{S_{SR}} > Q_{D_{SR}}$.

Businesses generally want to keep costs down, so in the long run they will try to reduce the amount they spend on labor. They might replace workers with machinery, shorten work hours, offer reduced customer service, or even relocate to countries that do not have minimum wage laws. As we move past the short run, more people will attempt to take advantage of higher minimum wages. Like firms, workers will adjust to the higher minimum wage over time. Some workers who might have decided to go to school full-time or remain retired, or who simply want some extra income, will enter the labor market because the minimum wage is now higher. As a result, minimum wage jobs will become progressively harder to find and unemployment will be magnified. The irony is that in the long run the minimum wage, just like any other price floor, has created two unintended consequences: a smaller demand for workers by employers ($Q_{D_{LR}}$ is significantly less than $Q_E$), and a larger supply of workers ($Q_{S_{LR}}$) looking for those previously existing jobs.

Proponents of minimum wage legislation are aware that it often creates unemployment. To address this problem, they support investment in training, education, and the creation of government jobs programs to provide more work opportunities. While jobs programs increase minimum wage jobs, training and additional education enable workers to acquire skills needed for jobs that pay more than the minimum wage. Economists generally believe that education and training programs have longer-lasting benefits to society as a whole since they enable workers to obtain better-paying jobs on a permanent basis.

## ECONOMICS IN THE REAL WORLD

### Wage Laws Squeeze South Africa's Poor

Consider this story that appeared in the *New York Times* in 2010.*

NEWCASTLE, South Africa—The sheriff arrived at the factory here to shut it down, part of a national enforcement drive against clothing manufacturers who violate the minimum wage. But women working on the factory floor— the supposed beneficiaries of the crackdown—clambered atop cutting tables and ironing boards to raise anguished cries against it. Thoko Zwane, 43, who has worked in factories since she was 15, lost her job in Newcastle when a Chinese-run factory closed in 2004. More than a third of South Africans are jobless. "Why? Why?" shouted Nokuthula Masango, 25, after the authorities carted away bolts of gaily colored fabric. She made just $36 a week, $21 less than the minimum wage, but needed the meager pay to help support a large extended family that includes her five unemployed siblings and their children.

The women's spontaneous protest is just one sign of how acute South Africa's long-running unemployment crisis has become. With their own economy saddled with very high unemployment rates, the women feared being out of work more than getting stuck in poorly paid jobs.

Trade-offs

*Celia W. Dugger, "Wage Laws Squeeze South Africa's Poor," *New York Times*, September 27, 2010.

South Africans wait in line for unemployment benefits.

In the years since the end of apartheid, the South African economy has grown, but not nearly fast enough to end an intractable unemployment crisis. For over a decade, the jobless rate has been among the highest in the world, fueling crime, inequality, and social unrest in the continent's richest nation. The global economic downturn has made the problem much worse, wiping out more than a million jobs. Over a third of South Africa's workforce is now idle. And 16 years after Nelson Mandela led the country to black majority rule, more than half of blacks ages 15 to 34 are without work—triple the level for whites.

"The numbers are mind-boggling," said James Levinsohn, a Yale University economist. ✳

## The Minimum Wage Is Often Nonbinding

Most people believe that raising the minimum wage is a simple step that the government can take to improve the standard of living of the working poor. However, in most places the minimum wage is often nonbinding and therefore has no impact on the market. Adjusting for inflation, the federal minimum wage was highest in 1968, so in real terms minimum wage workers are earning less today than they did almost half a century ago. Why would we have a minimum wage if it is largely nonbinding?

To help us answer this question, consider the two nonbinding minimum wage rates ($7 and $9) shown in Figure 4.10. A minimum wage of $7 per hour is far below the equilibrium wage of $10 ($W_E$), so at that point supply and demand push the equilibrium wage up to $10. Suppose that politicians decide to raise the minimum wage to $9. This new minimum wage of $9 would remain below the market wage, so there would be no impact on the labor market for workers who are willing to accept the minimum wage. Therefore, an increase in the minimum wage from $7 to $9 an hour will not create unemployment. Unemployment will occur only when the minimum wage rises above $10.

Politicians know that most voters have a poor understanding of basic economics. As a result, a politician can seek to raise the minimum wage with great fanfare. Voters would support the new rate because they do not know that it is likely to be nonbinding; they expect wages to rise. In reality, nothing will change, but the perception of a benevolent action will remain. In fact, since its inception in 1938, increases in the minimum wage in the United States have generally trailed the market wage and therefore have avoided creating unemployment. The minimum wage adjusts sporadically upward every few years but rarely rises enough to cause the market wage to fall below it. This creates the illusion that the minimum wage is lifting wages. However, it does not cause any of the adverse consequences of a binding minimum wage.

In an effort to raise the minimum wage beyond the national rate, a number of states have enacted higher minimum wage laws. Not surprisingly, some of the states with the highest minimum wage rates, like Washington, Oregon,

**FIGURE 4.10**

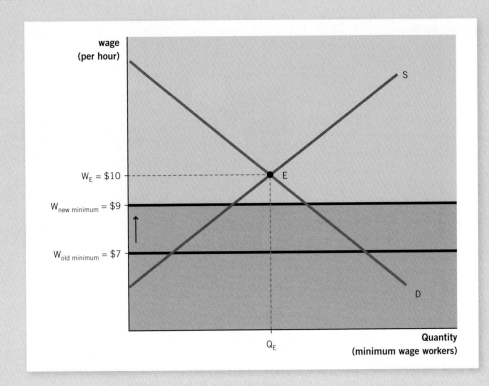

**A Nonbinding Minimum Wage**

An increase in the minimum wage from $7 to $9 remains nonbinding. Therefore, it will not change the demand for labor or the unemployment rate. If the minimum wage rises above the market wage, additional unemployment will occur.

and California, also have unemployment rates that are among the highest in the country—evidence that binding minimum wage rates can have serious consequences.

## ECONOMICS IN THE REAL WORLD

### A Sweet Deal, If You Can Get It

Sugar is one of life's small pleasures. It can be extracted and refined from sugar cane and sugar beets, two crops that can be grown in a variety of climates around the world. Sugar is both plentiful and cheap. As a result, Americans enjoy a lot of it—an average of over 60 pounds of refined sugar per person each year!

We would consume a lot more sugar if it was not subject to price controls. After the War of 1812, struggling sugar cane producers asked the government to pass a tariff that would protect domestic production. Over the years, price supports of all kinds have served to keep domestic sugar production high. The result is an industry that depends on a high price to survive. Under the current price-support system, the price of U.S.-produced sugar is roughly two to three times the world price. This has led to a bizarre set of incentives whereby U.S. farmers grow more sugar than they should and use land that is not well suited to the crop. For instance, sugar cane requires a subtropical climate, but most of the U.S. crop is grown in Louisiana, a region that is prone to hurricanes in the summer and killing freezes in the late fall. As a result, many sugar cane crops there are completely lost.

Incentives

## The Minimum Wage

### 30 Days

The (2005) pilot episode of this reality series focused on the minimum wage. Morgan Spurlock and his fiancée spend 30 days in a poor neighborhood of Columbus, Ohio. The couple attempt to survive by earning minimum wage (at that time, $5.15 an hour) in order to make ends meet. In addition, they are required to start off with only one week's minimum wage (about $300) in reserve. Also, they cannot use credit cards to pay their bills. They experience firsthand the struggles that many minimum wage households face when living paycheck to paycheck. *30 Days* makes it painfully clear how difficult it is for anyone to live on the minimum wage for a month, let alone for years.

A quote from Morgan Spurlock sums up what the episode tries to convey: "We don't see the people that surround us. We don't see the people who are struggling to get by that are right next to us. And I have seen how hard the struggle is. I have been here.

Could you make ends meet earning the minimum wage?

And I only did it for a month, and there's people who do this their whole lives."

After watching this episode of *30 Days*, it is hard not to think that raising the minimum wage is a good idea. Unfortunately, the economic reality is that raising the minimum wage does not guarantee that minimum wage earners will make more and also be able keep their jobs.

Which of these is the *real* thing? The Coke on the right, with high-fructose corn syrup, was made in the United States; the other, with sugar, was made in Mexico.

Why do farmers persist in growing sugar cane in Louisiana? The answer lies in the political process: sugar growers have effectively lobbied to keep prices high through tariffs on foreign imports. Since lower prices would put many U.S. growers out of business and cause the loss of many jobs, politicians have given in to their demands.

Meanwhile, the typical sugar consumer is largely oblivious to the political process that sets the price floor. It has been estimated that the sugar subsidy program costs consumers over one billion dollars a year. To make matters worse, thanks to corn subsidies high-fructose corn syrup has become a cheap alternative to sugar and is often added to processed foods and soft drinks. In 1980, Coca-Cola replaced sugar with high-fructose corn extract in the United States in order to reduce production costs. However, Coca-Cola continues to use sugar cane in many Latin American countries because it is cheaper. New research shows that high-fructose corn syrup causes a metabolic reaction that makes people who ingest it more inclined to obesity. Ouch! This is an example of an unintended consequence that few policymakers could have imagined. There is no reason why the United States must produce its own sugar cane. Ironically, sugar is cheaper in Canada primarily because Canada has no sugar growers—and thus no trade restrictions or government support programs. ✳

# Minimum Wage: Always the Same?

A minimum wage is a price floor, a price control that doesn't allow prices—in this case the cost of labor—to fall below an assigned value. Although the media and politicians often discuss the minimum wage in America as if there is only one minimum wage, it turns out that there are numerous minimum wages in the USA. In states where the state minimum wage is not the same as the federal minimum wage, the higher of the two wage rates takes effect.

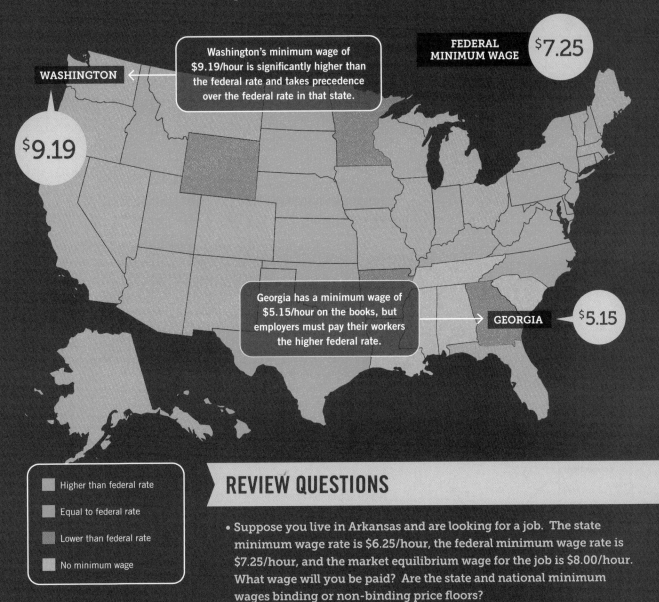

WASHINGTON

Washington's minimum wage of $9.19/hour is significantly higher than the federal rate and takes precedence over the federal rate in that state.

$9.19

FEDERAL MINIMUM WAGE  $7.25

Georgia has a minimum wage of $5.15/hour on the books, but employers must pay their workers the higher federal rate.

GEORGIA  $5.15

■ Higher than federal rate
■ Equal to federal rate
■ Lower than federal rate
■ No minimum wage

## REVIEW QUESTIONS

- Suppose you live in Arkansas and are looking for a job. The state minimum wage rate is $6.25/hour, the federal minimum wage rate is $7.25/hour, and the market equilibrium wage for the job is $8.00/hour. What wage will you be paid? Are the state and national minimum wages binding or non-binding price floors?

- Suppose Wisconsin increases its minimum wage from $7.25/hour, which is below the market wage for low-skill labor, to $11.00/hour, which is above the market wage. Using supply and demand curves, show how this might affect the number of employed workers.

# PRACTICE WHAT YOU KNOW

In today's Internet age, four degrees of separation are all that stand between you and the rest of the world.

## Price Ceilings and Price Floors: Would a Price Control on Internet Access Be Effective?

A recent study found the following demand and supply schedule for high-speed Internet access:

| Price of Internet | Connections demanded (millions of units) | Connections supplied (millions of units) |
|---|---|---|
| $60 | 10.0 | 62.5 |
| $50 | 20.0 | 55.0 |
| $40 | 30.0 | 47.5 |
| $30 | 40.0 | 40.0 |
| $20 | 50.0 | 32.5 |
| $10 | 60.0 | 25.0 |

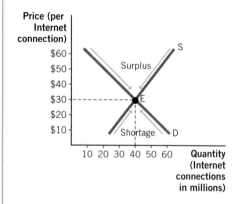

**Question: What are the equilibrium price and equilibrium quantity of Internet service?**

**Answer:** First, look at the table to see where supply and demand are equal. At a price of $30, consumers purchase 40 million units and producers supply 40 million units. Therefore, the equilibrium price is $30 and the equilibrium quantity is 40 million. At any price above $30, the quantity supplied exceeds the quantity demanded, so there is a surplus. The surplus gives sellers an incentive to cut the price until it reaches the equilibrium point, E. At any price below $30, the quantity demanded exceeds the quantity supplied, so there is a shortage. The shortage gives sellers an incentive to raise the price until it reaches the equilibrium point, E.

**Question: Suppose that providers convince the government that maintaining high-speed access to the Internet is an important element of technology infrastructure. As a result, Congress approves a price floor at $10 above the equilibrium price to help companies provide Internet service. How many people are able to connect to the Internet?**

**Answer:** Adding $10 to the market price of $30 gives us a price floor of $40. At $40, consumers demand 30 million connections. Producers provide 47.5 million connections. This is a surplus of 17.5 million units (shown). A price floor means that producers cannot cut the price below that point to increase the quantity that consumers demand. As a result, only 30 million units are sold. So only 30 million people connect to the Internet.

(CONTINUED)

*(CONTINUED)*

**Question:** When teachers realize that fewer people are purchasing Internet access, they demand that the price floor be repealed and a price ceiling be put in its place. Congress acts immediately to remedy the problem, and a new price ceiling is set at $10 below the market price. Now how many people are able to connect to the Internet?

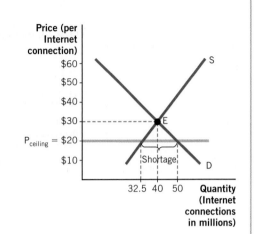

**Answer:** Subtracting $10 from the market price of $30 gives us a price ceiling of $20. At $20 per connection, consumers demand 50 million connections. However, producers provide only 32.5 million connections. This is a shortage of 17.5 million units (shown). A price ceiling means that producers cannot raise the price, which will cause an increase in the quantity supplied. As a result, only 32.5 million units are sold, so only 32.5 million people connect to the Internet.

**Question:** Which provides the greatest access to the Internet: free markets, price floors, or price ceilings?

**Answer:** With no government intervention, 40 million connections are sold. Once the price floor is established, there are 30 million connections. Under the price ceiling, 32.5 million connections exist. Despite legislative efforts to satisfy both producers and consumers of Internet service, the best solution is to allow free markets to regulate access to the good.

# Conclusion

Does the minimum wage help everyone earn a living wage? We learned that it is possible to set the minimum wage high enough to guarantee that each worker will earn a living wage. However, the trade-off in setting the minimum wage substantially higher is that it becomes binding and many workers will no longer have jobs. In other words, setting the minimum wage high enough to earn a living wage won't raise every worker out of poverty because many of those workers will no longer have jobs.

**Trade-offs**

The policies presented in this chapter—rent control, price gouging laws, the minimum wage, and agricultural price controls—create unintended consequences. Attempts to control prices should be viewed cautiously. When the price signal is suppressed through a binding price floor or a binding price ceiling, the market's ability to maintain order is diminished, surpluses and shortages develop and expand through time, and obtaining goods and services becomes difficult.

The role of markets in society has many layers, and we've only just begun our analysis. In the next chapter, we will develop a technique to measure the gains that consumers and producers enjoy in unregulated markets, and we will consider the distortions created by tax policy.

# ANSWERING THE BIG QUESTIONS

### When do price ceilings matter?

＊A price ceiling is a legally imposed maximum price. When the price is set below the equilibrium price, the quantity demanded will exceed the quantity supplied. This will result in a shortage. Price ceilings matter when they are set below the equilibrium price.

### What effects do price ceilings have on economic activity?

＊Price ceilings create two unintended consequences: a smaller supply of the good ($Q_S$) and a higher price for consumers who turn to the black market.

### When do price floors matter?

＊A price floor is a legally imposed minimum price. The minimum wage is an example of a price floor. If the minimum wage is set above the equilibrium wage, a surplus of labor will develop. However, if the minimum wage is nonbinding, it will have no effect on the market wage. Thus price floors matter when they are set above the equilibrium price.

### What effects do price floors have on economic activity?

＊Price floors lead to many unintended consequences, including surpluses, the creation of black markets, and artificial attempts to bring the market back into balance. For example, proponents of a higher minimum wage are concerned about finding ways to alleviate the resulting surplus of labor, or unemployment.

# Price Gouging: Disaster Preparedness

Disasters, whether natural or human-made, usually strike quickly and without warning. You and your family may have little or no time to decide what to do. That's why it is important to plan for the possibility of disaster and not wait until it happens. Failing to plan is planning to fail. In this box, we consider a few simple things you can do now to lessen the impact of a disaster on your personal and financial well-being.

During a disaster, shortages of essential goods and services become widespread. In the 30 states where price gouging laws are on the books, they prevent merchants from charging unusually high prices. If you live in one of these states, cash alone can't save you. You will have to survive on your own for a time before help arrives and communication channels are restored.

Taking measures to prepare for a disaster reduces the likelihood of injury, loss of life, and property damage far more than anything you can do after a disaster strikes. An essential part of disaster planning should include financial planning. Let's begin with the basics. Get adequate insurance to protect your family's health, lives, and property; plan for the possibility of job loss or disability by building a cash reserve; and safeguard your financial and legal records. It is also important to set aside extra money in a long-term emergency fund. Nearly all financial experts advise saving enough money to cover your expenses for six months. Most households never come close to reaching this goal, but don't let that stop you from trying.

Preparing a simple disaster supply kit is also a must. Keep enough water, nonperishable food, sanitation supplies, batteries, medications, and cash on hand for three days. Often, the power is out after a disaster, so you cannot count on ATMs or banks to be open. These measures will help you to weather the immediate impact of a disaster.

Finally, many documents are difficult to replace. Consider investing in a home safe or safe deposit box to ensure that your important records survive. Place your passports, Social Security cards, copies of drivers' licenses, mortgage and property deeds, car titles, wills, insurance records, and birth and marriage certificates out of harm's way.

Will you be ready if disaster strikes?

## CONCEPTS YOU SHOULD KNOW

black market (p. 109)
minimum wage (p. 124)
price ceiling (p. 108)

price control (p. 108)
price floor (p. 119)

price gouging laws (p. 115)
rent control (p. 114)

## QUESTIONS FOR REVIEW

1. Does a binding price ceiling cause a shortage or a surplus? Provide an example to support your answer.

2. Does a nonbinding price floor cause a shortage or a surplus? Provide an example to support your answer.

3. Will a surplus or a shortage caused by a price control become smaller or larger over time?

4. Are price gouging laws an example of a price floor or a price ceiling?

5. What will happen to the market price when a price control is nonbinding?

6. Why do most economists oppose attempts to control prices? Why does the government attempt to control prices anyway, in a number of markets?

## STUDY PROBLEMS (*solved at the end of the section)

1. In the song "Minimum Wage," the punk band Fenix TX comments on the inadequacy of the minimum wage to make ends meet. Using the poverty thresholds provided by the Census Bureau,* determine whether the federal minimum wage of $7.25 an hour provides enough income for a single full-time worker to escape poverty.

* 2. Imagine that the community you live in decides to enact a rent control of $700 per month on every one-bedroom apartment. Using the following table, determine the market price and equilibrium quantity without rent control. How many one-bedroom apartments will be rented after the rent-control law is passed?

| Monthly rent | Quantity demanded | Quantity supplied |
|---|---|---|
| $600 | 700 | 240 |
| $700 | 550 | 320 |
| $800 | 400 | 400 |
| $900 | 250 | 480 |
| $1,000 | 100 | 560 |

3. Suppose that the federal government places a binding price floor on chocolate. To help support the price floor, the government purchases all of the leftover chocolate that consumers do not buy. If the price floor remains in place for a number of years, what do you expect to happen to each of the following?

a. quantity of chocolate demanded by consumers
b. quantity of chocolate supplied by producers
c. quantity of chocolate purchased by the government

4. Suppose that a group of die-hard sports fans is upset about the high price of tickets to many games. As a result of their lobbying efforts, a new law caps the maximum ticket price to any sporting event at $50. Will more people be able to attend the games? Explain your answer. Will certain teams and events be affected more than others? Provide examples.

5. Many local governments use parking meters on crowded downtown streets. However, the parking spaces along the street are typically hard to find because the metered price is often set below the market price. Explain what happens when local governments set the meter price too low. Why do you think the price is set below the market-clearing price?

6. Imagine that local suburban leaders decide to enact a minimum wage. Will the community lose more jobs if the nearby city votes to increase the minimum wage to the same rate? Discuss your answer.

✳ 7. Examine the following graph, showing the market for low-skill laborers.

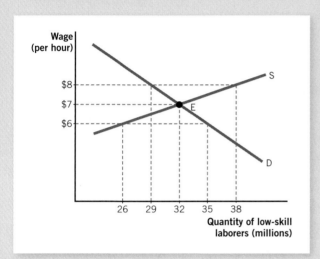

How many low-skill laborers will be unemployed when the minimum wage is $8 an hour? How many low-skill workers will be unemployed when the minimum wage is $6 an hour?

8. The demand and supply curves that we use can also be represented with equations. Suppose that the demand for low-skill labor, $Q_D$, is represented by the following equation, where W is the wage rate:

$$Q_D = 53,000,000 - 3,000,000\,W$$

The supply of low-skill labor, $Q_S$, is represented by the equation

$$Q_S = -10,000,000 + 6,000,000\,W$$

a. Find the equilibrium wage. (**Hint:** Set $Q_D = Q_S$ and solve for the wage, W.)
b. Find the equilibrium quantity of labor. (**Hint:** Now plug the value you got in part (a) back into $Q_D$ or $Q_S$. You can double-check your answer by plugging the answer from part (a) into both $Q_D$ and $Q_S$ to see that you get the same result.)
c. What happens if the minimum wage is $8? (**Hint:** Plug W = 8 into both $Q_D$ and $Q_S$.) Does this cause a surplus or a shortage?
d. What happens if the minimum wage is $6? (**Hint:** Plug W = 6 into both $Q_D$ and $Q_S$.) Does this cause a surplus or a shortage?

## SOLVED PROBLEMS

2. The equilibrium price occurs where the quantity demanded is equal to the quantity supplied. This occurs when $Q_D = Q_S = 800$. When the quantity is 800, the monthly rent is $800. Next, the question asks how many one-bedroom apartments will be rented after a rent-control law limits the rent to $700 a month. When the rent is $700, the quantity supplied is 320 apartments. It is also worth noting that the quantity demanded when the rent is $700 is 550 units, so there is a shortage of $550 - 320 = 230$ apartments once the rent-control law goes into effect.

7. How many low-skill laborers will be unemployed when the minimum wage is $8 an hour? The quantity demanded is 29M, and the quantity supplied is 38M. This results in $38M - 29M = 9M$ unemployed low-skill workers.

How many low-skill workers will be unemployed when the minimum wage is $6 an hour? Since $6 an hour is below the market-equilibrium wage of $7, it has no effect. In other words, a $6 minimum wage is nonbinding, and therefore no unemployment is caused.

# The Efficiency of Markets and the Costs of Taxation

**Raising tax rates always generates more tax revenue.**

Many people believe that if a government needs more revenue, all it needs to do is raise tax rates. If only it were that simple. Gasoline taxes demonstrate why this is a misconception.

**MIS CONCEPTION**

Most people find it painful to pay more than $3 a gallon for gas. In many places, sales and excise taxes add a significant amount to the price. For example, the price of gasoline throughout Europe is often more than double that in the United States, largely because of much higher gasoline taxes. Other countries, like Venezuela, Saudi Arabia, and Mexico, subsidize gasoline so that their citizens pay less than the market price. In countries where gasoline is subsidized, consumers drive their cars everywhere, mass transportation is largely unavailable, and there is little concern for fuel efficiency. In contrast, as you might imagine, in countries with high gasoline taxes consumers drive less, use public transportation more, and tend to purchase fuel-efficient vehicles.

How high do gasoline taxes have to rise before large numbers of people significantly cut back on their gasoline consumption? The answer to that question will help us understand the misconception that raising tax rates always generates more tax revenue.

In the previous chapter, we learned about the market distortions caused by price controls. We observed that efforts to manipulate market prices not only cause surpluses and shortages, but also lead to black markets. In this chapter, we will quantify how markets enhance the welfare of society. We begin with consumer surplus and producer surplus, two concepts that illustrate how taxation, like price controls, creates distortions in economic behavior by altering the incentives that people face when consuming and producing goods that are taxed.

How much do taxes cost the economy?

# BIG QUESTIONS

* What are consumer surplus and producer surplus?
* When is a market efficient?
* Why do taxes create deadweight loss?

## What Are Consumer Surplus and Producer Surplus?

**Welfare economics**
is the branch of economics that studies how the allocation of resources affects economic well-being.

Markets create value by bringing together buyers and sellers so that consumers and producers can mutually benefit from trade. **Welfare economics** is the branch of economics that studies how the allocation of resources affects economic well-being. In this section, we develop two concepts that will help us measure the value that markets create: *consumer surplus* and *producer surplus*. In competitive markets, the equilibrium price is simultaneously low enough to attract consumers and high enough to encourage producers. This balance between demand and supply enhances the welfare of society. That is not to say that society's welfare depends solely on markets. People also find satisfaction in many nonmarket settings, including spending time with their families and friends, and doing hobbies and charity work. For now, let's focus on how markets enhance human welfare.

### Consumer Surplus

**Willingness to pay**
is the maximum price a consumer will pay for a good.

Consider three students: Frank, Beanie, and Mitch. Like students everywhere, each one has a maximum price he is willing to pay for a new economics textbook. Beanie owns a successful business, so for him the cost of a new textbook does not present a financial hardship. Mitch is a business major who really wants to do well in economics. Frank is not serious about his studies. Table 5.1 shows the maximum value that each student places on the textbook. This value, called the **willingness to pay**, is the maximum price a consumer will pay for a good. The willingness to pay is also known as the reservation price. In an auction or a negotiation, the willingness to pay, or reservation price, is the price beyond which the consumer decides to walk away from the transaction.

Consider what happens when the price of the book is $151. If Beanie purchases the book at $151, he pays $49 less than the $200

How much will they pay for an economics textbook?

| TABLE 5.1 | |
|---|---|
| **Willingness to Pay for a New Economics Textbook** | |
| **Buyer** | **Willingness to pay** |
| Beanie | $200 |
| Mitch | $150 |
| Frank | $100 |

maximum he was willing to pay. He values the textbook at $49 more than the purchase price, so buying the book will make him better off.

**Consumer surplus** is the difference between the willingness to pay for a good and the price that is paid to get it. While Beanie gains $49 in consumer surplus, a price of $151 is more than either Mitch or Frank is willing to pay. Since Mitch is willing to pay only $150, if he purchases the book he will experience a consumer loss of $1. Frank's willingness to pay is $100, so if he buys the book for $151 he will experience a consumer loss of $51. Whenever the price is greater than the willingness to pay, a rational consumer will decide not to buy.

**Consumer surplus**
is the difference between the willingness to pay for a good and the price that is paid to get it.

## Using Demand Curves to Illustrate Consumer Surplus

In the previous section, we discussed consumer surplus as an amount. We can also illustrate it graphically with a demand curve. Figure 5.1 shows the demand curve drawn from the data in Table 5.1. Notice that the curve looks like a staircase with three steps—one for each additional textbook purchase. Each point on a market demand curve corresponds to one unit sold, so if we added more consumers into our example, the "steps" would become narrower and the demand curve would become smoother.

At any price above $200, none of the students wants to purchase a textbook. This relationship is evident on the x axis where the quantity demanded is 0. At any price between $150 and $200, Beanie is the only buyer, so the quantity demanded is 1. At prices between $100 and $150, Beanie and Mitch are each willing to buy the textbook, so the quantity demanded is 2. Finally, if the price is $100 or less, all three students are willing to buy the textbook, so the quantity demanded is 3. As the price falls, the quantity demanded increases.

We can measure the total extent of consumer surplus by examining the area under the demand curve for each of our three consumers, as shown in Figure 5.2. In Figure 5.2a the price is $175, and only Beanie decides to buy. Since his willingness to pay is $200, he is better off by $25; this is his consumer surplus. The green-shaded area under the demand curve and above the price represents the benefit Beanie receives from purchasing a textbook at a price of $175. When the price drops to $125, as shown in Figure 5.2b, Mitch also decides to buy a textbook. Now the total quantity demanded is 2 textbooks. Mitch's willingness to pay is $150, so his consumer surplus, represented by the red-shaded area, is $25. However, since Beanie's willingness to pay is $200, his consumer surplus rises from $25 to $75. So a textbook price of $125 raises the total consumer surplus to $100. In other words, lower prices create more consumer surplus in this market—and in any other.

## FIGURE 5.1

### Demand Curve for an Economics Textbook

The demand curve has a step for each additional textbook purchase. As the price goes down, more students buy the textbook.

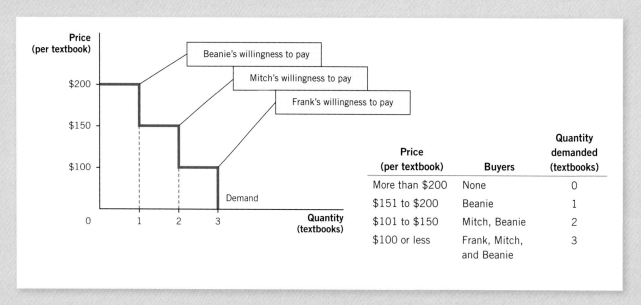

| Price (per textbook) | Buyers | Quantity demanded (textbooks) |
| --- | --- | --- |
| More than $200 | None | 0 |
| $151 to $200 | Beanie | 1 |
| $101 to $150 | Mitch, Beanie | 2 |
| $100 or less | Frank, Mitch, and Beanie | 3 |

## FIGURE 5.2

### Determining Consumer Surplus from a Demand Curve

(a) At a price of $175, Beanie is the only buyer, so the quantity demanded is 1. (b) At a price of $125, Beanie and Mitch are each willing to buy the textbook, so the quantity demanded is 2.

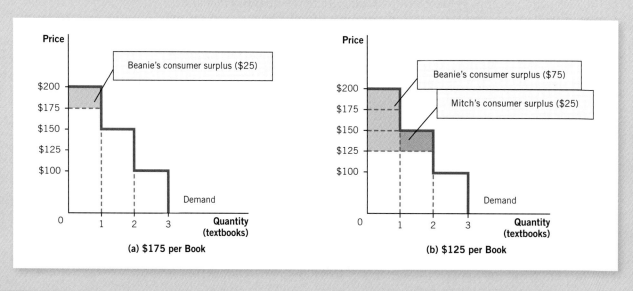

(a) $175 per Book

(b) $125 per Book

## Producer Surplus

Sellers also benefit from market transactions. In this section, our three students discover that they are good at economics and decide to go into the tutoring business. They do not want to provide this service for free, but each has a different minimum price, or *willingness to sell*. The **willingness to sell** is the minimum price a seller will accept to sell a good or service. Table 5.2 shows each tutor's willingness to sell his services.

Consider what happens at a tutoring price of $25 per hour. Since Frank is willing to tutor for $10 per hour, every hour that he tutors at $25 per hour earns him $15 more than his willingness to sell. This extra $15 per hour is his *producer surplus*. **Producer surplus** is the difference between the willingness to sell a good and the price that the seller receives. Mitch is willing to tutor for $20 per hour and earns a $5 producer surplus for every hour he tutors. Finally, Beanie's willingness to tutor, at $30 per hour, is more than the market price of $25. If he tutors, he will have a producer loss of $5 per hour.

How do producers determine their willingness to sell? They must consider two factors: the direct costs of producing the good and the indirect costs, or opportunity costs. Students who are new to economics often mistakenly assume that the cost of producing an item is the only cost to consider in making the decision to produce. But producers also have opportunity costs. Beanie, Mitch, and Frank each has a unique willingness to sell because each has a different opportunity cost. Beanie owns his own business, so for him the time spent tutoring is time that he could have spent making money elsewhere. Mitch is a business student who might otherwise be studying to get better grades. Frank is neither a businessman nor a serious student, so the $10 he can earn in an hour of tutoring is not taking the place of other earning opportunities or studying more to get better grades.

**Willingness to sell** is the minimum price a seller will accept to sell a good or service.

**Producer surplus** is the difference between the willingness to sell a good and the price that the seller receives.

Opportunity cost

## Using Supply Curves to Illustrate Producer Surplus

Continuing our example, the supply curve in Figure 5.3 shows the relationship between the price for an hour of tutoring and the quantity of tutors who are willing to work. As you can see on the supply schedule (the table within the figure), at any price less than $10 per hour no one wants to tutor. At prices between $10 and $19 per hour, Frank is the only tutor, so the

| TABLE 5.2 | |
|---|---|
| **Willingness to Sell Tutoring Services** | |
| **Seller** | **Willingness to sell** |
| Beanie | $30/hr |
| Mitch | $20/hr |
| Frank | $10/hr |

## FIGURE 5.3

**Supply Curve for Economics Tutoring**

The supply curve has three steps, one for each additional student who is willing to tutor. Progressively higher prices will induce more students to become tutors.

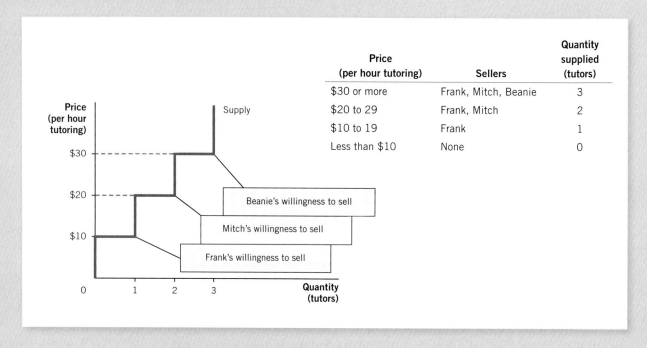

| Price (per hour tutoring) | Sellers | Quantity supplied (tutors) |
| --- | --- | --- |
| $30 or more | Frank, Mitch, Beanie | 3 |
| $20 to 29 | Frank, Mitch | 2 |
| $10 to 19 | Frank | 1 |
| Less than $10 | None | 0 |

quantity supplied is 1. Between $20 and $29 per hour, Frank and Mitch are willing to tutor, so the quantity supplied rises to 2. Finally, if the price is $30 or more, all three friends are willing to tutor, so the quantity supplied is 3. As the price they receive for tutoring rises, the number of tutors increases from 1 to 3.

What do these relationships between price and supply tell us about producer surplus? Let's turn to Figure 5.4. By examining the area above the supply curve, we can measure the extent of producer surplus. In Figure 5.4a, the price of an hour of tutoring is $15. At that price, only Frank decides to tutor. Since he would be willing to tutor even if the price were as low as $10 per hour, he is $5 better off tutoring. Frank's producer surplus is represented by the red-shaded area between the supply curve and the price of $15. Since Beanie and Mitch do not tutor when the price is $15, they do not receive any producer surplus. In Figure 5.4b, the price for tutoring is $25 per hour. At this price, Mitch also decides to tutor. His willingness to tutor is $20, so when the price is $25 per hour his producer surplus is $5, represented by the blue-shaded area. Since Frank's willingness to tutor is $10, at $25 per hour his producer surplus rises to $15. By looking at the shaded boxes in Figure 5.4b, we see that an increase in the rates for tutoring raises the combined producer surplus of Frank and Mitch to $20.

## FIGURE 5.4

**Determining Producer Surplus from a Supply Curve**

(a) The price of an hour of tutoring is $15. At this price, only Frank decides to tutor. (b) The price for tutoring is $25 per hour. At this price, Mitch also decides to tutor.

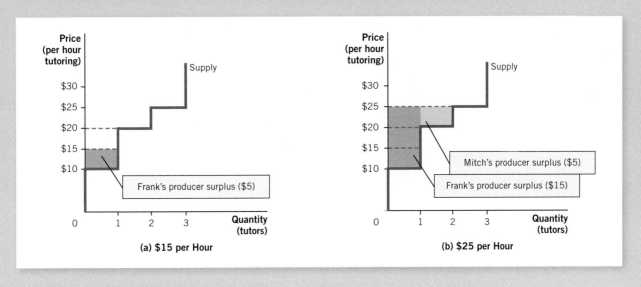

(a) $15 per Hour

(b) $25 per Hour

## PRACTICE WHAT YOU KNOW

### Consumer and Producer Surplus: Trendy Fashion

Leah decides to buy a new jacket from D&G for $80. She was willing to pay $100. When her friend Becky sees the jacket, she loves it and thinks it is worth $150. So she offers Leah $125 for the jacket, and Leah accepts. Leah and Becky are both thrilled with the exchange.

**Question: Determine the total surplus from the original purchase and the additional surplus generated by the resale of the jacket.**

Rachel Bilson wearing a D&G jacket

**Answer:** Leah was willing to pay $100 and the jacket cost $80, so she keeps the difference, or $20, as consumer surplus. When Leah resells the jacket to Becky for $125, she earns $25 in producer surplus. At the same time, Becky receives $25 in consumer surplus, since she was willing to pay Leah up to $150 for the jacket but Leah sells it to her for $125. The resale generates an additional $50 in surplus.

# When Is a Market Efficient?

**Total surplus,**
also known as **social welfare,**
is the sum of consumer surplus and producer surplus.

We have seen how consumers benefit from lower prices and how producers benefit from higher prices. When we combine the concepts of consumer and producer surplus, we can build a complete picture of the welfare of buyers and sellers. Adding consumer and producer surplus gives us **total surplus**, also known as **social welfare**, because it measures the welfare of society. Total surplus is the best way economists have to measure the benefits that markets create.

Figure 5.5 illustrates the relationship between consumer and producer surplus for a gallon of milk. The demand curve shows that some customers are willing to pay more for a gallon of milk than others. Likewise, some sellers (producers) are willing to sell milk for less than others.

Let's say that Alice is willing to pay $7.00 per gallon for milk, but when she gets to the store she finds it for $4.00. The difference between the price she is willing to pay, represented by point A, and the price she actually pays, represented by E (the equilibrium price), is $3.00 in consumer surplus. This is indicated by the blue arrow showing the distance from $4.00 to $7.00. Alice's friend Betty is willing to pay $5.00 for milk, but, like Alice, she finds it for $4.00. Therefore, she receives $1.00 in consumer surplus, indicated by the blue arrow at point B showing the distance from $4.00 to $5.00. In fact, all consumers who are willing to pay more than $4.00 are better off when they purchase the milk at $4.00. We can show this total area of consumer surplus on the graph as the blue-shaded triangle bordered by the demand curve, the $y$ axis, and the equilibrium price ($P_E$). At every point in this area, the consumers who are willing to pay more than the equilibrium price for milk will be better off.

Trade
creates
value

## FIGURE 5.5

**Consumer and Producer Surplus for a Gallon of Milk**

Consumer surplus is the difference between the willingness to pay along the demand curve and the equilibrium price, $P_E$. It is illustrated by the blue-shaded triangle. Producer surplus is the difference between the willingness to produce along the supply curve and the equilibrium price. It is illustrated by the red-shaded triangle.

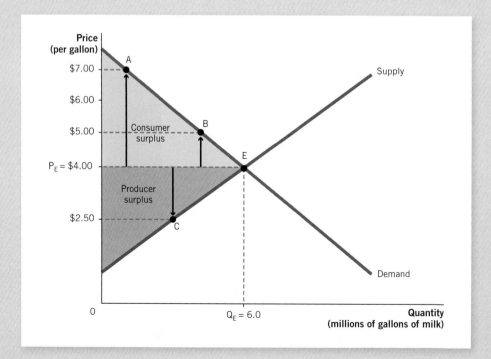

Continuing with Figure 5.5, producer surplus follows a similar process. Suppose that the Contented Cow dairy is willing to sell milk for $2.50 per gallon, represented by point C. Since the equilibrium price is $4.00, the business makes $1.50 in producer surplus. This is indicated by the red arrow at point C showing the distance from $4.00 to $2.50. If we think of the supply curve as representing the costs of many different sellers, we can calculate the total producer surplus as the red-shaded triangle bordered by the supply curve, the *y* axis, and the equilibrium price. The shaded blue triangle (consumer surplus) and the shaded red triangle (producer surplus) describe the increase in total surplus, or social welfare, created by the production and exchange of the good at the equilibrium price. At the equilibrium quantity of 6 million gallons of milk, output and consumption reach the largest possible combination of producer and consumer surplus. In the region of the graph beyond 6 million units, buyers and sellers will experience a loss.

The buyer and seller each benefit from this exchange.

When an allocation of resources maximizes total surplus, the result is said to be **efficient**. Efficiency occurs at point E when the market is in equilibrium. To think about why the market creates the largest possible total surplus, or social welfare, it is important to recall how the market allocates resources. Consumers who are willing to pay more than the equilibrium price will buy the good because they will enjoy the consumer surplus. Producers who are willing to sell the good for less than the market-equilibrium price will enjoy the producer surplus. In addition, consumers with a low willingness to buy (less than $4.00) and producers with a high willingness to sell (more than $4.00) do not participate in the market since they would be worse off. Therefore, the equilibrium output at point E maximizes the total surplus and is also an efficient allocation of resources.

An outcome is **efficient** when an allocation of resources maximizes total surplus.

## The Efficiency-Equity Debate

When economists model behavior, we assume that participants in a market are rational decision-makers. We assume that producers will always operate in the region of the triangle that represents producer surplus and that consumers will always operate in the region of the triangle that represents consumer surplus. We do not, for example, expect Alice to pay more than $7.00 for a gallon of milk or the Contented Cow dairy to sell a gallon of milk for less than $2.50 per gallon. In other words, for the market to work efficiently, voluntary instances of consumer loss must be rare. We assume that self-interest helps to ensure that all participants will benefit from an exchange.

Efficiency only requires that the pie gets eaten. Equity is a question of who gets the biggest share.

## ECONOMICS IN THE MEDIA

# Efficiency

### Old School

In the 2003 movie *Old School*, Frank tries to give away a bread maker he received as a wedding present. First he offers it to a friend as a housewarming gift, but it turns out that this is the friend who originally gave him the bread maker. Ouch! Later in the movie, we see Frank giving the bread maker to a small boy at a birthday party. Both efforts at re-gifting fail miserably.

From an economic perspective, giving the wrong gift makes society poorer. If you spend $50 on a gift and give it to someone who thinks it is only worth $30, you've lost $20 in value. Whenever you receive a shirt that is the wrong size or style, a fruitcake you won't eat, or something that is worth less to you than what the gift-giver spent on it, an economic inefficiency has occurred. Until now, we have thought of the market as enhancing efficiency by increasing the total surplus in society. But we can also think of the billions of dollars spent on mismatched gifts as a failure to maximize the total surplus involved in exchange. In other words, we can think of the efficiency of the gift-giving process as less than 100 percent.

Given what we have learned so far about economics, you might be tempted to argue that cash is the best gift you can give. When you give cash, it is never the wrong size or color, and the recipients can use it to buy whatever they want. However, very few people actually give cash (unless it is requested). Considering the advantages of cash, why don't more people give it instead of gifts? One reason is that cash seems impersonal. A second reason is that cash communicates exactly how much the giver spent. To avoid both problems, most people rarely give cash. Instead, they buy personalized gifts to communicate how much they care, while making it hard for the recipient to determine exactly how much they spent.

One way that society overcomes inefficiency in gifting is through the dissemination of information. For instance, wedding registries provide a convenient way for people who may not know the newlyweds very well to give them what they want. Similarly, prior to holidays many people tell each other what they would

Frank re-gifts a bread maker.

like to receive. By purchasing gifts that others want, givers can exactly match what the recipients would have purchased if they had received a cash transfer. This eliminates any potential inefficiency. At the same time, the giver conveys affection—an essential part of giving. To further reduce the potential inefficiencies associated with giving, many large families practice holiday gift exchanges. And another interesting mechanism for eliciting information involves Santa Claus. Children throughout the world send Santa Claus wish lists for Christmas, never realizing that the parents who help to write and send the lists are the primary beneficiaries.

To the economist, the strategies of providing better information, having gift exchanges, and sending wish lists to Santa Claus are just a few examples of how society tries to get the most out of the giving process—and that is something to be joyful about!

## PRACTICE WHAT YOU KNOW

### Total Surplus: How Would Lower Income Affect Urban Outfitters?

**Question:** If a drop in consumer income occurs, what will happen to the consumer surplus that customers enjoy at Urban Outfitters? What will happen to the amount of producer surplus that Urban Outfitters receives? Illustrate your answer by shifting the demand curve appropriately and labeling the new and old areas of consumer and producer surplus.

**Answer:** Since the items sold at Urban Outfitters are normal goods, a drop in income causes the demand curve (D) to shift to the left. The black arrow shows the leftward shift in graph (b) below. When you compare the area of consumer surplus (in blue) before and after the drop in income—that is, graphs (a) and (b)—you can see that it shrinks. The same is true when comparing the area of producer surplus (in red) before and after.

Does less income affect total surplus?

Your intuition might already confirm what the graphs tell us. Since consumers have less income, they buy fewer clothes at Urban Outfitters— so consumer surplus falls. Likewise, since fewer customers buy the store's clothes, Urban Outfitters sells less—so producer surplus falls. This is also evident in graph (b), since $Q_2 < Q_1$.

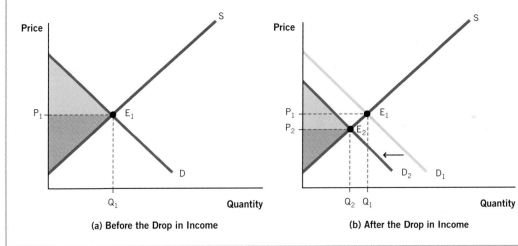

(a) Before the Drop in Income

(b) After the Drop in Income

However, the fact that both parties benefit from an exchange does not mean that each benefits equally. Economists are also interested in the distribution of the gains. **Equity** refers to the fairness of the distribution of benefits among the members of a society. In a world where no one cared about equity, only efficiency would matter and no particular division would be preferred. Another way of thinking about fairness versus efficiency is to consider a pie. If our only concern is efficiency, we will simply want to make sure that none of the pie goes to waste. However, if we care about equity, we will also want to make sure that the pie is divided equally among those present and that no one gets a larger piece than any other.

**Equity**
refers to the fairness of the distribution of benefits within the society.

In our first look at consumer and producer surplus, we have assumed that markets produce efficient outcomes. But in the real world, this is not always the case. Markets also fail; their efficiency can be compromised in a number of ways. Market failure is a topic of great importance in economics, but for now, all you need to know is that failure can occur.

# Why Do Taxes Create Deadweight Loss?

Taxes provide many benefits. They also remind us that "there is no free lunch"; for example, we don't pay the police dispatcher before dialing 911, but society has to collect taxes in order for the emergency service to exist. Taxes help to pay for many of modern society's needs—public transportation, schools, police, the court system, and the military, to name just a few. Most of us take these services for granted, but without taxes it would be hard to pay for them. How much does all of this cost? When you add all the federal, state, and local government budgets in the United States, you get five trillion dollars a year!

**Opportunity cost**

These taxes incur opportunity costs, since the money could have been used in other ways. In this section, we will use the concepts of consumer and producer surplus to explain the effect of taxation on social welfare and market efficiency. Taxes come in many sizes and shapes. Considering there are taxes on personal income, payroll, property, corporate profits, sales, and inheritances, the complexity makes it difficult to analyze the broad impact of taxation on social welfare and market efficiency. Fortunately, we do not have to examine the entire tax code all at once. In this chapter, we will explore the impact of taxes on social welfare by looking at one of the simplest taxes, the *excise tax*.

**Excise taxes**
are taxes levied on a particular good or service.

**Incidence**
refers to the burden of taxation on the party who pays the tax through higher prices, regardless of whom the tax is actually levied on.

## Tax Incidence

Economists want to know how taxes affect the choices that consumers and producers make. When a tax is imposed on an item, do buyers switch to alternative goods that are not taxed? How do producers respond when the products they sell are taxed? Since taxes cause prices to rise, they can affect how much of a good or service is bought and sold. This is especially evident with **excise taxes**, or taxes levied on one particular good or service. For example, all fifty states levy excise taxes on cigarettes, but the amount assessed varies tremendously. In New York, cigarette taxes are over $4.00 per pack, while in a handful of tobacco-producing states such as Virginia and North Carolina, the excise tax is less than $0.50. Overall, excise taxes, such as those on cigarettes, alcohol, and gasoline, account for less than 4% of all tax revenues. But because we can isolate changes in consumer behavior that result from taxes on one item, they help us understand the overall effect of a tax.

In looking at the effect of a tax, economists are also interested in the **incidence** of taxation, which refers to the burden of taxation on the party who pays the tax through

Why do we place excise taxes on cigarettes . . .     . . . and gasoline?

higher prices. To understand this idea, consider a $1.00 tax on milk purchases. Each time a consumer buys a gallon of milk, the cash register adds $1.00 in tax. This means that to purchase the milk, the consumer's willingness to pay must be greater than the price of the milk plus the $1.00 tax.

The result of the $1.00 tax on milk is shown in Figure 5.6. Because of the tax, the price of milk goes up and the demand curve shifts down (from $D_1$ to $D_2$). Why does the demand curve shift? Since consumers must pay the purchase price as well as the tax, the extra cost makes them less likely to buy milk at every price, which causes the entire demand curve to shift down. The intersection of the new demand curve ($D_2$) with the existing supply curve (S) creates a new equilibrium price of $3.50 ($E_2$), which is $0.50 lower than the original price of $4.00. But even though the price is lower, consumers are still worse off. Since they must also pay part of the $1.00 tax, the total price to them rises to $4.50 per gallon.

At the same time, because the new equilibrium price after the tax is $0.50 lower than it was before the tax, the producer splits the tax incidence with the buyer. The producer receives $0.50 less, and the buyer pays $0.50 more.

The tax on milk purchases also affects the amount sold in the market, which we also see in Figure 5.6. Since the after-tax equilibrium price ($E_2$) is lower, producers of milk reduce the quantity they sell to 750 gallons. Therefore, the market for milk becomes smaller than it was before the good was taxed.

Excise taxes paid by consumers are relatively rare because they are highly visible. If every time you bought milk you were reminded that you had to pay a $1.00 tax, it would be hard to ignore. As a result, politicians often prefer

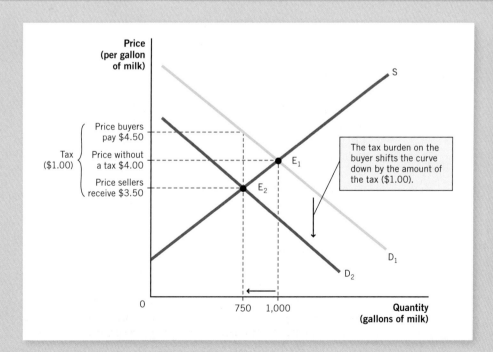

## FIGURE 5.6

**A Tax on Buyers**
After the tax, the new equilibrium price ($E_2$) is $3.50, but the buyer must also pay $1.00 in tax. Therefore, despite the drop in price, the buyer still owes $4.50. A similar logic applies to the producer. Since the new equilibrium price after the tax is $0.50 lower, the producer shares the tax incidence equally with the seller in this example. The consumer pays $0.50 more, and the seller nets $0.50 less.

to place the tax on the seller. The seller will then include the tax in the sale price, and buyers will likely forget that the sale price is higher than it would be without the tax.

Let's return to the $1.00 tax on milk. This time, the tax is placed on the seller. Figure 5.7 shows the result. First, look at the shift in the supply curve. Why does it shift? The $1.00 per gallon tax on milk lowers the profits that milk producers expect to make, which causes them to produce less milk at every price level. As a result, the entire supply curve shifts to the left in response to the tax that milk producers owe the government. The intersection of the new supply curve ($S_2$) with the existing demand curve creates a new equilibrium price ($E_2$) of $4.50—which is $0.50 higher than the original equilibrium price of $4.00 ($E_1$). This occurs because the seller passes part of the tax increase along to the buyer in the form of a higher price. However, the seller is still worse off. After the tax, the new equilibrium price is $4.50, but $1.00 goes as tax to the government. Therefore, despite the rise in price, the seller nets only $3.50, which is $0.50 less than the original equilibrium price.

The tax also affects the amount of milk sold in the market. Since the new equilibrium price after the tax is higher, consumers reduce the quantity demanded from 1,000 gallons to 750 gallons.

It's important to notice that the result in Figure 5.7 looks much like that in Figure 5.6. This is because it does not matter whether a tax is levied on the buyer or the seller. The tax places a wedge of $1.00 between the price that buyers ultimately pay ($4.50) and the net price that sellers ultimately receive ($3.50), regardless of who is actually responsible for paying the tax.

## FIGURE 5.7

**A Tax on Sellers**

After the tax, the new equilibrium price ($E_2$) is $4.50, but $1.00 must be paid in tax to the government. Therefore, despite the rise in price, the seller nets only $3.50. A similar logic applies to the consumer. Since the new equilibrium price after the tax is $0.50 higher, the consumer shares the $1.00/gallon tax incidence equally with the seller. The consumer pays $0.50 more, and the seller nets $0.50 less.

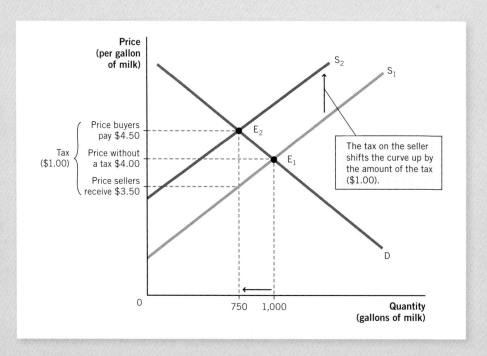

Continuing with our milk example, when the tax was levied on sellers, they were responsible for collecting the entire tax ($1.00 per gallon), but they transferred $0.50 of the tax to the consumer by raising the market price to $4.50. Similarly, when the tax was levied on consumers, they were responsible for paying the entire tax, but they essentially transferred $0.50 of it to the producer, since the market price fell to $3.50. Therefore, we can say that the incidence of a tax is independent of whether it is levied on the buyer or the seller. However, depending on the price elasticity of supply and demand, the tax incidence need not be shared equally, as we will see later. All of this means that the government doesn't get to determine whether consumers or producers bear the tax incidence—the market does!

## Deadweight Loss

Recall that economists measure economic efficiency by looking at total consumer and producer surplus. We have seen that a tax raises the total price consumers pay and lowers the net price producers receive. For this reason, taxes reduce the amount of economic activity. The decrease in economic activity caused by market distortions, such as taxes, is known as **deadweight loss**.

In the previous section, we observed that the tax on milk caused the amount purchased to decline from 1,000 to 750 gallons—a reduction of 250 gallons sold in the market. In Figure 5.8, the yellow triangle represents the deadweight loss caused by the tax. When the price rises, consumers who

**Deadweight loss**
is the decrease in economic activity caused by market distortions.

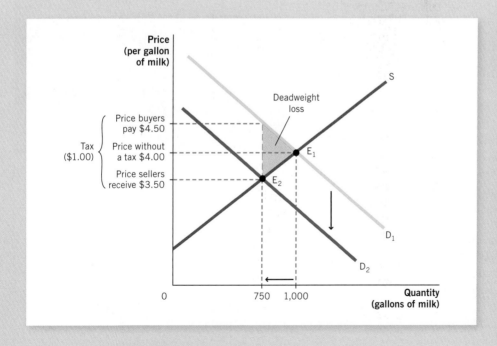

**FIGURE 5.8**

**The Deadweight Loss from a Tax**

The yellow triangle represents the deadweight loss caused by the tax. When the price rises, all consumers who would have paid between $4.00 and $4.49 no longer purchase milk. Likewise, the reduction in revenue the seller receives means that producers who were willing to sell a gallon of milk for between $3.51 and $4.00 will no longer do so.

would have paid between $4.00 and $4.49 will no longer purchase milk. Likewise, the reduction in the price the seller can charge means that producers who were willing to sell a gallon of milk for between $3.51 and $4.00 will no longer do so. The combined reductions in consumer and producer surplus equal the deadweight loss produced by a $1.00 tax on milk.

In the next sections, we will examine how differences in the price elasticity of demand lead to varying amounts of deadweight loss. We will evaluate what happens when the demand curve is perfectly inelastic, somewhat elastic, and perfectly elastic.

### Tax Revenue and Deadweight Loss When Demand Is Inelastic

Necessary goods and services—for example, water, electricity, and phone service—have highly inelastic demand. These goods and services are often taxed. For example, consider all the taxes associated with your cell phone bill: sales tax, city tax, county tax, federal excise tax, and annual regulatory fees. In addition, many companies add surcharges, including activation fees, local number portability fees, telephone number pooling charges, emergency 911 service, directory assistance, telecommunications relay service surcharges, and cancellation fees. Of course, there is a way to avoid all

**ECONOMICS IN THE MEDIA**

# Taxing Inelastic Goods

## "Taxman" by the Beatles

"Taxman" was inspired by the theme song from the popular 1960s television series *Batman*. The Beatles—especially George Harrison, who wrote the song—had grown quite bitter about how much they were paying in taxes. In the beginning of the song, Harrison sings, "Let me tell you how it will be. There's one for you, nineteen for me." This refers to the fact that the British government taxed high-wage earners £19 out of every £20 they earned. Since the Beatles' considerable earnings placed them in the top income tax bracket in the United Kingdom, a part of the group's earnings was subject to the 95% tax introduced by the government in 1965. As a consequence, the Beatles became tax exiles living in the United States and other parts of Europe, where tax rates were lower.

The inevitability of paying taxes is a theme that runs throughout the song. The lyrics mention that when you drive a car, the government can tax the "street"; if you try to sit, the government can tax "your seat"; if you are cold, the government can tax "the

The Beatles avoided high taxes by living outside the United Kingdom.

heat"; and if you decide to take a walk, it can tax your "feet"! The only way to avoid doing and using these things is to leave the country—precisely what the Beatles did. All these examples (streets, seats, heat, and walking) are necessary activities, which makes demand highly inelastic. Anytime that is the case, the government can more easily collect the tax revenue it desires.

these fees: don't use a cell phone! However, many people today feel that cell phones are a necessity. Cell phone providers and government agencies take advantage of the consumer's strongly inelastic demand by tacking on these extra charges.

Figure 5.9 shows the result of a tax on products with almost perfectly inelastic demand, such as phone service—something people feel they need to have no matter what the price. The demand for access to a phone (either a landline or a cell phone) is perfectly inelastic. Recall that whenever demand is perfectly inelastic, the demand curve is vertical. Figure 5.9a shows the market for phone service before the tax. The blue rectangle represents consumer surplus (C.S.), and the red triangle represents producer surplus (P.S.). Now imagine that a tax is levied on the seller, as shown in Figure 5.9b. The supply curve shifts from $S_1$ to $S_2$. The shift in supply causes the equilibrium point to move from $E_1$ to $E_2$ and the price to rise from $P_1$ to $P_2$, but the quantity supplied, $Q_1$, remains the same. We know that when demand is perfectly inelastic, a price increase does not alter how much consumers purchase. So the quantity demanded remains constant at $Q_1$ even after the government collects tax revenue equal to the green-shaded area.

There are two reasons why the government may favor excise taxes on goods with almost perfectly (or highly) inelastic demand. First, because these

How do phone companies get away with all the added fees per month? Answer: inelastic demand.

---

## FIGURE 5.9

**A Tax on Products with Almost Perfectly Inelastic Demand**

(a) Before the tax, the consumer enjoys the consumer surplus (C.S.) noted in blue, and the producer enjoys the producer surplus (P.S.) noted in red. (b) After the tax, the incidence, or the burden of taxation, is borne entirely by the consumer. A tax on a good with almost perfectly inelastic demand, such as phone service, represents a transfer of welfare from consumers of the good to the government, reflected by the reduced size of the blue rectangle in (b) and the creation of the green tax-revenue rectangle between $P_1$ and $P_2$.

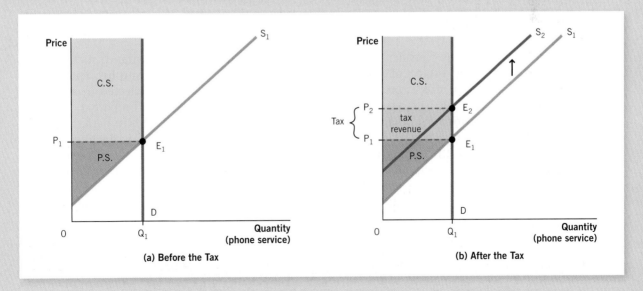

goods do not have substitutes, the tax will not cause consumers to buy less. Thus, the revenue from the tax will remain steady. Second, since the number of transactions, or quantity demanded ($Q_1$), remains constant, there will be no deadweight loss. As a result, the yellow triangle we observed in Figure 5.8 disappears in Figure 5.9 because the tax does not alter the efficiency of the market. Looking at Figure 5.9, you can see that the same number of transactions exist in (a) and (b). This means that the total surplus, or social welfare, is equal in both panels. You can also see this by comparing the shaded areas in both panels. The sum of the blue-shaded area of consumer surplus and the red-shaded area of producer surplus in (a) is equal to the sum of the consumer surplus, producer surplus, and tax revenue in (b). The green area is subtracted entirely from the blue rectangle, which indicates that the surplus is redistributed from consumers to the government. But society overall enjoys the same total surplus. Thus, we see that when demand is perfectly inelastic, the incidence, or the burden of taxation, is borne entirely by the consumer. A tax on a good with almost perfectly inelastic demand represents a transfer of welfare from consumers of the good to the government, reflected by the reduced size of the blue rectangle in (b).

### Tax Revenue and Deadweight Loss When Demand Is More Elastic

Now consider a tax on a product with more elastic demand, such as milk, the subject of our earlier discussion on calculating total surplus. The demand for milk is price sensitive, but not overly so. This is reflected in a demand curve with a typical slope as shown in Figure 5.10. Let's compare the after-tax price, $P_2$, in Figures 5.9b and 5.10b. When demand is almost perfectly inelastic, as it is in Figure 5.9b, the price increase from $P_1$ to $P_2$ is absorbed entirely by the consumer. But in Figure 5.10b, because demand is more sensitive to price, suppliers must absorb part of the tax, from $P_1$ to $P_3$, themselves. Thus, they net $P_3$, which is less than what they received when the good was not taxed. In addition, the total tax revenue generated (the green-shaded area) is not as large in Figure 5.9b as in Figure 5.10b, because as the price of the good rises some consumers no longer buy it and the quantity demanded falls from $Q_1$ to $Q_2$.

Notice that both consumer surplus (C.S.), the blue triangle, and producer surplus (P.S.), the red triangle, are smaller after the tax. Since the price rises after the tax increase (from $P_1$ to $P_2$), those consumers with a relatively low

## FIGURE 5.10

**A Tax on Products with More Elastic Demand**

(a) Before the tax, the consumer enjoys the consumer surplus (C.S.) noted in blue, and the producer enjoys the producer surplus (P.S.) noted in red. (b) A tax on a good for which demand and supply are each somewhat elastic will cause a transfer of welfare from consumers and producers to the government, the revenue shown as the green rectangle. It will also create deadweight loss (D.W.L.), shown in yellow, since the quantity bought and sold in the market declines (from $Q_1$ to $Q_2$).

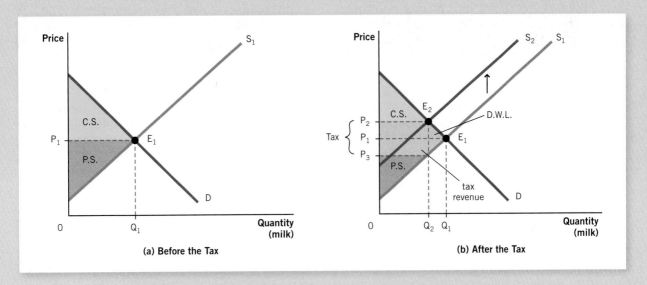

(a) Before the Tax

(b) After the Tax

willingness to pay for the good are priced out of the market. Likewise, sellers with relatively high costs of production will stop producing the good, since the price they net after paying the tax drops to $P_3$. The total reduction in economic activity, the change from $Q_1$ to $Q_2$, is the deadweight loss (D.W.L.) indicated by the yellow triangle.

The incidence of the tax also changes from Figure 5.9 to Figure 5.10. A tax on a good for which demand and supply are each somewhat elastic will cause a transfer of welfare from consumers and producers of the good to the government. At the same time, since the quantity bought and sold in the market declines, it also creates deadweight loss. Another way of seeing this result is to compare the red- and blue-shaded areas in Figure 5.10a with the red- and blue-shaded areas in Figure 5.10b. The sum of the consumer surplus and producer surplus in (a) is greater than the sum of the consumer surplus, tax revenue, and producer surplus in (b). Therefore, the total surplus, or efficiency of the market, is smaller. The tax is no longer a pure transfer from consumers to the government, as was the case in Figure 5.9.

### Tax Revenue and Deadweight Loss When Demand Is Highly Elastic

We have seen the effect of taxation when demand is inelastic and somewhat elastic. What about when demand is highly elastic? For example, a customer who wants to buy fresh lettuce at a produce market will find many local growers charging the same price and many varieties to choose from. If one of the vendors decides to charge $1 per pound above the market price, consumers will stop buying from that vendor. They will be unwilling to pay more when they can get the same product from another grower at a lower price; this is the essence of elastic demand.

Figure 5.11 shows the result of a tax on lettuce, a good with highly elastic demand. After all, when lettuce is taxed consumers can switch to other greens such as spinach, cabbage, or endive and completely avoid the tax. In this market, consumers are so price sensitive that they are unwilling to accept any price increase. And because sellers are unable to raise the equilibrium price, they bear the entire incidence of the tax. This has two effects. First, producers are less willing to sell the product at all prices. This shifts the supply curve from $S_1$ to $S_2$. Since consumer demand is highly elastic, consumers pay the same price as before ($P_1 = P_2$). However, the tax increase causes the producer to net less, or $P_3$. Since $P_3$ is substantially lower than the price before the tax, or $P_2$, producers offer less for sale after the tax is implemented. This is shown in Figure 5.11b in the movement of quantity demanded from $Q_1$ to $Q_2$. Since $Q_2$ is smaller than $Q_1$, there is also more deadweight loss than we observed in Figure 5.10b. Therefore, the total surplus, or efficiency of the market, is much smaller than before. Comparing the green-shaded areas of Figures 5.10b and 5.11b, you see that the size of the tax revenue continues

## FIGURE 5.11

**A Tax on Products with Highly Elastic Demand**

(a) Before the tax, the producer enjoys the producer surplus (P.S.) noted in red. (b) When consumer demand is highly elastic, consumers pay the same price after the tax as before. But they are worse off because less is produced and sold; the quantity produced moves from $Q_1$ to $Q_2$. The result is deadweight loss (D.W.L.), as shown by the yellow triangle in (b). The total surplus, or efficiency of the market, is much smaller than before. The size of the tax revenue (in green) is also noticeably smaller in the market with highly elastic demand.

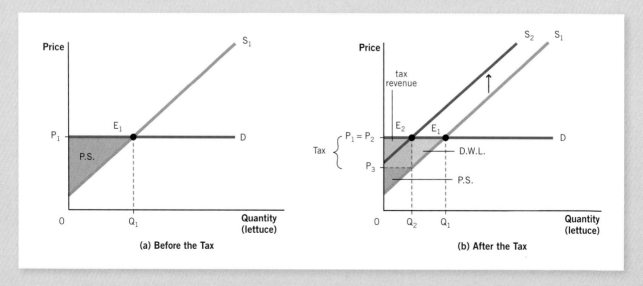

(a) Before the Tax

(b) After the Tax

to shrink. There is an important lesson here for policymakers—they should tax goods with relatively inelastic demand. Not only will this lessen the dead-weight loss of taxation, but it will also generate larger tax revenues for the government.

So far, we have varied the elasticity of the demand curve while holding the elasticity of the supply curve constant. What would happen if we did the reverse and varied the elasticity of the supply curve while keeping the elastic-ity of the demand curve constant? It turns out that there is a simple method for determining the incidence and deadweight loss in this case. The incidence of a tax is determined by the relative steepness of the demand curve compared to the supply curve. When the demand curve is steeper (more inelastic) than the supply curve, consumers bear more of the incidence of the tax. When the supply curve is steeper (more inelastic) than the demand curve, suppliers bear more of the incidence of the tax. Also, whenever the supply and/or demand curves are relatively steep, deadweight loss is minimized.

Let's explore an example in which we consider how the elasticity of demand and elasticity of supply interact. Suppose that a $3 per pound tax is placed on shiitake mushrooms, an elastic good. Given the information in Figure 5.12, we will compute the incidence, deadweight loss, and tax revenue from the tax.

Let's start with the incidence of the tax. After the tax is implemented, the market price rises from $7 to $8 per pound. But since sellers must pay $3 to the government, they keep only $5. Tax incidence measures the share of the tax paid by buyers and sellers, so we need to compare the incidence of the tax paid by each party. Since the market price rises by $1 (from $7 to $8), buyers are paying $1 of the $3 tax, or $\frac{1}{3}$. Since the amount the seller keeps falls

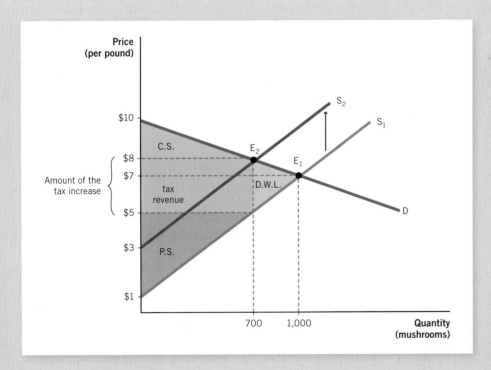

**FIGURE 5.12**

**A Realistic Example**

A $3 per pound tax is placed on mushroom suppliers. This drives the equilibrium price up from $E_1$ ($7) to $E_2$ ($8). Notice that the price only rises by $1. This means that the consumer picks up $1 of the $3 tax and the seller must pay the remaining $2. Therefore, most of the incidence is borne by the seller. Finally, neither the demand curve nor the supply curve is relatively inelastic, so the amount of deadweight loss (D.W.L.) is large.

How much would you pay per pound for these mushrooms?

by $2 (from $7 to $5), sellers are paying $2 of the $3 tax, or $\frac{2}{3}$. Notice that the demand curve is more elastic (flatter) than the supply curve; therefore, sellers have a limited ability to raise price.

Now let's determine the deadweight loss caused by the tax—that is, the decrease in economic activity. This is represented by the decrease in the total surplus found in the yellow triangle in Figure 5.12. In order to compute the amount of the deadweight loss, we need to determine the area of the triangle:

$$\text{The area of a triangle} = \frac{1}{2} \times \text{base} \times \text{height}$$

The triangle in Figure 5.12 is sitting on its side, so its height is $1000 - 700 = 300$, and its base is $\$8 - \$5 = \$3$.

$$\text{Deadweight loss} = \frac{1}{2} \times 300 \times \$3 = \$450$$

Finally, what is the tax revenue generated by the tax? In Figure 5.12, the tax revenue is represented by the green-shaded area, which is a rectangle. We can calculate the tax revenue by determining the area of the rectangle:

$$\text{The area of a rectangle} = \text{base} \times \text{height}$$

The height of the tax-revenue rectangle is the amount of the tax ($3), and the number of units sold after the tax is 700.

$$\text{Tax revenue} = \$3 \times 700 = \$2,100.$$

 **ECONOMICS IN THE REAL WORLD**

### The Short-Lived Luxury Tax

The Budget Reconciliation Act of 1990 established a special luxury tax on the sale of new aircraft, yachts, automobiles, furs, and jewelry. The act established a 10% surcharge on new purchases as follows: aircraft over $500,000; yachts over $100,000; automobiles over $25,000; and furs and jewelry over $10,000. The taxes were expected to generate approximately $2 billion a year. However, revenue fell far below expectations, and thousands of jobs were lost in each of the affected industries. Within three years, the tax was repealed. Why was the luxury tax such a failure?

When passing the Budget Reconciliation Act, lawmakers failed to consider basic demand elasticity. Because the purchase of a new aircraft, yacht, car, fur, or jewelry is highly discretionary, many wealthy consumers decided that they would buy substitute products that fell below the tax threshold or buy a used product and refurbish it. Therefore, the demand for these luxury goods turned out to be highly elastic. We have seen that when goods with elastic demand are taxed, the resulting tax revenues are small. Moreover, in this example the resulting decrease in purchases was significant. As a result, jobs were lost in the middle of an economic downturn. The combination of low revenues and crippling job losses in these industries was enough to convince Congress to repeal the tax in 1993.

The failed luxury tax is a reminder that the populist idea of taxing the rich is far more difficult to implement than it appears. In simple terms, it is nearly impossible to tax the toys that the rich enjoy because wealthy people can spend their money in so many different ways. In other words, they have options about whether to buy or lease, as well as many good substitutes to choose from. This means that they can, in many cases, avoid paying luxury taxes. ✳

If you were rich, would this be your luxury toy?

## Balancing Deadweight Loss and Tax Revenues

Up to this point, we have kept the size of the tax increase constant. This enabled us to examine the impact of the elasticity of demand and supply on dead-weight loss and tax revenues. But what happens when a tax is high enough to significantly alter consumer or producer behavior? For instance, in 2002 the Republic of Ireland instituted a tax of 15 euro cents on each plastic bag in order to curb litter and encourage recycling. As a result, consumer use of plastic bags quickly fell by over 90%. Thus, the tax was a major success because the government achieved its goal of curbing litter. In this section, we will consider how consumers respond to taxes of different sizes, and we will determine the relationship among the size of a tax, the deadweight loss, and tax revenues.

Incentives

Figure 5.13 shows the market response to a variety of tax increases. The five panels in the figure begin with a reference point, panel (a), where no tax is levied, and progress toward panel (e), where the tax rate becomes so extreme that it curtails all economic activity.

As taxes rise, so do prices. You can trace this rise from (a), where there is no tax and the price is $P_1$, all the way to (e), where the extreme tax causes the price to rise to $P_5$. At the same time, deadweight loss (D.W.L.) also rises. You can see this by comparing the sizes of the yellow triangles. The trade-off is striking. Without any taxes, deadweight loss does not occur. But as soon as taxes are in place, the market-equilibrium quantity demanded begins to decline, moving from $Q_1$ to $Q_5$. As the number of transactions (quantity demanded) declines, the area of deadweight loss rapidly expands.

Trade-offs

When taxes are small, as in Figure 5.13b, the tax revenue (green rectangle) is large relative to the deadweight loss (yellow triangle). However, as we progress through the panels, this relationship slowly reverses. In (c) the size of the tax revenue remains larger than the deadweight loss. However, in (d) the magnitude of the deadweight loss is far greater than the tax revenue. This means that the size of the tax in (d) is creating a significant cost in terms of economic efficiency. Finally, (e) shows an extreme case in which all market activity ceases as a result of the tax. Since nothing is produced and sold, there is no tax revenue.

FIGURE 5.13

**Examining Deadweight Loss and Tax Revenues**

The panels show that increased taxes result in higher prices. Progressively higher taxes also lead to more deadweight loss (D.W.L.), but higher taxes do not always generate more revenue, as evidenced by the reduction in revenue that occurs when tax rates become too large in panels (d) and (e).

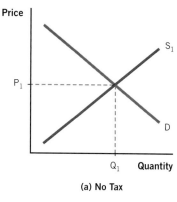

(a) No Tax

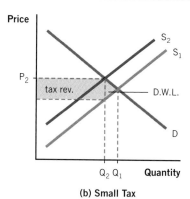

(b) Small Tax

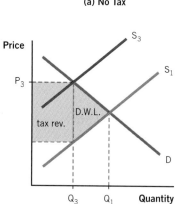

(c) Moderate Tax

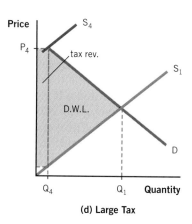

(d) Large Tax

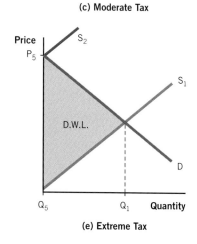

(e) Extreme Tax

# Bizarre Taxes

Governments tax their citizens for a variety of reasons. Often it's to raise revenue. Sometimes, taxes are levied to influence citizens' behavior. Occasionally, both of these reasons are in play. These two motivations have led to some very bizarre tax initiatives, as seen below. Though they all seem a bit unusual, these taxes get (or got) paid every single day.

## Flush Tax

Maryland's "Flush Tax," a fee added to sewer bills, went up from $2.50 to $5.00 a month in 2012. The tax is paid only by residents who live in the Chesapeake Bay Watershed, and it generates revenue for reducing pollution in Chesapeake Bay.

## Bagel Tax

New Yorkers love their bagels and cream cheese from delis. In the state, any bagel that has been sliced or has any form of spread on it (like cream cheese) is subject to a 9% sales tax on prepared food. Any bagel that is purchased "unaltered" is classified as unprepared and is not taxed.

## Playing Card Tax

The state of Alabama really doesn't want you playing solitaire. Buyers of playing cards are taxed ten cents per deck, while sellers must pay a $2 annual licensing fee. How much revenue does just a ten-cent tax generate? In 2011, it was almost $90,000.

## Tattoo Tax

Arkansas imposes a 6% tax on tattoos and body piercings to discourage this behavior, meaning that the people of Arkansas pay extra when getting inked or pierced.

## Window Tax

England passed a tax in 1696 targeting wealthy citizens—the more windows in one's house, the higher the tax. Many homeowners simply bricked over their windows. But they could not seal all of them, and the government did indeed collect revenue.

## Blueberry Tax

Maine levies a penny-and-a-half tax per pound on anyone growing, handling, processing, selling, or purchasing the state's delicious wild blueberries. The tax is an effort to make sure that the blueberries are not overharvested.

Maine produces 99% of the wild blueberries consumed in the USA, meaning that blueberry lovers have few substitutes available to avoid paying the tax and that demand is therefore inelastic.

Marylanders are being taxed on what's called a negative externality, a cost of their behavior that affects other people.

## REVIEW QUESTIONS

- Suppose that because of Alabama's playing card tax, fewer consumers purchase cards and fewer store owners sell them. What is this loss of economic activity called?

- Do you think the New York bagel tax is an effective tool to raise government revenue? Think about how the tax may or may not affect the purchasing behavior of New Yorkers.

# PRACTICE WHAT YOU KNOW

### Deadweight Loss of Taxation: The Politics of Tax Rates

Imagine that you and two friends are discussing the politics of taxation. One friend, who is fiscally conservative, argues that tax rates are too high. The other friend, who is more progressive, argues that tax rates are too low.

What is the optimal tax rate?

**Question: Is it possible that both friends could be right?**

**Answer:** Surprisingly, the answer is yes. When tax rates become extraordinarily high, the amount of deadweight loss dwarfs the amount of tax revenue collected. We observed this in the discussion of the short-lived luxury tax above. Fiscal conservatives often note that taxes inhibit economic activity. They advocate lower tax rates and limited government involvement in the market, preferring to minimize the deadweight loss on economic activity—see panel (b) in Figure 5.13. However, progressives prefer somewhat higher tax rates than fiscal conservatives, since a moderate tax rate—see panel (c)—generates more tax revenue than a small tax does. The additional revenues that moderate tax rates generate can fund more government services. Therefore, a clear trade-off exists between the size of the public sector and market activity. Depending on how you view the value created by markets versus the value added through government provision, there is ample room for disagreement about the best tax policy.

# Conclusion

Let's return to the misconception we started with: raising tax rates always generates more tax revenue. That's true up to a point. At low and moderate tax rates, increases do lead to additional tax revenue. However, when tax rates become too high, tax revenues decline as more consumers and producers find ways to avoid paying the tax.

In the first part of this chapter, we learned that society benefits from unregulated markets because they generate the largest possible total surplus. However, society also needs the government to provide an infrastructure for the economy. The tension between economic activity and the amount of government services needed is reflected in tax rates. The taxation of specific goods and services gives rise to a form of market failure called deadweight loss, which causes reduced economic activity. Thus, any intervention in the market requires a deep understanding of how society will respond to the incentives created by the legislation. In addition, unintended consequences can affect the most well-intentioned tax legislation and, if the process is not well thought through, can cause inefficiencies with far-reaching consequences. Of course, this does not mean that taxes are undesirable. Rather, society must balance (1) the need for tax revenues and the programs those revenues help fund, with (2) trade-offs in the market.

Incentives

Trade-offs

## ANSWERING THE BIG QUESTIONS

### What are consumer surplus and producer surplus?

✳ Consumer surplus is the difference between the willingness to pay for a good and the price that is paid to get it. Producer surplus is the difference between the willingness to sell a good and the price that the seller receives.

✳ Total surplus is the sum of consumer and producer surplus that exists in a market.

### When is a market efficient?

✳ Markets maximize consumer and producer surplus, provide goods and services to buyers who value them most, and reward sellers who can produce goods and services at the lowest cost. As a result, markets create the largest amount of total surplus possible.

✳ Whenever an allocation of resources maximizes total surplus, the result is said to be efficient. However, economists are also interested in the distribution of the surplus. Equity refers to the fairness of the distribution of the benefits among the members of the society.

### Why do taxes create deadweight loss?

✳ Deadweight loss occurs because taxes increase the purchase price, which causes consumers to buy less and producers to supply less. Deadweight loss can be minimized by placing a tax on a good or service that has inelastic demand or supply.

✳ Economists are also concerned about the incidence of taxation. Incidence refers to the burden of taxation on the party who pays the tax through higher prices, regardless of whom the tax is actually levied on. The incidence is determined by the balance between the elasticity of supply and the elasticity of demand.

ECONOMICS FOR LIFE

# Excise Taxes Are Almost Impossible to Avoid

The federal government collected $75 billion in excise taxes in 2011. Excise taxes are placed on many different products, making them almost impossible to avoid. They also have the added advantages of being easy to collect, hard for consumers to detect, and easier to enact politically than other types of taxes. You'll find excise taxes on many everyday household expenses—what you drink, the gasoline you purchase, plane tickets, and much more. Let's add them up.

1. **Gasoline.** 18.3 cents per gallon. This generates $37 billion and helps finance the interstate highway system.

2. **Cigarettes and tobacco.** $1 per pack and up to 40 cents per cigar. This generates $18 billion for the general federal budget.

3. **Air travel.** 7.5% of the base price of the ticket plus $3 per flight segment. This generates $10 billion for the Transportation Security Administration and the Federal Aviation Administration.

Data from Jill Barshay, "The $240-a-Year Bill You Don't Know You're Paying," *Fiscal Times*, Sept. 7, 2011.

4. **Alcohol.** 5 cents per can of beer, 21 cents per bottle of wine, and $2.14 for spirits. This generates $9 billion for the general federal budget.

These four categories account for $74 billion in excise taxes. You could still avoid the taxman with this simple prescription: don't drink, don't travel, and don't smoke. Where does that leave you? Way out in the country somewhere far from civilization. Since you won't be able to travel to a grocery store, you'll need to live off the land, grow your own crops, and hunt or fish.

But there is still one last federal excise tax to go.

5. **Hunting and fishing.** Taxes range from 3 cents for fishing tackle boxes to 11% for archery equipment. This generates $1 billion for fish and wildlife services.

Living off the land and avoiding taxes just got much harder, and that's the whole point. The government taxes products with relatively inelastic demand because most people will still purchase them after the tax is in place. As a result, avoiding excise taxes isn't practical. The best you can do is reduce your tax burden by altering your lifestyle or what you purchase.

Excise taxes are everywhere.

# CONCEPTS YOU SHOULD KNOW

consumer surplus (p. 139)
deadweight loss (p. 151)
efficient (p. 145)
equity (p. 147)

excise taxes (p. 148)
incidence (p. 148)
producer surplus (p. 141)
social welfare (p. 144)

total surplus (p. 144)
welfare economics (p. 138)
willingness to pay (p. 138)
willingness to sell (p. 141)

# QUESTIONS FOR REVIEW

1. Explain how consumer surplus is derived from the difference between the willingness to pay and the market-equilibrium price.

2. Explain how producer surplus is derived from the difference between the willingness to sell and the market-equilibrium price.

3. Why do economists focus on consumer and producer surplus and not on the possibility of consumer and producer loss? Illustrate your answer on a supply and demand graph.

4. How do economists define efficiency?

5. What type of goods should be taxed in order to minimize deadweight loss?

6. Suppose that the government taxes a good that is very elastic. Illustrate what will happen to the consumer surplus, producer surplus, tax revenue, and deadweight loss on a supply and demand graph.

7. What happens to tax revenues as tax rates increase?

# STUDY PROBLEMS (*solved at the end of the section)

1. A college student enjoys eating pizza. Her willingness to pay for each slice is shown in the following table:

| Number of pizza slices | Willingness to pay (per slice) |
|---|---|
| 1 | $6 |
| 2 | $5 |
| 3 | $4 |
| 4 | $3 |
| 5 | $2 |
| 6 | $1 |
| 7 | $0 |

a. If pizza slices cost $3 each, how many slices will she buy? How much consumer surplus will she enjoy?

b. If the price of slices falls to $2, how much consumer surplus will she enjoy?

2. A cash-starved town decides to impose a $6 excise tax on T-shirts sold. The following table shows the quantity demanded and the quantity supplied at various prices.

| Price per T-shirt | Quantity demanded | Quantity supplied |
|---|---|---|
| $19 | 0 | 60 |
| $16 | 10 | 50 |
| $13 | 20 | 40 |
| $10 | 30 | 30 |
| $ 7 | 40 | 20 |
| $ 4 | 50 | 10 |

a. What are the equilibrium quantity demanded and the quantity supplied before the tax is implemented? Determine the consumer and producer surplus before the tax.

b. What are the equilibrium quantity demanded and the quantity supplied after the tax is implemented? Determine the consumer and producer surplus after the tax.

c. How much tax revenue does the town generate from the tax?

3. Andrew paid $30 to buy a potato cannon, a cylinder that shoots potatoes hundreds of feet. He was willing to pay $45. When Andrew's friend Nick learns that Andrew bought a potato cannon, he asks Andrew if he will sell it for $60, and Andrew agrees. Nick is thrilled, since he would have paid Andrew up to $80 for the cannon. Andrew is also delighted. Determine the consumer surplus from the original purchase and the additional surplus generated by the resale of the cannon.

4. If the government wants to raise tax revenue, which of the following items are good candidates for an excise tax? Why?

a. granola bars
b. cigarettes
c. toilet paper
d. automobile tires
e. bird feeders

✳ 5. If the government wants to minimize the deadweight loss of taxation, which of the following items are good candidates for an excise tax? Why?

a. bottled water
b. prescription drugs
c. oranges
d. batteries
e. luxury cars

6. A new medical study indicates that eating blueberries helps prevent cancer. If the demand for blueberries increases, what will happen to the size of the consumer and producer surplus? Illustrate your answer by shifting the demand curve appropriately and labeling the new and old areas of consumer and producer surplus.

7. Use the graph at the top of p. 167 to answer questions a–f.

a. What area represents consumer surplus before the tax?
b. What area represents producer surplus before the tax?
c. What area represents consumer surplus after the tax?
d. What area represents producer surplus after the tax?
e. What area represents the tax revenue after the tax?
f. What area represents the deadweight loss after the tax?

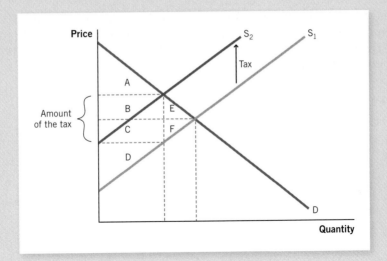

8. The cost of many electronic devices has fallen appreciably since they were first introduced. For instance, computers, cell phones, microwaves, and calculators not only provide more functions but do so at a lower cost. Illustrate the impact of lower production costs on the supply curve. What happens to the size of the consumer and producer surplus? If consumer demand for cell phones is relatively elastic, who is likely to benefit the most from the lower production costs?

9. Suppose that the demand for a concert, $Q_D$, is represented by the following equation, where P is the price of concert tickets and Q is the number of tickets sold:

$$Q_D = 2500 - 20P$$

The supply of tickets, $Q_S$, is represented by the equation:

$$Q_S = -500 + 80P$$

a. Find the equilibrium price and quantity of tickets sold. (**Hint:** Set $Q_D = Q_S$ and solve for the price, P, and then plug the result back into either of the original equations to find $Q_E$.)

b. Carefully graph your result in part a.

c. Calculate the consumer surplus at the equilibrium price and quantity. (**Hint:** Since the area of consumer surplus is a triangle, you will need to use the formula for the area of a triangle [$\frac{1}{2}$ × base × height] to solve the problem.)

10. In this chapter, we have focused on the effect of taxes on social welfare. However, governments also subsidize goods, or make them cheaper to buy or sell. How would a $2,000 subsidy on the purchase of a new hybrid vehicle impact the consumer surplus and producer surplus in the hybrid market? Use a supply and demand diagram to illustrate your answer. Does the subsidy create deadweight loss?

✳ 11. Suppose that a new $50 tax is placed on each cell phone. From the information in the graph below, compute the incidence, deadweight loss, and tax revenue of the tax.

a. What is the incidence of the tax?
b. What is the deadweight loss of the tax?
c. What is the amount of tax revenue generated?

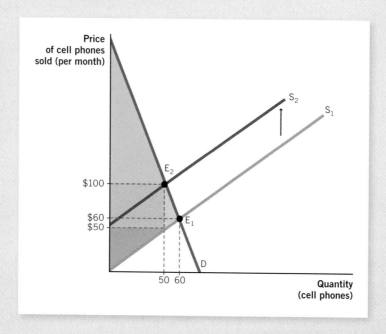

# SOLVED PROBLEMS

**5. a.** Many good substitutes are available: consumers can drink tap water, filtered water, or other healthy beverages instead of bottled water. Therefore, bottled water is not a good candidate for an excise tax.

**b.** Taxing prescription drugs will generate significant revenues without reducing sales much, if at all. There is almost no deadweight loss because consumers have few, if any, alternatives. Thus, prescription drugs are a good candidate for an excise tax.

**c.** Consumers can select many other fruits to replace oranges. The deadweight loss will be quite large. Therefore, oranges are not a good candidate for an excise tax.

**d.** Without batteries, many devices won't work. The lack of substitutes makes demand quite inelastic, so the deadweight loss will be small. Thus, batteries are an excellent candidate for an excise tax.

**e.** Wealthy consumers can spend their income in many ways. They do not have to buy luxury cars. As a result, the tax will create a large amount of deadweight loss. Therefore, luxury cars are a poor candidate for an excise tax.

**11. a.** After the tax is implemented, the market price rises from $60 to $100; but since sellers must pay $50 to the government, they net only $50. Tax incidence measures the share of the tax paid by buyers and sellers. Since the market price rises by $40 (from $60 to $100), buyers are paying $40 of the $50 tax, or $\frac{4}{5}$. Since the net price falls by $10 (from $60 to $50), sellers are paying $10 of the $50 tax, or $\frac{1}{5}$.

**b.** The deadweight loss is represented by the decrease in the total surplus found in the yellow triangle. In order to compute the amount of the deadweight loss, we need to determine the area inside the triangle. The area of a triangle is found by taking $\frac{1}{2} \times$ base $\times$ height. The triangle is sitting on its side, so the height of the triangle is 10 ($60 - 50$) and the base is $5 ($10 - $5). Hence the deadweight loss is $\frac{1}{2} \times 10 \times \$5 = \$25$.

**c.** The tax revenue is represented by the green-shaded area. You can calculate the tax revenue by multiplying the amount of the tax ($50) by the number of units sold after the tax (50). This equals $2,500.

# Macroeconomic BASICS

# Introduction to Macroeconomics and Gross Domestic Product

**There is no reliable way to gauge the health of an economy.**

You may notice that people often disagree on how the economy is doing. This might give you the impression that we aren't able to measure the

performance of the economy very well. But in fact, there is a reliable and objective measure of economic performance in a country. This measure is the primary focus of this chapter.

How can you tell if you have a good day at work or school? The answer is often tied to your productivity—how much you got done. Or the answer may be related to how much income you earned. Productivity and income are also useful measures for evaluating the performance of an entire economy, because a productive economy is a healthy economy and this is also an economy that generates income for its workers. This chapter describes how economists measure the health of an economy, using a measure of both output and income. This measure is gross domestic product, or GDP.

The U.S. economy produces almost one-fourth of all goods and services in the world.

# BIG QUESTIONS

✳ **How is macroeconomics different from microeconomics?**

✳ **What does GDP tell us about the economy?**

✳ **How is GDP computed?**

✳ **What are some shortcomings of GDP data?**

## How Is Macroeconomics Different from Microeconomics?

Macroeconomics is the study of the economy of an entire nation or society. This is different from microeconomics, which considers the behavior of individual people, firms, and industries. In microeconomics, you study what people buy, what jobs they take, and how they distribute their income between purchases and savings; you also examine the decisions of firms and how they compete with other firms. In macroeconomics, you will consider what happens when the national output of goods and services rises and falls, when overall national employment levels rise and fall, and when the overall price level goes up and down.

For example, in microeconomics you study the markets for salmon fillets (an example from Chapter 3). You study the behavior of people who consume salmon and firms that sell salmon—demanders and suppliers. Then you bring them together to see how the equilibrium price depends on the behavior of both demanders and suppliers.

Macroeconomics is the study of the broader economy. It looks at the big picture created by all markets in the economy—the markets for

A pink slip for one person is a microeconomic issue . . .

. . . but widespread unemployment is a macroeconomic issue.

| TABLE 6.1 | | |
|---|---|---|
| **Comparing the Perspectives of Microeconomics and Macroeconomics** | | |
| **Topic** | **Microeconomics** | **Macroeconomics** |
| Income | The income of a person or the revenue of a firm. | The income of an entire nation or a national economy. |
| Output | The production of a single worker, firm, or industry. | The production of an entire economy. |
| Employment | The job status and decisions of an individual or firm. | The job status of a national population, particularly the number of people who are unemployed. |
| Prices | The price of a single good. | The combined prices of all goods in an economy. |

salmon, coffee, computers, cars, haircuts, and health care, just to name a few. In macroeconomics, we examine total output in an economy rather than just a single firm or industry. We look at total employment across the economy rather than employment at a single firm. We consider all prices in the economy rather than the price of just one product, such as salmon. To illustrate these differences, Table 6.1 compares a selection of topics from the different perspectives of microeconomics and macroeconomics.

# What Does GDP Tell Us about the Economy?

Economists measure the total output of an economy as a gauge of its overall health. An economy that produces a large amount of valuable output is a healthy economy. If output falls for a certain period, there is something wrong in the economy. The same is true for individuals. If you have a fever for a few days, your output goes down—you don't go to the gym, you study less, and you might call in sick for work. We care about measuring our nation's economic output because it gives us a good sense of the overall health of the economy, much like a thermometer that measures your body temperature can give you an indication of your overall health. In this section, we introduce and explain our measure of an economy's output.

## Production Equals Income

This chapter is about the measurement of a nation's output, but it's also about the measurement of a nation's income. There's a good reason to cover output and income together: they are essentially the same thing. Nations and individuals that produce large amounts of highly valued output

Adding up the dollar sales is a way of measuring both production and income.

are relatively wealthy. Nations and individuals that don't produce much highly valued output are relatively poor. This is no coincidence.

Let's say you open a coffee shop in your college town. You buy or rent the equipment you need to produce coffee—everything from coffee beans and espresso machines to electricity. You hire the workers you need to keep the business running. Using these resources, you produce output such as cappuccinos, espressos, and draft coffee. On the first day, you sell 600 different coffee drinks at an average price of $4 each, for a total of $2,400. This dollar figure is a measure of your firm's production, or output, on that day, and it is also a measure of the income received.

You use the income to pay for your resources and to pay yourself. If you sell even more on the second day, the income generated increases. If you sell less, the income goes down.

**Gross domestic product (GDP)** is the market value of all final goods and services produced within a country during a specific period.

The same holds true for nations. **Gross domestic product (GDP)** is the market value of all final goods and services produced within a nation during a specific period of time—typically, a year. GDP is the primary measure used to gauge a nation's output. But it also measures a nation's income.

GDP is the sum of all the output from coffee shops, doctor's offices, software firms, fast-food restaurants, and all the other firms that produce goods and services within a nation's borders. The sale of this output becomes income to the owners of the firms and the resource suppliers. This dual function of GDP is part of the reason we focus on GDP as a barometer of the economy. When GDP goes up, national output and income are both higher. When GDP falls, the economy is producing less than before, and total national income is falling.

## Three Uses of GDP Data

Before analyzing the components of GDP, let's see why GDP is such an important indicator. In this section, we briefly explain the three primary uses of GDP data: to estimate living standards, to measure economic growth, and to determine whether an economy is experiencing recession or expansion.

### Measuring Living Standards

Imagine two very different nations. In the first nation, people work long hours in physically taxing labor, and yet their pay enables them to purchase only life's barest necessities—meager amounts of food, clothing, and shelter. In this nation, very few individuals can afford a high school education or health care from a trained physician. In the second nation, virtually no one starves, people tend to work in an air-conditioned environment, almost everyone graduates from high school, and many receive college degrees. The first nation experiences life similar to that in the United States two centuries ago; the second describes life in the United States today. Everyone would agree that living standards are higher in the United States today since most people can afford more of what they generally desire: goods, services, and leisure.

We can see these differences in living standards in GDP data. Indeed, GDP in modern America is much higher than it was in nineteenth-century America. Both output and income are higher, which indicates that living standards are also higher. While not perfect, GDP offers us a way of measuring living standards across both time and place.

Let's look at the nations with highest GDP in the world. Table 6.2 lists the world's largest economies by GDP in 2010. Column 3 shows GDP for the top 15 economies, giving a picture of the overall output and income of each of these nations. Total world GDP in 2010 was $63 trillion, which means that the United States alone produced almost 25% of all final goods and services in the world. The most significant recent movement on this list has occurred in China: in 1999, China ranked seventh, but by 2010 it had moved into second place.

Although total GDP is important, it is not the best indicator of living standards for a typical person. Table 6.2 reveals that in 2010, Japan and China had about the same amount of overall GDP. Yet the population of China was about 10 times the population of Japan. If we divide the GDP of each nation by its population, we find that in Japan there was about $43,000 worth of GDP (or income) for every person, and in China only about $4,300 per person.

## TABLE 6.2

### World's Largest Economies by GDP, 2010

| (1) Rank | (2) Country | (3) 2010 GDP (billions of dollars) | (4) Per capita GDP (dollars) |
|---|---|---|---|
| 1 | United States | $14,582 | $47,184 |
| 2 | China | 5,878 | 4,393 |
| 3 | Japan | 5,497 | 43,137 |
| 4 | Germany | 3,309 | 40,509 |
| 5 | France | 2,560 | 39,460 |
| 6 | United Kingdom | 2,246 | 36,100 |
| 7 | Brazil | 2,088 | 10,710 |
| 8 | Italy | 2,051 | 33,917 |
| 9 | India | 1,729 | 1,477 |
| 10 | Canada | 1,574 | 46,148 |
| 11 | Russian Federation | 1,480 | 10,440 |
| 12 | Spain | 1,407 | 30,542 |
| 13 | Mexico | 1,038 | 9,166 |
| 14 | South Korea | 1,015 | 20,757 |
| 15 | Australia | 925 | 42,131 |

*Source:* World Bank. All data are in 2010 U.S. dollars.

**Per capita GDP**
is GDP per person.

When we want to gauge living standards for an average person, we compute **per capita GDP**, which is GDP per person. That is, we divide the country's total GDP by its population. Per capita GDP is listed in the last column of Table 6.2.

## Measuring Economic Growth

We also use GDP data to measure economic growth. You can think of this as changes in living standards over time. When economies grow, living standards rise, and this outcome is evident in GDP data.

Figure 6.1 shows the change in per capita real GDP in the United States from 1960 to 2012. The overall positive slope of the curve indicates that living standards rose over the last 50 years in the United States, even though growth was not positive in every year. The data shows that income for the average person in 2010 was nearly three times what it was in 1960. So the typical person can now afford about three times as much education, food, vacation, air-conditioning, houses, and cars as the average person in 1960.

**Inflation**
is the growth in the overall level of prices in an economy.

**Real GDP**
is GDP adjusted for changes in prices.

Now, you might notice that in this section we have added the word "real" to our discussion of GDP. Figure 6.1 plots *real* per capita GDP. This is because we are now looking at data over time, so we have to adjust the GDP data for changes in prices that occur over time. Prices of goods and services almost always rise over time because of *inflation*. **Inflation** is the growth in the overall level of prices in an economy. Since GDP is calculated using market values (prices) of goods and services, inflation causes GDP to go up even if there is no change in the quantity of goods and services produced. Therefore, when we look at GDP data over time, we have to adjust it for the effects of inflation. **Real GDP** is GDP adjusted for changes in prices. The way we compute real GDP is discussed later in this chapter. For now, just note that any time we evaluate GDP figures over time, we must use real GDP, so that we account for inflation.

## FIGURE 6.1

**U.S. Per Capita Real GDP, 1960–2012**

The positive slope in this graph indicates increased living standards in the United States since 1960. It shows that the average person earns significantly more income today, even after adjusting for inflation. Over this period, real GDP per person increased by an average of 2% per year.

*Source:* U.S. Bureau of Economic Analysis; U.S. Census Bureau.

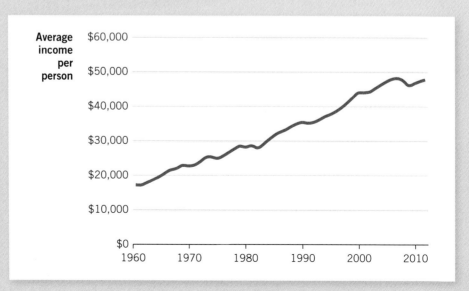

**Economic growth** is measured as the percentage change in real per capita GDP. Notice that this measure starts with GDP data but then adjusts for both population growth and inflation. Given this definition, you should view Figure 6.1 as a picture of economic growth in the United States. But despite what you see in the U.S. GDP data, you should not presume that economic growth is automatic or even typical. Figure 6.2 shows the experience of six other nations with six distinct experiences. The per capita real GDP in Poland, Turkey, and Mexico rose significantly over the period, more than doubling since 1950. India's remained very low for many years and then recently began to grow. Sadly, the data for Nicaragua and Somalia indicate that citizens in these nations are poorer now than they were in 1950.

Economic growth and its causes constitute one of the primary topics that macroeconomists study. In Chapter 12, we will consider the factors that lead to growth like that which the United States, Poland, Turkey, and Mexico have enjoyed—and, more recently, India. We will also consider why economies like those of Nicaragua and Somalia struggle to grow. Since real per capita GDP measures living standards, these issues are critical to real people's lives around the globe.

> **Economic growth** is measured as the percentage change in real per capita GDP.

## Measuring Business Cycles

We have seen that GDP data is used to measure living standards and economic growth. It is also used to determine whether an economy is expanding or contracting in the short run. In recent years, this use of GDP has received a lot of media attention because of concerns about *recessions*. **Recessions** are short-term economic downturns that typically last about 6 to 18 months. Even the mere threat of recession strikes fear in people's hearts, because income levels fall and many individuals lose their jobs or cannot find work during recessions. The U.S. recession that began in 2007 and lasted into 2009 has been

> A **recession** is a short-term economic downturn.

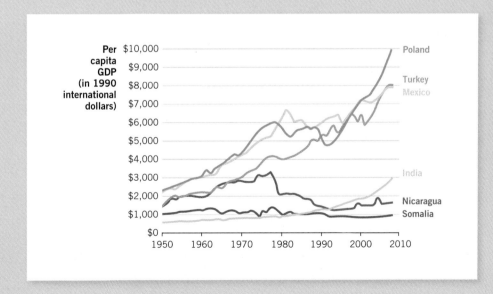

**FIGURE 6.2**

**Per Capita Real GDP in Six Nations, 1950–2008**

Growth in real per capita GDP in six nations shows that growth is not guaranteed. The levels for Poland, Turkey, and Mexico more than doubled since 1950. And while India began to grow more recently, both Nicaragua and Somalia have lost ground.

*Source:* Angus Maddison, *Statistics on World Population, GDP and Per Capita GDP, 1–2008 AD.*

The **Great Recession** was the U.S. recession lasting from December 2007 to June 2009.

A **business cycle** is a short-run fluctuation in economic activity.

An **economic expansion** is a phase of the business cycle during which the economy is growing faster than usual.

An **economic contraction** is a phase of the business cycle during which the economy is growing more slowly than usual.

dubbed the **Great Recession** because of its length and depth. It lasted for 19 months, and real GDP fell by almost 9% in the last three months of 2008. In addition, the recovery from the Great Recession has been very slow.

Even if an economy is expanding in the long run, it is normal for it to experience temporary downturns. **Business cycles** are short-run fluctuations in economic activity. Figure 6.3 illustrates a theoretical business cycle in relationship to a long-term trend in real GDP growth. The straight line represents the long-run trend of real GDP. The slope of the trend line is the average long-run growth of real GDP. For the United States, this is about 3% per year. But real GDP doesn't typically grow at exactly 3% per year. Instead of tracking exactly along the trend line, the economy experiences fluctuations in output. The wavy line represents the actual path of real GDP over time. It climbs to peaks when GDP growth is higher than usual and falls to troughs when output growth is lower than usual.

The peaks and troughs divide the business cycle into two phases: *expansions* and *contractions*. An **economic expansion** occurs from the bottom of a trough to the next peak, when the economy is growing faster than usual. After a certain period, the economy enters a recession, or an **economic contraction**—the period extending from the peak downward to the trough. During this phase, the economy is growing at a slower rate than usual. During expansions, jobs are relatively easy to find and average income levels climb. But during contractions, more people lose their jobs and income levels often fall.

Figure 6.3 makes it look like business cycles are uniform and predictable, but the reality is very different. Figure 6.4 plots U.S. real GDP over time, with contractionary periods—the recessions—shaded. GDP consistently declines during these recessionary periods, but they don't occur in a consistent, predictable pattern. You can easily spot the Great Recession, which began in December 2007 and lasted through June 2009.

## FIGURE 6.3

### The Business Cycle

The long-run trend shows consistent growth. The business cycle reflects the fluctuations that an economy typically exhibits. When the economy is growing faster than the long-run trend, it is in the expansion period of the business cycle. But when growth is slower than the trend, the economy is in a contraction. In real life, the cycle is not nearly as smooth and easy to spot as we picture here.

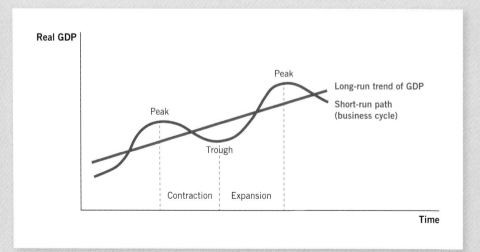

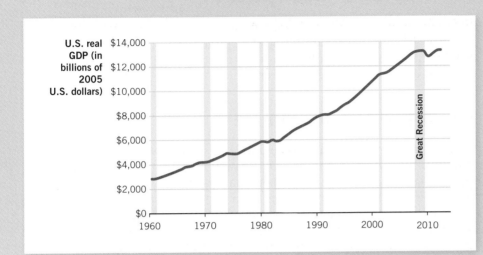

**FIGURE 6.4**

**U.S. Real GDP and Recessions, 1960–2012**

Over time, U.S. real GDP fluctuates. The shaded areas indicate periods of recession, when real GDP consistently declines. The Great Recession, which began in December 2007 and lasted through June 2009, was a particularly deep and lengthy modern recession.
*Source:* U.S. Bureau of Economic Analysis.

## PRACTICE WHAT YOU KNOW

### Three Uses of GDP Data: GDP as an Economic Barometer

Question: Which of the three uses of GDP data was applied in each particular case described below?

a. In 2011, many analysts claimed that the economy of India began slowing as GDP growth declined from 8.4% in 2010 to 6.9% in mid-2011.

b. Nicaragua and Haiti are the poorest nations in the Western Hemisphere, with annual 2010 per capita GDP of only $1,132 and $671, respectively.

c. The economy of Italy has slowed considerably over the past two decades, as evidenced by an average growth of real GDP of only 1.25% per year from 1990 to 2010.

What does GDP data tell us about Haiti?

Answers:

a. This case reflects a use of GDP data in terms of business cycles, indicating a potential recession. The statement describes a short-run window of data.

b. This statement uses data to show living standards. The figures indicate that average Nicaraguans and Haitians have to live on very small amounts of income each year.

c. This observation considers growth rates over almost 20 years, which means that GDP data were applied to look at long-run economic growth.

# How Is GDP Computed?

We have defined GDP as the market value of all final goods and services produced within a country during a specific period. In this section, we examine the definition more carefully in order to give you a deeper understanding of what goes into GDP and what does not.

## Counting Market Values

Nations produce a wide variety of goods and services, which are measured in various units. Computation of GDP literally requires the addition of apples and oranges, as well as every other final good and service produced in a nation. How can we add everything from cars to corn to haircuts to gasoline to prescription drugs in a way that makes sense? Certainly, we can't just add quantities. For example, in 2010 the United States produced about 8 million motor vehicles and about 12 billion bushels of corn. Looking only at quantities, one might conclude that because the nation produced about 1,500 bushels of corn for every car, corn production is much more important to the U.S. economy. But of course this is wrong; a bushel of corn is not worth nearly as much as a car.

To add corn and cars and the other goods and services in GDP, economists use market values. That is, we include not only the quantity data but also the price of the good or service. Figure 6.5 offers an example with fairly realistic data. If corn production is 12 billion bushels and these bushels sell for $5 each, the contribution of corn to GDP is $60 billion. If car production is 8 million vehicles and they sell for $30,000 each, the contribution of cars to GDP is $240 billion. If these were the only goods produced in a given year, GDP would be $300 billion.

As we have said, GDP reflects market values, and these values include both price and quantity information. Remember that the purpose of GDP data is to evaluate the health of an economy. But a nation's economic health depends on the total quantities of goods and services produced, as represented in the Quantity column of Figure 6.5. Market values enable us to add together many types of goods. At the same time, market values rely on prices, which can rise when inflation occurs. What if the prices of both cars and corn rise but the quantities produced remain unchanged? In that case, the GDP figure will rise even though the production level stays the same. This is why we compute real GDP by adjusting for inflation.

## Including Goods and Services

A **service** is an output that provides benefits without the production of a tangible product.

Physical goods are easy to visualize, but less than half of U.S. GDP comes from goods; the majority comes from *services*. **Services** are outputs that provide benefits without the production of a tangible product. Consider a service like a visit to your doctor for a physical. The doctor examines you and offers some medical advice, but you leave with no tangible output.

When considering the proportion of goods and services in U.S. GDP, it is important to note that the composition of U.S. GDP has evolved over time. In

**FIGURE 6.5**

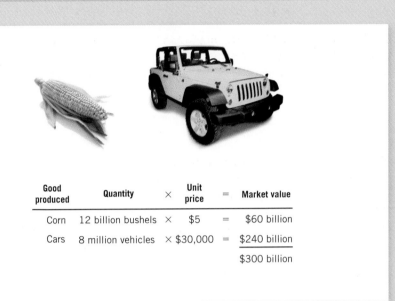

| Good produced | Quantity | × | Unit price | = | Market value |
|---|---|---|---|---|---|
| Corn | 12 billion bushels | × | $5 | = | $60 billion |
| Cars | 8 million vehicles | × | $30,000 | = | $240 billion |
| | | | | | $300 billion |

**Using Market Values to Compute GDP**

GDP reflects market values added together for many types of goods. In this simple example, the contribution to GDP from corn production is $60 billion and the contribution from car production is $240 billion.

the past, the dominant industries in the U.S. were manufactured goods such as autos, steel, and household goods. Today, a majority of U.S. GDP is service output such as medical, financial, transportation, education, and technology services. Figure 6.6 shows services as a share of U.S. GDP since 1960. As you can see, it grew from 50% in 1960 to about 70% in 2010.

Some people lament this move toward a service-dominated economy. They argue that manufacturing industries were a source of prosperity for our economy in the past and are still necessary for future growth. This is not a partisan issue; politicians from both major parties take this stand. However, this argument does not account for the nature of modern economic growth.

A century ago, the significant economic growth in the United States came from manufacturing output. But two centuries ago, the economic growth came from agricultural output. Economies evolve. Just because innovations in manufacturing spurred past growth does not mean that future growth should not occur through services.

When you visit the grocery store, you often purchase both goods (groceries) and services (clerking and bagging).

**FIGURE 6.6**

**Services as a Share of U.S. GDP, 1960–2010**

A century ago, the U.S. economy produced mostly manufactured goods; but this trend has shifted in recent decades, and now services account for most U.S. output.

*Source:* U.S. Bureau of Economic Analysis.

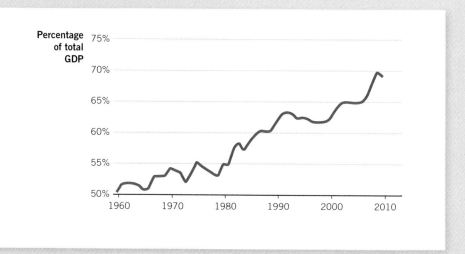

## Including Only Final Goods and Services

As we have said, GDP is the summation of spending on goods and services. But not all spending counts. To see why, consider all the spending involved in building a single good—a cell phone. Table 6.3 outlines some intermediate steps required to produce a cell phone that sells for $199. In the process of producing this phone, the manufacturer uses many *intermediate goods*. **Intermediate goods** are those that firms repackage or bundle with other goods for sale at a later stage. For example, the cellphone case and keyboard are intermediate goods because the phone manufacturer combines them with other intermediate goods, such as the operating system, to produce the cell phone, which is the *final good*. **Final goods** are goods that are sold to final users. The sale of the cell phone is included as part of GDP.

An **intermediate good** is a good that firms repackage or bundle with other goods for sale at a later stage.

A **final good** is a good sold to final users.

What happens if we count the value added during each intermediate step in making a cell phone? We start with the outer case and keyboard, which cost $5 to produce. Once the case and keyboard have been purchased, the component hardware, which costs $10, must be installed, bringing the value of the phone to $15. The operating system software, which costs $15, is then installed, raising the cost to $30. Next a cellphone provider purchases the phone and connects it to its network; this costs another $49, raising the phone's cost to $79. Finally, the phone is sold to the consumer for $199. The final value in this string of events, the retail price, is the true value that the cell phone creates in the economy. If we counted the value of each intermediate

This Intel processor is an intermediate good, buried inside your computer.

| TABLE 6.3 | | |
|---|---|---|
| **Intermediate Steps in Cellphone Production** | | |
| Steps | Value added during step (in dollars) | Prices of completed steps (in dollars) |
| 1. Assemble outer case and keyboard | $5 | $5 |
| 2. Prepare internal hardware | 10 | 15 |
| 3. Install operating system | 15 | 30 |
| 4. Connect to network | 49 | 79 |
| 5. Transact retail sale | 120 | 199 |
| Total | $199 | $338 |

step, we would arrive at a total of $338, which would overstate the phone's value in the economy.

One cannot get an accurate measure of GDP by summing all the sales made throughout the economy during the year, since many of them reflect intermediate steps in the production process. It is possible to get an accurate measurement of GDP by taking the sale price of the final good or by taking the value added at each step along the way, but not both; that would be double-counting.

## Within a Country

The word "domestic" in the phrase "gross domestic product" is important. GDP includes only goods and services produced domestically, or within the physical borders of a nation. The output of foreign-owned firms that is pro-

**Gross national product (GNP)** is the output produced by workers and resources owned by residents of the nation.

duced inside the United States is included in U.S. GDP, but the output of U.S. firms that is produced overseas is included in the GDP of the overseas nation. For example, Nike is a U.S. firm that produces shoes in Thailand. Thus, all the shoes produced in Thailand count as GDP for Thailand.

*Gross national product* is an alternative measure of national output that has been used in the past. **Gross national product (GNP)** is the output produced by workers and resources owned by residents of the nation. Thus, shoes produced by Nike in Thailand would count as part of U.S. GNP, since the owners of Nike are citizens (and residents) of the United States.

Nike shoes produced in Thailand count as GDP for Thailand.

# Including Only Production from a Particular Period

GDP only counts goods and services that are produced during a given period. Goods or services produced in earlier years do not count in a current year's GDP. For instance, when a new car is produced, it adds to GDP in the year it is sold. However, a used car that is resold does not count in current GDP since it was already counted in GDP for the year when it was produced and sold the first time. If we counted the used car when it was resold, we would be counting that car as part of GDP twice—double-counting—even though it was produced only once.

In addition, sales of financial assets such as stocks and bonds do not count toward GDP. After all, these kinds of sales, which we will discuss in Chapter 10, do not create anything new; they simply transfer ownership from one person to another. In this way, they are like used goods. However, brokerage fees do count as payment for the brokerage service, and they are included in GDP.

# Looking at GDP as Different Types of Expenditures

**Consumption (C)** is the purchase of final goods and services by households, excluding new housing.

In this section, we look more closely at different categories of goods and services included in GDP. The Bureau of Economic Analysis (BEA) is the U.S. government agency that tallies GDP data in a process called *national income accounting*. The BEA breaks GDP into four major categories: *consumption* (C), *investment* (I), *government purchases* (G), and *net exports* (NX). Using this framework, it is possible to express GDP as:

(Equation 6.1)

$$GDP = C + I + G + NX$$

Ice cream cones count as non-durable consumption goods.

Table 6.4 details the composition of U.S. GDP in 2012. For that year, total GDP was $15,684.8 billion, or over $15.5 trillion. To get a sense of what that amount represents, imagine laying 15.5 trillion one-dollar bills side-by-side—that would be enough to cover every U.S. highway, street, and county road more than twice! In addition, U.S. GDP is more than double the GDP of any other nation.

Looking at Table 6.4, you can see that consumption is by far the largest component in GDP, followed by government purchases and then by investment. Note that the value of net exports is negative. This occurs because the United States imports more goods than it exports. Let's take a closer look at each of these four components of GDP.

## Consumption (C)

**Consumption** (C) is the purchase of final goods and services by households, with the exception of new housing. Most people spend a large majority of their income on consumption goods and services. Consumption goods include everything from groceries to automobiles. You can see in Table 6.4 that services are a very big portion of consumption spending. They include things such as haircuts, doctor's visits, and help from a real estate agent.

TABLE 6.4

**Composition of U.S. GDP, 2012**

| Category | Individual expenditures (billions of dollars) | Total expenditures per category (billions of dollars) | Percentage of GDP |
|---|---|---|---|
| **Consumption (C)** | | $11,119.6 | 70.9% |
| Durable goods | $1,218.9 | | |
| Non-durable goods | 2,564.2 | | |
| Services | 7,336.5 | | |
| | | | |
| **Investment (I)** | | **2,062.3** | 13.1% |
| Fixed investment | 2,004.2 | | |
| Change in business inventories | 58.1 | | |
| | | | |
| **Government purchases (G)** | | **3,062.8** | 19.5% |
| Federal | 1,214.3 | | |
| State and local | 1,848.5 | | |
| | | | |
| **Net exports (NX)** | | **−559.9** | −3.6% |
| Exports | 2,184 | | |
| Imports | −2,744 | | |
| | | | |
| **Total GDP** | | **$15,684.8** | 100.0% |

*Source:* U.S. Bureau of Economic Analysis.

Refrigerators count as durable consumption goods.

Consumption goods can be divided into two categories: non-durable and durable. *Non-durable* consumption goods are consumed over a short period, and *durable* consumption goods are consumed over a long period. This distinction is important when the economy swings back and forth between good times and bad times. Sales of durable goods—for example, automobiles, appliances, and computers—are subject to significant cyclical fluctuations that correlate with the health of the economy. Since durable goods are generally designed to last for many years, consumers tend to purchase more of these when the economy is strong. In contrast, when the economy is weak, they put off purchases of durables and make those that they already have last longer—for example, working with an old computer for another year rather than replacing it with a new model right away. However, non-durables don't last very long, so consumers must often purchase them regardless of economic conditions.

## Investment (I)

When you hear the word "investment," you likely think of savings or stocks and bonds. But in macroeconomics, **investment (I)** refers to private spending on tools, plant, and equipment used to produce future output. Investment can be something as simple as the purchase of a shovel, a tractor, or a personal computer to help a small business produce goods and services for its customers. But investment also includes more complex endeavors such as the construction of large factories. For example, when Pfizer builds a new factory for the manufacturing of a new drug, it is making an investment. When Walmart builds a new warehouse, that expense is an investment. And when a family purchases a newly built house, that expense also counts as an investment. This may seem odd, since most of us think of a home purchase as something that is consumed; but in the national income accounts, such a purchase counts as an investment.

Investment also includes all purchases by businesses that add to their inventories. For example, in preparation for Christmas buying, an electronics retailer will order more TVs, cameras, and computers. GDP rises when business inventories increase. GDP is calculated this way because we want to measure output in the period it is produced. Investment in inventory is just one more way that firms spend today to increase output in the future.

## Government Spending (G)

National, state, and local governments purchase many goods and services, which are included in GDP as *government spending*. **Government spending (G)** includes spending by all levels of government on final goods and services. For example, every government employee receives a salary, which is considered a part of GDP. Similarly, governments spend money purchasing buildings, equipment, and supplies from private-sector firms. Governments also make expenditures on public works projects, including national defense, highway construction, schools, and post offices.

However, one form of government outlay does not count in GDP. *Transfer payments* that the government makes to households, such as welfare payments or unemployment insurance, are not direct purchases of new goods and services. These transfer payments merely move income from one group to another.

## Net Exports (NX)

The United States produces some goods and services that are exported to other countries, and it imports some goods and services that are produced elsewhere. Only exports are counted in GDP because they are produced in the United States. Imports, in contrast, are produced elsewhere but are used domestically within the United States. Since our goal is to measure domestic production accurately, GDP includes only **net exports (NX)**, which are exports minus imports of final goods and services. We can write this in equation form as:

$$\text{net exports (NX)} = \text{exports} - \text{imports}$$

When spending on imports is larger than spending on exports, net exports are negative. Net exports are typically negative for the United States.

Notice that imports enter the GDP calculations as a negative value: GDP = C + I + G + (exports − imports). From this, it would be easy to conclude that imports are harmful to an economy because they seem to reduce GDP. However, adding the different components together (C, I, G, and NX), in the process of national income accounting, really is just that— accounting. The primary goal is to keep a record of how people are buying the goods and services produced in the United States. More imports coming in means more goods and services for people in this nation. All other things being equal, this does not make us worse off.

## Real GDP: Adjusting GDP for Price Changes

According to the U.S. Bureau of Economic Analysis, in 2005 the nation's economy produced a GDP of $12.6 trillion. Just seven years later, in 2012, it produced over $15.5 trillion. That's a 24% increase in just seven years. Is that really possible? Think about that in long-run historical terms. Is it possible that the nation's economy grew to $12.6 trillion over more than two centuries, but then just seven years later grew to over $15.5 trillion? What's more, this happened in spite of the Great Recession of 2007–2009. If we look closer, we'll see that much of the recent increase in GDP is actually due to inflation.

The raw GDP data, based on market values, is computed on the basis of the prices of goods and services current at the time the GDP is produced. Economists refer to these prices as the *current prices*. The GDP calculated from current prices is called **nominal GDP**. Figure 6.7 compares U.S. nominal and real GDP from 2005 to 2012. Notice that nominal GDP rises much faster

**Nominal GDP is** GDP measured in current prices, and not adjusted for inflation.

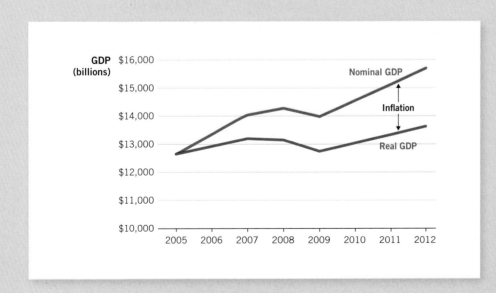

### FIGURE 6.7

**U.S. Nominal and Real GDP, 2005–2012**

Nominal GDP typically rises faster than real GDP since it rises with growth in both real production and growth in prices (inflation). From 2005 to 2012, nominal GDP in the United States rose by 24%, but three-fourths of that increase was due to inflation. The increase in real GDP during the same period was less than 8%. *Source:* U.S. Bureau of Economic Analysis.

A **price level** is an index of the average prices of goods and services throughout the economy.

than real GDP does. While nominal GDP rose by 24%, real GDP increased by less than 8%. The difference between these percentages reflects inflation.

Computing nominal GDP is straightforward: we add the actual prices of all final goods and services. But to compute real GDP, we also need a measure of overall prices, known as a *price level*. A **price level** is an index of the average prices of goods and services throughout the economy. It goes up when prices generally rise, and it falls when prices across the economy fall. Chapter 8 explores prices and the calculation of price levels. For now, just take the price data as given, and think of the price level as an indicator of changes in the general level of all prices across the economy.

The **GDP deflator** is a measure of the price level that includes prices of the final goods and services included in GDP.

The price level we use to adjust GDP data, known as the **GDP deflator**, includes the prices of the final goods and services counted in GDP. The GDP deflator serves to "deflate" all the price inflation out of nominal GDP so that we can see real GDP. Let's look at some actual data. Table 6.5 shows U.S. nominal GDP and price level data from 2000 to 2012. Looking at just two lines, for example, we can see that the price level was set at 100.0 in 2005 and rose to 103 in 2006. This indicates that, on average, prices across the economy rose by 3% between 2005 and 2006.

To compute real GDP, we extract the current prices of goods and services and then insert prices from a common time period, or *base period*, that has been agreed upon. We can do this in two steps:

1. **Filter out the current prices from the nominal GDP data.**
   We do this by dividing nominal GDP by the price level from the time period in which the GDP was produced.

| TABLE 6.5 |
|---|

### U.S. Nominal GDP and Price Level, 2000–2012

| Year | Nominal GDP (billions of dollars) | Price Level (GDP deflator) |
|---|---|---|
| 2000 | 9,952 | 89 |
| 2001 | 10,286 | 91 |
| 2002 | 10,642 | 92 |
| 2003 | 11,142 | 94 |
| 2004 | 11,853 | 97 |
| 2005 | 12,623 | 100 |
| 2006 | 13,377 | 103 |
| 2007 | 14,029 | 106 |
| 2008 | 14,292 | 109 |
| 2009 | 13,974 | 110 |
| 2010 | 14,499 | 111 |
| 2011 | 15,076 | 113 |
| 2012 | 15,865 | 115 |

*Source:* U.S. Bureau of Economic Analysis.

## 2. Put in the constant prices from the base period.

Now we just multiply by the price level (100) from the base period.

Putting these two steps together, we compute real GDP for any time period (t) as:

$$\text{real GDP}_t = \underbrace{\frac{\text{nominal GDP}_t}{\text{price level}_t}}_{\text{Step 1}} \underbrace{\times\ 100}_{\text{Step 2}} \qquad \text{(Equation 6.3)}$$

For example, nominal GDP in 2012 was $15,864.8 billion, and the price level was 115. To convert this to real GDP, we divide by 115 and multiply by 100:

$$\text{real GDP}_{2012} = \frac{\$15,864.8}{115} \times 100 = \$13,795.5 \text{ billion}$$

Table 6.6 illustrates both steps of this conversion.

The figure $13,795.5 billion is the U.S. GDP in 2012, adjusted for inflation. Economists and the financial media use other terms for real GDP; sometimes they might say "current year GDP in 2005 prices" or "GDP in constant 2005 dollars." Whenever you consider changes in GDP over time, you should look for these terms to ensure that your data is not biased by price changes.

## Growth Rates

For many macroeconomic applications, it is useful to calculate growth rates. For example, let's say you read that the GDP in Mexico in 2010 was about $1 trillion. You might consider this information to be troubling for the future of the Mexican economy, since $1 trillion is very small compared to U.S. GDP. But maybe you also read that Mexico's GDP grew by 18% in 2010 (it did!). In that case, you will probably get a different, and more positive, impression. In general, growth rates convey additional, often more illuminating, information.

| TABLE 6.6 |
| --- |

**Converting Nominal GDP into Real GDP**

**Data for 2012:**
**Nominal GDP = $15,864.8 billion**
**Price level (GDP deflator) = 115**

| General steps | Our example |
| --- | --- |
| Step 1: Filter out current prices. | $15,864.8 ÷ 115 = 137.955 |
| Step 2: Input base-period prices. | 137.955 × 100 = $13,795.5 |

Growth rates are calculated as percentage changes in a variable. For example, the growth of U.S. nominal GDP in 2012 is computed as:

(Equation 6.4)

$$\text{nominal GDP growth in 2012} = \frac{GDP_{2012} - GDP_{2011}}{GDP_{2011}} \times 100$$

Unless noted otherwise, the data comes from the end of the period. Therefore, the nominal GDP growth computed above tells us the percentage change in U.S. GDP from the end of 2011 to the end of 2012, or over the course of 2012. Using actual data, this is:

$$\text{nominal GDP growth in 2012} = \% \text{ change in nominal GDP}$$

$$= \frac{15{,}684.8 - 15{,}075.7}{15{,}075.7} \times 100 = 4.0\%$$

We can also compute the growth rate of the price level (GDP deflator) for 2012:

$$\text{price level growth rate} = \% \text{ change in price level}$$

$$= \frac{115 - 113}{113} \times 100 = 1.8\%$$

This means that throughout the U.S. economy in 2012, inflation was 1.8%.

Armed with these two computations, we can derive one more useful formula for evaluating GDP data. Recall that nominal GDP, which is the raw GDP data, includes information on both the price level and real GDP. When either of these factors changes, it affects nominal GDP. In fact, the growth rate of nominal GDP is approximately equal to the sum of the growth rates of these two factors:

(Equation 6.5)

$$\text{growth of nominal GDP} \approx \text{growth of real GDP} + \text{growth of price level}$$

Since growth rates are calculated as percentage changes, we can rewrite equation 6.5 as:

(Equation 6.6)

$$\% \text{ change in nominal GDP} \approx \% \text{ change in real GDP}$$
$$+ \% \text{ change in price level}$$

This equation gives us a simple way of dissecting the growth of GDP into its respective parts. For example, since we know that nominal GDP grew by 4% in 2012 and that the price level grew by 1.8%, the remaining nominal GDP growth of 2.2% is the result of growth in real GDP.

## What Are Some Shortcomings of GDP Data?

We began this chapter with a claim that GDP is the single best measure of economic activity. Along the way, we have learned that nominal GDP fails to account for changes in prices and that real GDP is a better measure of economic activity. We also talked about how real GDP per capita accounts for population

# PRACTICE WHAT YOU KNOW

### Computing Real and Nominal GDP Growth: GDP Growth in Mexico

The table below presents GDP data for Mexico. Use the data to answer the questions that follow.

**Question: What was the rate of growth of real GDP in Mexico in 2010?**

How much is Mexico's economy growing?

**Answer:** Using equation 6.6, we know:

$$\% \text{ change in real GDP} + \% \text{ change in price level}$$
$$\approx \% \text{ change in nominal GDP}$$

And rewriting the equation, we can solve for real GDP growth as:

$$\% \text{ change in real GDP} \approx \% \text{ change in nominal GDP}$$
$$- \% \text{ change in price level}$$

For 2010, we have:

$$\% \text{ change in real GDP} \approx 18 - 4.4 \approx 13.6$$

That's impressive.

**Question: Now how would you compute real GDP growth in Mexico in 2009?**

**Answer:** Using the 2009 data in the same equation, we get:

$$\% \text{ change in real GDP} \approx -19 - 4 = -23$$

This means that 2009 was a pretty rough year for the Mexican economy.

| Year | Nominal GDP growth rate | Price-level growth rate |
|------|------|------|
| 2007 | 9 | 6 |
| 2008 | 6 | 6 |
| 2009 | −19 | 4 |
| 2010 | 18 | 4.4 |

*Source:* World Bank.

# Looking at GDP in the United States

Gross domestic product (GDP) is the single most important indicator of macroeconomic performance. It gives us a snapshot of the overall health of the economy because it measures both output and income. These graphics illustrate the four pieces of GDP—consumption, investment, government spending, and net exports—and how these pieces changed from 1967 to 2011. On the bottom left, you can also see how real GDP has more than tripled since 1967.

| (In billions of 2011 dollars) | 1967 | 2011 |
| --- | --- | --- |
| TOTAL GDP | $4,466.1 | $15,075.7 |
| Consumption | $2,724.1 | $10,729.0 |
| Investment | $1,032.7 | $1,854.9 |
| Government | $689.9 | $3,059.8 |
| Net Exports | $19.3 | −$568.1 |

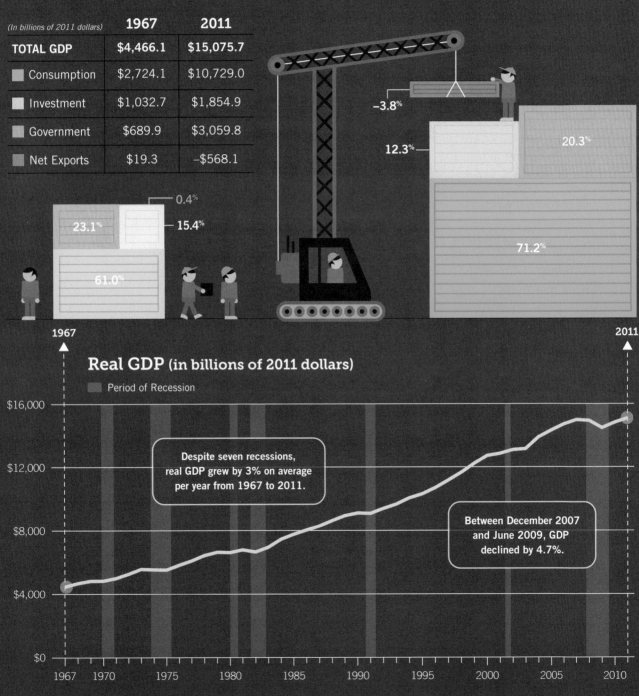

1967 — 23.1%, 15.4%, 0.4%, 61.0%

2011 — −3.8%, 12.3%, 20.3%, 71.2%

## Real GDP (in billions of 2011 dollars)

Period of Recession

Despite seven recessions, real GDP grew by 3% on average per year from 1967 to 2011.

Between December 2007 and June 2009, GDP declined by 4.7%.

$16,000 / $12,000 / $8,000 / $4,000 / $0

1967 1970 1975 1980 1985 1990 1995 2000 2005 2010

# Percentage Breakdowns, 1967 vs. 2011

By measuring the components of each piece of GDP, we can see how the makeup of the U.S. economy has changed over time.

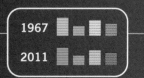

1967
2011

## Consumption

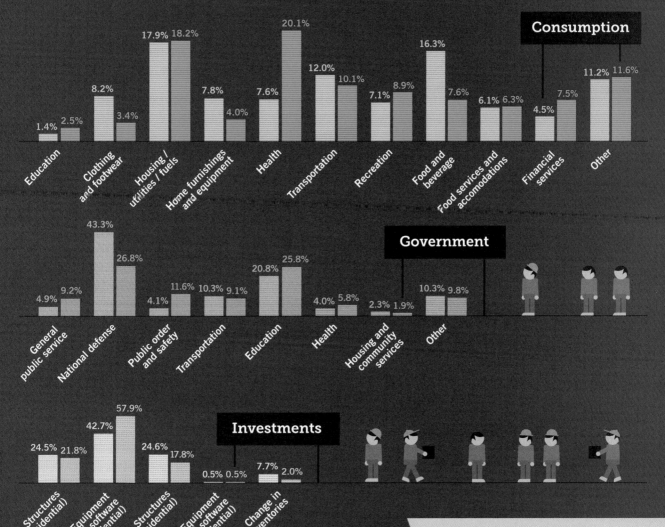

| Education | Clothing and footwear | Housing / utilities / fuels | Home furnishings and equipment | Health | Transportation | Recreation | Food and beverage | Food services and accomodations | Financial services | Other |
|---|---|---|---|---|---|---|---|---|---|---|
| 1.4% 2.5% | 8.2% 3.4% | 17.9% 18.2% | 7.8% 4.0% | 7.6% 20.1% | 12.0% 10.1% | 7.1% 8.9% | 16.3% 7.6% | 6.1% 6.3% | 4.5% 7.5% | 11.2% 11.6% |

## Government

| General public service | National defense | Public order and safety | Transportation | Education | Health | Housing and community services | Other |
|---|---|---|---|---|---|---|---|
| 4.9% 9.2% | 43.3% 26.8% | 4.1% 11.6% | 10.3% 9.1% | 20.8% 25.8% | 4.0% 5.8% | 2.3% 1.9% | 10.3% 9.8% |

## Investments

| Structures (non-residential) | Equipment and software (non-residential) | Structures (residential) | Equipment and software (residential) | Change in private inventories |
|---|---|---|---|---|
| 24.5% 21.8% | 42.7% 57.9% | 24.6% 17.8% | 0.5% 0.5% | 7.7% 2.0% |

## Net Exports

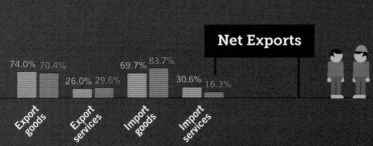

| Export goods | Export services | Import goods | Import services |
|---|---|---|---|
| 74.0% 70.4% | 26.0% 29.6% | 69.7% 83.7% | 30.6% 16.3% |

(% of total exports)    (% of total imports)

## REVIEW QUESTIONS

- What component of consumption do we spend a much greater percentage on now than in 1967?

- Why do economists stress real GDP rather than nominal GDP when looking at GDP changes over time?

Not counted in GDP: washing your own car.

differences. You will be relieved to learn that by now we have finished introducing new variations of GDP! However, there are some problems with relying on GDP data as a measure of a nation's well-being. In this section, we highlight four shortcomings that limit the effectiveness of GDP as a measure of the health of an economy. At the end of this section, we will consider why economists continue to rely on GDP.

## Non-Market Goods

Many goods and services are produced but not sold. Those goods and services are not counted in GDP data even though they create value for society. For instance, washing your own dishes, mowing your own grass, or washing your car are services produced, but they are not counted in GDP. When the non-market segment of an economy is large, there can be a dramatic undercounting of the annual output being produced. In less-developed societies where many households live off the land and produce goods for their own consumption, GDP—the measure of market activity—is a less reliable measure of the economic output.

## Underground Economy

The underground, or shadow, economy encompasses transactions that are not reported to the government, and therefore not taxed. Usually, these transactions are settled in cash. Some of these transactions are legal, such as when bartenders and waitresses collect tips, contractors build additions to homes, and landscapers cut lawns. But the underground economy also includes transactions like illegal exchanges of drugs. Transactions in the underground economy are not directly measurable because the income is not reported. Therefore, they are not included in official measures of GDP.

How big is the underground economy? No one is exactly sure. Economist Friedrich Schneider has estimated that for wealthy developed economies it is roughly 15% of GDP and that in transitioning economies the percentage rises to between 21% and 30% of GDP. However, in the world's most underdeveloped economies, like those of Nigeria or Armenia, the underground economy can be as much as 40% of GDP.

The United States is widely believed to have one of the smallest shadow economies in the world, with less than 10% of GDP unaccounted for in the official measurement. Why is the underground economy so small in the United States? The simple answer is that in the United States, and in many other developed economies, most citizens can earn more by legitimately participating in the economy than by engaging in illegal activities. In short, a strong economy that generates jobs and opportunities for advancement helps to reduce the size of the underground economy. In addition, corruption is much less common. This means that participants in the economy rarely face demands for bribes or kickbacks from authorities or organized crime. This is not the case in many developing nations, however. For example, Somalia, which ranks last on Transparency International's corruption index, has widespread piracy and virtually no formal economy that escapes bribery and thuggery.

## ECONOMICS IN THE REAL WORLD

### America's "Shadow Economy"

Journalist Taylor Barnes wrote about the U.S. underground economy in 2009. Barnes visited Malcolm X Boulevard on West 125th Street in New York City and reported several instances of underground transactions for services ranging from moving companies to sales of makeup, food stamps, and fake designer handbags.

According to Barnes, "Pinning down the informal economy is as tough as catching a fake Louis Vuitton vendor running from the police. But it's huge in the United States— larger than the official output of all but the upper crust of nations across the globe. And, due to the recent recession, it's growing."

Barnes cites the estimates of economist Friedrich Schneider, which put the size of the U.S. underground economy at around $1 trillion, or 8% of measured GDP. This estimate only includes legal activity; it excludes illegal activities such as drug deals. ✳

Not counted in GDP: sales of fake designer handbags.

## Quality of the Environment

Since GDP only measures the final amount of goods and services produced in a given period, it cannot distinguish how those goods and services are produced. Imagine two economies, both with the same real GDP per capita. One economy relies on clean energy for its production, and the other has lax environmental standards. Citizens in both countries enjoy the same standard of living, but their well-being is not the same. The lax environmental standards in the second economy lead to air and water pollution, as well as health problems for its citizens. Since there is more to quality of life than the goods and services we buy, using GDP to infer that both places are equally desirable would be inaccurate.

## Leisure Time

Not counted in GDP: a clean environment.

Since GDP only counts market activity, it fails to capture how long laborers work to produce goods and services. For most developed nations, according to the OECD, the average workweek is slightly over 35 hours. However, there are wide variations in how hard laborers work from one country to the next. At the high end, laborers in South Korea average 46 hours per week. In contrast, laborers in the Netherlands average fewer than 28 hours per week. This means that comparisons of GDP across countries are problematic because they do not account for the extra time available to workers in countries with substantially fewer hours worked. For example,

# The Underground Economy

## *Traffic*

*Traffic*, a crime film from 2000, looks at America's war on drugs through the lives of the people involved in it. The characters offer a fascinating range: from the nation's drug czar, to his cocaine-using daughter, to the cops who fight the war on both sides of the U.S./Mexican border, to the drug dealers who profit from trafficking the drugs.

In one scene, two agents from the Drug Enforcement Agency are interrogating a suspected drug trafficker. The suspect explains that the cocaine flow from Mexico into the United States cannot be stopped because there is too much demand in the United States and because Mexican dealers are willing to "throw supply at the problem." That is, the Mexican drug lords recognize that some of their shipments will be seized but that enough will get through to reach their customers in the United States to make the risks worthwhile.

One of the ironies about measuring GDP is that even though the drug trades are not part of GDP—because those illegal market transactions are not formally recorded—the people involved in fighting the war on drugs, as well as the sales of drug paraphernalia, are included in GDP.

How does more illegal drug traffic lead to higher GDP?

The movie also traces the life of a successful businessman who has made millions selling drugs. We see his estate, luxury cars, trophy wife, and all the accoutrements of success. His purchases, made from illegal sales, are counted in GDP because it measures the sales of final goods and services. Thus, while GDP cannot measure the economic activity in the underground economy, it can indirectly capture some of those transactions when the gains from selling drugs are used to purchase legal products.

in the United States the average workweek is 36 hours. A comparison with Japan, which also averages 36 hours per workweek, would be valid; but a comparison of the GDP in the United States with that of Sweden (31-hour workweek) or Greece (41-hour workweek) would be misleading.

Why don't economists correct some of the deficiencies of GDP by including them in their calculations? If we did, GDP might be a better gauge of well-being. For instance, in addition to the production of goods and services there are many other measurements that economists might use to determine whether a country is a good place in which to live: life expectancy, educational levels, access to health care, crime rates, or any of a host of other statistics.

One problem with including all the additional factors in GDP is that they are also difficult to measure. Moreover, the combined statistic that we would generate would be even more challenging to understand. Therefore, we limit GDP to measuring economic production, knowing that it is not a perfect measure of well-being. In addition, GDP is actually correlated with many of the variables we care about. In Chapter 11, we will present international data showing that increases in GDP are associated with increases in many measures of human welfare. After all, a country with a higher GDP per capita can focus on economic values beyond the basic necessities. Therefore, higher levels of GDP are highly correlated with a better environment, higher-quality and better access to health care, more education, more leisure time, and lower crime rates.

Not counted in GDP: extra time to relax.

## PRACTICE WHAT YOU KNOW

### Shortcomings of GDP Data: Use Caution in Interpreting GDP as an Economic Barometer

Some nations have more stay-at-home parents than others. How does this affect GDP comparisons?

In many parts of the world, a significant amount of effort goes into non-market production in the household, such as stay-at-home parenting. For example, Zimbabwe has a very high rate of non-market household production. In contrast, Canada has a low rate of non-market household production.

Question: How does the difference in non-market household production affect a comparison between Zimbabwe and Canada?

Answer: The GDP statistics for Zimbabwe are biased downward more than the statistics for Canada, since a larger portion of Zimbabwe's actual production goes unreported. As such, while Zimbabwe is actually a poorer nation than Canada, official statistics exaggerate the difference slightly.

# Conclusion

We began this chapter with the misconception that there is no reliable way to determine how well an economy is performing. But GDP is a measure that works well. In the short run, it helps us recognize business cycles. When the economy is struggling through a recession, this is evident in the GDP data. When the economy is healthy and expanding, GDP data reinforces this too. GDP also serves as a good indicator for living standards around the globe and over time. As we'll see in Chapter 11, nations with better living conditions are also nations with higher GDP. Thus, even though there are some short-comings in the GDP data, it is a sound indicator of the overall health of an economy.

In the next chapter, we will look at a second macroeconomic indicator—the unemployment rate. The unemployment rate and other job indicators give us an additional dimension on which to consider the health of an economy.

## ANSWERING THE BIG QUESTIONS

### How is macroeconomics different from microeconomics?

* Microeconomics is the study of individuals and firms, but macro-economics considers the entire economy.
* Many of the topics in both areas of study are the same; these include income, employment, and output. But the macro perspective is much broader than the micro perspective.

### What does GDP tell us about the economy?

* GDP measures both output and income in a macroeconomy.
* It is a gauge of productivity and the overall level of wealth in an economy.
* We use GDP data to measure living standards, economic growth, and business cycle conditions.

### How is GDP computed?

* GDP is the total market value of all goods and services produced in an economy in a given year.
* Economists typically compute GDP by adding four types of expendi-tures in the economy: consumption (C), investment (I), government spending (G), and net exports (NX).
* For many applications, it is also necessary to compute real GDP, or to adjust GDP for changes in prices.

### What are some shortcomings of GDP data?

* GDP data does not include the production of non-market goods, the underground economy, production effects on the environment, or the value placed on leisure time.

# Economic Growth Statistics: Deciphering Data Reports

Economics is all around us, and the topics of economics are constantly reported in the media. In addition to monthly reports on unemployment and inflation, there are monthly releases and revisions of GDP data for the United States and other nations. These updates often get a lot of attention. Unfortunately, media reports are not as careful with their economics terminology as we would like. Because they are not worded carefully, the reports can be misleading.

After learning about historical experiences with economic growth, you might find new interest in the economic growth reports that appear almost every month in the mainstream media. However, you must carefully evaluate the data they present. Now that you have perspective on growth statistics, you can determine for yourself whether economic news is positive or negative. For example, a *New York Times* article from April 2009 offers the following on economic growth in China for the previous quarter:

> China's economic output was 6.1 percent higher in the first quarter than a year earlier. . . . China's annual growth rate appeared slow in the first quarter after the 6.8 percent rate in the fourth quarter of 2008, partly because it was being compared with the economy's formidable output in the first quarter of last year.

Economic reports in the media are often misleading.

China's economy grew at over 6%, and yet this rate is taken as "slow." By now, you know that 6% is an incredibly fast rate of growth.

Good economists are very careful with language, and certain terms have very specific meanings. For example, we know that "economic growth" always refers to changes in *per capita* real GDP, not simply GDP or real GDP. But economic reports in mainstream media outlets often blur this distinction. That is exactly the case with the report in the *New York Times* article cited above.

Even though the author uses the term "annual growth rate," additional research reveals that he is talking about real GDP growth, but not adjusting the data for population changes. This is a fairly common occurrence, so you should watch out for it when you read economic growth reports. It turns out that the population growth rate in China was about 0.6% in 2009. This means that the growth rate of per capita real GDP in China was actually about 5.5%, which is still very impressive.

*Source:* Keith Bradsher, "China's Economic Growth Slows in First Quarter," *New York Times,* April 16, 2009.

ECONOMICS FOR LIFE

## CONCEPTS YOU SHOULD KNOW

business cycle (p. 180)
consumption (C) (p. 186)
economic contraction (p.180)
economic expansion (p. 180)
economic growth (p. 179)
final good (p. 184)
GDP deflator (p. 190)
government spending (G)
(p. 188)

Great Recession (p. 180)
gross domestic product (GDP)
(p. 176)
gross national product (GNP)
(p. 185)
inflation (p. 178)
intermediate good (p. 184)
investment (I) (p. 188)
net exports (NX) (p. 188)

nominal GDP (p. 189)
per capita GDP (p. 178)
price level (p. 190)
real GDP (p. 178)
recession (p. 179)
service (p. 182)

## QUESTIONS FOR REVIEW

1. Explain the relationship between output and income for both an individual and an entire economy.

2. What is the most important component (C, I, G, or NX) of GDP? Give an example of each component.

3. A farmer sells cotton to a clothing company for $1,000, and the clothing company turns the cotton into T-shirts that it sells to a store for a total of $2,000. How much did GDP increase as a result of these transactions?

4. A friend of yours is reading a financial blog and comes to you for some advice about GDP. She wants to know whether she should pay attention to nominal GDP or real GDP. Which one do you recommend, and why?

5. Is a larger GDP always better than a smaller GDP? Explain your answer with an example.

6. If Max receives an unemployment check, would we include that transfer payment from the government in this year's GDP? Why or why not?

7. Phil owns an old set of golf clubs that he purchased for $1,000 seven years ago. He decides to post them on Craigslist and quickly sells the clubs for $250. How does this sale affect GDP?

8. Real GDP for 2010 is less than nominal GDP for that year. But real GDP for 2000 is more than nominal GDP for that year. Why?

9. What are the four shortcomings with using GDP as a measure of well-being for the residents of a society?

## STUDY PROBLEMS (✴ solved at the end of the section)

1. A friend who knows of your interest in economics comes up to you after reading the latest GDP data and excitedly exclaims, "Did you see that nominal GDP rose from $17 trillion to $17.5 trillion?" What should you tell your friend about this news?

2. In the following situations, explain what is counted in this year's GDP:

   a. You bought a new Wii at GameStop last year and resold it on eBay this year.

   b. You purchase an *Investing for Dummies* book at Barnes & Noble.

   c. You purchase a historic home using the services of a real estate agent.

   d. You detail your car so it is spotless inside and out.

   e. You purchase a new hard drive for your old laptop.

   f. Your physical therapist receives $300 for physical therapy but reports only $100.

g. Apple buys 1,000 motherboards for use in making new computers.

h. Toyota produces 10,000 new Camrys that remain unsold at the end of the year.

3. To which component of GDP expenditure (C, I, G, or NX) does each of the following belong?

a. Swiss chocolates imported from Europe

b. a driver's license you receive from the Department of Motor Vehicles

c. a candle you buy at a local store

d. a new home

4. A mechanic builds an engine and then sells it to a customized body shop for $7,000. The body shop installs the engine in the car and resells it to a dealer for $20,000. The dealer then sells the finished vehicle for $35,000. A consumer drives off with the car. By how much does GDP increase? What is the value added at each step of the production process? How does the total value added compare with the amount by which GDP increased?

5. In this chapter, we used nominal GDP data from Table 6.5 to compute 2012 GDP in 2005 dollars. Using the same steps, use the data from Table 6.5 to compute 2011 GDP in 2005 dollars.

6. Many goods and services are illegally sold or legally sold but not reported to the government. How would increased efforts to count those goods and services affect our calculation of GDP?

7. Leisure time is not included in GDP, but what would happen if it was included? Would high-work countries like South Korea fare better in international comparisons of well-being, or worse?

*8. Fill in the missing data in the following table.

| Year | Nominal GDP | Real GDP | GDP deflator |
|---|---|---|---|
| 2007 | $100,000 | _____ | 100.0 |
| 2008 | _____ | $110,000 | 108.0 |
| 2009 | $130,000 | $117,000 | _____ |
| 2010 | $150,000 | _____ | 120.0 |
| 2011 | _____ | $136,000 | 125.0 |

*9. Consider an economy that only produces two goods: strawberries and cream. Use the table below to compute nominal GDP, real GDP, and the GDP deflator for each year. (Year 2010 is the base year.)

| Year | Price of strawberries (per pint) | Quantity of strawberries (pints) | Price of cream (per pint) | Quantity of cream (pints) |
|---|---|---|---|---|
| 2010 | $3.00 | 100 | $2.00 | 200 |
| 2011 | $4.00 | 125 | $2.50 | 400 |
| 2012 | $5.00 | 150 | $3.00 | 500 |

## SOLVED PROBLEMS

**8.**

| Year | Nominal GDP | Real GDP | GDP deflator |
|------|-------------|----------|--------------|
| 2007 | $100,000 | $100,000 | 100.0 |
| 2008 | $118,800 | $110,000 | 108.0 |
| 2009 | $130,000 | $117,000 | 111.1 |
| 2010 | $150,000 | $125,000 | 120.0 |
| 2011 | $170,000 | $136,000 | 125.0 |

To solve for the missing data, use the following equation (and 2007 as the base year):

$$\text{real GDP}_{year} = \frac{\text{nominal GDP}_{year}}{\text{price level}_{year}}$$
$$\times \text{ base year price level}$$

*For 2007:* real GDP$_{2007}$ = ($100,000 ÷ 100.0)
$$\times 100.0 = \underline{\$100,000}$$

*For 2008*: $110,000 = (nominal GDP$_{2008}$
$$÷ 108.0) \times 100.0$$

nominal GDP$_{2008}$ = ($110,000 ÷ 100.0)
$$\times 108.0 = \underline{\$118,800}$$

*For 2009*: $117,000 = ($130,000 ÷ GDP
$$\text{deflator}_{2009}) \times 100.0$$

GDP deflator$_{2009}$ = ($130,000 ÷ $117,000)
$$\times 100.0$$

GDP deflator$_{2009}$ = $\underline{111.1}$

*For 2010*: real GDP$_{2010}$ = ($150,000 ÷ 120.0)
$$\times 100.0$$

real GDP$_{2010}$ = $\underline{\$125,000}$

*For 2011*: $136,000 = (nominal GDP$_{2011}$
$$÷ 125.0) \times 100.0$$

nominal GDP$_{2011}$ = ($136,000 ÷ 100.0)
$$\times 125.0$$

nominal GDP$_{2011}$ = $\underline{\$170,000}$

**9.**

| Year | Nominal GDP | Real GDP | GDP deflator |
|------|-------------|----------|--------------|
| 2010 | $700 | $700 | 100.0 |
| 2011 | $1,500 | $1,175 | 127.7 |
| 2012 | $2,250 | $1,450 | 155.2 |

First, let's calculate nominal GDP for each of the three years by adding up the market values of the strawberries and cream produced during that year.

*For 2010*: nominal $GDP_{2010} = (\$3.00 \times 100) + (\$2.00 \times 200) = \$700$

*For 2011*: nominal $GDP_{2011} = (\$4.00 \times 125) + (\$2.50 \times 400) = \$1,500$

*For 2012*: nominal $GDP_{2012} = (\$5.00 \times 150) + (\$3.00 \times 500) = \$2,250$

Now, let's calculate real GDP in 2010 dollars by multiplying the quantities produced in each year by the 2010 prices.

*For 2010*: real $GDP_{2010} = (\$3.00 \times 100) + (\$2.00 \times 200) = \$700$

*For 2011*: real $GDP_{2011} = (\$3.00 \times 125) + (\$2.00 \times 400) = \$1,175$

*For 2012*: real $GDP_{2012} = (\$3.00 \times 150) + (\$2.00 \times 500) = \$1,450$

Finally, using the nominal GDP and real GDP numbers we calculated above, let's calculate the GDP deflator by using the following formula:

$$\text{GDP deflator}_{year} = \frac{\text{nominal GDP}_{year}}{\text{real GDP}_{year}} \times 100.0$$

GDP deflator$_{2010}$ = 100.0. Since 2010 is given as the base year, the GDP deflator must be 100.0.

*For 2011*: GDP deflator$_{2011} = (\$1,500 \div \$1,175) \times 100 = 127.7$

*For 2012*: GDP deflator$_{2012} = (\$2,250 \div \$1,450) \times 100 = 155.2$

# Unemployment

**We should aim for zero unemployment.**

Many people believe that even a small amount of unemployment is a sign of problems. This isn't true. On the one hand, it is never fun for any

person to search unsuccessfully for work. On the other hand, some unemployment is the result of positive changes in the economy that make us all better off in the long run. For this reason, economists agree that we can never eliminate unemployment entirely and that attempts to do so are misguided.

In this chapter, we will take a closer look at the topic of unemployment. Indeed, after GDP, the unemployment rate is the second most important indicator of economic health. We will examine the causes of unemployment and explain how it is measured. By looking at some historical data in context, we will begin to understand when unemployment is a matter of concern.

While some macroeconomic unemployment is natural, on the micro level, unemployment is not fun.

# BIG QUESTIONS

* What are the major reasons for unemployment?
* What can we learn from the employment data?

## What Are the Major Reasons for Unemployment?

**Unemployment**
occurs when a worker who is not currently employed is searching for a job without success.

Perhaps you know someone who has lost his or her job—a parent or a family friend. Losing a job is particularly difficult when a person is unable to easily transition to another one. After all, many of us depend on our jobs just to survive. There are few greater frustrations than this in a modern economy— being willing and able to work, but lacking an opportunity to do so. **Unemployment** occurs when a worker who is not currently employed is searching for a job without success. Unfortunately, the level of unemployment in the United States has been relatively high in recent years—during and after the Great Recession, which began at the end of 2007.

People leave their jobs for many reasons. Some do so voluntarily: they may choose to have children, return to school, or take another job. Others lose a job they wish to keep: an employee might be let go for poor performance or because the company is downsizing. When macroeconomists consider unemployment, they explicitly look at workers who seek employment yet are unable to secure it. We use the *unemployment rate* to monitor the level of unemployment in an economy. The **unemployment rate (u)** is the percentage of the labor force that is unemployed. Figure 7.1 plots the U.S. unemployment rate from 1960 to 2012. This visual graphic is one way of quickly measuring national economic frustration. As the unemployment rate climbs, people are more likely to be disappointed in their pursuit of a job.

The **unemployment rate (u)** is the percentage of the labor force that is unemployed.

Economists distinguish three types of unemployment: *structural, frictional,* and *cyclical*. You can think of each type as deriving from a different source. As it turns out, structural and frictional unemployment occur even when the economy is healthy and growing. For this reason, they are often called "natural unemployment." We consider them first.

### Structural Unemployment

Unemployment is difficult on households, and there is a waste of resources when idle workers sit on the sidelines. However, a dynamic, growing economy is an economy that adapts and changes. No one would consider it an improvement if we returned to the economy of early America, where 90% of Americans toiled in manual farm work and earned meager subsistence wages.

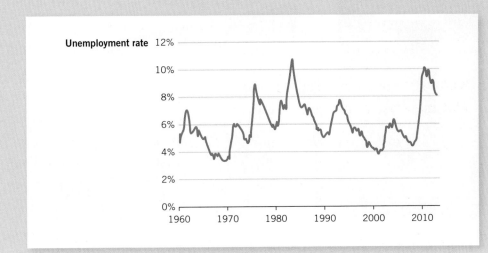

**FIGURE 7.1**

**U.S. Unemployment Rate, 1960–2012**
The unemployment rate is an important indicator of the economy's health. Since 1960, the average unemployment rate in the United States has been about 6%.

*Source:* U.S. Bureau of Labor Statistics.

The transformation to our modern economy has brought new jobs but also has required completely different skills. Some jobs have become obsolete, which has led inevitably to a certain amount of unemployment, even if just temporarily. And herein lies the dilemma. Dynamic, growing economies are also evolving economies. If we want an economy that adapts to changes in consumer demands and technology, we must accept some unemployment, at least temporarily, as a by-product of the growth.

Consider that in the past we produced no computers, cell phones, or polio vaccines. Subsequent inventions of new products and technologies enabled us to produce more and better output with fewer resources. But we also produced less of some other things—such as black and white televisions, cassette tapes, and typewriters. These kinds of structural changes left some workers unemployed, even if just temporarily.

## Creative Destruction

As new industries are created, some old ones are destroyed. The economist Joseph Schumpeter coined the term *creative destruction* to describe this process of economic evolution. **Creative destruction** occurs when the introduction of new products and technologies leads to the end of other industries and jobs, as some jobs become obsolete. This process leads to **structural unemployment**, which is caused by changes in the industrial makeup (structure) of the economy. Although structural unemployment can cause transitional problems, it is often a sign of a healthy, growing economy.

The retail book market provides a good example. In the 1980s and 1990s, the Borders book retailer grew from a small Ann Arbor, Michigan, bookseller to a national chain with 1,249 total locations. Borders' success came from innovation: the stores were physically much larger than earlier bookstores, offered four to five times as many titles, had comfortable reading areas, and

**Creative destruction**
occurs when the introduction of new products and technologies leads to the end of other industries and jobs.

**Structural unemployment**
is unemployment caused by changes in the industrial makeup (structure) of the economy.

Creative destruction in the retail book market means that when new products and jobs are created, other jobs are destroyed.

featured in-store cafés. These innovations led to the closure of many small independent booksellers, causing some temporary job shifts.

But innovations in the book market weren't over in the 1990s. The following decade saw greater competition from online booksellers like Amazon .com and the introduction of e-readers like the Kindle, Nook, and iPad. These changes led to the decline of Borders, which had 19,000 employees when it declared bankruptcy in 2011. At that point, Borders' employees found themselves structurally unemployed: they lost their jobs as a result of market innovations.

The steel industry provides another example. Steel helped to revolutionize life in the late nineteenth and early twentieth centuries. It is an essential component of automobiles, appliances, bridges, buildings, and even road construction. And while steel has been around for centuries, the number of workers needed to manufacture it has steadily dwindled. As recently as 1980, almost 500,000 people in the United States were employed making steel. That number fell to 225,000 in 2000 and declined again to about 150,000 in 2010. Where did all the jobs go? Advanced engineering made it possible for firms to replace workers with automated equipment. As a result, steel production has become much safer and more efficient. The trade-off—jobs in exchange for safety and efficiency—is reflected in the employment numbers for the industry.

From this, we can begin to understand why there is unemployment even in a healthy economy. For instance, in 2006—a typical year—real GDP in the United States grew by 2.7%, and 2 million new jobs were created. Yet there were approximately 5 million job separations, meaning people who either quit or were laid off, every month. In a dynamic economy, job turnover is normal.

## An Evolving Economy

In the long run, the evolving economy has led to drastic changes in the type of work Americans do. Figure 7.2 shows how jobs in the United States have evolved over the past two centuries. Two hundred years ago, over 90% of Americans worked in agriculture, either as farmers or as farm laborers. A century later, in 1900, only about half of U.S. workers were employed in farming. The rest were split between manufacturing (industry) jobs and service-related jobs. In 1900, a manufacturing job may have been in railroad or steel production, while a service job may have included a profession such as teaching or accounting. Today, five out of six American workers are employed in service-related jobs. Since 1979, manufacturing employment in the United States has fallen from almost 20 million jobs to just 11.5 million. Over the same period, employment in service industries has risen from 65 million to about 112 million. While we still need teachers and accountants, there are a multitude of new service jobs in fields such as engineering, finance, transportation, health, and government.

The trends presented in Figure 7.2 illustrate creative destruction: the structure of the economy evolves, which leads to different types of jobs. This long view presents the most positive angle on this process. After all, most of us would prefer working at modern jobs rather than toiling with simple farm tools in a field all day. But along the way, as jobs shift, some temporary structural unemployment inevitably occurs.

While structural unemployment can't be eliminated, it can be reduced in a number of ways. Workers must often retrain, relocate, or change their expectations in some way before they can work elsewhere. Lumberjacks may need to become computer repair specialists, or autoworkers may need to relocate from Michigan to Kentucky. Government can also enact policies to alleviate the pain of structural unemployment, such as by establishing job training programs and relocation subsidies.

## FIGURE 7.2

**The Evolution of Jobs in the United States**

Over the past two centuries, jobs in the United States have evolved from being primarily agricultural to industrial (manufacturing) and then to service.

*Source:* Federal Reserve Bank of Dallas.

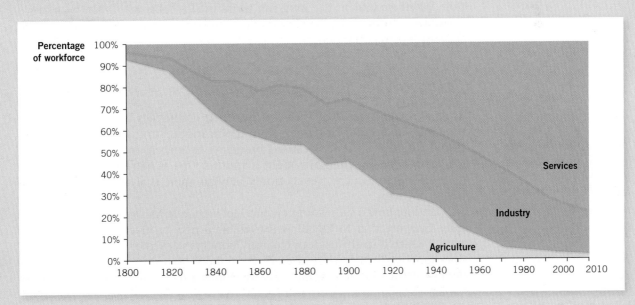

## ECONOMICS IN THE REAL WORLD

### Americans Don't Appear to Want Farm Work

In September 2010, Garance Burke of the Associated Press wrote an article about the frustration of U.S. farmers trying to find Americans to harvest fruit and vegetables. Even though the unemployment rate at the time was very high, Americans did not apply for available farm jobs. Burke notes that the few Americans who do take such jobs usually don't stay in the fields for long. The AP analysis showed that from January to June 2010, California farmers advertised 1,160 farm-worker jobs available to U.S. citizens and legal residents; only 36 were hired. One farmer named Steve Fortin noted problems with American workers: "A few years ago when domestic workers were referred here, we saw absentee problems, and we had people asking for time off after they had just started. Some were actually planting the plants upside down."

Why don't Americans want a career picking grapes?

Comedian Stephen Colbert partnered with the United Farm Workers (UFW) union in a "Take Our Jobs" campaign, aimed at getting farm jobs filled with American workers. Colbert even spent a day picking beans in a field, concluding that farm work is "really, really hard."

Ironically, during the 2007–2009 recession many migrant farm jobs were available for unemployed Americans, but they refused to apply for them. This lack of interest contrasts with events during the Great Depression more than 80 years earlier, when displaced farmers from the Great Plains states flooded California looking for work. So when some people today claim that immigrants are taking jobs away from American citizens, we can say that in the heart of the nation's biggest farming state this is certainly not true. In addition, when we look at the long-run trend in U.S. jobs, which shows a movement away from agricultural work and into service-sector jobs, we probably shouldn't be too alarmed. ✳

## Frictional Unemployment

**Frictional unemployment** is unemployment caused by delays in matching available jobs and workers.

Even when jobs are available and qualified employees live nearby, it takes time for workers and employers to find one another and agree to terms. **Frictional unemployment** is caused by delays in matching available jobs and workers. Frictional unemployment is another type of natural unemployment: no matter how healthy the economy may be, there is always some frictional unemployment.

Consider how a successful new product launch at McDonald's affects Burger King. Suppose that McDonald's introduces a new product called the "Quadstack," which is really just four Quarter Pounders stacked on top of one another. Also suppose that customers can't get enough of the new burger, and that because of the spike in new business, McDonald's needs to hire more employees.

At the same time, Burger King loses customers to McDonald's and decides to lay off some of its workers. Of course, the laid-off Burger King workers will take some time searching for new jobs. And McDonald's will take time deciding how many new workers it needs and which applicants to hire. Because some workers are unemployed during this transition, frictional unemployment results.

Frictional unemployment occurs even in the healthiest economy. Because we live in a world of imperfect information, there are incentives for employees to keep searching for the perfect job or for employers to search longer for the best employees. For example, as you approach graduation from college, you will probably take some time to search for a job and to determine which offer to accept; you won't be interested in just any job. Similarly, employers rarely hire the first applicant they see, though it may be costly to leave a position vacant. Even if there is a perfect job available for every worker, it will still take time to match workers and jobs. These time lags create friction in the labor market, and the result is temporary, frictional unemployment.

Even though frictional unemployment is natural, its level can rise or fall over time. Let's look at two causes of changes in frictional unemployment levels: information availability and government policies.

## Information Availability

Imagine looking for a job in the world without the Internet. You'd read a lot of newspaper ads, make dozens of phone calls, and probably make several in-person visits to firms where you think you might like to work. Yet after all that, you'd still have a great deal of uncertainty about the complete set of your job prospects.

Searching for a job has never been easier.

Today, most job searches are conducted online. For example, let's say you graduate with a degree in accounting and pass the CPA exam. You decide to search for a job online at Indeed.com. Even in 2012, with high overall unemployment, a nationwide search yields over 31,000 potential matches. Even narrowing this search to, say, the state of Virginia nets 1,200 potential jobs. The point is that the vast pool of information available through the Internet enables workers and companies to find one another more quickly and to make better matches with substantially lower costs. The result is lower frictional unemployment.

## Government Policies

Any factors that lengthen the job-search process increase frictional unemployment. These factors include government policies such as unemployment compensation and government regulations related to the hiring and firing of employees.

**Unemployment insurance,** also known as federal jobless benefits, is a government program that reduces the hardship of joblessness by guaranteeing that unemployed workers receive a percentage of their former income while they are unemployed. Governments provide unemployment insurance to workers for many reasons. The benefit cushions the economic consequences of being laid off, and it provides workers time to search for new employment. In addition, unemployment insurance can help contain macroeconomic problems before they spread to other industries. Consider what happens if the auto industry is

**Unemployment insurance** is a government program that reduces the hardship of joblessness by guaranteeing that unemployed workers receive a percentage of their former income while unemployed.

struggling and workers are laid off: the unemployed autoworkers will not be able to pay for goods and services that they previously purchased, and the reduction in their overall spending will hurt other industries. For example, if unemployed workers can't pay their mortgages, lenders will suffer and the downturn will spread to the financial industry. Viewed in this way, unemployment insurance serves to reduce the severity of the overall economic contraction.

## Incentives

Incentives

However, unemployment insurance also creates unintended consequences. For one thing, receiving the cushion of unemployment benefits makes some people feel less inclined to search for and take a job. These workers spend more time unemployed when they have insurance; without unemployment insurance, they are much more motivated to seek immediate employment. For example, in late 2007 the U.S. economy entered into the Great Recession, which ended in mid-2009. But several years after GDP growth resumed and the recession was declared over, the level of unemployment has remained high. Why? One reason might be the frictional unemployment that occurred because of special policies put in place during the recession. In November 2009, the U.S. government extended unemployment insurance to 99 weeks—that is, nearly 2 years, the highest level in history. While it certainly seems appropriate to help the jobless during recessions, this policy likely created an incentive to search longer for a new job, which, in turn, contributed to frictional unemployment.

Government regulations on hiring and firing also contribute to frictional unemployment. Regulations on hiring include restrictions on who can and must be interviewed, paperwork that employers must complete for new hires, and additional tax documents that must be filed for employees. Regulations on firing include mandatory severance pay, written justification, and government fines. And while these labor market regulations may be instituted to help workers by giving them greater job security, they have unintended consequences. When it is difficult to hire employees, firms take longer to do so, which increases frictional unemployment. When it is difficult to fire employees, firms take greater care in hiring them. Again, the longer search time increases frictional unemployment.

The United States has relatively few labor market regulations. In contrast, Germany and France have had especially stringent ones. For instance, if a French employer wishes to fire a worker who has been employed for two years or more, the employer must give three months' notice, pay a fine to the government, and offer the worker up to three years of severance pay. Figure 7.3 provides evidence of the unintended consequences of government labor regulations from 2000 to 2011 in three countries: France, Germany, and the United States. First, consider the significantly higher unemployment rates of France and Germany, compared to the United States, over most of the period shown. Much of this can be attributed to frictional unemployment as the result of labor market regulations. In 2005, Germany enacted labor market reforms which helped to bring their unemployment rate down. Toward the end of the decade, the unemployment rate in the United States rose dramatically. However, this was not a result of frictional unemployment; in the next section, we turn to the cause for that period of significant U.S. unemployment.

FIGURE 7.3

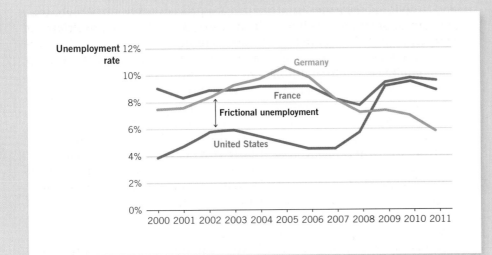

**Frictional Unemployment in France and Germany**

From 2000 to 2008, unemployment rates in France and Germany were much higher than those experienced in the United States. This was largely the result of labor market regulations. In 2005, reforms in Germany helped lead to lower rates.

*Source:* International Monetary Fund.

## ECONOMICS IN THE REAL WORLD

### Employment, Italian Style

The intention of labor market restrictions may be to help workers, but too often workers themselves bear the costs, as fewer jobs are created. Consider the labor market regulations in Italy, as reported in the *Wall Street Journal.** The key point of the article relates to the inability to draw the Italian economy out of stagnation in 2012. The authors point to hiring regulations as one significant problem impeding employment:

> Imagine you're an ambitious Italian entrepreneur, trying to make a go of a new business. You know you will have to pay at least two-thirds of your employees' social security costs. You also know you're going to run into problems once you hire your 16th employee, since that will trigger provisions making it either impossible or very expensive to dismiss a staffer.
>
> But there's so much more. Once you hire employee 11, you must submit an annual self-assessment to the national authorities outlining every possible health and safety hazard to which your employees might be subject. These include stress that is work-related or caused by

Italian firms like Fiat would hire many more employees if hiring regulations weren't so stringent.

* "Employment, Italian Style," *Wall Street Journal,* June 25, 2012.

age, gender and racial differences. You must also note all precautionary and individual measures to prevent risks, procedures to carry them out, the names of employees in charge of safety, as well as the physician whose presence is required for the assessment.

Now say you decide to scale up. Beware again: Once you hire your 16th employee, national unions can set up shop. As your company grows, so does the number of required employee representatives, each of whom is entitled to eight hours of paid leave monthly to fulfill union or works-council duties. Management must consult these worker reps on everything from gender equality to the introduction of new technology.

Hire No. 16 also means that your next recruit must qualify as disabled. By the time your firm hires its 51st worker, 7% of the payroll must be handicapped in some way, or else your company owes fees in-kind. During hard times, your company may apply for exemptions from these quotas—though as with everything in Italy, it's a toss-up whether it's worth it after the necessary paperwork.

Once you hire your 101st employee, you must submit a report every two years on the gender dynamics within the company. This must include a tabulation of the men and women employed in each production unit, their functions and level within the company, details of compensation and benefits, and dates and reasons for recruitments, promotions and transfers, as well as the estimated revenue impact.

From one view, regulations like these can be seen as helpful to employees. After all, we all want greater job benefits and protections. But such highly complex regulations clearly reduce an employer's incentives for hiring. The result is greater frictional unemployment. ✳

## Cyclical Unemployment

**Cyclical unemployment** is unemployment caused by economic downturns.

The third type of unemployment, **cyclical unemployment**, is caused by recessions, or economic downturns. This type of unemployment generates the greatest concern among economists and policymakers. It is the most serious type of unemployment because it means that jobs are not available for many people who want to work. And while both structural and frictional unemployment are consistent with a growing, evolving economy, the root cause of cyclical unemployment is an unhealthy economy. Unlike structural unemployment and frictional unemployment, cyclical unemployment is not considered a natural type of unemployment.

Although all three types of unemployment are temporary and disappear when workers are matched with jobs, the duration of cyclical unemployment is open-ended. No one knows how long a general macroeconomic downturn might last. Fortunately, recent recessions in the United States have been fairly short. The Great Recession of 2007–2009, for example, lasted for 19 months. This led to more cyclical unemployment than at any time in the previous 30 years.

During the Great Depression, almost all unemployment was cyclical.

# The Natural Rate of Unemployment

We have seen that there are three types of unemployment: structural, frictional, and cyclical. Figure 7.4 illustrates the relationship among these types of unemployment and both recessionary and healthy macroeconomic conditions. Notice that structural and frictional unemployment are always present. However, during healthy economic periods, cyclical unemployment falls toward zero.

This chapter began with the misconception that we should aim for zero unemployment. However, we have seen that some unemployment remains even during periods of economic expansion. Thus, zero unemployment is not attainable. Further, if policymakers consistently strive for zero unemployment, they may take actions that are harmful to the economy. For example, in the 1970s economic policymakers tried to push unemployment down past natural levels by putting more and more money into the economy. This strategy led to other complications like *inflation*, but it failed to reduce unemployment.

When we acknowledge a certain level of natural unemployment, we must also recognize a *natural rate of unemployment*. The **natural rate of unemployment (u\*)** is the typical rate of unemployment that occurs when the economy is growing normally. Maintaining this natural rate is a more appropriate goal for policymakers. As we have said, zero unemployment is not possible—there is always some amount. Economists never know the exact numerical value of the natural rate, in part because it changes over time. Currently, most economists feel that the natural rate of unemployment in the United States is near 5%.

When the unemployment rate is equal to its natural rate—that is, when no cyclical unemployment exists—the output level produced in the economy

The **natural rate of unemployment (u\*)** is the typical rate of unemployment that occurs when the economy is growing normally.

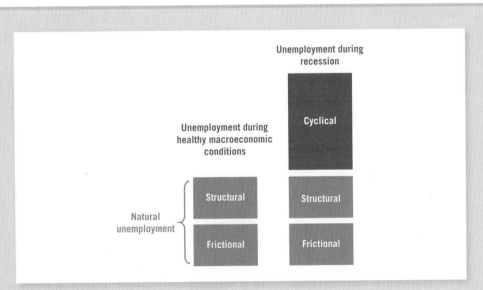

**FIGURE 7.4**

**Three Types of Unemployment**

During healthy macroeconomic conditions, both structural and frictional unemployment are present. During recessions, cyclical unemployment also appears.

**Full employment output (Y\*)** is the output level produced in an economy when the unemployment rate is equal to its natural rate.

is called **full employment output (Y\*)**. Recall from Chapter 6 that we measure economic output with real GDP, and our shorthand notation is this: real GDP = Y. An unemployment rate that is above the natural rate indicates cyclical unemployment, and at that point we say that the economy is producing at less than full employment output levels (Y < Y\*).

Sometimes, the actual unemployment rate is less than the natural rate (u < u\*). This can happen temporarily when the economy is expanding beyond its long-run capabilities. What conditions might bring this about? Demand for output might be so high that firms keep their factories open for an extra shift and pay their workers overtime. When output is at greater-than-full-employment output (Y > Y\*) and the unemployment rate is less than the natural rate (u < u\*), resources are being employed at levels that are not sustainable in the long run. To visualize this situation, consider your own productivity as deadlines approach. Perhaps you have several exams in one week, so you decide to set aside most other activities and study for 15 hours a day. Studying this much may yield good results, and you may be able to do it for a little while, but most of us cannot sustain such an effort over a long period.

Economists also refer to full employment output (Y\*) as *potential output* or *potential GDP*. This means that unless additional changes are made, the economy cannot sustain an output greater than Y\* in the long run. Table 7.1 summarizes the three possible macroeconomic conditions.

## What Can We Learn from the Employment Data?

Who exactly counts as "unemployed"? For example, many college students don't have jobs, but that doesn't mean they are officially unemployed. Before examining historical unemployment rates in detail, we need to understand how unemployment is measured in the official employment statistics. In this section, we will also look at some challenges of measuring unemployment.

**TABLE 7.1**

**The Natural Rate of Unemployment and Full Employment Output**

|  | Healthy economy | Recession | Exceptional expansion |
|---|---|---|---|
| Where is the unemployment rate (u) relative to the natural rate of unemployment (u\*)? | u = u\* | u > u\* | u < u\* |
| Where is economic output (Y) relative to full employment output (Y\*)? | Y = Y\* | Y < Y\* | Y > Y\* |
| What is the level of cyclical unemployment? | Cyclical unemployment is zero. | Cyclical unemployment is positive. | Cyclical unemployment is negative. |

## PRACTICE WHAT YOU KNOW

### Three Types of Unemployment: Which Type Is It?

Question: In each of the following situations, is the unemployment that occurs a result of cyclical, frictional, or structural changes? Explain your responses.

How long will you search for work?

**a.** Workers in a high-end restaurant are laid off when the establishment experiences a decline in demand during a recession.

**b.** A group of automobile workers lose their jobs as a result of a permanent reduction in the demand for automobiles.

**c.** A new college graduate takes three months to find his first job.

Answers:

**a.** *Cyclical changes.* Short-run fluctuations in the demand for workers are often the result of the ebb and flow of the business cycle. When the economy picks up, the laid-off workers can expect to be rehired.

**b.** *Structural changes.* Since the changes described here are long-run in nature, these workers cannot expect their old jobs to return. Therefore, they must engage in retraining in order to re-enter the labor force. Since they will be unable to find work until the retraining process is complete, this represents a fundamental shift in the demand for labor.

**c.** *Frictional changes.* The recent college graduate has skills that the economy values, but finding an employer still takes time. This short-run job search process is a perfectly natural part of finding a job.

## The Unemployment Rate

Earlier in this chapter, we defined the unemployment rate (u) as the percentage of the labor force that is unemployed. We measure this as follows:

$$\text{unemployment rate} = u = \frac{\text{number unemployed}}{\text{labor force}} \times 100$$

(Equation 7.1)

Let's look at this definition more closely. To be officially unemployed, a person has to be in the *labor force*. A member of the **labor force** is defined as someone who is already employed or actively seeking work. If a jobless person has not sought a job in four weeks, that person is not counted in the unemployment statistics. Individuals not included in the official definition

The **labor force** includes people who are already employed or actively seeking work.

include retirees, stay-at-home parents, people who are in jail, military personnel, children under age 16, and many full-time students.

Figure 7.5 provides recent data for the different groups. Starting with the relevant U.S. population (244,663,000), we find that approximately two-thirds of it is counted in the labor force (155,654,000). Of this, in January 2013, fully 12,332,000 were unemployed. Plugging these numbers in to equation 7.1 yields:

$$u = \frac{12{,}332{,}000}{155{,}654{,}000} = 7.9\%$$

This is a relatively high unemployment rate.

## Historical Unemployment Rates

We now turn to historical data. One of our goals is to give you a good sense of normal conditions. It's also helpful to examine periods when particularly high unemployment rates prevailed. In Chapter 13, we will discuss possible reasons for these difficult periods. Figure 7.6 shows the U.S. unemployment rate from 1960 to 2012, with the blue-shaded vertical bars representing periods of recession.

The average unemployment rate in the United States since 1960 has been about 6%. On average, there is a small amount of cyclical unemployment,

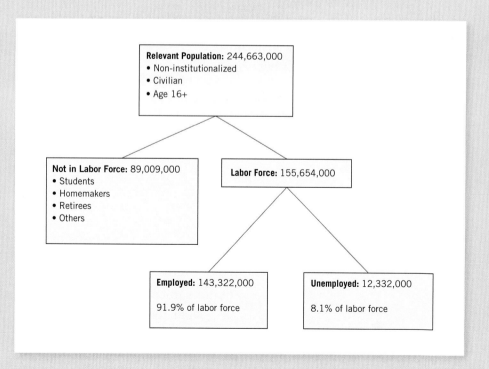

so this number is above the natural rate. But 6% is a good reference point to use when comparing unemployment rates across time and across nations. Rates above 6% are high by historical U.S. standards; rates under 6% are low.

Notice how the U.S. unemployment rate consistently spikes during recessions. This pattern vividly illustrates cyclical unemployment. Also note how long it takes for unemployment to return to the natural level of about 5% after a recession ends. As you can see, some unemployment always remains, no matter how significant or prolonged the economic expansion. This occurs because structural and frictional unemployment are always positive. For example, in early 2000 real GDP for the United States was expanding at a very significant 6.4% and the unemployment rate (as Figure 7.6 shows) was 3.8%. That's the lowest U.S. unemployment rate since 1970—but still above zero.

## Shortcomings of the Unemployment Rate

The unemployment rate, released monthly, is a timely and consistent indicator of the health of the macroeconomy. However, it has two shortcomings as an economic indicator. Let's look at each in turn.

**FIGURE 7.6**

**U.S. Unemployment Rate and Recessions, 1960–2012**

The U.S. unemployment rate consistently spikes during recessions, which are indicated here by the blue-shaded bars. During recessions, cyclical unemployment rises. During non-recessionary periods, the unemployment rate drops toward the natural rate of approximately 5%, and only structural and frictional unemployment remain.

*Source:* U.S. Bureau of Labor Statistics.

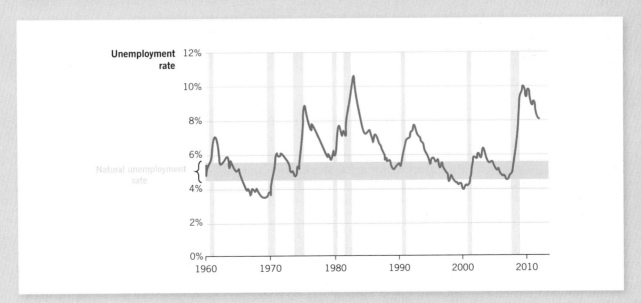

# Structural Unemployment

## *The Office*

In the TV show *The Office*, Angela, Kevin, and Oscar are accountants at the Scranton branch office of Dunder-Mifflin, a paper company. In one episode from 2007, a representative from the corporate office (which oversees all branches) unveils a new accounting system that is being installed. Ryan, from corporate, explains to Angela, Kevin, and Oscar that the new system automates most of the billing process, so that when a customer places an order it gets emailed to the warehouse and a copy goes directly to the customer's inbox.

Angela then asks, "How do we bill them?" and Ryan responds, "You don't. The invoicing, account reconciliation, and all the follow-up claims just go right to your BlackBerry." At this point, Oscar says, "So what do the accountants do?" Ryan responds, "Well, unless there is a real problem client, nothing."

Angela and Oscar immediately understand that their jobs are becoming obsolete. But Kevin still doesn't understand. So after Ryan has left the room, he crows, "This is the greatest thing that has ever happened to us!" Angela responds, "No, it's not." Kevin still doesn't get it, jumping in with, "Are you kidding me?" Oscar then delivers the bad news: "It

Is technical progress always good news?

was already a stretch that they needed three of us. Now they don't even need one."

In this story, you might think that technology is putting the accountants out of work. This is true in a short-run sense because less labor is needed to complete the billing process. However, the structural unemployment that is about to occur is a necessary by-product of a dynamic and growing economy. The workers who are no longer needed in accounting will become available to perform other jobs in the economy where human capital is needed. However, they may need retraining first.

---

**Discouraged workers** are those who are not working, have looked for a job in the past 12 months and are willing to work, but have not sought employment in the past 4 weeks.

**Underemployed workers** are those who have part-time jobs but who would prefer to work full-time.

The first shortcoming of the unemployment rate is related to exclusions. People who are unemployed for a long time may just stop looking for work—not because they don't want a job, but because they get discouraged. When they stop looking for work, they fall out of the labor force and no longer count as unemployed; in other words, they are excluded from the statistics. **Discouraged workers** are defined as those who are not working, have looked for a job in the past 12 months and are willing to work, but have not sought employment in the past 4 weeks.

Another group not properly accounted for are **underemployed workers**, defined as workers who have part-time jobs but who would like to have full-time jobs. These workers are not counted as unemployed. In fact, the official unemployment rate includes only workers who have no job and who are actively seeking work. This definition excludes both discouraged and

## FIGURE 7.7

**A Broader Measure of U.S. Labor Market Problems, 1994–2012**

The orange line includes workers who are officially unemployed, discouraged workers who have given up the job search, and workers who are underemployed, or working part-time when they would rather work full-time. The gap between this broader measure and the official unemployment rate, shown by the blue line, grows when the economy enters a recession. The most recent gap is particularly evident beginning in 2008.

*Source:* U.S.Bureau of Labor Statistics.

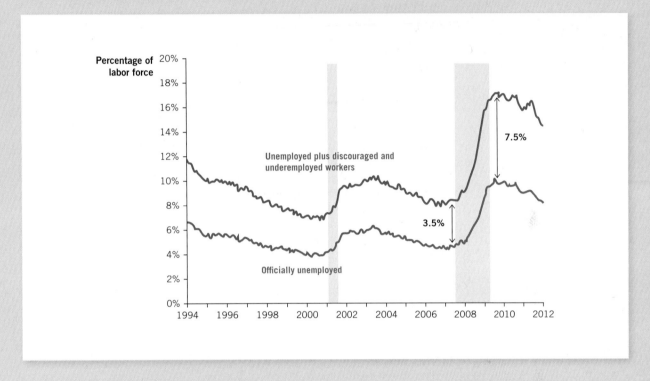

underemployed workers, groups that increase during economic downturns. Figure 7.7 shows the official U.S. unemployment rate for the period 1994–2012 versus an alternative measure that includes discouraged and underemployed workers. Not only does the alternative measure show a much higher rate than the unemployment rate, but the difference expands significantly during and after recessions (the blue-shaded regions).

The second shortcoming of the official measurement of unemployment is that it does not answer another important set of questions about who is unemployed or how long they have been out of work. Are people unemployed for short spells, or is the duration of their joblessness long-term? If most unemployment is short-term, we might not be as concerned with a higher unemployment rate, since it indicates that the unemployment is a temporary situation rather than a long-term problem for workers. To help fill in this part of the unemployment picture, the Bureau of Labor Statistics keeps

| TABLE 7.2 |
| --- |

**Duration of Unemployment in the United States, 2007 and 2011**

| | Percentage of total unemployed | |
| --- | --- | --- |
| Duration | 2007 | 2011 |
| Short-term | 67.4% | 41.3% |
| Less than 5 weeks | 35.9 | 19.5 |
| 5 to 14 weeks | 31.5 | 21.8 |
| Long-term | 32.6 | 58.7 |
| 15 to 26 weeks | 15.0 | 15.0 |
| 27 weeks and over | 17.6 | 43.7 |

*Source:* U.S. Bureau of Labor Statistics.

an alternative measure of unemployment that tracks the length of time workers have been unemployed.

Table 7.2 shows the duration of unemployment in the United States in 2007 and 2011. The year 2007 came at the end of a long expansionary period in the U.S. economy. At that time, more than two-thirds of total unemployment was short-term (14 weeks or less), and just 17.6% of those unemployed were out of work for longer than 27 weeks. In contrast, consider 2011, after the U.S. economy experienced a significant recession. There we see a big increase in the percentage of those unemployed for the very long term—27 weeks or more—which was more than 43% of total unemployment in 2011.

## Other Labor Market Indicators

Macroeconomists use several other indicators to get a more complete picture of the labor market. These include the labor force participation rate and statistics on gender and race.

### Labor Force Participation

The size of the labor force is itself an important macroeconomic statistic. To see why, consider two hypothetical island economies that differ only in the size of their labor forces. These two islands, called "2K" and "2K12," each have a population of one million people and are identical in every way except in the size of their labor forces. On the first island, 2K, the labor force is 670,000. On the second island, 2K12, the labor force is just 630,000 workers. Island 2K has 40,000 more workers to produce goods and services for a population that is exactly the same size as that of island 2K12. This is why economists watch the *labor force participation rate*. The **labor force participation rate** is the portion of the population that is in the labor force:

The **labor force participation rate** is the percentage of the population that is in the labor force.

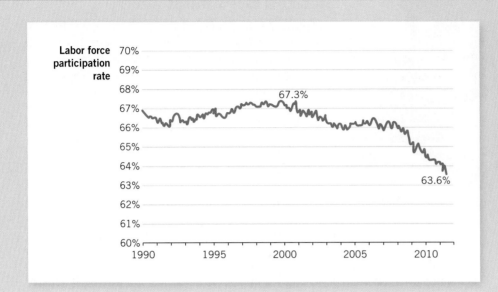

**FIGURE 7.8**

**U.S. Labor Force Participation Rate, 1990–2012**

The labor force participation rate in the United States peaked at 67.3% in 2000, but it has subsequently fallen below 64%.

*Source:* U.S. Bureau of Labor Statistics.

labor force participation rate = (labor force ÷ population) × 100

On 2K, the labor force participation rate is 67%; but on 2K12, the labor force participation rate is just 63%.

By now, you may have guessed that these are the labor force participation rates for the U.S. economy in the years 2000 and 2012. Figure 7.8 shows the evolution of the labor force participation rate in the United States from 1990 to 2012. You can see that it peaks at 67.3% in 2000 but then falls to 63.6% in 2012. All else being equal, this means that in 2012 there were fewer people working relative to the overall population in the United States than in any of the previous years shown in the graph, including the year 2000.

The changing demographics of the U.S. population is likely to reduce the labor force participation rate even further over the coming decades. The term "baby boom" refers to the period after the end of World War II when U.S. birth rates temporarily rose dramatically. The U.S. Census Bureau pegs this period at 1946–1964. So there is now a bubble in the U.S. population known as the "baby boomers." (This group most likely includes your parents.) But now, as the oldest baby boomers begin to retire, the labor force participation rate will fall. All else being equal, fewer workers will produce less GDP. And at the same time, federal expenses allocated toward retirees—for example, Social Security and Medicare—will rise. As you can see in Figure 7.8, these demographic changes are coming at a time when the labor force participation rate in the United States is declining.

The baby boom is a topic that resurfaces often in macroeconomics. In Chapter 9, we'll consider the effects of these demographic changes on interest rates and the market for savings; in Chapter 15, we'll cover the effects on the federal budget deficit.

Compared to two generations ago, men are more likely to stay at home today.

## Gender and Race Statistics

As Figure 7.9 indicates, the composition of the U.S. labor force today is markedly different from that of two generations ago. Not only are more women working (from 32% in 1948 to almost 60% today), but male labor force participation has fallen dramatically (from over 87% to just 70%). Men still remain more likely to participate in the labor force than women, but the participation gap has significantly narrowed. These changes are a function of shifting social attitudes.

How do we explain the fact that fewer males are working? There are a number of reasons for the decline. Men are living longer, acquiring more education, and spending more time helping to raise families. Since men who are retired, in school, or staying at home to care for children are not counted as part of the labor force, these shifts have lowered the labor force participation rate for males.

Unemployment rates also vary widely across ages and races. Table 7.3 breaks down these statistics by age, race, and gender. Looking first at unemployment rates, in April 2012 the overall unemployment rate was 8.1%. But this ranges from a low of 6.8% for both white males and females (over 20 years old) to a high of 39.6% for black teenage males. Notice also that labor force participation rates are very low among teenagers, with white teenagers at about 37% but black teenagers at just 25%.

## FIGURE 7.9

**Trends in U.S. Labor Force Participation, 1948–2012**

Over the past 65 years, the composition of the U.S. labor force has shifted drastically. While more women have entered the labor force, the percentage of men in the labor force has dropped from almost 90% to just 70%.

*Source:* U.S. Bureau of Labor Statistics.

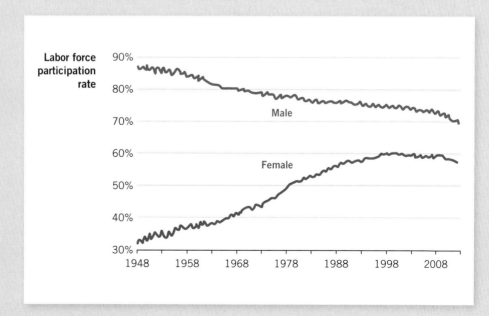

## TABLE 7.3

**U.S. Unemployment and Labor Force Participation Rates by Gender and Race, April 2012**

| Group | Unemployment rate | Labor force participation rate |
|---|---|---|
| Overall | 8.1% | 63.7% |
| Adults (age 20+) | | |
| Black males | 13.6 | 67.3 |
| Black females | 10.8 | 62.8 |
| White males | 6.8 | 73.5 |
| White females | 6.8 | 58.8 |
| Teenagers (age 16–19) | | |
| Black males | 39.6 | 25.7 |
| Black females | 36.8 | 24.5 |
| White males | 25.3 | 36.6 |
| White females | 20.3 | 36.7 |

*Source:* U.S. Bureau of Labor Statistics.

# Case Study: Unemployment in the Great Recession

> By now, it's clear to everyone that we have inherited an economic crisis as deep and dire as any since the days of the Great Depression. Millions of jobs that Americans relied on just a year ago are gone; millions more of the nest eggs families worked so hard to build have vanished. People everywhere are worried about what tomorrow will bring.
> —President Obama, February 5, 2009

The recession of 2007–2009 has been dubbed the Great Recession. The implication, of course, is that the depth of the contraction can only be compared to that of the Great Depression that spanned the 1930s. As a college student, the Great Recession may be the only significant economic downturn you recall. Now that we've studied both real GDP growth and unemployment, it is a good time to put the recent recession into perspective.

In the quote above, dated just two weeks after President Obama took office for his first term, he declares that the recession is as bad as any since the Great Depression. But while the Great Recession was certainly a rough patch for the U.S. economy, it wasn't nearly as severe as the Great Depression, which lasted for most of the 1930s. We'll look more carefully at the Great Depression when we get to Chapter 14.

There was also a relatively mild recession in 2001 and another in 1990. But it turns out that the contraction from July 1981 to November 1982 (let's call it the "1982 recession") is similar to the Great Recession, which

# Unemployment and the Labor Force

The unemployment rate is a primary economic indicator. Many people view it as particularly important because it measures a level of hardship that is not necessarily conveyed in GDP statistics. Every 1% jump in the U.S. unemployment rate means an additional 1.5 million jobs are lost. These effects are not spread equally over society, and there can be great variation across races and other demographic categories. For an example of a demographic comparison, rates are shown here for white and black men and women.

The labor force participation rate tells a vivid story about the United States over the course of the twentieth and early twenty-first centuries. As more and more women have entered, men have also exited, so that the two rates have converged.

## Unemployment Rate by Demographic, 1972–2012

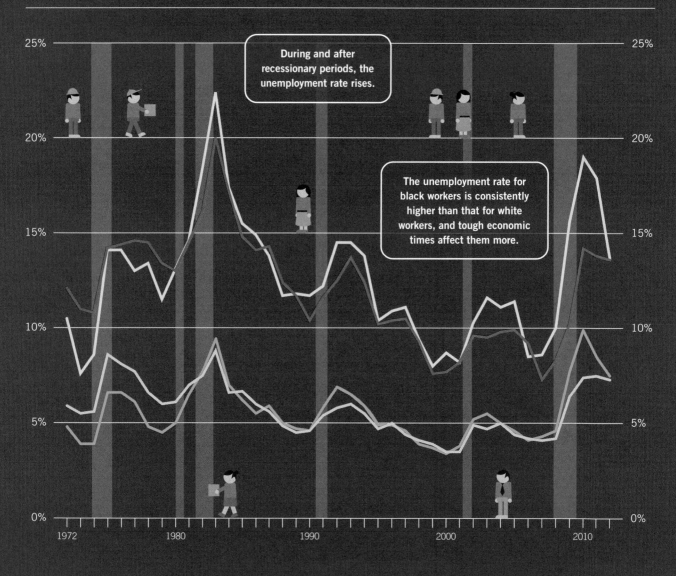

During and after recessionary periods, the unemployment rate rises.

The unemployment rate for black workers is consistently higher than that for white workers, and tough economic times affect them more.

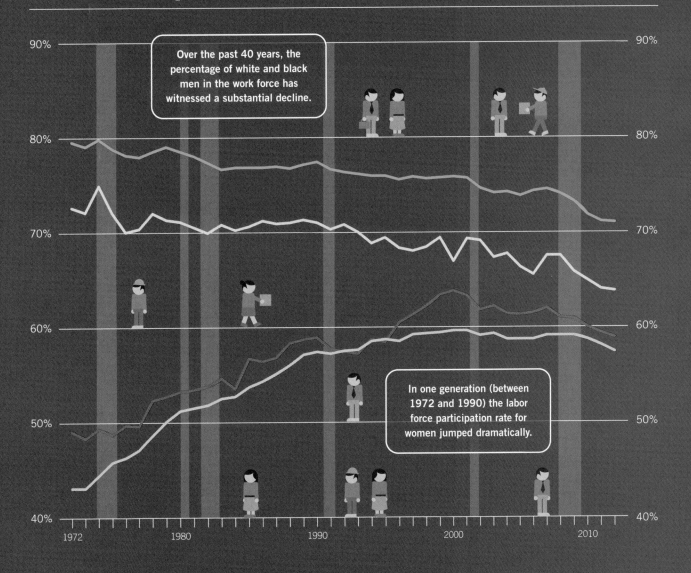

## REVIEW QUESTIONS

- In the Great Recession of the late 2000s, roughly how many percentage points did the unemployment rate of black men rise?

- How do you explain the labor force participation rate changes between men and women?

## Labor Force Participation Rate by Demographic, 1972–2012

Over the past 40 years, the percentage of white and black men in the work force has witnessed a substantial decline.

In one generation (between 1972 and 1990) the labor force participation rate for women jumped dramatically.

90%

80%

70%

60%

50%

40%

1972    1980    1990    2000    2010

## PRACTICE WHAT YOU KNOW

This German worker is employed at a textile plant.

### Unemployment and Labor Force Participation Rates: Can You Compute the Rates?

The following data is from Germany in 2010:

$$\text{Working-age population} = 70{,}856{,}000$$
$$\text{Labor force} = 41{,}189{,}000$$
$$\text{Employed} = 38{,}209{,}000$$

**Question: Using the data, how would you compute the number of unemployed workers, the unemployment rate, and the labor force participation rate for Germany in 2010?**

Answer: The unemployment rate is the total number of unemployed as a percentage of the labor force. First, determine the number of unemployed as the total labor force minus the number of employed:

$$\text{unemployed} = \text{labor force} - \text{employed} = \underline{2{,}980{,}000}$$

Use this to determine the unemployment rate, which is the number of unemployed divided by the labor force:

$$\text{unemployed} \div \text{labor force} = 2{,}980{,}000 \div 41{,}189{,}000 = \underline{7.2}$$

Finally, the labor force participation rate is the labor force as a percentage of the working-age population:

$$
\begin{aligned}
\text{labor force participation rate} &= \text{labor force} \div \text{working-age population} \\
&= 41{,}189{,}000 \div 70{,}856{,}000 \\
&= \underline{58.1\%}
\end{aligned}
$$

You might notice that this rate is significantly below 63.6%, which is the 2012 labor force participation rate for the United States.

officially lasted from December 2007 to June 2009. In this section, we compare the Great Recession to the 1982 recession. We find similarities and differences.

First, consider real GDP growth over the course of both recessions. Figure 7.10 compares quarterly GDP growth rates beginning near the official start of each recession. The two recessions were similar in duration: the 1982 recession lasted for 16 months, and the Great Recession lasted for 19 months. They were also similar in depth: the worst quarter during the 1982 recession witnessed –6.4% growth, while the 2008 recession saw

FIGURE 7.10

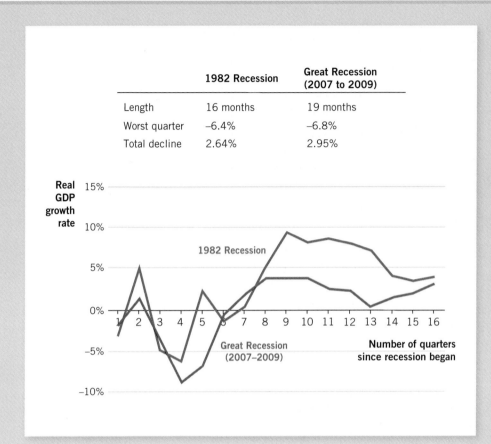

|  | 1982 Recession | Great Recession (2007 to 2009) |
|---|---|---|
| Length | 16 months | 19 months |
| Worst quarter | –6.4% | –6.8% |
| Total decline | 2.64% | 2.95% |

**Real GDP Growth Rates for the United States during Two Recessions**

The quarterly changes in real GDP for the United States were very similar over the course of the 1982 recession and the Great Recession of 2007–2009. However, real GDP rebounded to very high growth rates after the recession was over at the end of 1982. When the Great Recession ended in 2009, the growth rates were much lower and remained low for much longer.

*Source:* U.S. Bureau of Economic Analysis.

–8.9% growth in its worst quarter. If this quarterly rate had lasted for an entire year, the U.S. economy would have produced almost 9% less GDP than it did in the year before. However, the big difference between the two episodes is in the economic recovery after the recessions officially ended. In 1982 and 1983, the economy rebounded with growth rates of almost 10%. But following the Great Recession, in 2010 and 2011 real GDP growth rates were only 2% to 3%.

Now let's compare unemployment rates for the two recessions, as shown in Figure 7.11. The unemployment rate in the 1982 recession was consistently higher during the actual recession period, which lasted for 16 months. But the real difference is in the slow recovery following the Great Recession. In particular, excess unemployment, clearly above the natural rate of 5%, persisted for more than three years (36 months) after the end of the official recession period.

The unemployment data is consistent with the GDP data. Both show two recessions similar in depth and duration. But the 1982 recession was followed by a swift recovery, while the effects of the more recent recession have lingered for several years afterward. How do these compare to the

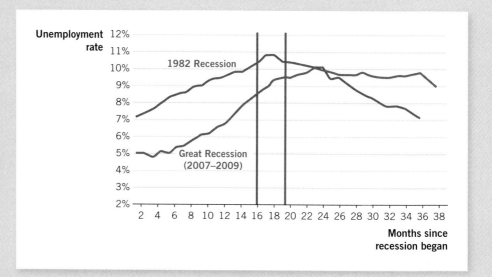

**U.S. Unemployment Rates during Two Recessions**

The 1982 recession and the Great Recession of 2007–2009 both led to unemployment rates above 10%. However, in each case the recovery, indicated by vertical lines, was very different. The most recent recession has left lingering unemployment above 8% for several years.

*Source:* U.S. Bureau of Labor Statistics.

Great Depression from the 1930s? Consider this: during the Great Depression, real GDP fell by 30% over three years, and the unemployment rate, which actually topped 25% at one point, remained higher than 15% for almost an entire decade. Thankfully, we haven't seen conditions that bad at any time since.

## Conclusion

This chapter began with the misconception that we should aim for zero unemployment. However, during the course of the chapter you have learned that even a growing economy has some unemployment. We considered why policymakers shouldn't aim for zero unemployment—because some unemployment is natural. People pay attention to the unemployment rate because it can affect them personally, but economists monitor the unemployment rate as an important macroeconomic indicator. In addition to real GDP, we use the unemployment rate to assess the position of the economy relative to the business cycle. Because employment data is released more frequently than GDP data, it offers a timelier picture of current conditions. For this reason, the first Friday of every month, when the employment data is released, tends to be a nervous day, especially during turbulent economic times.

In the next chapter, we will look more closely at a third important macroeconomic indicator—inflation.

# Finish Your Degree!

College students often fret over which major will lead to the best chance of getting a job. Your major certainly matters for getting the job you want, and it may also affect your future income. But the figure below shows just how important it is to finish your degree, no matter what your major may be.

The chart plots unemployment rates by level of educational attainment. This data is from April 2012, but you can find current data by visiting the Bureau of Labor Statistics (BLS) at www.bls.gov. Notice how the unemployment rate drops as the level of educational attainment increases. This pattern holds true across all majors. In particular, look at the big drop in the unemployment rate for those who complete a bachelor's degree or higher. The unemployment rate is about half that of those who have some college but do not complete a bachelor's degree. It turns out that the most important major is the one that holds your interest long enough to guarantee that you graduate!

Want to give yourself the best chance of getting a job?

ECONOMICS FOR LIFE

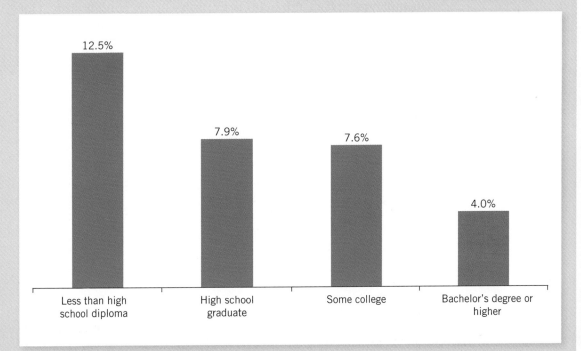

U.S. unemployment rate by educational attainment, April 2012

## ANSWERING THE BIG QUESTIONS

### What are the major reasons for unemployment?

* There are three types of unemployment: structural unemployment, frictional unemployment, and cyclical unemployment.
* Structural unemployment is caused by changes in the structure of the economy that make some jobs obsolete.
* Frictional unemployment is caused by imperfect information, which leads to increased search time in the job market.
* Cyclical unemployment is caused by recessionary conditions that eliminate jobs during a downturn in the business cycle.

### What can we learn from the employment data?

* The unemployment rate, one of the most reliable indicators of an economy's health, reflects the portion of the labor force that is not working and is unsuccessfully searching for a job.
* The labor force participation rate reflects the portion of the population that is working or searching for work.
* Unemployment data enables economists to examine social trends and identify where the labor market conditions are particularly strong or weak.
* Unemployment data also helps to evaluate current conditions in a long-run historical perspective. For example, the case study in this chapter helps us view the recent Great Recession in the context of earlier economic downturns.

# CONCEPTS YOU SHOULD KNOW

creative destruction (p. 209)
cyclical unemployment (p. 216)
discouraged workers (p. 222)
frictional unemployment
(p. 212)
full employment output
(p. 218)

labor force (p. 219)
labor force participation rate
(p. 224)
natural rate of unemployment
(p. 217)
structural unemployment
(p. 209)

underemployed workers
(p. 222)
unemployment (p. 208)
unemployment insurance
(p. 213)
unemployment rate (p. 208)

# QUESTIONS FOR REVIEW

1. Until the late 1960s, most economists assumed that less unemployment was always preferable to more unemployment. Define and explain the two types of unemployment that are consistent with a dynamic, growing economy.

2. Is there any unemployment when an economy has "full employment?" If so, what type(s)?

3. The news media almost always bemoans the current state of the U.S. economy. How does the most recent unemployment rate relate to the long-run average?

4. What type of unemployment is affected when online job search engines reduce the time necessary for job searches? Does this outcome affect the natural rate of unemployment? If so, how?

5. What groups does the Bureau of Labor Statistics count in the labor force? Explain why the official unemployment rate tends to underestimate the level of labor market problems.

6. Does the duration of unemployment matter? Explain your answer.

# STUDY PROBLEMS (✳ *solved at the end of the section*)

1. In his song "Allentown," Billy Joel sings about the demise of the steel and coal industry in Pennsylvania. Why do you think the loss of manufacturing jobs was so difficult on the workers in areas like Allentown and other parts of the Midwest where manufacturing was once the largest employer? What type of unemployment is the song about?

2. In January 2008, the U.S. unemployment rate dropped to 4.9%. Oddly, employment also fell from the prior month. How was this possible?

3. A country with a civilian population of 90,000 (all over age 16) has 70,000 employed and 10,000 unemployed persons. Of the unemployed, 5,000 are frictionally unemployed and another 3,000 are structurally unemployed.

On the basis of this data, answer the following questions:

a. What is the size of the labor force?
b. What is the unemployment rate?
c. What is the natural rate of unemployment for this country?
d. Is this economy in recession or expansion? Explain.

4. Visit www.bls.gov and search through the tables on unemployment to answer the following questions:

a. What is the current national unemployment rate for the United States?
b. What is the current unemployment rate among people most like you? (Consider your age, sex, and race.)

5. Consider a country with 300 million residents, a labor force of 150 million, and 10 million unemployed. Answer the following questions:

   a. What is the labor force participation rate?
   b. What is the unemployment rate?
   c. If 5 million of the unemployed become discouraged and stop looking for work, what is the new unemployment rate?
   d. Suppose instead that 30 million jobs are created and this attracts 20 million new people into the labor force. What would be the new rates for labor force participation and unemployment?

✳ 6. Consider the following hypothetical data from the peaceable nation of Adirolf, where there is no military, the entire population is over the age of 16, and no one is institutionalized for any reason. Then answer the questions.

| Classification | Number of people |
| --- | --- |
| Total population | 200 million |
| Employed | 141 million |
| Full-time students | 10 million |
| Homemakers | 25 million |
| Retired persons | 15 million |
| Seeking work but without a job | 9 million |

   a. What is the unemployment rate in Adirolf?
   b. What is the labor force participation rate in Adirolf?

For questions c through f: assume that 15 million Adirolfian homemakers begin seeking jobs and that 10 million find jobs.

   c. Now what is the rate of unemployment in Adirolf?
   d. How does this change affect cyclical unemployment in Adirolf?
   e. What will happen to per capita GDP?
   f. Is the economy of Adirolf better off after the homemakers enter the labor force? Explain your response.

✳ 7. In each of the following situations, determine whether or not the person would be considered unemployed.

   a. A 15-year-old offers to pet-sit, but no one hires her.
   b. A college graduate spends the summer after graduation touring Europe before starting a job search.
   c. A part-time teacher is only able to work two days a week, even though he would like a full-time job.
   d. An automobile worker becomes discouraged about the prospects for future employment and decides to quit looking for work.

## SOLVED PROBLEMS

6a. The unemployment rate in Adirolf is 6%. To calculate the unemployment rate, use:

   unemployment rate = u = (number unemployed ÷ labor force) × 100
   • The number of unemployed: 9 million
   • Labor force can be calculated in two ways:
     • Employed plus unemployed: 141 million + 9 million = 150 million
     • Total population minus those not in labor force (students, homemakers, retirees):

   200 million − (10 million + 25 million + 15 million) = 150 million

   Note: because the total population is only composed of non-institutionalized civilians over the age of 16, we can use this (200 million) as the relevant population.

   Unemployment rate = u = (number unemployed ÷ labor force) × 100 = (9 ÷ 150) × 100 = 6%

b. The labor force participation rate in Adirolf is 75%. To calculate the labor force participation rate, use:

labor force participation rate = (labor force ÷ population) × 100

- Labor force (calculated above): 150 million
- Population: 200 million

labor force participation rate = (labor force ÷ population) × 100 = (150 ÷ 200) × 100 = 75%

c. Now the rate of unemployment in Adirolf is 8.5%. To calculate the new unemployment rate, use the same equation as above. However, the figures have changed with new entrants to the labor force:
- The new number of unemployed: 9 million + 5 million = 14 million
- The new number of employed: 141 million + 10 million = 151 million
- The new labor force can be calculated in three ways:
  - Previous labor force plus new entrants: 150 million + 15 million = 165 million
  - Employed plus unemployed: 151 million + 14 million = 165 million
  - Total population minus those not in labor force (students, homemakers, retirees):

200 million − (10 million + 10 million + 15 million) = 165 million

unemployment rate = u = (number unemployed ÷ labor force) × 100 = (14 ÷ 165) × 100 = 8.5%

Note: even though the number of employed increased, because the size of the labor force increased by more, the unemployment rate has increased.

d. The change does not affect cyclical unemployment, which is generally associated with economic downturns. Instead, the entrance of new workers into the labor force represents a change in the labor force participation rate. In general, the entry of new workers to the labor force is associated with good economic times. Because most of the housewives were able to find jobs, we can conclude that the economy of Adirolf is growing.

e. With an increase in the number of employed workers, total output in the economy will increase. However, the size of the population has not changed. Thus, per capita GDP will increase as a result of the change.

f. Adirolf has a stronger economy with more working housewives. Even though the unemployment rate has increased as a result of many housewives entering the labor force, the increase in unemployment is not the result of economic downturn; rather, it is a sign of a growing economy. Adirolf has a stronger economy with higher GDP per capita and a greater labor force participation rate as a result of this change.

7a. No. The relevant population used to measure unemployment and the labor force comprises individuals 16 years of age or older. This 15-year-old is not part of the relevant population, so she is not considered unemployed.

b. No. To be counted in the unemployment statistics, an individual must have made efforts to get a job in the past four weeks. This college graduate is not actively seeking work during the summer, so he is not counted as an unemployed individual.

c. No. This part-time teacher is underemployed because he would prefer a full-time position, but under the unemployment rate measurements he is considered to be employed.

d. No. The automobile worker is a discouraged worker if he has searched for work in the past year but has stopped looking for work over four weeks ago. However, since he is not actively looking for work now, he is no longer considered to be part of the labor force.

# The Price Level and Inflation

**Inflation is no big deal.**

For the last 30 years, inflation has been under control in the United States. As a college student, you have probably never experienced

significant inflation. Sure, you may notice that many prices rise from year to year, but these are slow, steady, often predictable increases. However, as recently as the 1980s the annual inflation rate in the United States was close to 15%—about five times the average inflation rate over the last two decades. And 15% is low by international standards. So it may appear that inflation is not a significant problem. But it certainly has been in the past, and there is no guarantee that we are safe from it in the future. Moreover, looking around the world, we can see that inflation is still an important issue for many countries. In Zimbabwe, for example, the rate of inflation was so high in 2008 that prices were doubling every day! Zimbabwean dollars became worthless by the thousand, million, and even billion, before the currency was effectively abandoned in 2009. High inflation can cause the destruction of wealth across an entire economy, and equally important, unpredictable inflation can wreak havoc within an economy—as we will see in the pages ahead.

Zimbabweans show off devalued currency at a 2008 political rally. How is it possible to have 1 billion dollars and not be able to afford dinner?

# BIG QUESTIONS

＊ **How is inflation measured?**

＊ **What problems does inflation bring?**

＊ **What is the cause of inflation?**

## How Is Inflation Measured?

You might notice inflation on a routine shopping trip or especially when you see a reference to prices in an old book or movie. For example, in the 1960 movie *Psycho*, a hotel room for one night was priced at just $10. In Chapter 6, we defined inflation as the growth in the overall level of prices in an economy—so inflation occurs when prices rise throughout the economy. When overall prices rise, this affects our budget; it limits how much we can buy with our income. When overall prices fall, our income goes farther and we can buy more goods.

Imagine an annual inflation rate of 100%. At this rate, prices would double every year. How would this affect your life? Would it change what you buy? Would it change your savings plans? Would it change the salary you negotiate with your employer? Yes, it would change your life on a daily basis. Now imagine that prices double *every day*. This was the situation in Zimbabwe in 2008 when the inflation rate reached almost 80 billion percent per month! This is an example of what economists call *hyperinflation*, an extremely high rate of inflation, and it completely stymies economic activity. In Zimbabwe, for example, average citizens could barely afford necessities like bread and eggs.

Figure 8.1 shows inflation in the United States from 1960 to 2012. The long-run average over this period was 4%, a good benchmark for evaluating current inflation rates. In the 1970s and early 1980s, there were periods of very high inflation. At one point in 1980, the inflation rate was almost 15%. But since the early 1980s, inflation seems well controlled in the United States. Looking again at Figure 8.1, you might notice a brief spell of *deflation* in 2009. **Deflation** occurs when overall prices fall; it is negative inflation. Notice, too, that periods of recessions—the blue-shaded vertical bars in Figure 8.1—often coincide with falling inflation rates. While this is not always true, you can see it in both 1982 and 2009.

**Deflation**
occurs when overall prices fall.

Measuring inflation is a straightforward goal, but requires great care. First, prices don't all move together; some prices fall even when most others rise. Second, some prices affect consumers more than others: for example, a 10% increase in the cost of housing is significantly more painful than a 10% increase in the cost of hot dogs. Before we arrive at a useful measure of inflation, we have to agree on what prices to monitor and how much weight we'll give to each price. In the United States, the Bureau of Labor Statistics (BLS) measures reports and inflation data. In this section, we describe how the BLS estimates the overall price level. (Remember from Chapter 6 that the price level is an index of the average prices of goods and services throughout an economy.) The BLS's goal is to (1) determine the prices of all the goods and services that a typical consumer buys, and (2) identify how much of a typical consumer's budget is spent on these particular items.

The **consumer price index (CPI)** is a measure of the price level based on the consumption patterns of a typical consumer.

## The Consumer Price Index (CPI)

We start by looking at the most common price level used to compute inflation. The **consumer price index (CPI)** is the measure of the price level based on the consumption patterns of a typical consumer. When you read or hear about inflation in the media, the report almost certainly focuses on this measure. The CPI is essentially the price of a typical "basket" of goods purchased by a representative consumer in the United States. What's in that basket? In addition to groceries, there is clothing, transportation, housing, medical care, education, and many other goods and services. The idea is to include everything a typical consumer buys. This gives us a realistic measure of a typical consumer's cost of living.

Figure 8.2 displays how the CPI was allocated among major spending categories in March 2012. There are prices for very specific goods inside these categories. For example, "Food and beverages" includes prices for everything from potato chips to oranges (both Valencia and navel) to flour (white, all purpose, per pound). These are goods in a "basket" that typical American consumers buy.

While the CPI is the predominant measure of the general price level, it is not the only one. For example, in Chapter 6 we saw that when computing real GDP data the best choice is the GDP deflator, which includes prices from all the final

The CPI is based on prices from a typical "basket" of all consumer goods.

---

FIGURE 8.1

**Inflation in the United States, 1960–2012**

From 1960 to 2012, inflation rates in the United States averaged 4%. This number is high because of excessive inflation in the 1970s. The inflation rate peaked at over 14% in 1980. More recently, inflation rates have averaged between 2% and 3%.

*Source:* U.S. Bureau of Labor Statistics.

Inflation rate

Long-run average = 4%

goods and services that constitute GDP. Remember that GDP includes not only consumer goods but also services that consumers never actually purchase, like large farm equipment and wind turbines. The GDP deflator is too broad for our purposes here, because we are focusing on the prices of goods and services purchased by typical American consumers.

Of course, none of us is exactly typical in our spending. College students allocate significantly more than 6.4% of their spending on education, senior citizens spend a lot more than average on medical care, a fashionista spends more than average on clothing, and those with lengthy commutes spend more than average on transportation. The CPI reflects the overall rise in prices for consumers *on average*.

## Computing the CPI

Each month, the BLS conducts surveys by sending employees into stores in 38 geographic locations to gather and input price information on over 8,000 goods. The BLS estimates prices on everything from apples in Chicago, Illinois, to electricity in Scranton, Pennsylvania, to gasoline in San Diego, California. In addition to inputting price information, the BLS surveyors estimate how each good and service affects a typical consumer's budget. Once they do this, they attach a weight to the price of each good in the consumer's "basket." For example, Figure 8.2 indicates that the typical consumer spends 17% of his or her budget on transportation. Therefore, transportation prices receive 17% of the total weight in the typical consumer's basket of goods. Once the BLS has compiled the prices and budget allocation weights, it can construct the CPI.

To illustrate how this works, let's build a price index using just three goods. Imagine that when you go to the movies you notice that you are spending

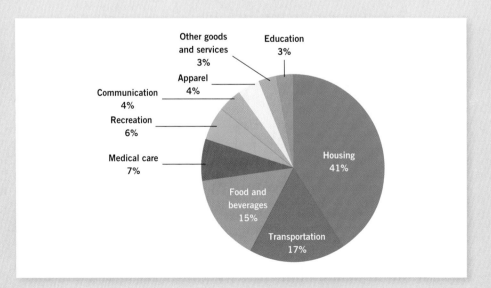

## FIGURE 8.2

**The Pieces of the Consumer Price Index, March 2012**

The weights assigned to the different categories of expenditures are based on the spending patterns of a typical American. For example, 17% of a typical American's spending is on transportation; this includes car payments and fuel, among other expenses.

*Source:* U.S. Bureau of Labor Statistics.

more for that outing than you did last year. You decide to construct a price index to see exactly how the price increases are affecting your budget. You decide to name your index the EPI (entertainment price index). For the sake of this example, assume that a typical night at the movie theater includes a movie ticket, two boxes of popcorn, and two medium Cokes. This is the basket of three goods included in your EPI.

The first four columns in Figure 8.3 show your EPI data for the first year, 2014. The second column shows the respective quantities of goods in your basket, and the third column displays the unit prices of these goods. The price of popcorn is $4 per box, the Cokes are $4 each, and the movie ticket is $8. The fourth column shows how much you pay in total for each good; this is price multiplied by quantity. For example, in 2014 the price of popcorn was $4 per box, so you paid a total of $8 for two boxes of popcorn. Adding all the goods together, we get the total price for your basket of goods in 2014, which was $24. This is how much you spent for all the goods in your EPI in 2014.

Let's now move to 2015. First, note that your consumption pattern hasn't changed; you still buy the same basket of goods. But some of the prices did change in 2015. Popcorn is now priced at $6 per box, and the movie ticket costs $10. But note that not all prices changed. The cost of a Coke remained the same.

To see how the new 2015 prices affect your spending, we compute the total cost required to consume the same goods in the same quantities. The last column shows the costs of each component in your basket. The sum of these is now $30.

| | | 2014 | | 2015 | |
| Good | Quantity | Unit price | Total cost | Unit price | Total cost |
| --- | --- | --- | --- | --- | --- |
| Popcorn | 2 | $4 | $8 | $6 | $12 |
| Coke | 2 | $4 | $8 | $4 | $8 |
| Movie ticket | 1 | $8 | $8 | $10 | $10 |
| Basket price | | | $24 | | $30 |
| Index (EPI) | | $\frac{\$24}{\$24} \times 100 = 100$ | | $\frac{\$30}{\$24} \times 100 = 125$ | |

**FIGURE 8.3**

**Calculating a Simple Price Index**

In calculating this entertainment price index (EPI), we use the same steps that the Bureau of Labor Statistics does when calculating the CPI. First, we determine the typical basket of goods. Then we calculate the total price of the basket in a base year, 2014 in this example, and set that base year at 100 (creating an index). For subsequent years, we add up the new prices for the same basket of goods and then divide by the original basket price to determine the new index number.

The final step is to create an index. You need an index because, in the real world, adding a lot of prices together yields a huge number that would be difficult to work with. So we create an index that is equal to 100 at a fixed point in time—your base year. In our example, 2014 can be your base year. To convert, we divide all years by the basket price value from the base year and multiply by 100:

(Equation 8.1)

$$\text{price index} = \frac{\text{basket price}}{\text{basket price in base year}} \times 100$$

Using this formula, you can confirm that the EPI for 2014 is 100 and that the EPI for 2015 is 125.

When the Bureau of Labor Statistics computes the CPI for the United States, it follows the same basic steps:

1. Define the basket of goods and services and their appropriate weights.
2. Determine the prices of goods across periods.
3. Convert to the index number for each period.

## ECONOMICS IN THE REAL WORLD

### Sleuthing for Prices

The government considers prom dresses to be a typical consumer item.

Tracking the prices in the CPI requires a great deal of effort and precision. In September 2007, Nancy Luna of the *Orange County Register* followed one of the 350 employees of the Bureau of Labor Statistics who is charged with finding current prices of the goods included in the CPI. The BLS employee, Frank Dubich, traveled 800 miles per month tracking prices.

The items to be priced were very specific. For example, Dubich was asked to visit a grocery store to find the price of "an 18.5-ounce can of Progresso Rich & Hearty creamy chicken soup with wild rice," which turned out to be $1.98. Dubich also had to note that this was a sale price.

In another instance, Dubich was embarrassed to be seen pricing because the item was a prom dress. He noticed several clerks staring at him as he hunted for the price tag, so he quickly recorded the price and left.

In macroeconomics, we generally see one single number that indicates how much prices have changed. But it's important to remember that there are thousands of prices tracked each month by government workers like Frank Dubich. ✳

## Measuring Inflation Rates

Once the CPI is computed, economists use it to measure inflation rates. The inflation rate (i) is calculated as the percentage change in the price level (P). Using the CPI as the price level, the inflation rate from period 1 to period 2 is:

(Equation 8.2)

$$\text{inflation rate (i)} = \frac{P_2 - P_1}{P_1} \times 100$$

Note that this is a growth rate, computed just like the growth rate of GDP in Chapter 6. In our entertainment price index example above, the CPI rose from 100 to 125 in one year. So the inflation for that year was 25%, computed as:

$$\text{inflation rate (i)} = \frac{125-100}{100} \times 100 = 25\%$$

The BLS releases CPI estimates every month. Normally, inflation rates are measured over the course of a year, showing how much the price level grows in 12 months. Figure 8.4 shows the historical relationship between the U.S. inflation rate and the CPI. Panel (a) plots the U.S. CPI from 1960 to 2012. The base period for the CPI is set for 1982–1984, so it goes through 100 in mid-1983. The CPI was just 30 in 1961 and rose to 230 by 2011. This means that the typical basket of consumer goods rose in price more than sevenfold between 1960 and 2012.

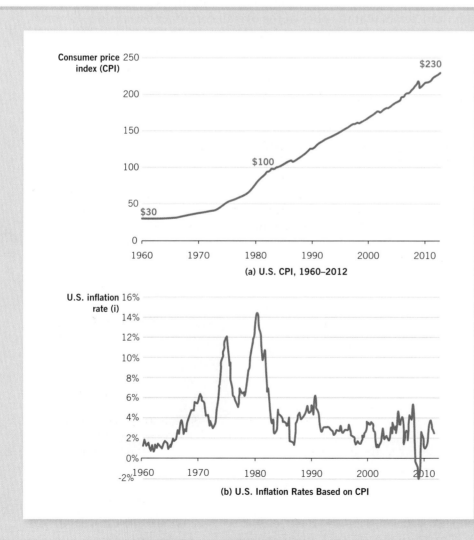

(a) U.S. CPI, 1960–2012

(b) U.S. Inflation Rates Based on CPI

## FIGURE 8.4

**The CPI and Inflation, 1960–2012**

Panel (a) shows the CPI since 1960. The index of prices for a typical consumer's basket of goods was at 30 in 1961 but rose to 230 by 2012. Panel (b) shows the U.S. inflation rate, computed as the growth rate of the CPI. A rapidly rising CPI, like we see in panel (a) during the 1970s, is reflected in the inflation rate.

*Source:* U.S. Bureau of Labor Statistics.

Panel (b) of Figure 8.4 plots inflation rates based on the CPI data in panel (a). The inflation graph reveals a number of historical observations that are important to our study of macroeconomics. For example, when you look at the graph you might wonder what was going on in the 1970s. Before and after the 1970s, inflation was relatively stable and the rate averaged less than 3%. But from 1970 to 1981, the inflation rate averaged 8%, including the year between April 1979 and March 1980 when it was over 14.5%. We'll explain the reasons for these historically high rates in Chapter 18. For now, in comparing the two graphs in Figure 8.4, notice that the CPI increased more rapidly from 1979 to 1980 than in any other period shown. Overall, the long-run average rate of inflation in the United States is about 4%.

## ECONOMICS IN THE REAL WORLD

### Prices Don't All Move Together

While it's clear that prices generally rise, not all prices go up. When the CPI rises, it indicates that the price of the overall consumer basket rises. However, some individual prices stay the same or even fall. For example, consumer electronic prices almost always fall. When flat-panel plasma TVs were introduced in the late 1990s, a 40-inch model cost more than $7,000. Fifteen years later, 50-inch flat-panel TVs are available for less than $500. This is the result of technological advancements: as time passes, it often takes fewer resources to produce the same item or something better.

Computers are another example. In 1984, Apple introduced the Macintosh computer at a price of $2,495. The CPU for the Macintosh ran at 7.83 MHz, and the 9-inch monitor was black and white. Today, you can buy an Apple iMac for less than $2,000. This new Apple computer has a quad-core processor that runs at a total of 11,200 MHz, and the monitor is 27 inches (color, of course). The new computer is better by any measure, yet it costs less than the early model. These kinds of changes in quality make it difficult to measure the CPI over time. ✳

The 1984 Macintosh price was $2,495 . . .   . . . but this 2011 Apple iMac cost just $1,999.

# Using the CPI to Equate Dollar Values over Time

Prices convey a lot of information, but prices from different periods can be quite confusing. For example, in 1924 a consumer could buy a fully constructed, 1,600-square-foot home through Sears at a price of just $1,969. But how does that price compare to today's prices? In addition to measuring inflation rates, we can use the CPI to answer these types of questions.

To compare the prices of goods over time, we convert all prices to today's prices, or "prices in today's dollars." Here is the formula:

$$\text{price in today's dollars} = \text{price in earlier time} \times \frac{\text{price level today}}{\text{price level in earlier time}}$$

(Equation 8.3)

Following this formula, we can compute the 2012 price of the 1924 Sears home. The CPI in 2012 was 230, and the CPI in 1924 was 17, so the computation is:

$$\text{price in } 2012 = \$1,969 \times \frac{230}{17} = \$26,639$$

In fact, the 1924 Sears price would be pretty low even today.

Table 8.1 takes past prices from some iconic foods and converts them into today's dollars. For example, the price of a one-pound bag of Oreo cookies was 32 cents in 1922. But, using Equation 8.3, we multiply $0.32 by the modern price level (230) and divide by the 1922 price level (17) to determine the old price in today's dollars. It turns out that, once converted, the old price is $4.33, which is much higher than today's actual price of $2.99. The price in today's dollars corrects for the overall amount of inflation since 1942, helps make sense of historical prices, and dispels the notion that everything was less expensive in the past. This observation is nominally true but not especially interesting. Adjusting for inflation provides a real comparison, which is what good economists always look for.

## TABLE 8.1

### Converting Past Prices into Modern Dollar Values

| | Product | Year | Price | Conversion | Today's dollars (2012) | Today's actual price |
|---|---|---|---|---|---|---|
| | Coca-Cola (12 oz.) | 1942 | $0.05 | **$0.05 × (230 ÷ 16)** | $0.72 | $0.63 |
| | Hershey's chocolate bar (1 oz.) | 1921 | $0.05 | **$0.05 × (230 ÷ 18)** | $0.64 | $0.69 |
| | McDonald's hamburger | 1955 | $0.15 | **$0.15 × (230 ÷ 27)** | $1.28 | $0.89 |
| | Nabisco's Oreo cookies (1 lb.) | 1922 | $0.32 | **$0.32 × (230 ÷ 17)** | $4.33 | $2.99 |

# Inflation and the Consumer Price Index

Inflation is a concern for everyone, not just economists. When inflation occurs, the purchasing power of a dollar's worth of income falls, so inflation can eat into the real purchasing power of an individual's income. If unexpected, or significantly different from what was expected, inflation can cause serious harm to an economy. The inflation rate is measured as the percentage change in the overall price level. The price level we often use to measure inflation is the Consumer Price Index (CPI), which is driven by the prices paid by a typical American consumer.

## Rate of Inflation and CPI, 1960–2012

Although inflation varied quite a bit over the last 50-plus years, the price of the typical consumer basket rose gradually and consistently.

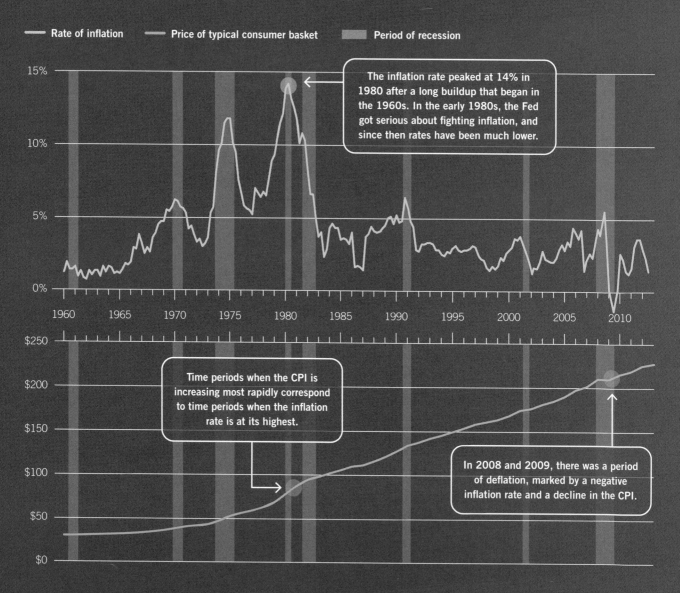

— Rate of inflation    — Price of typical consumer basket    ▮ Period of recession

The inflation rate peaked at 14% in 1980 after a long buildup that began in the 1960s. In the early 1980s, the Fed got serious about fighting inflation, and since then rates have been much lower.

Time periods when the CPI is increasing most rapidly correspond to time periods when the inflation rate is at its highest.

In 2008 and 2009, there was a period of deflation, marked by a negative inflation rate and a decline in the CPI.

# The Pieces of the CPI, December 2012

The data below shows the various categories in which U.S. citizens spend their income.

## PIECES OF THE CPI
### DECEMBER 2012

| Category | Percent |
|---|---|
| HOUSING | 41.0% |
| TRANSPORTATION | 16.8% |
| FOOD AND BEVERAGES | 15.3% |
| MEDICAL CARE | 7.2% |
| EDUCATION AND COMMUNICATION | 6.8% |
| RECREATION | 6.0% |
| APPAREL | 3.6% |
| OTHER | 3.4% |

| HOUSING | 41.0% | | MEDICAL CARE | 7.2% |
|---|---|---|---|---|
| Shelter | 31.7% | | Medical care services | 5.4% |
| Fuels and utilities | 5.3% | | Drugs and supplies | 1.7% |
| Furnishings and other | 4.0% | | | |
| | | | RECREATION | 6.0% |
| TRANSPORTATION | 16.8% | | Video and audio | 1.9% |
| Private transportation | 15.7% | | Pets and pet care | 1.1% |
| Public transportation | 1.2% | | Other | 3.0% |
| FOOD AND BEVERAGE | 15.3% | | APPAREL | 3.6% |
| Food at home | 8.6% | | Women's / girls' apparel | 1.5% |
| Food away from home | 5.7% | | Men's / boys' apparel | 0.9% |
| Alcoholic beverages | 0.9% | | Footwear and other | 1.2% |
| EDUCATION AND COMMUNICATION | 6.8% | | OTHER | 3.4% |
| Communication | 3.5% | | Personal care | 2.6% |
| Tuition and supplies | 3.3% | | Tobacco products | 0.8% |

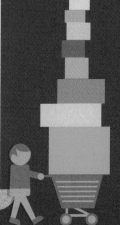

## REVIEW QUESTIONS

- When was the last time the inflation rate exceeded 5% in the United States?

- Explain why television and computer prices continue to fall but we still observe increases in the CPI.

## Which Movies Are Most Popular?

Is *Avatar* really the most successful movie of all time?

After a successful new movie comes out, the film industry totals up box office receipts and other revenue to see how well the movie has done. But since the receipt data are tied to the period in which the movie was released, they are nominal receipts, not receipts adjusted for inflation.

For example, *Avatar* is now the highest-grossing film of all time, meaning that it earned more revenue than any film from the past. *Titanic* held the top spot from 1998 to 2009, and *Star Wars* held the top spot from 1977 to 1997. Table 8.2 ranks the top seven movies of all times first by total receipts. The list of movies may not surprise you—there are several modern movies there that you've probably seen. However, you may find it odd to think of *Shrek 2* as the seventh most popular movie of all time.

The second-to-last column shows total receipts adjusted for inflation in 2012. After this adjustment, you can see that *Avatar* is no longer number 1 and in fact produced only about half the real revenue as the original *Star Wars* movie, which was released in 1977. The last column shows the rank of these movies once inflation is accounted for. Notice that *Avatar* falls to number 14 and *Shrek 2* falls to number 31. So what is the absolute top movie of all time, based on total inflation-adjusted receipts? The answer is *Gone with the Wind*, released in 1939, with inflation-adjusted receipts of over $1.6 billion. ✳

## The Accuracy of the CPI

We have seen that computing the CPI is not simple. Yet in order to understand what is happening in the macroeconomy, it is important that the CPI be accurate. For example, sometimes a rapid fall in inflation signals a recession, as it did in 1982 and 2008. Like real GDP and the unemployment rate, inflation is an indicator of national economic conditions.

But there is another reason the CPI needs to be accurate: when employers adjust wages for inflation, they generally use the CPI. For example, when the United Auto Workers (UAW) union signs a wage agreement with General Motors, the agreement specifies wages for autoworkers several years in advance. Since future inflation is unknown and the UAW wants to protect its workers from excess inflation, the agreement stipulates that wages will be tied to the CPI. Therefore, when the CPI rises, wages rise; when the CPI falls, wages fall. So if the CPI overstates inflation, the miscalculation can cost companies millions of dollars. If the CPI understates inflation, this hurts workers, since their wages will not rise as much as they should.

Wage contracts for over 200,000 UPS employees are adjusted for inflation in reference to the CPI.

How accurate is the CPI? If consumers always bought the same goods from the same suppliers, it would be extremely accurate, and economists would be able to compare the changes in price from one year to the next very easily. But this is not realistic. Consumers buy different goods from different stores at different locations, and the quality of goods changes over time. Because the typi-

## TABLE 8.2

### Top Movies of All Time, Ranked by Total U.S. Receipts

| Movie | Year | Receipts | Receipts adjusted for inflation, 2012 | Adjusted rank |
|---|---|---|---|---|
| 1. *Avatar* | 2009 | $760,508,000 | $770,262 | 14 |
| 2. *Titanic* | 1997 | $658,547,000 | $1,074,258 | 5 |
| 3. *The Dark Knight* | 2008 | $533,345,000 | $588,314 | 28 |
| 4. *Star Wars Episode I— The Phantom Menace* | 1999 | $474,544,000 | $715,277 | 16 |
| 5. *The Avengers* | 2012 | $472,240,000 | $472,240 | 58 |
| 6. *Star Wars* | 1977 | $460,998,000 | $1,410,707 | 2 |
| 7. *Shrek 2* | 2004 | $441,226,000 | $562,723 | 31 |

cal basket of consumer goods keeps changing, it is difficult to measure its price. The most common concern is that the CPI overstates true inflation. There are three reasons for this concern: the substitution of different goods and services, changes in quality, and the availability of new goods, services, and locations.

## Substitution

When the price of a good rises, consumers instinctively look to substitute less expensive alternatives. This makes CPI calculations difficult because the typical consumer basket changes. Earlier, when we calculated an entertainment price index, we assumed that you always bought the same quantities of all goods, even when the price of popcorn rose and the price of Coke remained the same. However, it is more realistic to assume that if the price of popcorn

# Equating Dollar Values through Time

## *Austin Powers: International Man of Mystery*

The Austin Powers series is a hilarious spoof of the James Bond films. In *International Man of Mystery* we are introduced to British secret agent Austin Powers, who was cryofrozen at the end of the 1960s. Thirty years later, Austin Powers is thawed to help capture his nemesis, Dr. Evil, who was cryofrozen at the same time as Austin and has now stolen a nuclear weapon to hold the world hostage.

Being frozen for 30 years causes Dr. Evil to underestimate how much he should ask for in ransom money: "Gentlemen, it's come to my attention that a breakaway Russian republic called Kreplachistan will be transferring a nuclear warhead to the United Nations in a few days. Here's the plan. We get the warhead, and we hold the world ransom . . . FOR ONE MILLION DOLLARS!"

There is an uncomfortable pause.

Dr. Evil's Number Two speaks up: "Don't you think we should ask for more than a million dollars? A million dollars isn't that much money these days. Virtucon alone makes over nine billion dollars a year."

Dr. Evil responds (pleasantly surprised): "Oh, really? ONE HUNDRED BILLION DOLLARS!"

"ONE HUNDRED BILLION DOLLARS!"

*International Man of Mystery* takes place in 1997, and Dr. Evil was frozen in 1967. How much did the price level rise over those 30 years? The CPI was 33.4 in 1967 and 160.5 in 1997. Dividing 160.5 by 33.4 yields a ratio of 4.8. So if Dr. Evil thought that $1 million was a lot of money in 1967, an equivalent amount in 1997 would be $4.8 million. Dr. Evil does not let that stop him from asking for more!

rises, then some people will choose a less expensive snack. In other words, they find a substitute for popcorn. But when consumers substitute less expensive goods, that change alters the weights of all the goods in the typical consumption basket. Without acknowledging the substitution of less expensive items, the CPI would exaggerate the effects of the price increase, leading to upward bias. Since 1999, the BLS has used a formula that accounts for both the price increase and the shift in goods consumption.

## Changes in Quality

Over time, the quality of goods generally increases. For example, the movie theater you frequent may soon begin to offer all movies in 3D. Because this technology is more expensive than the older technology, the price of a ticket might rise from $10 to $12. The increase will seem like inflation, since ticket prices will go up. And yet, consumers will be getting "more" movie for their buck, since the quality will have improved. If the CPI did not account for quality changes, it would have an upward bias. But the BLS also uses an adjustment method to account for quality changes.

## New Products and Locations

In a dynamic, growing economy, new goods are introduced and new buying options become available. For example, tablet computers, flash drives, and even cell phones weren't in the typical consumer's basket 20 years ago. In addition, Amazon.com and eBay weren't options for consumers to make purchases before the 1990s.

Traditionally, the BLS updated the CPI goods basket only after long time delays. This strategy biased the CPI in an upward direction for two reasons. First, the prices of new products typically drop in the first few years after their introduction. If the CPI basket doesn't include the latest prices, this price drop is lost. Second, new retail outlets such as Internet stores typically offer lower prices than traditional retail stores do. If the BLS continued to check prices only at traditional retail stores, it would overstate the price that consumers actually pay for goods and services.

In an effort to measure this upward bias, the BLS began computing a *chained CPI* in 2000. The **chained CPI** is a measure of the CPI in which the typical consumer's basket of goods is updated monthly. While it's more difficult to measure and takes longer to estimate, the chained CPI is a better indicator of inflation for the typical consumer. Figure 8.5 shows the two CPI measures together. The vertical distance between the two lines indicates the upward bias of the traditional CPI, which updates the basket of goods less often. Notice that the distance grows over time.

The **chained CPI** is a measure of the CPI in which the typical consumer's "basket" of goods considered is updated monthly.

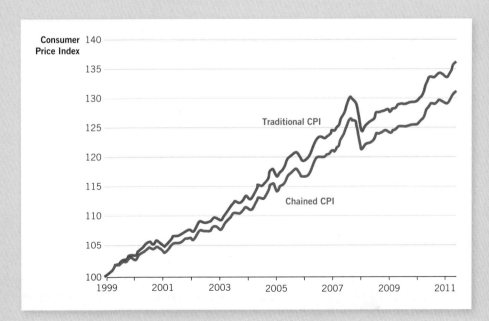

**FIGURE 8.5**

**The Chained CPI versus the Traditional CPI**

The chained CPI reduces the upward bias of the traditional CPI by updating the consumer's basket of goods every month. This single correction accounts for price reductions that typically occur during the first few years after a new product has been introduced.

*Source:* U.S. Bureau of Labor Statistics.

**ECONOMICS IN THE REAL WORLD**

## The Billion Prices Project

The Billion Prices Project (BPP) is an academic initiative at the Massachusetts Institute of Technology that monitors daily price fluctuations of approximately 5 million items sold by roughly 300 online retailers in more than 70 countries. The BPP is different than the CPI in that it only tracks the prices of goods that are sold online, and it does not weight those prices to reflect their importance in a typical consumer basket. However, even given these differences, the BPP tracks the CPI rather closely. Figure 8.6 shows the BPP index along with the CPI. Obviously, they look very similar, but the BPP series consistently estimates slightly more inflation than the CPI does since the end of 2009.

Why would researchers create an alternative measure to the CPI? The answer, in part, is because having access to the Internet makes the gathering of real-time price data extremely easy. With time, researchers hope to be able to examine over a billion prices each day across every major sector of the economy. Since the BPP is based only on online sales, there are limitations in generalizing its findings to the entire economy. However, the BPP data tracks the CPI quite closely. In relatively stable environments with low inflation, the BPP and CPI are not likely to be very different. But that is not likely to be the case in high-inflation environments, and certainly not when hyperinflation is present. When inflation is high (or highly variable), the BPP has the potential to point out meaningful trends in prices long before the CPI data can capture those changes. ✳

---

**The Billion Prices Project**

The Billion Prices Project is an independent index that tracks prices across the Internet as an alternative to the CPI. As the data lines indicate, the BPP index looks very similar to the CPI; however, it is compiled exclusively from online retail prices and requires no input from government workers.

*Source:* BPP - PriceStats - State Street http://bpp.mit .edu/usa/.

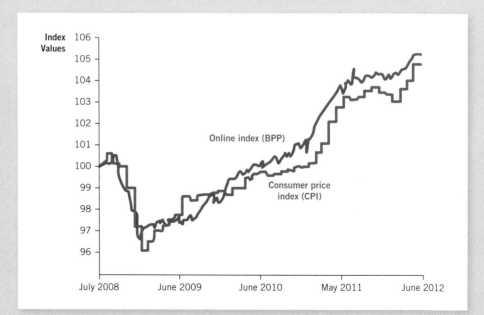

## PRACTICE WHAT YOU KNOW

### Using the CPI to Equate Prices over Time: How Cheap Were the First Super Bowl Tickets?

Ticket prices to America's premier sporting event, the Super Bowl, were much lower when it was first played in 1967. In fact, you could have bought a ticket for as little as $6. This seems very low by today's prices. In 2012, many seats sold for more than $2,500 each.

Question: If the CPI from 1967 was 33 and the CPI for 2012 was 230, how would you convert the price of a $6 ticket in 1967 into 2012 dollars?

Answer: For this question, we need to use equation 8.3:

$$\text{price in today's dollars} = \text{price in earlier time} \times \frac{\text{price level today}}{\text{price level in earlier time}}$$

The earlier price was $6, so we substitute this price and the two price levels from above to get:

$$\text{price in today's dollars} = \$6 \times (230 \div 33) = \$41.82$$

It turns out that the old Super Bowl tickets were indeed cheap—you'd be lucky to get a hot dog and a soda at a modern Super Bowl for $41.82.

A 1967 Super Bowl ticket.

# What Problems Does Inflation Bring?

Many people believe that inflation is most harmful because it reduces the purchasing power of their income. For example, consider that prices were much lower in the 1970s; therefore, it's easy to think that an annual salary of $10,000 at that time could buy a lot more than it can today. Well, this would be true if all else were equal. But salaries are prices too (prices for labor), and inflation causes them to rise as well. Remember: inflation is an overall rise in prices throughout the economy.

But this does not mean that inflation is harmless. Indeed, inflation does impose many costs on an economy. In this section, we discuss these costs. They include shoeleather costs, money illusion, menu costs, uncertainty over future price levels, wealth redistribution, and price confusion.

When inflation reaches the levels witnessed in Zimbabwe in 2008, shoeleather costs are significant.

**Shoeleather costs**
are the resources that are wasted when people change their behavior to avoid holding money.

**Money illusion**
occurs when people interpret nominal changes in wages or prices as real changes.

A worker's **nominal wage** is his or her wage expressed in current dollars.

## Shoeleather Costs

Inflation is costly for society when it causes people to do things they wouldn't do in an environment of price stability. After all, the higher the rate of inflation, the more likely people are to change their normal patterns of spending and money-holding. The reason is that inflation is essentially a tax on holding money. As the prices of goods and services rise with inflation, the value of dollars in people's wallets falls. This problem is not currently severe in the United States because inflation rates are very low. But hyperinflation means that the value of dollars falls daily.

In order to avoid the "tax" on holding money, people hold less money, which means more trips to the bank to make withdrawals. This is where the term *shoeleather costs* comes from: **shoeleather costs** are the resources that are wasted when people change their behavior to avoid holding money. In times past, these costs referred to the actual expense of replacing shoes that might get worn out as a result of making many trips to the bank. Today, these include fuel costs and the time and effort that people expend when they make multiple trips to a bank or ATM.

## Money Illusion

The second problem that inflation imposes is among the least understood. Even when people know that inflation has occurred, they do not always react rationally. So although wages and prices might rise because of inflation, people frequently respond as if the prices are higher in real terms. For example, if the price of a movie goes up by 10% but our wages and all other prices go up by a similar amount, nothing has changed in real terms. But many people mistakenly conclude that movies have become more expensive. If they treat a price increase from inflation as a change in relative price, they may go see fewer movies or make other decisions based on the new price. Economists call this *money illusion*. **Money illusion** occurs when people interpret nominal changes in wages or prices as real changes.

Money illusion is an easy trap to fall into. Let's see if we can trick you into it. Consider the cost-of-living data presented in Table 8.3. The index scores show relative living costs for an average inhabitant of various U.S. cities. The index is set so that 100 is the cost of living in an average U.S. city.

For this example, let's focus on two particular cities: Philadelphia, Pennsylvania, and Charlotte, North Carolina. The index score for Philadelphia is 126.5; for Charlotte, it is 93.2. These index scores imply that a salary of $93,200 for a person living in Charlotte is equivalent to a salary of $126,500 for a person living in Philadelphia. The difference is more than $30,000.

Now imagine that you are living in Charlotte and earning $93,200, but your firm offers to relocate you to Philadelphia at a pay rate of $100,000. Doesn't that seem like a pretty large raise? You might be excited to call your parents and tell them you'll be making "six figures." But, in fact, it is actually a real pay cut since you can buy less with $100,000 in Philadelphia than you can with $93,200 in Charlotte. Money illusion makes it feel like a raise.

The key distinction in this situation is between *real wages* and *nominal wages*. A worker's **nominal wage** is his or her wage expressed in current dollars. The nominal wage is similar to nominal GDP. It is the wage expressed in

## TABLE 8.3

### The Cost of Living in Selected U.S. Cities

| City | Cost-of-living index number |
|------|------------------------------|
| New York (Manhattan) | 216.7 |
| San Francisco, CA | 164.0 |
| Washington, DC | 140.1 |
| Los Angeles, CA | 136.4 |
| Boston, MA | 132.5 |
| **Philadelphia, PA** | **126.5** |
| Seattle, WA | 121.4 |
| Chicago, IL | 116.9 |
| Richmond, VA | 104.5 |
| Phoenix, AZ | 100.7 |
| Detroit, MI | 99.4 |
| Atlanta, GA | 95.6 |
| **Charlotte, NC** | **93.2** |
| Dallas, TX | 91.9 |

*Source*: C2ER, Arlington, VA, ACCRA Cost of Living Index, Annual Average 2010.

current dollars, like $60 per hour or $120,000 per year. The **real wage** is the nominal wage adjusted for changes in the price level. The real wage is more informative because it describes what the worker earns in terms of purchasing power. So while a salary of $100,000 a year may sound high, if the CPI doubles, that salary will not go very far.

The **real wage** is the nominal wage adjusted for changes in the price level.

Significant macroeconomic problems arise if workers fall victim to money illusion when they interpret the value of their wages, because the illusion causes them to focus on their nominal wage instead of their real wage. For example, when prices fall, any given nominal wage is worth more in real terms. In Chapter 13, we'll see that macroeconomic adjustments can depend on whether workers are willing to let wages fall when other prices fall. Money illusion causes these adjustments to take longer than they should, and this delay tends to lengthen economic downturns.

## Menu Costs

The act of physically changing prices is also costly. **Menu costs** are the costs of changing prices. While some businesses can change prices easily—for

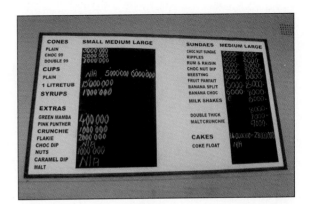

Chalk menus are one way to limit menu costs. This menu is from an ice cream parlor in Zimbabwe during its 2008 hyperinflation. Notice that the price of a small chocolate cone is 5 million Zimbabwean dollars.

**Menu costs**
are the costs of changing prices.

example, gas pumps and signs at gas stations are designed for this purpose— businesses such as restaurants can find it expensive to print new menus when their prices change.

Other costs considered in this category are not directly related to menus. For example, changing prices can make regular customers angry enough to take their business elsewhere. Think about your favorite lunch spot. Perhaps you regularly buy a bagel and an iced tea for $4 at Bodo's Bagels. What if the price for this combination suddenly increases to $5? You might be annoyed enough to go somewhere else next time.

Menu costs discourage firms from adjusting prices quickly. When some prices are slow to respond, the effects of macroeconomic disturbances are magnified. We'll talk about this more in Chapter 13.

## Uncertainty about Future Price Levels

Imagine you decide to open a new coffee shop in your college town. You want to produce espressos, café mochas, and cappuccinos. Of course, you hope to sell these for a profit. But before you can sell a single cup of coffee, you have to spend funds on your resources. You have to buy (that is, invest in) capital goods like an espresso bar, tables, chairs, and a cash register. You also have to hire workers and promise to pay them. All firms, large and small, face this situation. Before any revenue arrives from the sales of output, firms have to spend on resources. This also applies to the overall macroeconomy: in order to increase GDP in the future, firms must invest today. The funds required to make these investments are typically borrowed from others.

**Output**
is the production that a firm creates.

The timeline of production shown in Figure 8.7 illustrates how this process works. At the end, the firm sells its *output*. **Output** is the production that a firm creates. The important point is that in a normal production process, funds must be spent today and then repaid in the future—after the output sells. But for this sequence of events to occur, businesses must make promises

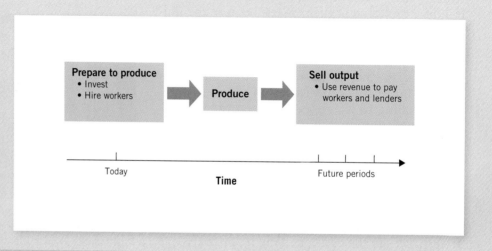

## FIGURE 8.7

**The Timeline of Production**

The way output is typically produced begins with preparation that includes purchases of equipment, labor, and other resources. Actual output and revenue from the sale of output come later. Thus, the firm can only begin production with promises of future payments to resource suppliers.

to deliver payments in the future: these include payments to workers and lenders. Thus, two types of long-term agreements form the foundation for production: wage and loan contracts. Both of these involve agreements for dollars to be delivered in future periods.

But inflation affects the real value of these future dollars. When inflation confuses workers and lenders, these essential long-term agreements seem risky and people are less likely to enter into them. Chapter 9 focuses on the market for loans in an economy, and we cover this at a deeper level there. For now, we note that inflation can cripple loan markets because people don't know what future price levels will be. When firms cannot borrow money or hire long-term workers, future production is limited. Thus, inflation risk can lead to lower economic output, which is GDP.

## Wealth Redistribution

Inflation can also redistribute wealth between borrowers and lenders. Returning to the coffee shop example above, imagine that you borrow $50,000 to start your business. You borrow this sum from a bank with the promise of paying back $60,000 in five years. Now if inflation unexpectedly rises during those five years, the inflation will devalue your future payment to the bank— as a result, you will be better off, but the bank will be worse off. Thus, surprise inflation redistributes wealth from lenders to borrowers.

If both you and the bank fully expect the inflation to occur, the bank will require more in return for the loan, so the inflation will not be a problem. In the United States, inflation has been low and steady since the early 1980s. Therefore, surprises are rare. But nations with higher inflation rates also have a higher variability of inflation, which makes it difficult to predict the future. This is one more reason why high inflation increases the risk of making the loans that are an important source of funding for business ventures.

## Price Confusion

Market prices are signals to consumers and firms—signals that help allocate resources in a market economy. For example, if demand increases, prices rise and firms have an incentive to increase the quantity of output that they supply. All else equal, firms take rising prices as a signal to increase output and falling prices as a signal to decrease output. But inflation also shows up as rising prices. If firms cannot determine which price changes are due to inflation, resources may be misdirected in the economy.

Figure 8.8 illustrates the dilemma that firms face in this context. Initially, it may appear that output prices are rising as a result of an increase in demand. But if the cause is inflation, then prices throughout the economy will rise and the optimal output for the firm should remain at the original output level. If firms always react to price changes by increasing their output, they run the risk of over-building. This can be painful later.

The housing market in the United States provides a good example of price confusion. In 2005, housing prices were high and rising. We can look back now and recognize a price bubble that did not reflect real long-run increases in demand. It appears now that rising housing prices reflected inflation.

However, high prices at the time spurred many builders to develop more properties. When housing prices later fell, many of those builders declared bankruptcy. The crash in housing prices was one of the contributing factors to the recent Great Recession, which began at the end of 2007.

## Tax Distortions

Even if inflation caused all prices to rise uniformly, there would still be distortionary effects. These would occur because tax laws do not typically account for inflation. One area in which particularly distortionary effects occur is *capital gains taxes*.

**Capital gains taxes** are taxes on the gains realized by selling an asset for more than its purchase price. For example, if your parents bought a house in 1980 for $80,000 and then sold it in 2012 for $230,000, they made a $150,000 capital gain on the sale of the house, and this capital gain is taxed. However, it turns out that the CPI rose by exactly the same amount between 1980 and 2012: as we saw in Figure 8.4, the CPI was 80 in 1980 and climbed to 230 by 2012. Therefore, the value of your parents' house just kept pace with inflation. In real terms, the value of their house did not climb. But they would still be required to pay a significant tax upon the sale of their home. As it turns out, the amount of their tax is determined by inflation and not by the tax laws; if there had been no inflation, your parents would have owed no tax.

Capital gains are realized on more than just home sales. Capital gains also arise with the sales of stocks, bonds, and other financial securities. As we will discuss in Chapter 10, these securities are a crucial ingredient to a growing and expanding economy. But inflation combined with a capital gains tax means that most people will be less likely to make these kinds of purchases. One possible solution is to rewrite the tax laws to take account of inflation's effects.

As the previous discussion points out, inflation imposes specific costs on an economy. Table 8.4 summarizes these costs.

> **Capital gains taxes** are taxes on the gains realized by selling an asset for more than its purchase price.

---

**FIGURE 8.8**

**"Why Did My Price Change?"**

Price changes send information, or signals, to businesses. However, higher prices can be the result of either a real increase in demand or inflation. If upward pressure on prices is the result of greater demand, the profit-maximizing firm should increase its output. But if the price increase is the result of inflation, the firm should not change its level of output.

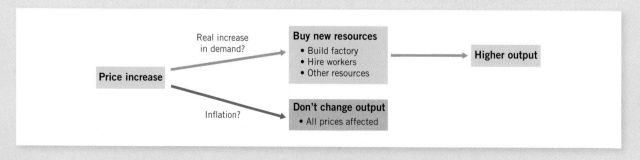

## TABLE 8.4

### The Costs of Inflation

| Cost of inflation | Description |
| --- | --- |
| Shoeleather costs | Time and resources are spent to guard against the effects of inflation. |
| Money illusion | Consumers misinterpret nominal changes as real changes. |
| Menu costs | Inflation means that firms must incur extra costs to change their output prices. |
| Uncertainty about future price levels | Long-term agreements may not be signed if lenders, firms, and workers are unsure about future price levels. |
| Wealth redistribution | Surprise inflation redistributes wealth between borrowers and lenders. |
| Price confusion | Inflation makes it difficult to read price signals, and this confusion can lead to a misallocation of resources. |
| Tax distortions | Inflation makes capital gains appear larger and thus increases tax burdens. |

# PRACTICE WHAT YOU KNOW

### Problems with Inflation: How Big Is Your Raise in Real Terms?

Your boss calls you into his office and tells you he has good news. Because of your stellar performance and hard work, you have earned a 3% raise for next year. But when you think about your future pay, you should also know how much inflation has eroded your current pay. For example, if the inflation rate is 3% per year, then you need a 3% raise just to keep pace with inflation.
Note that you can see inflation rates for yourself by visiting the Bureau of Labor Statistics web site (www.bls.gov). Once there, look up inflation rates based on the CPI.

Question: In what situation would a 3% raise signify a lower real wage?

Answer: If the inflation rate is greater than 3%, then a 3% raise would actually be a decline in your real wage.

Question: What inflation problem must you overcome to correctly see the value of your raise?

Answer: *Money illusion.* You must evaluate the real, rather than the nominal, value of your pay.

The printing press: the cause of inflation.

# What Is the Cause of Inflation?

Since inflation presents these serious macroeconomic costs, you might assume that there is significant debate about the causes. But that assumption would be incorrect. Economist Milton Friedman famously said, "inflation is always and everywhere a monetary phenomenon." What he meant is that inflation is consistently caused by increases in a nation's money supply relative to the quantity of real goods and services in the economy.

Figure 8.9 shows average inflation rates and the money supply growth rates across 160 nations for the years 1991–2011. For practically all nations, the relationship appears to be almost one-to-one. The blue line is a hypothetical one-to-one line, where a nation's average inflation rate is exactly equal to the average money supply growth rate. It is difficult to distinguish all 160 nations, because almost all of the data points are right on this one-to-one line, with inflation rates of less than 200%. The United States, for example, has an average inflation rate of 5.7% and a money supply growth rate of 5.5%. In contrast, the few nations with even higher average inflation rates are easy to pick out. For example, in this sample the average inflation rates in Brazil were 323% per year (this is not a typo!), and that inflation stemmed from monetary growth rates of about 331%.

## FIGURE 8.9

### Inflation and Money Growth Rates in 160 countries, 1991–2011

The relationship between inflation rates and money growth rates is virtually one-to-one for many countries over long periods of time. This applies to nations with low inflation rates and to nations with high inflation rates.

*Source:* World Bank.

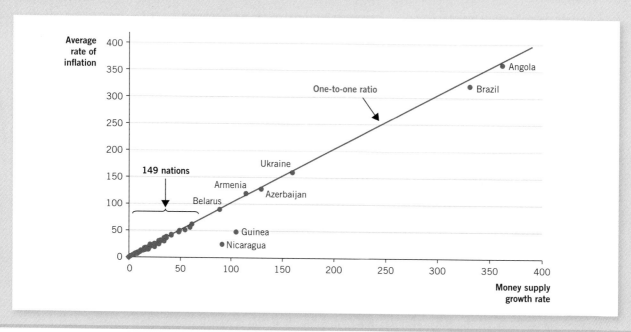

In Chapter 18, we will address this question more formally; we will use a macroeconomic model to show how monetary expansion translates into inflation. But the intuition is straightforward: when the supply of money in an economy grows *relative to the quantity of goods and services,* then it takes more money to buy any particular good or service. Money then becomes less valuable relative to goods and services—and this relationship constitutes inflation. The principle holds true regardless of the type of money used. For example, when Spanish conquistadors brought gold back to Europe from Latin America in the sixteenth century, the supply of money (gold) in Europe increased, and this led to inflation.

## The Reasons Governments Inflate the Money Supply

In this chapter, we discussed several problems that stem from inflation: shoe-leather costs, money illusion, menu costs, uncertainty over future price levels, wealth redistribution, price confusion, and tax distortions. And yet we know what causes inflation. Thus, it is reasonable to wonder why inflation is often still a macroeconomic problem. We point to two reasons: large government debts and short-term gains.

First, large government debts often spur governments to choose to increase the money supply rapidly. When a government owes large sums and also controls the supply of money, there is a natural urge to print more money to pay off debts. After World War I, the German government owed billions of dollars to other nations and to its workers, so it resorted to printing more money—and this action led to inflation rates of almost 30,000% in late 1923.

Second, surprise increases in the money supply can temporarily stimulate an economy toward more rapid growth rates. We'll look at this issue very closely in Chapter 18, but it is a constant temptation for governments that can be shortsighted and focused on a quick economic boost. The problems from inflation are often long term and difficult to overcome. But the short-term economic boost can be very tempting for governments. Unfortunately, to realize any benefits from inflation, the government has to keep surprising people in the economy. As a result, in attempting to stay ahead of expectations, inflation can spiral out of control.

# Conclusion

This chapter began with a common misconception—that inflation is no big deal. But we have seen that inflation and the problems it imposes can be severe. And while inflation rates have been low in the United States for several years now, at times in the past they have been very high—such as during the 1970s. In addition, inflation rates in some other nations remain high.

Inflation, along with the unemployment rate and changes in real GDP, is an important indicator of overall macroeconomic conditions. Now that we have covered these three, we move next to savings and the determination of interest rates.

# Inflation Devalues Dollars: Preparing Your Future for Inflation

In this chapter, we talked about how inflation deval-ues the money you currently hold and the money you've been promised in the future. One problem you may encounter is how to prepare for retirement in the face of inflation. Perhaps you are not worried about this, since the inflation rate in the United States over the past 50 years has averaged 4%, and more recently the average has been only 2%. But even these low rates mean that dollars will be worth significantly less 40 years from now.

One way to think about the effect of inflation on future dollars is to ask what amount of future dollars it will take to match the real value of $1.00 today. The graph below answers this question based on a retirement date of 40 years in the future. The differ-ent inflation rates are specified at the bottom.

Thus, if the inflation rate averages 4% over the next four decades, you'll need $4.80 just to buy the same goods and services you can buy today for $1.00.

What does this mean for your overall retirement plans? Let's say you decide you could

How many nest eggs will you need to put aside to keep pace with inflation?

live on $50,000 per year if you retired today. If the inflation rate is 4% between now and your retirement date, you would need enough sav-ings to supply yourself with 50,000 × $4.80, or $240,000 per year, just to keep pace with inflation.

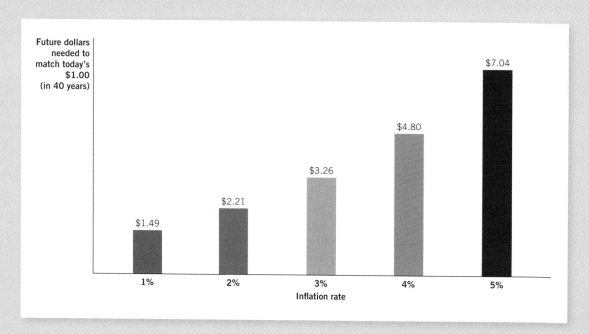

# ANSWERING THE BIG QUESTIONS

## How is inflation measured?

⁂ Inflation rates are calculated as the percentage change in the overall level of prices.

⁂ Economists use the CPI to determine the general level of prices in the economy.

⁂ Determining which prices to include in the CPI can be challenging for several reasons: consumers change what they buy over time, the quality of goods changes, and new products and sales locations are introduced.

## What problems does inflation bring?

⁂ Inflation imposes shoeleather costs: it causes people to waste resources as they seek to avoid holding money.

⁂ Inflation can cause people to make decisions based on nominal rather than real monetary values, a problem known as money illusion.

⁂ Inflation adds menu costs.

⁂ Inflation introduces uncertainty about future price levels. Because this makes it difficult for consumers and producers to plan, it impedes economic progress.

⁂ Unexpected inflation redistributes wealth from lenders to borrowers.

⁂ Inflation makes it difficult for producers to read price signals correctly; this is known as price confusion.

⁂ Inflation distorts people's tax obligations.

## What is the cause of inflation?

⁂ Inflation occurs when governments increase a nation's money supply too quickly.

⁂ Governments often increase the money supply too quickly when they are in debt or when they desire a short-run stimulus for the economy.

## CONCEPTS YOU SHOULD KNOW

capital gains taxes (p. 260)
chained CPI (p. 253)
consumer price index (CPI)
(p. 241)

deflation (p. 240)
menu costs (p. 258)
money illusion (p. 256)
nominal wage (p. 256)

output (p. 258)
real wage (p. 257)
shoeleather costs (p. 256)

## QUESTIONS FOR REVIEW

1. The price of a typical laptop computer has fallen from $2,000 in 1985 to $800 today. At the same time, the consumer price index has risen from 100 to 250. Adjusting for inflation, how much did the price of laptops change? Does this answer seem right to you, or is it missing something? Explain your response.

2. What three issues are at the center of the debate regarding the accuracy of the CPI? Please give an example of each issue.

3. If the prices of homes go up by 5% and the prices of concert tickets rise by 10%, which will have the larger impact on the CPI? Why?

4. If a country is experiencing a relatively high rate of inflation, what impact will this have on the country's long-term rate of economic growth?

5. In a sentence or two, evaluate the accuracy of the following statement, including a clear and precise statement of historical comparison: *Inflation in the United States last year was 0%. This is close to the historical level.*

6. Wage agreements and loan contracts are two types of multi-period agreements that are

important for economic growth. Suppose you sign a two-year job contract with Wells-Fargo stipulating that you will receive an annual salary of $93,500 plus an additional 2% over that in the second year to account for expected inflation.

a. If the inflation rate turns out to be 3% rather than 2%, who will be hurt by this? Why?

b. If the inflation rate turns out to be 1% rather than 2%, who will be hurt by this? Why?

Suppose that you also take out a $1,000 loan at the Cavalier Credit Union. The loan agreement stipulates that you must pay it back with 4% interest in one year, and again, the inflation rate is expected to be 2%.

c. If the inflation rate turns out to be 3% rather than 2%, who will be hurt by this? Why?

d. If the inflation rate turns out to be 3% rather than 2%, who will be helped by this? Why?

7. What are the seven problems caused by inflation? Briefly explain each one.

## STUDY PROBLEMS (*solved at the end of the section*)

1. In 1991, the Barenaked Ladies released their hit song "If I Had a Million Dollars." How much money would the group need in 2012 to have the same amount of real purchasing power in 2012? Note that the consumer price index in 1991 was 136.2 and in 2012 it was 230.

2. Visit the Bureau of Labor Statistics website for the CPI, www.bls.gov/cpi, and find the latest news release. Table 1 in that release presents

CPI data for all items and also for many individual categories.

a. How much has the entire index changed (in percentage terms) in the past year?

b. Now pick out the five individual categories that have increased the most in the past year.

3. While rooting through the attic, you discover a box of old tax forms. You find that your grandmother made $75 working part-time

during December 1964 when the CPI was 31.3. How much would you need to have earned in January of this year to have at least as much real income as your grandmother did in 1964? To determine the CPI for January of this year, you can visit the Bureau of Labor Statistics website (www.bls.gov).

✳ **4.** Suppose that the residents of Greenland play golf incessantly. In fact, golf is the only thing that they spend their money on. They buy golf balls, clubs, and tees. In 2010, they bought 1,000 golf balls for $2.00 each, 100 clubs for $50.00 each, and 500 tees for $0.10 each. In 2011, they bought 1,100 golf balls for $2.50 each, 75 clubs for $75.00 each, and 1,000 tees for $0.12 each.

**a.** What was the CPI for each year?

**b.** What was the inflation rate in 2011?

✳ **5.** If healthcare costs make up 10% of total expenditures and they rise by 15% while the other components in the consumer price index remain constant, by how much will the price index rise?

## SOLVED PROBLEMS

**4. a.** We'll use the quantities from the first year to designate the weights. In order to build a price index, we first need to choose which year we will use as the base year. Let 2010 be the base year. Next we define our basket as the goods consumed in 2010: 1,000 golf balls, 100 clubs, and 500 tees.

In 2010, this basket cost as follows:

$$(1,000 \times \$2.00) + (100 \times \$50.00)$$
$$+ (500 \times \$0.10) = \$7,050.00$$

In 2011, this basket cost as follows:

$$(1,000 \times \$2.50) + (100 \times \$75.00)$$
$$+ (500 \times \$0.12) = \$10,060.00$$

Dividing the cost of the basket in each year by the cost of the basket in the base year and multiplying by 100 gives us the CPI for each year.

For 2010, the CPI is calculated as:
$$(\$7,050 \div \$7,050) \times 100 = 100$$

For 2012, the CPI is calculated as:
$$(\$10,060 \div \$7,050) \times 100 = 142.7$$

**b.** The inflation rate is defined as $[(CPI_2 - CPI_1) \div CPI_1] \times 100$. Plugging the values from part (a) into the formula, we get an inflation rate of 42.7%:

$$[(142.7 - 100) \div 100] \times 100 = 42.7$$

**5.** The CPI will rise by 1.5%. Suppose the CPI in the first year is 100. If healthcare costs are 10% of total expenditures, then they account for 10 of the 100 points, with the other 90 points falling in other categories. If healthcare costs rise by 15% in the second year, then those 10 points become 11.5 points. Since the prices of the other categories have not changed, the CPI now stands at 101.5, since $11.5 + 90 = 101.5$.

Using our formula for calculating the inflation rate, the rise in healthcare costs has raised the overall price level by 1.5%:
$$[(101.5 - 100) \div 100] \times 100 = 1.5.$$

# Savings, Interest Rates, and the Market for Loanable Funds

**The government sets interest rates.**

Just about anything you read or hear about interest rates in the popular media leaves you with the impression that the government sets interest

**MISCONCEPTION**

rates. This isn't exactly true. For sure, the government can influence many rates. But almost all interest rates in the U.S. economy are determined privately—on the basis of the interaction between the market forces of supply and demand. In fact, you can understand why interest rates rise and fall by applying supply and demand analysis to the market for loans. That's what we will do in this chapter. Along the way, we'll also consider the many factors that influence savers and borrowers.

In this chapter, we discuss many of the same topics you might study in a course on banking or financial institutions, but our emphasis is different. We are interested in studying how financial institutions and markets affect the macroeconomy. When we are finished, you will understand why interest rates rise and fall, and you will also appreciate the necessity of the loanable funds market in the larger macroeconomy.

These traders play one of many important roles in the market for loanable funds.

# BIG QUESTIONS

＊ **What is the loanable funds market?**

＊ **What factors shift the supply of loanable funds?**

＊ **What factors shift the demand for loanable funds?**

＊ **How do we apply the loanable funds market model?**

## What Is the Loanable Funds Market?

The **loanable funds market** is the market where savers supply funds for loans to borrowers.

Financial markets are where firms and governments obtain funds, or *financing,* for their operations. These funds come primarily from household savings across the economy. In economics, we analyze financial markets in the context of a *loanable funds market.* The **loanable funds market** is the market where savers supply funds for loans to borrowers.

This market is not a single physical location but includes places like stock exchanges, investment banks, mutual fund firms, and commercial banks. In this section, we explain the particular characteristics of the loanable funds market and the significant role it plays in the overall economy.

Figure 9.1 illustrates the role of the loanable funds market. Savings flow in and become loans for borrowers. We could call it the market for savings, or even the market for loans. The term *loanable funds* captures the information in both.

---

### FIGURE 9.1

**The Role of the Loanable Funds Market**

The market for loanable funds is where savers bring funds and make them available to borrowers. Households (private individuals and families) are the primary suppliers of loanable funds. Firms are the primary demanders, or borrowers, of loanable funds. When this market is functioning well, firms get the funds necessary for production and savers are paid for lending.

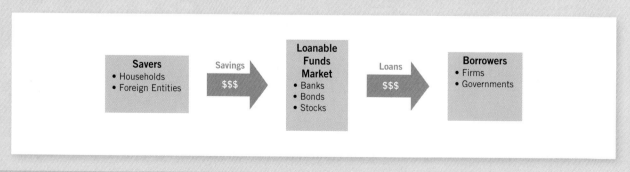

On the left side of the figure, the suppliers of funds—those who save—include households and foreign entities. Households are private individuals and families. Foreign entities include foreign governments, firms, and private citizens that choose to save in the United States. For most of the applications we discuss, we focus on households as the primary suppliers of loanable funds. If you have a checking or savings account at a bank, you are a supplier of loanable funds. You deposit funds into your bank account, but these funds don't just sit in a vault; banks loan out the majority of these funds. Household savings in retirement accounts, stocks, bonds, and mutual funds are other big sources of loanable funds.

The demanders, or borrowers, of loanable funds include firms and governments. In this chapter, we focus on firms as the primary borrowers of loanable funds. To reinforce the significance of this market, think about why borrowing takes place: firms borrow to invest. That is, firms looking to produce output in the future must borrow in order to pay their expenses today.

Figure 9.2 shows the production timeline that we introduced in Chapter 8. At the end of the timeline is output, or GDP. When this output is sold, it produces revenue for the firms, and the revenue serves to pay bills. But future GDP depends on spending today for necessary resources. This spending comes before any revenue is gained from the sale of output. Therefore, firms must borrow in order to generate future GDP—that's how important the loanable funds market is to the entire economy. Without a well-functioning loanable funds market, future GDP dries up.

Imagine that you are an entrepreneur who decides to start a company that will produce and sell college apparel. If you succeed, you will contribute to national GDP. But you don't really think of it this way; you simply hope that you have discovered a great business opportunity. Now before you ever sell your first shirt, hat, or sweatpants, you have to spend money on the resources you'll use in the production process. For example, if you plan on silk-screening your college logo onto hooded sweatshirts, you have to buy

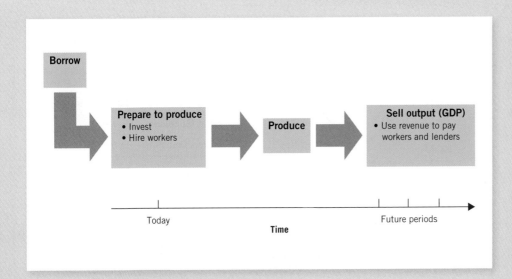

## FIGURE 9.2

### The Timeline of Production

The production timeline illustrates that GDP depends critically on the loanable funds market. At the end of the production timeline we see output, or GDP. But before a firm can produce output, it must purchase resources. Since these purchases occur before the revenue comes in, firms must borrow at the beginning of the timeline.

Before you can sell college apparel, you have to buy equipment and other supplies.

sweatshirts, paint, and a screen printing press. Here is where the loanable funds market comes into play: since you have no revenue yet, you need to borrow in order to make these investments.

Borrowing fuels investment, which creates future output. But notice that *every dollar borrowed requires a dollar saved*. Without savings, we cannot sustain future production. If you want to borrow to buy the resources you need to produce college apparel, someone else has to save. Working backward, the chain of crucial relationships looks like this: output (GDP) requires investment; investment requires borrowing; borrowing requires savings. And all the links in this chain require a loanable funds market that efficiently channels funds from savers to borrowers.

We will study this crucial market from the perspective of prices, quantities, supply, and demand—like any other market. The good in this market is loanable funds. The demanders (or consumers) are borrowers; the suppliers are savers. Figure 9.3 presents a picture of supply (Savings, or S) and demand (Investment, or D) for loanable funds, along with a summary of the distinctions of the loanable funds market.

An **interest rate**
is a price of loanable funds, quoted as a percentage of the original loan amount.

One advantage of this demand and supply approach is that it clarifies the role of interest rates. An **interest rate** is a price of loanable funds. It is like the price of toothpaste or computers or hoodies; it is simply quoted differently—as a percentage of the original loan amount. People who are thinking about planning for retirement or making a big purchase such as a house or a car worry about interest rate fluctuations but do not necessarily understand why interest rates rise and fall. If we acknowledge that an interest rate is just the price of loanable funds, we can use supply and demand to reveal the factors that make interest rates rise and fall.

We now turn to the two different views of interest rates: the view of the saver and the view of the borrower.

## FIGURE 9.3

### The Loanable Funds Market

Savings (S) is channeled into investment (D) in the loanable funds market. In this market, loanable funds are the goods that are bought and sold. The price is an interest rate. This price, like any other market-determined price, is determined by the interaction between supply and demand.

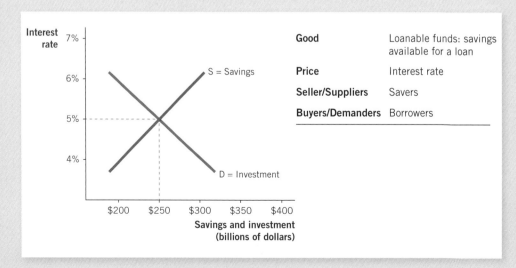

| Good | Loanable funds: savings available for a loan |
| **Price** | Interest rate |
| **Seller/Suppliers** | Savers |
| **Buyers/Demanders** | Borrowers |

# Interest Rates as a Reward for Saving

If you are a saver, the interest rate is the return you get for supplying funds. For example, let's say your parents gave you some cash when you came to college this semester. After buying textbooks, groceries, and other supplies, you have $1,000 left, which you consider saving. You go to a bank near campus and inquire about opening a new account. In this transaction, the bank is the buyer, and it offers a certain price for the use of your savings. When it does offer a price, it is not in dollars. The bank quotes a price in interest rates, or as a percentage of how much you save. But it communicates the same information. So if you are saving $1,000, the bank might tell you, "We'll pay you 6% if you save that money for a year." Since 6% of $1,000 is $60, this is equivalent to saying, "We'll pay you $60 if you save that money for a year."

If you save $1,000 for one year with an interest rate of 6%, this brings you $1,060 next year, which is computed as:

$$\$1,000 + (6\% \text{ of } \$1,000) = \$1,000 + \$60 = \$1,060$$

Banks are willing to pay you for your savings. The price they pay is the interest rate.

For savers, the interest rate is a reward. Every dollar saved today returns more in the saver's account in the future. The higher the interest rate, the greater the return will be in the future. Table 9.1 illustrates how interest rates affect $1,000 worth of savings. An interest rate of 4% yields $1,040 one year later; an interest rate of 10% yields $1,100.

Think of the interest rate as the opportunity cost of consumption. Consider the $1,000 savings in Table 9.1. With a 4% interest rate and a $1,000 purchase today, you are giving up the $40 you would make by saving that $1,000. But at an interest rate of 10%, using the $1,000 for consumption today means giving up an additional $100 next year. Interest rates on savings accounts in the United States today are typically less than 2%. But imagine an interest rate of 10% for a savings account. This was actually the situation in the United States in the 1980s. With an interest rate that high, even college students find a way to save.

As we have mentioned, savings constitutes the supply of loanable funds. The higher the interest rate, the greater is the incentive to save. This is the loanable funds version of the law of supply: the quantity of savings rises when the interest rate rises. This positive relationship between interest rates and savings is reflected in the slope of the supply curve (S), illustrated in Figure 9.3. When the interest rate is 4%, the quantity of loans supplied is $200 billion per year; at 5% the quantity supplied increases to $250 billion, and at 6% it increases to $300 billion.

Incentives

| TABLE 9.1 | |
|---|---|
| **Higher Interest Rates and Greater Future Returns** | |
| **Interest rate** | **Value of $1,000 after 1 year** |
| 4% | $1,040 |
| 5% | 1,050 |
| 6% | 1,060 ◀ |
| 10% | 1,100 |

If you save $1,000 for one year at an interest rate of 6%, this yields $1,060 next year, computed as:

$$\$1,000 + (6\% \text{ of } \$1,000)$$
$$= \$1,000 + (0.06 \times \$1,000)$$
$$= \$1,000 + \$60$$
$$= \$1,060$$

## Interest Rates as a Cost of Borrowing

We now turn to the demand, or borrowing, side of the loanable funds market. For this, we shift to the firm's perspective and return to your plan to produce college apparel. Recall that you need to buy the sweatshirts, paint, and screen printing press to produce hoodies and other products with a college logo. Assume that you need $100,000 to start your business. If you borrow $100,000 for one year at an interest rate of 6%, you'll need to repay $106,000 in one year. It makes sense to do this only if you expect to earn more than 6%, or $6,000, on this investment.

For borrowers, the interest rate is the cost of borrowing. Firms borrow only if they expect the return on their investment to be greater than the costs of the loan. For example, at an interest rate of 6% a firm would borrow only if it expected to make more than a 6% return with its use of the funds. Let's state this as a rule:

*Profit-maximizing firms borrow to fund an investment if and only if the expected return on the investment is greater than the interest rate on the loan.*

The lower the interest rate, the more likely a business will succeed in earning enough to exceed the interest it will owe at the end of the year. For example, if your firm can borrow at an interest rate of just 4%, you'll need to make a return greater than 4%. There are probably several investments available today that would pay more than a 6% return; but there are even more that would yield returns greater than 4%, and more still that would pay greater than 2%. If we apply our rule from above, we'll see a larger quantity of loans demanded as the interest rate drops. This gives us the inverse relationship between interest rate and quantity demanded of loans that is reflected in the slope of the demand curve for loanable funds.

The graph of the loanable funds market in Figure 9.3 illustrates the demand curve (D) for loanable funds across the entire U.S. economy. At an interest rate of 6%, the quantity of loans demanded by all business firms in the economy is $200 billion. This indicates that firms believe only $200 billion worth of investment will pay returns greater than 6%. At an interest rate of 5%, firms estimate that another $50 billion worth of total loans will earn between 5% and 6%, and the quantity of loans demanded rises to $250 billion. Lower interest rates lead to a greater quantity of demand for loanable funds.

## How Inflation Affects Interest Rates

If you save $1,000 for a year at an interest rate of 6%, your reward for saving is $60. But inflation affects the real value of this reward. For example, imagine that the inflation rate is exactly 6% during the year you save. This inflation means that next year it will take $1,060 to buy the same quantity of goods and services that you are able to buy this year for $1,000. In this case, your interest rate of 6% and the inflation rate of 6% cancel each other out. You break even, and that's no reward.

When making decisions about saving and borrowing, people care about the *real interest rate*, not the *nominal interest rate*. The **real interest rate** is the interest rate that is corrected for inflation; it is the rate of return in terms of real purchasing power. In contrast, the **nominal interest rate** is the interest rate before it is corrected for inflation; it is the stated interest rate. In our

The **real interest rate** is the interest rate that is corrected for inflation.

The **nominal interest rate** is the interest rate before it is corrected for inflation.

example, the interest rate of 6% is the nominal interest rate. But with 6% inflation, the real return on your savings disappears, and the real interest rate is zero—or 0%. In general, we can approximate the real interest rate by subtracting the inflation rate from the nominal interest rate in an equation known as the **Fisher equation**:

The **Fisher equation** states that the real interest rate equals the nominal interest rate minus the inflation rate.

$$\text{real interest rate} = \text{nominal interest rate} - \text{inflation rate}$$ (Equation 9.1)

For example, if the inflation rate this year is 2%, a nominal interest rate of 6% on your savings yields a 4% real interest rate. The Fisher equation is named after economist Irving Fisher, who formulated the relationship between inflation and interest rates.

Savers and borrowers care about the real rate of interest on a loan because this is the rate that describes how the real purchasing power of their funds changes over the course of the loan. Since interest rates are a result of supply and demand in the market for loanable funds, higher inflation rates lead to higher nominal interest rates in order to compensate lenders for the loss of purchasing power. We can rewrite the Fisher equation to see how inflation generally increases nominal interest rates:

$$\text{nominal interest rate} = \text{real interest rate} + \text{inflation rate}$$ (Equation 9.2)

For a given real interest rate, the higher the rate of inflation, the higher the nominal interest rate will be. Table 9.2 shows how the nominal interest rate rises with inflation rates for a given level of real interest rates. If the real interest rate is 4% and there is no inflation, then the nominal interest rate is also 4%. But if the inflation rate rises to 2%, the nominal interest rate increases to 6%. If the inflation rate rises further to 4%, then the nominal interest rate rises to 8%.

We can picture the Fisher equation by looking at real and nominal interest rates over time. Figure 9.4 plots real and nominal interest rates in the United States from 1960 to 2012. The difference between them is the inflation rate. Notice that this gap was particularly high during the inflationary 1970s but that it narrowed considerably as inflation rates fell in the 1980s. After 2008, nominal interest rates in the United States were less than 1%. Given that inflation rates were around 2%, this implies negative real interest rates.

Unless otherwise stated, in this text we will use nominal interest rates. We do this for two reasons. First, nominal interest rates are the stated interest rates— the rates you read about and consider in actual financial transactions. Second, low and steady inflation means that the difference between real and nominal interest rates doesn't fluctuate much. That is, while we recognize that savers and borrowers care about the real interest rate, the current inflationary environment

| TABLE 9.2 | | | | | |
|---|---|---|---|---|---|
| **How Inflation Affects Nominal Interest Rates** | | | | | |
| Inflation rate | | Real interest rate | | Nominal interest rate | |
| 0% | + | 4% | = | 4% | |
| 2% | + | 4% | = | 6% | |
| 4% | + | 4% | = | 8% | |

## FIGURE 9.4

**Real and Nominal Interest Rates, 1960–2012**

The difference between real and nominal interest rates is the rate of inflation. The experience of the 1970s illustrates that nominal interest rates are historically high when inflation is also high.

*Sources:* Federal Reserve Bank of St. Louis FRED database; Bureau of Labor Statistics.

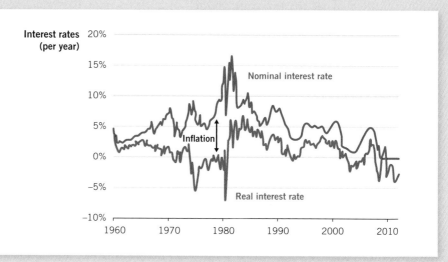

throughout much of the developed world leaves little to be gained by focusing on the real interest rate through the applications we discuss in this text.

In the next two sections, we consider the factors that cause shifts in the supply and demand for loanable funds.

As India grows from poor to rich, much of the funds that its citizens save find their way into the U.S. loanable funds market.

# What Factors Shift the Supply of Loanable Funds?

Recall that the supply of loanable funds comes from savings. If you have either a savings or a checking account, you are a participant in this market. We turn now to three factors that determine the level of the supply curve for loanable funds: income and wealth, time preferences, and consumption smoothing. When these factors change, the supply curve shifts.

## Income and Wealth

Imagine that a distant relative passes away and you inherit $20,000. What will you do with these unexpected funds? You might celebrate with a fancy meal and a shopping spree. But most of us would also save some of this newfound wealth. All else equal, people prefer to have more savings. Thus, increases in income generally produce increases in savings. If income declines, people save less. These changes shift the loanable funds supply curve.

The relationship between income and savings is true across the globe. As nations gain wealth, they save more.

## PRACTICE WHAT YOU KNOW

### Interest Rates and Quantity Supplied and Demanded: U.S. Interest Rates Have Fallen

In 1981, many interest rates in the United States were 15%, but the inflation rate was 10%. In 2012, many interest rates were less than 1%, and the inflation rate was 2%.

**Question:** What were the real interest rates in 1981 and 2012?

**Answer:** Using equation (9.1), we compute the real interest rate as:

$$\text{real interest rate} = \text{nominal interest rate} - \text{inflation rate}$$

For 1981, the real interest rate was: $15\% - 10\% = 5\%$

For 2012, the real interest rate was: $1\% - 2\% = -1\%$

**Question:** All else equal, how does the drop in interest rates between 1981 and 2012 affect the quantity of loanable funds supplied?

**Answer:** The quantity supplied decreases along the supply curve. Lower interest rates reduce the incentive to save.

---

Over the past 20 years, the increase in foreign savings has often made its way into the U.S. loanable funds market. For example, a businessman in Mumbai, India, may find himself with extra savings. He will probably put some into an Indian bank and some into Indian stocks and bonds. But there's a good chance he'll also channel some of his savings into the United States. Historically, U.S. financial markets have offered relatively greater returns than markets in other countries. In addition, the U.S. financial markets are often considered less risky than other global markets because of the size and relative robustness of the U.S. economy. Therefore, as global economies have grown, there has been an increase in savings in the United States.

The increase in foreign savings came at a good time for the United States because domestic savings began falling in the 1980s. Without the influx of foreign funds, U.S. firms would have had difficulty funding investment. Of course, there is no guarantee that foreign savings will continue to flow into the United States at the same rates. But as long as some foreign funds still enter the U.S. financial markets, their presence will ensure continued opportunities for domestic firms to borrow for investment.

## Time Preferences

Imagine that your parents promised you a cash reward for getting a good grade in economics. Does it matter if they pay immediately or wait until you graduate? Yes, it matters—you want the money as soon as you earn it. This is

The term **time preferences** refers to the fact that people prefer to receive goods and services sooner rather than later.

Do you care when a friend repays your loan?

not unusual. People always prefer to receive funds sooner than later, and the same applies to goods and services; economists call this general tendency *time preferences*. The term **time preferences** refers to the fact that people prefer to receive goods and services sooner rather than later. Because people have time preferences, someone must pay them to save. While time preferences are generally stable over time, if the rate of time preference in a society changes, the supply of loanable funds shifts.

While we all prefer sooner to later, some people have greater time preferences than others. Think of those with the strongest time preferences as being the least patient: they *strongly* prefer now to later. Someone with weaker time preferences has more patience. All else equal, people with stronger time preferences save less than people with weaker time preferences.

There are other ways that time preferences can be observed. For example, people with very strong time preferences may not even go to college, since the returns to getting a college education are not typically realized until years later. Time spent in college is time that could have been spent earning income. The fact that you are a college student demonstrates that you are more patient than some others who choose instead to work for more income now.

You'll be happy to know that there is a definite payoff to getting a college education. College graduates earn significantly more than high school graduates. Figure 9.5 shows median annual salary in the United States by educational attainment. Some college dropouts—for example, Mark Zuckerberg—earn millions of dollars a year. But the figure's data shows that the median worker with a basic college degree earns about $15,000 more a year than those who don't graduate from college. Patience pays off!

## FIGURE 9.5

**Median Annual Salary and Educational Attainment**

It takes patience, or relatively low time preferences, to stay in school. But annual earnings based on years of schooling shows that education pays off for most graduates.

*Source:* Bureau of Labor Statistics.

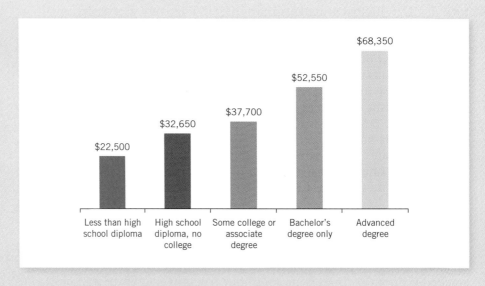

# Consumption Smoothing

Over the course of a typical lifetime, income varies drastically. Early in life, income levels are relatively low, but income generally rises through midlife. As people near retirement, their income levels fall again. Figure 9.6 illustrates a typical economic life cycle. Income (the green line) is highest in the middle "prime earning years" and lower at both the beginning and end of an individual's work life.

But no one wants to *consume* according to this pattern over their lifetime; most people prefer to consume in a more consistent way throughout their life. Thus, when we are young, we often borrow and spend more than we are earning. We may borrow for college education or to buy our first home. Also, when we retire, our income levels fall, but we don't want our spending to fall just as much. So we generally smooth our consumption over the course of our life. The blue line in Figure 9.6 represents a normal consumption pattern, which is smoother than the income pattern. This **consumption smoothing** is accomplished with the help of the loanable funds market.

Early in life, we spend more than we earn. Therefore, we have to borrow. In Figure 9.6, borrowing is the shaded vertical area between income and consumption in early life. Midlife, or the prime earning years, is the time to repay loans and save for retirement. During this period of the life cycle, the income line exceeds the consumption line. Later in life, when people retire and their income falls, they tend to live on their savings. Economists call this *dissaving*. **Dissaving** occurs when people withdraw funds from their previously accumulated savings. Figure 9.6 shows dissavings as the shaded vertical area between income and consumption in later life.

We can use the concept of consumption smoothing to clarify a situation that is currently affecting the U.S. economy. If we have a steady flow of

**Consumption smoothing** occurs when people borrow and save in order to smooth consumption over their lifetime.

**Dissaving** occurs when people withdraw funds from their previously accumulated savings.

**FIGURE 9.6**

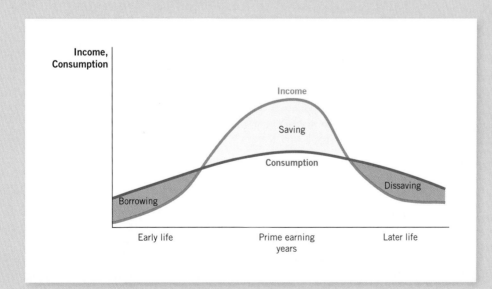

### Savings over a Typical Life Cycle

For most people, income is relatively low in early life, rises in their prime earning years, and falls in later life. But people generally prefer to smooth their consumption over the course of their life. This means that they borrow early in life for items like education and their first home; save during midlife when their income is highest; and finally, draw down savings when they retire.

# Time Preferences

### *Confessions of a Shopaholic*

This movie from 2009 follows a shopping junkie, Becky Bloomwood, who must come to terms with her exploding debt. Becky has very strong time preferences: she can't stop spending even though she owes almost $20,000 on her credit cards. When she finally realizes the mess she is in, she attends a Shopaholics Anonymous meeting. This is where the fun really begins.

Becky, like many other first-time visitors to the support group, is reluctant to tell her story. But after listening to others speak of their trials during the past week, the leader turns to Becky, who begins to tell her story. The pure joy she experiences while shopping is immediately obvious to the other members of the support group. As they listen to her describe the fantastic feeling she gets from making new purchases, they long to feel the same way. Her story is not as much about repentance as it is about the need to shop more. This creates a euphoric response from the group. After talking for a short time, Becky has convinced herself—and most of the group—to go on a shopping spree. She bolts from the meeting and races home to her apartment, where she keeps one last credit card in the freezer for emergencies. Gleefully, she takes the card and heads off to find something new to purchase.

This film conveys how easy it is to get into unmanageable debt and how hard it is to break the cycle. Do you know of any friends or relatives—maybe even you yourself—who carry a large amount

Economists would say that Becky has very strong time preferences.

of credit card debt? Can you imagine how many people in the entire United States might be in a similar situation? Now think about how those people prefer to borrow rather than save. This perspective helps us to see that in the nation's macroeconomy the desire to borrow, driven by time preferences, reduces the supply of loanable funds.

people moving into each life stage, the amount of savings in the economy is stable and there will be a steady supply in the market for loanable funds. But if a significant portion of the population leaves the prime earning years at the same time, overall savings will fall. As it turns out, this is the current situation in the United States because the baby boomers are now retiring from the labor force. The oldest members of this group reached retirement age in 2011. Over the next 10 to 15 years, U.S. workers will enter retirement in record numbers. This means an exit from the prime earning years and, consequently, much less savings. We'll come back to this issue in the last section of this chapter.

Figure 9.7 illustrates the effect on the supply of loanable funds when there are changes in income and wealth, time preferences, or consumption smoothing. The initial supply of loanable funds is represented by $S_1$. The supply of loanable funds increases to $S_2$ if there is a change that leads to an increase in savings at all levels of interest rates. For example, an increase in foreign income and wealth would increase the supply of savings. Similarly, if people's time preferences fell—if they became more patient—the supply of loanable funds would increase. Finally, if a relatively large portion of the population moves into midlife, when savings is highest, this would also increase savings from $S_1$ to $S_2$.

At other, times, however, the supply of loanable funds might decrease. For example, if income and wealth decline, people would save less across all interest rates. This is illustrated as a shift from $S_1$ to $S_3$ in Figure 9.6. Also, if time preferences increase, people would become more impatient, which would reduce the supply of loanable funds. Finally, if a relatively large population group moves out of their prime earning years and into retirement, the supply of loanable funds would decrease. This last example describes what is happening in the United States right now.

Table 9.3 summarizes our discussion of the factors that either increase or decrease the supply of loanable funds.

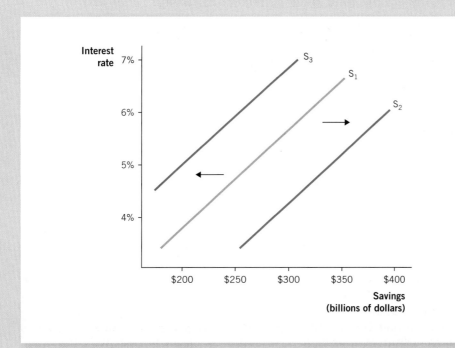

**FIGURE 9.7**

**Shifts in the Supply of Loanable Funds**

The supply of loanable funds shifts to the right when there are decreases in time preferences, increases in foreign income and wealth, and more people in midlife, when savings is highest. The supply of loanable funds shifts to the left when there are increases in time preferences, decreases in foreign income and wealth, and fewer people in midlife, when savings is highest.

| TABLE 9.3 | | |
|---|---|---|
| **Factors That Shift the Supply of Loanable Funds** | | |
| Factor | Direction of effect | Explanation |
| Income and wealth | • *Increases* in income and wealth *increase* the supply of loanable funds.<br>• *Decreases* in income and wealth *decrease* the supply of loanable funds. | Savings is more affordable when people have greater income and wealth. |
| Time preferences | • *Increases* in time preferences *decrease* the supply of loanable funds.<br>• Decreases in time preferences increase the supply of loanable funds. | Lower time preferences indicate that people are more patient and more likely to save for the future. |
| Consumption smoothing | • If *more* people are in midlife and their prime earning years, savings is *higher*.<br>• If *fewer* people are in midlife, savings is *lower*. | Income varies over the life cycle, but people generally like to smooth their consumption. |

## ECONOMICS IN THE REAL WORLD

### Why Is the Savings Rate in the United States Falling?

Are Americans becoming increasingly short-sighted? Many people believe that Americans' time preferences are indeed climbing, because savings rates have fallen significantly over the past few decades. Figure 9.8 shows the savings rate in the United States since 1960. The **savings rate** is personal saving as a portion of disposable (after-tax) income. As you can see, the U.S. savings rate fell consistently for almost 30 years, beginning in the early 1980s. In 1982, the savings rate was almost 11%. The decline continued until about 2005, when the savings rate bottomed out at just 1.5%. We are now in a position to consider possible causes. In particular, is this decline due to changes in income and wealth, time preferences, or consumption smoothing?

We can rule out a decline in income and wealth as a cause of the savings decline. In fact, the decline began and continued throughout the 1980s and 1990s, which were both decades of significant income growth. In addition, the savings rate increased during the Great Recession that began in late 2007. Second, we can rule out the idea that the savings rate declined as consumption smoothing occurred. After all, during the period of savings decline, the baby-boom population was a significant part of the labor force. Consumption smoothing would imply an increase in savings rates through the 1980s and 1990s, given that the baby boomers were working throughout this period.

Many people believe that savings have dropped because time preferences have risen. Perhaps you have heard older Americans talking about the impatience of today's younger workers. If today's working Americans are more

*The **savings rate** is personal saving as a portion of disposable (after-tax) income.*

focused on instant gratification, they save less. Is this really the cause of the savings decline? If so, why did it happen? Economists don't have consistent answers to these questions.

A closer look at the data indicates that there may be something else behind the decline in personal savings—it could just be a measurement issue. In reality, there are several alternative ways to *save* for the future, not all of which are counted in the official definition of "personal savings." For example, let's say you buy a house for $200,000 and the value of the house rises to $300,000 in just a few years. This means you now have gained $100,000 in personal wealth. The gain in the value of your house helps you prepare for the future just like increased savings

Is your generation too short-sighted?

would. But gains of this nature are not counted as personal savings. In addition to real estate gains, the gains from purchases of stocks and bonds are also not counted in personal savings.

Here is an alternative view of the recent trends. From 1980 to 2007, real estate and stock market values rose significantly. Recognizing this as an alternative path to future wealth, many people shifted their personal savings into these assets. The result is that personal savings rates, as officially measured, plummeted. Not convinced yet? Look what happened to personal savings rates in 2008 and 2009, as both real estate and stock prices tumbled: personal savings rates climbed to almost 6%.

Are today's Americans less patient than earlier generations? Perhaps. But given the way personal savings rates are measured, it is difficult to determine a clear answer to this question. ✳

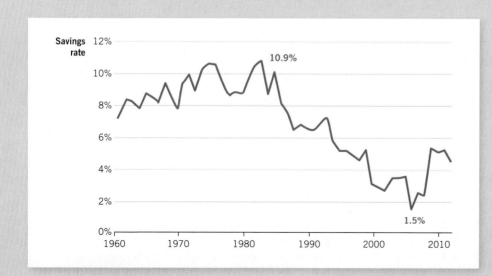

## FIGURE 9.8

**Savings Rate in the United States, 1960–2012**

In the United States, the savings rate (savings as a portion of disposable income) has fallen significantly over the past three decades. In 1982, the savings rate was 10.9%; but it fell to just 1.5% in 2005.

*Source:* U.S. Bureau of Economic Analysis.

# A Map of the Loanable Funds Market

The loanable funds market is really a picture of financial markets. Savers are the sellers in this market, while borrowers are the buyers. Firms borrow to fund investment in buildings, equipment, and inventory. Governments borrow to pay for public goods like roads, bridges, and national defense, in addition to wealth transfer programs. Every dollar borrowed requires a dollar saved, so we need savings to fund the private and public sector investments that help increase GDP in the future.

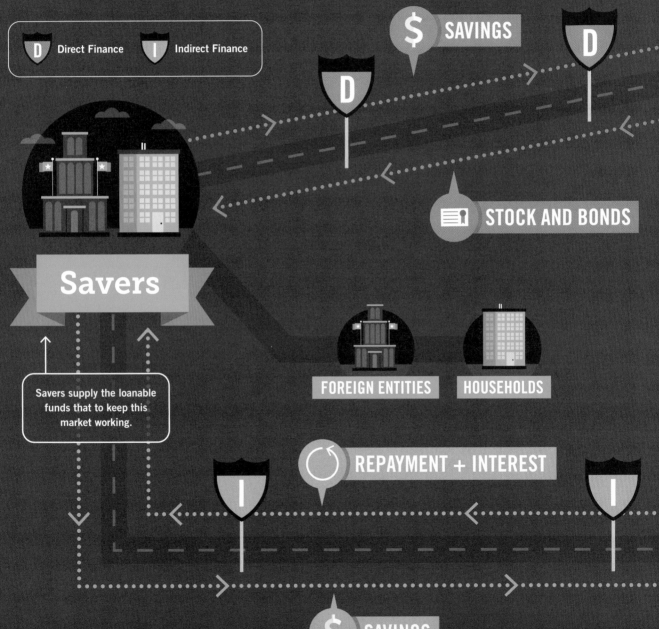

**D** Direct Finance  **I** Indirect Finance

**$ SAVINGS**

**D**

**D**

**STOCK AND BONDS**

**Savers**

Savers supply the loanable funds that to keep this market working.

**FOREIGN ENTITIES**  **HOUSEHOLDS**

**REPAYMENT + INTEREST**

**I**

**I**

**$ SAVINGS**

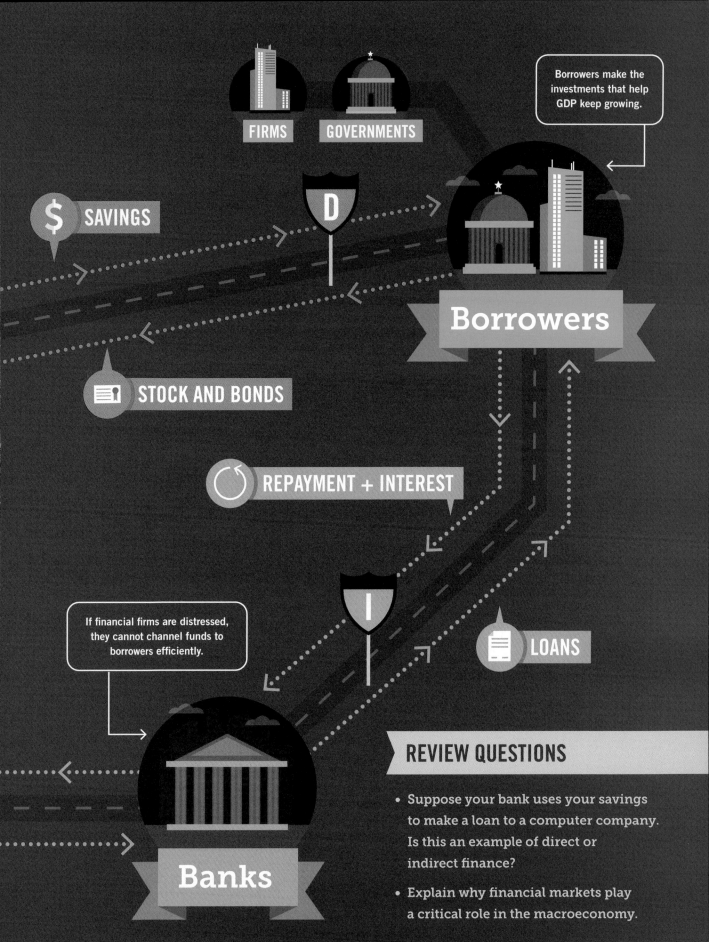

FIRMS

GOVERNMENTS

Borrowers make the investments that help GDP keep growing.

$ SAVINGS

D

Borrowers

STOCK AND BONDS

REPAYMENT + INTEREST

I

If financial firms are distressed, they cannot channel funds to borrowers efficiently.

LOANS

REVIEW QUESTIONS

• Suppose your bank uses your savings to make a loan to a computer company. Is this an example of direct or indirect finance?

• Explain why financial markets play a critical role in the macroeconomy.

Banks

## PRACTICE WHAT YOU KNOW

### Time Preferences: HIV in Developing Nations

The worldwide AIDS pandemic is an especially bad problem in developing nations, where infection rates can be extremely high. For example, in 2003, almost 40% of people age 15 to 49 in the nation of Botswana were living with HIV/AIDS, and life expectancy at birth was below 35 years. There are many terrible effects of a situation like this. For now, let's focus on how a pandemic affects people's time preferences.

**Question: How does a drop in life expectancy affect time preferences and the supply of loanable funds?**

**Answer:** With life expectancy plummeting to under 35 years, people are less likely to plan for the future. As time preferences increase, the supply of loanable funds goes down. Thus, when a nation is hit hard by a pandemic such as HIV/AIDS, one side effect is lower savings, which means a reduced supply of loanable funds—which in turn leads to lower economic output in the future.

*Source:* IndexMundi.com.

A man wears a T-shirt for AIDS awareness in Lagos, Nigeria. How does a pandemic affect the market for loanable funds?

# What Factors Shift the Demand for Loanable Funds?

To look at the demand side, we shift perspectives to those who borrow in the loanable funds market. As we have seen, the demand for loanable funds derives from the desire to invest or purchase capital goods that aid in future production. We know that the interest rate matters and that this relationship is reflected in the slope of the demand curve. We now turn to factors that cause shifts in the demand for loanable funds. We focus on two: the productivity of capital and investor confidence.

## Productivity of Capital

Consider a firm that is trying to decide whether to borrow for an investment. Perhaps your own firm is trying to decide whether to borrow to buy a new silk-screening machine, the SS-1000, for your college clothing business. This machine is capital, and its purchase counts as an investment. To determine whether you should take a loan, recall our rule: a firm should borrow to fund an investment only if the expected return is greater than the interest rate on the loan. Therefore, if the interest rate on the loan is 6%, you will borrow to buy the SS-1000 only if you expect to earn more than a 6% return from it.

Let's say that after crunching the numbers on expected costs and sales from the SS-1000, you estimate a return of just 4% from an investment in the SS-1000. You decide not to buy the new machine.

But then something changes. That something is the availability of the brand-new SS-2000. The SS-2000 is an improved machine that prints T-shirts at double the rate of the SS-1000. Given this new machine, which is slightly more expensive, you calculate that your expected return will be 7%, so you decide to take the loan and buy the machine. Thus, your demand for loanable funds has increased as a direct result of the availability of the new machine, which is twice as productive as the earlier machine.

What are the implications for the macroeconomy? Remember that firms borrow in order to finance capital purchases. Therefore, the level of demand for loans depends on the productivity of capital. Changes in capital productivity shift the demand for loanable funds. If capital is more productive, the demand for loans increases; if capital is less productive, the demand for loans decreases.

Productivity can change for a number of reasons. Consider the impact of the Internet. A connection to the Internet provides quick access to data and networking capabilities that people only dreamed about 20 years ago. The Internet also increases the productivity of computers, which are a major capital expense. Over the past 20 years, an increase in expected returns associated with the Internet has made investment in computer equipment (capital) more attractive. This means that investment in capital yields greater returns, which in turn increases the demand for loans. When capital is more productive, firms are more likely to borrow to finance purchases of this type of capital.

This screwdriver is a picture of capital . . .

. . . and this one represents an increase in capital productivity.

**Investor confidence** is a measure of what firms expect for future economic activity.

## Investor Confidence

The demand for loanable funds also depends on the beliefs or expectations of the investors at business firms. If a firm believes its sales will increase in the future, it invests more today to build for future sales. If, instead, it believes its future sales will fall, it invests less today. **Investor confidence** is a measure of what firms expect for future economic activity. If confidence is high, they are more likely to borrow for investment at any interest rate. Economist John Maynard Keynes referred to an investor's drive to action as "animal spirits," meaning that investment demand may not even be based on rational decisions or real factors in the economy.

Figure 9.9 illustrates shifts in the demand for loanable funds. If capital productivity increases, demand for investment increases from $D_1$ to $D_2$—that is, demand is higher across all interest rates. Similarly, if investor confidence rises, demand for loanable funds increases from $D_1$ to $D_2$. In contrast, if capital productivity or investor confidence falls, the demand for loanable funds falls from $D_1$ to $D_3$.

## FIGURE 9.9

**Shifts in the Demand for Loanable Funds**

Increases in capital productivity and investor confidence lead to an increase in the demand for loanable funds at all interest rates, shifting demand from $D_1$ to $D_2$. Decreases in capital productivity and investor confidence decrease the demand for loanable funds from $D_1$ to $D_3$.

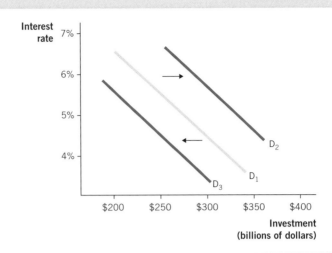

---

## PRACTICE WHAT YOU KNOW

### Demand for Loanable Funds: SpongeBob and Loanable Funds

**Question: Which of the following changes would affect the demand for loanable funds, and how?**

**a.** Research shows that watching the cartoon *SpongeBob SquarePants* can shorten a child's attention span. Now assume that an entire generation of children grows up watching this cartoon and becomes less patient, or their time preferences increase.

**b.** A technological advance leads to greater capital productivity.

**c.** The interest rate falls.

How dangerous is this sponge?

**Answers:**

**a.** This factor would not affect the demand for loanable funds, but it would affect the supply of loanable funds. Less patience means that time preferences increase and the supply of loanable funds declines.

**b.** Yes, this increases the demand for loanable funds.

**c.** The falling interest rate would lead to a movement along the demand curve, rather than a shift in loanable funds. This can be caused by an increase in the supply of loanable funds.

# How Do We Apply the Loanable Funds Market Model?

We are now ready to begin using the loanable funds market to study applications we see in the real world. First, we consider the implications of equilibrium in this market. After that, we examine past and future views of the U.S. loanable funds market.

## Equilibrium

Equilibrium in the loanable funds market occurs at the interest rate where the plans of savers match the plans of borrowers—that is, where quantity supplied equals quantity demanded. In Figure 9.10, this occurs at an interest rate of 5%, where savers are willing to save $250 billion and borrowers desire $250 billion in loans (in other words, they seek to invest $250 billion). At interest rates above 5%, the quantity of loanable funds supplied exceeds the quantity demanded, and this imbalance leads to downward pressure on the interest rate. At interest rates below 5%, the quantity demanded exceeds the quantity supplied, and this imbalance leads to upward pressure on interest rates.

The loanable funds market, like other markets, naturally tends to move toward equilibrium, where supply is equal to demand. This equilibrium condition reinforces a key relationship between savings and investment. Equilibrium occurs when:

$$Savings = Investment$$

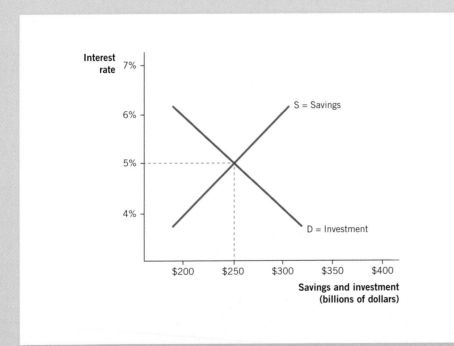

**FIGURE 9.10**

**Equilibrium in the Market for Loanable Funds**

Equilibrium in the loanable funds market occurs where supply equals demand, at an interest rate of 5% and a quantity of $250 billion. Because investment is limited by savings, exactly $250 billion is saved and $250 billion is invested.

In Figure 9.10, households and foreign entities have decided to save a combined total of $250 billion at an interest rate of 5%. Subsequently, firms borrow this $250 billion for investment. Thus, dollars that are saved make their way into the loanable funds market and are then channeled to firms for investment purposes.

Equilibrium also helps to clarify an important principle we'll return to often in this text. Investment requires saving because:

*Every dollar borrowed requires a dollar saved.*

If an economy is to grow over time, someone has to invest in capital that helps to produce more in the future. But investment requires savings. Without savings, the economy cannot grow.

Equilibrium is a helpful starting point for understanding how the loanable funds market functions. But in the real world, financial market conditions change frequently. We can account for these changes in our model by using shifts in the supply and demand curves. Let's consider two examples: a decline in investor confidence and a decrease in the supply of loanable funds.

## A Decline in Investor Confidence

When the overall economy slows, firms often reduce investment since they expect reduced sales in future periods; this move reflects a decline in investor confidence. This happened recently in the United States during the Great

## FIGURE 9.11

**A Decline in Investment Demand**

(a) When decision-makers at firms lose confidence in the future direction of the economy, investment demand declines and lower investment results. (b) In the United States, real investment declined during both recessions that occurred between 2000 and 2012.

*Source:* Panel (b): U.S. Bureau of Economic Analysis.

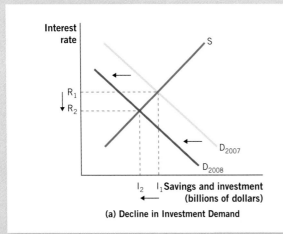

(a) Decline in Investment Demand

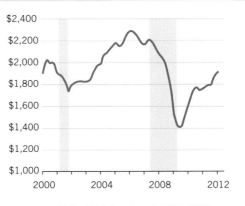

(b) Real U.S. Investment, 2000–2012

Recession that began at the end of 2007. Panel (a) of Figure 9.11 shows how a decline in investor confidence affects the loanable funds market. When investment demand declines (shown in the figure as the change between $D_{2007}$ and $D_{2008}$), the loanable funds model predicts lower interest rates (a drop from $R_1$ to $R_2$) and a lower equilibrium level of investment (a drop from $I_1$ to $I_2$). Panel (b) of Figure 9.11 shows that investment fell during both recessions (the blue-shaded bars) in the years shown. During the Great Recession, real investment fell from $2.2 trillion to just $1.4 trillion—a 60% drop in less than two years.

## A Decrease in the Supply of Loanable Funds

Let's now return to the potential effects of the baby boomers' retirement over the next 10 to 15 years. As we saw in the discussion of consumption smoothing, this will likely lead to a decrease in the supply of loanable funds in the United States. Figure 9.12 illustrates this kind of change. The curve labeled $S_{2015}$ represents the supply of loanable funds in 2015. But as the baby boomers retire, supply may shift back to $S_{2025}$ one decade later.

All else equal, this shift means lower investment (in the figure, a drop from $I_1$ to $I_2$) and lower GDP growth going forward. However, many other factors may change over the next few years to increase savings in the United States. For example, as other nations grow, foreigners may continue to increase their savings in the United States. Or perhaps savings rates in the United States will continue their recent rise. These increases could offset the effects of the baby boomers' retirement and keep interest rates low for U.S. firms.

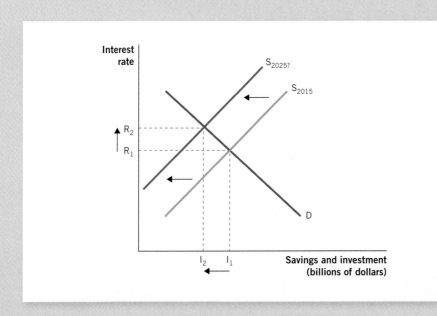

## FIGURE 9.12

**The Possible Future of the U.S. Loanable Funds Market**

As baby boomers retire and draw down their savings, supply in the loanable funds market will decrease. Without increases in savings from other sources, we will see higher interest rates and lower levels of investment.

# PRACTICE WHAT YOU KNOW

## Working with the Loanable Funds Model: Foreign Savings in the United States

Recently, the economies of China and India have begun to grow very rapidly. This increases the income and wealth of their citizens. In turn, these citizens increase their savings in their country and also in the United States.

How does foreign economic growth affect the U.S. loanable funds market?

**Question:** When foreign savings enter the U.S. loanable funds market, which curve is affected—supply or demand? How is this curve affected?

**Answer:** The supply of loanable funds increases as savings increase.

**Question:** How would you graph the U.S. loanable funds market both before and after the increase in foreign savings?

**Answer:**

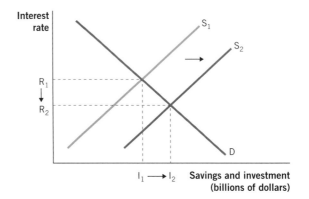

Before the increase in foreign savings, supply is designated as $S_1$ and demand as D. These imply interest rate $R_1$ and savings/investment amount $I_1$. When new foreign savings enter the market, supply increases to $S_2$, which decreases the interest rate to $R_2$ and increases the savings/investment amount to $I_2$.

**Question:** How does the change in foreign savings affect both investment and future output in the United States?

**Answer:** When the interest rate falls, the quantity of investment increases. Firms can afford to borrow more to build and expand their businesses. This increase in investment means that future output, or GDP, will be higher in the United States.

# Conclusion

We began this chapter with the misconception that interest rates are set by the government. To be sure, the government influences interest rates, a topic we'll discuss further in Chapter 17. But interest rates are actually set in the market through the interaction of supply and demand. The discussion in this chapter has provided the foundation we need to discuss interest rates and financial markets further.

In macroeconomics, few topics are more important than investment. And investment is the result of equilibrium in the market for loanable funds. Savers supply the funds that support loans; borrowers are investors who demand the loans. Equilibrium determines the quantity of investment and the interest rate in an economy.

In the next chapter, we extend our analysis of the market for loanable funds by looking at other methods for borrowing and lending. These include stocks, bonds, and other financial securities.

## ANSWERING THE BIG QUESTIONS

### What is the loanable funds market?

* The loanable funds market connects savers with borrowers.
* Savers are suppliers of loanable funds, and they earn interest as a reward for saving.
* Borrowers are the buyers of loanable funds, and they pay interest as the cost of borrowing.

### What factors shift the supply of loanable funds?

* Changes in income and wealth shift the supply of loanable funds.
* Changes in time preferences also affect the supply of loanable funds.
* Consumption smoothing is another factor that shifts the loanable funds supply.

### What factors shift the demand for loanable funds?

* Capital productivity is the main determinant of the demand for loanable funds.
* Investor confidence also affects the demand for loanable funds.

### How do we apply the loanable funds market model?

* We can use the loanable funds market model to examine real-world changes in both supply and demand for loanable funds.
* The loanable funds model also clarifies the important implication that every dollar borrowed requires a dollar saved.

ECONOMICS FOR LIFE

# Compound Interest: When Should You Start Saving for Retirement?

When you graduate from college, get a job, and start earning a steady income, you'll have several choices to make. Should you buy or lease a car? Should you buy or rent a home? Should you donate money or time to charity? Regardless of your decisions on issues such as these, you should always make room in your budget for savings.

We know that everyone has positive time preferences, so all else equal, you probably would rather consume now than later. But all else is not equal. That is, a little less consumption now will lead to a lot more consumption later, even under assumptions of very reasonable interest rates. The return to savings is like an exponential function: the longer you save, the greater your return to savings, even at a constant interest rate. The reason is based on compound interest, which implies that the interest you earn becomes savings—which also bears interest. Let's see how this works.

Consider two people who choose alternate paths. Dirk understands the power of compound interest and chooses to start saving $100 per month when he is 25 years old. Lee has stronger time preferences and decides to wait until age 45 to start saving $100 per month. If both Dirk and Lee work until they are 65 years old, Dirk saves for 40 years and Lee saves for 20.

You might guess that Dirk will end up with twice as much in his retirement account, since he saved twice as long. But you'd be wrong. It turns out that Lee's retirement savings will increase to $53,988. That's not too bad, considering he saved just $100 per month over 20 years, or 240 months—the interest payments certainly helped. But what about Dirk? His retirement savings will increase to $281,767! That's more than five times the size of Lee's, and Dirk only made twice as many payments.

What did we assume to get these returns? We assumed a 7% interest rate, which is the long-run historical real rate of return on a diversified stock portfolio. But any interest rate would illustrate the key point here: compound interest increases the value of your savings exponentially. So even with very strong time preferences, it makes sense to start saving early.

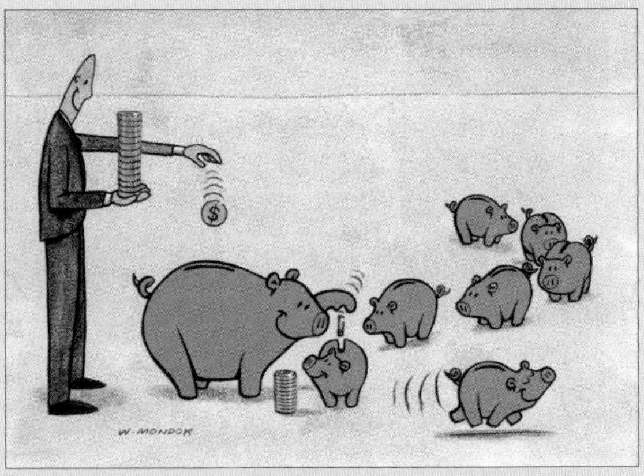

Compound interest produces more interest income.

The graph illustrates the returns to saving $100 per month at an average annual return of 7% until retirement. The only difference is when you start saving. Notice that as you move along the horizontal axis, for each additional five years' worth of savings the amount by which total savings grows will increase.

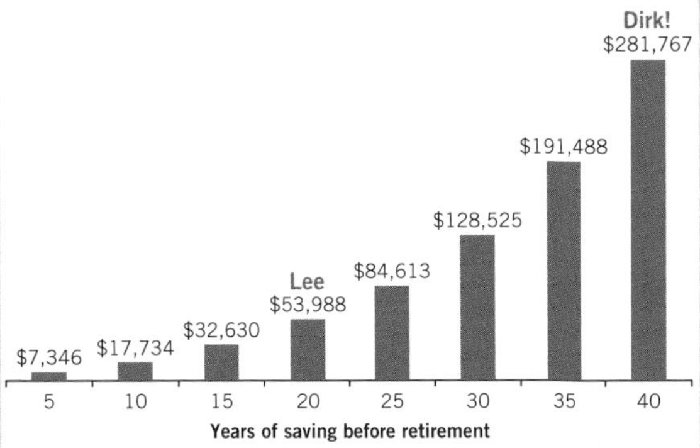

## CONCEPTS YOU SHOULD KNOW

consumption smoothing (p. 279)   investor confidence (p. 286)   savings rate (p. 282)
dissaving (p. 279)               loanable funds market (p. 270)  time preferences (p. 278)
fisher equation (p. 275)         nominal interest rate (p. 274)
interest rate (p. 272)           real interest rate (p. 274)

## QUESTIONS FOR REVIEW

1. Explain the importance of the loanable funds market to basic GDP in a macroeconomy.

2. All else equal, what does a lower interest rate mean for firms? What does a lower interest rate mean for savers?

3. Consider two alternatives to prepare for retirement: (1) saving in a bank where your funds earn interest, and (2) buying fine art that rises in value over time. Each grows your retirement account over time.

   a. If the rates of return on fine art purchases fall, how would you expect the allocation of retirement funds to change across the macroeconomy?

   b. If the national savings rate is based only on the first option (saving in a bank), then what happens to the national savings rate when the allocation of retirement funds shifts as you describe in your response to part (a)?

4. List the factors that affect the supply side of the loanable funds market. Which factor(s) determine the slope of the supply curve? Which factor(s) affect the level of the curve?

5. List the factors that affect the demand side of the loanable funds market. Which factor(s) determine the slope of the demand curve? Which factor(s) impact the level of the curve?

6. Why does inflation have a positive effect on nominal interest rates?

## STUDY PROBLEMS (✳ *solved at the end of the section*)

1. Assume that the residents of a nation become more patient (experience a reduction in their time preferences).

   a. What will happen to the interest rate in that nation? What will happen to the equilibrium level of investment in that nation? Explain your answers.

   b. In the long run, how will the lower time preferences affect the levels of capital and income growth in that nation?

2. Many interest rates in the United States recently fell. Which of the following factors could have been the cause?

   a. increase in the demand for loanable funds
   b. decrease in the demand for loanable funds
   c. increase in the supply of loanable funds
   d. decrease in the supply of loanable funds

3. Use the Fisher equation to fill in the blanks in the following table:

| Inflation rate | Real interest rate | Nominal interest rate |
| --- | --- | --- |
| _____ | 2% | 7% |
| _____ | 0% | 7% |
| 2% | _____ | 6% |
| 9% | _____ | 6% |
| 2% | 2% | _____ |
| 10% | 2% | _____ |

✳ 4. Consider two hypothetical nations: Wahooland and Wildcat Island. Initially, these nations are identical in every way. In particular, they are the same with regard to population size and age, income and wealth, and time preferences.

They also have the same interest rates, saving, and investment.

a. Suddenly, in the year 2015, the interest rate in Wahooland rises. After some investigating, economists determine that nothing has happened to the supply of loanable funds. Therefore, what are the possible reasons for this rise in interest rates in Wahooland?

b. Given your answer to part (a), what can you say about the level of investment in Wahooland relative to that in Wildcat Island in 2015? What can you say about future income levels in Wahooland versus Wildcat Island?

c. Often, we think of lower interest rates as always being preferable to higher interest rates. What has this question taught us about that idea?

✳ 5. Some people have proposed an increase in retirement ages for Americans. Consider the effects of this proposed new policy.

a. Show how the change would affect supply and demand in the market for loanable funds.

b. How would this change affect the equilibrium interest rate and investment?

c. In the long run, how would this affect real GDP in the United States?

# SOLVED PROBLEMS

**4. a.** If supply does not change, the rise in interest rates must be due to a change in demand. If rates went up, then demand must have increased. An increase in the demand for loanable funds occurs from one or both of the following: (1) an increase in the productivity of capital; (2) an increase in investor confidence.

**b.** Investment will be higher in Wahooland than in Wildcat Island. Future GDP will be higher in Wahooland, and this means that income will be higher.

**c.** Higher interest rates could be caused by very productive capital. Thus, an innovative nation that tends to have new productive ideas and then high capital productivity might also have higher interest rates. These interest rates can indicate very high returns to capital investment, which is certainly not bad for an economy.

**5. a.** The key is to examine how the policy change would affect savings through people's preferences for consumption smoothing. If Americans start working longer, this would delay the dissaving period in their life and increase their savings. So supply would increase (shift outward). Demand would not change.

**b.** The equilibrium interest rate would fall, and investment would increase.

**c.** Real GDP would be greater, all else equal, due to the increase in investment. Basically, the new savings would become investment in capital. Thus, in the future there would be more tools for production in the United States, and output would be higher.

# Financial Markets and Securities

**Borrowing from foreign countries is harmful to the economy.**

Many people are concerned that foreign nations own significant amounts of U.S. national debt. China, in particular, owns more U.S. debt than any other foreign nation. The worry is that since we owe them money, these nations can control us. But think of the situation in terms of loanable funds. From this perspective, the Chinese are lenders who are sending their savings into the United States. These Chinese savings keep our interest rates lower than they would otherwise be. This helps both our government and private firms in the United States.

**MIS CONCEPTION**

The financial vehicles that we discuss in this chapter are necessary for economic growth and development. These include stocks, bonds, home mortgages, and other financial instruments. Even though we are covering financial topics, macroeconomics is the common thread that weaves throughout these topics—each of these helps you gain a more detailed understanding of the factors that impact the overall economy. We can minimize the negative effects of recessions and experience economic growth only when financial markets function efficiently. When there are problems in financial markets, economic growth is impossible.

Would we ever have to sell U.S. landmarks to China to help pay the debt?

# BIG QUESTIONS

* How do financial markets help the economy?
* What are the key financial tools for the macroeconomy?

## How Do Financial Markets Help the Economy?

In financial markets, borrowers and lenders come together. The buyers (or borrowers) in financial markets are firms and governments in search of funds to undertake their daily operations. The sellers (or lenders) are savers looking for opportunities to earn a return on their savings. In Chapter 9, we introduced the loanable funds market as a way of thinking about financial markets through the lens of supply and demand. In this chapter, we present an *institutional* view of financial markets. That is, we consider what types of firms operate in the middle of financial markets and what types of tools they use to facilitate the exchanges between savers and borrowers.

The major players in the middle of financial markets are called *financial intermediaries*. **Financial intermediaries** are firms that help to channel funds from savers to borrowers. *Banks* are one example of a financial intermediary. **Banks** are private firms that accept deposits and extend loans. Banks and other financial intermediaries are important for the macroeconomy because they are at the center of financial markets: they help connect borrowers with savers.

**Financial intermediaries** are firms that help to channel funds from savers to borrowers.

**Banks** are private firms that accept deposits and extend loans.

### Direct and Indirect Financing

When firms seek funding to pay for resources for production, they go to the loanable funds market. There are two different paths through the loanable funds market: *indirect* and *direct finance*. **Indirect finance** occurs when savers lend funds to financial intermediaries, which then loan these funds to borrowers. In this case, savers are indirectly financing the investments of firms.

**Direct finance** occurs when borrowers go directly to savers for funds. If you want a loan to start or expand a small business, you might go to a bank. But large established firms can skip financial intermediaries and go directly to the lenders when they need funds.

**Indirect finance** occurs when savers deposit funds into banks, which then loan these funds to borrowers.

**Direct finance** occurs when borrowers go directly to savers for funds.

Figure 10.1 shows the two alternate routes through the loanable funds market. The top half illustrates indirect finance, in which banks and other financial intermediaries facilitate the exchanges between lenders (that is, savers) and borrowers. If you have a savings or checking account at a bank, you participate in the loanable funds market as a lender. Banks package together the savings of many depositors like you to extend loans. The bottom half of Figure 10.1 illustrates direct finance, in which borrowers bypass financial intermediaries and go directly to lenders for funds.

To undertake direct finance, firms need a contract that specifies the terms and conditions of the loan. These contracts usually take the form of a *security*. A **security** is a tradable contract that entitles its owner to certain rights. For example, a **bond** is a security that represents a debt to be paid. If you own a bond, it means that someone owes you money—it is a formal IOU. Bonds are a tool of direct finance because they enable borrowers to go directly to savers for funds. If a firm sells a bond to an individual, it is borrowing funds that will be repaid at a later date. For example, in 2012 the Target Corporation had $14.4 billion in bonds outstanding. This means that the Target Corporation owed $14.4 billion to the owners of those bonds.

A **security** is a tradable contract that entitles its owner to certain rights.

A **bond** is a security that represents a debt to be paid.

## The Importance of Financial Markets

Financial markets play a vital role in the macroeconomy. Macroeconomic growth is based on the production of GDP across the economy. This production comes from individual firms such as cupcake shops, department stores, computer producers, and airplane manufacturers. But these firms need funding to build and buy the resources they use to produce their goods and services. These funds come from financial markets.

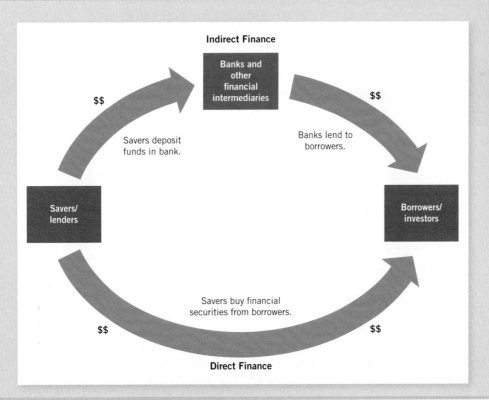

### FIGURE 10.1

**Direct versus Indirect Finance**

Funds make their way through the loanable funds market through two distinct paths. Indirect finance occurs when savers and borrowers utilize banks or other financial intermediaries. Alternatively, direct finance occurs when borrowers go directly to savers for their funds.

Consider what happens when financial markets break down. In 2007, several U.S. financial institutions began faltering. In September 2008, Lehman Brothers, a financial intermediary with over $600 billion in assets, actually went bankrupt. As a result, financial intermediaries all over the world became less inclined to extend loans. Since firms found it more difficult to borrow, economic contraction was inevitable. This contraction was the Great Recession that lasted through mid-2009.

## ECONOMICS IN THE REAL WORLD

### Why Bail Out the Big Rich Banks?

After the Lehman Brothers bankruptcy, it appeared there might be a domino effect that would lead to the collapse of many large banks. To avoid this potential disaster, the U.S. government implemented the Troubled Asset Relief Program—which came to be known as TARP—in October 2008. The TARP program allocated $700 billion to help keep banks from failing. The money was used to aid banks that had made bad loans.

Do America's wealthiest banks really need taxpayer-funded bailouts?

This program was very controversial from the beginning. On the one hand, the government was clearly bailing out big banks after many had made poor business decisions. It didn't seem right for the government to use taxpayer funds to help banks that seemed to contribute to the recession, especially since most people in the general population were still struggling financially.

But we can also make an argument in favor of the TARP program. Think of financial intermediaries as the bridge to future GDP. When the bridge is strong and safe, savers can lend to borrowers and then firms can invest in future GDP. But if the bridge collapses, output grinds to a halt. If firms aren't producing, they certainly don't need workers. GDP falls and unemployment rises. That's how important the bridge is.

Economists are not in complete agreement about the need for the TARP program; some still feel that it was misguided. But economists do agree on the necessity of healthy financial institutions. ✳

# What Are the Key Financial Tools for the Macroeconomy?

In this section, we begin exploring the many tools used in financial markets to help fund investment. We focus on tools that matter for the macroeconomy, including bonds, stocks, Treasury securities, home mortgages, and private-sector securities created by the process of securitization. We start with bonds.

## PRACTICE WHAT YOU KNOW

### Direct versus Indirect Finance: Which Is It?

Your friend Krista wants to open a cupcake shop. She needs to buy many resources before she can sell cupcakes and earn revenue. She is uncertain as to whether she should use direct or indirect financing.

These are some of the resources necessary to produce Lemon Bliss cupcakes.

**Question:** For each of the following alternatives, is the financing considered direct or indirect?

**a.** Krista borrows money from a friend.

**b.** Krista takes a loan from her small local bank.

**c.** Krista arranges a loan from a large national bank.

**d.** Krista issues bonds and sells them to people in her neighborhood.

**Answers:**

**a.** This is direct finance: Krista, the borrower, goes directly to the lender without the aid of a financial intermediary.

**b.** This is indirect finance: the bank makes the loan to Krista from the funds of various savers.

**c.** This is also indirect finance; the size of the bank does not matter.

**d.** This is direct finance: Krista goes directly to the lenders. It doesn't matter if the bonds are sold to people she happens to know.

## Bonds

Firms issue several types of securities to raise funds, but we can view them all as variations of a basic corporate bond.

Let's say your friend Kara wants to open a new website design business. But first she needs a loan to buy computers and software. Initially, Kara goes to a bank for a loan, but it turns her away since her company is new and viewed as very risky. So Kara comes to you and asks for a one-year loan. You know Kara well, so you agree to loan her some money with the understanding that she will repay the funds plus interest exactly one year later.

To formalize your agreement, you decide to draw up an IOU contract like the one presented in Figure 10.2. This is the contract you sign with your friend, Kara Alexis. When you "buy" this contract from Kara, you are lending her funds with the promise that she'll pay you $10,000 in one year. The contract is essentially the same as a corporate or government bond, and it serves the same purpose. This is an example of direct finance, with the borrower going directly to the lender.

# Direct Finance

### *Boiler Room*

This movie, a drama from 2000, starts off as a potential success story for the main character, Seth Davis, who is played by Giovanni Ribisi. Davis is a college dropout who manages to land a job with an investment firm called J.T. Marlin. Davis's job at Marlin is to sell securities. Davis is right in the middle of direct finance: firms come to Marlin so that Davis can sell their securities to lenders.

Unfortunately, it turns out that Marlin is selling securities for firms that don't exist. Marlin is essentially stealing from lenders, rather than channeling the funds to actual firms. When Davis figures this out, the action in the movie really heats up. The FBI has been tracking the firm for a period of time. The company is actually a brokerage firm that runs a scheme known as a "pump and dump," using its brokers to create artificial demand in the stock of expired or fake companies. When the firm is done pumping the stock up, the investors have no one in the market to sell their shares to, and the price of the stock crashes.

When the FBI catches Seth in the scheme, they instruct him to return to work the next day so that

Davis finds himself caught in a web of dishonest direct finance.

they can set up a sting to bring the entire operation down. Seth is granted immunity as long as he follows the FBI's directions. As the sting takes place, we see Seth leaving the building as several police cars and prison buses speed into the parking lot. The FBI agents emerge, ready to raid the building. Direct finance plays an important role in the macroeconomy, so it is very dangerous to tamper with it.

---

The **maturity date** of a bond is the date on which the loan repayment is due.

**Face value**, or **par value** ($p_m$), of a bond is the value of the bond at maturity—the amount due at repayment.

Like any bond, your contract contains three important pieces of information: the name of the borrower, the repayment date, and the amount due at repayment. In this example, the name of the borrower is Kara Alexis; the repayment date is February 20, 2015. The date on which the loan repayment is due is the **maturity date**. Finally, every bond contract also specifies the *face value*, or *par value*, of the bond. The **face value** ($p_m$), or **par value**, of the bond is the value of the bond at maturity—the amount due at repayment. For notation purposes, we'll call the face value $p_m$ since it is the price, or value, of the bond at maturity.

Perhaps you noticed in Figure 10.2 that we gave the face value of the bond, but not the amount of the initial loan. In fact, you and Kara must come to an agreement about how much you will loan her. But with a bond agreement, the face value is typically set at a round number like $10,000. When you and Kara settle on the initial loan amount, you are agreeing to the dollar price of the bond (p). The price of the bond is the original dollar amount of the loan. For example, if you agree on a price of $8,000 for Kara's bond, that is the amount you loan her. From your perspective, you loan her $8,000 today for the promise that she'll pay you $10,000 in one year. From Kara's perspec-

**FIGURE 10.2**

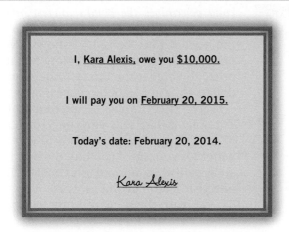

**A Basic Bond Security**
A simple IOU contract between two friends is like a bond. It specifies three things: (1) the name of the borrower (here, Kara Alexis); (2) the repayment date (February 20, 2015); (3) the amount due at repayment ($10,000).

tive, she now has $8,000 she can use to buy computers and software for her website design business, and she can begin producing GDP. But in one year she has to repay $10,000.

That's how a basic bond security works. Many bonds also include *coupons* that specify periodic interest payments to the bond owner. That distinction is not important for our purposes, so we focus on bonds that entail a single payment when the bond matures.

We now build on this foundation by discussing how interest rates relate to bond prices and how default risk affects the price of a bond.

### The Bond Dollar Price and Interest Rate

In the discussion above, we described Kara's bond in dollar prices. But loan prices are generally quoted in interest rates. Therefore, we need to consider how the dollar price (p) is related to the interest rate (R) of a bond. To determine the interest rate on this bond, we have to find the rate of return on the dollars that are loaned. For example, you "buy" Kara's bond for $8,000, and one year later the bond is worth $10,000. In percentage terms, the value of the bond increased by 25 percent. Thus, the rate of return, or interest rate, is computed as a growth rate, where the price of the bond is growing from its initial value ($p_0$):

$$\text{interest rate} = R = \frac{\text{face value} - \text{initial price}}{\text{initial price}} = \frac{p_m - p_o}{p_o} \qquad \text{(Equation 10.1)}$$

If the price of the bond is $8,000, the interest rate is computed as:

$$R = \frac{p_m - p_o}{p_o} = \frac{\$10,000 - \$8,000}{\$8,000} = 25\%$$

We used growth rates when we discussed GDP growth and inflation. Here, the interest rate is computed as a growth rate; it is the rate of growth of the original funds invested.

---

**Inside the bond (Figure 10.2 note):**

I, Kara Alexis, owe you $10,000.

I will pay you on February 20, 2015.

Today's date: February 20, 2014.

Kara Alexis

## TABLE 10.1

**Dollar Price and Interest Rate for a $10,000 One-Year Bond**

| Dollar price ($p_0$) | Interest rate (R) |
|---|---|
| $9,000 | 11% |
| $8,000 | 25% |
| $7,500 | 33% |
| $5,000 | 100% |

With bonds, the face value is fixed—it is printed on the front of the bond. Thus, *the dollar price of a bond determines the bond's interest rate.* If you know the dollar price of a given bond, you can determine the interest rate. Table 10.1 shows several alternative prices for a $10,000 bond. Notice that the lower the price, the higher the interest rate, since it takes fewer dollars to earn $10,000 one year later.

Each price implies a different interest rate. For example, if Kara sells you the $10,000 bond for only $7,500, the interest rate rises to 33%. This is much better for you, since you buy the bond for $7,500 and are repaid that amount plus $2,500 in interest only one year later. But this is worse for Kara because she is getting just $7,500 this year, with the same promise to repay you $10,000 next year.

Notice that as the price of the bond drops, the interest rate on the bond rises. If the bond price drops to $5,000, the interest rate climbs to 100%. This relationship holds by definition: *the dollar price and interest rate of a bond have an inverse relationship.*

In Chapter 9, we saw that the interest rate on a loan is the cost of borrowing and the reward for saving. Higher interest rates (lower dollar prices) hurt borrowers and help lenders. As a lender, you want to buy bonds for the lowest price possible because you want the highest possible interest rate on your savings. The borrower wants to sell her bonds for the highest price possible so that she can pay the lowest possible interest rate.

A primary factor in determining the interest rate on bonds is the default risk of the borrower, a topic to which we now turn.

## FIGURE 10.3

**Two Possible Outcomes with a Bond**

With a bond, both the maturity date and the face value are certain. Thus, there are only two possible outcomes if a bond owner holds the bond until maturity: either the borrower will pay the face value, or she will default. Because these are the only two possible outcomes, default risk is the primary concern of a bond owner.

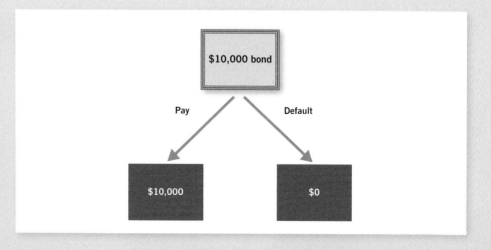

## Default Risk

Some financial transactions are very complex and potentially lead to many different outcomes. But bonds are fairly straightforward. If the bond owner holds the bond until maturity, there are two basic outcomes: the borrower pays the maturity value of the bond, or the borrower defaults on the loan. These possibilities are illustrated in Figure 10.3. For the bond owner, then, the risk of default is the primary concern. **Default risk** is the risk that the borrower will not pay the face value of the bond on the maturity date.

All else equal, the greater the default risk, the lower the price of a bond. Consider Kara's bond that she is selling to finance her startup website design company. If you really trust Kara and believe that her business will succeed, you might buy her $10,000 bond for $9,500. At this price, she promises to pay you about 5.25% interest for the use of your funds for a year. However, if you are skeptical about either Kara's integrity or the prospects for her business success, you may be willing to pay only $8,000 for the bond. At this price, she will pay 25% interest for the loan instead. This scenario illustrates an important bond price principle: *bond interest rates rise with default risk*.

Consider bonds offered by the Target Corporation. Target is a large company with many capital investments. As we said previously, the Target Corporation had $14.4 billion in bonds outstanding in 2012. This means that there is a significant market for Target bonds. Let's imagine hypothetical supply and demand for one-year $100,000 Target bonds, illustrated in Figure 10.4. Initially, with the demand curve at $D_1$ and supply at S, the equilibrium price is $98,000.

Now let's assume that something negative happens to the future prospects of Target's business. Perhaps Walmart attracts customers away from Target. This news reduces the probability that Target will pay off its bonds as they mature; in other words, it increases Target's default risk. As such, the demand for Target bonds declines from $D_1$ to $D_2$. As demand declines, the market price of Target bonds falls from $98,000 to $97,000, which means that the interest rate rises (since the dollar price and interest rate on a bond always move

**Default risk**
is the risk that the borrower will not pay the face value of a bond on the maturity date.

## FIGURE 10.4

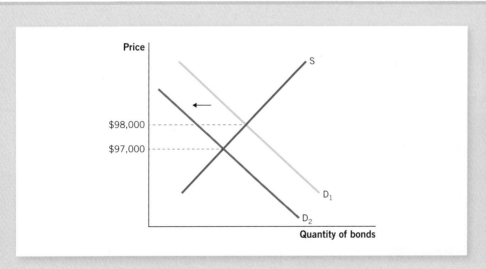

### How Increased Default Risk Affects the Market for $100,000 Target Bonds

The initial price in the market for Target bonds is $98,000. But an increase in default risk reduces the demand for Target bonds, resulting in a lower price and a higher interest rate. This outcome drives up the borrowing costs for Target.

in opposite directions). As a result, we can generalize to say that increases in default risk (1) cause a drop in the price that firms can charge for their bonds and (2) cause an increase in their interest rates.

## Bond Ratings

Default risk is important to bond holders, and it helps to determine the price of the bond. But typical individuals have difficulty judging the default risk of any one company, let alone the thousands of firms that sell bonds in a developed economy. To address this problem, private rating agencies evaluate and then grade the default risk of borrowing entities. They give a grade that reflects the likelihood of default. Three ratings agencies are particularly prominent in the United States: Moody's, Standard and Poor's, and Fitch. The ratings systems are similar for all three firms, so we'll choose Standard and Poor's (S&P) for explanatory purposes.

The most stable firms, those most likely to pay their debts, are given a rating of AAA. In the recent past, firms like Johnson & Johnson and Microsoft have achieved AAA ratings. A high rating is desirable because it directly translates into higher prices and lower interest rates on the firm's bonds. Moreover, the firm's operating costs are directly affected by its bond rating, since the interest rate is the cost of a key resource for its production. If Microsoft's bond rating falls from AAA to AA, this change increases the company's cost in the same way that its costs would rise if its employees negotiated higher wages, or another key resource became more expensive.

Table 10.2 shows selected bond ratings from 2011. As we move down the table, the grade falls and the default risk increases. All grades below medium (BB and lower) are called *non-investment grade*. They are also known as *junk bonds*. Non-investment-grade bonds have lower ratings, and these lower ratings mean higher interest rates for the borrowing firms, such as General Motors and Delta Airlines. In an attempt to spin this positively, bond salesmen prefer to call these bonds *high yield securities*, because the higher interest rates mean higher yields to lenders when the firms do not default.

**Stocks**
are ownership shares in a firm.

You can own part of Google! To see its current share price, type its ticker symbol (Goog) into a search engine.

## Stocks

Stock securities offer another option for firms that need funding to finance their production of output. **Stocks** are ownership shares in a firm. From the firm's point of view, stocks offer a new financing avenue, but they also involve ceding some ownership of the firm. In this important sense, stocks are very different from bank loans or bonds: owners of stock securities are actual owners of the firm. In contrast, when a firm sells bonds, it does not cede direct control of the firm to new owners.

Why would a firm sell stocks instead of bonds? One reason is that bond financing leaves the firm with a lot of bills that must be paid. For example, when IBM sells $10 million worth of 10-year bonds, the company takes on the obligation to pay $10 million in 10 years. If the firm cannot pay these bills, the owners may need to declare bankruptcy and lose the firm altogether. With stocks, however, the owners can sell shares of the firm to others and move forward without the burden of debt.

| TABLE 10.2 | | |
|---|---|---|
| **Sample Bond Ratings** | | |
| **S&P\*** | **Grade** | **Examples** |
| AAA | Prime | Microsoft, Johnson & Johnson, University of Virginia, Harvard University |
| AA | High | Berkshire Hathaway, Toyota, Walmart, Coca-Cola, University of North Carolina, Duke University |
| A | Upper medium | AT&T, McDonald's, Target, Dell, Disney, Nike, Bank of America, Home Depot, Intel, Anheuser-Busch |
| BBB | Lower medium | Washington Post, Hewlett-Packard, Mary's, Spain, Time Warner, MolsonCoors, Nissan |
| BB | Non-investment or speculative | Dillard's, General Motors, Best Buy, Ford, Goodyear, Turkey |
| B | Highly speculative | Sprint-Nextel, Jetblue, E-trade, Delta Airlines, New York Times, Greece, JCPenney, Dave & Buster's |
| CCC | Extremely speculative | RadioShack, Cyprus, Reader's Digest, Sears, James River Coal |
| D | In default | American Airlines |

\*as of January 2013.

From the lender's perspective, stock ownership is also different from bond ownership. Since stock owners (shareholders) are owners of the firm, they have some influence in the operations of the firm. In fact, a shareholder who owns more than 50% of the shares of the firm is the majority shareholder and controls more than 50% of the ownership votes. A majority shareholder can determine the direction of the company, an influence that is not available to bond holders.

## Secondary Markets

Most people who purchase stocks and bonds use brokers, who buy the stocks and bonds in *secondary markets*. **Secondary markets** are markets in which securities are traded after their first sale. Secondary markets are like used car markets, but the "used" assets are securities. There's nothing wrong with a used security; it just means that the buyer is not purchasing the security directly from the firm whose name is on it. You will probably recognize the names of some important secondary stock markets. They include the New York Stock Exchange (NYSE) and the NASDAQ (National Association of Securities Dealers Automated Quotations).

**Secondary markets** are markets in which securities are traded after their first sale.

The NYSE is the largest secondary stock market in the world.

The existence of a secondary market for a given security will increase the demand for that security. Consider the difference between a Target Corporation bond and the hypothetical bond you bought from Kara Alexis to help fund her website design company. Whoever buys the Target bond can sell it with a quick call to a broker or with the click of a mouse. The ease of resale is valuable and therefore worth a higher price. But when you buy Kara's bond, you have to hold on to it until you can personally locate another buyer. This sort of complication greatly limits the demand for bonds that cannot be re-sold in secondary markets, which lowers the price (that is, it raises the interest rate).

Figure 10.5 illustrates the impact that secondary markets have on security prices. If a secondary market exists for a security, then the demand for the security increases (from $D_1$ to $D_2$); in turn, the increased demand causes the price of the security to rise (from $p_1$ to $p_2$), all else equal. For the firm, this is helpful as it lowers the interest rate the firm pays on its bonds and, therefore, its cost of borrowing.

Secondary markets are a valuable institution of market economies because they lower the costs of borrowing. This is true for any asset. For example, let's say you are considering buying a particular home. Your real estate agent tells you that the price is very reasonable, but there is one unusual stipulation: you can never sell the home once you buy it. Of course, this is not a realistic stipulation, but think about how that would affect your willingness to buy the home. The purchase would be more risky, and no buyer would pay as much for that home as for one that could be re-sold. Secondary markets, by offering future sale opportunities for securities, increase the demand for them.

## FIGURE 10.5

### The Effect of Secondary Markets on Security Prices

The existence of secondary markets increases the demand for securities. When demand increases, the price rises (and the interest rate falls). Secondary markets allow firms to borrow at lower interest rates.

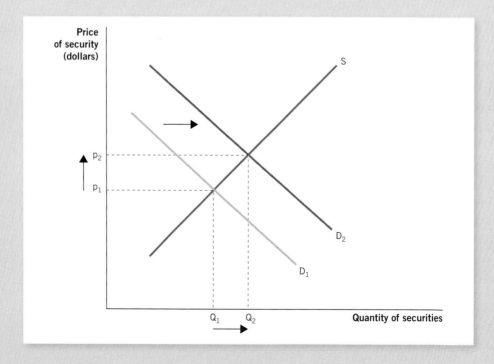

## ECONOMICS IN THE REAL WORLD

### Stock Market Indexes: Dow Jones versus S&P

Media reports about the stock market tend to focus on stock price indexes like the Dow Jones Industrial Average and the S&P 500. Just as the consumer price index (CPI) tracks general consumer prices, these stock market indexes track overall stock prices. Recall that the CPI is a weighted average of all consumer prices, where the weights are determined by the portion of the typical consumer budget that is spent on any given item. When the CPI rises, it indicates a corresponding rise in the general level of consumer prices. Similarly, when the stock indexes rise and fall, it indicates a corresponding rise and fall in the general level of stock prices.

The best-known stock index is the Dow Jones Industrial Average (the Dow). When the Dow was first published in 1896, it tracked 12 companies. Today, it tracks 30 companies selected by the editors of the *Wall Street Journal*. The editors maintain the index so that it represents companies in all the important sectors of the economy. To stay up to date, the Dow must occasionally change the companies it indexes. For example, when the technology sector came to the forefront in the late 1990s, Intel and Microsoft were added.

One of the advantages of the Dow is that it provides historical data all the way back to May 26, 1896. At that time, the calculation was very simple: an investor added the price of all 12 stocks and divided the sum by 12 to compute a simple average. Today, the Dow incorporates 30 stock prices in the average, but it is essentially computed in the same way. This means that the Dow tracks only the price of the stock, not the overall value of a company or the relative values of the companies in the stock market.

The S&P 500 index weights the stock prices by the *market value* of the companies it tracks. The market value is the total number of stock shares multiplied by the price per share. Under a market value–weighted index, the stock prices of large companies have a greater impact than those of smaller companies. For instance, Apple (with a market value of $542 billion in 2012) weighs much more heavily than Facebook (with a market value of $66 billion in 2012). Moreover, there is another difference between the S&P 500 and the Dow Jones index: while the Dow tracks only 30 companies, the S&P 500 tracks 500 companies, thus providing a much broader representation of the stock market.

In many respects, the Dow is an artifact of simpler times, when computing a broadly based index was time-intensive. Today, spreadsheets can crunch all the stock price data in milliseconds. Nevertheless, the Dow has been a very reliable measure of market performance, and it also provides a continuous record of historical information that cannot be replaced by more recent indexes. In addition, investors are accustomed to the Dow, and its simplicity makes it easy to understand and follow.✷

Is it good news when the Dow Jones Industrial Average goes up?

# The Dow Jones Industrial Average

The Dow Jones Industrial Average is perhaps the most closely watched financial market indicator. The Dow tracks average stock prices of 30 firms that represent major industries in the U.S. economy; these include Coca-Cola, Walmart, Disney, Microsoft, Bank of America, and Boeing. Since the Dow represents a broad array of industries, movements indicate changes in private investors' expectations about the future direction of the macroeconomy. Increases in the Dow generally reflect confidence in the future of the U.S. economy; decreases mean people are pessimistic. While other economic indicators take months to measure, the Dow is an instantaneous indicator of how private investors view future economic conditions.

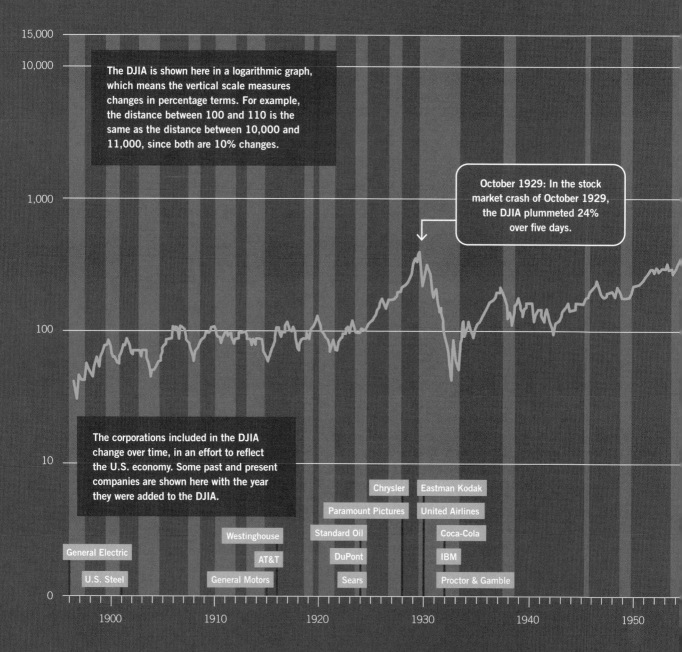

The DJIA is shown here in a logarithmic graph, which means the vertical scale measures changes in percentage terms. For example, the distance between 100 and 110 is the same as the distance between 10,000 and 11,000, since both are 10% changes.

October 1929: In the stock market crash of October 1929, the DJIA plummeted 24% over five days.

The corporations included in the DJIA change over time, in an effort to reflect the U.S. economy. Some past and present companies are shown here with the year they were added to the DJIA.

Chrysler · Eastman Kodak
Paramount Pictures · United Airlines
Standard Oil · Westinghouse · Coca-Cola
General Electric · DuPont · IBM · AT&T
U.S. Steel · General Motors · Sears · Proctor & Gamble

## Key

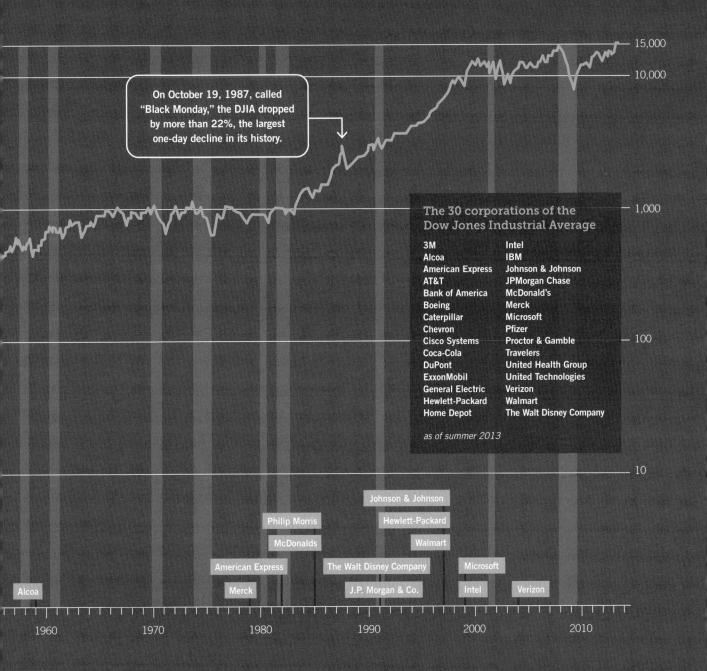

- **Dow Jones Industrial Average**
- **Period of recession**

## REVIEW QUESTIONS

- Approximately how long did it take the Dow to rise from 1,000 to 10,000? From 10,000 to 15,000?

- Why do movements in overall stock prices indicate something about the entire macroeconomy?

On October 19, 1987, called "Black Monday," the DJIA dropped by more than 22%, the largest one-day decline in its history.

**The 30 corporations of the Dow Jones Industrial Average**

| | |
|---|---|
| 3M | Intel |
| Alcoa | IBM |
| American Express | Johnson & Johnson |
| AT&T | JPMorgan Chase |
| Bank of America | McDonald's |
| Boeing | Merck |
| Caterpillar | Microsoft |
| Chevron | Pfizer |
| Cisco Systems | Proctor & Gamble |
| Coca-Cola | Travelers |
| DuPont | United Health Group |
| ExxonMobil | United Technologies |
| General Electric | Verizon |
| Hewlett-Packard | Walmart |
| Home Depot | The Walt Disney Company |

*as of summer 2013*

15,000

10,000

1,000

100

10

Johnson & Johnson

Philip Morris

Hewlett-Packard

McDonalds

Walmart

American Express

The Walt Disney Company

Microsoft

Merck

J.P. Morgan & Co.

Intel

Verizon

Alcoa

1960     1970     1980     1990     2000     2010

U.S. Treasury securities are used to pay for government spending when tax revenue falls short.

**Treasury securities**
are the bonds sold by the U.S. government to pay for the national debt.

# Treasury Securities

So far in our discussion, we have considered firms as the major borrowing entity in an economy. But governments are significant borrowers too. For example, according to the U.S. Treasury Department, the United States federal government has about $16 trillion worth of debt—that's about $50,000 per citizen. All this borrowing takes place through bond sales. The U.S. government bonds are called *Treasury securities*. **Treasury securities** are the bonds sold by the U.S. government to pay for the national debt.

Treasury securities are sold through auctions to large financial firms. The auction price determines the interest rate. After a Treasury security is sold the first time, anyone can buy it in the large and active secondary market for U.S. Treasury securities.

U.S. Treasury securities are generally considered less risky than any other bond, because no one expects the U.S. government to default on its debts. Of course, there are times, in the midst of heated political debate, when politicians threaten actions that could lead to default. But this is generally considered just political rhetoric. In fact, global financial turmoil would certainly follow a debt default by the U.S. government.

Because Treasury bonds are safe, firms and governments from all over the world buy U.S. Treasury securities as a way to limit risk. In 2011, approximately $4.5 trillion (about 32%) of U.S. federal debt was held by foreigners. Figure 10.6 shows the breakdown of foreign ownership of U.S. Treasury securities.

## FIGURE 10.6

**Major Foreign Holders of U.S. Treasury Securities, 2011 (in billions of dollars)**

Of the $16 trillion of U.S. government debt, foreigners hold approximately 32%. China alone owns $1.3 billion of our national debt, but this represents less than 9% of the total outstanding.

*Source:* U.S. Treasury Department.

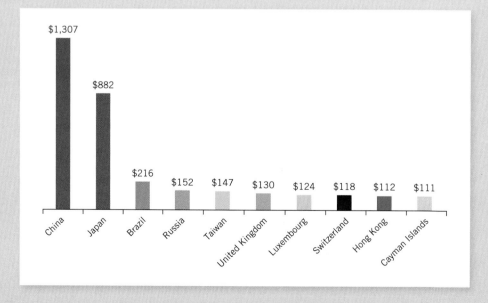

As we noted in the opening "misconception" statement of this chapter, many people are concerned that nations like China will exert undue influence on the U.S. government if we owe them money. But this perspective misses a key point: foreign savings keep interest rates lower in the United States than they would otherwise be. This means that U.S. firms and governments can undertake their activities at lower costs. In turn, lower interest rates mean more investment and greater future GDP. That is a clear benefit of foreign investment in the United States.

Treasury securities play many roles in the macroeconomy. For example, they are used when the government alters the supply of money in the economy, which we will discuss in Chapter 17. In addition, if the government decides to increase spending without raising taxes, it must pay for the additional spending by borrowing, or by selling bonds. We will explore this role of Treasury securities in Chapter 15.

## Home Mortgages

Another important borrowing tool in the United States is the home mortgage loan, which individuals use to pay for homes. The most common mortgage loan lasts 30 years from inception and is paid off with 360 monthly payments. These mortgages are really just variations on the basic bond security we have described in this chapter. When a family wants to buy a home, they take on a mortgage loan, which is a contract that states their willingness to repay the loan over several years—just like a firm signing a bond contract.

The macroeconomic significance of home mortgages has grown over time, as more and more people own homes. Figure 10.7 shows the growth in the U.S. mortgage market over the past 30 years. The graph plots the total size of the U.S. mortgage market in real dollars. The home mortgage market in the United States expanded greatly leading up to the recession in 2008. In 1982, there was about $2.2 trillion in home mortgages in the United States. By 2008, the market had expanded to over $10 trillion.

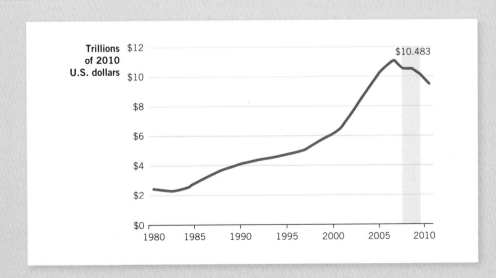

**FIGURE 10.7**

**Total Size of U.S. Mortgage Market, 1980–2011**

The home mortgage market in the United States expanded greatly leading up to the recession in 2008. In 1982, there was about $2.2 trillion worth of home mortgages in the United States. But by 2008, this amount expanded to over $10 trillion.

*Source:* Federal Reserve.

# PRACTICE WHAT YOU KNOW

Could both of these flags fly over Washington someday?

## The Effects of Foreign Investment: What If We Limit Foreign Ownership of Our National Debt?

Imagine that a new law significantly limits foreign ownership of U.S. Treasury bonds.

**Question:** How would you graph the market for Treasury bonds showing how the new law will affect demand?

**Answer:** Demand will decline since the new law limits foreign demand.

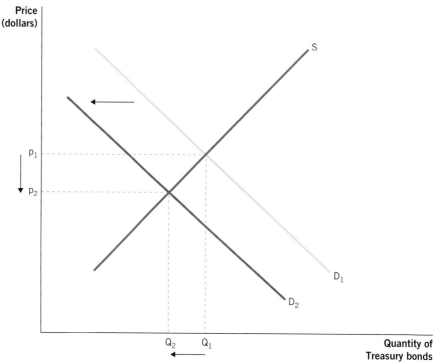

**Question:** What will happen to Treasury bond prices?

**Answer:** The price of Treasury bonds will decline. When demand falls, the new equilibrium price will be lower.

**Question:** What will happen to interest rates on Treasury bonds?

**Answer:** The interest rates on Treasury bonds will increase, since dollar price and the interest rate move in opposite directions. A lower price means that the government will sell each bond for fewer dollars, so it will be paying higher interest to the bond owner.

In the end, restrictions on foreign investment will lead to higher domestic interest rates.

# Securitization

Bonds, stocks, mortgages, and other financial securities channel funds from savers to borrowers. Opportunities for both firms and individuals expand when credit is available. In addition, lower borrowing costs certainly help borrowers. When interest rates are lower, investment opportunities expand for everything from factories to roads to homes to education. And, as we noted above, secondary markets reduce borrowing costs. For this reason, there are incentives to create new markets for all varieties of loan agreements. These new markets make it easier and less expensive for firms to borrow to fund investment. And, all else equal, lower investment costs mean more GDP for the nation in the future.

Consider two common personal loans: home mortgages and student loans. The United States has secondary markets in which home mortgages and student loans are bought and sold daily. This activity lowers interest rates on home and education loans, which directly benefits homeowners and students. But these markets would not exist if the individual personal loans hadn't been *securitized*. **Securitization** is the creation of a new security by combining otherwise separate loan agreements.

**Securitization**
is the creation of a new security by combining otherwise separate loan agreements.

Figure 10.8 illustrates how mortgage-backed securities are created. Each mortgage-backed security is a combination, or bundle, of mortgages. The new security is then available for resale in secondary markets. In a few years, you may use a mortgage to buy a home. There is a chance your mortgage will be bundled together with others into a big security that can be bought and sold. The mere existence of this market means that you'll pay lower interest rates on your mortgage loan.

Indeed, securitization lowers interest rates for borrowers. It also offers new opportunities for lenders. For example, people from all over the globe can now buy securities tied to the U.S. mortgage market. But this also means that lenders need to correctly evaluate the risk associated with these newly

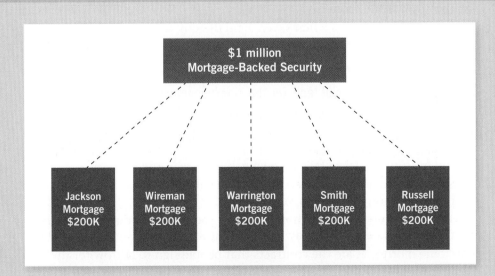

## FIGURE 10.8

**Securitization**
Securitization is the creation of a new security by combining otherwise separate loan agreements. For example, it is possible to create a $1 million mortgage-backed security by buying five separate $200,000 mortgages and then selling them together as a bundle.

created securities. When the U.S. home mortgage market began collapsing in 2007, the negative reverberations were felt worldwide. For example, because Icelandic banks owned a large number of securities tied to the U.S. home mortgage market, both the economy and government of Iceland collapsed in 2008 and 2009.

# Conclusion

We began this chapter with the misconception that borrowing from foreign countries—that is, foreign ownership of the national debt—is harmful to the economy. However, we have seen that this is not the case. Funds flowing into the U.S. loanable funds market help lead to economic expansion, no matter where they originate. One of the themes throughout this chapter has been the importance of savings and lending to the macroeconomy. With indirect finance, banks and financial intermediaries help channel funds from savers to borrowers. With direct finance, firms sell securities such as stocks and bonds directly to savers. These securities enable savers to earn returns on their savings while also giving firms access to funds for investment.

In the chapters that follow, we'll see that these financial institutions play a major role in the macroeconomy.

## ANSWERING THE BIG QUESTIONS

### How do financial markets help the economy?

* Financial markets help channel funds to investment opportunities throughout the economy.
* Direct finance occurs when savers lend directly to borrowers; indirect finance occurs when savers and borrowers go through financial intermediaries.

### What are the key financial tools for the macroeconomy?

* Bonds serve as a basic instrument of direct finance: they provide a tool with which firms and governments can finance their activities.
* Stocks are an additional source of funds for firms, but one that enables the security-holder to take an ownership share in the firm.
* Secondary markets make securities more valuable and offer more avenues for funds to flow to investors.
* Treasury securities are the bonds sold by the U.S. government to finance the national debt. They play a prominent role in macroeconomic policy.
* Home mortgages are the contracts that people sign to borrow for the purchase of a home. Because the mortgage market is so large, the entire macroeconomy is affected by its condition.

# Long-Run Returns for Stocks versus Bonds

In this chapter, we have focused on the importance of stocks and bonds for financing the activities of firms and governments. But you may be wondering which of these instruments would best serve your own personal savings.

Let's begin by looking at the historical returns for stocks versus bonds. The bar graph below, based on data from the Bureau of Labor Statistics, shows that from 1960 to 2011 the average inflation-adjusted return for long-term Treasury bonds was 3.18%. But over the same period, stocks yielded 6.67%. Thus, the return to stocks was more than twice the return to bonds.

Perhaps this doesn't seem like a huge difference to you. After all, 3% and 6% both seem small. But think of it this way: what if your grandparents had put $100 into both stocks and bonds for you in 1960? After adjusting for inflation, by 2011 your savings in bonds would have yielded $2,735.63, but the $100 in stocks would have generated a return of $10,027.78. These alternatives are plotted in the graph on the right.

Which should you choose: stocks or bonds?

To be sure, stocks are riskier. In our example in the figure, just look at how the value of your savings would have fluctuated over the years. With stocks, the value of your savings would have sometimes climbed or fallen by more than $1,000 a year. With bonds, the fluctuations would have been much smaller. Therefore, if you are extremely averse to risk, you might choose bonds. But in the long run, your risk aversion will cost you dearly.

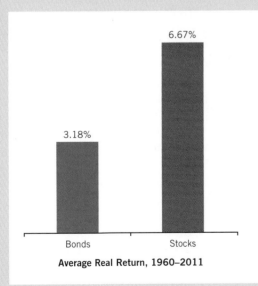

**Average Real Return, 1960–2011**

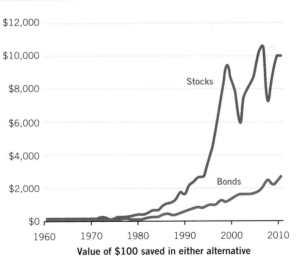

**Value of $100 saved in either alternative**

ECONOMICS FOR LIFE

## CONCEPTS YOU SHOULD KNOW

banks (p. 300)
bond (p. 301)
default risk (p. 307)
direct finance (p. 300)
face value or par value ($p_m$)
(p. 304)

financial intermediaries
(p. 300)
indirect finance (p. 300)
maturity date (p. 304)
secondary markets (p. 309)
securitization (p. 317)

security (p. 301)
stocks (p. 308)
Treasury securities (p. 314)

## QUESTIONS FOR REVIEW

1. What is the difference between direct and indirect finance? Discuss the reasons why a firm (a borrower) might choose each method. Discuss the reasons why a saver might choose each.

2. What is securitization? Discuss how securitization benefits borrowers.

3. One principle we learned in this chapter is that the dollar price and the interest rate on a bond move in opposite directions. Why is this always the case?

4. What is the primary use of U.S. Treasury securities? Why are the interest rates on Treasury securities so low? If people worried about the United States defaulting on the national debt, what would you expect to happen to interest rates on U.S. Treasury securities? Why?

5. Why might a firm prefer to finance its investments with bonds rather than stocks? Alternatively, why might a firm prefer stocks to bonds?

## STUDY PROBLEMS (* solved at the end of the section)

1. Toyota bonds are currently rated AA, and Ford bonds are rated BB. Suppose the price of a $1,000 one-year Toyota bond is $970.

   a. What is the rate of return on the one-year Toyota bond?
   b. The price of a $1,000 one-year Ford bond must be:
      i. less than $970.
      ii. greater than $970.
      iii. $970.
      iv. There is insufficient information to answer this question.
   c. The rate of return of a $1,000 one-year Ford bond must be:
      i. less than the return on the Toyota bond.
      ii. greater than the return on the Toyota bond.
      iii. the same as the return on the Toyota bond.
      iv. There is insufficient information to answer this question.

* 2. In 2008, when the U.S. automobile industry was struggling, the price of Ford Motor Company bonds rose. In this question, you need to calculate how the price increase also affects the interest rate.

   a. What is the interest rate on a one-year Ford bond with a face value of $5,000 and a price of $4,750?
   b. What is the new interest rate on a one-year Ford bond with a face value of $1,000 and a price of $4,950?

* 3. Let's say you own a firm that produces and sells Ping-Pong tables. The name of your company is iPong because your tables have a plug-in jack for all Apple products. To finance a new factory, you decide to sell bonds. Your bonds are rated BBB.

   a. Draw supply and demand curves for your iPong bonds. (The quantity of bonds is measured along the x axis, and the price along the y axis.) Label the supply curve S, the demand curve D, and the equilibrium price p.

b. How will the demand for iPong bonds be affected if a new secondary market agrees to buy and sell iPong bonds? Illustrate the new demand curve in the graph above, and label it $D_{SM}$. How will this affect the price and interest rate on iPong bonds?

4. This question involves the hypothetical iPong firm from question 3.

  a. How will demand be affected if a ratings agency upgrades your bond rating to AA?
  b. How will the ratings upgrade affect the price of your bond?
  c. How will the ratings upgrade affect your cost of borrowing?

5. Use supply and demand curves to illustrate how default risk affects both the price and the interest rate of a bond.

6. In this chapter, we discussed Target Corporation bonds to illustrate the effect of default risk on the price of a bond. In particular, when the default risk rises, the demand for a bond falls and then the equilibrium price falls. In our example, the price of a $100,000 Target bond fell from $98,000 to $97,000.

  a. What is the interest rate on a one-year $100,000 bond that sells for $98,000?
  b. What is the interest rate on a one-year $100,000 bond that sells for $97,000?

# SOLVED PROBLEMS

2. a. Use the formula:

$$R = \frac{P_m - P_o}{P_o}$$

Then compute: $R = (\$5,000 - \$4,750) \div \$4,750 = \$250 \div \$4,750 = 5.26\%$

b. $R = (\$5,000 - \$\$4,950) \div \$4,950 = \$50 \div \$4,950 = 1.01\%$

Therefore, when the price of the bond rose by $200, this reduced the interest rate from 5.26% to just 1.01%.

3. a.

b. If a secondary market is available to sell bonds, the demand for the bonds will increase since the bonds will become more attractive to buyers. When a secondary market exists, you can always re-sell any bond you own. If there is no secondary market, you are stuck with it once you have it.

In the figure above, demand increases and price rises. This means lower interest rates for your iPong firm.

# The Long and Short of
# MACROECONOMICS

# CHAPTER 1

# Economic Growth and the Wealth of Nations

**Natural resources are the key to economic prosperity.**

Many people believe that natural resources such as trees, oil, and farmland are the primary sources of economic growth. They believe that

nations like the United States and Australia are prosperous because they have vast natural resources that can be used to produce goods and services. A variation on this idea emphasizes geography—that nations with the best shipping locations and the mildest climates have more prosperous economies. But what about the two Koreas? North and South Korea have the same natural resources, yet the two economies are as different as night and day. Over the course of the next two chapters, we will explore what economics has to say about differences in economic growth across nations.

Striving for economic growth is not only about accumulating more wealth. Yes, economic growth brings iPads and Jet Skis, but it's much more important than that. Economic growth means that more women and infants survive childbirth, more people have access to clean water and better sanitation, and people live healthier, longer, and more educated lives.

In this chapter, we begin by looking at the implications of economic growth for human welfare. We then consider the impact of an economy's resources and technology on economic growth. Finally, we discuss the key elements that an economy needs in order to grow.

The two Koreas at night: South Korea bursting with light, and North Korea mired in economic darkness.

# BIG QUESTIONS

* Why does economic growth matter?
* How do resources and technology contribute to economic growth?
* What institutions foster economic growth?

# Why Does Economic Growth Matter?

In 1900, life expectancy in the United States was 47 years. Income—adjusted for inflation—was less than $5,000 per person. About 140 of every 1,000 children died before their first birthday. Only about one-third of American homes had running water. Most people lived less than a mile from their job, and almost nobody owned an automobile. Yes, this is a description of life in the United States in 1900, but it is also a description of life in many poor countries today. What happened in the United States since 1900? Economic growth.

In this section, we examine how economic growth impacts the lives of average people around the world. We also examine the historical data on economic growth and explain some mathematics of growth rates.

## Some Ugly Facts

Before looking at data on growth, we need to recall how economists measure economic growth. In Chapter 6, we defined *economic growth* as the percentage change in real per capita GDP. We know that real per capita GDP measures the average level of income in a nation. But for most people, life is not all about the pursuit of more income. The fact remains that economic growth alleviates human misery and lengthens lives. Wealthier societies provide better living standards, which include better nutrition, educational opportunities, health care, freedom, and even sources of entertainment.

Let's look around the world and compare life in poor countries with life in rich countries. Table 11.1 presents human welfare indicators for a selection of rich and poor countries. Among the poor nations are Bangladesh, Haiti, North Korea, Niger, Liberia, Tanzania, Nepal, Ethiopia, and Zimbabwe. The wealthy nations include Australia, Denmark, Israel, Japan, Germany, South Korea, and the United States, among others.

Consider the first group of indicators, which are related to mortality. In poor countries, 76 out of every 1,000 babies die at birth or in the first year of their life, while in rich nations the number is only 5 out of every 1,000. This means infants are 15 times more likely to die in poor nations. Those that survive one year in poor nations are about 20 times more likely to die before

| TABLE 11.1 | | |
|---|---|---|
| **Human Welfare in Poor versus Rich Nations** | | |
| Life indicators | Poor nations | Rich nations |
| GDP per capita, PPP (2005 international $)* | $1,095 | $32,971 |
| Infant mortality rate (per 1,000 live births) | 76 | 5 |
| Under-5 mortality rate (per 1,000) | 118 | 6 |
| Life expectancy at birth (years) | 57 | 80 |
| Physicians (per 10,000 people) | 1.8 | 29.3 |
| Births attended by skilled health staff (%) | 41 | 100 |
| Access to improved water source (%) | 64 | 100 |
| Access to improved sanitation (%) | 35 | 100 |
| Personal computers (per 100 people) | 1.7 | 70 |
| Internet users (per 100 people) | 2.7 | 74 |
| Motor vehicles (per 1,000 people) | 12 | 638 |
| Mobile cellular subscriptions (per 100 people) | 27 | 108 |
| Literacy rate, adult male (%) | 69 | 99 |
| Literacy rate, adult female (%) | 55 | 99 |
| Ratio of female to male secondary enrollment (%) | 84 | 99 |
| Ratio of female to male post-secondary enrollment (%) | 64 | 121 |

*Source*: World Bank. Poor nations are 40 poorest; rich nations are 31 high-income OECD nations.

*GDP data is from 2010 and is adjusted for prices across the different nations using a purchasing power parity (PPP) method. Other indicators are from 2008 and 2009.

their fifth birthday, as indicated by the under-5 mortality rates. Overall, life expectancy in poor nations is 57 years, while in wealthy nations it is 80 years. Just being born in a wealthy nation adds almost a quarter century to an individual's life.

The second group of indicators in Table 11.1 helps to explain the mortality data. Rich nations have about 15 times as many doctors per person: 30 physicians per 10,000 people versus 2 per 10,000. Clean water and sanitation are available to only a fraction of people in poor nations, while these are generally available to all in rich nations. Children in poor nations die every year because they can't get water as clean as the water that comes out of virtually any faucet in the United States. This leads to common ailments like tapeworms and diarrhea that are life-threatening in poor nations. In fact, in 2010 the World Health Organization estimated that 3.6 million people die each year from waterborne diseases.

The third group of indicators lists a selection of nonessential conveniences that we in the United States often take for granted. In wealthy nations, there are 70 personal computers

Clean water, even in a bag, saves lives.

for every 100 people; in poor nations, the number is only 1.7 per 100 people. Fully 74 people out of every 100 use the Internet in rich nations, but only 2.7 people per 100 are able to use it in poor nations. Rich nations have about 50 times more motor vehicles per 1,000 people and 4 times as many cell-phone subscriptions.

The last group of indicators in Table 11.1 tells the sobering story about education. First, notice that literacy rates in poor countries are significantly lower than literacy rates in wealthy countries. But there is also a significant difference in literacy rates between men and women in poor nations. Furthermore, women have less access to both secondary and post-secondary education than men in poor nations; equal access would imply an enrollment ratio of 100%. So while education opportunities are more rare for all people in poor nations, women fare the worst.

The data in Table 11.1 support our contention that per capita GDP matters—not for the sake of more income per se, but because it correlates with better human welfare conditions, which matter to everyone.

## Learning from the Past

We can learn a lot about the roots of economic growth by looking at historical experiences. Until very recently, the common person's existence was devoted to subsistence, which involved simply trying to find enough shelter, clothing, and nourishment to survive. As we saw in the previous section, even today many people still live on the margins of subsistence. What can history tell us about how rich nations achieved economic development? The answer will help to clarify possible policy alternatives going forward.

### We Were All Poor Once

When you look around the globe today, you see rich nations and poor nations. You can probably name many rich nations: the United States, Japan, Taiwan, and the Western European nations, among others. You might also know the very poor nations: almost all of Africa, much of Latin America, and significant parts of Asia. But the world was not always this way. If we consider the longer history of humankind, only recently did the incomes of common people rise above subsistence level. The Europe of 1750, for instance, was not noticeably richer than Europe at the time of the birth of Jesus of Nazareth.

Consider the very long run. Angus Maddison, a noted economic historian, estimated GDP levels for many nations and for the whole world back to the year AD 1. Figure 11.1 plots Maddison's estimates of per capita GDP, in 2010 U.S. dollars. Clearly, there was a historical break around 1800 that dramatically changed the path of average world living standards.

Maddison estimated that the average level of income in the world in 1350 was about $816. Given that the number is adjusted to 2010 prices, this would be comparable to you having an annual income of about $800. If you had $816 to live on for an entire year, it's clear that your solitary focus would be on basic necessities like food, clothing, and shelter. Of course, there were certainly rich individuals over the course of history, but until relatively recently the average person's life was essentially one of subsistence living. Consider Alice Toe, the Liberian girl profiled in the Economics in the Real World feature on p. 332. This type of life, where even meals are uncertain, was the basic experience for the average person *for nearly all of human history.*

Of course, there were global variations in income before 1700. For example, average income in Western Europe in 1600 was about $1,400, while in Latin America it was less than $700. This means that Western Europeans were twice as wealthy as Latin Americans in 1600. But average Europeans were still very poor!

The Industrial Revolution, during which many economies moved away from agriculture and toward manufacturing in the 1800s, is at the very center of the big break in world income growth. Beginning with the Industrial Revolution, the rate of technical progress became so rapid that it was able to outpace population growth. The foundation for the Industrial Revolution was laid in the preceding decades, and this included private-property protection and several technological innovations. We don't claim that the Industrial Revolution was idyllic for those who lived through it, but the legal and technological innovations of that era paved the way for the unprecedented gains in human welfare that people have experienced since.

This data doesn't imply that life is always easy and predictably comfortable for everyone in the modern world. But the opportunities afforded to the

## FIGURE 11.1

### Long-Run World Per Capita Real GDP (in 2010 U.S. dollars)

Historical accounts often focus on monarchs and other wealthy people. But for the average person, living standards across the globe didn't change considerably from the time of Jesus to the time of Thomas Jefferson. The data plotted here is per capita GDP in 2010 U.S. dollars, which is adjusted for prices across both time and place.

*Source:* Angus Maddison, *Statistics on World Population, GDP and Per Capita GDP, 1–2008 AD.* All figures converted to 2010 U.S. dollars.

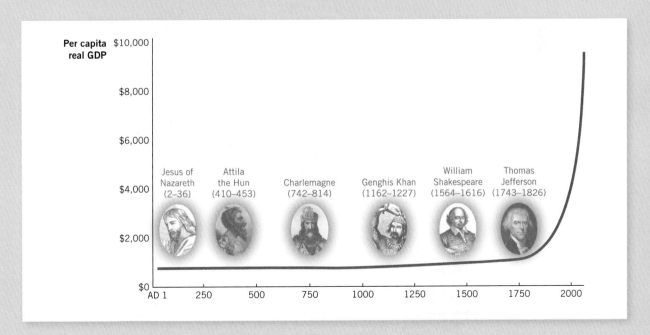

average person alive today are very different from those afforded to the average person in past centuries. Table 11.2 lists a sampling of some of the major innovations that have taken place in the past 150 years. Try to imagine life without any of these, and you'll get a sense of the gains we've made since the Industrial Revolution.

## Some Got Rich, Others Stayed Poor

Although wealth has increased over the past two centuries, it is not evenly distributed around the globe. Figure 11.2 shows per capita real GDP (in 2010 U.S. dollars) for various world regions. In 1800, the income of the average U.S. citizen was just less than $2,000 (in year 2010 dollars). Imagine trying to live on $3 per day in today's world—that is, $3 to buy all the food, clothing, shelter, education, transportation, and anything else you might need to purchase. That was life in the United States in 1800, and it's comparable to life in many nations today.

## TABLE 11.2

### Important Inventions since the U.S. Civil War

| | | | |
|---|---|---|---|
| Typewriter | 1867 | Electron microscope | 1939 |
| Sheep shears | 1868 | Electric clothes dryer | 1940 |
| Telephone | 1876 | Nuclear reactor | 1942 |
| Phonograph | 1877 | Microwave oven | 1945 |
| Milking machine | 1878 | Cruise control | 1945 |
| Two-stroke engine | 1878 | Computer | 1946 |
| Blowtorch | 1880 | Xerography | 1946 |
| Slide rule | 1881 | Videotape recorder | 1952 |
| Arc welder | 1886 | Airbags | 1952 |
| Diesel engine | 1892 | Satellites | 1958 |
| Electric motor (AC) | 1892 | Laser | 1960 |
| X-ray machine | 1895 | Floppy disk | 1965 |
| Electric drill | 1895 | Microprocessor | 1971 |
| Radio | 1906 | Personal computer | 1975 |
| Assembly line | 1908 | Fiberoptic cables | 1977 |
| Cash register | 1919 | Fax machine | 1981 |
| Dishwasher | 1924 | Camcorder | 1982 |
| Rocket | 1926 | Cell phone | 1983 |
| Television | 1926 | Compact disk | 1983 |
| Antilock brakes | 1929 | GPS | 1989 |
| Radar | 1934 | Laser eye surgery | 1989 |
| Tape recorder | 1935 | Internet | 1991 |
| Jet engine | 1939 | | |

*Source*: Michael Cox and Richard Alm, *Myths of Rich and Poor* (New York: Basic Books, 1999), and miscellaneous other sources.

## FIGURE 11.2

### Per Capita Real GDP over 200 Years (in 2010 U.S. dollars)

Two hundred years ago, all regions and nations were poor. The modern differences in wealth that we see around the world today began to emerge before 1900. But the twentieth century saw unprecedented growth take hold in the United States and Western Europe. Unfortunately, some parts of the globe today are no better off than the United States and Western Europe were in 1800.

*Source:* Angus Maddison, *Statistics on World Population, GDP and Per Capita GDP, 1–2008 AD.* All figures converted to 2010 U.S. dollars.

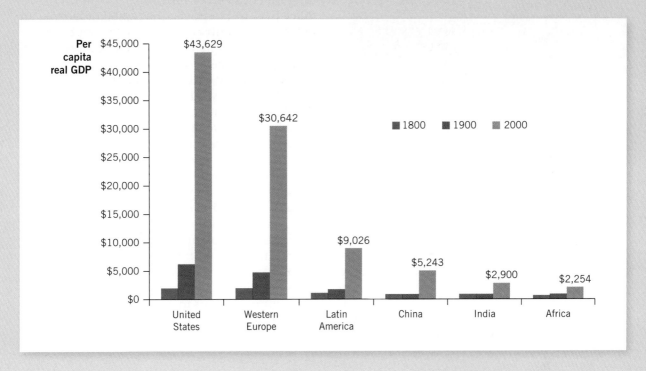

By 1900, some regions had broken the stranglehold of poverty. In 1900, per capita real GDP in Western Europe was $4,701; in the United States, it was $6,153. Prior to 1900, general income levels this high had never been experienced. But in China, India, and Africa, the averages were still less than $1,000 in 1900. The twentieth century proved to be even more prosperous for some, as the income gap widened between the United States and Western Europe and the rest of the world. Unfortunately, per capita real income on the African continent today is still less than that of the United States in 1850, which was $2,768.

While many of the current disparities between nations began about 200 years ago, some nations have moved from poor to rich as recently as the past few decades. In 1950, for example, South Korea, with per capita real GDP of just $1,309, was poorer than Liberia, at $1,617. Today, South Korea is one of the wealthiest countries in the world, with a per capita income of more than $30,000, while Liberia is near $1,200 in per capita income.

Alice and her brother Reuben search for crabs in Monrovia, Liberia.

### One Child Who Needs Economic Progress

This is a true story about a girl named Alice Toe, who is four years old. In her photo, you can see from her eyes that she is mischievous and has a sparkling personality. When this picture was taken, she was digging for crabs for the sole purpose of frightening a visiting American economist.

Alice lives in Monrovia, the capital of Liberia, an impoverished country in West Africa about the size of the state of Virginia. She was three years old when she contracted tapeworms by drinking water from the neighborhood well. Unfortunately, her family could not afford to send her to a doctor. Her stomach became enlarged and her hair bleached—indicators of malnutrition caused by tapeworms. Filtered water, which costs about $3 per gallon in Liberia, is too expensive for most families and must be transported by foot.

Tapeworm infection is easily treated with a pill that costs less than 25 cents and lasts for six months. But Alice and her grandfather could not afford even this inexpensive treatment—that's how poor they were. Fortunately, an American missionary happened to meet Alice and made sure that she received the treatment she needed. Without help, she probably would have died.

Alice's story is not unusual. Many thousands of children die each year from illnesses like tapeworm infection. Worldwide, 122 of every 1,000 children born in the poorest nations do not reach the age of five, although many could be saved with treatments that literally cost pennies. The good news is that economic growth can bring improvements in quality of life. For the sake of Alice Toe and other children like her, let's hope that economic progress will take root in Liberia. ✳

| TABLE 11.3 | |
|---|---|

**World Economic Growth for Different Historical Eras**

| Years | Growth rate |
|---|---|
| AD 1–1800 | 0.02% |
| 1800–1900 | 0.64% |
| 1900–1950 | 1.04% |
| 1950–2000 | 2.12% |

*Source*: Angus Maddison, *Statistics on World Population, GDP and Per Capita GDP, 1–2008 AD*. All figures converted to 2010 U.S. dollars.

## Measuring Economic Growth

Overall, people today are much wealthier than they were 200 years ago. However, this prosperity did not occur overnight. Rather, income grew a little bit each year. There is a striking mathematical truth about growth: small differences in growth rates lead to large differences in wealth levels over time. In this section, we explain how growth rates are computed, and we consider the level of growth a nation needs for its population to experience significant improvements in living standards.

### The Mathematics of Growth Rates

The big break out of poverty began during the nineteenth century. Table 11.3 shows data on world economic growth in different periods. From 1800 to

1900, average world GDP growth was only 0.64%. From 1900 to 1950, world economic growth increased to about 1%. The difference between roughly 0% and 1% might seem trivial; it certainly doesn't seem like much if your exam grade goes from 85 to 86. But when economic growth increases by 1%, it makes a big difference. In this section, we show how growth is calculated.

We have seen that economic growth is the annual growth rate of per capita real GDP. It is our measure of how an average person's income changes over time, including an allowance for price changes. But the government reports overall GDP data in nominal terms. Therefore, to get an accurate growth rate, we need to account for both inflation and population growth. We can use the following equation to approximate economic growth, where %Δ indicates the percentage change in a variable:

economic growth ≈ %Δ in nominal GDP – %Δ price level – %Δ population        (Equation 11.1)

Let's walk through the equation for economic growth using actual U.S. data as shown in Table 11.4. Starting with nominal GDP data for 2011 and 2012, we compute nominal GDP growth as 4.0%. But part of the increase in nominal GDP is due to inflation. In 2012, the price level, as measured by the GDP deflator, grew by 1.8%. We subtract this inflation from nominal GDP growth to get real GDP growth of 2.2%. This number applies to the entire nation, but population also increased by 1% in 2012. When we subtract population growth, we are left with 1.2% as the rate of economic growth for the United States in 2012. This growth rate was lower than normal: since 1950, average economic growth in the United States has been about 2.1%.

A word of caution about terminology is in order. There's a big difference between nominal GDP growth, real GDP growth, and real per capita GDP growth. Looking at Table 11.4, you can see these terms highlighted in orange letters. But sloppy economic reporting sometimes confuses the terms. You may read something like "the U.S. economy grew by 2.2% in 2012," which often refers to real GDP growth and is not calculated on a per capita basis. It would be an even bigger mistake to claim that U.S. economic growth in

| **TABLE 11.4** | |
|---|---|
| **Computing an Economic Growth Rate** | |
| U.S. GDP in 2011 (millions of $) | $15,075,700 |
| U.S. GDP in 2012 (millions of $) | $15,684,800 |
| Nominal GDP growth | 4.0% |
| − Price growth (inflation) | 1.8% |
| = Real GDP growth | 2.2% |
| − Population growth | 1.0% |
| = Real per capita GDP growth | 1.2%   = Economic growth |

*Source*: GDP data, U.S. Bureau of Economic Analysis; population data, U.S. Census Bureau, www.census.gov/popest/states/NST-ann-est.html.

2012 was 4.0%, a number that is not adjusted for either population growth or inflation. Such confusing wording is a common mistake in reports on international economic growth statistics.

## Growth Rates and Income Levels

Before we consider policies that might aid economic growth, we need to look more closely at how growth rates affect income levels.

First, consider how significant it is when income doubles, or increases by 100%. If your income doubled today—all else equal—you could afford twice as much of everything you are currently buying. Now imagine what would happen if income doubled for an entire country or even for all countries. In the United States, per capita real GDP more than doubled in the 40 years between 1970 and 2010. This means that the average person living in the United States in 2010 could afford twice as much food, clothing, transportation, education, and even government services as the average U.S. resident in 1970. That's quite a difference.

But increasing real income by 100% in a single year is not realistic. Let's pick a number closer to reality—say, 2%, which is a normal rate of economic growth for the United States. With a growth rate of 2%, how long would it take to double your income? For example, let's say you graduate and, given your expertise in economics, you get several job offers. One offer is for $50,000 per year with a guaranteed raise of 2% every year. How long before your salary is $100,000?

The first answer that pops into your head might be 50 years (based on the idea that 2% growth for 50 years adds up to 100% growth). But this answer would be wrong because it ignores the fact that growth compounds over time. As your salary grows, 2% growth leads to larger and larger dollar increases. Because of this compounding effect, it actually would take only about 35 years to double income at a 2% growth rate.

Table 11.5 illustrates the process of compounding over time by showing the increase from year to year. Income starts at $50,000 in year 1, and a 2% increase yields $1,000, so that one year of growth results in income of $51,000. Subsequent 2% growth in the second year yields $1,020 of new income (2% of $51,000), so after two years income is $52,020. Looking at year 3, the 2% increase yields $1,040.40. Each year, the dollar increase in income (the green column) gets larger, as 2% of a growing number continues to grow.

## TABLE 11.5

### Compound Growth

| | Income | 2% increase in income | Income in next year |
|---|---|---|---|
| Year 1 | $50,000.00 | $1,000.00 | $51,000.00 |
| Year 2 | $51,000.00 | $1,020.00 | $52,020.00 |
| Year 3 | $52,020.00 | $1,040.40 | $53,060.40 |
| Year 4 | $53,060.40 | $1,061.21 | $54,121.61 |
| Year 5 | $54,121.61 | $1,082.43 | $55,204.04 |
| ... | | | |
| Year 35 | $100,000 | | |

In fact, at a growth rate of 2% it takes only 35 years for income to double. This scenario corresponds with the experience of the U.S. economy. Since 1970, per capita real GDP in the United States has more than doubled. Yet this jump occurred while U.S. economic growth rates averaged "only" about 2%. Think about that: during your parents' lifetime, average real income levels in the United States doubled.

## The Rule of 70

In the example above, we saw that when income grows at 2% per year it doubles in just 35 years. A simple rule known as the *rule of 70* determines the length of time necessary for a sum of money to double at a particular growth rate. According to the **rule of 70**:

> *If the annual growth rate of a variable is x%, the size of that variable doubles every 70 ÷ x years.*

The rule of 70 is an approximation, but it works well with typical economic growth rates.

Table 11.6 illustrates the rule of 70 by showing how long it takes for each $1.00 of income to double in value, given different growth rates. At a growth rate of 1%, each dollar of income will double every 70 ÷ 1 years. If growth increases to 2%, then a dollar of income will double every 70 ÷ 2 = 35 years. Consider the impact of a 4% growth rate. If this can be sustained, income doubles every 72 ÷ 4 = 17.5 years. In 70 years, income doubles 4 times, ending up at 16 times its starting value! China has been recently growing at almost 10% per year, and indeed its per capita income has been doubling about every seven years—a remarkable rate of growth.

The rule of 70 shows us that small and consistent growth rates, if sustained for a decade or two, can greatly improve living standards. Over the long course of history, growth rates were essentially zero and the general human condition was poverty. But over the past two centuries we have seen small, consistent growth rates, and the standard of living for many has increased dramatically.

We can look at actual growth rates of various countries over a long period to see the impact on income levels. Table 11.7 presents growth rates of several countries over 58 years from 1950 to 2008. Let's start with Nicaragua and

The **rule of 70** states that if the annual growth rate of a variable is *x*%, the size of that variable doubles every 70 ÷ *x* years.

## TABLE 11.6

### A Dollar of Income at Different Growth Rates

| Annual growth rate | Years to double | Value after 70 years (approximate) |
| --- | --- | --- |
| 0% | Never | $1.00 |
| 1% | 70 | $2.00 |
| 2% | 35 | $4.00 |
| 3% | 23.3 | $8.00 |
| 4% | 17.5 | $16.00 |

## TABLE 11.7

### Economic Growth, 1950–2008

| Average annual growth rate (%) | | Real per capita GDP in 1950 | Real per capita GDP in 2008 |
|---|---|---|---|
| **less than 1% growth** | −1.4 Dem. Republic Congo | 873 | 382 |
| | −0.7 Haiti | 1,610 | 1,051 |
| | 0.1 Nicaragua | 2,476 | 2,565 |
| | 0.2 Zimbabwe | 1,074 | 1,194 |
| | 0.5 North Korea | 1,309 | 1,719 |
| **about 1% growth** | 1.0 Tanzania | 649 | 1,141 |
| | 1.1 Lebanon | 3,722 | 6,824 |
| | 1.1 Rwanda | 838 | 1,563 |
| | 1.2 El Salvador | 2,282 | 4,507 |
| | 1.2 Nigeria | 1,154 | 2,336 |
| **about 2% growth** | 2.1 United States | 14,654 | 47,784 |
| | 2.1 Mexico | 3,625 | 12,228 |
| | 2.1 Australia | 11,359 | 38,777 |
| | 2.1 United Kingdom | 10,635 | 36,388 |
| | 2.1 Chile | 5,624 | 20,208 |
| **greater than 2% growth** | 2.7 India | 949 | 4,559 |
| | 2.8 Turkey | 2,487 | 12,363 |
| | 4.4 Japan | 2,944 | 34,967 |
| | 4.5 Singapore | 3,401 | 43,077 |
| | 4.8 China | 687 | 10,307 |
| | 5.5 Taiwan | 1,404 | 32,072 |
| | 5.6 South Korea | 1,309 | 30,061 |

*Source*: Angus Maddison, *Statistics on World Population, GDP and Per Capita GDP, 1–2008 AD.* All figures converted to 2010 U.S. dollars.

Turkey. In 1950, both nations had roughly the same income per person. But Turkey grew at over 2% annually, and Nicaragua didn't experience any net growth. As a result, the average income in Turkey is now four to five times the average income in Nicaragua.

Further down Table 11.7, you see other nations that grew at rates faster even than Turkey. In 1950, Japan's per capita income was similar to Turkey's. Yet 4.4% growth led to income of $35,000 per person by 2008 in Japan. Taiwan, with 5.5% growth over the entire period, moved from being among the world's poorest economies to being among the richest.

Perhaps the biggest recent growth story is China's. Only 20 years ago, it was among the world's poorer nations. Over the past 20 years, China has

This entire Shanghai skyline was built in the past 20 years, testament to an astonishing rate of growth.

grown at nearly 10% a year. Even if its astonishing growth slows considerably, China will still move into the group of the wealthiest nations in the coming decades.

Clearly, economic growth experiences have varied widely across time and place. But relatively small and consistent growth rates are sufficient to move a nation out of poverty over the period of a few generations. And this movement out of poverty really matters for the people who live in these nations.

## ECONOMICS IN THE REAL WORLD

### How Does 2% Growth Affect Average People?

We have seen that economic growth in the United States has averaged 2% per year over the past 50 years. What does this mean for a typical person's everyday life? We've assembled some basic data on economic aspects of life in the United States for an average person in 1960. This may be about the time your grandparents were your age.

Today, average real income is four times the level of 1960. Americans live 10% longer, have twice as many doctors, live in houses that are twice as big, enjoy more education, and own more and better cars and household appliances. We work 15% fewer hours and hold jobs that are physically less taxing. In 1960, there were no cell phones, and roughly three out of four homes had a single telephone. Today, there are more telephones than there are people in the United States. In addition, many modern amenities were not available in 1960. Can you imagine life without a personal computer and the Internet, DVDs, microwave ovens, and central air conditioning? Take a look at Table 11.8 to see a striking contrast. ✳

How different was life when your grandparents were your age?

### TABLE 11.8

#### The United States: 1960 versus 2010

| General Characteristics | 1960 | 2010 |
|---|---|---|
| Life expectancy | 69.7 years | 78.3 years |
| Physicians per 10,000 people | 14.8 | 27 |
| Years of school completed | 10.5 (median) | 12 (average) |
| Portion of income spent on food | 27% | 8% |
| Average workweek | 40.9 hours | 34 hours |
| Workforce in agriculture or manufacturing | 37% | 19% |
| Home ownership | 61.9% | 67.4% |

**New Home**

| | 1960 | 2010 |
|---|---|---|
| Size | 1,200 square feet | 2,457 square feet |
| Bedrooms | 2 | 3 |
| Bathrooms | 1 | 2.5 |
| Central air conditioning? | no | yes |

**Best-Selling Car**

| | 1960 | 2010 |
|---|---|---|
| Model | Chevrolet Impala | Toyota Camry |
| Price (2010 dollars) | $19,753 | $26,640 |
| Miles per gallon | 13–16 | 20–29 |
| Horsepower | 135 | 268 |
| Air conditioning? | optional | standard |
| Automatic transmission? | optional | standard |
| Airbags? | no | standard |
| Power locks and windows? | no | standard |

**TV**

| | 1960 | 2010 |
|---|---|---|
| Size | 23 inches | 50 inches |
| Display | black & white | high-definition color |
| Price (2010 dollars) | $1,391 | $700 |

*Source*: U.S. Census Bureau, *Statistical Abstract of the United States*, and U.S. Bureau of Labor Statistics.

## PRACTICE WHAT YOU KNOW

### Computing Economic Growth: How Much Is Brazil Growing?

GDP in Brazil has grown rapidly in recent years. But historically Brazil is a country that has struggled with inflation rates. The table below gives 2010 statistics for Brazil.

| Nominal GDP growth rate | GDP deflator growth rate | Population growth rate |
|---|---|---|
| 15.73% | 8.23% | 0.9% |

**Question:** What was the rate of economic growth for Brazil in 2010?

**Answer:** First, recall equation 11.1:

$$\text{economic growth} = \%\Delta\,\text{nominal GDP} - \%\Delta\,\text{price level}$$
$$- \%\Delta\,\text{population}$$

Now, for Brazil, we have:

$$\text{economic growth} = 15.73 - 8.23 - 0.9 = 6.6\%$$

How much does inflation affect Brazil's growth data?

**Question:** If Brazil continues to grow at 6.6% per year, how long will it take to double the level of per capita real GDP?

**Answer:** Use the rule of 70:

$$70 \div 6.6 = 10.6 \text{ years}$$

Clearly, the growth of GDP in Brazil in 2010 was significant, even after accounting for both inflation and population growth.

*Data source*: International Monetary Fund, World Economic Outlook, April 2012.

# How Do Resources and Technology Contribute to Economic Growth?

At this point, you may wonder what can be done to provide the best opportunity for economic growth. We see economic growth in many, though certainly not all, nations. But even in those that have grown in the past, future growth is not assured. So now we turn to the major sources of economic growth.

Economists continue to debate the relative importance of the factors that lead to economic growth. However, there is a general consensus on the significance of three factors for economic growth: *resources*, *technology*, and *institutions*. In this section, we examine the first two; in the final section of the chapter, we look at institutions.

# Economic Growth

Economic growth, measured as the growth rate of per capita real GDP, is the key determinant of living standards in nations across time. The map shows the average annual growth rates of nations across the globe from 1950 to 2008. On the right, we give a snapshot of the differences in living conditions between wealthy nations and poor nations.

| ● Negative – 0.9% growth | | ● 1% – 1.9% growth | | ● 2% – 2.9% growth | | ● 3% + growth | |
|---|---|---|---|---|---|---|---|
| *With 0% growth, nations are no better off than they were in 1950.* | | *With 1% growth, living standards nearly doubled over 58 years.* | | *With 2% growth, living standards almost quadrupled over 58 years.* | | *With 3% growth, some of the poorest nations are now among the richest.* | |
| Dem. Rep. Congo | −1.41 | Lebanon | 1.05 | United States | 2.06 | Israel | 3.24 |
| Haiti | −0.73 | Cuba | 1.06 | Mexico | 2.12 | Japan | 4.36 |
| Liberia | −0.47 | South Africa | 1.10 | Canada | 2.17 | China | 4.78 |
| Iraq | −0.45 | Nigeria | 1.22 | Pakistan | 2.17 | Taiwan | 5.54 |
| Zimbabwe | 0.18 | Bangladesh | 1.31 | Chile | 2.23 | South Korea | 5.55 |

● Incomplete Data

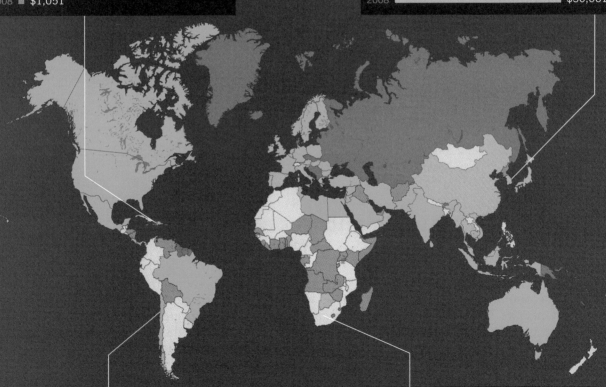

**Haiti Real Per Capita GDP**
1950 $1,610
2008 $1,051

**South Korea Real Per Capita GDP**
1950 $1,309
2008 $30,061

**Chile Real Per Capita GDP**
1950 $5,624
2008 $20,208

**South Africa Real Per Capita GDP**
1950 $3,885
2008 $7,346

# Human Welfare: Poor vs. Rich Nations

● Poor Nation  ● Rich Nation

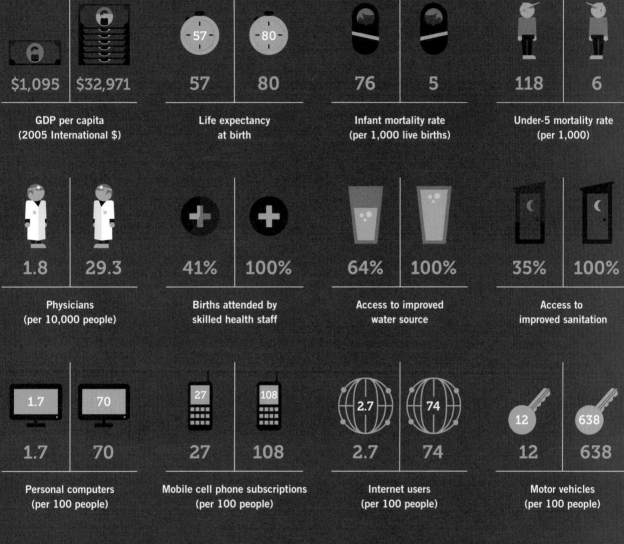

| $1,095 | $32,971 |
|---|---|

GDP per capita
(2005 International $)

| 57 | 80 |
|---|---|

Life expectancy
at birth

| 76 | 5 |
|---|---|

Infant mortality rate
(per 1,000 live births)

| 118 | 6 |
|---|---|

Under-5 mortality rate
(per 1,000)

| 1.8 | 29.3 |
|---|---|

Physicians
(per 10,000 people)

| 41% | 100% |
|---|---|

Births attended by
skilled health staff

| 64% | 100% |
|---|---|

Access to improved
water source

| 35% | 100% |
|---|---|

Access to
improved sanitation

| 1.7 | 70 |
|---|---|

Personal computers
(per 100 people)

| 27 | 108 |
|---|---|

Mobile cell phone subscriptions
(per 100 people)

| 2.7 | 74 |
|---|---|

Internet users
(per 100 people)

| 12 | 638 |
|---|---|

Motor vehicles
(per 100 people)

| 69% | 99% |
|---|---|

Literacy rate
(adult male)

| 55% | 99% |
|---|---|

Literacy rate
(adult female)

## REVIEW QUESTIONS

- On average, how much longer do people live in rich versus poor nations?

- If a growth rate of 1.1% persists in South Africa, how long it will take for income to double? Use the Rule of 70.

*Poor nations are the 40 poorest; rich nations are 31 high-income OECD nations. GDP data is from 2010 and is adjusted for prices across the different nations using a purchasing power parity (PPP) method. Other indicators are from 2008 and 2009.*

# Resources

Resources, also known as factors of production, are the inputs used to produce goods and services.

All else being equal, the more *resources* there are available to a nation, the more output that nation can produce. **Resources**, also known as **factors of production**, are the inputs used to produce goods and services. The discovery or cultivation of new resources is a source of economic growth. Economists divide resources into three major categories: natural resources, physical capital, and human capital.

## Natural Resources

Diamonds may be a girl's best friend, but are they essential for economic growth?

Natural resources include physical land and the inputs that occur naturally in or on the land. Coal, iron ore, diamonds, and lumber are examples of natural resources. Less obvious examples are mountains, beaches, temperate weather patterns, and scenic views—resources that residents enjoy consuming and that sometimes lead to tourism as a major industry.

Natural resources are an important source of economic wealth for nations. For example, the United States has fertile farmland, forests, coal, iron ore, and oil; the United States supplies about 9% of the world's oil.

Geography, or the physical location of a nation, is also a natural resource that can contribute to economic growth. Geographic location facilitates trade and affects other important variables such as weather and disease control. The world map in Figure 11.3 shows global GDP per square kilometer. As you can see, locations on coasts or along rivers have developed more rapidly than areas inland. These are the locations that were more naturally suited to trade in the days before railroads, trucks, and airplanes.

Natural resources clearly help to increase economic development, but they are not enough to make a nation wealthy. After all, many poor nations are rich in natural resources. For example, Liberia has mahogany forests, iron ore deposits, rubber tree forests, diamonds, and a beautiful coastline along the Atlantic Ocean. Yet with all these natural resources, Liberia is still poor. In contrast, think about Hong Kong, which is very small and densely populated with few natural resources. Yet the citizens of Hong Kong are among the wealthiest people in the world.

## Physical Capital

The second category of resources is physical capital, or just capital. Recall that capital comprises the tools and equipment used in the production of goods and services. Examples of capital include factories, tractors, roads and bridges, computers, and shovels. The purpose of capital is to aid in the production of future output.

Consider the shipping container, a basic tool that has aided the movement of goods around the globe. The shipping container is a standard-size (20- or 40-foot-long) box used to move goods worldwide. In 1954, a typical cargo ship traveling from New York to Germany might have carried as many as 194,582 individual items. The transportation involved bags, barrels, cartons, and many other different means of packaging and storing goods. Loading and unloading the ship required armies of men working long hours for days on end. Not surprisingly, shipping goods from one country to another was expensive.

**FIGURE 11.3**

GDP per square kilometer
- $ 0 - 499
- $ 500 - 1,099
- $ 1,100 - 2,999
- $ 3,000 - 8,099
- $ 8,100 - 21,199
- $ 22,000 - 59,999
- $ 60,000 - 162,999
- $ 163,000 - 441,999
- $ 442,000 - 546,000,000
- ||||| No Data

### Global GDP Density

The world's wealthiest areas (shown in darker colors on this map) are often those located near natural shipping lanes along coasts and rivers, where trade naturally flowed. This pattern is evidence that geography matters in economic development.

*Source:* John Luke Gallup, Jeffrey D. Sachs, and Andrew D. Mellinger, "Geography and Economic Development," Working Paper No. 1, Center for International Development at Harvard University, March 1999.

The standardized shipping container was first used in 1956. Suddenly, it was possible to move cargo around the globe without repacking every time the mode of transportation changed. Once a cargo ship enters the port, cranes lift the containers 200 feet in the air and unload about 40 large boxes each hour. Dozens of ships can be unloaded at a time, and most of the operation is run by computers. A container full of iPods can be loaded on the back of a truck in Shenzhen, China, transported to port, and loaded onto a ship that carries 3,000 containers. The ship can bring the iPods to the United States, where the containers are loaded onto a train and, later, a truck. This movement happens without anyone touching the contents. Clearly, the shipping container is a tool that has revolutionized world trade and improved lives.

As the quantity of physical capital per worker rises, so does output per worker. Of course, workers are more productive with more and better tools. Look around the world: the productive nations have impressive roads, bridges, buildings, and factories. In poor nations, paved roads are nonexistent or in disrepair, vehicles are of lower quality, and computers are a luxury. Even public electricity and sewage treatment facilities are rare in many developing nations.

Because of the obvious correlation between tools and wealth, many of the early contributions to growth theory focused on the role of physical capital goods. As a result, much international aid went

This cargo ship, bearing hundreds of individual shipping containers, is arriving in San Francisco with goods from Asia.

into the building of roads and factories, in the hope that prosperity would follow automatically. But today most people understand that capital alone is not sufficient to produce economic growth. Factories, dams, and other large capital projects bring wealth only when they mesh well with the rest of the economy. A steel factory is of little use in a region better suited for growing corn. Without a good rail network or proper roads, a steel factory cannot get the tools it needs and cannot easily sell its products. Dams that are not maintained fall into disrepair within years. Water pipes are a wonderful modern invention, but if they are not kept in good shape, human waste from toilets contaminates the water supply. The point is that simply building new capital tools in a nation does not ensure future sustained economic growth.

## Human Capital

**Human capital**
is the resource represented by the quantity, knowledge, and skills of the workers in an economy.

The output of a nation also depends on people to use its natural resources. **Human capital** is the resource represented by the quantity, knowledge, and skills of the workers in an economy. It is possible to expand human capital by increasing the number of workers available, by educating the existing labor force, or both.

We often think in terms of the sheer quantity of workers: all else being equal, a nation with more workers produces more output. But more output does not necessarily mean more economic growth. In fact, economic growth requires more output *per capita*. Adding more workers to an economy may increase total GDP without increasing per capita GDP. However, if more workers from a given population enter the labor force, GDP per capita can increase. For example, as we discussed in Chapter 7, women have entered the U.S. labor force in record numbers over the past 50 years. This change certainly contributed to increases in measured GDP and per capita GDP. When the primary output of adult women in the United States was non-market output such as homemaking services, it was not counted in the official GDP statistics. As more women join the official labor force, their output increases both GDP and per capita GDP.

There is another important dimension of human capital: the knowledge and skills of the workers themselves. In this context, it is possible to increase human capital through education and training. Training includes everything from basic literacy to college education, and from software competencies to specific job training.

Not many people would doubt that a more educated labor force is more productive. And certainly, to boost per capita output, educating the labor force is more helpful than merely increasing the quantity of workers. But education alone is not enough to ensure economic progress. For many years, for example, India struggled with economic growth, even while its workers were among the most educated in the world.

Education enhances human capital, but is it the key ingredient to economic growth?

## PRACTICE WHAT YOU KNOW

### Resources: Growth Policy

Many policies have been advocated to help nations escape poverty, and the policies often focus on the importance of resources.

**Question: For each policy listed below, which resource is the primary focus?**

a. international loans for infrastructure like roads, bridges, and dams
b. mandated primary education
c. restrictions on the development of forested land
d. population controls
e. international aid for construction of a shoe factory

The Akosombo Dam in Ghana was built with international aid funds.

**Answers:**

a. Infrastructure is physical capital.
b. Education involves human capital.
c. These restrictions focus on maintaining a certain level of natural resources.
d. Population controls often result from a short-sighted focus on physical capital per capita. The fewer people a nation has, the more tools there are per person.
e. The focus here is on physical capital.

# Technology

We all know that the world would be much poorer without computers, automobiles, electric light bulbs, and other goods that have resulted from productive ideas. **Technology** is the knowledge that is available for use in production. Though technology is often embodied in machines and productive techniques, it is really just knowledge. New technology enables us to produce more while using fewer of our limited resources. A **technological advancement** introduces new techniques or methods so that firms can produce more valuable outputs per unit of input. We can either produce more with the same resources or use fewer resources to produce the same quantity.

For example, the assembly line was an important technological advance. Henry Ford adopted and improved the assembly line method in 1913 at the Ford Motor Company. In this new approach to the factory, workers focused on well-defined jobs such as screwing on individual parts. The conveyor belt moved the parts around the factory to workers' stations. The workers themselves, by staying put rather than moving around the production floor, experienced a lower rate of accidents and other mishaps.

**Technology**
is the knowledge that is available for use in production.

A **technological advancement**
introduces new techniques or methods so that firms can produce more valuable outputs per unit of input.

Agriculture is a sector where technological advances are easy to spot. For example, we know that land resources are necessary to produce corn. But technological advances mean that over time it has become possible to grow and harvest more corn per acre of land. In fact, in the United States the corn yield per acre is now six times what it was in 1930. In 1930, we produced about 25 bushels of corn per acre, but now the yield is consistently over 150 bushels per acre. How is this possible? Through technology that has produced hybrid seeds, herbicides, fertilizers, and irrigation techniques.

Figure 11.4 presents another agricultural example of technological advancement. There are now significantly fewer milk cows in the United States than at any time since 1920. But total milk output is at historic highs because dairy farmers can now get about four times as much milk out of each cow. For example, farmers now line the cows' stalls with six to eight inches of sand. The sand is comfortable to lie on, it offers uniform support, and it stays cooler in the summer. In the end, the cows produce more milk. This is one simple example of how new ideas or technological advancements enable us to produce more while using fewer resources.

Like capital, technology produces value only when it is combined with other inputs. For example, simply carrying plans for a shoe factory to Haiti would not generate much economic value. The mere knowledge of how to produce shoes, while important, is only one piece of the growth puzzle. An economy must have the physical capital to produce shoes, must have the human capital to man the factory and assembly line, and must create favor-

## FIGURE 11.4

**Fewer Cows, But More Milk**

Wisconsin dairy cow populations continue to decline, but the average cow now produces four times more milk than in 1924. This means that, even with fewer cows, Wisconsin farmers produce two and a half times more milk than they did in 1924.

*Source:* Kate Golden, "Wisconsin's Ever-More-Efficient Milk Industry," WisconsinWatch.org, May 6, 2010.

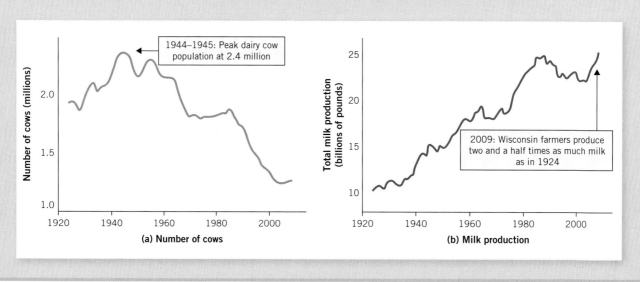

(a) Number of cows

(b) Milk production

able conditions and incentives for potential investors. Economic growth occurs when all these conditions come together. That is one reason why it is incorrect to identify technological innovations as the sole cause of differences in wealth across nations.

Moreover, technological innovations do not occur randomly across the globe. Some places produce large clusters of such innovations. Consider that information technology largely comes from MIT and Silicon Valley, movie and television ideas generally come from Hollywood, and new fashion designs regularly come from Paris, Milan, Tokyo, and New York. Technological innovations tend to breed more innovations. This leads us to reword an earlier question: Why do some regions innovate (and grow) more than others? A large part of the answer lies in our next subject, institutions.

# What Institutions Foster Economic Growth?

In 1950, residents in the African nation of Liberia were wealthier than those on the Southeast Asian island of Taiwan. Today, however, per capita GDP in Taiwan is more than 20 times that of Liberia. Yes, much of this wealth gap stems from obvious current differences in physical capital, human capital, and technology. But we must ask how these differences came about. Without a doubt, the biggest difference between Taiwan and Liberia since 1950 is the final growth factor we consider in this chapter: *institutions*.

An **institution** is a significant practice, relationship, or organization in a society. Institutions are the official and unofficial conditions that shape the environment in which decisions are made. Discussions often focus on institutions such as the laws and regulations in a nation. But other institutions such as social mores and work habits are also important.

An **institution** is a significant practice, relationship, or organization in a society.

Institutions are not always tangible physical items that we can look at or hold. There might be a physical representative of an institution, such as the U.S. Constitution or the building where the Supreme Court meets, but the essence of an institution encompasses expectations and habitual practices. The rules and the mindset within the Supreme Court are what is important, not the building or the chairs.

In this section, we consider the most significant institutions that affect production and income in a nation. These include private property rights, political stability and the rule of law, open and competitive markets, efficient taxes, and stable money and prices. Many of these are examined in detail elsewhere in this book, so we cover them only briefly here.

## Private Property Rights

The single greatest incentive for voluntary production is ownership of what you produce. The existence of **private property rights** means that individuals can own property—including houses, land, and other resources—and that when they use their property in production, they own the resulting output.

**Private property rights** encompass the rights of individuals to own property, to use it in production, and to own the resulting output.

Think about the differences in private property rights between Liberia and Taiwan. In Liberia, the system of ownership titles is not dependable. As a result, Liberians who wish to purchase land often must buy the land multiple times from different "owners," because there is no dependable record of true ownership. Taiwan, in contrast, has a well-defined system of law and property rights protection. Without such a system, people have very little incentive to improve the value of their assets.

In the past two decades, the government of China has relaxed its laws against private property ownership. This move has led to unprecedented growth. These market reforms stem from a risky experiment in the rural community of Xiaogang. In 1978, the heads of 21 families in Xiaogang signed an agreement that became the genesis of private property rights in China. This remarkable document read:

> December 1978, Mr. Yan's Home. We divide the field (land) to every household. Every leader of the household should sign and stamp. If we are able to produce, every household should promise to finish any amount they are required to turn in to the government, no longer asking the government for food or money. If this fails, even if we go to jail or have our heads shaved, we will not regret. Everyone else (the common people who are not officers and signees of this agreement) also promise to raise our children until they are eighteen years old. First signer: Hong Chang Yan.*

The agreement stipulated that each family would continue to produce the government quota for their agricultural output. But they would begin keeping anything they produced above this quota. They also agreed to stop taking food or money from the government. This agreement was dangerous in 1978—so dangerous that they stipulated that they would raise one another's children if any of the signees were put in jail.

The Xiogang agreement led to an agricultural boom that other communities copied. Seeing the success of this property rights experiment, Deng Xiaoping and other Chinese leaders subsequently instituted market reforms in agriculture in the 1980s, and then in manufacturing in the 1990s. China's economy is growing rapidly today not because the Chinese found new resources or updated their technology. They are wealthier because they now recognize private property rights in many different industries.

## Political Stability and the Rule of Law

To understand the importance of political stability and the rule of law, consider again Liberia and Taiwan. Before 2006, Liberia endured 35 years of political unrest. Government officials assumed office through the use of violence, and national leaders consistently used their power to eradicate their

Bullet casings litter the street in Monrovia, Liberia, in 2003.

* Literal translation by Chuhan Wang.

opponents. In contrast, Taiwan's political climate has been relatively stable since 1949. If you were an entrepreneur deciding where to build a factory, would you want to invest millions of dollars in a country with constant violent unrest, or would you choose a peaceful country instead? Which nation would you predict is more likely to see new factories and technological innovation?

Political instability is a disincentive for investment. After all, investment only makes sense if there is a fairly certain payoff at the end. In an environment of political instability, there is no incentive to invest in either human or physical capital because there is no predictable future payoff.

Consistent and trustworthy enforcement of a nation's laws is crucial for economic growth. Corruption is one of the most common and dangerous impediments to economic growth. When government officials steal, elicit bribes, or hand out favors to friends, this behavior reduces incentives for private investment. If individuals cannot count on consistent returns to investment in human or physical capital, investment declines. And this decline reduces future growth.

The World Justice Project has collected data on the rule of law across the world. Figure 11.5 shows the nations broken down into five groups, based on consistent enforcement of the rule of law. It is no surprise that nations scoring in the top group on this index are also the nations with the highest levels of per capita GDP. The most corrupt nations are also those with the lowest levels of income.

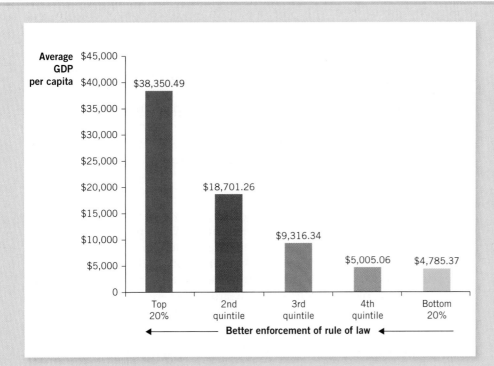

## FIGURE 11.5

**The Rule of Law and Per Capita Income**

Consistent and fair enforcement of a nation's laws pays off with economic growth. The nations with the least corruption have average per capita GDP of $38,350, but the most corrupt nations have average per capita GDP of just $4,785.

*Source*: World Justice Project, Annual Report 2011. GDP figures are adjusted using PPP (constant 2005 international $), 2005–2009.

## ECONOMICS IN THE REAL WORLD

### What Can Parking Violations Teach Us about International Institutions?

Would you get more parking tickets if you weren't compelled to pay for them?

Until 2002, diplomatic immunity protected United Nations diplomats in New York City from fines or arrest because of parking violations. This gave economists Raymond Fisman and Edward Miguel the idea for a unique natural experiment: they studied how officials responded to the lack of legal consequences for violating the law. Parking violations under these conditions are an example of corruption because they represent the abuse of power for private gain. Therefore, by comparing the level of parking violations of diplomats from different societies, the economists created a way to compare corruption norms among different cultures.

Fisman and Miguel compared unpaid parking violations with existing survey-based indices on levels of corruption across nations. They found that diplomats from high-corruption nations accumulated significantly more unpaid parking violations than those from low-corruption nations. Among the worst offenders were diplomats from Kuwait, Egypt, Chad, Sudan, and Bulgaria. Among those with zero unpaid parking violations were Australia, Canada, Denmark, Japan, and Norway.

This finding suggests that cultural or social norms related to corruption are quite persistent: even when stationed thousands of miles away, diplomats behave as if they are at home. Norms related to corruption are apparently deeply ingrained.

Incentives

In 2002, enforcement authorities acquired the right to confiscate the diplomatic license plates of violators. And guess what? Unpaid violations dropped by almost 98%. This outcome illustrates the power of incentives in influencing human behavior. ✳

## Competitive and Open Markets

In this section, we take a quick look at three institutions that are essential for economic growth: competitive markets, international trade, and flow of funds across borders. These market characteristics are covered in detail elsewhere in this book.

### Competitive Markets

In Chapter 3, we explored how competitive markets ensure that consumers can buy goods at the lowest possible prices. When markets aren't competitive, people who want to participate face barriers to entry. This inhibits competition and innovation. Yet many nations monopolize key industries by preventing competition or by establishing government ownership of industries. This strategy limits macroeconomic growth.

### International Trade

Trade creates value

Recall from Chapter 2 that trade creates value. International trade is very much like trade between individuals in the same country. In some cases, trade enables nations to consume goods and services that they would not produce on their own. Specialization and trade makes all nations better off because each can produce goods for which it enjoys a comparative advantage.

Output increases when nations (1) produce the goods and services for which they have the lowest opportunity cost, and (2) trade for the other goods and services they might wish to consume.

International trade barriers reduce the benefits available from specialization and trade. Chapter 19 is devoted to the study of international trade.

### Flow of Funds across Borders

In Chapter 9, we talked about the importance of savings for economic growth. For example, the inflow of foreign savings has helped to keep interest rates low in the United States even as domestic savings rates have fallen. If firms and individuals are to invest in physical or human capital, someone has to save. Opportunities for investment expand if there is access to savings from around the globe. That is, if foreigners can funnel their savings into your nation's economy, your nation's firms can use these funds to expand. However, many developing nations have restrictions on foreign ownership of land and physical plant within their borders. Restrictions on the flow of capital across borders handcuff domestic firms because they are forced to seek funds solely from domestic savers.

## Efficient Taxes

On the one hand, taxes must be high enough to support effective government. Political stability, the rule of law, and private property rights protection all require strong and consistent government. And taxes provide the revenue to pay for government services. On the other hand, if we tax activities that are fundamental to economic growth, there will be fewer of these activities. In market economies, output and income are strictly intertwined. If we tax income, we are taxing output, and that is GDP. So although taxes are necessary, they can also reduce incentives for production.

Before the federal government instituted an income tax, government services were largely funded by taxes on imports. But international trade is also an essential institution for economic growth. So taxes on imports also impede growth.

Efficient taxes are taxes sufficient to fund the activities of government while impeding production and consumption decisions as little as possible. It is not easy to determine the efficient level of taxes or even to determine what activities should be taxed. We will discuss this issue further in Chapter 16, when we discuss fiscal policy.

## Stable Money and Prices

High and variable inflation is a sure way to reduce incentives for investment and production. In Chapter 9, we saw that inflation increases uncertainty over future price levels. When people are unsure about future price levels, they are certainly more reluctant to sign contracts that deliver dollar payoffs in the future. Because of this, unpredictable inflation diminishes future growth possibilities. In the United States, the Federal Reserve (Fed) is charged with administering monetary policy. The Fed is designed to reduce incentives for politically motivated monetary policy, which typically leads to highly variable inflation rates. We cover the Fed in greater detail in Chapter 17.

# PRACTICE WHAT YOU KNOW

## Institutions: Can You Guess This Country?

**Question:** The following is a list of characteristics for a particular country. Can you name it?

1. This country has almost no natural resources.
2. It has no agriculture of its own.
3. It imports water.
4. It is located in the tropics.
5. It has four official languages.
6. It occupies 710 square kilometers.
7. It has one of the world's lowest unemployment rates.
8. It has a literacy rate of 96%.
9. It had a per capita GDP of $35,500 in 2009.
10. It has one of the densest populations per square mile on the planet.

Hint: the nation's flag is one of those shown here.

**Answer:** Congratulations if you thought of Singapore! At first blush, it seems almost impossible that one of the most successful countries on the planet could have so little going for it.

**Question: How could a country with so few natural resources survive, let alone flourish? How can an economy grow without any agriculture or enough fresh water?**

**Answer:** What Singapore lacks in some areas it more than makes up for in others. Singapore has a lot of human capital from a highly educated and industrious labor force. It has been able to attract plenty of foreign financial funds by creating a stable and secure financial system that protects property rights and encourages free trade. Singapore also has a strategically situated deep-water port in Southeast Asia that benefits from proximity to the emerging economies of China and India.

# Conclusion

We began this chapter with the misconception that natural resources are the primary source of economic growth. While it doesn't hurt to have more resources, they are certainly not sufficient for economic growth. Modern economics points instead to the institutions that frame the environment within which business and personal decisions are made.

## Learning More and Helping Alleviate Global Poverty

ECONOMICS FOR LIFE

The information presented in this chapter reveals a picture of significant and persistent poverty across much of the globe. It is possible that this discussion and your classroom lectures have inspired you to learn more about global poverty or even to try to help those who are less fortunate around the globe. Toward those ends, we can give a little advice.

The surest way to learn about world economic reality is to travel to a developing nation. We suggest taking an alternative spring break or even studying abroad for an entire semester in a developing nation. These are costly ventures, but they will almost certainly change your perspective on life. If you get the chance to travel, be sure to speak directly to people on the streets and ask them to share their personal stories with you. Talk to small business owners, parents, and children. If possible, try to speak to people who have nothing to gain by sharing their story.

It is possible that you wish to give financially to help the less fortunate around the globe. There are many international aid charities, but unfortunately not all are truly helpful or even completely honest. We recommend visiting the website for Givewell (www.givewell.org), which researches charitable organizations from around the world and recommends a few that have proven to be honest and effective.

If you want to study more about growth economics, you should start with two books. The first book is by economist William Easterly, titled *The Elusive Quest for Growth: Economists' Adventures and Misadventures in the Tropics*. In this book, Easterly weaves personal narrative and economic theory together in a unique way to help you understand how economic theories regarding growth have evolved through the years. He both explains past failures and argues compellingly for future policy proposals. The second book, by economists Daron Acemoglu and

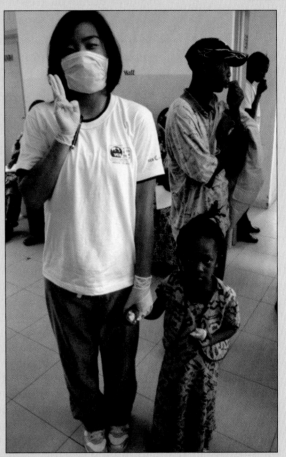

A University of Virginia student helps with eye surgeries in Tema, Ghana.

James Robinson, is called *Why Nations Fail: The Origins of Power, Prosperity, and Poverty*. This book presents the very best arguments for institutions as the primary source of economic growth. Even though this book is written by leading macroeconomists, it is enjoyable reading for mass audiences.

This chapter helps set a framework for thinking about growth policies. Many of the issues we touch on will see deeper treatment in later chapters. In particular, Chapter 12 presents the theory of economic growth. The current chapter has served as a catalyst to deepen your understanding of the theories behind those ideas.

# ANSWERING THE BIG QUESTIONS

## Why does economic growth matter?

* Economic growth affects human welfare in meaningful ways.
* Historical data shows that sustained economic growth is a relatively modern phenomenon.
* Relatively small but consistent growth rates are the best path out of poverty.

## How do resources and technology contribute to economic growth?

* Natural resources, physical capital, and human capital all contribute to economic growth.
* Technological change, which leads to the production of more valuable output per unit of input, also sustains economic growth.

## What institutions foster economic growth?

* Private property rights secure ownership of what an individual produces, creating incentives for increased output.
* Political stability and the rule of law allow people to make production decisions without concern for corrupt government.
* Competitive and open markets allow everyone to benefit from global productivity.
* Efficient taxes are high enough to support effective government, but low enough to provide positive incentives for production.
* Stable money and prices allow people to make long-term production decisions with minimal risk.

# CONCEPTS YOU SHOULD KNOW

factors of production (p. 342)
human capital (p. 344)
institution (p. 347)

private property rights (p. 347)
resources (p. 342)
rule of 70 (p. 335)

technological advancement
(p. 345)
technology (p. 345)

# QUESTIONS FOR REVIEW

1. What are the three factors that influence economic growth?

2. What is human capital, and how is it different from strictly the quantity of workers available for work? Name three ways to increase a nation's human capital. Is an increase in the size of the labor force also an increase in the human capital? Explain your answer.

3. How is economic growth measured?

4. Describe the pattern of world economic growth over the past 2,000 years. Approximately when did economic growth really take off?

5. List five human welfare conditions that are positively affected by economic growth.

6. Many historical accounts credit the economic success of the United States to its abundance of natural resources.

   a. What is missing from this argument?
   b. Name five poor nations that have significant natural resources.

7. The flow of funds across borders is a source of growth for economies. Use what you learned

about loanable funds in Chapter 9 to describe how foreign funds might expand output in a nation.

8. In 2011, when the U.S. unemployment rate was over 9%, President Barack Obama said, "There are some structural issues with our economy where a lot of businesses have learned to become much more efficient with a lot fewer workers. You see it when you go to a bank and you use an ATM, you don't go to a bank teller, or you go to the airport and you're using a kiosk instead of checking in at the gate." Discuss the president's quote in terms of both short-run unemployment and long-run growth.

9. The difference between 1% growth and 2% growth seems insignificant. Explain why it really matters.

10. What do economists mean by the term "institutions"? Name five different laws that are institutions that affect production incentives. Name three social practices that affect production in a society.

# STUDY PROBLEMS (✱ solved at the end of the section)

✱ 1. Real per capita GDP in China in 1959 was about $350, but it doubled to about $700 by 1978, when Deng Xiao Ping started market reforms.

a. What was the average annual economic growth rate in China over the 20 years from 1959 to 1978?
b. Chinese per capita real GDP doubled again in only seven years, reaching $1,400 by 1986. What was the average annual economic growth rate between 1979 and 1986?

* 2. The table below presents long-run macroeconomic data for two hypothetical nations, A and B.

| | A | B |
|---|---|---|
| Nominal GDP growth | 12% | 5% |
| Inflation | 10% | 2% |
| Nominal interest | 4% | 4% |
| Unemployment rate | 12% | 5% |
| Population growth | 1.5% | 1% |

Assume that both nations start with real GDP of $1,000 per citizen. Fill in the blanks in the table below, assuming the data above applies for every year considered.

| | A | B |
|---|---|---|
| Economic growth rate | _____ | _____ |
| Years required for real per capita GDP to double | _____ | _____ |
| Real per capita GDP 140 years later | _____ | _____ |

3. Let's revisit the data from Table 11.3, showing the following world economic growth rates for specific historical eras:

| Years | Growth rate |
|---|---|
| AD 1–1800 | 0.02% |
| 1800–1900 | 0.64% |
| 1900–1950 | 1.04% |
| 1950–2000 | 2.12% |

How many years will it take for average per capita real GDP to double at each of those growth rates?

4. Use the data in the table below to compute economic growth rates for the United States for 2008, 2009, and 2010. Note that all data is from the end of the year specified.

| Date | Nominal GDP (billions of current $) | GDP deflator | Population growth |
|---|---|---|---|
| 2007 | $14,061.8 | 106.30 | 1.01% |
| 2008 | 14,369.1 | 108.62 | 0.93% |
| 2009 | 14,119.0 | 109.61 | 0.87% |
| 2010 | 14,660.4 | 110.66 | 0.90% |

5. The rule of 70 applies in any growth rate application. Let's say you have $1,000 in savings and you have three alternatives for investing these funds:

- a savings account earning 1% interest per year
- a U.S. Treasury bond mutual fund earning 3% interest per year
- a stock market mutual fund earning 8% interest per year

How long would it take to double your savings in each of the three accounts?

6. Assume that you plan to retire in 40 years and are evaluating the three different accounts in the question above. How much would your $1,000 be worth in 40 years under each of the three alternatives?

# SOLVED PROBLEMS

**1a.** The rule of 70 tells us that we can divide 70 by the rate of growth to get the number of years before a variable doubles. Therefore, if we know the number of years that a variable actually did take to double, we can rearrange the rule of 70 to determine the average growth rate, $x$:

$$70 \div x = 20$$
$$70 \div 20 = x$$
$$= 3.5$$

Therefore, China grew an average of 3.5% over the 20-year period from 1959 to 1978.

**b.** Now, with real per capital GDP doubling in just 7 years, the rule of 70 implies:

$$70 \div 7 = 10$$

Therefore, China grew an average of 10% over the seven-year period from 1979 to 1986.

**2.** To determine economic growth rate, we use the approximations formula:

nominal GDP growth rate
− inflation
− population growth rate
―――――――――――――
economic growth rate

For nation A: 12% − 10% − 1.5% = 0.5%

For nation B: 5% − 2% − 1% = 2%

To determine the years required for real per capita GDP to double, we use the rule of 70:

For nation A: 70 ÷ 0.5 = 140

For nation B: 70 ÷ 2 = 35

To determine real per capita GDP 140 years later, use the rule of 70 results. Nation A's level doubles in exactly 140 years, so it will be two times the original level of $1,000, so $2,000. Nation B's level doubles after 35 years and then doubles again after 35 more. So after 70 years its level of real per capita GDP is four times the original level. It doubles again in 35 years, so after 105 years it is eight times the original level. Then it doubles again in 35 more years, so after 140 years its real per capita GDP is 16 times the original level, $16,000.

|  | A | B |
|---|---|---|
| Economic growth rate | 0.5% | 2% |
| Years required for real per capita GDP to double | 140 | 35 |
| Real per capita GDP 140 years later | $2,000 | $16,000 |

**The essential ingredient for economic growth is physical capital such as factories, infrastructure, and other tools.**

Looking around the world, you see many rich nations and many poor nations. Rich developed nations have impressive capital including highways, factories, and office buildings. Poor under-developed nations have more unpaved roads and fewer modern factories and buildings. Many people see that capital and wealth seem to go hand in hand and conclude that capital is the source of wealth. From this view, if poor nations could just acquire bigger and better tools, they too could be wealthy. But correlation does not prove causation. Modern economic growth theory indicates that capital is the result of growth, rather than the cause of it, and that the key to economic growth is institutions.

**MIS CONCEPTION**

In the last chapter, we saw that economic growth can transform lives. Consistent economic growth, even at relatively small rates, is the pathway out of poverty. In this chapter, we shed light on the causes of economic growth by examining growth theory. We also discuss policies that foster growth.

As the chapter title implies, much of the content of this chapter is theoretical. Yet because of the relationship between economic growth and human welfare, the theory is never far from the real world. We begin the chapter with a brief description of how economic theories develop. After that, we consider the evolution of growth theory starting with the Solow growth model. After discussing the theory and implications of the Solow model, we consider modern growth theory and the implied policy prescriptions.

Modern roads speed productivity, but are they a sure route to wealth?

# BIG QUESTIONS

* How do macroeconomic theories evolve?
* What is the Solow growth model?
* How does technology affect growth?
* Why are institutions the key to economic growth?

## How Do Macroeconomic Theories Evolve?

This chapter marks our first major step into macroeconomic theory, or modeling. In Chapter 2, we discussed how economic models are built: good models are simple, flexible, and able to make powerful predictions. In this chapter, we present a model of economic growth that simplifies from the real world yet also helps us make powerful predictions about economic growth. The stakes are high: growth theory and policy have significant impacts on human lives. Therefore, it's important to consistently re-evaluate growth theory in light of real-world results.

Today, economists agree that economic growth is determined by a combination of resources, technology, and institutions. But this consensus is the result of an evolution in growth theory that started almost 60 years ago, with the contributions of economist Robert Solow. Although the theory has changed significantly over the past two decades, Solow's growth model still forms the nucleus of modern growth theory.

In many academic disciplines, new theories are fodder for intellectual debates, with no direct impact on human lives. But in economics, theories are put to the test in the real world, often very soon after they are first articulated. Figure 12.1 illustrates the relationship between economic ideas and real-world events. At the top of the circle, we begin with observations of the real world, which inform a theory as it develops. Once an economic theory is developed, it can influence the policies that are used to pursue certain economic goals. These policies affect the daily lives and well-being of real people. Finally, as economists observe the effects of policy in the real world, they continue to revise economic theory.

Economic growth models affect the welfare of billions of people worldwide. The results can be beneficial. But if growth theory is wrong or incomplete, it can lead to faulty policy prescriptions that result in poverty. We will revisit this point toward the end of the chapter.

### The Evolution of Growth Theory

In 1776, Adam Smith published his renowned book *An Inquiry into the Nature and Causes of the Wealth of Nations*. This book was the first real economics textbook and, as the title indicates, it focused on what makes a nation wealthy.

**FIGURE 12.1**

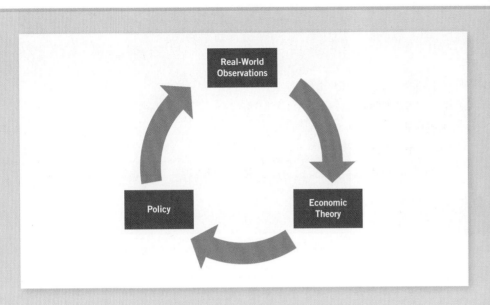

**The Interplay between the Real World and Economic Theory**
Observations of the real world shape economic theory. Economic theory then informs policy decisions that are designed to meet certain economic goals. Once these policies are implemented, they affect the real world. Further real-world observations contribute to additional advances in economic theory, and the cycle continues.

The central question, paraphrased from the title, is this: why do some nations prosper while others do not? More than two centuries later, we still grapple with the nature and causes of the wealth of nations.

Economists are not alone in their pursuit of answers to this question. Perhaps you or someone you know has visited a developing country. As travel becomes easier and the world economy becomes more integrated, people are more exposed to poverty around the globe. Many college students today ask the same questions as economists: why are so many people poor, and what can be done about it?

This link between economic theory and human welfare is what drives many scholars to study the theory of economic growth. As the Nobel Prize–winning macroeconomist Robert Lucas wrote in 1988:

> Is there some action a government of India could take that would lead the Indian economy to grow like Indonesia's or Egypt's? If so, what exactly? If not, what is it about the "nature of India" that makes it so? The consequences for human welfare involved in questions like these are simply staggering: *Once one starts to think about them it is hard to think of anything else.*

Economic growth has not always been the primary focus of macroeconomics. After the Great Depression in the 1930s, macroeconomics shifted to the study of business cycles, or short-run expansions and contractions. In the 1980s and 1990s, recessions rarely occurred, and so the primary focus of macroeconomics returned to long-run growth.

Growth theory began with the Solow model, which was developed in the 1950s and still serves as the foundation for growth theory, both in method and in policy. Therefore, while growth theory has evolved, it is helpful to consider the Solow model as both a starting point and the nucleus of current theory.

Why are some nations rich, like Malaysia . . .          . . . while other nations remain poor, like Uganda?

# What Is the Solow Growth Model?

If you travel around the globe and visit nations with different levels of income, you will notice significant differences in the physical tools available for use in production. Wealthy nations have more factories, better roads, more and better computers—they have more capital. Simply viewing the difference in capital, it is easy to conclude that capital automatically yields economic growth.

This was the basic premise of early growth theory: there are rich nations and there are poor nations, and the rich nations are those that have capital. Throughout this chapter, we will often refer to capital as *physical capital* to distinguish it from human capital. Natural resources and human capital are also important in the Solow growth model, but the focus is primarily on physical capital, or just capital. We begin by looking at a nation's production function, which describes how changes in capital affect real output.

## A Nation's Production Function

A **production function** for a firm describes the relationship between the inputs the firm uses and the output it creates.

The Solow model starts with a *production function* for the entire economy. In microeconomic theory, a firm's **production function** describes the relationship between the inputs a firm uses and the output it creates. For example, at a single McDonald's restaurant the daily output depends on the number of employees; anything needed to make the final product such as hamburger patties, French fries, and so on; and the capital tools that employees have to work with, including things such as space for cooking, cash registers, and drink dispensers. In equation form, the production function for a single firm is:

(Equation 12.1) $$q = f(\text{human capital, physical capital})$$

where q is the output of the firm. Equation 12.1 says that output *is a function of* the quantities of human and physical capital that the firm uses. For McDonald's, the output is the number of meals produced.

In macroeconomics, we extend the production function to an entire nation or macroeconomy. The **aggregate production function** describes the relationship among all the inputs used in the macroeconomy and the total output of that economy, where GDP is output. In its simplest form, the aggregate production function tells us that GDP is a function of three broad types of resources, or factors of production, which are the inputs used in producing goods and services. These inputs are physical capital, human capital, and natural resources. We can state it in equation form as:

$$GDP = Y = F(\text{physical capital, human capital, natural resources})$$

(Equation 12.2)

The **aggregate production function** describes the relationship among all the inputs used in the macroeconomy and the total output (GDP) of that economy.

where Y is real output, or GDP.

We can think about the relationship between input and output in a very simple economy. Consider a situation in which there is only one person in the macroeconomy—for example, Chuck Noland from the 2000 movie *Cast Away*. Chuck's individual, or microeconomic, decisions are also macroeconomic decisions, because he is the only person in the economy. The GDP of Chuck's island includes only what he produces with his resources. Let's say that Chuck spends his days harvesting fruit on the island. In this case, GDP is equal to whatever fruit Chuck harvests. Table 12.1 shows Chuck's production function and some of the resources he has available.

Chuck's output is the fruit he harvests from around his island. His resources include his human capital, the physical capital of a bamboo ladder, and the island's natural resources such as bamboo and fruit trees. All else equal, the more Chuck has of any of these resources, the more GDP he can produce. Economic growth occurs if Chuck produces more fruit per week.

Chuck's individual, or microeconomic, decisions are also macroeconomic decisions, because he is the only person in the economy.

The production function for a large developed macroeconomy like that of the United States is the same as Chuck Noland's in many ways. Output depends on the resources available for production. The United States has significant natural resources such as oil, iron ore, coal, timber, and farmland. In terms of human capital, the United States has a large labor force composed of over 155 million workers. Of those workers age 25 and over, more than 90% have graduated from high school. Finally, the United States has built

## TABLE 12.1

### Chuck Noland's Production Function

**Production function**

$GDP = f(\text{natural resources, human capital, physical capital resources})$

| GDP | Resources | Example |
|-----|-----------|---------|
| | Natural resources | Fruit trees and bamboo |
| Fruit | Human capital | Chuck's time and knowledge |
| | Physical capital | Bamboo ladder |

up a very large stock of physical capital. All of these resources enable the nation to produce an annual GDP of more than $16 trillion.

## The Focus on Capital Resources

The early Solow model focused on capital goods. As we noted in the chapter opener, early growth theorists saw that capital resources in wealthy nations far exceed those available in developing nations. After all, there are more factories, highways, bridges, and dams in wealthy nations. It seemed logical to conclude that capital is the key to growth.

In addition, periods of investment growth in developed economies are also periods of economic expansion. Figure 12.2 plots quarterly U.S. economic growth rates with investment growth rates from 1960 to 2011. The data shows a clear positive correlation between real GDP growth and the rate of investment growth. This is another reason to believe that investment and capital are the primary sources of economic growth.

## FIGURE 12.2

### U.S. Investment and GDP Growth, 1960–2011

Growth in real investment is positively correlated with growth in real GDP. The big question is whether this implies causation.

*Source:* Bureau of Economic Analysis.

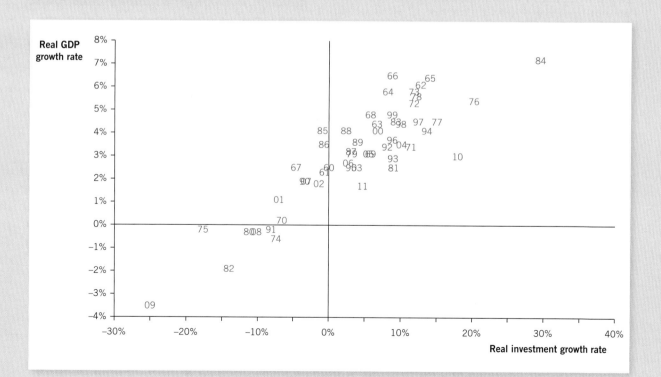

Earlier, we noted the interplay of theory and real-world observations. This is one example. Capital *appears* to cause economic growth because there is such a strong correlation between wealth and output. And, certainly, no one would dispute that workers are more productive when they have more tools. For now, we will continue our focus on capital. Later, we will explore some of the missing pieces that contemporary growth theory has contributed.

## Diminishing Marginal Products

Chuck Noland would be happy if he found a new grove of mangoes on his island, and his newfound resources would increase his GDP. Resources also help actual large macroeconomies. For example, the discoveries of natural gas in the United States have increased dramatically over the past two decades. This new energy resource enables the United States to produce more with cheaper resources, because natural gas is less expensive than crude oil. To quantify how helpful a resource may be, economists employ the concept of *marginal product*. The **marginal product** of an input is the change in output divided by the change in input. More formally:

$$MP_{input\ x} = \text{change in output from a change in input x}$$

More resources increase output, so we say the marginal product of each resource is positive.

The **marginal product** of an input is the change in output divided by the change in input.

### Diminishing Marginal Product in a One-Person Economy

Let's take a closer look at Chuck Noland's production function. Initially, Chuck produces GDP by climbing trees and picking fruit. With this method, he is able to gather 1 bushel of fruit in a week. He produces this weekly GDP without the aid of any physical capital. Then Chuck decides to build a bamboo ladder. Building the ladder is a costly investment because it takes him away from producing fruit for a whole week. But then, after he has the ladder as physical capital, his weekly output grows to 4 bushels. Using the language we defined above, we say that the marginal product (MP) of his ladder is 3 bushels of fruit per week:

$$MP_{capital} = \text{change in output from a change in capital} = 3$$

Chuck is so happy with his ladder that he builds a second ladder so that he can leave one on each side of the island. Now his weekly output climbs to 6 bushels of fruit. Because he produces 4 bushels with one ladder and 6 bushels with two ladders, the marginal product of the second ladder is 2 bushels. Note that while the marginal product of the second ladder is positive, it is less than the marginal product of the first ladder. The marginal product of the second ladder is not as large because while the first ladder completely altered the way Chuck harvests fruit, the second ladder just makes his job a little easier.

Figure 12.3 shows a hypothetical relationship between Chuck's output and the number of ladders he uses. Looking first at the table on the right, note that the second column shows total output (bushels per week), which depends on the number of ladders. The third column shows the marginal product of each ladder. Notice that the marginal product per ladder declines as more ladders are added. This reflects the principle of **diminishing marginal product**, which states that the marginal product of an input falls as the quantity of the

A ladder would help!

**Diminishing marginal product** occurs when the marginal product of an input falls as the quantity of the input rises.

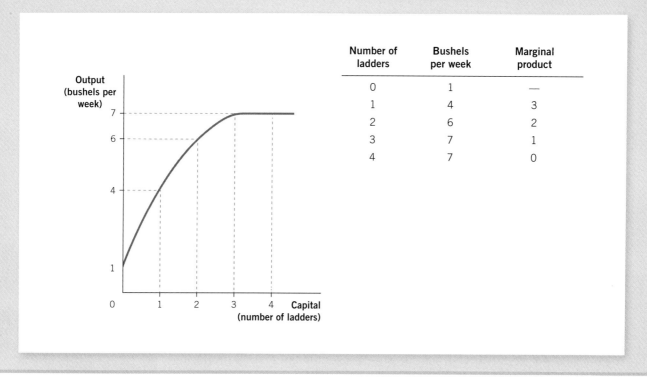

## FIGURE 12.3

### Chuck Noland's Production Function

The table shows how output (bushels per week) increases as the number of ladders increases; it describes the relationship between output and capital inputs. The graph is a picture of the production function. Output increases with capital, but each unit of capital yields less additional output. The shape of the production function, in which the slope is declining, illustrates the diminishing marginal product of capital.

| Number of ladders | Bushels per week | Marginal product |
|---|---|---|
| 0 | 1 | — |
| 1 | 4 | 3 |
| 2 | 6 | 2 |
| 3 | 7 | 1 |
| 4 | 7 | 0 |

input rises. Diminishing marginal product generally applies across all factors of production at both the microeconomic and the macroeconomic levels.

The left side of Figure 12.3 is a graph of Chuck's production function: it plots the points from the first two columns of the table on the right. With no ladders, the production function indicates 1 bushel of fruit; but then as ladders are added, output climbs along the curve. The slope of the curve flattens out because the marginal product of the added ladders diminishes.

This principle of diminishing marginal productivity is not special to our example of one man alone on an island. It is a phenomenon that holds for resources in a macroeconomy in general, and it is a cornerstone insight of the Solow growth model. Sometimes, this principle is referred to as *diminishing returns*. The discussion below places this concept in the macroeconomic context of the U.S. interstate highway system.

### U.S. Interstate Highways and the Aggregate Production Function

In the United States, we have a system of interstate highways that the federal government has built. This highway system is essentially a 50,000-mile capital good that we use to help produce GDP. The network of highways con-

How much would GDP fall without our interstate highways?

nects the major cities of the United States. These highways increase GDP in the United States—they enhance our ability to transport goods and services across the nation. For example, a couch manufactured in High Point, North Carolina, can be transported exclusively by interstate highway to Cleveland, Ohio, in less than eight hours. Before the construction of the interstate system, the same trip between High Point and Cleveland would have taken twice as long, required more gasoline due to inefficient speeds, and caused much more wear and tear on the vehicles used.

Our system of highways is a significant resource that contributes to our nation's GDP. On the one hand, if the interstate highway system were somehow to close down completely, GDP would immediately fall. On the other hand, what would happen to GDP if the government created a second interstate highway system with 50,000 miles of additional roads crisscrossing the United States? That is, what would be the marginal product of an additional interstate highway system? The impact would be positive, but much smaller than that of the original network. This illustrates diminishing returns: the marginal product of highways declines as more and more become available. The production relationship is just like that of Chuck Noland's ladders.

Figure 12.4 is a picture of the aggregate production function—the production function for the entire economy. On the vertical axis, we have output for the macroeconomy, which is real GDP (Y). Economic growth is represented as movements upward along the vertical axis. On the horizontal axis, capital resources (K) increase from left to right. Notice that the slope of the function is positive, which indicates positive marginal product. But the marginal impact of capital also declines as more is added. For example, the difference in output from the increase in capital from $K_1$ to $K_2$ is larger than the change in output from a change in capital from $K_3$ to $K_4$. This outcome illustrates the declining marginal product of capital.

The aggregate production function forms the basis for most discussions in growth theory since 1956. Economic growth is represented by upward

**FIGURE 12.4**

**The Aggregate Production Function**

The aggregate production function graphs the relationship between output (real GDP) and capital inputs. The shape of the production function illustrates two important features of production. First, the marginal production of resources is positive, as indicated by the positive slope. Second, the marginal product of additional resources declines as more resources are added. This is evident in the declining slope of the function.

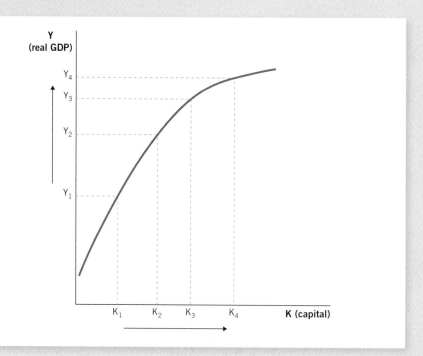

movement along the vertical axis. Indeed, if we focus *only* on this simple formulation, economic growth happens only with investment in capital. Diminishing returns, or declining marginal productivity, is the key assumption of the Solow model. As we shall see, this single assumption leads to striking implications for the macroeconomy.

## Implications of the Solow Model

We can use the basic framework of the production function with an emphasis on capital and diminishing returns to flesh out the two important implications of the Solow model: the conditions of a *steady state* and *convergence*.

### The Steady State

How many ladders should Chuck Noland build? It takes a week to build each ladder, and each additional ladder adds less output than the one before. Therefore, at some point Chuck has no incentive to build additional ladders. Perhaps this happens after he builds two ladders. Looking back at Figure 12.3, you can see that a third ladder yields only 1 more bushel of fruit. Let's assume that Chuck decides it is not worth a week of work (to build a ladder) for 1 more bushel of fruit. Therefore, he builds only two ladders. This means that his output remains at 6 bushels a week. At this point, economic growth for Chuck stops.

An economy at the steady state is like an airplane at its cruising altitude.

The Solow model implies the same outcome for large macroeconomies. Because the marginal product of capital decreases, at some point there is no reason to build (that is, invest in) more capital. Perhaps this occurs at $K_3$ in Figure 12.4. This means there is no incentive to build additional capital beyond the level of $K_3$ because the benefits in terms of additional output no longer exceed the cost of building capital. Since there is no incentive to build capital past $K_3$, and since we are assuming that capital is the source of growth, the economy stops growing once it reaches $K_3$. This is called the economy's *steady state*. The **steady state** is the condition of a macroeconomy when there is no new net investment.

The **steady state** is the condition of a macroeconomy when there is no new net investment.

Once an economy reaches the steady state, there is no change in either capital or real income. The steady state is a direct implication of diminishing returns: when the marginal return to capital declines, at some point there is no incentive to build more capital. And this is not a very encouraging situation. You can think of the steady state as the "stagnant state," because when the economy reaches its steady state, real GDP is no longer increasing and economic growth stops.

It is important to distinguish between investment and net investment. Over time, capital wears out: roads get potholes, tractors break down, and factories become obsolete—this is known as capital *depreciation*. **Depreciation** is a fall in the value of a resource over time. Depreciation is natural with capital, and it erodes the capital stock. Without new investment, capital declines over time, so some positive investment is needed to offset depreciation. But if investment is exactly enough to replace depreciated items, the capital stock will not increase—and this means no *net investment*. **Net investment** is investment minus depreciation. In order to increase the capital stock, net investment must be positive.

**Depreciation** is a fall in the value of a resource over time.

**Net investment** is investment minus depreciation.

This distinction between investment and net investment is important when we consider the steady state. In the steady state, net investment equals zero. There may be positive investment, but this is investment to replace worn-out machines and tools. So when an economy reaches its steady state, the capital stock stays constant. For example, if three ladders represent a steady-state condition on Chuck Noland's island, he may repair his ladders periodically. Repairing the ladders to maintain a level of capital counts as investment, but not as net investment.

# PRACTICE WHAT YOU KNOW

The Japanese government estimated total damages of $309 billion from the 2011 earthquake and tsunami.

## Changes in Resources: Natural Disasters

In 2011, a major earthquake and tsunami in Japan destroyed significant physical capital, including roads, homes, factories, and bridges.

Question: How would you use an aggregate production function to illustrate the way a major destruction of capital affects a macroeconomy in the short run?

Answer:

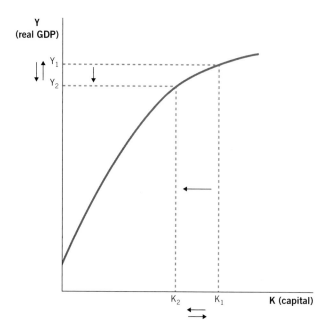

This is an unusual situation in which the level of capital in a nation actually falls. Since capital (K) is on the horizontal axis of the production function, the decline in capital moves Japan back along its production function. This means less GDP for Japan (Y falls) until the nation can get its capital rebuilt.

Question: With no further changes, what happens to real GDP in the long run?

Answer: With no further changes, real GDP returns to the steady-state output level in the long run. At the new level of capital ($K_2$), the marginal product of additional capital is relatively high, so there is a greater return to building new capital. But in the long run, since there was no shift in the production function, the level of capital returns to the steady-state level ($K_1$), which means that output also returns to its steady-state level ($Y_1$).

## Convergence

If nations with large stocks of capital stop growing, then nations with less capital can catch up if they are adding to their capital stock. This means that nations all over the globe could potentially converge to the same level of wealth. **Convergence** is the idea that per capita GDP levels across nations will equalize as nations approach the steady state. Here is the logic of the Solow model: rich nations are rich because they have more capital. But as these nations approach their steady state, the returns to capital decline and the growth slows. When a nation reaches a steady state, its economic growth stops. But if a nation has not yet reached the steady state, adding capital still leads to growth in that nation. Therefore, investment in developing nations should yield relatively greater returns, and this outcome should lead to more capital in developing nations.

Consider the United States and China. In 1980, the United States was wealthy, but China was poor. Figure 12.5 shows both nations as they might have appeared on a production function in 1980. Yet since 1980, growth rates in China have exceeded growth rates in the United States. This blast of growth in China has been accompanied by rapid industrialization—that is, the creation of new physical capital. According to the Solow model, the new capital in China yields greater returns because the nation started with less capital.

If this basic model were always true to reality, new factories would typically yield higher returns in poor nations than in rich nations. Investors seeking to build new factories would turn to nations like Haiti, Nicaragua, and North Korea—nations with relatively small capital stocks.

**Convergence**
is the idea that per capita GDP levels across nations will equalize as nations approach the steady state.

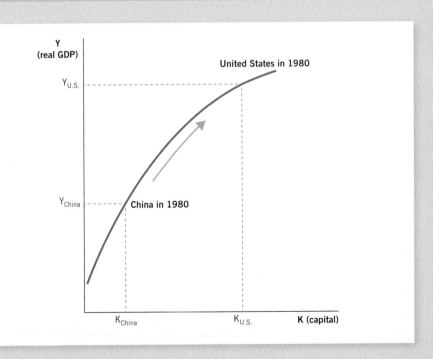

**FIGURE 12.5**

**Convergence**
In 1980, the United States had much more capital than China did; this was one reason why real GDP for the United States was much higher. But in the years since, China has increased its capital stock substantially and has grown much more rapidly than the United States. The Solow model implies that the United States is closer to its steady state and therefore grows more slowly than China.

Convergence argues that the hare and the tortoise will end up at the finish line together.

According to the Solow theory, developing nations should catch up because the older, developed economies have already made new discoveries and have documented mistakes to avoid in the development process. Developing nations can jump right into acquiring the best equipment, tools, and practices. For example, if they are building cars, they don't have to start with a Model T and a basic labor-intensive assembly line; they can immediately establish a modern plant resembling those of, say, Honda and Volkswagen.

But reality is much different. First, although we see cases of rapid growth in poor nations, convergence is rare. Some poor nations have grown rapidly over the past few decades. In addition to China, the nations of South Korea, Singapore, India, Chile, and others have done well. But they are exceptions. Most poor nations continued to stagnate at the turn of the twenty-first century. Second, growth in developed nations hasn't stopped. For example, Figure 12.6 shows U.S. economic growth rates in 20-year time windows since 1820. If anything, growth was accelerating even as Solow wrote his papers in the 1950s. Taken together, these observations give no evidence of either catching up or slowing down.

Given that we have no evidence of either a steady state or of convergence, it is time to re-assess the model. In particular, we need to answer the question of why we see sustained growth in wealthy nations. In the next section, we consider whether technology is the answer.

## FIGURE 12.6

### U.S. Economic Growth Rates since 1820

The Solow model implies that growth in the United States should slow down over time. However, there is little evidence of the United States reaching a steady state.

*Source:* U.S. Bureau of Economic Analysis.

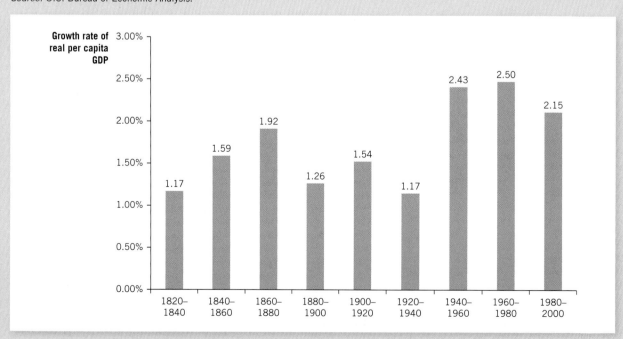

# How Does Technology Affect Growth?

In this section, we consider how technological innovations affect the Solow model. We also address assumptions about the way they occur.

## Technology and the Production Function

In 1994, Intel introduced a revolutionary computer chip for personal computers—the Pentium chip. The Pentium could perform 188 million instructions per second and was more than three times faster than its predecessor chip. But by 2011, just 19 years later, Intel's new chip, the Core i7 3960x, could perform 178 *billion* instructions per second. The new chip costs less and uses less energy than the old chip, yet it is almost a thousand times faster!

These Intel chips give us a good picture of what technology does. A computer chip is physical capital—it is a tool that helps us produce. When we get faster chips, we can produce even more with the same amount of capital.

Now let's see how new technology affects the Solow growth model. First, consider the production function. Figure 12.7 shows two production functions: $F_1$ is the initial production function, when computers are running on Pentium chips; $F_2$ is the production function after faster chips become available. Note that the new production function is steeper than the old. The slope is determined by the marginal product of capital, and the new computer chips make capital more productive at all levels. For any given level of capital, real GDP is higher. These are the kinds of changes that fuel sustained economic growth.

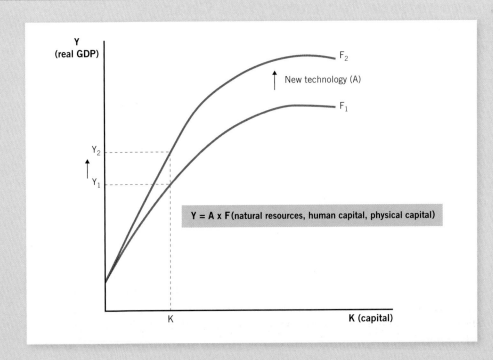

**FIGURE 12.7**

**New Technology and the Production Function**

New technology increases the slope of the production function as the marginal product of capital increases. The old production function is shown as $F_1$ and the new production function as $F_2$. After the technological innovation (represented by A in the equation), capital is more productive, and this outcome leads to new economic growth. If technology continues to advance, economic growth can be sustained.

Y = A x F (natural resources, human capital, physical capital)

Older map technology took lots of time . . .        . . . but the new map technology is faster.

We can also see how the production function is altered in equation form. The aggregate production function now includes an allowance for technological advancement:

(Equation 12.3)    $Y = A \times F$(natural resources, human capital, physical capital)

where the letter *A* accounts for technological change. This small addition to the basic model helps to explain continued economic growth. Without new technology, the economy eventually reaches a steady state, and growth stops. But new technology means that output is higher for any given level of capital, because the capital, which embeds the new technology, is more productive. The new technology shifts real output, and therefore income, up to new levels.

Before looking at policy implications that derive from the Solow model, we need to look more closely at how technological change occurs in the model.

## Exogenous Technological Change

Why do people innovate? What drives them to create better ways of producing? If technology is the source of sustained growth, then the answer to this question is critical.

In the Solow model, there is no real answer to the question of what causes technological innovation. The model assumes that technical change occurs *exogenously*. Recall from Chapter 2 that exogenous factors are the variables not accounted for in a model. For our purposes here, this means that technological innovations just happen—they are not based on economics. In this sense, technological innovations occur randomly. If technology is exogenous, it is like rainfall: sometimes you get a lot, and sometimes you don't get any. If some nations get more technological innovations than others, then that is just their good fortune.

But if technology is the source of sustained growth, and if technology is exogenous, then economic growth is also exogenous. **Exogenous growth** is growth that is independent of any factors in the economy. When we see innovation occurring in the same places over and over, the Solow model chalks it up to luck. In this view, the innovations are not due to any inherent characteristics of the economies that experience them. Similarly, in this view, poor nations are poor because the random technology innovations happened elsewhere.

**Exogenous growth** is growth that is independent of any factors in the economy.

# PRACTICE WHAT YOU KNOW

## Technological Innovations: How Is the Production Function Affected?

When new technology is introduced, it makes capital more productive. For example, modern tractors are faster and more powerful than tractors of old.

**Question: How does this type of change affect the production function?**

This tractor was state-of-the-art technology in 1910.

**Answer:** The production function gets steeper at each point. For example, when the level of capital is K, the slope of production function $F_2$ is steeper than the slope of $F_1$. The reason is that capital is now more productive at every level. The first unit of capital adds more to output than before, and the 500th unit of capital adds more to output than before. The marginal product of capital, which is embedded in the slope of the production function, is now higher at all levels.

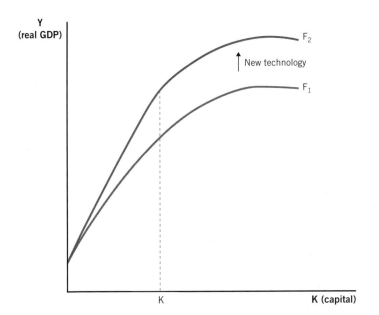

# Technological Change

## *Modern Marvels*

*Modern Marvels* is a television series on the History Channel. It often showcases technological innovations that have revolutionized the way goods and services are produced. In Season 13, an episode titled "Harvesters 2" included a look at cranberry harvesting around the globe.

Cranberries are grown on low-lying vines. In the past, cranberry harvesting involved many workers carefully hand-harvesting the berries. But cranberries also have air pockets inside them, and these pockets enable farmers to employ a wet harvest. The big innovation in harvesting occurred when farmers began flooding the fields and then knocking the cranberries off the bushes with water-reel harvesters called beaters. This innovation meant that just a few workers could harvest 10 acres of cranberries in a single day, saving hundreds of hours of labor.

The beaters make the harvest go quickly, but they also tend to damage some of the berries. Recently, Habelman Brothers, a cranberry farm in Tomah, Wisconsin, began using a gentler method than the water-reel so as not to damage the cranberries. Their harvesters use waterwheels with wooden panels to

Cranberries don't grow in water, but they float to the top when farmers flood the fields.

knock the berries off the vines, damaging fewer berries in the process.

These two innovations—water-harvesting and the new, gentler waterwheel—are both examples of innovations caused by incentives. The first innovation cut harvesting costs significantly, and the second increased the return from the harvest. The innovators are the farmers—those who have the most to gain. Technology is not random; it is a result of individuals responding to incentives.

The discovery of the glue used for Post-it Notes was accidental. When the notes are used to paper a friend's car, it is normally premeditated.

If you question the assumption that technological advance is a matter of pure luck, you are right. But why did the Solow growth model make this assumption? First, technological progress is tied to scientific advancements, and at times scientific discoveries seem to happen by chance. One classic example is the invention of Post-it Notes. Researchers at 3M accidentally stumbled onto a formula for glue that made Post-it Notes possible.

Second, most economic models are developed mathematically. The assumption of exogenous technical change made the theoretical growth models simpler to solve because it ruled out a very complicated factor. But in the 1980s, economists developed other models to help incorporate technical change into the heart of the original model.

## Policy Implications of the Solow Model

At the beginning of this chapter, we noted that macroeconomic theory has strong implications for policy; it translates into policy recommendations. What policy prescriptions follow from the Solow growth model?

If you believe the Solow model and its conclusions, then the policy implications are straightforward. Wealth comes from capital and modern technology. Therefore, developing nations need the latest technology embedded in capital goods. Furthermore, wealthy nations and individuals around the globe who wish to help poor nations should funnel aid to the poor countries for use in purchasing the latest capital.

Two specific types of aid developed during the 1950s and 1960s to implement this approach. First, actual capital goods were built with aid from developed nations. For example, in 1964, with funding from the United States, Great Britain, and the World Bank, the Akosombo Dam was built in the West African nation of Ghana. The hydroelectric dam was intended to produce several benefits. It formed a lake that could be used for water transportation and a fishing industry. The dam could also generate electricity. But even a gift of this magnitude failed to jump-start the Ghanaian economy. Forty-three years after the dam was completed, average income levels in Ghana have risen by just $300 per person.

Second, billions of dollars of international aid went to developing nations to help them fund investment in infrastructure such as highways, bridges, and modern ports, as well as other types of capital. These aid payments were intended to help poor nations build capital infrastructure that would pave the way to economic growth.

However, even after billions of dollars in aid, nations such as Zimbabwe, Liberia, Nicaragua, and Haiti are just as poor today as they were in 1960. In contrast, Taiwan, Chile, China, and India received almost no international aid, yet they have grown rapidly.

The application of the Solow model via growth policy was not always successful. In fact, most of the twentieth century witnessed faulty policy, based on incomplete growth theory. It resulted in very few success stories and a series of failures. Consider the continent of Africa, where policies based on Solow growth models were applied consistently. Solow's growth model was developed in 1956. Thirty-seven African nations achieved independence from 1956 to 1977, so these newly independent and poverty-stricken nations offered a unique opportunity to apply the Solow model. Yet now, half a century later, it is clear that these policies failed across the continent. Many African nations are no better off now than they were 50 years ago, even while much of the rest of the globe has experienced significant economic gains. These real-world observations led to a re-examination of growth theory in the late twentieth century.

# Why Are Institutions the Key to Economic Growth?

Over the past 20 years, a resurgence in growth theory has been spurred by the belief that *some economies grow faster for reasons particular to those economies.* In some nations, and even in pockets within nations, technological advances arrive more rapidly. Growth is sustained through technological innovation,

**Endogenous growth**
is growth driven by factors
inside the economy.

Endogenous growth origi-
nates inside an economy, as
it does inside an organism.

but these innovations do not occur randomly. Rather, economic growth is
*endogenous*. **Endogenous growth** is growth driven by factors inside the economy. There must be some reason that assembly lines, sewing machines, air
conditioning, personal computers, and the Internet were all developed in
the United States. These advances spurred economic growth and improved
people's lives. Why did they all occur here? Modern growth theory seeks to
understand why such innovations occur in one place and not another.

Nowadays, many economists stress the importance of institutions. We
introduced institutions in Chapter 11. In this section, we develop a framework for thinking about which institutions best foster growth.

## The Role of Institutions

Consider the city of Nogales, which straddles the border of the United States
in Arizona and Mexico. Average income in the northern half of the city is
three times that in the southern half. The education level on the northern
side is much higher, the roads are much better, and infant mortality much
lower. The two halves of the city have the same geography, ethnicity, and
weather. Why are the two sides so different? According to economist Daron
Acemoglu, who wrote about the city in *Esquire* magazine in 2009:

> The key difference is that those on the north side of the border enjoy law
> and order and dependable government services—they can go about their
> daily activities and jobs without fear for their life or safety or property
> rights. On the other side, the inhabitants have *institutions* that perpetu-
> ate crime, graft, and insecurity. [emphasis added]

Institutions are the final ingredient in our list of factors that affect economic growth. Recall from Chapter 11 that institutions are significant
organizations, laws, and social mores in society that frame the incentive
structure within which individuals and business firms act. Institutions are
the rules of the game, both formal and informal. They frame the environment within which production takes place. They help determine the costs
and benefits of production. Table 12.2 lists the institutions that are important for growth.

If we include institutions in the aggregate production function, we have:

(Equation 12.4)    $Y = A \times F(\text{natural resources, human capital, physical capital, } \textbf{institutions})$

| TABLE 12.2 |
|---|
| **Institutions That Foster Economic Growth** |

| | |
|---|---|
| 1. Political stability and the rule of law | 5. The flow of funds across borders |
| 2. Private property rights | 6. Efficient taxes |
| 3. Competitive markets | 7. Stable money and prices |
| 4. International trade | |

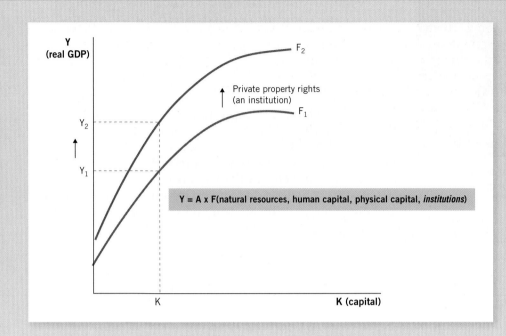

**FIGURE 12.8**

**Efficient Institutions and the Production Function**

The adoption of efficient institutions shifts a nation's production function upward. Efficient institutions (such as private property rights, shown here) make it possible for nations to produce more for any given level of resources, and they increase incentives for technological innovation.

Certain institutions lay the groundwork for natural endogenous growth. With these institutions in place, there are incentives for new technology to emerge and drive growth.

Figure 12.8 shows how institutions can affect the production function, causing it to rise from $F_1$ to $F_2$. Consider the shift toward private property rights that occurred in China since the 1980s. As we talked about in Chapter 11, the shift toward private property rights changed incentives for producers, who now get to keep much of their output. This change is behind the exploding growth we now see in China.

Incentives

Modern growth theory builds on the Solow model. The aggregate production function is still the core of all growth theory. Resources and technology are also considered important contributors to economic growth. But the fundamental characteristic of modern growth theory is the focus on institutions.

## Institutions Determine Incentives

As you know by now, GDP is production. To determine what leads to endogenous economic growth, we need to consider how institutions affect production decisions. Let's focus on the decision to produce for an individual firm. Imagine you are considering whether to open a new website design business. You decide that you will only open such a business if you expect to at least break even—that is, your payoff must cover your costs. This is not unusual. We can state this condition as follows:

Hard work, sacrifice, and patience are required before your firm can produce output.

Voluntary investment and production occurs only if
*expected payoff ≥ costs*.

The payoffs come later than the costs and are uncertain, which is why we call them *expected payoffs*.

No matter what your output—website design, college gear, cupcakes, or tractors—the payoffs come after production and after sales. The exact time lag depends on the type of output, but the payoffs from all output come sometime after the expenditures on resources. Because of the delay and the resources required, firms need to believe that the sacrifice, patience, and effort will offer a real payoff in the future.

Consider your decision to invest in your human capital by attending college. Why are you and your family voluntarily spending so much of your resources on human capital? The answer must be that you expect the return to be greater than the cost. That is, you expect to gain more from your college education than you pay for it. And you probably will, even if it takes a few years to realize the greatest monetary returns.

Investment and production occur naturally if future payoffs are significant and predictable—if the incentives for them are strong enough. These incentives are determined by a nation's institutions. For example, if people are allowed to own private property and use it for personal gain, they have strong incentives to use their resources wisely. In contrast, if the government or a group owns property, there is less incentive to care for the property. For example, consider how you might care for your dorm room compared to a room in a house that you or your parents own. People are generally less care-

## FIGURE 12.9

**Institutions, Incentives, and Endogenous Growth**

The goal is economic growth, but it all starts with institutions. Institutions provide the incentives that motivate choices made by people in an economy. The right institutions provide incentives for people to invent new technology and to invest in human and physical capital. These actions lead to economic growth.

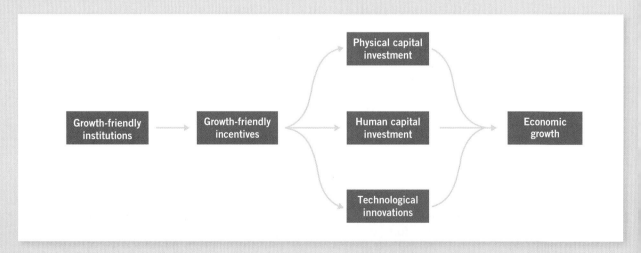

ful with rental property than with their own property. This is why security deposits are standard policy for rentals.

Institutions that foster growth are institutions that create incentives for endogenous or natural growth. In Chapter 11, we saw that the institutions most important for growth include private property rights, political stability and the rule of law, competitive and open markets, efficient taxes, and stable money and prices. These institutions create incentives for technological innovation and investments in both human and physical capital. Figure 12.9 illustrates this relationship between institutions and economic growth. Institutions create incentives for production and investment. If the right incentives are in place, production and investment occur naturally, and the result is more human capital, more physical capital, and technological advancement—all of which lead to economic growth.

Some institutions also act to reduce expected payoffs. Among these are corruption, political instability, high and variable inflation, and high tax rates. One of the keys to sustained growth is to eliminate these barriers to natural growth. Figure 12.10 illustrates how inefficient institutions can impede growth. Since payoffs from productive actions come in the future, anything that reduces the likelihood of these payoffs reduces the incentive for investment today.

We can now understand why we don't see convergence across all economies: different institutions lead to different rates of growth. Resources and technology are not enough. Nations grow faster when they have more efficient institutions. Others grow slowly because they don't. Unless institutions are the same across nations, we should not expect to see convergence.

Modern growth theory acknowledges the core truths of the Solow model: resources and technology are sources of economic growth. But it also recognizes the importance of institutions. This emphasis on institutions matters for policy. For example, international aid, even aid that is directed for capital goods, cannot lead to growth if the recipient nation does not have efficient institutions. Institutions are the key ingredient to long-run growth.

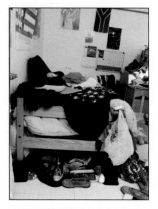

Would you take better care of your dorm room if it was your personal property?

## FIGURE 12.10

**Institutions That Inhibit Endogenous Growth**

People must work and invest today in order to get payoffs from output in the future. Inefficient institutions (such as political instability, corruption, inflation, and high tax rates) reduce the expected future payoffs and thus reduce the incentives for production. Growth-fostering institutions are those that maximize expected future payoffs for producers.

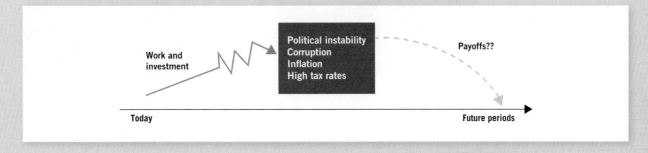

## ECONOMICS IN THE REAL WORLD

### Chile: A Modern Growth Miracle

Several nations, after struggling for centuries with little economic growth, have recently begun to grow at impressive rates. The best-known examples are China and India. Less well known is the recent economic growth in Chile.

Since 1985, the growth of real per capita GDP in Chile has averaged 4.3%. The rule of 70 (see Chapter 11) tells us that it only takes about 16 years to double living standards at that rate. In fact, real GDP for Chile rose from $7,709 per person to over $20,000 per person in the 23 years from 1985 to 2008. You can see this in the per capita real GDP shown in panel (a) of Figure 12.11. Notice also the change from Chile's past experience. Chile grew by less than 1% from 1900 to 1985.

As we have seen, economic growth means that most lives change for the better. One vivid indicator of these changes is life expectancy. Panel (b) of Figure 12.11 shows that life expectancy in Chile increased from 57 years in 1960 to 78 years by 2009. This increase of 21 years in average lifespan moved Chile ahead of many of its Latin American neighbors.

What is the cause of growth for Chile? In a word—institutions. In 1973, Chile began significant economic reforms. In addition to lowering trade barriers and instituting monetary and price stability (inflation was 665% in 1974), the government privatized many state-owned businesses and removed controls on wages and prices. These institutional reforms paved the way for the historic economic growth happening now in Chile. ✷

Chile's recent growth is as breathtaking as the view from Santiago.

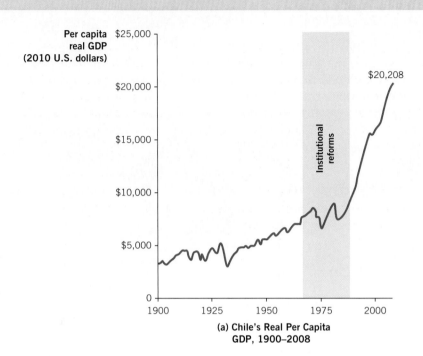

(a) Chile's Real Per Capita
GDP, 1900–2008

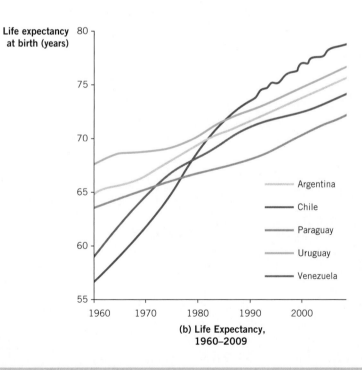

(b) Life Expectancy,
1960–2009

**FIGURE 12.11**

**Economic Growth and
Life Expectancy in
Chile**

Institutional reforms in
Chile have led to historic
economic growth, which has
helped the people of Chile
in many ways. One clear
improvement is the increase
in life expectancy.

*Source:* (a) Angus Maddison,
*Statistics on World Popula-
tion, GDP and Per Capita GDP,
1–2008 AD.* All figures converted to 2010 dollars.
(b) Gapminder.org.

# Institutions and Growth

The three sources of economic growth are resources, technology, and institutions. Institutions provide the framework within which production and work decisions are made. Efficient institutions provide the necessary foundation for natural endogenous growth, leading to better uses of resources and maximizing the incentives for technological innovations.

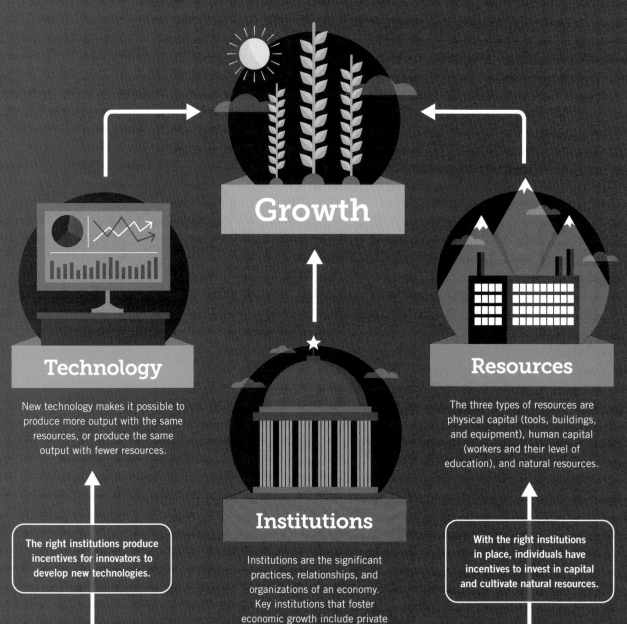

**Growth**

**Technology**

New technology makes it possible to produce more output with the same resources, or produce the same output with fewer resources.

**Institutions**

Institutions are the significant practices, relationships, and organizations of an economy. Key institutions that foster economic growth include private property rights, limited corruption, open international trade and financial capital markets, efficient taxes, competitive markets, and stable money and prices.

**Resources**

The three types of resources are physical capital (tools, buildings, and equipment), human capital (workers and their level of education), and natural resources.

The right institutions produce incentives for innovators to develop new technologies.

With the right institutions in place, individuals have incentives to invest in capital and cultivate natural resources.

# Inefficient Institutions

## Corruption

Corrupt governments reduce honest physical and human capital investment, as the expected returns to these investments fall or become riskier.

## Government control of industries

Public control of key resources and industries reduces the incentive for efficient and productive investment.

## Political instability

There is no natural incentive to invest, work, and produce if people are not sure which government controls the future. War and violence reduce that incentive, too.

## Rampant inflation

High and variable inflation rates increase the risk of current investments, since firms and workers cannot know for sure the real value of their future returns.

# Efficient Institutions

## Private property rights

When individuals personally gain from their effort and personal resources, they have the strongest incentive to use them productively.

## Consistent government

Predictable laws and enforcement strengthen incentives for long-term production and investment.

## Open trade

International trade allows nations to specialize in production and expand their consumption possibilities.

## Stable money and prices

Low and stable inflation rates reduce the risk of long-term investment and production.

# REVIEW QUESTIONS

- How does private property ownership (versus government ownership) affect the incentives for productive use of resources?

- How does technological progress aid resources to promote growth?

# PRACTICE WHAT YOU KNOW

## Solow Growth Theory versus Modern Growth Theory: What Policy Is Implied?

**Question:** Below is a list of policy proposals that have been advanced to help the economies of developing nations. Determine whether each proposal is consistent with the Solow model, modern growth theory, neither, or both.

**a.** unrestricted international aid to help build a power plant

**b.** aid for a power plant that is dependent on democratic reforms

**c.** microfinance (very small short-term loans for small businesses)

**d.** reductions in trade restrictions

**Answers:**

**a.** This is consistent with the Solow model: physical capital leads to growth.

**b.** This is consistent with both Solow and modern growth theory. The power plant is physical capital, but the aid is dependent on institutional reform.

**c.** Neither. This kind of program does not directly address the need for resources or the need for institutional reform.

**d.** This is consistent with modern growth theory. Open trade is institutional reform that leads to greater competition and more options for citizens in developing nations.

This cargo ship brings goods from Asia to the United States. Which growth model would encourage this kind of international trade?

## Institutions of Growth: Applying for a Patent

The late Apple CEO Steve Jobs is famous for having his name on well over 300 different patents. This means he is credited with participation in all of those new inventions. Inventions are technological innovations, and we've seen that these are a source of economic growth.

Patent laws are an important institution that has helped to pave the way for many technological advancements. Patents create a 20-year monopoly for the inventor or owner of the patent. This monopoly is an incentive that encourages innovation. Patent laws are thus an institution that serves to encourage new inventions that shift the economy's production function upward.

If you have an idea that you'd like to patent, you need to apply for your patent through the U.S. Patent Office. In addition to a detailed description of your patent, you'll need to create a drawing that specifies exactly how your idea is new and different. Finally, it is a good idea to hire a patent attorney to edit your patent application so you can reduce the chances that someone will copy your idea later.

Steve Jobs was one of the great innovators.

Even if you don't have the resources to capitalize on your invention, you can always try to sell your patent to someone who can.

You may not be as successful as Steve Jobs, but you can be sure that patents are a legal way to make monopoly profit.

# Conclusion

We opened this chapter with the misconception that physical capital is the essential economic growth ingredient. We have seen that while capital is helpful, it is clear that physical tools are not enough to ensure long-run growth. The same applies to other resources and technology. Without institutions that promote the incentive to produce, sustained endogenous growth does not take root.

Many people think that macroeconomics is all about business cycles and recessions. Our goal in this chapter has been to present the ideas behind long-run growth theory, rather than short-run cycles. In Chapter 13, we present a model that economists use to study short-run business cycles.

# ANSWERING THE BIG QUESTIONS

### How do macroeconomic theories evolve?

* Macroeconomic theories evolve in relationship to observations in the real world. Policies often follow from theory. Policies produce results, which, in turn, influence revisions of economic theory.

### What is the Solow growth model?

* The Solow growth model is a model of economic growth based on a production function for the economy.
* The key feature of the production function is diminishing returns.
* The Solow growth model posits that diminishing returns lead economies toward a zero-growth steady state.
* The Solow growth model further posits that given steady states, economies tend to converge over time.

### How does technology affect growth?

* Technology is a source of sustained economic growth.
* In the Solow model, technology is exogenous.

### Why are institutions the key to economic growth?

* Modern growth theory emphasizes institutions as the key source of growth.
* Institutions determine incentives for production.
* Efficient institutions can lead to endogenous growth.

## CONCEPTS YOU SHOULD KNOW

aggregate production function (p. 363)

convergence (p. 371)

depreciation (p. 369)

diminishing marginal product (p. 365)

endogenous growth (p. 378)

exogenous growth (p. 374)

marginal product (p. 365)

net investment (p. 369)

production function (p. 362)

steady state (p. 369)

## QUESTIONS FOR REVIEW

1. Modern economic theory points to three sources of economic growth. What are these three sources? Give an example of each.

2. About 50 years ago, Robert Solow contributed two significant papers to the literature on economic growth theory. What are the two key properties of the aggregate production function at the center of Solow's first contribution?

3. Explain why a nation cannot continue to grow forever by just adding more capital.

4. The Solow model assumes that technology changes are exogenous. What does this mean? Why does this matter for growth policy? What does this assumption imply about growth rates across nations over time?

5. China is a land of vast resources. In addition, technology is easily transportable across international borders. If we rule out these two sources of growth, to what can we attribute the economic growth in China since 1979?

6. The basic Solow growth model implies convergence. What is convergence? What key assumption about the marginal product of capital implies convergence?

7. How can an increase in educational opportunities increase growth? Use a graph to illustrate how educational opportunities affect a nation's production function.

## STUDY PROBLEMS (*solved at the end of the section*)

1. The Solow model focuses on how resources affect output. In this chapter, we focused on capital.

   a. Name the other two major categories of resources.

   b. Draw an aggregate production function with a typical shape; label this function F.

   c. Draw a second production function that indicates a technological advancement; label this new function $F_1$.

2. Define human capital. Draw a graph that illustrates an increase in effective labor on a production function.

3. Suppose the people in the United States increase their savings rate. How will this affect the rate of economic growth in the United States?

✳ **4.** Economic growth derives from many sources. Some of these cause a parallel shift in a nation's production function, while others change the slope of the production function. Below is a graph of three different production functions: $F_1$, $F_2$, and $F_3$. Assume that a nation begins with production function $F_1$. Production function $F_2$ is a parallel shift upward from $F_1$; in contrast, $F_3$ is an increase in the slope from $F_1$.

For each of the following scenarios, determine which of the two new production functions, $F_2$ or $F_3$, best illustrates how the scenario would affect production.

**a.** Human capital rises through education.

**b.** Technological advancement occurs.

**c.** New natural gas reserves are found.

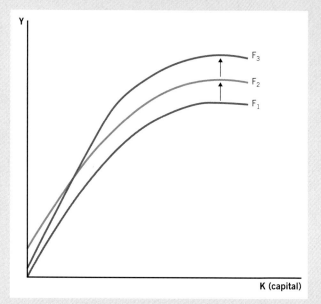

# SOLVED PROBLEM

**4. a.** The shift would be to $F_2$, since it represents more output at all levels of capital.

 **b.** The shift would be to $F_3$, since the marginal product of capital increases.

 **c.** The shift would be to $F_2$, since it represents more output at all levels of capital.

# The Aggregate Demand–Aggregate Supply Model

**Recessions are inevitable and occur every few years.**

Many people believe that every few years the economy plunges into a recession and then, after a short period of slow growth, rebounds for a period of expansion. They consider this pattern to be inevitable, with recessions happening every six to eight years. The term "business cycle" is a popular way to describe the recession-expansion phenomenon because so many people are convinced that the recession-expansion pattern occurs in a regular cycle.

**MIS CONCEPTION**

But, in fact, recessions are rarer today than at any other time in our nation's history: while there have been 22 U.S. recessions since 1900, there have been just three since 1982. In addition, no two recessions are alike in either cause or effect.

If you came to macroeconomics with a desire to learn more about recessions and their causes, this is the chapter for you. Chapters 11 and 12 focused on long-run economic growth. In this chapter and the next, we focus on short-run fluctuations in the macroeconomy. We begin by building a model of the economy that we can use to consider the causes of business-cycle fluctuations. In Chapter 14, we'll examine historical events in the context of the model and also consider some of the major debates in macroeconomics, which can be framed in terms of our short-run model.

Worldwide recession from 2007 to 2009 left many economic resources underutilized, like these homes in Spain.

# BIG QUESTIONS

* What is the aggregate demand–aggregate supply model?
* What is aggregate demand?
* What is aggregate supply?
* How does the aggregate demand–aggregate supply model help us understand the economy?

## What Is the Aggregate Demand–Aggregate Supply Model?

In macroeconomics, there are two different paths of study. One direction explores long-run growth and development. The second direction examines short-run fluctuations, or business cycles. The two paths are complementary: both study GDP growth, employment, and the people, firms, and governments that impact the economy. But the paths are also different. Growth economics focuses on longer time horizons—say, five to ten years or more. Business-cycle theory typically focuses on time horizons of five years or less.

In Chapter 6, we presented the idea of a basic business cycle, in which real GDP increases for a while during the expansionary phase and then decreases during the contractionary, or recessionary, phase. The business cycle is most evident in real GDP growth and unemployment rates. During recessions, real GDP growth slows and the unemployment rate rises. During expansions, real GDP growth expands and the unemployment rate falls.

Panel (a) of Figure 13.1 shows real GDP growth rates by quarter for the United States from 1985 to 2012. The blue-shaded vertical bars indicate the three recessions during this period. During each recession, real GDP growth slowed and even turned negative. The fourth quarter of 2008 registered −8.9% growth, making it the worst quarter since 1958. Panel (b) plots the unemployment rate over the same period. The unemployment rate rose sharply during each of the recessions and then slowly fell afterward. The highest unemployment rate during this period was 10% in October 2009.

**Aggregate demand** is the total demand for final goods and services in an economy.

**Aggregate supply** is the total supply of final goods and services in an economy.

The model we use to study business cycles is the *aggregate demand–aggregate supply* model. At the core of the model are the concepts of demand and supply, which are already familiar to you. In earlier chapters, we looked at the demand and supply of a single good, like savings. But now we look at the demand and supply of all final goods and services in an economy—the demand and supply of GDP. **Aggregate demand** is the total demand for final goods and services in an economy. **Aggregate supply** is the total supply of final goods and services in an economy. The word *aggregate* means total.

We consider each side of the economy separately before bringing them together. The next section explains aggregate demand; after that, we will look at aggregate supply.

# What Is Aggregate Demand?

We have an experiment for you to try. Ask five people the following question: *How can you personally help our economy?* We predict that most responses will focus on buying something or spending money somewhere. In our model of the economy, this is demand. Aggregate demand is the spending side of the economy. When people spend on goods and services, aggregate demand increases, and most people believe that this spending is what drives the economy. We'll see later that this is only partially true.

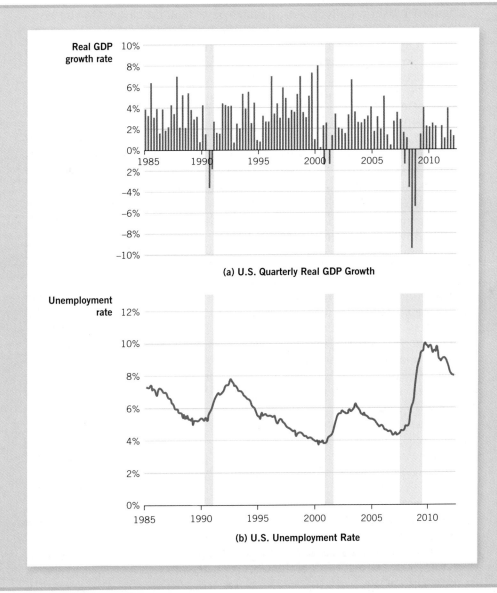

**FIGURE 13.1**

**U.S. Real GDP Growth, Unemployment Rates, and Recessions, 1985–2012**

Business cycles are readily observable in real GDP growth and unemployment rates. Panel (a) shows that quarterly real GDP growth often declines during recessionary periods. Panel (b) shows how the unemployment rate spikes up during recessions, then gradually falls as the economy expands.

*Sources*: (a) U.S. Bureau of Economic Analysis; (b) U.S. Bureau of Labor Statistics.

(a) U.S. Quarterly Real GDP Growth

(b) U.S. Unemployment Rate

To determine aggregate demand, we sum up spending from different sources in the economy. These sources include private domestic consumers who buy cars, food, clothing, education, and many other goods and services. Business firms are another major group; they buy resources needed to produce output. The government is a large purchaser of labor and other resources used to produce government services. Finally, foreign consumers buy many goods and services produced in the United States. These four major groups constitute the four pieces of aggregate demand: consumption (C), investment (I), government (G), and net exports (NX). The total of these four yields aggregate demand (AD) in a given period:

(Equation 13.1) $$AD = C + I + G + NX$$

As we study aggregate demand, we'll consider factors that affect each of these sources.

Figure 13.2 shows a graph of the aggregate demand curve. On the horizontal axis, we plot quantities of all final goods and services, which constitute real GDP. On the vertical axis, we measure the overall price level (P) in the economy. This is not the price of any particular good or service, but a general level of prices for the whole economy. Since we are looking at all final goods and services, the correct price index to use is the GDP deflator (see Chapter 6). The GDP deflator is set at 100 in a particular period of time and then fluctuates from that level. A rise in P indicates inflation in the economy.

On the graph in Figure 13.2, we have labeled a particular point where the price level is 100 and the quantity of aggregate demand is $16 trillion, which was the size of the U.S. economy in 2012. The negative slope of the aggregate demand curve means that increases in the price level lead to decreases in the quantity of aggregate demand. Similarly, when the price level falls, the quantity of aggregate demand rises. But be careful here: aggregate demand does not slope downward for the same reason that individual good demand curves slope downward. In the case of a particular good, an increase in price leads

## FIGURE 13.2

**The Aggregate Demand Curve**

The aggregate demand curve shows the inverse relationship between the quantity demanded of real GDP and the economy's price level (P).

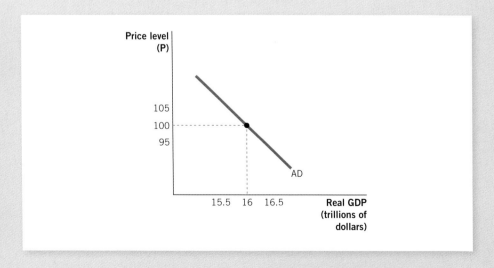

consumers to substitute out of consumption for that good and into consumption for other goods. But the aggregate demand curve indicates demand for all goods in an economy, so there is no corresponding substitution effect. In the next section, we explain the reasons for the negative slope.

## The Slope of the Aggregate Demand Curve

All else being equal, increases in the economy's price level lead to decreases in the quantity of aggregate demand. You might agree with this statement without closely evaluating it, because it sounds like the relationship between the quantity demanded of a single good and its price. But now we are evaluating the whole economy. Remember that the price level is the price of all final goods and services. Aggregate demand and aggregate supply don't just measure the quantity of pizzas demanded and supplied; they measure the production of all the firms in all the markets that constitute the economy. Therefore, substitutions from one market to another have no effect on the total amount of output, or real GDP. Substituting out of pizza and into chicken nuggets doesn't change GDP.

There are three reasons for this inverse relationship between the quantity of aggregate demand and the price level: the *wealth effect*, the *interest rate effect*, and the *international trade effect*.

### The Wealth Effect

If you wake up tomorrow morning and all prices have suddenly doubled, you'll be poorer, in real terms, than you are today. Your consumption will fall because your *wealth* has fallen. **Wealth** is the value of one's accumulated assets. Your wealth is the total value of everything you own, including the money in your wallet and in your bank accounts. The **wealth effect** is the change in the quantity of aggregate demand that results from wealth changes due to price-level changes.

Wealth is the value of one's accumulated assets.

The **wealth effect** is the change in the quantity of aggregate demand that results from wealth changes due to price-level changes.

For example, if you and your friends have $60 to buy pizza, you can afford to buy four $15 pizzas. But if inflation causes the price of pizzas to rise to $20, you can only afford three pizzas. Similarly, a rise in prices all over the economy reduces real wealth in the economy, and then the quantity of aggregate demand falls. In contrast, if prices fall, real wealth increases, and then the quantity of aggregate demand also increases.

If you hold money as part of your wealth, the price level affects its real value.

### The Interest Rate Effect

If the price level rises and real wealth falls, people also save less. Therefore, in addition to the wealth effect, an increase in the price level affects people's savings. Let's say that you are on a budget that allows you to buy groceries and save a little each month. If the price level rises, you'll probably cut back on both areas. When you spend less on groceries, your actions are reflecting the wealth effect. When you cut back on savings, your action leads to the *interest rate effect*. The **interest rate effect** occurs when a change in the price level leads to a change in interest rates and, therefore, in the quantity of aggregate demand. Remember that every dollar borrowed requires

The **interest rate effect** occurs when a change in the price level leads to a change in interest rates and, therefore, in the quantity of aggregate demand.

a dollar saved. Therefore, when savings declines, the quantity of investment must also decline, which affects aggregate demand.

Figure 13.3 shows the loanable funds market before and after a decrease in savings. Initially, the demand and supply of loanable funds are indicated by curves D and $S_1$ and the equilibrium interest rate is 5%. If the economy's price level rises, people save less, which shifts supply to $S_2$. The reduction in supply leads to a higher interest rate of 6%, at which point the quantity of investment falls from $I_1$ to $I_2$. Because investment is one piece of aggregate demand, a decrease in investment decreases overall aggregate demand. Thus, a change in the price level initiates a cascade of events with the result that firms invest less at higher interest rates because individuals are saving less.

The **international trade effect** occurs when a change in the price level leads to a change in the quantity of net exports demanded.

## The International Trade Effect

In our model, the price level and real GDP represent the domestic market. In the context of the world economy, we must also consider the prices of goods from the United States *relative to* the prices of goods from other countries. When the U.S. price level rises, all else being equal, U.S. goods are relatively more expensive than goods from other countries, and the quantity demanded of U.S. goods falls. The **international trade effect** occurs when a change in the price level leads to a change in the quantity of net exports demanded.

Consider two similar sport utility vehicles: a Jeep Wrangler and a Toyota FJ Cruiser. The Jeep is produced in the United States in Toledo, Ohio. The Toyota is produced in a suburb of Tokyo, Japan. When the prices of U.S. goods rise relative to the prices of Japanese goods, consumers are more likely to

Jeep Wrangler: produced in Toledo, Ohio.

## FIGURE 13.3

**The Interest Rate Effect in the Loanable Funds Market**

If the economy's price level rises, people save less. The decline in savings from $S_1$ to $S_2$ leads to an increase in the interest rate from 5% to 6%. At this higher interest rate, the quantity of investment falls from $I_1$ to $I_2$ because investment is more costly. Since investment is a component of aggregate demand, a fall in equilibrium investment that occurs with a rise in price level causes the quantity of aggregate demand to fall.

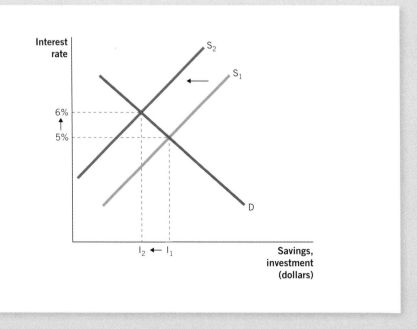

choose the Toyota, so U.S. exports fall and imports rise.

Figure 13.4 shows how the wealth effect, the interest rate effect, and the international trade effect work together to influence the quantity of aggregate demand. Each effect begins with a change in the economy's price level. When the price level rises from 100 to 110, consumption (C) declines from the wealth effect, investment (I) declines via the interest rate effect, and net exports (NX) fall due to the international trade effect. In reality, the three effects do not influence aggregate demand equally. The international trade effect is relatively small because exports are a relatively small part of GDP. Since consumption is by far the largest component of GDP, the wealth effect is the most significant.

Toyota FJ Cruiser: produced near Tokyo, Japan.

It is important to distinguish between *shifts in* versus *movements along* the aggregate demand curve. In this section, we have identified three effects related to movements along the aggregate demand curve. These three effects originate with a change in the economy's price level. In contrast, shifts in the demand curve occur when people demand more goods and services at a given price level. These shifts can come from any of the components of aggregate demand: consumption, investment, net exports, and government spending. In the next section, we look at five factors that shift aggregate demand.

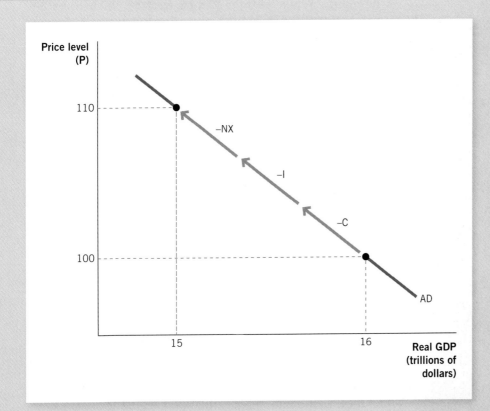

## FIGURE 13.4

### The Slope of the Aggregate Demand Curve

When the price level rises, the quantity of aggregate demand falls. This negative relationship is due to three different effects: (1) the wealth effect implies a lower quantity of consumption (C) demand because real wealth falls at higher price levels; (2) the interest rate effect implies a lower quantity of investment (I) demand due to higher interest rates; (3) the international trade effect implies a lower quantity of net export (NX) demand due to relatively higher domestic prices. Each effect focuses on a different component of aggregate demand.

# Shifts in Aggregate Demand

The price level is not the only factor that affects aggregate demand. When people demand more goods and services at all price levels, aggregate demand shifts in a positive direction. In this section, we consider five causes of aggregate demand shifts: changes in real wealth, expected income, expected future prices, foreign income and wealth, and the value of the dollar.

## Real Wealth

One determinant of people's spending habits is their current wealth. If your great-aunt died and left you $1 million, you'd probably start spending more

right away: you'd eat out tonight, upgrade your wardrobe, and maybe even shop for some bigger-ticket items. This observation also applies to entire nations. When national wealth increases, aggregate demand increases. If wealth falls, aggregate demand declines.

For example, many people own stocks or mutual funds that are tied to the stock market. So when the stock market fluctuates, the wealth of a large portion of the population is affected. When overall stock values rise, wealth increases, which increases aggregate demand. However, if the stock market falls significantly, then wealth declines and aggregate demand decreases. Widespread changes in real estate values also affect wealth. Consider that for many people a house represents a large portion of their wealth. When real estate values rise and fall, individual wealth follows, and this outcome affects aggregate demand.

Median home prices fell from $248,000 to $222,000 between 2007 and 2010. That roughly 10% drop led to a significant decrease in many people's wealth, as well as a decline in aggregate demand.

Before moving on, note that in this section we are talking about changes in individuals' real wealth *not* caused by changes in the price level. When we discussed the slope of the aggregate demand curve, we distinguished the wealth effect, which is caused by changes in the economy's price level (P).

## Expected Income

Expected future income also affects aggregate demand. If people expect higher income in the future, they spend more today. For example, graduating college seniors often begin spending more as soon as they secure a job offer, even though the job and the corresponding income don't start until months later. But expectations aren't always right. We consume today based on what we anticipate for the future, even though the future is uncertain. Still, the entire economy can be affected by just a change in the general sentiment of consumers.

How much income does your future hold?

Perhaps you've heard of the consumer confidence or consumer sentiment index. This index uses survey data to estimate how consumers feel about the future direction of the economy. Confidence, or lack of confidence, in the future of the economy changes consumer spending today. Consumer confidence can swing up and down with unpredictable events such as national elections or international turmoil. When these sentiments change, they shift aggregate demand.

## Changes in Wealth

### *Dumb and Dumber*

In this comedy from 1994, two likeable but incredibly simpleminded friends, Harry and Lloyd, try to return a suitcase to its owner. For most of the movie, they have no idea that the suitcase they are trying to return is filled with a million dollars.

When they accidentally open the case while en route to Aspen, Colorado, the friends discover the cash and decide to spend the money freely by writing IOUs and placing them in the suitcase to be repaid later. The newfound money creates a change in Harry and Lloyd's wealth. The two friends immediately enjoy their unexpected wealth by staying at a lavish hotel, giving away $100 bills as tips for the staff, and even using money to wipe their noses when they can't find ordinary tissues to do the job.

What kind of tuxedo would you buy if you had a suitcase full of money?

In one sense, Harry and Lloyd are much like the rest of us. If our wealth changes, it affects our demand for goods and services (via the wealth effect). But Harry and Lloyd are dumb and dumber in that their spending is completely based on someone else's wealth.

### Expected Prices

Expectations also matter when it comes to future prices. When people expect higher prices in the future, they are more likely to spend today, so current aggregate demand increases. Consider a nation with rampant inflation. When people in this nation get paid, they will spend their income quickly to take advantage of today's lower prices. If, instead, people expect lower prices in the future, today's aggregate demand will decline.

### Foreign Income

When the income of people in foreign nations grows, their demand for U.S. goods increases, and this activity increases aggregate demand. In contrast, if a foreign nation goes into recession, its demand for U.S. goods and services falls. One recent positive example is the growth of large emerging economies and their demand for U.S. goods. As nations like Brazil, China, and India have grown wealthier, their demand for U.S. goods and services has increased.

## ECONOMICS IN THE REAL WORLD

### General Motors Sales Up in China, but Down in Europe

General Motors, one of the world's largest car manufacturers, now sells over 200,000 vehicles a month in China alone. According to a July 6, 2012, article in the online news site chinadaily.com.cn, GM delivered 1.42 million cars and minivans in the first six months of 2012. Sales to China are growing at more

Buick: more popular in China than in the United States.

than 10% per year thanks in part to the growing incomes of many Chinese citizens. The GM product line Buick does particularly well in China. Buick now sells about four times as many cars in China as in the United States. In 2010, Buick sold 550,010 cars in China and only 155,289 in the United States.

Increased sales in China have been offset by slowing sales in Europe, where many economies were in recession in 2012. In the second quarter of 2012, GM reported a loss of $361 million in its European division alone. ✳

### Value of the Dollar

Exchange rates are another international factor that shifts aggregate demand. We'll cover these fully in Chapter 20. For now, think in terms of the value of the dollar in world markets. When the value of the dollar rises relative to the currency of other nations, Americans find that imports are less expensive. At the same time, it becomes more expensive for other nations to buy our exports. These two factors combine to reduce net exports, so a stronger dollar leads to a decline in net exports, which reduces aggregate demand.

## FIGURE 13.5

**Factors That Shift the Aggregate Demand Curve**

The aggregate demand curve shifts to the right with *increases* in real wealth, expected income, expected future prices, and foreign income and wealth, or with a *decrease* in the value of the dollar. The aggregate demand curve shifts to the left with *decreases* in real wealth, expected income, expected future prices, and foreign income and wealth, or with an *increase* in the value of the dollar.

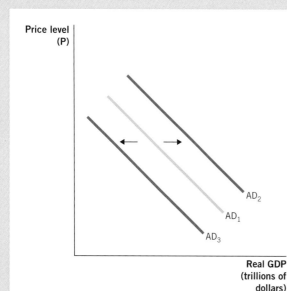

| Shift factor | Increase in factor leads to: | Decrease in factor leads to: |
|---|---|---|
| Real wealth | Increase to $AD_2$ | Decrease to $AD_3$ |
| Expected income | Increase to $AD_2$ | Decrease to $AD_3$ |
| Expected price level | Increase to $AD_2$ | Decrease to $AD_3$ |
| Foreign income | Increase to $AD_2$ | Decrease to $AD_3$ |
| Value of the dollar | Decrease to $AD_3$ | Increase to $AD_2$ |

Figure 13.5 summarizes the effects of the five factors that shift aggregate demand. On the graph, initially aggregate demand is shown as $AD_1$. Aggregate demand shifts to the right (to $AD_2$) with *increases* in real wealth, expected income, expected future prices, and foreign income and wealth, or with *decreases* in the value of the U.S. dollar. In contrast, aggregate demand shifts to the left (to $AD_3$) with *decreases* in real wealth, expected income, expected future prices, and foreign income and wealth, or with *increases* in the value of the U.S. dollar.

## PRACTICE WHAT YOU KNOW

### Aggregate Demand: Shifts in Aggregate Demand versus Movements along the Aggregate Demand Curve

One of the challenges in applying the aggregate demand–aggregate supply model is knowing when to distinguish shifts in aggregate demand from movements along the aggregate demand curve. Here we present four scenarios.

Question: For each scenario below, does it cause a movement along the curve or a shift in the curve? Explain your response each time.

Textile workers in Nicaragua depend on the export economy as a source of jobs.

1. Consumers read positive economic news and then expect strong future economic growth.

2. Due to an increase in the price level in the United States, consumers substitute out of clothes made in the United States and into clothes made in Nicaragua.

3. Several European economies go into recession.

4. A decrease in the price level leads to greater real wealth and more savings, which reduces the interest rate and increases investment.

Answers:

1. This scenario involves an increase in expected future income, which increases aggregate demand and causes a positive shift in the curve.

2. This scenario begins with a change in the price level, so we know it will involve a movement along the curve. Here the price level rises, so it is a movement back along the curve, signaling a decrease in the quantity of aggregate demand.

3. Foreign recession leads to lower foreign income and wealth, an outcome that decreases the demand for goods and services made in the United States. Less demand for U.S. products causes a decrease in aggregate demand in the United States. This leads to a negative shift in the aggregate demand curve.

4. Since this scenario involves a change in the price level, it will lead to a movement along the aggregate demand curve. In this case, the lower prices lead to the interest rate effect and an increase in the quantity of aggregate demand.

# What Is Aggregate Supply?

We have seen that aggregate demand embodies the spending desires of an economy. It tells us how many goods and services people want at different price levels. But peoples' wants and desires alone do not determine GDP. We must also consider the supply side of the economy, which tells us about the willingness and ability of producers to supply GDP.

Most of us relate easily to the demand side because we are used to buying things on a daily basis. To understand the supply side of the economy, we need to think from the perspective of those who produce and sell goods and services. For example, imagine you own a coffee shop where you produce drinks such as espressos, lattes, and iced coffee. Your inputs include workers, coffee beans, milk, water, and espresso machines. You buy inputs and combine them in a particular way to produce your output.

Figure 13.6 presents an overview of the basic function of the firm. In the middle is the firm, where inputs are turned into output. The input prices, such as wages and interest rates on loans, help to determine the firm's costs. The output prices, such as the cost of an espresso, determine the firm's revenue.

In order to understand aggregate supply, we need to consider how changes in the overall price level (P) affect the supply decisions of the firm. But the influence of the price level on aggregate supply depends on the time frame we are considering. The *long run* in macroeconomics is a period of time sufficient for all prices to adjust. The long run doesn't arrive after a set period of time; it arrives when all prices have adjusted. However, in the *short run*, only some

## FIGURE 13.6

**The Function of the Firm**

The firm uses inputs, or factors of production, to produce its output in a particular way. Input prices, such as wages for workers, affect the firm's costs. Output prices affect the firm's revenue.

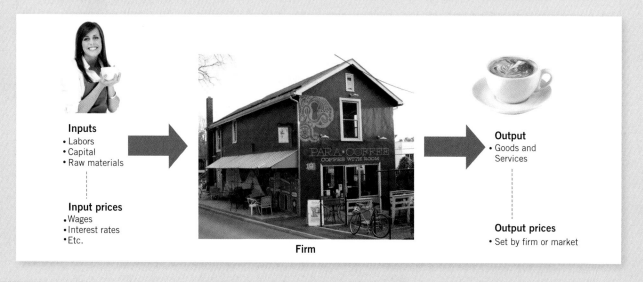

**Inputs**
• Labors
• Capital
• Raw materials

**Input prices**
• Wages
• Interest rates
• Etc.

**Firm**

**Output**
• Goods and Services

**Output prices**
• Set by firm or market

prices can change. In macroeconomics, the short run is the period of time in which some prices have not yet adjusted.

## Long-Run Aggregate Supply

As we've discussed several times in this text, the long-run output of an economy depends on resources, technology, and institutions. In the short run there may be fluctuations in real GDP, but in the long run the economy moves toward full employment output ($Y^*$). The price level does not affect long-run aggregate supply. Think of it this way: in the long run, the number of paper dollars we exchange for our goods and services does not impact our ability to produce.

Figure 13.7 plots the economy's long-run aggregate supply curve (LRAS). Notice that since we plot this with the economy's price level (P) on the vertical axis and real GDP (Y) on the horizontal axis, long-run aggregate supply is a vertical line at $Y^*$, which is full employment output. In Chapter 7, we defined full employment output as the output produced in the economy when unemployment (u) is at the natural rate ($u^*$). This is the output level that is sustainable for the long run in the economy. Because prices don't affect full employment output, the LRAS curve is a vertical line at $Y^*$. If the price level is 100, the quantity of aggregate supply is equal to $Y^*$. If the price level rises to 110 or falls to 90, output in the long run is still $Y^*$.

### Shifts in Long-Run Aggregate Supply

The long-run aggregate supply curve shifts when there is a long-run change in a nation's ability to produce output, or a change in $Y^*$. The factors that shift long-run aggregate supply are the same factors that determine economic growth: resources, technology, and institutions.

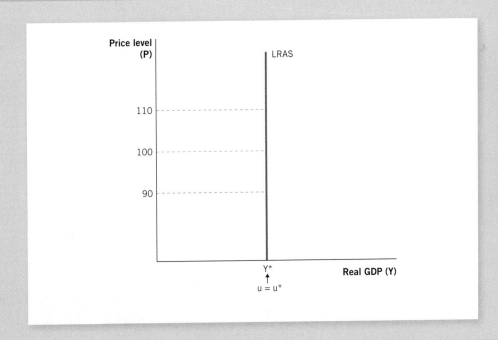

**FIGURE 13.7**

**The Long-Run Aggregate Supply Curve**

The LRAS curve is vertical at $Y^*$ because in the long run the price level does not affect the quantity of aggregate supply. $Y^*$ is full employment output, where the unemployment rate (u) is equal to the natural rate ($u^*$).

# The Business Cycle

Since 1970, the U.S. economy has experienced seven recessions. These business cycle fluctuations are most visible in observations of real GDP growth and the unemployment rate. During recessions, real GDP typically falls and the unemployment rate climbs. During expansions, real GDP expands and the unemployment rate falls back toward the natural rate.

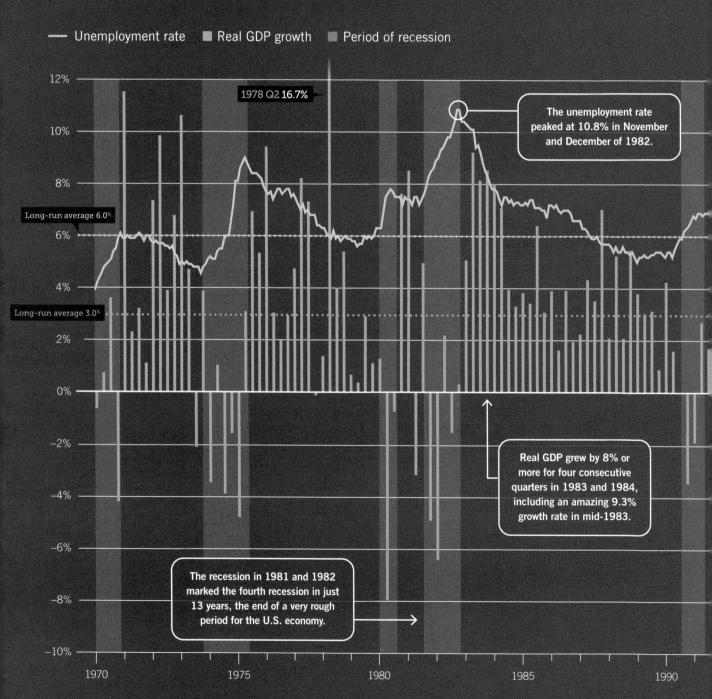

— Unemployment rate     ■ Real GDP growth     ■ Period of recession

1978 Q2 **16.7%**

Long-run average 6.0%

Long-run average 3.0%

The unemployment rate peaked at 10.8% in November and December of 1982.

Real GDP grew by 8% or more for four consecutive quarters in 1983 and 1984, including an amazing 9.3% growth rate in mid-1983.

The recession in 1981 and 1982 marked the fourth recession in just 13 years, the end of a very rough period for the U.S. economy.

12%

10%

8%

6%

4%

2%

0%

−2%

−4%

−6%

−8%

−10%

1970          1975          1980          1985          1990

- Looking at the year immediately following each recession, can you determine which economic recovery was most difficult? On what do you base your answer?

- If the unemployment rate was below the natural rate in 2000, what does this imply about aggregate demand?

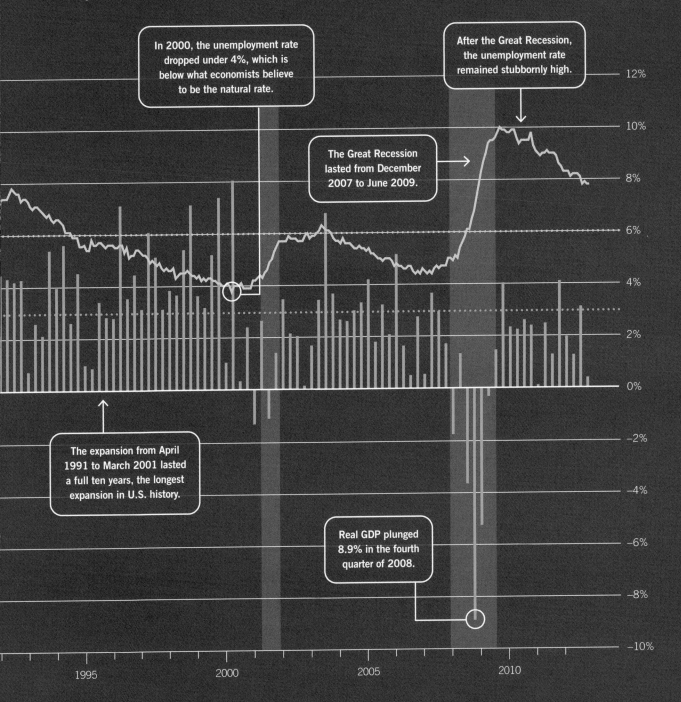

In 2000, the unemployment rate dropped under 4%, which is below what economists believe to be the natural rate.

After the Great Recession, the unemployment rate remained stubbornly high.

The Great Recession lasted from December 2007 to June 2009.

The expansion from April 1991 to March 2001 lasted a full ten years, the longest expansion in U.S. history.

Real GDP plunged 8.9% in the fourth quarter of 2008.

If hovercraft worked on land too, traffic would subside and the economy's LRAS curve would shift to the right.

For example, new technology leads to increases in long-run aggregate supply. Consider what would happen if a firm develops a safe, effective, and affordable hovercraft that enables people to travel more quickly and frees up congestion on the roads. This new technology would lead to an increase in long-run aggregate supply because it would increase productivity in the economy: we would now produce more with our limited resources.

Figure 13.8 illustrates a shift in long-run aggregate supply. Initially, the LRAS curve is vertical at $Y^*$, which depends on resources, technology, and institutions. After the new hovercraft technology is introduced, $LRAS_1$ shifts to the right (to $LRAS_2$) because now the full employment output in the economy is greater than before. Notice that both before and after the shift, the unemployment rate is at the natural rate ($u^*$). The new technology does not reduce the unemployment rate, but workers in the economy are more productive. The new output rate, $Y^{**}$, is designated with asterisks because it represents a new full employment output rate.

We can illustrate economic growth by using the long-run aggregate supply curve. As the economy grows over time, full employment output increases and the LRAS curve shifts to the right. But the $LRAS_3$ curve can also shift to the left (to $LRAS_3$). This would occur with a permanent decline in the economy's resources or with the adoption of inefficient institutions.

## FIGURE 13.8

### Shifts in Long-Run Aggregate Supply

Shifts in the long-run aggregate supply curve occur when there is a change in an economy's resources, technology, or institutions. A technological advance moves an economy from $LRAS_1$ to $LRAS_2$. This is a picture of economic growth. When the LRAS curve shifts to the right, this movement also indicates a change in the economy's full employment output level from $Y^*$ to $Y^{**}$. The unemployment rate does not change, but workers are more productive.

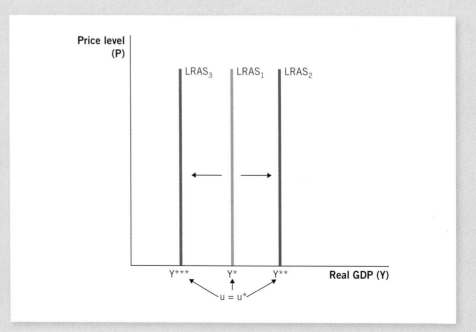

# Short-Run Aggregate Supply

We just saw that the price level does not impact aggregate supply in the long run. However, in the short run there is a positive relationship between the price level and the quantity of aggregate supply. There are three reasons for this relationship: inflexible input prices, menu costs, and money illusion.

First, consider input prices. At your coffee shop, you pay the baristas a particular wage, and this wage is set for a period of time. In addition, interest rates for your loans are normally fixed. Economists say that these input prices are *sticky*, since they take time to change. In contrast, output prices tend to be more flexible. Whereas input prices are typically set in a written contract, output prices are often easy to change. For example, coffee shop prices are often written on a chalkboard, which makes it pretty easy to change them from day to day.

The distinction between sticky input prices and flexible output prices is at the center of our discussion of aggregate supply because it affects the way firms react when prices do move. Think of this in terms of your coffee shop. You negotiate one-year contracts with your workers. Your coffee bean suppliers fix their prices for a certain period as well. If inflation begins to push up all prices in the macroeconomy, you pull out your chalkboard eraser and raise the price of lattes, espressos, and mochas; these are output prices, and they are very flexible. But your input prices are sticky (the coffee beans still cost the same, and you have to pay your employees the same amount)—at least for a while. Therefore, your costs remain the same. And here is the link to aggregate supply: because your costs don't rise but your revenues do, it makes sense for you to increase output. When you and other firms raise output, GDP rises.

The dynamic between sticky input prices and flexible output prices explains the positive slope of the short-run aggregate supply curve. Figure 13.9 shows the short-run aggregate supply curve, labeled as SRAS. When the price level rises from 100 to 110, firms produce more in the short run because input prices are sticky, and real GDP rises from $16 trillion to $17 trillion. When the price level falls to 90, firms produce less in the short run because flexible output prices fall but sticky input prices stay relatively high. This leads to a decrease in real GDP to $15 trillion.

There are other reasons why aggregate supply might be positively related to the price level in the short run. Menu costs, which we introduced in Chapter 8, are another factor that affects short-run aggregate supply. If the general price level is rising but a firm decides not to adjust its prices because of menu costs, customers will want more of its output. If firms decide to increase output rather than print new menus, the quantity of aggregate supply increases. So again, output is positively related to the price level in the short run.

We also talked about the problem of money illusion in Chapter 8. Recall that money illusion occurs when people interpret nominal values as real values. In terms of aggregate supply, if output prices are falling but workers are reluctant to accept nominal pay decreases, they reinforce the stickiness of input prices. As we said

These output prices are very flexible—they can be changed with the push of a button.

above, if input prices don't fall with output prices, firms reduce output in response to general price-level changes.

Any type of price stickiness leads to a positively sloped aggregate supply curve in the short run. But keep in mind that since all prices can change in the long run, the long-run aggregate supply curve is vertical at the full employment output level.

## Shifts in Short-Run Aggregate Supply

When the long-run aggregate supply curve shifts, it signals a permanent change that affects the long run and the short run. Therefore, all long-run aggregate supply curve shifts also cause the short-run aggregate supply curve to move. In addition to the factors that shift long-run aggregate supply, we can single out three factors that shift only short-run aggregate supply: temporary *supply shocks*, changes in expected future prices, and errors in past price expectations.

## Supply Shocks

In December 2010, frigid temperatures across most of Florida caused orange crops to freeze. The freeze reduced total orange output in the state by 450 million pounds for the season. As a result, the price of oranges in grocery stores rose by more than 10%. Surprise events that change a firm's production costs are called **supply shocks**. When supply shocks are temporary, they shift only the short-run aggregate supply curve. But supply shocks can be negative or positive. Negative supply shocks lead to higher production costs; positive supply shocks reduce production costs.

A price change in an important factor of production is another supply shock. For example, in the year between July 2007 and July 2008 oil prices

A **supply shock** is a surprise event that changes a firm's production costs.

---

**FIGURE 13.9**

**The Short-Run Aggregate Supply Curve**

The positive slope of the short-run aggregate supply curve indicates that increases in the economy's price level lead to an increase in the quantity of aggregate supply in the short run. For example, if the price level rises from 100 to 110, the quantity of aggregate supply rises from $16 trillion to $17 trillion in the short run. The reason is that some prices are sticky in the short run.

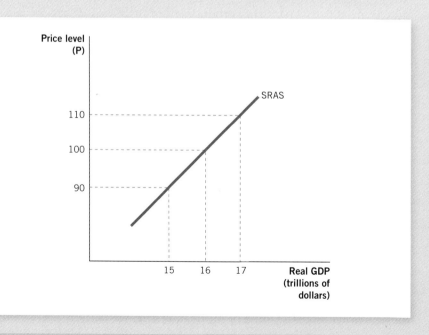

in the United States doubled from $70 a barrel to over $140 a barrel. You may recall this period because gas prices rose from about $2 per gallon to more than $4 per gallon in the summer of 2008. Figure 13.10 plots the price of oil from 2004 to 2012. Oil is an important input to many productive processes, so when its price doubles, a macroeconomic supply shock occurs.

Freezing temperatures shock not only the orange crop but also the price in grocery stores.

## Expected Future Prices

If you are going to sign a long-term wage contract, you'll want to form some expectation about future prices. After all, the real value of your future income depends on prices in the future. All else being equal, when workers and firms expect higher prices in the future, they negotiate higher wages. This leads to higher labor costs, which reduces firms' profitability and makes them less willing to produce at any price level. Therefore, higher expected future prices lead to a lower quantity of aggregate supply.

The process works in reverse if workers and firms expect a lower price level. Subsequent negotiations produce a labor agreement with lower wages, which reduces labor costs. When labor costs fall, additional production is more profitable at any price level, and the short-run aggregate supply curve shifts to the right.

## Corrections of Past Errors in Expectations

We have seen that workers and resource suppliers sign contracts on the basis of some expectation of future prices. But these expectations are not always correct. When the expectations turn out to be wrong, workers will want to renegotiate or adjust their wages in later periods. This affects costs, which in turn affects short-run aggregate supply. For example, let's say you sign a wage contract under the assumption that the inflation rate will be about 2% in the

**FIGURE 13.10**

### Price of Crude Oil

The increase in crude oil prices is an example of a supply shock, since production costs for firms throughout the economy rise drastically.

*Source*: U.S. Energy Information Administration.

next year, but it turns out to be 5%. At the end of the year, you need to renegotiate with your employer. When workers renegotiate their wages upward, this action reduces short-run aggregate supply. If workers renegotiate their wages downward, this action increases short-run aggregate supply.

Figure 13.11 summarizes the three factors that shift short-run aggregate supply. The short-run aggregate supply curve increases, or shifts to the right (to SRAS$_2$), with the following changes: positive supply shocks, expectations of future prices being lower, and adjustments to lower price expectations. The short-run aggregate supply curve decreases, or shifts to the left (to SRAS$_3$), with the following changes: negative supply shocks, expectations of future prices being higher, and adjustments to higher price expectations.

## How Does the Aggregate Demand–Aggregate Supply Model Help Us Understand the Economy?

In a market economy, output is determined by exchanges between buyers and sellers. As we shall see, this means that the economy will tend to move to the point at which aggregate demand is equal to aggregate supply. In this section, we bring aggregate demand and aggregate supply together and then consider how changes in the economy affect real GDP, unemployment, and the price level.

### FIGURE 13.11

**Factors That Shift the Short-Run Aggregate Supply Curve**

The short-run aggregate supply curve shifts to the right when there are positive supply shocks, decreases occur in expected price levels, and anticipated price levels turn out to be too high. The curve shifts to the left when there are negative supply shocks, increases occur in expected future prices, and anticipated price levels turn out to be too low.

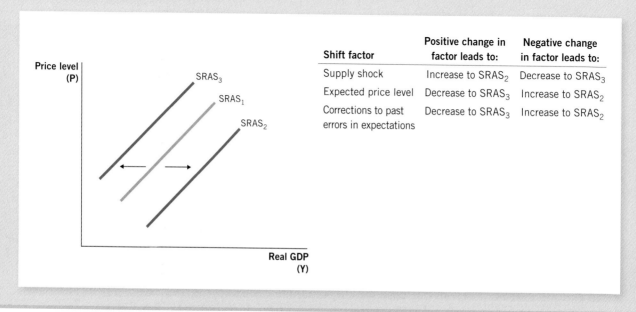

| Shift factor | Positive change in factor leads to: | Negative change in factor leads to: |
|---|---|---|
| Supply shock | Increase to SRAS$_2$ | Decrease to SRAS$_3$ |
| Expected price level | Decrease to SRAS$_3$ | Increase to SRAS$_2$ |
| Corrections to past errors in expectations | Decrease to SRAS$_3$ | Increase to SRAS$_2$ |

# PRACTICE WHAT YOU KNOW

## Long-Run Aggregate Supply and Short-Run Aggregate Supply: Which Curve Shifts?

In the real world, change is typical. In our aggregate demand–aggregate supply model, change means that the curves shift. Careful application of the model requires that you be able to determine which curve shifts, and in which direction, when real-world events occur.

Question: In each of the scenarios listed below, is there a shift in the long-run aggregate supply curve, the short-run aggregate supply curve, both, or neither? Explain your answer each time.

This oil rig sits atop the Bakken shale formation in North Dakota, where vast new shale gas resources have been discovered.

1. New shale gas deposits are found in North Dakota.
2. Hot weather leads to lower crop yields in the Midwest.
3. The Organization of Petroleum Exporting Countries (OPEC) meets and agrees to increase world oil output, leading to lower oil prices for six months.
4. U.S. consumers expect greater income in 2014.

Answers:

1. This scenario leads to an increase in both long-run aggregate supply and short-run aggregate supply. The shale gas discovery represents new resources, which shifts the long-run aggregate supply curve to the right. In addition, every long-run aggregate supply curve shift affects the short-run aggregate supply curve.
2. The lower crop yields are not permanent, so only the short-run aggregate supply curve shifts to the left. After the bad weather passes, the short-run aggregate supply curve shifts back to the right.
3. This scenario causes a short-run aggregate supply curve shift, because it doesn't represent a permanent change in oil quantities.
4. Neither the short-run aggregate supply curve nor the long-run aggregate supply curve shift. A change in expected income shifts the aggregate demand curve.

## Equilibrium in the Aggregate Demand–Aggregate Supply Model

Figure 13.12 plots the aggregate demand and the aggregate supply curves in the same graph. The point where they intersect, A, is the equilibrium point at which the opposing forces of supply and demand are balanced. At point A, the price level is P* and the output level is Y*. Prices naturally adjust to move the economy toward this equilibrium point.

To understand why the economy tends toward equilibrium at price level P*, consider other possible price levels. For example, if the price level is $P_H$, which is higher than P*, aggregate supply will be greater than aggregate demand. In this case, producers are producing more than consumers desire at current prices. Therefore, prices naturally begin to fall to eliminate a potential surplus of goods and services. As prices fall, the quantity of aggregate demand increases and the economy moves toward a new equilibrium at P*.

In contrast, if the price level is $P_L$, which is lower than P*, aggregate demand will exceed aggregate supply. At those prices, buyers desire more than producers are willing to supply. Because demand exceeds supply, prices rise and the price level moves toward P*. The only price level at which the plans of suppliers and demanders match is P*. Market forces automatically push the economy to the price level at which aggregate demand is equal to aggregate supply.

We can also describe this equilibrium in equation form. Therefore, in equilibrium, both long-run and short-run aggregate supply are equal to aggregate demand:

(Equation 13.2)

$$LRAS = SRAS = AD$$

Aggregate supply is the real GDP produced, which we indicate as Y. Aggregate demand derives from four components: C, I, G, and NX. Therefore, we can rewrite equation 13.2 as:

(Equation 13.3)

$$Y = C + I + G + NX$$

Now we know what equilibrium looks like in our model. This is our reference point for thinking about the economy at a particular point in time.

In the real world, things are always changing: everything from technology to weather to wealth and expectations can change. Now that we've built our model of the macroeconomy, we can use it to examine how changes in the real world affect the economy.

## FIGURE 13.12

**Equilibrium in the Aggregate Demand–Aggregate Supply Model**

Forces in the economy naturally move it toward equilibrium at point A, where aggregate supply is equal to aggregate demand, $P = P^*$, $Y = Y^*$, and $u = u^*$. At $P_H$, aggregate supply exceeds aggregate demand, which puts downward pressure on prices and moves the economy toward equilibrium at $P^*$. At $P_L$, where aggregate demand exceeds aggregate supply, upward pressure on prices moves the economy toward equilibrium at $P^*$.

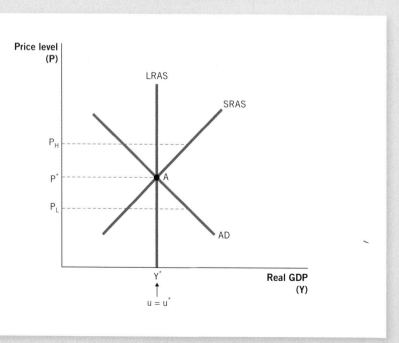

In what follows, both in this chapter and for the remainder of the book, we consider many real-world factors that lead to changes in the macroeconomy. When we consider a change, we follow a particular sequence of steps that help lead us to the new equilibrium. Once we determine the new equilibrium, we can assess the impact of the change on real GDP, unemployment, and the price level. The five steps are as follows:

1. Begin with the model in long-run equilibrium.
2. Determine which curve(s) are affected by the change(s), and identify the direction(s) of the change(s).
3. Shift the curve(s) in the appropriate direction(s).
4. Determine the new short-run and/or long-run equilibrium points.
5. Compare the new equilibrium(s) with the starting point.

Next we consider shifts in all three curves: long-run aggregate supply, short-run aggregate supply, and aggregate demand.

## Adjustments to Shifts in Long-Run Aggregate Supply

We have seen that technological advances increase full employment output and shift long-run aggregate supply to the right. For example, the Internet is a new and important technology that was extended to the general public in the 1990s. The Internet makes millions of workers more productive. The effect on the macroeconomy is illustrated in Figure 13.13. We begin at long-run equilibrium point A, with the full employment output ($Y^*$) and the price

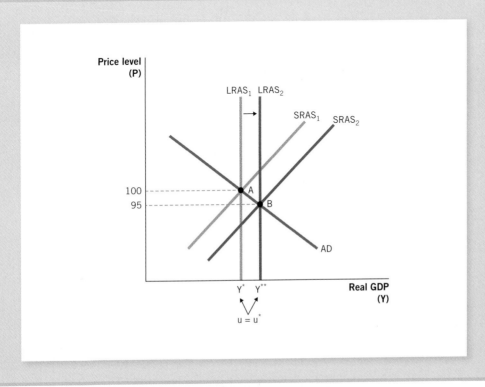

### FIGURE 13.13

**How Long-Run Aggregate Supply Shifts Affect the Economy**

Beginning at long-run equilibrium point A, the price level is at 100 and output is at the natural rate ($Y^*$). New technology shifts long-run aggregate supply positively from $LRAS_1$ to $LRAS_2$ because the economy can now produce more at any price level. The new long-run equilibrium is at point B, and there is now a new, higher natural rate of output ($Y^{**}$). Note that the unemployment rate (u) is equal to the natural rate ($u^*$) both before and after the shift.

level 100. But the introduction of new technology means that the long-run aggregate supply curve shifts from LRAS$_1$ to LRAS$_2$. Recall that changes in long-run aggregate supply also affect the short run, so the short-run aggregate supply shifts from SRAS$_1$ to SRAS$_2$. Assuming that this is the only change in the economy, we move to long-run equilibrium at point B. Notice that at point B the economy has a new full employment output level at Y$^{**}$.

All else being equal, technological change leads to more output and a lower price level. Before the Internet, the unemployment rate was at the natural rate (u$^*$). After the new technology becomes available, employment remains at the same level; but because we have better tools, workers are more productive. This analysis also applies to anything that increases the long-run aggregate supply curve, such as the discovery of new resources or the introduction of new institutions that are favorable for growth.

## Adjustments to Shifts in Short-Run Aggregate Supply

Now let's examine the effects of a change in short-run aggregate supply. Consider what happens when there is a short-run supply disruption caused by an oil pipeline break. This is an example of a supply shock. Since oil is a resource that is used in many production processes, the disruption temporarily reduces the ability of the economy to produce goods. We show this in Figure 13.14 by shifting the short-run aggregate supply curve to the left, from SRAS$_1$ to SRAS$_2$. The new equilibrium is at point b, with a higher price level (105) and a lower level

## FIGURE 13.14

**How Short-Run Aggregate Supply Shifts Affect the Economy**

A temporary negative supply shock shifts short-run aggregate supply from SRAS$_1$ to SRAS$_2$. In the short run, this moves the economy to equilibrium at point b (denoted with a lowercase letter to distinguish from long-run equilibrium). This equilibrium entails higher prices, lower real GDP, and higher unemployment. In the long run, the economy returns to equilibrium at point A.

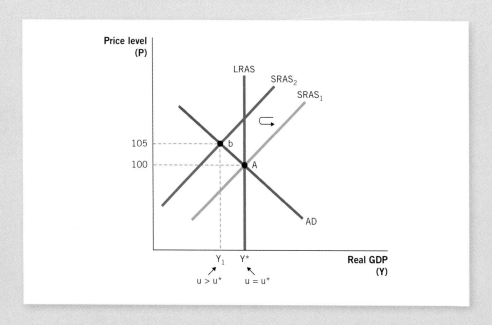

of output ($Y_1$). Because this is a short-run equilibrium, we use the lowercase b. The lower output means increased unemployment in the short run ($u > u^*$). Notice that nothing happened to long-run aggregate supply—in the long run, the pipeline will be fixed and oil can be produced at output level $Y^*$ again.

Since the disruption is temporary, eventually the short-run aggregate supply curve will shift back to the right until it reaches SRAS again. Short-run disruptions in aggregate supply do not alter the long-run equilibrium in the economy; eventually the price level, output, and the unemployment rate return to their long-run equilibrium levels at point A. But in the short run, an economic downturn brings higher unemployment and lower real GDP.

## ECONOMICS IN THE REAL WORLD

### The Drought of 2012 Sends Prices Higher

According to an Associated Press article in August 2012, the summer of 2012 was the hottest on record for the United States. High temperatures led to extremely low yields in both corn and soybean crops: the USDA projected 123 bushels per acre of corn in 2012, down from 147 bushels in 2011.

According to the AP article, economist Rick Whitacre projected higher prices for many different consumer goods such as cereal, soda, cake mixes, candy bars, and even makeup. Since corn is an important feed source for cattle, Whitacre projected a 4% to 6% rise in beef and pork prices.

This is a classic example of supply shock, and the result is exactly what the aggregate demand–aggregate supply model predicts: short-run aggregate supply shifts to the left, which leads to higher prices throughout the economy. ✳

These Iowa fields were supposed to be much greener in July 2012.

# Adjustments to Shifts in Aggregate Demand

Aggregate demand shifts for many reasons. Some shifts occur because of expectations rather than actual events, yet they still affect the macroeconomy. For example, let's say that consumer confidence rises unexpectedly: consumers wake up one morning with expectations of higher future income. This change causes increased aggregate demand because consumers start spending more. Can this kind of change have real effects on the economy? That is, will a change in consumer confidence affect unemployment and real GDP? Let's look at the model.

Figure 13.15 illustrates the changes in the economy from the increased consumer confidence. We start with long-run equilibrium at point A, where the price level is 100, real GDP is at full employment output $Y^*$, and unemployment is equal to the natural rate ($u = u^*$). Then aggregate demand shifts from $AD_1$ to $AD_2$. This moves the economy to short-run equilibrium at point b. The short-run equilibrium is associated with higher prices (P = 105) and higher real GDP ($Y_1$). In addition, the unemployment rate drops to $u_1$, which is less than $u^*$. Thus, changes in aggregate demand do affect the real economy, at least in the short run.

## FIGURE 13.15

### How Aggregate Demand Shifts Affect the Economy

An increase in aggregate demand moves the economy from the initial equilibrium at point A to a new short-run equilibrium at point b. The positive aggregate shift increases real GDP and decreases unemployment in the short run ($u < u^*$). In the short run, prices adjust—but only partially, since some prices are sticky. In the long run, when all prices adjust, the short-run aggregate supply curve shifts to $SRAS_2$ and the economy moves to long-run equilibrium at point C, where $Y = Y^*$ and $u = u^*$.

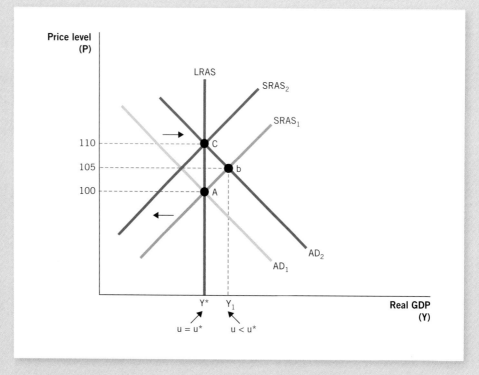

## PRACTICE WHAT YOU KNOW

### Using the Aggregate Demand–Aggregate Supply Model: The Japanese Earthquake and Tsunami of 2011

In 2011, a record-breaking earthquake hit Japan and was followed immediately by a tsunami. This natural disaster destroyed significant capital in Japan, including roads, buildings, and even nuclear power plants.

**Question:** How would you use the aggregate demand–aggregate supply model to illustrate the effect of this disaster on the Japanese economy?

**Answer:** People often think that natural disasters affect only short-run aggregate supply, because the effects are temporary. But if a disaster is so severe that it destroys resources, the long-run aggregate supply will also decline.

These devastating tsunami waves permanently destroyed many capital goods along part of Japan's seacoast.

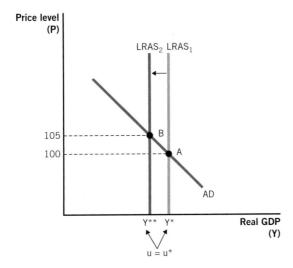

Notice that the unemployment rate (u) is equal to the natural rate (u*) both before and after the shift. Jobs remain because there is plenty of work to do in the aftermath of a natural disaster. However, in the long run Japan has fewer resources after the earthquake than it had before, and this outcome limits the nation's economic growth.

**Question:** How does this affect the U.S. economy?

**Answer:** Real foreign income falls in Japan, which leads to a decline in aggregate demand for U.S. goods and services.

| TABLE 13.1 |
| --- |

**Summary of Results from Aggregate Demand Shifts**

| | Increase in aggregate demand | | Decrease in aggregate demand | |
| --- | --- | --- | --- | --- |
| | Short run | Long run | Short run | Long run |
| **Real GDP** | Y rises | Y returns to original level | Y falls | Y returns to original level |
| **Unemployment** | u falls | u returns to original level | u rises | u returns to original level |
| **Price level** | P rises | P rises even further | P falls | P falls even further |

Our example presents a positive result—after all, unemployment falls and real GDP rises. Now let's complete this example by following through to long-run equilibrium. Recall the difference between the long run and the short run: in the long run, all prices adjust. As all prices adjust, the short-run aggregate supply curve shifts to the left from SRAS₁ to SRAS₂. This moves us to long-run equilibrium at point C. Notice that at C we are back to the original output level (Y*) and unemployment level (u*), but prices are higher (P = 110). The model is telling us that demand changes have no real effects in the long run because only the price level, a nominal variable, is affected.

What are the consequences of this move to long-run equilibrium, and how does it compare to the short-run equilibrium? At point b, real GDP is up and unemployment is down. But not everyone is happy. For example, workers with sticky wages are now paying more for their final goods and services, but their wages did not adjust upward in the short run. In fact, any sellers with sticky prices are hurt in the short run when other prices rise.

Because everyone can adjust their prices eventually, there is a movement to point C in the long run. Thinking about your coffee shop, in the long run you can renegotiate wages and all other long-term contracts. Thus, if there is a 10% increase in prices throughout the economy, both input and output prices rise by 10%. The price of a $4 latte rises to $4.40, and the barista wage of $10 per hour rises to $11 per hour. When input prices rise to match output price changes, the short-run aggregate supply curve shifts to SRAS₂. In the long run, once all prices adjust, the price level does not affect the quantity of output supplied. This is why output returns to Y*, the full employment level.

Table 13.1 summarizes the economic effects of aggregate demand changes in both the short run and the long run. The last two columns summarize the effects of negative decreases in aggregate demand. These decreases in aggregate demand are a particular source of debate among macroeconomists. In Chapter 14, we'll look closely at negative aggregate demand shifts during both the Great Depression of the 1930s and the Great Recession of 2007–2009.

## Recession-Proof Your Job

Recessions are hard on almost everyone in an economy, but there are ways you can shield yourself from unemployment.

The first thing you need is a college degree. As we showed in Chapter 8, the unemployment rate in April 2012 was 8.1% for the entire labor force, but just 4% for college graduates.

One lesson we learned in this chapter is that unemployment persists in the macroeconomy when wages are inflexible downward. This outcome applies to individuals too. If you do happen to lose your job, you may need to consider accepting a lower wage or even a change of career so as to obtain another job. The more flexible your wage range, the less likely you are to experience long-term unemployment.

Finally, if you lose your job, be sure to take advantage of all the modern job-search tools available today. There are millions of jobs available, even when unemployment rates are very high—you just need to know how to find those jobs. For example, the web-

Don't let this happen to you!

site indeed.com turns up thousands of job vacancies for almost any job description. As of August 2012, searching for either "accountant" or "CPA" yielded over 30,000 results, a search for "civil engineer" yielded 10,605 results, and "marketing" yielded 253,467 results.

**ECONOMICS FOR LIFE**

# Conclusion

We began this chapter with the misconception that recessions are normal occurrences that happen every few years. In fact, they are anything but normal. They occur with unpredictable frequency and are caused by many different factors. Recessions in business cycles are often caused by changes in aggregate demand, but the same symptoms can also reflect short-run aggregate supply shifts.

This chapter introduced the aggregate demand–aggregate supply model of the economy, which helps us understand how changes in the real world affect the macroeconomy. In the next chapter, we'll use the model to evaluate the two biggest macroeconomic disturbances of the past century: the Great Depression of the 1930s and the Great Recession of 2007–2009.

# ANSWERING THE BIG QUESTIONS

### What is the aggregate demand–aggregate supply model?

* The aggregate demand–aggregate supply model is the model that economists use to study short-run fluctuations in the economy.

### What is aggregate demand?

* Aggregate demand represents the spending side of the economy. It includes consumption, investment, net exports, and government spending.
* The slope of the aggregate demand curve is negative due to the wealth effect, the interest rate effect, and the international trade effect.
* The aggregate demand curve shifts when there are changes in real wealth, expected income, expected future prices, foreign income and wealth, and the value of the dollar.

### What is aggregate supply?

* Aggregate supply represents the producing side of the economy.
* Long-run aggregate supply is relevant when all prices are flexible. This curve is vertical at full employment output and is not influenced by the price level.
* In the short run, when some prices are sticky, the short-run aggregate supply curve is relevant. This curve indicates a positive relationship between the price level and real output supplied.

### How does the aggregate demand–aggregate supply model help us understand the economy?

* We can use the aggregate demand–aggregate supply model to see how changes in either aggregate demand or aggregate supply affect real GDP, unemployment, and the price level.

## CONCEPTS YOU SHOULD KNOW

aggregate demand (p. 394)  international trade effect (p. 398)  wealth effect (p. 397)
aggregate supply (p. 394)  supply shock (p. 410)
interest rate effect (p. 397)  wealth (p. 397)

## QUESTIONS FOR REVIEW

1. What are three reasons the aggregate demand curve slopes downward? Name at least three factors that cause the aggregate demand curve to shift.

2. What are three reasons the short-run aggregate supply curve slopes upward? Name at least three factors that cause the short-run aggregate supply curve to shift.

3. How are the factors that shift the long-run aggregate supply curve different from those that shift the short-run aggregate supply curve?

4. Why is the long-run aggregate supply curve vertical?

5. How does strong economic growth in China affect aggregate demand in the United States?

6. Suppose the economy is in a recession caused by lower aggregate demand. If no policy action is taken, what will happen to the price level, output, and employment in the long run?

7. Consider two economies, both in recession. In the first economy, all workers have long-term contracts that guarantee high nominal wages for the next five years. In the second economy, all workers have annual contracts that are indexed to changes in the price level. Which economy will return to the natural rate of output first? Explain your response.

## STUDY PROBLEMS (✱ *solved at the end of the section*)

1. Describe whether the following changes cause the short-run aggregate supply to increase, decrease, or neither.

   a. The price level increases.
   b. Input prices decrease.
   c. Firms and workers expect the price level to fall.
   d. The price level decreases.
   e. New policies cause an increase in the cost of meeting government regulations.
   f. The number of workers in the labor force increases.

2. Describe whether the following changes cause the long-run aggregate supply to increase, decrease, or neither.

   a. The price level increases.
   b. The stock of capital in the economy increases.
   c. Natural resources increase.
   d. The price level decreases.
   e. Firms and workers expect the price level to rise.
   f. The number of workers in the labor force increases.

3. On the following graph, illustrate the short-run and long-run effects of an increase in aggregate demand. Describe what happens to the price level, output, and employment.

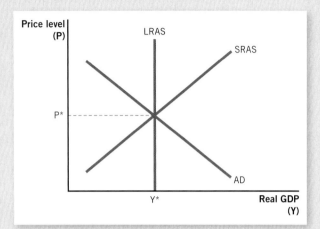

4. How does a lower price level in the United States affect the purchases of imported goods? Explain, using aggregate demand.

✳5. Describe whether the following changes cause the aggregate demand curve to increase, decrease, or neither.

   a. The price level increases.
   b. Investment decreases.
   c. Imports decrease and exports increase.
   d. The price level decreases.
   e. Consumption increases.
   f. Government purchases decrease.

✳6. Suppose that a sudden increase in aggregate demand moves the economy from its long-run equilibrium.

   a. Illustrate this change using the aggregate demand–aggregate supply model.
   b. What are the effects of this change in the short run and the long run?

7. In the summer of 2008, global oil prices spiked to extremely high levels before coming down again at the end of that year. This temporary event had global effects, because oil is an important resource in the production of many goods and services. Focusing only on the U.S. economy, determine how this kind of event affects the price level, unemployment rate, and real GDP in both the short run and the long run. Assume the economy was in long-run equilibrium before this change and consider only this stated change.

✳8. You work for Dr. Zhang, the autocratic dictator of Zhouland. After taking an economics course, you decide that devaluing your currency (Zhoullars) is the way to increase GDP. Following your advice, Dr. Zhang orders massive increases in the supply of Zhoullars, which reduces the value of Zhoullars in world markets. Use the AD-AS model to determine the effects to real GDP, unemployment, and the price level in Zhouland in both the short run and the long run. Assume the economy was in long-run equilibrium before this change and consider only this stated change.

# SOLVED PROBLEMS

**5. a.** Neither. A change in the price level (P) leads to a movement along the AD curve. When the price level rises, the quantity of aggregate demand declines along the curve.

**b.** Investment (I) is one component of aggregate demand, so a decrease in investment decreases aggregate demand.

**c.** Net exports (NX) is another component of aggregate demand. An increase in exports and a decrease in imports imply that net exports rise, so aggregate demand increases.

**d.** Aggregate demand neither increases nor decreases with a change in the price level (P). A change in the price level leads to movement along the AD curve. When the price level decreases, the quantity of aggregate demand declines along the curve.

**e.** Consumption (C) is a component of aggregate demand, so an increase in investment means an increase in aggregate demand.

**f.** Government purchases (G) are a component of aggregate demand, so a decrease in government purchases causes a decrease in aggregate demand.

**6. a.** Aggregate demand increases from $AD_1$ to $AD_2$. In the short run, equilibrium will be at point b. In the long run, equilibrium will move to point C.

**b.** In the short run, real GDP rises, the unemployment rate falls, and the price level rises. In the long run, real GDP goes back to the full employment level, the unemployment rate returns to the natural rate, and the price level rises further.

**8.** The reduction in the value of the Zhoullar means an increase or positive shift in the aggregate demand curve. This creates the same scenario pictured in the solution to problem #6; please refer again to that figure.

   In the short run, there is greater real GDP, lower unemployment, and a higher price level. This short-run equilibrium is pictured as point b in the figure.

   In the long run, the only change is an increase in the price level (P), as indicated by the new long-run equilibrium at point C in the figure. Note that this is consistent with the discussion of inflation in Chapter 9. That is, the cause of inflation is monetary expansion. When Dr. Zhang commanded that the number of Zhoullars should increase, this meant that inflation would eventually arrive.

# The Great Recession, the Great Depression, and Great Macroeconomic Debates

**The Great Recession was comparable to the Great Depression.**

The Great Recession that started at the end of 2007 was a very difficult period for both the United States and the global economy. By most any

measure, it was the worst recession since the Great Depression of the 1930s. But many people have the false impression that this recession was nearly as difficult as the Great Depression. It wasn't even close. The effects on real GDP and unemployment were significantly smaller in the more recent contraction. Furthermore, living standards in the twenty-first century are much higher than they were during the Great Depression era.

In this chapter, we take a closer look at both of these infamous economic contractions. We first consider them in the context of the aggregate demand–aggregate supply model. We then give an overview of the major debates of macroeconomics and how they relate to the two contractions, again in the context of aggregate demand and aggregate supply.

On Inauguration Day in 2009, the U.S. economy was mired in the Great Recession.

# BIG QUESTIONS

* Exactly what happened during the Great Recession and the Great Depression?
* What are the big disagreements in macroeconomics?

# Exactly What Happened during the Great Recession and the Great Depression?

The Great Recession and the Great Depression are the two most significant economic downturns of the past 100 years in the United States. In this section, we examine both downturns with two goals in mind. First, we will briefly put each one in historical perspective, in terms of both depth and duration. Second, we will examine them in the context of the aggregate demand–aggregate supply model (see Chapter 13). Analyzing these two crucial real-world events demonstrates the power of the aggregate demand–aggregate supply framework. We begin with the Great Recession.

## The Great Recession

In December 2007, the U.S. economy entered the recession we now call the "Great Recession." Some analysts adopted the name Great Recession because the downturn was longer and deeper than typical recessions, so many people wanted to tie it to the Great Depression, which lasted throughout much of the 1930s. In addition, many people acknowledged early on that there were significant problems in the financial markets—another similarity with the Great Depression. Finally, the title stuck when the effects of the recession refused to subside for several years after the recession was officially over. Before discussing the causes of the Great Recession, let's look more closely at just how serious the contraction was.

### The Depth and Duration of the Great Recession

The official duration of the Great Recession was 18 months (December 2007 to June 2009), making it the longest of all recessions since World War II. But even this length understates the full amount of time during which the economic downturn affected the U.S. economy. For several years after the recession was officially over, unemployment remained high and real GDP grew slowly.

One way to grasp the depth and duration of the Great Recession is to compare it with the other recessions that have occurred since World War II. Figure 14.1 shows comparative data on real GDP and the unemployment rate. Panel (a) compares the pattern of real GDP during the Great Recession and an average pattern of the other recessions since World War II. To illustrate the two paths of GDP, we set them to 100 at the onset of the contraction. Notice that during a typical recession, real GDP falls slightly and then comes back to its original level after about a year and a half. In contrast, during the Great Recession output fell significantly and then recovered more slowly. In fact, it took nearly four years for real GDP to reach its pre-recession level in the third quarter of 2011.

Panel (b) shows the monthly unemployment rate for the Great Recession as compared to an average unemployment rate across the other post–World War II recessions. For a typical recession, the unemployment rate climbed to around 7% and then declined after about 12 to 15 months. But for the Great Recession, the unemployment rate climbed to 10% in October 2009 (22 months after the recession began) and remained at or near 8% even 5 years after the recession began. Taken together, panels (a) and (b) indicate that the Great Recession was more severe than a typical recession.

We now turn to the aggregate demand–aggregate supply model to examine the factors that contributed to the Great Recession.

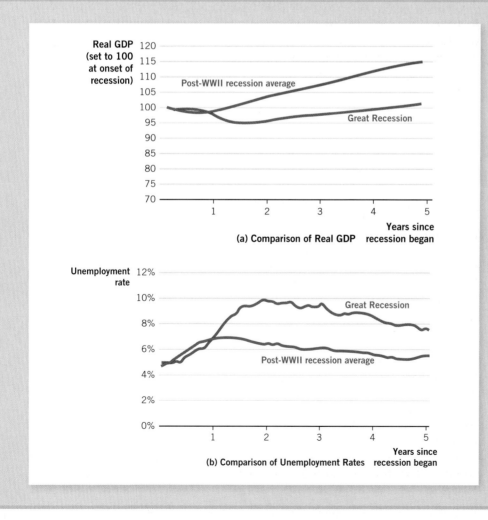

**FIGURE 14.1**

**Unemployment Rate and Real GDP, Great Recession versus All Other Post-WWII Recessions**

(a) During the Great Recession, real GDP fell further and rebounded more slowly than it otherwise would during a normal postwar recession.

(b) Also, the unemployment rate rose to levels far higher than have occurred in typical postwar recessions, and it remained high long after the rate typically falls.

*Sources*: Panel (a): U.S. Bureau of Economic Analysis; panel (b): U.S. Bureau of Labor Statistics.

## Using Aggregate Demand and Aggregate Supply to Analyze the Great Recession

In considering the causes of the Great Recession, most economists and policymakers initially assumed it was caused by a significant decline in aggregate demand. And while aggregate demand did indeed fall, it is clear in hindsight that aggregate supply also fell. We can now look more closely at this very difficult economic period in the context of the aggregate demand–aggregate supply model. We begin with the changes in aggregate supply.

The decline in aggregate supply was caused by problems with a key economic institution: the loanable funds market. In 2007, it became clear that there was trouble brewing in U.S. financial markets. Much of the trouble stemmed from the declining values of U.S. real estate. Figure 14.2 plots an index of U.S. house purchase prices from 2001 to 2012, with the Great Recession period shaded as a vertical blue bar. You can see that home prices began to fall in the months before the Great Recession, with the decline accelerating rapidly through 2008.

You might recall from Chapter 10 that at this time home mortgages had become securitized into mortgage-backed securities and that significant quantities of these securities were held by most of the largest financial institutions in the United States. Thus, when real estate values fell, that event led to a systemic problem in U.S. financial markets. Because of the financial firms' interdependence, the problem quickly spread throughout the United States and then to the rest of the world. Financial crisis signals a breakdown in the loanable funds market. When the loanable funds market does not function properly, firms cannot get funding to produce output, and aggregate supply falls.

A crucial issue as we analyze the Great Recession is identifying whether the decline in aggregate supply was temporary or permanent. Recall that in the aggregate demand–aggregate supply model, there are very different effects from changes in short-run and long-run aggregate supply. If the effect of the financial crisis was temporary, then we would view it as a short-run supply shock, illustrated in the aggregate demand–aggregate supply model with a leftward shift in the short-run aggregate supply curve. In this scenario, after the financial turmoil ends, the economy returns to its natural rate of output. (See Figure 13.14 on p. 416 for a refresher.)

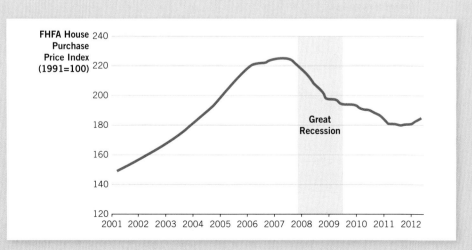

**FIGURE 14.2**

**U.S. House Purchase Price Index, 2001–2012**

U.S. home prices began falling in mid-2007 and then fell consistently through the Great Recession period.

*Source*: Federal Housing Finance Agency.

But, in fact, the crisis in the loanable funds market had permanent effects. Why? Because it led to the enactment of new financial regulations. The **Dodd-Frank Act**, signed in July 2010, is the primary regulatory response to the financial turmoil that contributed to the Great Recession. This act established several new oversight bodies and regulations on financial institutions with the stated aim of reducing risk in financial markets. While we certainly hope that the new regulations will inhibit future financial turmoil, most economists also recognize that the burdens they impose on financial firms will also inhibit the ability of these firms to provide funding for investment opportunities in the economy. This represents a permanent change in financial institutions, which shifts the long-run aggregate supply curve.

The **Dodd-Frank Act** is the primary regulatory response to the financial turmoil that contributed to the Great Recession.

Consider the following analogy. Financial markets are like a bridge between savers and borrowers in an economy. If the economy is to grow, firms must be able to borrow, and so the bridge must be safe and efficient. But during the period of the Great Recession, there were several accidents on the bridge, disrupting the flow of traffic and temporarily slowing the economy. The new financial regulations are like a stricter speed limit imposed on the bridge to make it safer. There will be fewer accidents in the future (we hope), but traffic will move less efficiently across the bridge from now on. Therefore, we illustrate the permanent effects of the financial crisis and changes in institutions as a decline in long-run aggregate supply.

But aggregate demand was negatively affected as well. At least two factors contributed to a large decline in aggregate demand. The first was a fall in wealth: people's homes are often the largest piece of their overall wealth, so when real estate values fell, people's wealth dropped. (See again Figure 14.2.) In addition, U.S. stocks lost one-third of their value during 2008. For millions of people, this meant seeing their retirement savings drop by a full one-third. Both of these situations contributed to large declines in wealth, so aggregate demand declined significantly.

Aggregate demand also fell because of a decline in expected income. Beginning in 2007, consumers realized that the economy was undergoing a downturn. Figure 14.3 shows the related Consumer Sentiment Index, which also

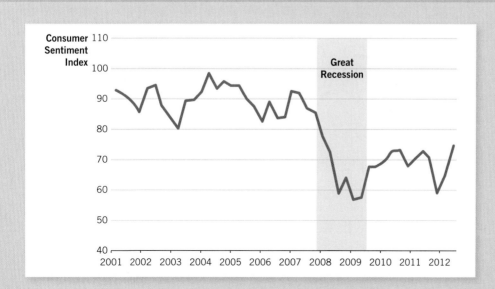

## FIGURE 14.3

**Consumer Sentiment Index, 2001–2012**

The Consumer Sentiment Index is a measure of consumers' confidence about their own financial situation and the future direction of the economy. This index began falling in 2007 and then fell significantly during the Great Recession.

*Source*: St. Louis Federal Reserve FRED database. The Consumer Sentiment Index was developed at the University of Michigan.

began falling ahead of the recession and then fell significantly during 2008. Together, these two factors—a decline in wealth and a decline in expected income—led to a decline in aggregate demand.

Let's now consider the aggregate demand–aggregate supply model to see the implications of these shifts for the macroeconomy. Figure 14.4 shows a decline in both aggregate demand and aggregate supply from 2007 to 2008. Aggregate demand shifted from $AD_{2007}$ to $AD_{2008}$, and long-run aggregate supply shifted from $LRAS_{2007}$ to $LRAS_{2008}$. In 2007, the economy was in equilibrium at point A; at that time, the unemployment rate (not pictured in Figure 14.4) was below 5% and real GDP was growing at a 3.6% rate in the second quarter of 2007. Then housing prices fell, leading to financial market turmoil, lower real wealth, and then lower consumer confidence. The declines in aggregate demand and long-run aggregate supply moved the economy to a new equilibrium at point b. During this time, the unemployment rate climbed to 10%, and by the last quarter of 2008 real GDP had shrunk by 8.9% (on an annual basis).

One reason this recession has been called "Great" is that the decline in real GDP and the increase in the unemployment rate were large by historical standards. But another reason is that symptoms of the recession dragged on for several years after the recession was officially over. In 2012, real GDP was still expanding at less than 2% and the unemployment rate remained at 8%. In response, the government employed many different tools to try to move the economy back to normal growth and lower levels of unemployment. We will discuss these tools over the next four chapters. But the tools focused primarily on aggregate demand.

World financial institutions remained in poor health for quite a while, thus impacting aggregate supply—and this outcome kept many economies from quickly returning to previous output levels. Figure 14.5 shows U.S. real GDP from 1993 to 2012. In addition, we plot a dashed trend line that indicates the general path of real GDP prior to the Great Recession. This figure indicates that something permanent happened to the U.S. economy during the Great

## FIGURE 14.4

**The Decline in Both Long-run Aggregate Supply and Aggregate Demand, 2007–2008**

Financial market turmoil and lower consumer confidence led to decreases in both long-run aggregate supply and aggregate demand. The result was a new, lower level of real GDP and a higher rate of unemployment.

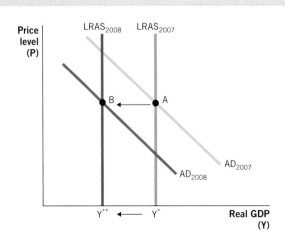

## PRACTICE WHAT YOU KNOW

### The Great Recession: What Made It "Great"?

Question: What are three reasons why the 2007–2009 recession came to be known as the Great Recession?

Answer:

1. Initially, the name appeared because the recession was clearly worse than a typical recession. For example, real GDP fell by an annual rate of 8.9% in the fourth quarter of 2008.

2. There was noticeable stress in financial markets, making the downturn similar to that aspect of the Great Depression.

3. The effects of the Great Recession, in terms of both high unemployment rates and slow real GDP growth, persisted long after the recession was officially over.

Recession. Long-run aggregate supply declined. The economy began growing again, but from a lower baseline level after the Great Recession.

## The Great Depression

We have seen that the Great Recession was much worse than typical U.S. recessions. However, even though it has been termed "Great," we should not make the mistake of equating it with the Great Depression. In this section, we first examine

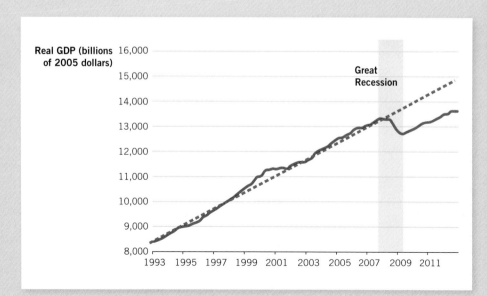

**FIGURE 14.5**

**Real GDP versus the Previous Trend**

There was a significant decline in real GDP during the Great Recession. But, in addition, there seems to be no tendency for the economy to return to its former trend line. This indicates that there was a permanent decline in long-run aggregate supply. In essence, the Great Recession led to a permanent loss of real GDP that it may never recover.

economic indicators during the Great Depression era, and then we consider the severe contraction in terms of the aggregate demand–aggregate supply model.

## The Magnitude of the Great Depression

To convey a sense of the historic magnitude of the Great Depression, we have plotted long-run U.S. real GDP data in Figure 14.6. The data goes all the way back to 1870, but it is easy to identify the Great Depression—the significant drop in real GDP beginning in 1930. There have been several contractions in the U.S. economy since 1870, but none as severe as the Great Depression. During that period, real GDP fell from $977 billion in 1929 to $716 billion in 1933 (both equated to 2005 dollars). Imagine an economic contraction so severe that after four years the economy is producing almost 30% less than it was when the contraction started!

During the Great Depression, shantytowns dubbed "Hoovervilles," after President Hoover, sprang up outside major U.S. cities.

Furthermore, even though their names are similar, the Great Recession pales in comparison to the Great Depression. Figure 14.7 shows real GDP growth rates and unemployment rates beginning with the start of the two contractions. Panel (a) plots real GDP over the two contractions. Even though we earlier observed that the Great Recession was severe in comparison to typical U.S. recessions, when we compare it to the Great Depression it looks like a harmless temporary decline. Real GDP fell by nearly 30% over the four years from 1929 to 1933, and it took seven years for real GDP to return to its pre-recession level.

Panel (b) plots the unemployment rates. In 1929, the unemployment rate was just 2.2%, but by 1933 (four years later) it had climbed to over 25%! In other words, by 1933 one out of four workers was without a job. Particularly alarming was the length of

## FIGURE 14.6

**Real U.S. GDP, 1870–2012**

When we look at U.S. real GDP growth over the long run, the Great Depression is easy to spot, since it is the severe decline that occurred during the 1930s. To normalize across percentage changes, the plotted data is the logarithm of real GDP.

*Source*: U.S. Bureau of Economic Analysis.

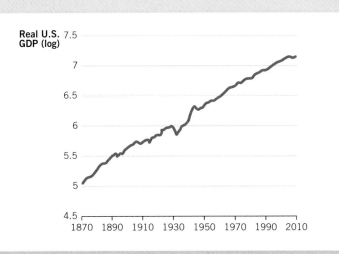

the contraction: the unemployment rate remained above 15% for almost the entire decade of the 1930s.

## Using Aggregate Demand and Aggregate Supply to Explain the Great Depression

The Great Depression was unusual because it was so deep and lasted so long. In fact, it was actually two separate recessions (August 1929 to March 1933, and May 1937 to June 1938). But the Great Depression was also characterized by another striking condition: prices across the economy declined throughout the course of the decade. In fact, at the end of the 1930s the general price level, as measured by the GDP deflator, was still 20% lower than it had been in 1929. The decline in prices indicates that the primary cause of the Great Depression was a decline in aggregate demand.

Figure 14.8 illustrates how a significant decline in aggregate demand affects the macroeconomy. In 1929, the economy was in equilibrium at point A, with aggregate demand designated as $AD_{1929}$. Then a significant decline in aggregate demand occurred for several years, as indicated by a shift to

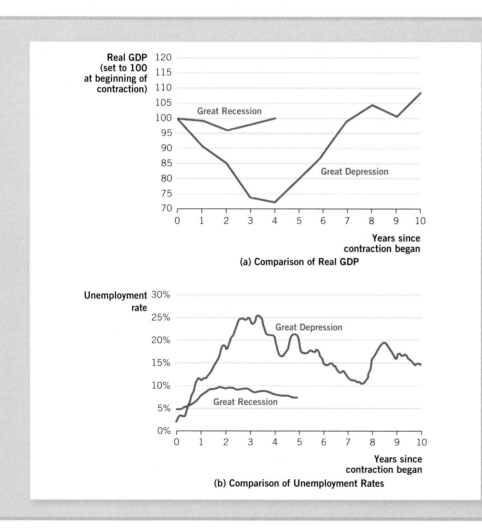

**FIGURE 14.7**

**Unemployment Rate and Real GDP for the Great Recession and the Great Depression**

(a) During the Great Depression, real GDP fell by almost a third, and it took seven years to return to its pre-recession level. In comparison, the decline in real GDP during the Great Recession seems meager. (b) During the Great Depression, the unemployment rate climbed to over 25% and remained over 15% for most of the entire decade of the 1930s. These levels far exceed the unemployment rates experienced during the Great Recession of 2007–2009.

*Source*: Panel (a): U.S. Bureau of Economic Analysis; panel (b): U.S. Bureau of Labor Statistics.

(a) Comparison of Real GDP

(b) Comparison of Unemployment Rates

**Macroeconomic policy** encompasses government acts to influence the macroeconomy.

**Fiscal policy** comprises the use of government's budget tools, government spending, and taxes to influence the macroeconomy.

**Monetary policy** involves adjusting the money supply to influence the macroeconomy.

$AD_{1930+}$. As we have seen in our study of macroeconomics, lower aggregate demand leads to lower real GDP (shown in the figure as $Y_1$), higher unemployment rates (25%), and a lower price level (shown here as a decline from 100 to 80). These match the symptoms of the Great Depression.

What caused the decline in aggregate demand? Unfortunately, it turns out that much of the decline was caused by faulty *macroeconomic policy*. **Macroeconomic policy** encompasses government acts to influence the direction of the overall economy. Economists also distinguish two different types of macroeconomic policy: *fiscal policy* and *monetary policy*. **Fiscal policy** comprises the use of government's budget tools, government spending, and taxes to influence the macroeconomy. **Monetary policy** involves adjusting the money supply to influence the economy. We are not yet ready to talk in detail about macroeconomic policies (those are the topics of the next section of this textbook), but we can outline the major determinants of the Great Depression based on aggregate demand and aggregate supply.

First, a stock market crash on October 29, 1929, is generally viewed as the beginning of the Great Depression. The day the stock market crashed has come to be known as Black Thursday. But the economy did not crash just because the stock market experienced a severe downturn. A significant reaction to this event was a change in people's expectations for the future. In particular, expected future income declined—and we know that this factor decreases aggregate demand. Between 1929 and 1932, stock prices (as measured by the Dow Jones Industrial Average) fell by almost 90%.

What was the government's policy reaction? The federal government purposefully reduced the quantity of money in the economy in 1928 and 1929 in hopes of controlling stock prices, which policymakers thought were too high. As we will

Was the stock market crash the only cause of the Great Depression?

---

## FIGURE 14.8

### The Decline in Aggregate Demand during the Great Depression

A significant decline in aggregate demand after 1929 can help to explain all three symptoms of the Great Depression: a decline in real GDP (from $Y^*$ to $Y_1$), an increase in the unemployment rate (from 3% to 25%), and a decrease in the price level (from 100 to 80).

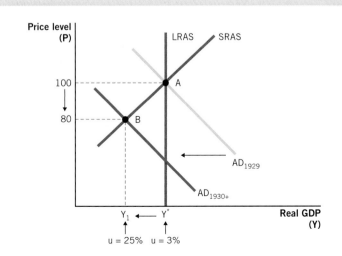

see in Chapter 18, tighter money (that is, a reduced money supply) leads to lower aggregate demand. In this context, the biggest policy error involved the banks. As financial panic spread across the country, people began withdrawing their deposits from banks. As a result, between 1930 and 1933 more than 9,000 banks failed in the United States. And while the government had the ability to lend to these ailing banks, it failed to do so. This policy led to even larger declines in the money supply. In fact, between 1929 and 1933 the quantity of money in the U.S. economy declined by one-third. Economists today agree that these policy failures and the resulting decline in the money supply led to a significant decline in aggregate demand and were thus the primary contributors to the beginning of the Great Depression.

There were other reasons as well why the economy dragged through recession for so long. For example, in the early 1930s Presidents Hoover and Roosevelt raised taxes in attempts to balance the federal budget. And as we'll see in Chapter 16, higher taxes also reduce aggregate demand. Another policy blunder affected aggregate supply: in 1930, Congress passed the Smoot-Hawley Tariff Act. This legislation imposed tariffs on thousands of imported goods and set off a global trade war as other nations reacted by imposing tariffs on U.S. exports.

In the end, most analysts agree that the economic contraction was primarily characterized by a significant decline in aggregate demand. In this context, the Great Depression was an event that reshaped the way both economists and non-economists think about the economy. In the next section, we consider how the Great Depression changed economic thought.

# What Are the Big Disagreements in Macroeconomics?

Here we consider the major debates in macroeconomics by building on the previous discussion of the Great Depression. Most economists agree with the basic implications of the aggregate demand–aggregate supply model. However, economists disagree about the role of government in the economy and whether the economy can correct itself. In this section, we try to clarify the disagreements.

One of the most contentious issues among economists involves the economy's adjustment to long-run equilibrium. Some economists believe that adjustment can and should occur naturally. This group is known as **classical economists**. Others see the return to long-run equilibrium as an adjustment that occurs unpredictably and often with much delay; this group, known as **Keynesian economists**, calls for the government to speed the process back to full employment. While not every economist fits completely in either camp, these distinctions help to clarify the debate.

**Classical economists** stress the importance of aggregate supply and generally believe that the economy can adjust back to full employment equilibrium on its own.

**Keynesian economists** stress the importance of aggregate demand and generally believe that the economy needs help in moving back to full employment equilibrium.

## Classical Economics

At the beginning of the twentieth century, economics was essentially focused on microeconomic issues. Economists had a good sense of the merits of supply and demand analysis for individual markets. As you know, when we consider basic supply and demand, the price of the good adjusts to draw the

# Great Recession vs. Great Depression

The U.S. recession from December 2007 to June 2009 has been named the Great Recession. This name seems appropriate because it was the longest and most severe recession since the 1930s. But the name also ties it to the Great Depression era of the 1930s, and this comparison is misleading. While these two infamous contractions have similarities, they are drastically different in their economic impact. In terms of both real GDP and unemployment rates, the negative effects of the Great Depression dwarfed those of the Great Recession.

## Real GDP

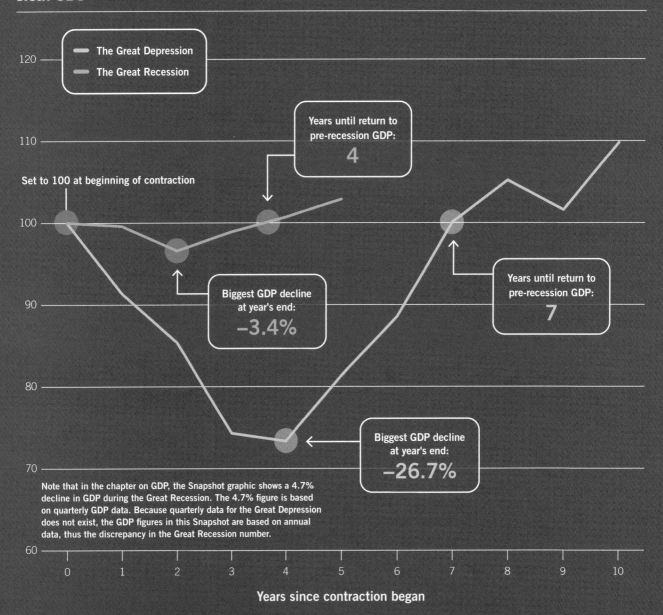

- The Great Depression
- The Great Recession

Set to 100 at beginning of contraction

Years until return to pre-recession GDP:
**4**

Biggest GDP decline at year's end:
**−3.4%**

Years until return to pre-recession GDP:
**7**

Biggest GDP decline at year's end:
**−26.7%**

Note that in the chapter on GDP, the Snapshot graphic shows a 4.7% decline in GDP during the Great Recession. The 4.7% figure is based on quarterly GDP data. Because quarterly data for the Great Depression does not exist, the GDP figures in this Snapshot are based on annual data, thus the discrepancy in the Great Recession number.

Years since contraction began

- If we assume a natural rate of unemployment equal to 5%, how much cyclical unemployment existed during the worst parts of the Great Recession and the Great Depression?

- Name two actions—or inactions—by the government that economists agree contributed to the depth and duration of the Great Depression.

## Unemployment

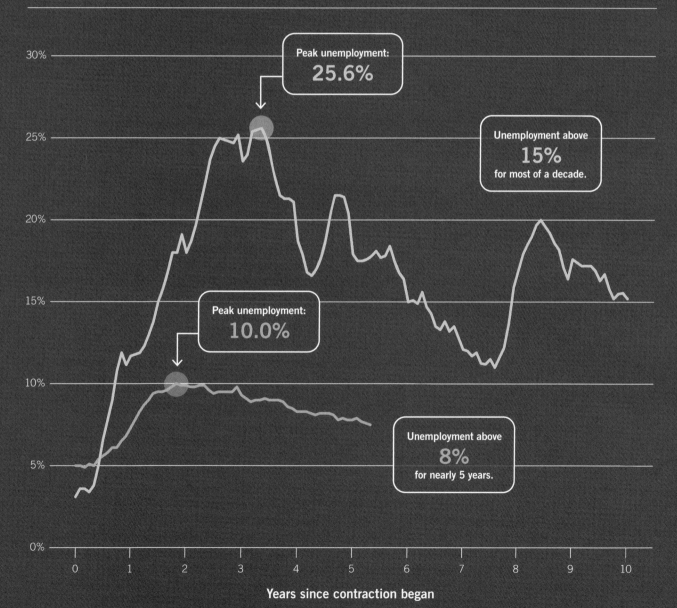

Peak unemployment:
**25.6%**

Unemployment above
**15%**
for most of a decade.

Peak unemployment:
**10.0%**

Unemployment above
**8%**
for nearly 5 years.

Years since contraction began

market toward equilibrium. To the extent that these economists considered macroeconomic issues, they extended their ideas from microeconomic analysis. In particular, they believed that since prices for individual goods are flexible, then prices across the economy are also flexible.

The classical economists dominated this era. One tenet of classical economics is the assumption that prices are flexible throughout the economy. Now if prices are completely flexible, then the economy is essentially self-correcting: no matter what factors change in the economy, no matter what curves shift, the economy automatically comes back to full employment. Figure 14.9 illustrates the classical view. Initially, the economy is in long-run equilibrium at point A. If aggregate demand increases from AD$_1$ to AD$_2$, price flexibility means that the economy moves to a new equilibrium at point B. At point B, real GDP is at full employment output (Y*) and the unemployment rate is at the natural rate (u = u*). In short, the shift in aggregate demand is barely noticeable in the economy because prices adjust.

The results are not much different when aggregate demand declines. If aggregate demand falls from AD$_1$ to AD$_3$, price flexibility implies that the economy moves to long-run equilibrium at point C. (This is very different from the actual experience we showed in Figure 14.7.) When prices are completely flexible, the economy comes back to full employment output and the natural rate of unemployment relatively quickly. Classical economists probably slept well at night, without worries about long-term economic contractions.

Because they believed the economy is self-correcting, classical economists were essentially pro-market, or laissez-faire, in their policy recommendations. Because they had faith that market adjustments would take place quickly, they saw no significant role for a government macroeconomic policy focusing on short-run fixes when the economy is under- or over-performing.

## FIGURE 14.9

**The Classical View of the Macroeconomy**

In the classical view, prices adjust quickly in both directions. Therefore, shifts in aggregate demand do not lead to changes in output or employment because the output level stays at full employment. When prices are completely flexible, aggregate demand becomes less relevant and changes in long-run aggregate supply are primarily considered the source of economic prosperity.

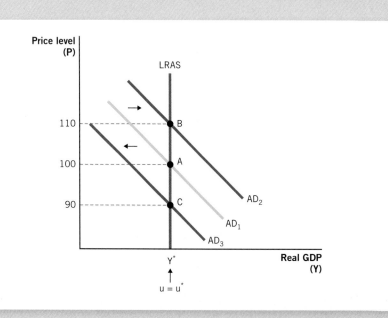

Today, some economists are still in the classical camp. They don't worry much about aggregate demand shifts. These economists focus on economic policies designed to promote long-run growth; their main focus is on shifting long-run aggregate supply. Given this perspective, they see savings as a crucial positive factor in the economy: savings is translated into investment, which increases capital and causes long-run aggregate supply to shift to the right.

# Keynesian Economics

While the classical economists dominated economics during the first part of the twentieth century, the Great Depression challenged the predominant view. It fact, the Great Depression set the stage for a new approach to macroeconomics. John Maynard Keynes, a British economist, formulated this new approach. In 1936, Keynes published *The General Theory of Employment, Interest, and Money*. This book vaulted him into the forefront of macroeconomic debates because it offered a theory about why cyclical unemployment might persist. Indeed, the title of the book—*The General Theory*—implies that Keynes believed that an economy out of long-run equilibrium is not unusual.

*Keynesian economists* emphasize that wages do not adjust downward quickly enough during recessions—in other words, are "sticky downward"—perhaps because of the presence of long-term contracts and money illusion (see Chapter 8). As a result, high real wages prevent the labor market from reaching equilibrium and restoring full employment. This outcome leads to prolonged recessions. Keynes believed that short-run economic circumstances could be improved through government intervention. He argued that the government should try to shift the aggregate demand curve back to its initial level. According to Keynes, it is foolish to wait for long-run adjustments—as he famously put it, "In the long run we are all dead."

Keynesian economists assume that prices are sticky downward, so they focus on the demand side of the economy as the source of instability. Look back at Figure 14.8, showing the decline in aggregate demand between 1929 and 1930. This large decline was due to a fall in consumer confidence and also the policy blunders of the 1930s. Notice that aggregate demand shifts from $AD_{1929}$ to $AD_{1930+}$. According to Keynesian theory, individuals and firms both stopped spending as the stock market dropped in 1929, and firms became wary of future returns from capital—with the result that consumption and investment both fell significantly.

But if wages are sticky, there is no underlying tendency for the economy to return to full employment equilibrium. In essence, the equilibrium at B is a long-run equilibrium in the Keynesian model. What is the source of the extreme price stickiness? Keynesian economists have posited that resource prices such as wages are very sticky downward, especially when negotiated through collective bargaining agreements by unions. Certainly, unions were very strong in the 1930s, and this fact could have added to the wage rigidity. But money illusion may also have played a role. Consider yourself an employee in the midst of the Great Depression: times are tough, and now your employer is asking you to take a wage decrease. This would be a tough pill to swallow even if it were not a *real* wage decrease, so some might refuse a wage decrease.

Keynes recommended that the British and U.S. governments take action to increase aggregate demand. If aggregate demand is too low because individuals and firms are reluctant to spend, Keynes argued, the government might fill the void by increasing the government-spending piece of aggregate demand. We will cover this topic in more detail in Chapter 16.

The Keynesian view of the economy offered an explanation for the Great Depression. In fact, after the nation emerged from the Great Depression, Keynesian theory became entrenched in the field of economics.

Table 14.1 summarizes the major differences between classical and Keynesian economists. Today, the profession is mixed on whether this is the correct approach; economists debate the importance of sticky prices and the merits of government policy based on the Keynesian model.

## PRACTICE WHAT YOU KNOW

### The Big Debates: Guess Which View

Question: Below, we give four statements. Which type of economist, Keynesian or classical, would likely support each statement? Explain your choice each time.

**a.** "If you want to help the economy, you should increase your spending."

**b.** "If you want to help the economy, you should increase your savings."

Which type of economist would recommend this shopping trip?

**c.** "Government policy should focus on counteracting short-run fluctuations in the economy."

**d.** "Government policy should not intervene in the business cycle since the economy can correct itself."

Answer:

**a.** *Keynesian.* The Keynesian approach focuses on spending, or aggregate demand, as the fundamental factor in the economy.

**b.** *Classical.* The classical approach focuses on long-run aggregate supply as the primary source of economic prosperity. In this view, increases in savings are necessary for investment, and this shifts out long-run aggregate supply.

**c.** *Keynesian.* The Keynesian approach emphasizes inherent instability in the macroeconomy and the resulting need for government action to counteract the business cycle.

**d.** *Classical.* The classical approach emphasizes price flexibility, which means that the economy can correct itself and naturally move back to full employment output levels.

## TABLE 14.1

### Classical versus Keynesian Economics

| | Classical economics | Keynesian economics |
|---|---|---|
| **Key time period** | Long run | Short run |
| **Price flexibility** | Prices are flexible | Prices are sticky |
| **Savings** | Crucial to growth | A drain on demand |
| **Key side of market** | Supply | Demand |
| **Market tendency** | Stability, full employment | Instability, cyclical unemployment |
| **Government intervention** | Not necessary | Essential |

# Conclusion

We began this chapter with the misconception that the Great Recession is comparable to the Great Depression. But we have seen that other than having similar names, the two economic contractions were not much alike. The Great Depression lasted much longer and had a much greater impact on unemployment and real GDP. The two contractions are the two largest in the U.S. economy over the past 100 years, but the Great Depression was significantly more severe.

Going forward, we can use the aggregate demand–aggregate supply model as a tool for analyzing government policy. Most economists believe that the macroeconomy needs at least a little help from government. This help comes in the form of monetary policy, which adjusts the money supply, and fiscal policy, which adjusts government taxes and spending. Over the next four chapters, we will evaluate these policy alternatives and use the aggregate demand–aggregate supply model to understand how government policy affects the economy.

## ANSWERING THE BIG QUESTIONS

### Exactly what happened during the Great Recession and the Great Depression?

 * The Great Recession was characterized by shifts in both long-run aggregate supply and aggregate demand.
 * The Great Recession was deeper and longer than typical U.S. recessions.
 * The Great Depression was significantly worse than the Great Recession.
 * Many factors contributed to the Great Depression, but most significant was a large and persistent decline in aggregate demand.

### What are the big disagreements in macroeconomics?

 * The big debates in macroeconomics focus on the flexibility of prices.
 * If prices are assumed to be flexible, the implication is a generally stable macroeconomy without significant need for government help.
 * If prices are assumed to be sticky, the implication is an inherently unstable economy in need of government assistance.

# The Big Disagreements in Macroeconomics

## "Fear the Boom and the Bust"

This highly original rap video imagines what two giants of economics, F. A. Hayek and John Maynard Keynes, would have to say to defend their ideas. F. A. Hayek represents the classical economists. Here is one of the best lines:

> We've been going back and forth for a century
> **[KEYNES]** I want to steer markets,
> **[HAYEK]** I want them set free
> There's a boom and bust cycle and good reason to fear it

F. A. Hayek was the twentieth century's most significant defender of free markets. In 1943 he wrote *The Road to Serfdom*, a book that cautions against central planning. Hayek characterizes markets as having the ability to organize spontaneously, to the benefit of an economy. *The Road to Serfdom* appeared in print just a few years after John Maynard Keynes published his *General Theory* in 1936. How could these two giants of economics see the world so differently?

Hayek, who received the 1974 Nobel Prize in Economics, lived long enough to observe that economics had come full circle. His Nobel acceptance speech was titled "The Pretense of Knowledge." In the talk, he criticized the economics profession for being too quick to adopt Keynesian ideas. Keynes had argued that the economy moves slowly to long-run equilibrium. Hayek countered that efforts to stimulate demand presume that economists know what they are doing; he argued that just because

It's Keynes versus Hayek!

we can build elaborate macroeconomic models does not mean that the models can anticipate every change in the economy. Hayek pointed to the high inflation rates and high unemployment rates of the 1970s as evidence that the Keynesian model was incomplete. Accordingly, he concluded, it would be best to put our faith in the one thing all economists generally agree on: that eventually the economy will naturally return to full employment output levels.

"Fear the Boom and the Bust" presents the views of Hayek and Keynes to make you think. While there are many references in the rap that you might not "get" just yet, watch it anyway (and tell your friends to watch it). The subject it treats is an important, ongoing debate, and one of the goals of your study of economics is to acquire the information you need to decide for yourself what approach is best for the economy.

# Understanding the Great Depression in Today's Context

You lived through the Great Recession. Perhaps it affected you personally. Certainly, many people experienced hardships as a result of the economic downturn. However, very few of us were forced to move into shanties on the street as a result of the downturn.

But the Great Depression was different. Living through it literally scarred an entire generation of Americans. Perhaps your great-grandparents were part of this generation. Now might be a good time to talk to them and ask how their life changed during the 1930s.

Many American families lost their homes and jobs during the Depression. The best remaining alternative for many in some parts of the country was sharecropping, or living on a farm and harvesting the crops on behalf of the owners. For some other families, the best available living arrangement was in shantytowns outside of major cities. These shantytowns became known as Hoovervilles, named after President Hoover. Although homelessness and unemployment are still issues for some people in the United States, the extent of the problems is far smaller today—and was far smaller during the Great Recession—than it was during the Great Depression.

We can use a familiar consumer item to illustrate the difference between the two contractions. During the Great Recession years of 2007–2009, the number of Starbucks locations in the United States grew from 10,684 to 11,128.[*] Thus, a chain of coffee shops that sell basic drinks for about $4 each actually expanded during the Great Recession. Yes, the coffee is very good, but that could never have happened during the Great Depression.

Now think again about how the Great Recession affected you or someone you know. How much more extreme might those effects have been during the Great Depression?

---

[*] "Starbucks Company Statistics," Statistic Brain, published September 2012. statisticbrain.com

ECONOMICS FOR LIFE

Unemployed workers gather together in New York City, December 1937. They have a Christmas tree near their shanty.

Stores like this one would not have survived the Great Depression.

## CONCEPTS YOU SHOULD KNOW

classical economists (p. 437)          fiscal policy (p. 436)                    macroeconomic policy (p. 436)
Dodd-Frank Act (p. 431)               Keynesian economists (p. 437)            monetary policy (p. 436)

## QUESTIONS FOR REVIEW

1.  What were the cause(s) of the long-run aggregate supply shift during the Great Recession? What were the cause(s) of the aggregate demand shift during the Great Recession?

2.  What specific numerical evidence would you give to explain why the Great Depression was so much worse than the Great Recession?

3.  What is the key side (supply or demand) of the economy for Keynesian economists? What assumption about prices leads them to this emphasis? What is the key side (supply or demand) of the economy for classical economists? What assumption about prices leads them to this emphasis?

## STUDY PROBLEMS (∗ solved at the end of the section)

∗ 1.  Explain whether each of the following statements is more likely to come from a classical economist or a Keynesian economist:
    a. "The recent decline in consumer confidence will likely spell disaster for the economy."
    b. "Business managers making investment decisions play a crucial role in the short-run economy."
    c. "Consumer spending is down, but that is good news because it means that savings is up."
    d. "In the long run we are all dead."
    e. "There is no reason to believe that most prices will take more than several months to adjust in either direction."

2.  For this problem, we want to practice working with the aggregate demand–aggregate supply model.
    a. Set up two separate aggregate demand–aggregate supply models in long-run equilibrium, with both short-run and long-run aggregate supply curves and an aggregate demand curve. Label the equilibrium price level as P* and the equilibrium level of real GDP as Y*.

    b. Using the first set of curves you drew in part (a), now assume that aggregate demand and aggregate supply (both short-run and long-run) decline. If all curves shift by the same amount, what is the resulting change in real GDP and the price level? What is the implied change in the unemployment rate?
    c. Now, using the second set of curves from part (a), let aggregate demand decline by a large amount while the aggregate supply curves decline by a relatively small amount. What are the resulting short-run changes in real GDP and the price level? What is the implied short-run change in the unemployment rate?
    d. Parts (b) and (c) describe the two different conditions of the Great Recession and the Great Depression. Which part refers to the Great Recession? Which part refers to the Great Depression?

# SOLVED PROBLEM

1. a. *Keynesian.* The key here is that Keynesian economists emphasize the role of aggregate demand, which depends on consumer confidence.

   b. *Keynesian.* The key here is the emphasis on the short run. Investment is a component of aggregate demand and can have an impact on spending in the short run.

   c. *Classical.* The key here is the classical emphasis on savings, which can lead to greater levels of lending in the loanable funds market—an outcome that increases capital in the long run.

   d. *Keynesian.* In fact, this is a direct quote from John Maynard Keynes himself. The key here is that the quote de-emphasizes the long run in favor of the short run.

   e. *Classical.* The key here is the emphasis on price flexibility.

# Fiscal
# POLICY

**Governments never balance their budgets.**

You don't have to look far to read about government budget problems. Does *any* government have enough money to pay its bills? Debt

problems seem to be mounting all over the globe, including in various U.S. states and localities. Nationally, the U.S. budget has seen record deficits in recent years, with spending vastly surpassing revenue. Given the current budget environment, one might assume that governments never balance their budgets. But, in fact, the United States had a balanced budget as recently as 2001.

So deficits are not inevitable. But then why are they so rampant? In this chapter, we examine the causes of budget problems and consider whether they can be avoided in the future. The primary goal of the chapter is to equip you with the knowledge you need to critically examine fiscal policy options. We will frame the recent government budget struggles in their proper context, so you have a better sense of the magnitude of these problems both historically and globally.

Of all the chapters in this text, this and the following chapter on government policy responses to the business cycle are among the most important for your post-college life. Though most people do not actually work on government budgets, if you vote or otherwise participate in the political process, you'll need to decide what tax and spending plans endorsed by the various candidates make the most sense to you.

In this chapter, we first consider the spending side of the government budget. We then move to the revenue side, where we look closely at taxes. Finally, we bring these together to examine budget deficits and government debt.

Budgets for the U.S. government are the result of negotiations between Congress and the president.

# BIG QUESTIONS

* How does the government spend?
* How does the government tax?
* What are budget deficits, and how bad are they?

# How Does the Government Spend?

We live in interesting and historic macroeconomic times. Since the onset of the global financial crisis in 2007, federal budget crises have arisen in nations around the globe, including the United States, Japan, Greece, Italy, Peru, and Argentina. Government budgets have moved into the spotlight mainly because so many governments are deeply in debt. Here in the United States, the federal government budget deficits are a constant topic of political and economic debate.

A government budget is a *plan* for both spending and raising funds for the government. In this way, it is similar to a budget plan you may create for your own personal finances. There are two sides to a budget: the sources of funds (income or revenue) and the uses of funds (spending or outlays). We start with the spending side. If we were looking at your personal budget, these categories might be items such as tuition, books, food, and housing.

## Government Outlays

The U.S. government now spends over $3.5 trillion each year—more than $10,000 for every citizen. Figure 15.1 shows real U.S. government outlays from 1960 to 2012. Notice how steep the line gets around the year 2000. Between 2000 and 2010, real outlays grew by more than 50%. There are many reasons for this rapid growth in government spending. Much of the increase was due to spending during and after the Great Recession of 2007–2009, in an effort to keep the economy from sinking further. But, there have also been significant spending increases in government programs such as Social Security and Medicare.

**Transfer payments** are payments made to groups or individuals when no good or service is received in return.

**Government outlays** are the part of the government budget that includes both spending and transfer payments.

When you think of U.S. government spending, your mind probably jumps to goods and services like roads, bridges, military equipment, and government employees. These are the government spending component (G) in gross domestic product. But as we examine the total government budget, we must also include *transfer payments*. **Transfer payments** are payments made to groups or individuals when no good or service is received in return. With a transfer payment, the government transfers funds from one group in society to another. These include income assistance (welfare) and Social Security payments to retired or disabled persons. As we'll see later in this chapter, transfer payments constitute a large and growing share of

U.S. federal outlays. When looking at government budgets, we include both spending and transfer payments in the broader category called *government outlays*. **Government outlays** are the part of the government budget that includes both spending and transfer payments.

Table 15.1 shows the major divisions in U.S. government outlays in 2012. We divide the outlays into three groups: *mandatory outlays*, *discretionary spending*, and interest payments. By far the largest portion of the federal budget is dedicated to **mandatory outlays**, which constitute government spending that is determined by ongoing programs like Social Security and Medicare. These programs are mandatory because existing laws mandate government funding for them. Mandatory outlays are not generally altered during the budget process; they require changes to existing laws, which take a long time to accomplish. Sometimes, these programs are known as *entitlement* programs, since citizens who meet certain requirements are then entitled to benefits under current laws. We talk more about these mandatory programs in the next section.

**Mandatory outlays** comprise government spending that is determined by ongoing long-term obligations.

Government spending includes purchases of military equipment.

## FIGURE 15.1

**U.S. Government Outlays, 1960–2012 (in millions of 2012 dollars)**

Total outlays represent the spending side of the government budget. This graph shows real outlays (in millions of 2012 dollars) since 1960. In the decade between 2000 and 2010, real outlays grew by more than 50%. Total outlays are now over $3.5 trillion per year, or $10,000 per U.S. citizen.

*Source*: U.S. Office of Management and Budget. Figures are converted to 2012 dollars using GDP deflator for government expenditures from the Bureau of Economic Analysis.

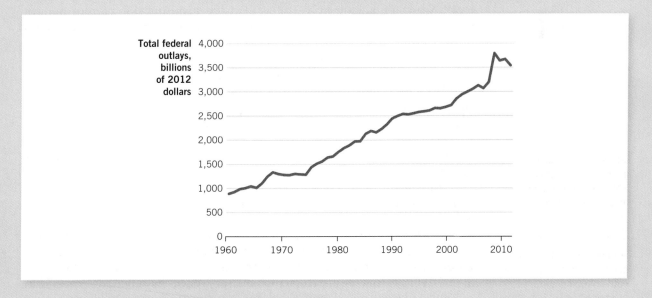

| TABLE 15.1 | | | |
|---|---|---|---|
| **2012 U.S. Government Outlays** | | | |
| Category | 2012 outlays (billions of dollars) | Percentage of total | |
| Social Security | $767.7 | 21.7% | |
| Medicare | 551.0 | 15.6% | **Mandatory** |
| Income assistance | 604.3 | 17.1% | |
| Other plus receipts | 107.6 | 3.0% | |
| Interest | 222.5 | 6.3% | **Interest** |
| Defense | 670.3 | 18.9% | **Discretionary** |
| Non-defense discretionary | 615.0 | 17.4% | |
| **Total** | **$3,538.5** | | |

*Source*: Congressional Budget Office.

**Discretionary outlays** comprise spending that can be altered when the government is setting its annual budget.

**Discretionary outlays** comprise government spending that can be altered when the government is setting its annual budget. Examples of discretionary spending include monies for bridges and roads, payments to government workers, and defense spending. When you think of examples of government spending, you may think of these discretionary items. But total discretionary spending accounts for less than 40% of the U.S. government budget.

The final category singled out in Table 15.1 is interest payments. These are payments made to current owners of U.S. Treasury bonds. Such payments are not easy to alter, given a certain level of debt, so they are also essentially mandatory payments.

To clarify these three categories, consider how your monthly budget might look after you graduate from college. On the spending side of your budget, you'll need to plan for groceries, gasoline, car payments, housing payments, utility bills, and perhaps some college debt payments. Some of these categories will be discretionary—that is, you'll be able to alter them from month to month. These include groceries, gas, and utilities. Some categories will be mandatory, with a level that is pre-determined each month. Mandatory categories include your monthly housing and car payments. Finally, payments on your college debt will be much like mandatory interest payments, because your student loan has a specific interest rate that does not change.

We clarify the distinction between mandatory and discretionary spending because it's important to note that certain categories are pre-determined and not negotiable from year to year. The distinctions also help us understand the recent growth of government spending in many nations. It turns out that much of the growth has been in mandatory spending. Returning to Table 15.1, we see that mandatory spending

Dining out on steak might be important to you, but it is not actually a mandatory category in your budget.

constituted 57.4% of the U.S. budget in 2012. In fact, if we include interest payments as obligatory, that leaves just 36.3% of the U.S. budget as discretionary. You might remember this the next time you read or hear about budgetary negotiations. While much of the debate focuses on discretionary spending items, like bridges or environmental subsidies or defense items, the majority of the budget goes to mandatory spending categories.

It wasn't always this way. Figure 15.2 plots U.S. federal budget categories as portions of total outlays for the years 1962–2012. The yellow-shaded categories represent mandatory spending. Fifty years ago, mandatory spending was less than one-third of the U.S. federal budget. The cause of this growth is largely political: more programs have been added to the government outlay budget. Miscellaneous mandatory spending programs include unemployment compensation, income assistance (welfare), and food stamps. Medicare was added in 1966 and then expanded in 2006. In 2012, Social Security and Medicare together accounted for more than one-third of the U.S. federal budget, up from only 13% in 1962. Part of this increase was due to expanded benefits, such as Medicare coverage of prescription drug costs and increasing Social Security payments to retirees. In addition, as we shall see, the changing demographics of the U.S. population have contributed to the growth in mandatory spending.

## Social Security and Medicare

Because of the growing size of the Social Security and Medicare programs, it is important to understand what they are and why so many resources are devoted to these programs in the United States.

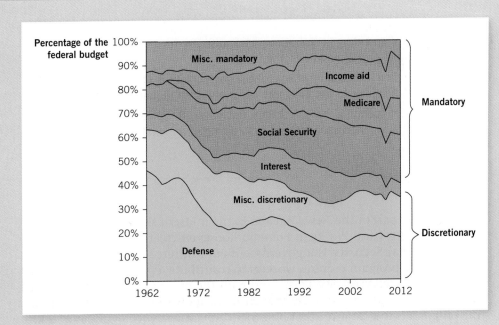

**FIGURE 15.2**

**Historical Federal Outlay Shares, 1962–2012**

The percentage of the budget allocated to mandatory spending programs has almost doubled since 1962. In contrast, discretionary spending is a shrinking part of the federal budget.

*Source*: Congressional Budget Office.

# PRACTICE WHAT YOU KNOW

Is your mobile phone bill mandatory or discretionary?

## Mandatory versus Discretionary Spending

Question: Of the following types of private spending, which ones are discretionary and which ones are mandatory components of a consumer's budget? Explain your response for each.

**a.** groceries

**b.** car payment

**c.** cell phone monthly fee

Answer:

**a.** This type of spending is discretionary. Even though groceries are a necessity, consumers can increase or decrease their spending on this budget component.

**b.** This is typically mandatory, as the consumer has signed a long-term agreement that entails monthly payments.

**c.** This type of payment is mandatory if the consumer has a long-term contract but discretionary if the phone plan is pay-as-you-go.

Question: Of the following types of spending, which ones are discretionary and which ones are mandatory components of a government budget? Explain your response for each.

**a.** a new interstate highway

**b.** Medicare

**c.** international aid

Answer:

**a.** This type of spending is discretionary because the government can choose not to fund a new interstate highway.

**b.** This spending is mandatory because the government is obligated via previously enacted laws to pay Medicare expenses when recipients qualify.

**c.** This type of spending is discretionary. Each year, the government can choose how much to spend on aid to foreign governments.

---

**Social Security** is a government-administered retirement funding program.

In 1935, as part of the New Deal and in the midst of the Great Depression, the U.S. Congress and President Franklin Roosevelt created the *Social Security* program. **Social Security** is a government-administered retirement funding program. The program requires workers to contribute a portion of their earnings into the Social Security Trust Fund with the promise that they'll receive these back (including a modest growth rate) upon retirement. The goal of the program is to guarantee that no American worker retires without at least some retirement income.

To understand our nation's current budget situation, it helps to consider the Social Security program over time. In the beginning, there were no retirees receiving Social Security and many workers contributing to Social Security. This meant that payments into the Trust Fund began to pile up, even though at that time Social Security taxes were only 2% of wages. However, as time went on, more and more workers retired and became eligible for benefits. Thus, as workers retire and draw benefits from the program, the balance of the Trust Fund declines. In order to keep the Trust Fund from running out of funds, Social Security tax rates have increased. The tax rate is now up to 12.4%.

**Medicare** is a mandated federal program that funds health care for retired persons. This program

FDR signed the Social Security Act in 1935.

was established in 1965 with the goal of providing medical insurance for all retired workers. Like Social Security, the law requires current workers to pay Medicare taxes with the promise of receiving insurance upon retirement. In 2003, Medicare was extended into reimbursements for prescription drugs for retirees as well.

**Medicare**
is a mandated federal program that funds health care for retired people.

Both Medicare and Social Security are concentrated on the elderly population and so are impacted greatly as population demographics shift. Given that these programs now account for nearly 40% of all federal outlays, we need to consider the demographic changes before we can completely understand the ongoing dynamics of the federal budget.

## Demographics

Entitlement programs have come to dominate the federal budget, with Social Security and Medicare taking up ever-expanding shares. There are three natural demographic reasons for this. First, people are living longer today than ever before, which means that they draw post-retirement benefits for longer periods. In 1930, life expectancy after age 60 was less than 13.7 years. The amount of time that retirees would collect Social Security benefits was therefore limited. Today, Americans live an average of 22.6 years after age 60. This is a big change from the assumptions on which the system was founded.

Second, those who paid into the programs for many years are now retired and drawing benefits. To be eligible for Social Security and Medicare payments, workers have to pay taxes out of their earnings while they work. Thus, when Social Security and Medicare were first established, no workers were eligible for payouts, but millions of workers were paying in. So both programs naturally generated substantial tax revenue with very few outlays for many years. But the honeymoon is over.

Third, in addition to a normal flow of retirees, the baby boomers (people born between 1946 and 1964) are now retiring. Thus, over the next 15 to 20 years, workers will retire in record numbers. This demographic shift will require record spending on the mandatory programs.

Panel (a) of Figure 15.3 shows the U.S. population age 65 and over by decade since 1900. Notice how in each decade a larger portion of the population is older than 65—and eligible for mandatory benefits from Social Security and Medicare. This portion will grow even larger over the next two decades as the baby boomers retire. Going forward, the United States will have fewer and fewer workers paying into system, and more and more retirees drawing out. Panel (b) of Figure 15.3 shows the change in the number of U.S. workers per Social Security beneficiary, beginning in 1960. As you can see, in 1960 there were more than five workers per beneficiary in the Social Security system. With that number, it wasn't very difficult to accumulate a large trust fund. But now there are fewer than three workers per beneficiary, and as the baby boomers retire this is set to fall to just above two, as indicated by the projections for the years 2030 and 2050.

Let's summarize the effects of these mandatory spending programs on the U.S. government budget. In 1962, mandatory spending made up less than one-third of the U.S. budget. By 2010, mandatory spending grew to more than half of the budget. As we shall see, any discussion about the national debt and deficits must necessarily focus on these programs. If we are serious about reducing the national debt, we cannot ignore them.

## FIGURE 15.3

**The Effects of an Aging Population on Social Security, 1900–2010**

Panel (a) shows how the U.S. population is aging, with an increasing percentage being age 65 and older. With the baby boomers now reaching this age, the percentage will increase even further in coming years. This also means that there will be fewer and fewer workers per Social Security beneficiary, as panel (b) illustrates.

*Sources*: U.S. Census Bureau and Social Security Administration.

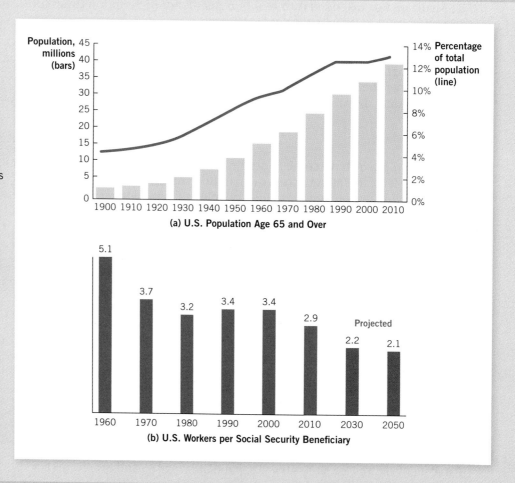

(a) U.S. Population Age 65 and Over

(b) U.S. Workers per Social Security Beneficiary

## ECONOMICS IN THE REAL WORLD

### Are There Simple Fixes to the Social Security and Medicare Funding Problems?

Either Social Security and Medicare programs must be revamped, or the U.S. government budget will be swamped by obligations to these programs in the future. But some people feel that a few relatively minor tweaks can solve the problems. Robert Powell, writing for *MarketWatch* in July 2010, explored potential solutions to the Social Security and Medicare funding problems. According to Powell, the budget problems can be largely alleviated with a few creative solutions. These solutions include the following:

1. *Increasing the retirement age from 67 to 70.* In general, people are living longer and healthier lives than when these retirement programs were implemented. If people were to work three years longer, this would mean three more years of saving for retirement and three fewer years of drawing benefits.
2. *Adjusting the benefits computation to the consumer price index.* Benefit payments to retirees are adjusted for inflation on the basis of average wage levels when they retire. This policy is in place to ensure that workers' benefits keep up with standard-of-living changes during their working years. Currently, these benefit payments are adjusted on the basis of an average wage index, which has historically increased faster than the CPI. If, instead, the CPI were used to adjust benefits payments, the payments would not grow as fast and would still account for inflation.
3. *Means-testing for Medicare and Social Security benefits.* As it stands now, retirees receive benefits from Medicare and Social Security regardless of whether they are able to pay on their own. Thus, one suggestion is to decrease the benefits paid to wealthier recipients who can afford to pay for their own retirement and medical care.

While these three proposed solutions may help to shore up the federal budget, each one would involve a change in existing law. Moving the retirement age to 70 years would alter the labor force going forward, but it would mean billions of dollars in savings for these federal programs. In contrast, changing the benefits indexation from the average wages to the CPI would yield mixed effects; the CPI has actually increased more rapidly than average wages in recent years. Finally, if means-testing were to be implemented, it would completely change incentives going forward. Means-testing would punish retirees who have saved on their own and can therefore afford more in retirement. In addition, Medicare and Social Security are mandatory programs that all workers must pay into during their time in the labor force. Means-testing implies that some workers wouldn't receive the benefits from a program they were required to pay into.

These three simple solutions might reduce the benefits paid out in the short run and, in so doing, reduce pressure on the federal budget. But means-testing would likely lead to greater problems in the long run because of the incentive problem. ✳

## Spending and Current Fiscal Issues

Before turning our attention to the revenue side of the budget, we should take a look at the recent history with regard to U.S government outlays. Figure 15.4 shows real federal government outlays from 1990 to 2012. In the figure, you can clearly see that federal government spending began growing quickly around 2001. And while there are many reasons for the increased spending, we can identify three major factors:

1. *Increased spending on Social Security and Medicare.* As we have seen, spending on these programs has grown significantly in recent years.
2. *Defense spending in the wake of the terrorist attacks of September 11, 2001.* Prior to 2001, defense spending had consistently declined as a portion of the federal budget since the fall of the Soviet Union in 1991, to just 16.5% by 2001. But by 2010, defense spending constituted 19.1% of the federal budget.
3. *Government responses to the Great Recession, beginning with fiscal policy in 2008.* We'll cover these policy responses (including their rationale) more fully in Chapter 16, but it's important to note that outlays increased from $2.87 trillion in 2007 to $3.58 trillion in 2009. That's a 25% increase in just two years.

# How Does the Government Tax?

Governments have several avenues to raise revenues. Fees assessed for government services—for example, admission fees to national parks—contribute small amounts of revenue. However, virtually all government revenue is raised through taxes.

## FIGURE 15.4

**U.S. Government Outlays, 1990–2012 (in millions of 2012 dollars)**

The rate of growth of U.S. government outlays has increased significantly in recent years. This graph shows a clear increase in spending after the terrorist attacks on September 11, 2001, as well as large spending increases during and after the Great Recession.

*Source*: U.S. Office of Management and Budget.

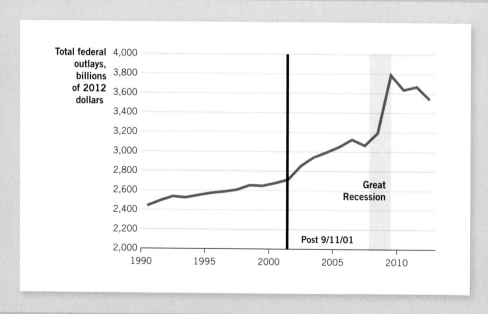

No one enjoys paying taxes, but government activity must be funded. If we want the government to provide Social Security, Medicare, national defense, highways, and public education, then we all have to pay taxes. In this section, we detail the principal means by which the federal government raises tax revenue.

## Sources of Tax Revenue

Figure 15.5 shows the sources of tax revenue for the U.S. government in 2012. The two largest sources are individual income taxes and social insurance (Social Security and Medicare) taxes. Together, these two categories accounted for 81% of all federal tax revenue in the United States in 2012. Both of these taxes are deducted from workers' paychecks, so they are referred to as *payroll taxes*.

The other major types of taxes together produced just 19% of the federal revenue. The largest of these is taxes on the income of corporations, which yielded $242.3 billion in 2012, or 10% of the total revenue. Estate and gift taxes are levied when property is gifted to others, particularly as an inheritance. Excise taxes are taxes on a particular good or commodity such as cigarettes or gasoline. The federal excise tax on cigarettes is $1.01 per pack, and the tax on gasoline is 18.4 cents per gallon. Altogether, excise taxes yielded

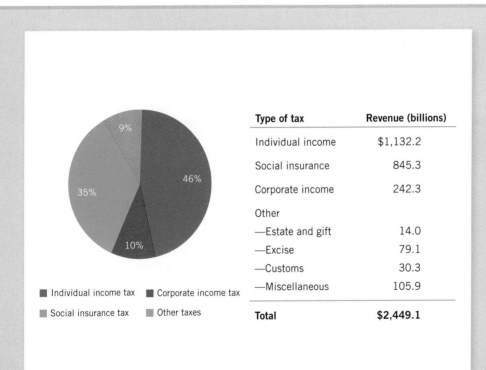

**FIGURE 15.5**

**U.S. Federal Tax Revenue Sources, 2012**

The major sources of tax revenue for the U.S. government begin with the two payroll taxes: individual income taxes and social insurance (Social Security and Medicare) taxes. Together, these two categories accounted for 81% of all tax revenue in 2012. Total tax revenue in 2012 was about $2.5 trillion.

*Source*: Congressional Budget Office, Historical Budget Data.

| Type of tax | Revenue (billions) |
| --- | --- |
| Individual income | $1,132.2 |
| Social insurance | 845.3 |
| Corporate income | 242.3 |
| Other | |
| —Estate and gift | 14.0 |
| —Excise | 79.1 |
| —Customs | 30.3 |
| —Miscellaneous | 105.9 |
| **Total** | **$2,449.1** |

- ■ Individual income tax
- ■ Social insurance tax
- ■ Corporate income tax
- ■ Other taxes

$79.1 billion in tax revenue in 2012. Customs taxes are taxes on imports, and these yielded just $30.3 billion in 2012. Because of the relative importance of payroll taxes to the financing of the U.S. government, we discuss them in greater detail in the next section.

# Payroll Taxes

When you graduate from college and get a full-time job, you'll probably receive bigger paychecks than any you have previously received. But those paychecks will probably be smaller than you expect. Remember, the government pays for activities with tax revenue predominantly raised from income. Payroll taxes include social insurance taxes and individual income taxes.

## Social Insurance Taxes

Earlier in this chapter, we discussed Social Security and Medicare. You will recall that over one-third of the U.S. federal government's outlays are for these two programs. And these programs are paid for with taxes on employees' pay; the benefits that a retiree receives depends on the taxes paid in during his or her time in the labor force. Currently, the tax for these two programs amounts to 15.3% of a worker's pay. This is typically split in half, with 7.65% paid by the employee and 7.65% paid by the employer. People who are self-employed pay the full amount. This tax is applicable to the first $110,100 an individual earns. These dollars go into the Social Security and Medicare trust funds that serve to provide income and health care assistance to retirees.

## Income Tax

A **progressive income tax system** is one in which people with higher incomes pay a larger portion of their income in taxes than people with lower incomes do.

The **marginal tax rate** is the tax rate paid on an individual's next dollar of income.

U.S. federal income taxes are set according to a scale that increases with income levels. This is known as a *progressive tax system*. In a **progressive income tax system**, people with higher incomes pay a larger percentage of their income in taxes than people with lower incomes do. Figure 15.6 shows 2012 U.S. federal tax rates for single individuals. Notice that the tax rate climbs with income level.

The tax rates specified in Figure 15.6 are *marginal tax rates*. A **marginal tax rate** is the tax rate paid on an individual's next dollar of income. Let's say your first full-time job after college offers you a salary of $60,000. For simplicity, we'll also assume you have no tax deductions, so your entire salary is taxable income. In terms of the tax rates presented in Figure 15.6, this income level puts you in the 25% tax bracket. This doesn't mean that you'll pay 25% of all your income in taxes; it only means that you'll pay 25% on every dollar of income *above $35,350*. You'll pay 10% on income up to $8,700 and 15% on the income between $8,700 and $35,350.

When we consider fiscal policy in Chapter 16, it will be critical to understand the way income tax rates affect an individual's total tax bill. For this reason, we will now go through a more extended example in which we compute a person's tax bill based on the marginal tax rates shown in Figure 15.6. Let's use these rates to compute your tax bill based on a taxable income of $60,000.

Before we go through the math, note that you'll pay three different tax rates: 10% on income up to $8,700; 15% on income between $8,700 and $35,350; and 25% on income above $35,650. Your total tax bill will be determined as:

$$
\begin{array}{rcl}
0.10 \times \$8,700 & = & \$870.00 \\
+\ 0.15 \times (\$35,350 - \$8,700) & = & \$3,997.50 \\
+\ 0.25 \times (60,000 - \$35,350) & = & \$6,162.50 \\
\hline
\text{Total} & = & \$11,030.00
\end{array}
$$

Therefore, your $60,000 income will accrue a federal income tax bill of $11,030, which will be about 18.4% of your income. This 18.4% will be your *average tax rate*. An **average tax rate** is the total tax paid divided by the amount of taxable income. Notice that the average tax rate is below the marginal tax rate. This is generally the case in a progressive tax system, and it is due to the fact that the marginal tax rate applies to the last few dollars taxed, but not to all income.

The **average tax rate** is the total tax paid divided by the amount of taxable income.

**2012 U.S. Federal Tax Rates**

These tax rates are marginal tax rates, which means that they apply only to dollars within the specified income ranges. For example, all income earned between $35,350 and $85,650 is taxed at 25%; but if someone earns $85,651, that last dollar is taxed at the 28% rate.

*Source*: Internal Revenue Service.

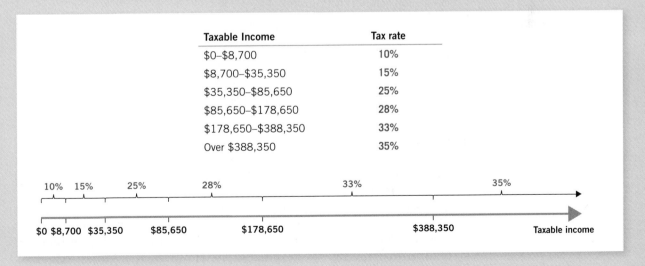

| Taxable Income | Tax rate |
| --- | --- |
| $0–$8,700 | 10% |
| $8,700–$35,350 | 15% |
| $35,350–$85,650 | 25% |
| $85,650–$178,650 | 28% |
| $178,650–$388,350 | 33% |
| Over $388,350 | 35% |

## PRACTICE WHAT YOU KNOW

### Government Revenue: Federal Taxes

Assume that your taxable income is $100,000. Use the 2012 marginal tax rates from Figure 15.6 to determine your taxes.

Figuring out your income tax bill involves some basic math.

**Question: How would you compute your federal income tax?**

**Answer:** Looking at Figure 15.6, keep in mind that the different rates apply only to the income in the specified bands. For example, the first tax rate of 10% applies only to income up to $8,700. Income between $8,700 and $35,350 is taxed at 15%. Use this pattern to determine the tax paid on all income up to $100,000. Multiply these rates by the income in the respective brackets, and sum these to get the total income tax:

|  |  |  |
|---|---|---|
| $0.10 \times \$8,700$ | = | $870.00 |
| $+\ 0.15 \times (\$35,350 - \$8,700)$ | = | $3,997.50 |
| $+\ 0.25 \times (\$85,650 - \$35,350)$ | = | $12,575.00 |
| $+\ 0.28 \times (\$100,000 - \$85,650)$ | = | $4,018.00 |
| **Total** | = | **$21,460.50** |

**Question: How would you compute your Social Security and Medicare tax? (The relevant tax rate is 7.65%.)**

**Answer:** You compute your tax as:

$$\$100,000 \times 0.0765 = \$7,650.00$$

## Historical Income Tax Rates

Though taxes may seem like a fact of life now, the income tax is only about 100 years old in the United States. Prior to 1913, there was no income tax in the United States; most tax revenues were generated by taxes on imports. But import taxes were set to decline, so the government looked to income taxes as another source of revenue. The following page shows the actual Form 1040 from 1913—the form individuals submit to the IRS when they file their tax returns. In 1913, this form was essentially one page for all income-earners. The original income tax in the United States was similar to the current tax system, in that the rates were progressive. However, the highest marginal tax rate in 1913 was just 6%, which only applied to income greater than $500,000—over $11 million in today's dollars. Very few people were making this kind of income in 1913.

TO BE FILLED IN BY COLLECTOR.

**Form 1040.**

TO BE FILLED IN BY INTERNAL REVENUE BUREAU.

List No. ..........................

.............. District of ..........................

Date received ..........................

## INCOME TAX.

**THE PENALTY**
FOR FAILURE TO HAVE THIS RETURN IN
THE HANDS OF THE COLLECTOR OF
INTERNAL REVENUE ON OR BEFORE
MARCH 1 IS $20 TO $1,000.
(SEE INSTRUCTIONS ON PAGE 4.)

File No. ..........................

Assessment List ..........................

Page ..................... Line ..............

**UNITED STATES INTERNAL REVENUE.**

## RETURN OF ANNUAL NET INCOME OF INDIVIDUALS.

(As provided by Act of Congress, approved October 3, 1913.)

**RETURN OF NET INCOME RECEIVED OR ACCRUED DURING THE YEAR ENDED DECEMBER 31, 191....**

(FOR THE YEAR 1913, FROM MARCH 1, TO DECEMBER 31.)

Filed by (or for) .................................................. of ..................................................

(Full name of individual.)      (Street and No.)

in the City, Town, or Post Office of .................................................. State of ..........................

(Fill in pages 2 and 3 before making entries below.)

1. GROSS INCOME (see page 2, line 12) .................................. $

2. GENERAL DEDUCTIONS (see page 3, line 7) .................................. $

3. NET INCOME .................................................. $

Deductions and exemptions allowed in computing income subject to the normal tax of 1 per cent.

4. Dividends and net earnings received or accrued, of corporations, etc., subject to like tax. (See page 2, line 11).......... $

5. Amount of income on which the normal tax has been deducted and withheld at the source. (See page 2, line 9, column A)...

6. Specific exemption of $3,000 or $4,000, as the case may be. (See Instructions 3 and 19) ..................................

Total deductions and exemptions. (Items 4, 5, and 6).......... $

7. TAXABLE INCOME on which the normal tax of 1 per cent is to be calculated. (See Instruction 3).. $

8. When the net income shown above on line 3 exceeds $20,000, the additional tax thereon must be calculated as per schedule below:

| | | | | INCOME. | TAX. |
|---|---|---|---|---|---|
| 1 per cent on amount over $20,000 and not exceeding $50,000.... | | | | $ | $ |
| 2 " " 50,000 " " 75,000.... | | | | | |
| 3 " " 75,000 " " 100,000.... | | | | | |
| 4 " " 100,000 " " 250,000.... | | | | | |
| 5 " " 250,000 " " 500,000.... | | | | | |
| 6 " " 500,000.... | | | | | |

Total additional or super tax ..................................... $

Total normal tax (1 per cent of amount entered on line 7).... $

Total tax liability.................................................. $

In 1913, Form 1040 was only a page long.

Once the income tax was instituted, marginal tax rates rose quickly. In fact, by 1918 the top marginal rate rose to 77%. This applied only to income over $2 million, but it meant that every dollar earned yielded only 23 cents to the income-earner. Figure 15.7 plots the top marginal income tax rates in the United States from 1913 to 2012. Note that while this figure shows only the top rate, it is a good indicator of the general level of rates over time.

There are several important dates in the evolution of income tax rates. During the 1930s, in the throes of the Great Depression, income tax revenues naturally fell. Presidents Hoover and Roosevelt, in attempts to balance the federal budget, pressed Congress to increase top marginal rates to 80%. Later, in 1963, with top marginal rates over 90%, President Kennedy pushed for rate reductions that led to the top rate falling to 70%. Then, in the 1980s, President Reagan led the push to lower marginal tax rates even further. By the end of that decade, the top marginal rate was just 28%. In 1993, President Clinton proposed higher rates, and the top rate rose to 39.6%. President George W. Bush pushed through a temporary decrease in this top rate in 2003, and the lower rate of 35% persisted for ten years, before the rate returned to 39.6% in 2013. Over the course of a century, there was a great deal of fluctuation in marginal tax rates. Going forward, it is not likely that rates will ever return to the levels witnessed prior to 1980.

## Who Pays for Government?

In a progressive tax system, wealthy citizens pay more than poor citizens for government services. Of course, the very wealthy pay most of all. In the United States, the wealthiest 20% of all households paid 94% of all income taxes in 2009; the poorest 40% actually "pay" negative taxes due to various tax credits and income assistance. Figure 15.8 plots the shares of income tax

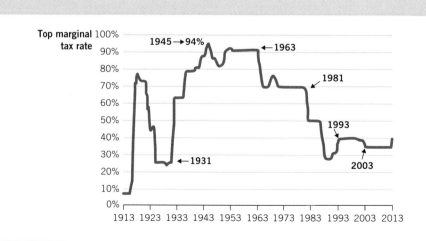

### FIGURE 15.7

**Historical Top U.S. Marginal Tax Rates, 1913–2012**

Marginal rates are a good indicator of overall tax rates since 1913. There are several key historical dates. For example, in 1931, marginal tax rates increased significantly. Major downward revisions occurred in 1963 and in the 1980s.

*Source*: Internal Revenue Service.

liability by U.S. household income levels from 1980 to 2009. Notice that the top 1% of all households alone paid about 40% of all income taxes in 2009.

# What Are Budget Deficits, and How Bad Are They?

We are now ready to bring both sides of the budget together. Doing this enables us to examine the differences between spending and revenue. In this section, we define budget deficits and debt and also consider these in a long-run historical context.

## FIGURE 15.8

**Percentage of Total Federal Taxes Paid by Various Income Groups, 1980–2009**

In 2009 the middle-income group in the United States (labeled as Middle 20%) paid less than 10% of all income taxes paid. The wealthiest 20% (the top line) of income-earners paid 94% of all income taxes in 2009. Digging deeper into this top 20%, we can see that the top 1% of all income-earners paid nearly 40% of all income taxes collected in 2009. The bottom 40% of income earners actually "pay" negative taxes due to various tax credits and income assistance.

*Source*: Tax Policy Center.

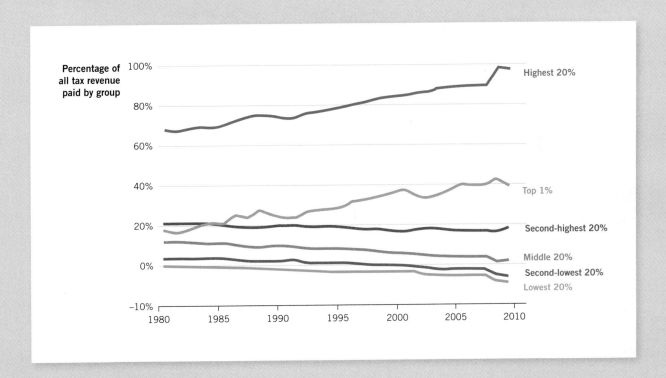

# Deficits

A **budget deficit** occurs when government outlays exceed revenue.

A **budget surplus** occurs when government revenue exceeds outlays.

A **budget deficit** occurs when government outlays exceed revenue. Panel (a) of Figure 15.9 plots U.S. budget outlays and revenues from 1960 to 2012, in millions of 2012 dollars. Outlays, displayed in orange, have grown rapidly, especially since 2001. Over the long run, revenue has grown, but it has declined since 2007. You can see that outlays have generally exceeded revenue for much of the recent past. For example, in 2010 total outlays were almost $3.5 trillion, while revenue was about $2.2 trillion. The difference, $1.3 trillion, is the budget deficit for that year.

It is also possible for the government to have a **budget surplus**, which occurs when revenue exceeds outlays. The most recent federal budget surpluses came

---

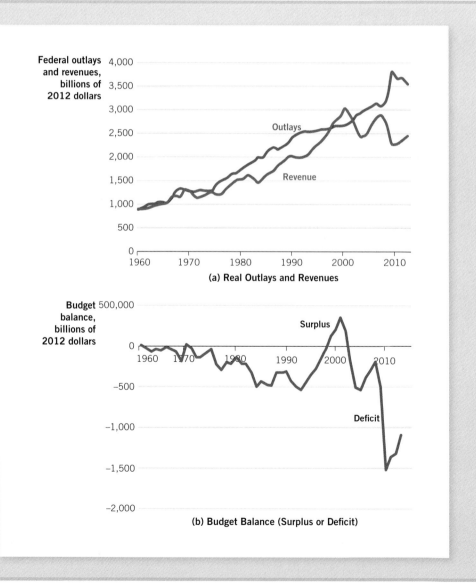

**FIGURE 15.9**

**U.S. Federal Budget Data, 1960–2012 (in millions of 2012 dollars)**

(a) Real outlays are shown in orange, and revenue in blue, for the U.S. federal government budget since 1960. When the outlays exceed revenue, the budget has a deficit for that year.

(b) In the plot of the real budget balance, negative values indicate a deficit. The Great Recession of 2007–2009 and the government's response to it helped to create the 2009 deficit of $1.5 trillion (in 2012 dollars), the largest in U.S. history.

*Source*: U.S. Office of Management and Budget.

**(a) Real Outlays and Revenues**

**(b) Budget Balance (Surplus or Deficit)**

in the four years from 1998 to 2001. Panel (b) of Figure 15.9 graphs the budget balance from 1960 to 2012. When the budget is in deficit, the balance is negative; when the budget is in surplus, the balance is positive.

The Great Recession and government responses during the recession helped to create the 2009 deficit of $1.4 trillion, the largest in U.S. history. This deficit is larger than the deficits generated during World War II in the 1940s. But dollar values for government budget figures are misleading over the long run, since the population and the size of the economy change. To control for both population and economic growth, economists look at the deficit as a portion of GDP. When we divide budget data by GDP, we essentially scale it to the size of the economy. Figure 15.10 shows the U.S. federal outlays and revenue, both as a fraction of GDP, from 1960 to 2012. Over the entire period, outlays averaged 20% of GDP and revenues averaged 17.5% of GDP. These averages are shown as dashed lines in the figure. The long-run averages can be viewed as a target benchmark for future budgets.

The blue-shaded vertical bars in Figure 15.10 indicate economic recessions. Since the onset of the Great Recession at the end of 2007, outlays, revenues, and deficits have all reached historic magnitudes. Both outlays and revenues currently lie well outside their long-run averages. When recessions hit, tax revenue, which is largely tied to income, declines. In addition, for reasons we cover in the next chapter, government outlays

## FIGURE 15.10

### U.S. Federal Outlays and Revenue as a Percentage of GDP, 1960–2012

The deficit-to-GDP ratio is a more informative gauge of the magnitude of deficits over time, because it accounts for changes in population and economic growth. Here we illustrate outlays (orange) and revenue (blue) as a percentage of GDP. The deficit is the vertical distance between the lines. Dashed lines indicate long-run averages. These show us that recent spending has been above the long-run average and recent revenue has been below the long-run average. The blue-shaded bars indicate recessionary periods. As you can see, deficits grow during recessions.

*Source*: U.S. Office of Management and Budget.

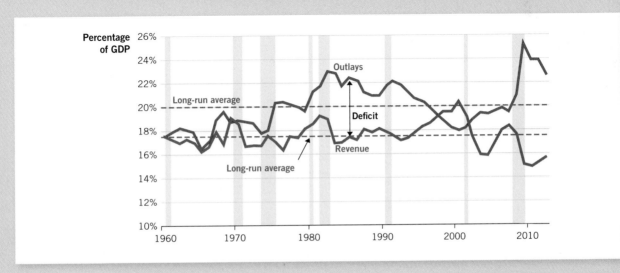

often increase during recessions. Together these two results cause deficits to increase during recessions.

When the budget is in deficit, the government must borrow funds to pay for the difference between outlays and revenue. In Chapter 10, we introduced U.S. Treasury bonds as important financial assets in the loanable funds market. Now we can understand how those bonds originate: when tax revenues fall short of outlays, the government sells Treasury bonds to cover the difference.

## Deficits versus Debt

In your personal budget, it might happen that your spending (outlays) in a given month exceeds your income. In other words, you find that you have a deficit. You might rely on funds from parents or grandparents to make up the difference, but this money counts either as income (if it's a gift) or as a loan (if you have to repay it). Often, you will have to borrow, perhaps using a credit card. A loan, whether it is from a friend, relative, or credit card company, is a debt that must be paid.

A **debt** is the sum total of accumulated budget deficits.

It's easy to confuse the terms "deficit" and "debt." A deficit is a shortfall in revenue for a particular year's budget. A **debt** is the total of all accumulated

### FIGURE 15.11

**U.S. National Debt, 1990–2010 (in billions of 2010 dollars)**

The total amount of U.S. federal government debt (shown in blue) has grown to over $14 trillion in recent years, even exceeding annual GDP in the United States. But much of this is owned by agencies of the government itself (the government owes money to itself), so many economists focus instead on the debt that is held publicly (by anyone besides the federal government). This amount (shown in orange) is still less than $10 trillion and constitutes about 60% of U.S. GDP. If you are curious about the current size of the U.S. national debt, you can visit the web site www.usdebtclock.org.

*Source*: U.S. Treasury, *Treasury Bulletin*.

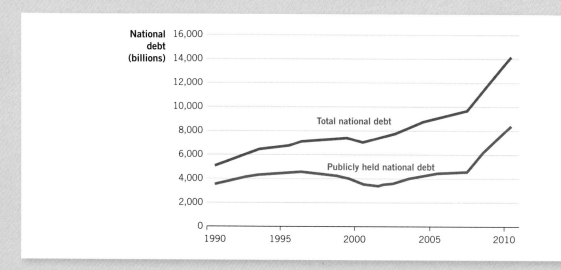

and unpaid deficits. Consider your tuition bill over the course of your time in college. If you borrow $5,000 to help pay for your first year of college, that is your first-year deficit. If you borrow another $5,000 for your second year, you have a $5,000 deficit for each year, and your debt grows to $10,000.

Figure 15.11 shows the U.S. national debt (in real terms) from 1990 to 2010. Notice that we distinguish between total debt and debt held by the public. The difference between these is debt owned internally by one of the many branches of the U.S. government. Sometimes, a given federal agency will purchase Treasury bonds. For example, as part of its mandate to control the money supply, the Federal Reserve typically holds billions of dollars' worth of Treasury securities. Thus, it can be helpful to distinguish total government debt that is not also owned by the government itself, and this is the portion that is publicly held. Figure 15.11 indicates that both measures have risen in recent years, caused by the large budget deficits.

Credit cards make it easy to let spending grow beyond income.

While the U.S. national debt is historically large, relative to the size of the economy, it is still smaller than that of many other nations, including many wealthy ones. Figure 15.12 shows publicly held debt-to-GDP ratios for several nations in 2010. The United States came in at about 61%, but Japan's ratio was over 180%.

## FIGURE 15.12

**International Debt-to-GDP Ratios, 2010 Publicly Held Debt**

While the U.S. debt-to-GDP ratio has grown to over 60% in recent years, this is still smaller than that of some other developed nations.

*Source*: Organisation for Economic Co-operation and Development.

Japan, Greece, Italy, Belgium, Portugal, United Kingdom, Israel, France, United States, Ireland, Netherlands, Spain, Poland, Germany, Turkey, Finland, Denmark, Canada, Sweden, Korea, Mexico, Norway, Switzerland, Australia, Chile

Debt-to-GDP ratio
0% 20% 40% 60% 80% 100% 120% 140% 160% 180% 200%

# The Federal Budget Deficit

The U.S. federal government has run a budget deficit for almost the entire past half-century. The graph below plots federal revenue against outlays as a percentage of GDP, a measurement that stays consistent as the size of the economy changes. The light green line underneath shows the deficit as a percentage of GDP. Note that the deficit is particularly likely to increase during recessions, as tax revenue declines and spending often jumps. The bottom of the page shows which political party controls the White House and each house of Congress. As you can see, budget deficits are very much a bipartisan affair.

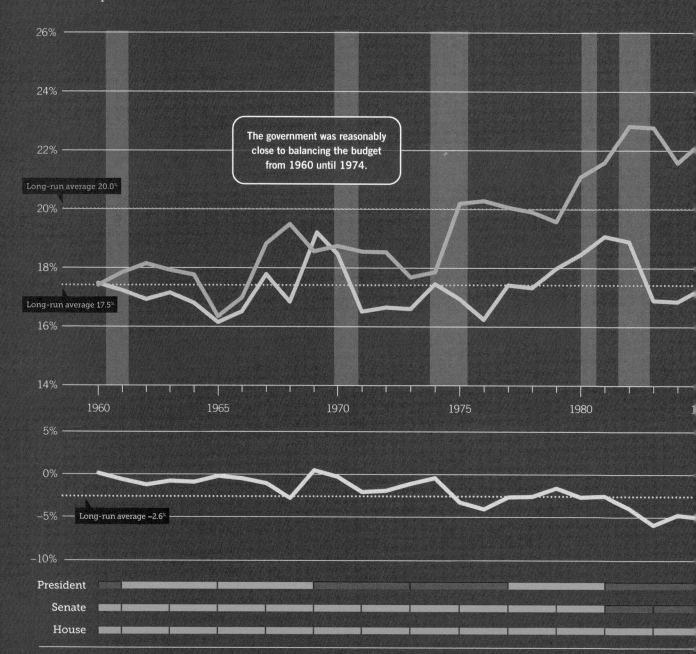

The government was reasonably close to balancing the budget from 1960 until 1974.

Long-run average 20.0%

Long-run average 17.5%

Long-run average −2.6%

President
Senate
House

## Key

— Outlays as % of GDP
— Tax revenue as % of GDP
— Deficit as % of GDP
◼ Democratic control
◼ Republican control
◼ Period of recession

## REVIEW QUESTIONS

- The single worst deficit since 1960 occurred in 2009. When was the worst deficit since 1960 and prior to 2009?

- Reference this graph as you describe how our different political parties would act to balance our current budget.

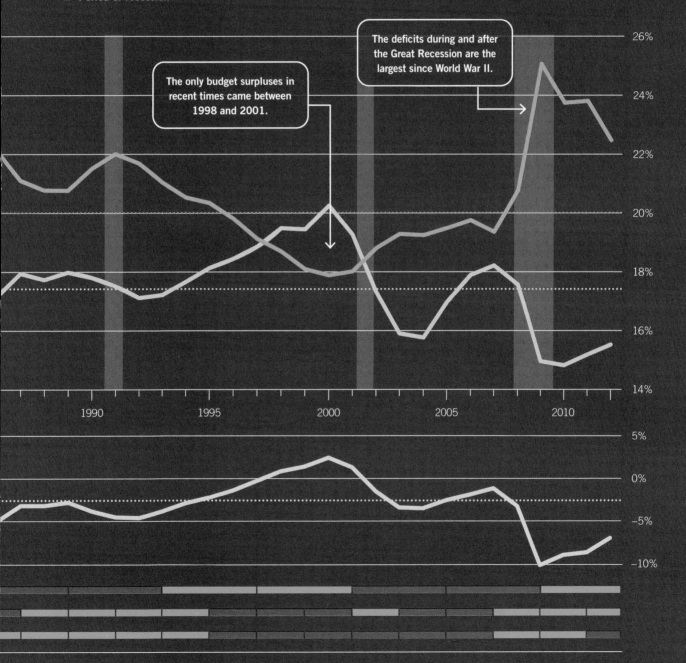

The only budget surpluses in recent times came between 1998 and 2001.

The deficits during and after the Great Recession are the largest since World War II.

## ECONOMICS IN THE REAL WORLD

### Several European Nations Are Grappling with Government Debt Problems

In the summer of 2011, Greece erupted in a series of demonstrations, some marked by violent encounters between citizens and their national police. The issue at the heart of these protests was the Greek national debt, which climbed to almost 150% of their GDP in 2010 (see Figure 15.13). In order to avert a Greek debt default, other members of the European Union and the International Monetary Fund forged together aid packages of $146 billion in 2010 and $165 billion in 2011.

But the aid from Europe was granted only with strict *austerity* requirements. In this context, **austerity** involves strict budget regulations aimed at debt reduction. These austerity measures are what drove the Greek citizens to protest, because the measures included wage cuts and pension freezes for public workers, as well as an increase in the sales tax to 23%. The Greek government had agreed to these requirements in order to secure international aid and avert a default, but the Greek citizens rose up against their government after the agreements were signed.

Greece is not the only European nation with very high sovereign (national) debt. As of 2012, Italy and Spain, the eighth and twelfth largest economies in the world, were both facing default and severe austerity measures. In September 2012, Spanish rioters hurled gasoline bombs at police to protest the austerity measures their government had adopted. The fear of the other European nations is that there will be a domino effect, because much of Greece's sovereign debt is owned by other European governments and private banks. Therefore, if Greece defaults on its sovereign debt, the outcome will be damaging to Spain. And if Spain then defaults, others might also—and so on. All this international worry and unrest derive from excessive government debt. ✳

**Austerity**
involves strict budget regulations aimed at debt reduction.

Spanish police attempt to control demonstrators who oppose austerity measures in 2012.

# Foreign Ownership of U.S. Federal Debt

As we saw in Chapter 10, many people are concerned about foreign owner-ship of U.S. debt. The concern stems from a fear that foreigners who own U.S. debt will control the country politically as well as economically. How-ever, according to the U.S. Treasury, as of November 2011 about 70% of U.S. national debt was held domestically, and just 30% internationally. China, Japan, and the United Kingdom are the major foreign holders of U.S. debt.

Figure 15.13 shows foreign and domestic ownership of total U.S. debt from 1990 to 2010. Total national debt grew from about $5 trillion to over $14 trillion. However, domestic investors and U.S. government agencies were the purchasers of most of the new debt. Still, the portion of U.S. government debt that is foreign owned doubled from about 15% to near 30% over that 20-year period.

While this foreign ownership of U.S. government debt is troubling for many Americans, it is important to realize the importance of the foreign funds to the U.S. loanable funds market. As we discussed in Chapter 10, foreign lending increases the supply of loanable funds in the United States, which helps keep interest rates low. Lower interest rates mean that firms and governments in the United States can borrow at lower cost. Furthermore, the increase in foreign ownership is a natural byproduct of emerging foreign economics—as they get wealthier, they buy more U.S. Treasury bonds.

## FIGURE 15.13

**Foreign and Domestic Ownership of U.S. Government Debt, 1990–2010 (in billions of 2010 dollars)**

Most U.S. government debt is owned by Americans or by the U.S. government itself. This graph shows total national debt and internationally owned debt. The percentage owned internationally has grown in recent years, but it is still less than one-third of the total.

*Source*: U.S. Treasury, *Treasury Bulletin*.

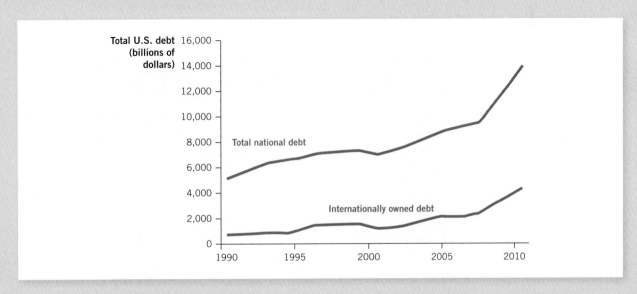

# PRACTICE WHAT YOU KNOW

## Federal Budgets: The U.S. Debt Crisis

The U.S. national debt grew substantially in the first decade of this century. The table below shows the data on the national debt from both 2001 and 2010.

| Year | Total U.S. debt (billions of $) | Nominal GDP (billions of $) |
|------|------|------|
| 2001 | $5,807 | $10,286 |
| 2010 | $13,561 | $14,499 |

**Question:** Using the data, how would you compute the U.S. debt-to-GDP ratio in both 2001 and 2010?

**Answer:** For the year 2001, you compute the debt-to-GDP ratio as:

$$\$5,807 \div \$10,286 = 0.56$$

For the year 2010, you compute the debt-to-GDP ratio as:

$$\$13,562 \div \$14,499 = 0.94$$

**Question:** What are the major reasons why the national debt increased so much between 2001 and 2010?

**Answer:** First, on the outlay side, U.S. government spending increased due to higher costs for Social Security and Medicare, additional defense spending in the wake of the terrorist attacks of September 11, 2001, and government responses to the Great Recession beginning with fiscal policy in 2008.

Second, on the revenue side, tax receipts declined sharply during and after the Great Recession.

This running national debt clock is posted near Times Square in New York City.

## ECONOMICS IN THE REAL WORLD

### Does China Own the United States?

In a July 2011, article in *GlobalPost*, Tom Mucha addressed the question of who owns the U.S. government debt.* The United States now has more than $15 trillion in debt, and many people fear that the owners of the bonds will have disproportionate influence on the activities of the U.S. government. According to Mucha:

> Many people—politicians and pundits alike—prattle on that China and, to a lesser extent Japan, own most of America's $14.3 trillion in government debt. But there's one little problem with that conventional wisdom: it's just not true. While the Chinese, Japanese, and plenty of other foreigners own substantial amounts, it's really Americans who hold most of America's debt.

Here's a breakdown by total amount held and percentage of total U.S. debt, according to *Business Insider*:

China owns 8% of the U.S. national debt.

- Mutual funds: $300.5 billion (2.0%)
- Commercial banks: $301.8 billion (2.1%)
- State, local, and federal retirement funds: $320.9 billion (2.2%)
- Money market mutual funds: $337.7 billion (2.4%)
- United Kingdom: $346.5 billion (2.4%)
- Private pension funds: $504.7 billion (3.5%)
- State and local governments: $506.1 billion (3.5%)
- Japan: $912.4 billion (6.4%)
- U.S. households: $959.4 billion (6.6%)
- China: $1.16 trillion (8%)
- U.S. Treasury: $1.63 trillion (11.3%)
- Social Security Trust Fund: $2.67 trillion (19.0%)

So the United States owes foreigners about $4.5 trillion in debt. But the United States owes itself $9.8 trillion. ✳

# Conclusion

We started this chapter with the misconception that governments never balance their budgets. Certainly, given the current size of U.S. budget deficits and the sovereign debt problems around the world, it would be natural to assume that national budgets are never balanced. But, in fact, as we have seen, the United States had a balanced federal budget as recently as 2001.

This chapter lays the groundwork for us to examine fiscal policy in Chapter 16. Much of the debt and deficits we've observed are a direct result of government budgetary maneuvers to affect the macroeconomy. Going forward, we now understand the institutions of fiscal policy. In Chapter 16, we'll learn about the economic theories that support fiscal policy.

---

*Thomas Mucha, "Who Owns America? Hint: It's Not China," *GlobalPost*, July 20, 2011, GlobalPost.com.

ECONOMICS FOR LIFE

# Budgeting for Your Take-Home Pay

Most college students have not yet held full-time jobs. So you are probably still planning for that day when you graduate and get your first big paycheck. We certainly don't want to discourage you, but we will offer a few words of caution for when you are budgeting your major expenses.

Let's say you graduate and obtain a good job in the city of your choice. You agree to a salary of $60,000 per year. This is a good starting salary (probably due to the economics courses you took!), so you start thinking about your budget for the future. Consider a few of the biggest questions: How much can you afford for your monthly housing payment? How large a car payment can you afford? How much can you spend on groceries or dining out? How much should you save each month?

It's a smart move to think about these questions ahead of time. But when you plan, be sure to recognize that your take-home pay will be far less than $60,000. It is tempting to make a monthly budget based on the $5,000 per month that your basic salary promises. In the table below, we estimate the actual size of your paycheck.

First, we subtract federal income tax. Based on the 2012 tax rates, we determine that your annual payment will be $11,030. Next we subtract 7.65% for Social Security and Medicare. After that, we subtract 5% each for state income taxes (this is about average), benefits (like health insurance, dental, and optical), and retirement contributions.

After these deductions, you are left with less than $3,000 per month! Your take-home pay is about 40% less than your salary.

Therefore, when you are making major spending decisions about things such as housing and car payments, be sure to budget based on this much-smaller figure. If, instead, you budget based on your salary, you won't be able to save, and you may even become dependent on credit cards.

|  | Monthly | Yearly |
| --- | --- | --- |
| Salary | $5,000.00 | $60,000 |
| Federal income tax | $919.00 | $11,030 |
| Social Security/Medicare tax | $382.50 | $4,590 |
| State income tax | $250.00 | $1,200 |
| Benefits | $250.00 | $3,000 |
| Retirement | $250.00 | $3,000 |
| Take-home pay | $2,948.50 | $37,180 |

When you put together your budget, be sure to account for all the deductions from your paycheck.

## ANSWERING THE BIG QUESTIONS

### How does the government spend?

* Government spending has grown sharply since 2000, and it is now about $3.5 trillion.
* Mandatory spending programs now constitute more than 50% of government spending at the U.S. national level. These mandatory programs include Social Security, Medicare, and welfare programs.
* Interest on the national debt is nearly 10% of federal spending. Defense spending is almost 20% of federal spending. The remaining 20% of the budget goes to discretionary government spending like highways, bridges, and the salaries of many government employees.

### How does the government tax?

* The U.S. government raises over 80% of its revenues through payroll taxes: income taxes and taxes for Social Security and Medicare. The income tax yields about $1 trillion in revenue per year. It is a progressive tax, so wealthier Americans pay more in taxes than the poor do.

### What are budget deficits, and how bad are they?

* If total government outlays exceed revenue in a given year, the budget is in deficit.
* Deficits add to the national debt, which is the accumulated deficit over time. Recently, the U.S. government has tallied deficits of more than $1 trillion per year. This amounts to almost 10% of GDP and cannot be sustained indefinitely.

## CONCEPTS YOU SHOULD KNOW

austerity (p. 474)
average tax rate (p. 463)
budget deficit (p. 468)
budget surplus (p. 468)
debt (p. 470)

discretionary outlays (p. 454)
government outlays (p. 452)
mandatory outlays (p. 453)
marginal tax rate (p. 462)
Medicare (p. 457)

progressive income tax system
(p. 462)
Social Security (p. 456)
transfer payments (p. 452)

## QUESTIONS FOR REVIEW

1. Since the 1960s, Social Security and Medicare have grown as portions of U.S. government spending.

   a. What major categories have shrunk during the same period?
   b. Has the U.S. budget become more or less flexible as a result of the growth in the mandatory programs? Explain your response.

2. Explain the difference between a budget deficit and the national debt.

3. Going back to 1960, there have been a few years in which the U.S. government budget was in surplus. What years were these? Why do you think those surpluses disappeared when they did? Figure 15.10 might be helpful in answering this question.

4. This question refers to Figure 15.10, which shows the U.S. outlays and spending as portions of GDP.

   a. List three periods when the U.S. budget deficit was relatively large.
   b. What historical events were taking place in the United States during these three periods that may have led to these large deficits? Be specific.

5. Explain why mandatory outlays are predicted to grow (as a portion of the total budget) over the next decade.

6. Explain the difference between average tax rates and marginal tax rates. Is it possible for a person's average tax rate to equal his or her marginal tax rate? If so, how?

## STUDY PROBLEMS (✱ *solved at the end of the section*)

1. Use the marginal income tax rates in Figure 15.6 (see p. 463) to compute the following:
   a. tax due on taxable income of $100,000, $200,000, and $500,000
   b. average tax rate on taxable income of $100,000, $200,000, and $500,000

2. Greece, Ireland, Portugal, and Spain all went through national budget difficulties in recent years. Use the data below to answer questions regarding the sovereign debts of these nations. (All data comes from the OECD and is in billions of current U.S. dollars.)

| | 2000 | | 2010 | |
| --- | --- | --- | --- | --- |
| | **Debt** | **GDP** | **Debt** | **GDP** |
| Greece | $138 | $127 | $455 | $308 |
| Ireland | $34 | $98 | $124 | $206 |
| Portugal | $62 | $118 | $203 | $231 |
| Spain | $292 | $586 | $734 | $1,420 |

   a. Compute the debt-to-GDP ratio for all four nations in both 2000 and 2010.
   b. Compute the average yearly budget deficit for each of the nations over this period.

c. In your judgment, which of the four nations was in the worst fiscal shape in 2010? Use your computations from above to justify your answer.

3. There are three different ways to report budget deficit data: nominal deficits, real deficits, and deficit-to-GDP ratios. Which of the three is most informative? Why?

✳4. Greece is a nation that has been through significant national budget turmoil. In 2010, it was discovered that the government had been concealing the true size of the national debt for several years. The data in the table below reveals just how much the nation's officially reported national debt grew between 2000 and 2010. The data is in billions of U.S. dollars. Use the data to answer the questions that follow.

| 2000 | | 2010 | |
|---|---|---|---|
| **Debt** | **GDP** | **Debt** | **GDP** |
| $138 | $127 | $455 | $308 |

a. What was the average annual increase in the Greek debt over the 10-year span?
b. What was the average annual budget deficit for Greece over this period?

✳5. Use the data in the table above to compute the debt-to-GDP ratio for Greece in both 2000 and 2010.

## SOLVED PROBLEMS

4. a. The debt grew from $138 billion to $455 billion over 10 years, which was an increase of $31 billion, or an average of $31.7 billion per year.

b. Given that the debt increased by $31.7 billion per year, this number was also the figure for the average annual deficit over this period.

5. For 2000: $138 \div 127 = 1.09$
For 2010: $455 \div 308 = 1.48$

# Fiscal Policy

**Government spending is a simple tool for fighting recessions.**
Many people believe that the government can quickly and predictably
offset economic downturns. The belief that the government can increase

spending and decrease taxes in order to safely evade recessions is common among much of the media, among many
politicians, and in many historical accounts of past economic
troubles. But if past experience has taught us anything, it is that government actions have uneven and unpredictable effects on the economy.
While it's true that the government may be able to influence the macroeconomy, many government spending initiatives have failed to quickly
revive an ailing economy.

In this chapter, we examine the case for fiscal policy, which includes
both government spending and taxes. We begin by framing fiscal policy
in the aggregate demand–aggregate supply model. We examine both
expansionary and contractionary policies. We then consider potential
shortcomings of fiscal policy and conclude with a view from the supply-
side perspective.

The American Recovery and Reinvestment Act, which entailed almost $1 trillion in government spending, was passed to help the economy recover from the Great Recession.

# BIG QUESTIONS

* What is fiscal policy?
* What are the shortcomings of fiscal policy?
* What is supply-side fiscal policy?

# What Is Fiscal Policy?

When the economy falters, people often look to the government to help push the economy forward again. In fact, the government uses many different tools to try to affect the economy. Economists classify these tools on the basis of two different types of policy: *monetary policy* and *fiscal policy*. Monetary policy is the use of the money supply to influence the economy. We will study monetary policy in Chapter 18. Fiscal policy is the use of government spending and taxes to influence the economy. Fiscal policy, the topic of this chapter, makes use of the tools of the federal budget to affect the economy. In the United States, tax and spending changes are legislated and approved by both Congress and the president.

In this section, we first describe how the government can use fiscal policy to try to stimulate the economy; then we discuss how fiscal policy might be used to slow down rapid growth. Along the way, we consider how this strategy affects government budget deficits and debt. Finally, we examine the multiplier process, which describes the way in which the effects of fiscal policy ripple through the economy.

## Expansionary Fiscal Policy

In the fall of 2007, the U.S. economy was slipping into recession. This led many people to think that the government should do something to keep the recession at bay. In particular, many expected the government to step in with tax reductions or spending programs to help stimulate the economy. **Expansionary fiscal policy** occurs when the government increases spending or decreases taxes to stimulate the economy toward expansion. In this section, we use the aggregate demand–aggregate supply model to examine the effects of expansionary fiscal policy.

In Chapter 13, we introduced the aggregate demand–aggregate supply model. In that model, we showed that recession can occur as a result of a drop in aggregate demand. In theory, the economy can move itself back to full employment in the long run, when all prices adjust. Consider the example presented in Figure 16.1. Initially, the economy is in long-run equilibrium at point A, with $P = 100$, $Y = Y^*$ (full employment), and $u = u^*$ (the natural rate). If aggregate demand declines to $AD_2$, the economy moves to

**Expansionary fiscal policy** occurs when the government increases spending or decreases taxes to stimulate the economy toward expansion.

short-run equilibrium at point b, with output at $Y_1$, which is less than full employment output, and an unemployment rate greater than the natural rate.

At equilibrium point b, government officials can wait for the economy to adjust back to full employment equilibrium at point C. This adjustment occurs when all prices adjust downward and short-run aggregate supply (SRAS) shifts downward. But prices can take a while to adjust. In addition, recessions are difficult times for many people, and they expect the government to take action to ease their plight. Thus, government officials often choose to use fiscal policy to try to shift aggregate demand back to its original level. If this works, the economy resumes full employment equilibrium at point A.

Fiscal policy can make use of either government spending or taxes, or a combination of the two tools. First, government spending (G) is one component of aggregate demand. Therefore, increases in G directly increase aggregate demand. When private spending (consumption, investment, and net exports) is low, government can increase demand directly by increasing G. Fiscal policy can also focus on consumption (C) by decreasing taxes. Decreases in taxes can increase aggregate demand because people have more of their income left to spend after paying their taxes. If people keep more of their paycheck, the theory goes, they can afford more consumption.

Recent history in the United States offers two prominent examples of expansionary fiscal policy. In the next section, we review these examples to clarify how both government spending and taxes are used in fiscal policy.

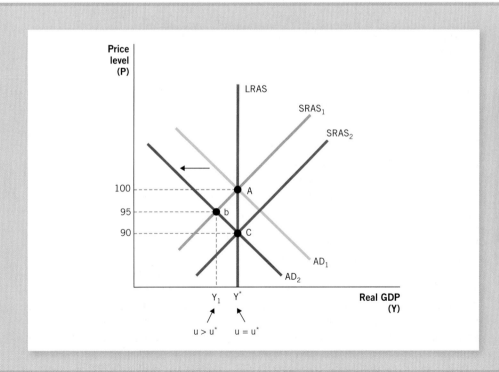

**FIGURE 16.1**

**Expansionary Fiscal Policy**

A decrease in aggregate demand moves the economy from point A to equilibrium at point b, with less than full employment output ($Y_1$), and unemployment (u) being greater than the natural rate ($u^*$). In the long run, all prices adjust, moving the economy back to full employment equilibrium at point C. The goal of expansionary fiscal policy is to shift aggregate demand back to $AD_1$ so that the economy returns to full employment without waiting for long-run adjustments.

## Fiscal Policy during the Great Recession

In the fall of 2007, the U.S. unemployment rate climbed from 4.6% to 5%. Thus, as it became clearer that economic conditions were worsening in the United States, the government took action. Political leaders decided that fiscal policy could help. Figure 16.2 shows real GDP growth and the unemployment rate in the United States over the period of the Great Recession and beyond. The official period of the recession is shaded blue. The top panel shows quarterly real GDP growth over the period, which fell to −1.8% at the beginning of 2008. The bottom panel shows the monthly unemployment rate, which began climbing in late 2007 and remained at high levels through 2011, well after the recession officially ended.

Surrounded by congressional leaders, President Bush signed the Economic Stimulus Act of 2008 . . .

In this context, the government enacted two significant fiscal policy initiatives. The first, signed in February 2008 by President George W. Bush, was the Economic Stimulus Act of 2008. The cornerstone of this act was a tax rebate for Americans. They had already paid their taxes for 2007, and the stimulus act included a partial rebate of those previously paid taxes. The government actually mailed rebate checks to taxpayers! And these refunds were not insignificant: a typical four-person family received a rebate check for $1,800 ($600 per adult and $300 per child). The overall cost of this action to government was $168 billion; it refunded about one of every seven dollars paid in individual income taxes for 2007. The expectation was that American taxpayers would spend rather than save most of this $168 billion, thereby increasing aggregate demand and stimulating the economy.

However, after the first fiscal stimulus was passed, economic conditions worsened. In Figure 16.2, notice that real GDP growth plummeted and the unemployment rate rose significantly in 2008 after the first fiscal stimulus legislation. National elections at the end of 2008 brought Barack Obama to the White House and changed the balance of power in Washington. In February 2009, less than one month after taking office, the new president signed the American Recovery and Reinvestment Act of 2009. The focus of this second act shifted to government spending. In addition, the size of this second fiscal stimulus—$787 billion—was much larger than the first.

These two major pieces of legislation illustrate the tools of fiscal policy: taxes and spending. The first focused on taxes; the second on government spending. The two acts may seem very different, but both sought to increase aggregate demand—they are based on the analysis we presented in Figure 16.1.

Fiscal policy generally focuses on aggregate demand. At the end of this chapter, we'll consider an alternative approach—one that uses government spending and taxes to affect aggregate supply in the long run.

. . . and one year later, President Obama signed the much larger American Recovery and Reinvestment Act of 2009.

## Fiscal Policy and Budget Deficits

We have seen that the typical prescription for an ailing economy is to increase government spending, decrease taxes, or both. You may be wondering how the government pays for all the spending or deals with the shortfall in tax revenue. The answer is through borrowing.

## FIGURE 16.2

### Major Fiscal Policy Initiatives during the Great Recession

The Great Recession began in December 2007. In February 2008, President Bush signed the Economic Stimulus Act of 2008, which introduced tax cuts to stimulate the economy and avoid recession. But during 2008 the economy sunk deeper into recession. In February 2009, President Obama signed the American Recovery and Reinvestment Act of 2009, which focused on government spending programs.

*Source*: GDP data is from the U.S. Bureau of Economic Analysis; unemployment rate data is from the U.S. Bureau of Labor Statistics.

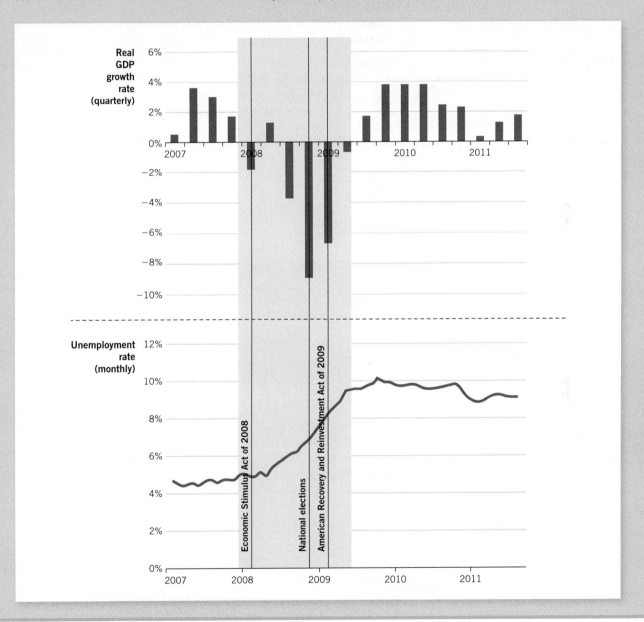

# Recession, Stimulus, Reinvestment

The U.S. government reacted to the Great Recession with two of the most important fiscal policy initiatives in history. The Economic Stimulus Act of 2008, signed by President Bush that February, sought to stimulate aggregate demand by issuing rebate checks to taxpayers. A year later, conditions had worsened, and the newly elected President Obama signed the much larger American Recovery and Reinvestment Act of 2009. This act also was an effort to increase aggregate demand, but mainly by boosting government spending instead of personal consumption. But, while these two acts may have lessened the economic decline, neither delivered the kind of turnaround that was promised.

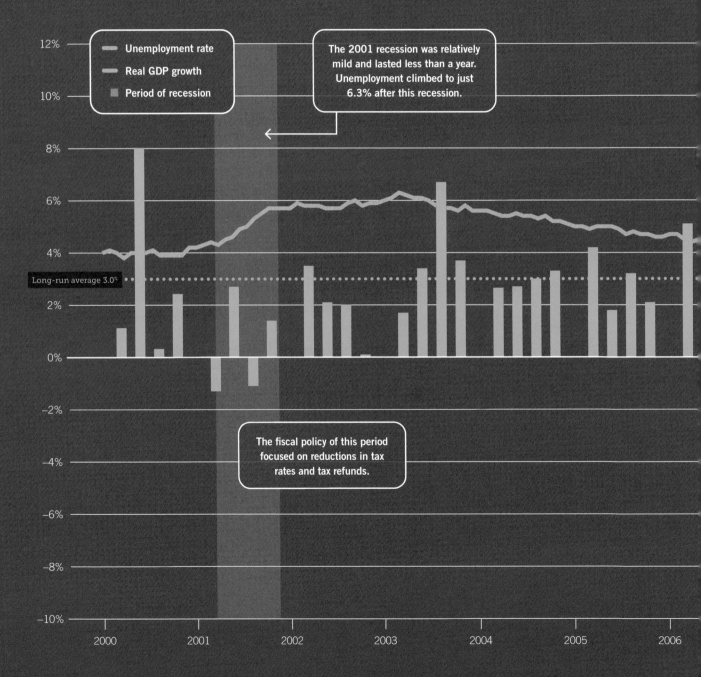

Legend:
- Unemployment rate
- Real GDP growth
- Period of recession

The 2001 recession was relatively mild and lasted less than a year. Unemployment climbed to just 6.3% after this recession.

Long-run average 3.0%

The fiscal policy of this period focused on reductions in tax rates and tax refunds.

- The GDP growth numbers from 2010 onward are similar to the GDP numbers from 2002 to 2008. What is not similar?

- What other factors beyond GDP growth might account for the historically high unemployment numbers since late 2008?

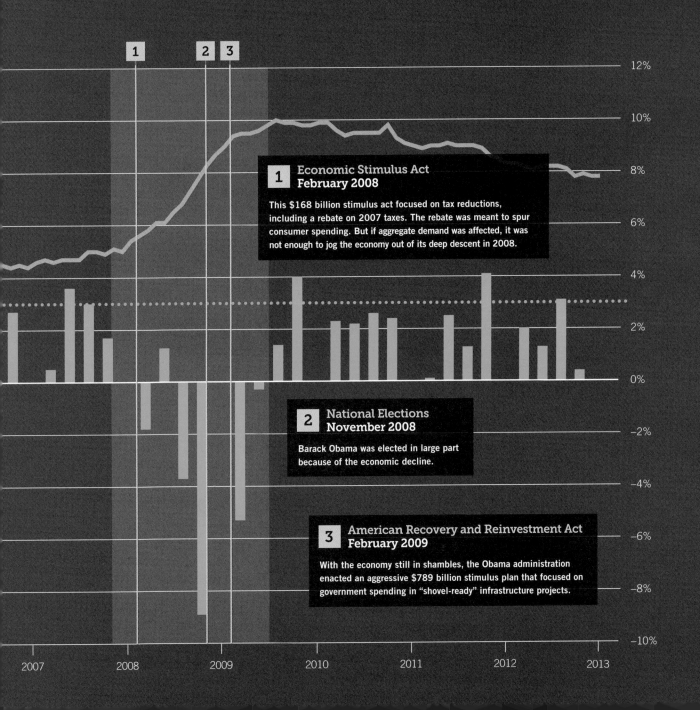

**1** **Economic Stimulus Act**
**February 2008**

This $168 billion stimulus act focused on tax reductions, including a rebate on 2007 taxes. The rebate was meant to spur consumer spending. But if aggregate demand was affected, it was not enough to jog the economy out of its deep descent in 2008.

**2** **National Elections**
**November 2008**

Barack Obama was elected in large part because of the economic decline.

**3** **American Recovery and Reinvestment Act**
**February 2009**

With the economy still in shambles, the Obama administration enacted an aggressive $789 billion stimulus plan that focused on government spending in "shovel-ready" infrastructure projects.

2007   2008   2009   2010   2011   2012   2013

Let's start with a simplified example. Assume at the start that the government is currently balancing the national budget so that outlays equal tax revenue. Then the economy slips into recession, and the government decides to increase government spending by $100 billion. The government must pay for this by borrowing; it must sell $100 billion worth of Treasury bonds. As a result, the federal budget is in deficit by $100 billion.

But that's only part of the story. In reality, the deficit will rise by more than $100 billion because tax revenue will fall. Recall from Chapter 15 that more than 80% of U.S. tax revenue derives from payroll taxes. In a recession, with income down and unemployment up, the amount of revenue that the government takes in from taxes falls, even if the tax rate stays the same.

It is easy to verify both of these phenomena by looking at recent U.S. recessions. Figure 16.3 shows U.S. federal outlays and tax revenue from 1985 to 2012, with recessionary periods shaded as vertical blue bars. First, look at the period of the Great Recession of 2007–2009. Note how spending (outlays) increased sharply in 2009, the year of the $787 billion fiscal stimulus. But falling income also led to less income tax revenue. Looking back over the three recessions shown in this graph, we see that spending increased but that tax revenue fell during each one.

The bottom line is clear: expansionary fiscal policy inevitably leads to increases in budget deficits and the national debt during economic downturns. This policy prescription may seem odd to you. After all, if you personally fell on rough economic times, you might (reasonably) react differently. For example, if your employer were to cut you back to part-time employment, would it seem like a good idea to go on a spending binge? It might make you feel better while you were shopping, but it wouldn't help your financial situation much. In a macroeconomic perspective, however, one reason why expansionary fiscal policy might work for the overall economy is that spending by one person becomes income to another, which can snowball into income increases throughout the economy. We discuss this aspect later in the chapter in the section on multipliers.

## FIGURE 16.3

### Real U.S. Outlays and Revenue, 1985–2012

The use of expansionary fiscal policy to counteract economic downturns leads to greater budget deficits. During recessionary periods, outlays increase and tax revenue falls. In 2001, these strategies erased the budget surplus; in 1990 and 2008, these strategies expanded the size of the deficit.

*Source:* Office of Management and Budget.

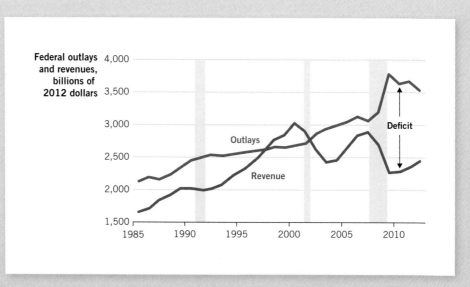

# Contractionary Fiscal Policy

We have seen that expansionary fiscal policy is often used to try to increase aggregate demand during economic downturns. But there are also times when *contractionary* fiscal policy is used to reduce aggregate demand. **Contractionary fiscal policy** occurs when the government decreases spending or increases taxes to slow economic expansion.

There are two reasons why a government might want to reduce aggregate demand. First, as we discussed above, expansionary fiscal policy creates deficits during recessions. An increase in taxes or a decrease in spending during an economic expansion can work to eliminate the budget deficit and pay off some of the government debt. For example, the U.S. government ran budget surpluses from 1998 to 2001, at the end of an extended period of economic expansion. These surpluses were not large enough to pay off the national debt entirely, but they did shrink it somewhat.

Second, the government might want to reduce aggregate demand if it believes that the economy is expanding beyond its long-run capabilities. Full employment output ($Y^*$) is considered the highest level of output sustainable in the long run. But if the unemployment rate falls below the natural rate ($u^*$), it indicates that output may be above $Y^*$. Some analysts then worry that the economy may "overheat" from too much spending, which can lead to inflation. Figure 16.4 illustrates this possibility, beginning at short-run equilibrium point a, with aggregate demand equal to $AD_1$. Notice that this level of aggregate demand leads to short-run equilibrium where real GDP is higher than its full employment level ($Y_1 > Y^*$). In addition, at point a the unemployment rate is below the natural rate ($u < u^*$), which is not sustainable in the long run.

When aggregate demand is high enough to drive unemployment below the natural rate, there is upward pressure on the price level, which is at 105

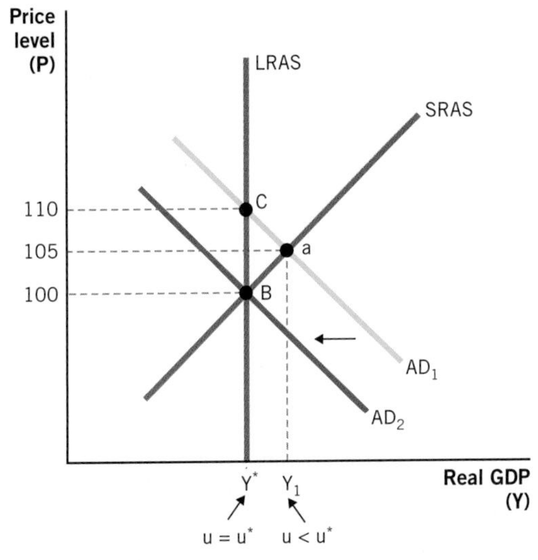

**Contractionary fiscal policy** occurs when the government decreases spending or increases taxes to slow economic expansion.

## FIGURE 16.4

**Contractionary Fiscal Policy**

When policymakers believe the economy is producing beyond its long-run capacity ($Y_1 > Y^*$), fiscal policy can be used to reduce aggregate demand. Contractionary fiscal policy moves the economy from short-run equilibrium at point a to equilibrium at point B, thus avoiding the inflationary outcome at point C.

at short-run equilibrium point a. Further, without a reduction in aggregate demand, the economy naturally moves toward equilibrium at point C in the long run, as prices fully adjust. But this equilibrium implies even more inflation. Thus, in order to avoid inflation, fiscal policy can be used to try to reduce aggregate demand from $AD_1$ to $AD_2$. This strategy moves the economy back to long-run equilibrium with price stability at point B.

Together, contractionary and expansionary fiscal policy can serve to counteract the ups and downs of business cycles. We examine this combination more closely in the next section.

### Countercyclical Fiscal Policy

All else being equal, people generally prefer smoothness and predictability in their financial affairs. In Chapter 9, we talked about this characteristic in reference to consumption smoothing; in Chapter 10, we considered how people are risk averse. Along these lines, an economy that grows at a consistent rate is preferable to an economy that grows in an erratic fashion. For these and other reasons, politicians generally employ fiscal policy to counteract the business cycle.

> **Countercyclical fiscal policy** is fiscal policy that seeks to counteract business-cycle fluctuations.

The use of fiscal policy to counteract business-cycle fluctuations is known as **countercyclical fiscal policy**. It consists of using expansionary policy during economic downturns and contractionary policy during economic expansions. Figure 16.5 illustrates the goals of countercyclical fiscal policy. The natural path of the economy (without countercyclical fiscal policy) includes business cycles during which income and employment fluctuate. The hope is that countercyclical fiscal policy can reduce the fluctuations inherent in a business cycle.

You might recall from Chapter 14 that Keynesian economists focus on aggregate demand (total spending) in the economy. Keynesian economics provides the theoretical foundation for countercyclical fiscal policy. In fact, Keynes's ideas provided a theoretical foundation for the New Deal government spending programs implemented in the United States in 1933 and 1935. But these ideas are also behind the very recent fiscal policy initiatives of both 2008 and 2009.

## FIGURE 16.5

**Countercyclical Fiscal Policy and the Business Cycle**

The goal of countercyclical fiscal policy is to smooth out the fluctuations in the business cycle.

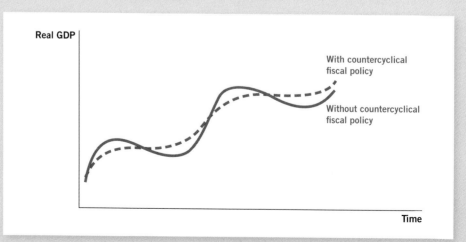

| TABLE 16.1 | | | |
|---|---|---|---|
| **Countercyclical Fiscal Policy Tools** | | | |
| **Fiscal policy action** | **Timing** | **Objective: How it affects aggregate demand (AD)** | **Byproduct: How it affects the budget deficit** |
| **Expansionary** | | | |
| ↑ Government spending (G) | When the economy is contracting | G is one component of AD, so increases in G directly increase AD. | Increases budget deficit |
| ↓ Taxes (T) | | Decreasing T leaves more funds in the hands of consumers, who then spend more on consumption (C). When C rises, AD rises. | |
| **Contractionary** | | | |
| ↓ Government spending (G) | When the economy is expanding | Decreases in G directly decrease AD. | Decreases budget deficit |
| ↑ Taxes (T) | | Increasing T leaves fewer funds in the hands of consumers, who then spend less on consumption (C). When C falls, AD falls. | |

Table 16.1 summarizes the tools of countercyclical fiscal policy, including the timing and effects of the policy on aggregate demand as well as its effects on the government budget deficit.

## Multipliers

The tools of fiscal policy are even more powerful than our initial discussion reveals. This is because the initial effects can snowball into further effects. When fiscal policy shifts aggregate demand, some effects are felt immediately. But a large share of the impact occurs later, as spending effects ripple throughout the economy. To see this clearly, we need to build on two concepts— one is review, the other is new.

First, the review concept: recall from Chapter 6 that what one person spends becomes income to others. This is true not only for private spending but also for government spending. For example, if the government uses fiscal policy to increase spending on new roads, the dollars spent on these roads become income to the suppliers of all the resources that go into the production of the roads. Now the new concept: increases in income generally lead to increases in consumption. When a person's income rises, he or she might save some of this new income but might be just as likely to spend part of it too. The **marginal propensity to consume (MPC)** is the portion of additional income that is spent on consumption:

The **marginal propensity to consume (MPC)** is the portion of additional income that is spent on consumption.

$$\text{MPC} = \frac{\text{change in consumption}}{\text{change in income}}$$

(Equation 16.1)

For example, say you earn $400 in new income, and you decide to spend $300 and save $100. Your marginal propensity to consume is then

Spend or save? What is your marginal propensity to consume?

$300 ÷ $400 = 0.75. In other words, you spend 75% of your new income. The MPC isn't constant across all people, but it is a fraction between 0 and 1:

$$0 \leq MPC \leq 1$$

Let's consider a simple example of how spending changes affect the economy. For this example, let's say that the government decides to increase spending by $100 billion and spends all of the funds on salaries for government workers. This government spending becomes new income for the government workers. Now let's assume that these workers spend about 75 cents of each dollar of their new income, or that their MPC is 0.75. In total, the government workers spend $75 billion and save $25 billion of their new income. The government workers' spending becomes $75 billion worth of income to others in the economy. (Thus, in sum, we now have $175 billion in new income.) If the recipients of that $75 billion income also spend 75% of it, they create another $56.25 billion in new income for others in the economy, for a total of $231.25 billion.

It's clear that the initial $100 billion in government spending can create more than $100 billion in income; this occurs through the "multiplying" effect we just described. The effect continues on, round after round, as new income-earners turn around and spend a portion of their income.

The multiplying effect is significant when we focus on aggregate demand in the economy. Each time people earn new income, they spend part of it. After all the dust settles, the total impact is a multiple of the original spending created by the fiscal policy. Figure 16.6 illustrates this multiplier process for our current example. The table part of the figure shows how spending becomes income and then how part of the new income is spent. The first round represents the government's initial spending of $100 billion. The following rounds represent the new income generated by consumption spending. Since the MPC is 0.75 in this example, each round generates 75% of the income produced in the preceding round.

In the graph, we show aggregate demand. Each time spending increases, aggregate increases (shifts outward). The initial aggregate demand is labeled $AD_1$. Each round of spending shifts aggregate demand to the right. Finally, aggregate demand settles at $AD_N$, where N represents the completion of the multiplier process.

To determine the total impact on spending from any initial government expenditures, we need to use a formula known as the *spending multiplier*. The **spending multiplier ($m^s$)** tells us the total impact on spending from an initial change of a given amount. The multiplier depends on the marginal propensity to consume: the greater the marginal propensity to consume, the greater the spending multiplier. The formula for this spending multiplier is:

The **spending multiplier ($m^s$)** is a formula to determine the total impact on spending from an initial change of a given amount.

(Equation 16.2)

$$m^s = \frac{1}{(1 - MPC)}$$

Since the MPC is a fraction between 0 and 1, the multiplier is generally larger than 1. For example, if the marginal propensity to consume is 0.75, the multiplier is determined as:

$$m^s = \frac{1}{(1 - MPC)} = \frac{1}{1 - 0.75} = \frac{1}{0.25} = 4$$

## FIGURE 16.6

### The Spending Multiplier Process

Assume that MPC = 0.75 and the government increases spending by $100 billion. In the table, you can see how the spending multiplies throughout the economy; each round is 75% of the prior round. In the end, the total spending increase is four times the initial change in government spending. The graph illustrates the shifting aggregate demand curve, as the spending multiplies throughout the economy.

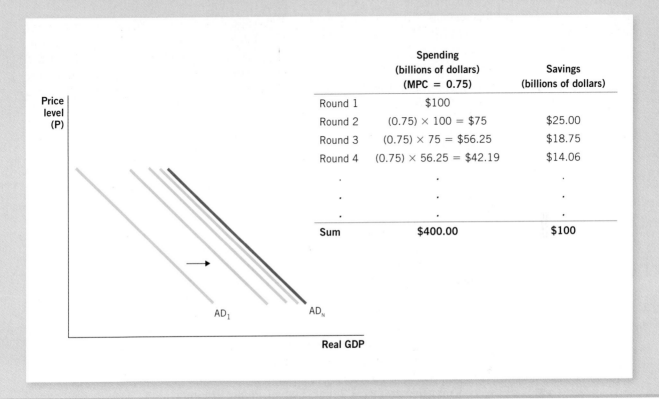

| | Spending (billions of dollars) (MPC = 0.75) | Savings (billions of dollars) |
|---|---|---|
| Round 1 | $100 | |
| Round 2 | (0.75) × 100 = $75 | $25.00 |
| Round 3 | (0.75) × 75 = $56.25 | $18.75 |
| Round 4 | (0.75) × 56.25 = $42.19 | $14.06 |
| | . | . |
| | . | . |
| | . | . |
| Sum | $400.00 | $100 |

Price level (P)

AD₁    ADₙ

Real GDP

Sometimes, this multiplier is called the *Keynesian* or *fiscal multiplier*.

Note that the multiplier concept applies to all spending, no matter whether that spending is public or private. In addition, there is a multiplier associated with tax changes. A reduction in the tax rate leaves more income for consumers to spend. This spending multiplies throughout the economy in much the same way as government spending multiplies.

The multiplier process also works in reverse. If the government reduces spending or increases taxes, people have less income to spend, shifting the aggregate demand curves to the left. In terms of the aggregate demand curve in Figure 16.6, the initial decline in government spending leads to subsequent declines as the effects reverberate through the economy.

The spending multiplier implies that the tools of fiscal policy are very powerful. Not only can the government change its spending and taxing, but also multiples of this spending then ripple throughout the economy over several periods.

The multiplier effects of fiscal policy on an economy are similar to the rippling effects of a stone thrown into water.

## Spending Multiplier

### *Pay It Forward*

In this movie, a drama from 2000, a young boy named Trevor (played by Haley Joel Osment) comes up with an idea that he thinks can change the world. Instead of paying people back for good deeds, Trevor suggests a new approach called "pay it forward." The idea is for him to help three people in some way. According to Trevor, "it has to be really big, something they can't do by themselves."

Then each of those three people helps three more. You can see how this idea leads to a multiplication of people helping other people.

Trevor's scheme is both similar to and different from the spending multiplier at the center of Keynesian fiscal policy. It is similar in that one person's "spending" leads to "spending" by others.

But we have seen that the spending multiplier is driven by the marginal propensity to consume, which

Trevor explains his good-deed pyramid scheme.

is a fraction between 0 and 1, as people generally save part of any new income they earn. So the spending multiplication process slows down and eventually dies out.

However, the multiplier in *Pay it Forward* exceeds 1 because each person can help many people. In Trevor's scheme, the multiplier is 3. So the good deeds can continue to expand to more and more good deeds.

## PRACTICE WHAT YOU KNOW

Some government spending projects are more shovel-ready than others.

### Expansionary Fiscal Policy: Shovel-Ready Projects

In early 2009, with the U.S. economy in deep recession, newly elected President Obama vowed to use fiscal stimulus spending on "shovel-ready" projects. The projects were deemed shovel-ready because they had already been approved and were just waiting for funding. Obama hoped his stimulus plan would create new jobs with minimal delays.

Question: Assume the economy is in short-run equilibrium with output being less than full employment output. Also assume, for this entire question, that the marginal propensity to consume (MPC) is equal to 0.50. What is the value of the government spending multiplier in this case?

Answer: Equation 16.2 gives us the formula for the spending multiplier:

$$m^s = \frac{1}{(1 - MPC)} = \frac{1}{(1 - 0.5)} = \frac{1}{0.5} = 2$$

Question: Given the size of the multiplier, what would be the implied change in income (GDP) from stimulus spending of $800 billion?

Answer: The total implied impact would be: $2 \times \$800$ billion $= \$1.6$ trillion

# What Are the Shortcomings of Fiscal Policy?

At this point, you may wonder why fiscal policy doesn't always work perfectly in the real world. If activist fiscal policy is as simple as tweaking G and T and letting the multiplier go to work, why do recessions still happen? Unfortunately, the real world isn't so simple. Millions of people make individual decisions that affect the entire economy. How much fiscal policy is enough? How much will people save? Economists can't know the answers to these questions ahead of time.

But there are also more formal shortcomings of activist fiscal policy. In this section, we consider three issues that arise in the application of activist fiscal policy: time lags, crowding-out, and savings shifts.

## Time Lags

Both fiscal and monetary policies are intended to smooth out the economic variations that accompany a business cycle. So timing is important. But there are three lags that accompany policy decisions: recognition lag, implementation lag, and impact lag.

1. *Recognition lag.* In the real world, it is difficult to determine when the economy is turning up or down. GDP data is released quarterly, and the final estimate is not known until three months after the period in question. Unemployment rate data tends to lag even further behind. In addition, growth is not constant: one bad quarter does not always signal a recession, and one good quarter is not always the beginning of an expansion. All these factors make it very difficult to recognize when expansion or contraction starts.
2. *Implementation lag.* It takes time to implement fiscal policy. In most nations, one or more governing bodies must approve tax and spending legislation. In the United States, such legislation must pass both houses of Congress and receive presidential approval before becoming law. For this reason, fiscal policy takes much longer to implement than monetary policy does. For example, as we discussed earlier in this chapter, the Economic Stimulus Act of 2008 entailed sending tax rebate checks to U.S. taxpayers. The act passed in early February, yet most checks did not go out until about six months later. This delay occurred even though the recipients were known ahead of time—that's about as "shovel-ready" as a project can get.
3. *Impact lag.* Finally, it takes time for the complete effects of fiscal or monetary policy to materialize. The multiplier makes fiscal policy powerful, but it takes time to ripple through the economy.

If lags cause the effects of fiscal policy to be delayed for a year or 18 months, there is a risk that the policy can actually magnify the business cycle. That is, if the effects of expansionary fiscal policy hit when the economy is already expanding, it may lead to excessive aggregate demand and inflation. Then, if contractionary fiscal policy is implemented with delays, the effects could lead to even deeper recessions.

How would you like it if your medications only worked with an 18-month lag?

**ECONOMICS IN THE REAL WORLD**

### Recognizing Lags

Hindsight is 20-20. But in reality, it is very difficult to determine instantaneously how the economy is performing. Looking back now, we know that the U.S. economy entered a recession in December 2007. But this development was far from clear at the time. In fact, as Edmund Andrews pointed out in a *New York Times* article in February 2008, the Bush administration was not convinced that the economy was in a recession. Reporting on February 12, Andrews wrote:

> The White House predicted on Monday that the economy would escape a recession and that unemployment would remain low this year, though it acknowledged that growth had already slowed. "I don't think we are in a recession right now, and we are not forecasting a recession," said Edward P. Lazear, chairman of the White House Council of Economic Advisers. . . . The administration's forecast calls for the economy to expand 2.7 percent this year and for unemployment to remain at 4.9 percent.

It's not inconceivable that this forecast was biased by political considerations, but, according to Andrews, even independent economists were predicting a 1.7% growth rate for 2008. In reality, real GDP fell by 3.5% and the unemployment rate rose to 7.3% by the end of 2008. As this example demonstrates, it is very difficult to accurately recognize current economic conditions. ✳

### Automatic Stabilizers

**Automatic stabilizers** are government programs that automatically implement countercyclical fiscal policy in response to economic conditions.

One possibility for alleviating the lag problem is to put in place programs that automatically adjust government spending and taxes when economic conditions change. **Automatic stabilizers** are government programs that automatically implement countercyclical fiscal policy in response to economic conditions. Given that the prescription is to increase spending and decrease taxes during downturns, and to decrease spending and increase taxes during expansions, there are several government programs that accomplish this automatically:

- *Progressive income tax rates* guarantee that individual tax bills fall when incomes fall (during recessions) and rise when incomes rise (during expansions).
- *Taxes on corporate profits* lower total tax bills when profits are lower (during contractions) and raise tax bills when profits are higher (typically during expansions).
- *Unemployment compensation* increases government spending automatically when the number of unemployed people rises and decreases government spending when fewer people are unemployed.
- *Welfare programs* also increase government spending during downturns and decrease government spending when the economy is doing better.

In short, automatic stabilizers can eliminate recognition lags and implementation lags, and thereby alleviate some concerns of destabilizing fiscal policy.

## Crowding-Out

The second shortcoming of activist fiscal policy addresses the actual impact of government spending and the multiplier effects. This critique is based on the idea that government spending may be a substitute for private spending.

When this is the case, the impact on aggregate demand is smaller. Economists call this *crowding-out*. **Crowding-out** occurs when private spending falls in response to increases in government spending.

For example, say the government starts a new program in which it buys a new laptop computer for every college student in America. (Don't get too excited, this is just hypothetical.) But if the government is buying computers for students, then students won't buy as many computers for themselves. People may continue to spend on other items, but they might save, too. When private spending falls in response to increases in government spending, we say that crowding-out has occurred. When private spending falls in response to an increase in government spending, then aggregate demand does not increase and the fiscal policy becomes ineffective.

Let's look more closely at how crowding-out works. Assume that the government has a balanced budget. Then the government increases spending by $100 billion but does not raise taxes. This means that it has to borrow the $100 billion in the loanable funds market. But, as we know, every dollar borrowed requires a dollar saved. So when the government borrows $100 billion, the money has to come from $100 billion in savings.

Figure 16.7 illustrates what happens when the government enters the loanable funds market to borrow $100 billion. The graph shows that initially the

**Crowding-out**
occurs when private spending falls in response to increases in government spending.

If the government bought you a new laptop, would you spend your income on another one too?

## FIGURE 16.7

**Crowding-Out in the Loanable Funds Market**
Initially, at point A, private savings of $100 billion all becomes private investment of $250 billion. But government borrowing shifts the demand for loans from $D_1$ to $D_2$. The new demand for loans leads to equilibrium at point B, with a higher interest rate. At the new equilibrium there is $300 billion in private savings ($S_B$ in the table), but $100 billion goes to the government ($G_B$) and $200 billion is left for private investment ($I_B$).

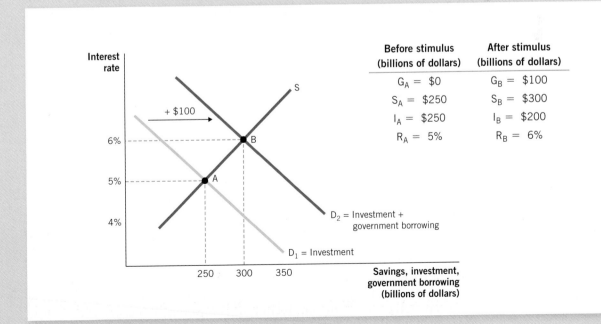

| | Before stimulus (billions of dollars) | After stimulus (billions of dollars) |
|---|---|---|
| | $G_A$ = $0 | $G_B$ = $100 |
| | $S_A$ = $250 | $S_B$ = $300 |
| | $I_A$ = $250 | $I_B$ = $200 |
| | $R_A$ = 5% | $R_B$ = 6% |

The crowding-out view: fiscal policy essentially takes water out of the deep end and then pours it into the shallow end. Does this change the water level in the pool?

market is in equilibrium at point A with demand for loans designated as $D_1$ (that is, investment). The initial interest rate is 5%, and at this rate there is $250 billion worth of savings. This amount of savings funds $250 billion in private borrowing. The table in Figure 16.7 summarizes these initial values in the column labeled "Before stimulus (A)."

Now when the government borrows, the demand for loans increases by $100 billion at all points. This is indicated on the graph as a shift from $D_1$ to $D_2$. But the new demand for loans completely changes the equilibrium in the market. The increased demand drives the interest rate up from 5% to 6%, and the new equilibrium quantity of loanable funds increases to $300 billion, shown as point B on the graph. The interest rate rises because of the increase in demand for loans caused by government borrowing.

To demonstrate the overall effects of this new government borrowing, we compare the values of private savings and investment at the two equilibrium points. These are displayed in the table in Figure 16.7. The new equilibrium quantity of loans is $300 billion, but the government has borrowed $100 billion ($G_B$). This means that borrowing for private investment spending ($I_A$) declines to $200 billion ($I_B$). Essentially, the higher interest rate discourages some private purchases; thus, the government purchases crowd out private spending.

Finally, note that private savings increases from $250 billion ($S_A$) to $300 billion ($S_B$)—that is, by $50 billion—because the higher interest rate ($R_B$) has caused more individuals to devote more of their income to savings. But if savings rises by $50 billion, then consumption must fall by $50 billion. This is a direct relationship. The end result is that an increase of $100 billion in deficit-financed government spending leads to $100 billion less of private spending—$50 billion from investment and $50 billion from savings.

In this example, we have complete crowding-out: every dollar of government spending crowds out a dollar of private spending. In reality, crowding-out may be less than complete, but this example does illustrate an important caveat regarding the effects of fiscal policy.

 **ECONOMICS IN THE REAL WORLD**

### Did Government Spending Really Surge in 2009?

Economist and *New York Times* editorial writer Paul Krugman is an ardent defender of Keynesian countercyclical fiscal policy. During the course of the Great Recession, Krugman used his column to consistently advocate for more and more government spending.

Yet, after the historically large fiscal stimulus in 2009, many people were baffled as to why the economy struggled with high unemployment rates and slow real GDP growth even through 2012. In a February 14, 2011, post on his blog, Krugman argued that the increase in federal spending was offset by reductions on spending at the state government level. According to Krugman, "Once you take state and local cutbacks into account, there was no surge of government spending."

In a sense, even though he didn't identify it as such, Krugman was pointing out a variation of crowding-out. Technically, crowding-out occurs when private individuals substitute government (federal, state, and local) spending in place of

Why should states build new highways when the federal government offers to do it for them?

their private spending. But Krugman's complaint is that the crowding-out occurred in the government sector. Federal government spending rose, and then state and local government spending fell. Most states were facing crises of their own as a result of the recession. Thus, they substituted federal spending for state spending. This strategy helped them to balance their budgets during the recession. But it also meant that total government spending did not rise as much as the federal government intended. And this may help explain why the 2009 fiscal stimulus failed to push the U.S. economy back to full employment. ✳

## Savings Shifts

If your new income is temporary, are you more inclined to save it?

Imagine that you get a $1,000 check in the mail from the business office at your college. You would probably wonder why you got the check and whether you would have to return it. But you might also get excited and begin thinking about all the goods and services you could buy. How much would you spend, and how much would you save?

Let's consider two different scenarios as to the source of these funds. First, imagine that you are awarded a $1,000 scholarship after your tuition bill is already paid. Thus, the money is yours to keep. In this case, you might spend much or all of the $1,000. But if, instead, the funds were sent to you in error, then you would have to repay them. In this second scenario, you probably wouldn't spend any of the $1,000 you got from the college.

In some ways, government spending in the economy is similar to the second scenario. New spending today has to be paid for someday. This means that taxes must rise sooner or later. The **new classical critique** of fiscal policy asserts that increases in government spending and decreases in taxes are largely offset by increases in savings, because people know they'll have to pay higher taxes eventually. But if savings increases, then consumption falls, and this outcome mitigates the effects of the government spending.

Table 16.2 summarizes the three shortcomings of fiscal policy. Time lags can cause fiscal policy to magnify business cycles, crowding-out can lead to lower private spending when the government spends, and the new classical critique implies that savings rises when people anticipate higher future taxes. Each of these factors can diminish the effects of fiscal policy.

The **new classical critique** of fiscal policy asserts that increases in government spending and decreases in taxes are largely offset by increases in savings.

## TABLE 16.2

### Summary of Fiscal Policy Shortcomings

| Shortcoming | Summary | Result |
|---|---|---|
| Time lags | The effects of fiscal policy may be delayed by lags in recognition, implementation, and effectiveness. | If lags are significant, fiscal policy can be destabilizing and magnify business cycles. |
| Crowding-out | Government spending can serve as a substitute for private spending. | Even partial crowding-out reduces the impact of fiscal stimulus. |
| Savings shifts | In response to increases in government spending or lower taxes, people may increase their current savings to help pay for inevitably higher future taxes. | If current savings increases by the entire amount of the federal stimulus, the effects of the stimulus are negated. |

## PRACTICE WHAT YOU KNOW

### Crowding-Out: Does Fiscal Policy Lead to More Aggregate Demand?

Without crowding-out, a statue of economist Adam Smith could stimulate the economy.

Imagine that the country is in recession and the government decides to increase spending. It commissions a very large statue for $50 million. To pay for the statue, the government borrows all of the $50 million.

After the government borrows the $50 million, the interest rate rises from 3% to 4% and the equilibrium quantity of loanable funds increases from $500 million to $530 million.

Question: How would you sketch a graph of the loanable funds market representing this scenario? Be sure to indicate on this graph all the changes that take place after the borrowing.

Answer: Originally, the market is in equilibrium at point A with an interest rate of 3% and savings and investment being equal at $500 million. Then the demand for loans increases by $50 million at all points when the government borrows $50 million. This change moves the market to a new equilibrium at point B.

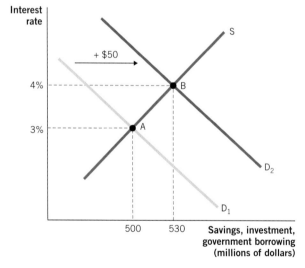

Question: Using the above information, and assuming complete crowding-out, what would you predict will happen to C, I, G, and total aggregate demand (AD) in response to the government's action?

Answer: Government spending (G) will increase by $50 million. Total savings will increase to $530 million, which means that consumption (C) will fall by $30 million. But since the government is borrowing $50 million of the savings, private investment (I) will fall to $480 million, a decrease of $20 million. All of this means a net change of zero in aggregate demand. These changes are summarized in the table below.

| Component | C | I | G | AD |
|---|---|---|---|---|
| Change (millions of dollars) | $ −30 | $ −20 | $ +50 | — |

# What Is Supply-Side Fiscal Policy?

We have considered typical fiscal policy, which focuses squarely on aggregate demand. It is also possible to implement fiscal policy with the intent of affecting the supply side of the economy. In this section, we begin by describing the supply-side perspective and certain popular supply-side policy proposals. We then look more closely at marginal tax rates and consider how changes in tax rates can affect the economy.

## The Supply-Side Perspective

We can illustrate the supply-side perspective in the aggregate demand–aggregate supply model. For most of this chapter, we have focused on shifting the demand curve with fiscal policy. Now we will explore how taxes and government spending can affect long-run aggregate supply. **Supply-side fiscal policy** involves the use of government spending and taxes to affect the supply, or production, side of the economy. In Figure 16.8, this is indicated as a shift from $LRAS_1$ to $LRAS_2$. When long-run aggregate supply shifts, this means a shift to a new level of full employment output; in the figure, this is shown as a move from $Y^*$ to $Y^{**}$.

Recall from Chapter 13 that shifts in long-run aggregate supply are caused by changes in resources, technology, and institutions. For example, we know that technological advances increase long-run aggregate supply: a technological advancement allows production of a greater quantity of output using the same or fewer resources. In the long run, much economic growth derives from technological advances. The government can implement fiscal policy and use the tax code to encourage technological advancement. For example, since 1981 in the United States, businesses have received tax credits for expenses related to research and development: firms that spend on research and development of new technology pay lower taxes than firms that don't. This is a significant incentive that encourages innovation and ultimately generates a

**Supply-side fiscal policy** involves the use of government spending and taxes to affect the production (supply) side of the economy.

## FIGURE 16.8

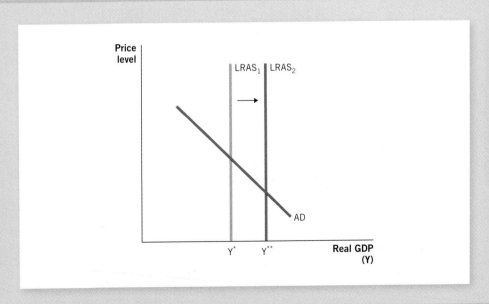

**Supply-Side Fiscal Policy**

Typical (demand-side) fiscal policy involves the use of government spending and taxes to shift aggregate demand. In contrast, supply-side fiscal policy involves the use of government spending and taxes to shift long-run aggregate supply (from $LRAS_1$ to $LRAS_2$), which moves the economy from one full employment output level ($Y^*$), to a new full employment output level ($Y^{**}$).

Subsidies for college education are a type of supply-side fiscal policy.

greater supply of output. Thus, the goal of this fiscal policy is to shift long-run aggregate supply.

There are many fiscal policy initiatives that focus on the supply side of the economy. These include:

1. *Research and development (R&D) tax credits.* Reduced taxes are available for firms that spend resources to develop new technology.

2. *Policies that focus on education.* Subsidies or tax breaks for education expenses create incentives to invest in education. One example is the Pell grant, which helps to pay for college expenses. Eventually, education and training increase effective labor resources and thus increase aggregate supply.

3. *Lower corporate profit tax rates.* Lower taxes increase the incentives for corporations to undertake activities that generate more profit.

4. *Lower marginal income tax rates.* Lower income tax rates create incentives for individuals to work harder and produce more, since they get to keep a larger share of their income. We will discuss this further below.

All of these initiatives share two characteristics. First, they increase the incentives for productive activities. Second, each initiative takes time to affect aggregate supply. For example, education subsidies may encourage people to go to college and learn skills that will help them to succeed in the workplace. But the full impact of that education won't be felt until after the education is completed. For this reason, supply-side proposals are generally emphasized as long-run solutions to growth problems.

## PRACTICE WHAT YOU KNOW

With congressional leaders at his side, President Bush signed a law that reduced top income tax rates from 39.6% to 35%.

### Supply Side versus Demand Side: The Bush Tax Cuts

In mid-2001, the Bush administration won congressional approval for lower income tax rates. One stipulation of this rate cut was that the rates also be applied retroactively to taxes from the year 2000.

Question: Would you consider this fiscal policy to be demand-side focused, supply-side focused, or both? Explain your response.

Answer: Both! Tax rate cuts are generally supply-side initiatives, since they frame incentives for production going forward. So the rate cuts applying to income taxes for 2001 and beyond were focused on the supply side.

But the Bush tax cuts also applied to taxes already paid. This meant that refund checks were mailed to taxpayers, refunding part of the taxes they had paid for the year 2000. This provision was clearly demand-focused, as the government hoped that taxpayers would use the funds to increase spending—that is, aggregate demand.

# Marginal Income Tax Rates

We have noted that lowering marginal income tax rates is one way in which fiscal policy can affect the supply side of the economy. However, the relationship between tax rates and tax revenue is one of the most highly controversial in politics. Economists are not as divided over the issue as the public at large is. But you don't often hear or read the entire explanation, perhaps because it doesn't consistently line up nicely with either political side on the issue.

## Tax Rates and Tax Revenue

Some politicians always advocate for tax rate cuts, no matter how large the budget deficit. They claim that a tax rate cut always leads to an increase in tax revenues. How can this be? They argue that a tax rate cut can be creative; it can stimulate work effort, employment, and income, and then generate more income tax revenue for the government. Tax revenue rises because more people are employed and income levels are higher.

Consider the following quote:

> The worst deficit comes from a recession. And if we can take the proper action in the proper time, this can be the most important step we can take to prevent another recession. That is the right time to make tax cuts, both for your family budget, and the national budget, resulting from a permanent basic reform and reduction in our rate structure. A creative tax cut, creating more jobs and income and, eventually, more revenue.
>
> *—35th president of the United States*

You may be surprised to learn that the president quoted is John F. Kennedy. He made this statement in 1962, when marginal tax rates were as high as 91%. Consider what a 91% marginal tax rate means: you would get to keep only nine cents from an additional dollar's worth of income. That certainly diminishes incentives for work effort and production! And that is the world in which JFK gave his speech. Most people would agree that 91% marginal tax rates stifle economic growth. So, although it may seem counterintuitive, it is possible to lower tax rates and increase overall tax revenue.

In contrast, at low initial tax rates an increase in the tax rate leads to an increase in tax revenue. For example, there was no income tax in the United States in 1912. As we saw in Chapter 15, the United States instituted the income tax in 1913 with a top marginal rate of just 6%. Of course, income tax revenue rose between 1912, when there was no income tax, and 1913, when a modest tax was introduced. At low tax rates, increases lead to revenue increases.

JFK: Early supply-sider?

## The Laffer Curve

Let's clarify the relationship between tax rates and tax revenue. Total income tax revenue depends on the level of income and the tax rate:

$$\text{income tax revenue} = \text{tax rate} \times \text{income}$$

(Equation 16.3)

**Incentives**

The **Laffer curve** is an illustration of the relationship between tax rates and tax revenue.

This equation is straightforward. But because human beings react to incentives, it is not always easy to predict how tax revenue will change when tax rates change. The **Laffer curve**, named after economist Arthur Laffer and shown in Figure 16.9, illustrates the relationship between tax rates and tax revenue. Notice that we have labeled two regions of the Laffer curve. Region I, in blue, illustrates that increasing tax rates leads to increasing tax revenues:

$$\uparrow\text{income tax revenue} = \uparrow\text{tax rate} \times \text{income}$$

But at some point, tax rates become so high that they provide significant disincentives for earning income. This is the case in Region II, shown in orange, where decreases in the tax rate lead to more tax revenue. The United States was in Region II in 1962, when some marginal tax rates were above 90% and President Kennedy gave his speech. At this point, an increase in the tax rate reduces income enough so that net tax revenue falls (illustrated below by the double downward-pointing arrows):

$$\downarrow\text{income tax revenue} = \uparrow\text{tax rate} \times \downarrow\downarrow\text{income}$$

In Region II of the Laffer curve, decreases in tax rates lead to increases in tax revenue. At the lower rate, people have greater incentives to work and earn more income. Thus, the lower tax rates stimulate the economy and lead to more tax revenue overall.

At some specific tax rate, tax revenue is maximized. In Figure 16.9, this rate is labeled $t^*$. Economists don't know exactly what this amount is. But there is evidence from the United States that $t^*$ is below 70%. The evidence comes from the 1980s. Recall from Chapter 15 that in 1980 marginal tax rates on the wealthiest Americans were 70%. But in the 1980s, marginal rates fell across all income brackets. This was a very highly controversial political issue at the time. We now have the advantage of hindsight to determine what happened to tax revenue during the 1980s.

Considering all U.S. taxpayers, average tax revenue (adjusted for both inflation and the number of returns) went from $6,954 to $6,202 between 1980 and

## FIGURE 16.9

**The Laffer Curve**

In Region I of the Laffer curve, where tax rates are relatively low, increases in tax rates lead to increases in tax revenue. In Region II, where tax rates are relatively high, increases in tax rates decrease tax revenue. Economists disagree over the size of $t^*$, the tax rate that separates the regions.

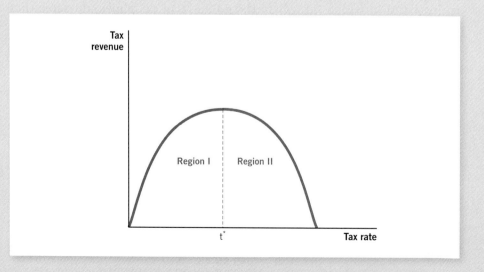

| TABLE 16.3 |

| TABLE 16.3 | | | |
|---|---|---|---|
| **U.S. Income Tax Revenue for Different Income Levels, 1980 and 1991** | | | |
| | Income tax revenue per return (2009 dollars) | | |
| | All taxpayers | Bottom 50% | Top 1% |
| 1980 | $6,954 | $1,005 | $131,307 |
| 1991 | $6,202 | $692 | $153,675 |

1991. Many analysts point to these figures and designate them as proof that the Laffer curve doesn't exist, or even that supply-side economics lacks merit.

But remember the two distinct regions of the Laffer curve. A careful look at the data shows that the rate reductions led to less tax revenue both overall and for those who were paying relatively low taxes in 1980. But, for the wealthiest Americans, a rate reduction did lead to an increase in revenue. Table 16.3 shows data for U.S. taxpayers for both 1980 and 1991. Rate reductions led to greater revenue only for the top taxpayers. Overall, revenues declined when we adjust for both inflation and population.

The point to be taken from Table 16.3 is that data from the 1980s confirms there really are two regions on the Laffer curve. Generally, conservative public figures tend to stress Region II, where tax rate reductions lead to increased revenue. Liberals emphasize Region I, where rate increases lead to more revenue. Both regions are important for economic policy.

# Conclusion

We began the chapter with the misconception that government spending is a tool for fighting recessions—in other words, that government policy can quickly and predictably counteract business-cycle fluctuations. It is certainly true that reductions in private demand accompany economic downturns. It is also true that government is able to use fiscal policy to increase expenditures or stimulate private spending through tax reductions. But the complete effects are difficult to predict. Recent experiences confirm this difficulty.

Looking ahead, we turn our attention next to monetary policy. In Chapter 17, we cover money and the Federal Reserve; in Chapter 18, we discuss how monetary policy affects the economy.

## ANSWERING THE BIG QUESTIONS

### What is fiscal policy?

* Fiscal policy is the use of government spending and taxes to affect the macroeconomy, generally through aggregate demand.

## Planning for Your Future Taxes

The U.S. national debt is currently over $16 trillion, or more than $50,000 per person. In 2007, the national debt per person was only $30,000. Thus, we can infer that the increase is directly attributable to the Great Recession and the fiscal policy undertaken during that period.

What does this mean for you? It means that your taxes are going to be higher in the future. All Americans will need to contribute to pay down this large national debt. So taxes in the future will surely be higher, and you should plan for this.

In addition, economic growth will likely be lower until the debt is paid down. We know that higher income taxes reduce incentives for production, so it is safe to say that economic growth will be lower until this debt is paid off and taxes can come down again.

However, you can take actions to lower your future tax bills. First, you probably ought to budget for higher taxes. This may mean saving more now than you would have saved otherwise. Second, in terms of personal investments, you might consider

Government spending on highway projects was part of fiscal policy legislated during the Great Recession.

buying securities that provide tax-free income. For example, the interest on municipal bonds (bonds issued by state and local governments) is not federally taxed. These simple steps might turn out to be significant when your future tax bills arrive.

---

* Countercyclical fiscal policy is designed to counteract business-cycle fluctuations by increasing aggregate demand during downturns and decreasing aggregate demand during expansionary periods.

### What are the shortcomings of fiscal policy?

* Fiscal policy is subject to three significant lags: a recognition lag, an implementation lag, and an impact lag.
* In addition, crowding-out can diminish the effects of fiscal policy.
* Finally, according to the new classical critique, savings adjustments by private individuals can further diminish the stimulating effects of fiscal policy.

### What is supply-side fiscal policy?

* The supply-side approach to fiscal policy focuses on how government spending and tax policy influence peoples' incentives to work and produce. This is a long-run view that concentrates on institutional changes.
* A key proposal of supply-side fiscal policy is that lower marginal income tax rates can actually lead to greater tax revenue when tax rates are currently at a high level.

## CONCEPTS YOU SHOULD KNOW

automatic stabilizers (p. 498)
contractionary fiscal
    policy (p. 491)
countercyclical fiscal
    policy (p. 492)
crowding-out (p. 499)

expansionary fiscal
    policy (p. 484)
Laffer curve (p. 506)
marginal propensity to
    consume (MPC) (p. 493)

new classical
    critique (p. 501)
spending multiplier (p. 494)
supply-side fiscal
    policy (p. 503)

## QUESTIONS FOR REVIEW

1. How are government budget balances affected by countercyclical fiscal policy? Be sure to describe the effects of both expansionary and contractionary fiscal policy.

2. Using the aggregate demand–aggregate supply model, one might argue that the economy will adjust on its own when aggregate demand drops. How does this adjustment work? Why might this adjustment take some time? (We discussed this in Chapter 14.)

3. Explain why the government budget deficit increases during a recession even without countercyclical fiscal policy.

4. Explain the difference among the three types of fiscal policy lags. What are automatic stabilizers? Which lags do automatic stabilizers affect?

5. In what circumstances would contractionary fiscal policy be recommended? How might you implement this type of policy? Why would you implement this policy—what are the reasons why it might make sense to slow the economy through government policy?

## STUDY PROBLEMS (✷ *solved at the end of the section*)

1. Explain the difference between typical demand-side fiscal policy and supply-side fiscal policy. For each of the following fiscal policy proposals, determine whether the primary focus is on aggregate demand or aggregate supply:
   a. a $1,000 per person tax reduction
   b. a 5% reduction in all tax rates
   c. Pell grants, which are government subsidies for college education
   d. government-sponsored prizes for new scientific discoveries
   e. an increase in unemployment compensation

2. To explore crowding-out, let's set up a simple loanable funds market in initial equilibrium.

   a. Draw a graph showing initial equilibrium in the loanable funds market at $800 million and an interest rate of 4%. Label your initial supply and demand curves as $S_1$ and $D_1$.
   b. Now assume that the government increases spending by $100 million that is entirely deficit-financed. Show the new equilibrium in the loanable funds market. (Note: there is a range of possible numerical answers for this question. You should choose one number and then be sure the rest of your answer is consistent with this number.)

c. Write the new equilibrium interest rate and quantity of loanable funds in the blanks below:
New interest rate: _____
New quantity of loanable funds: _____

d. If we assume there was no government debt prior to the fiscal stimulus, determine the new quantities for the blanks below:
Savings: _____
Investment: _____
Government spending: _____

e. How much did private consumption change as a result of the change in the quantity of savings?

3. The new classical critique of activist fiscal policy is theoretically different from the crowding-out critique. Explain the difference by using a graph of the loanable funds market.

✳ 4. Fill in the blanks in the table below. Assume that the MPC is constant over everyone in the economy.

| MPC | Spending multiplier | Change in government spending | Change in income |
|------|------|------|------|
| _____ | 5 | $100 | _____ |
| _____ | 2.5 | _____ | −$250 |
| 0.5 | _____ | $200 | _____ |
| 0.2 | _____ | _____ | $1,000 |

# SOLVED PROBLEM

4.

| MPC | Spending multiplier | Change in government spending | Change in income |
|-----|---------------------|-------------------------------|------------------|
| _0.8_ | 5 | $100 | _$500_ |
| _0.6_ | 2.5 | _−$100_ | −$250 |
| 0.5 | _2_ | $200 | _$400_ |
| 0.2 | _1.25_ | _$800_ | $1,000 |

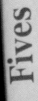

# Monetary POLICY

PART

5

**It's easy to control the amount of money in an economy.**

Most people believe that controlling the amount of money in the economy is a simple task. After all, there is a fixed number of "green

**MIS CONCEPTION**

pieces of paper" floating around the economy, and only the government has the authority to print more. But the job is actually very difficult. In fact, banks and private individuals influence the money supply with their daily private decisions. That's right: even *you* can make the money supply rise or fall.

We begin this chapter by looking closely at what defines money. It turns out that money is more than just currency and coins. Because banks also play an integral role in the money supply process, we will discuss how they operate and how their decisions affect the amount of money in the economy. Finally, we look at the role of the Federal Reserve System and examine how it oversees the amount of money in the economy. This background provides essential preparation for the discussion of monetary policy that comes in Chapter 18.

Money is more than just green paper!

# BIG QUESTIONS

* **What is money?**
* **How do banks create money?**
* **How does the Federal Reserve control the money supply?**

## What Is Money?

It probably seems strange to ask, "what is money?" After all, we use money all the time. Even children know we use money to buy goods and services. But what is included in this? Certainly, the green pieces of paper we call *currency* are included. **Currency** is the paper bills and coins that are used to buy goods and services. But people also make many purchases without using currency.

The quantity of money in an economy affects the ease with which individuals and firms can make purchases. It also affects the price level. For these reasons, we need to understand what constitutes money. In this section, we define the functions of money and then explain how the quantity of money is measured.

**Currency**
is the paper bills and coins that are used to buy goods and services.

## Three Functions of Money

Money has three functions: as a medium of exchange, as a unit of account, and as a store of value. Let's look at each function in turn.

### A Medium of Exchange

If you want to buy groceries, you offer money in exchange for them; if you work, you accept money as payment for your services. Money is a common **medium of exchange**—that is, it is what people trade for goods and services.

Modern economies generally have a government-provided medium of exchange. In the United States, the government provides our dollar currency. But even in economies without government provision, a preferred medium of exchange usually emerges. For example, in colonial Virginia, before there was any government mandate regarding money, tobacco became the accepted medium of exchange. Economist Milton Friedman wrote this about tobacco's use: "It was the money that the colonists used to buy food, clothing, to pay taxes—even to pay for a bride."

Invariably, some medium of exchange evolves in any economy; the primary reason is the inefficiency of money's alternative: *barter*. **Barter** involves individuals trading some good or service they already have for something else that they want; there is no commonly accepted medium of exchange. If you want food in a barter economy, you must find a grocer who also happens to want whatever you have to trade. Maybe you can only offer your labor services, but the grocer wants a cash register. In that case, you have to

**A medium of exchange** is what people trade for goods and services.

**Barter**
involves the trade of a good or service without a commonly accepted medium of exchange.

try to find someone who has a cash register and also wants to trade it for your labor. This takes more than a coincidence; it takes a double coincidence. Barter requires a **double coincidence of wants**, in which each party in an exchange transaction happens to have what the other party desires. A double coincidence is pretty unusual, and this is why a medium of exchange naturally evolves in any exchange environment.

Without money, what would you trade for this coffee and bagel?

Historically, the first medium of exchange in an economy has been a commodity that is actually traded for goods and services. **Commodity money** involves the use of an actual good in place of money. In this situation, the good itself has value apart from its function as money. Examples include gold, silver, and the tobacco of colonial Virginia. But commodities are often difficult to carry around when the holder needs to make purchases. Thus, due to transportation costs, money evolved into certificates that represented a fixed quantity of the commodity. These certificates became the medium of exchange but were still tied to the commodity, since they could be traded for the actual commodity if the holder demanded it.

**Commodity-backed money** is money that can be exchanged for a commodity at a fixed rate. For example, until 1971, U.S. dollars were fixed in value to specific quantities of silver and gold. When seen in a picture, a one-dollar U.S. silver certificate looks much like dollar bills in circulation today, but the print along the bottom of the note reads, "one dollar in silver payable to the bearer on demand." Until 1964, we also had actual commodity coins in the United States. U.S. quarters from 1964 look like the same quarters we use today, but unlike today's they are made of real silver.

While commodity money and commodity-backed money evolve privately in all economies, the type of money used in most modern economies depends on government. In particular, most modern economies make use of *fiat money* for their medium of exchange. **Fiat money** is money that has no value except as the medium of exchange; there is no inherent or intrinsic value to the currency. In the United States, our currency is physically just pieces of green paper. This paper has value because the government has mandated that we can use the currency to pay our debts. On U.S. dollar bills, you can read the statement "This note is legal tender for all debts, public and private."

There are advantages and disadvantages to fiat and commodity monies. On the one hand, commodity-backed money ties the value of the holder's money to something real. If the government is obligated to trade silver for

A **double coincidence of wants** occurs when each party in an exchange transaction happens to have what the other party desires.

**Commodity money** involves the use of an actual good in place of money.

**Commodity-backed money** is money that can be exchanged for a commodity at a fixed rate.

**Fiat money** is money that has no value except as the medium of exchange; there is no inherent or intrinsic value to the currency.

The money pictured here looks much like our modern money, but the dollar bill is a commodity-backed silver certificate from 1957. At that time, it could be traded for a dollar's worth of actual silver. The quarter from 1964 is made of real silver.

every dollar in circulation, this certainly limits the number of dollars it can print, which probably limits inflation levels. Fiat money offers no such constraint on the expansion of the money supply. Rapid monetary expansion and then inflation often occur without a commodity standard that ties the value of money to something real.

On the other hand, tying the value of a nation's currency to a commodity is dangerous when the market value of that commodity fluctuates. Imagine how a new discovery of gold affects prices in a nation with gold-backed currency. An increased supply of gold reduces gold prices, and therefore more gold is required in exchange for all other goods and services. This situation constitutes inflation: the price of everything in terms of the money (gold) rises. And this is exactly what occurred in Europe as Spanish conquistadors brought back tons of gold from Central and South America between the mid-fifteenth and the mid-seventeenth centuries. Because a change in the value of a medium of exchange affects the prices of all goods and services in the macroeconomy, it can be risky to tie a currency to a commodity.

## A Unit of Account

A **unit of account** is the measure in which prices are quoted.

Money also serves as a *unit of account*. A **unit of account** is the measure in which prices are quoted. Money enables you and someone you don't know to speak a common language. For example, when the cashier says that the mangoes you want to buy cost 99 cents each, she is communicating the value of mangoes in a way you understand. Consider a world without an accepted unit of account. In that world, goods would be priced in multiple ways. Theoretically, this means you might go shopping and find goods priced in terms of any possible currency or even other goods. Imagine how difficult it would be to shop! Using money as a unit of account is so helpful that a standard unit of account generally evolves, even in small economies.

Thank goodness each of these fruits is priced in a common unit of account.

Expressing the value of something in terms of dollars and cents also enables people to make accurate comparisons between items. Thus, money also serves as a measuring stick and recording device. Think of your checkbook for a moment. You don't write down in the ledger that you bought a bagel and coffee; instead, you write down that you spent $4. You tally the debits and credits to keep track of your account and to record transactions in a consistent manner.

## A Store of Value

A **store of value** is a means for holding wealth.

Money's third function is as a *store of value*. A **store of value** is a means for holding wealth. Traditionally, money served as an important store of value. Think of bags of gold coins from the Middle Ages. In both fiction and nonfiction stories, forbidden treasures or pirate's treasures are generally represented by gold; this precious metal was the vehicle for storing great values. But in modern economies, this function is much less important. Today, we have other options for holding our wealth, many of which offer greater returns than keeping dollar bills in a sock drawer or stuffed under a mattress. We can easily put our dollars into bank accounts or investment accounts that earn interest. These options have caused money's role as a store of value to decline.

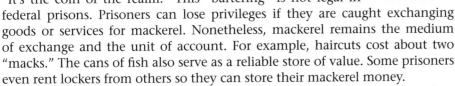

## ECONOMICS IN THE REAL WORLD

### The Evolution of Prison Money

In the past, cigarettes were often the preferred unit of account and medium of exchange in prisons. This commodity money was useful as currency in addition to its manufactured purpose. But in 2004 the U.S. government outlawed smoking in federal prisons, and this decision led to the development of a new medium of exchange.

The evolution of prison money.

In an October 2008 *Wall Street Journal* article, Justin Scheck reported on one federal facility where cans of mackerel had taken over as the accepted money. According to one prisoner, "It's the coin of the realm." This "bartering" is not legal in federal prisons. Prisoners can lose privileges if they are caught exchanging goods or services for mackerel. Nonetheless, mackerel remains the medium of exchange and the unit of account. For example, haircuts cost about two "macks." The cans of fish also serve as a reliable store of value. Some prisoners even rent lockers from others so they can store their mackerel money.

But while mackerel is popular, it is not the only commodity used as money in federal prisons. In some prisons, protein bars or cans of tuna serve as money. One reason why mackerel is preferred to other alternatives is that each can costs about one dollar—so it's a simple substitute for U.S. currency, which inmates are not allowed to carry. ✳

## Measuring the Quantity of Money

Now that we have defined the three functions of money, we need to consider how money is actually measured. As we saw in Chapter 8, the quantity of money in an economy affects the overall price level. In particular, a nation's inflation rate is dependent on the rate of growth of its quantity of money. In addition, in Chapter 18 we'll see that the quantity of money can influence real GDP and unemployment rates. Therefore, since money has such profound macroeconomic influences, it is important to measure it accurately. But doing so is not quite as simple as just adding up all the green pieces of paper in an economy.

To get a sense of the difficulties of measuring the money supply, think about all the different ways you make purchases. You might hold some currency for emergencies, to make a vending machine purchase, or to do laundry. On top of this, you might write a check to pay for your rent, school bill, or utilities bills. Moreover, you probably carry a debit card that enables you to automatically withdraw from

If you keep your money in your sock drawer, you incur an opportunity cost of foregone interest from a bank account.

your savings or checking accounts. To measure the quantity of money in an economy, we must somehow find the total value of all these alternatives that people like you use to buy goods and services. Clearly, currency alone is not enough—people buy things all the time without using currency. Currency is money, but it constitutes only a small part of the total money supply.

**Checkable deposits**
are deposits in bank accounts from which depositors may make withdrawals by writing checks.

**M1**
is the money supply measure that is essentially composed of currency and checkable deposits.

**M2**
is the money supply measure that includes everything in M1 plus savings deposits, money market mutual funds, and small-denomination time deposits (CDs).

(Equation 17.1)

## M1 and M2

As we broaden our definition of money beyond currency, we first acknowledge bank deposits for which checks can be written. **Checkable deposits** are deposits in bank accounts from which depositors may make withdrawals by writing checks. These deposits represent purchasing power that is very similar to currency, since personal checks are accepted at many places. Adding checkable deposits to currency essentially gives us a money supply measure known as *M1*. **M1** is the money supply measure that is composed of currency and checkable deposits. M1 also includes traveler's checks, but these account for a very small portion of M1.

A broader measure of the money supply, **M2**, includes everything in M1 plus savings deposits. M2 also includes two other types of deposits: money market mutual funds and small-denomination time deposits (certificates of deposit). The key point to remember is that the money supply in an economy includes both currency and bank deposits:

$$\text{money supply (M)} = \text{currency} + \text{deposits}$$

Equation 17.1 is an approximation of the general money supply. Actual data for both M1 and M2 is regularly published by the Federal Reserve. Figure 17.1 shows the components of M1 and M2 as of July 2012. Notice that currency in

## FIGURE 17.1

**Measures of the U.S. Money Supply, 2012**

M1 and M2 are the most common measures of the money supply. M1 includes currency and checking deposits. M2 includes everything in M1 plus savings deposits, small time deposits, and money market mutual funds.

*Source*: Federal Reserve, Money Stock Measures.

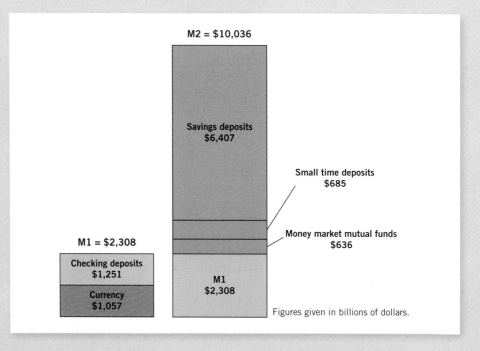

the United States is about $1 trillion. Adding checkable deposits of another $1 trillion yields M1 of about $2 trillion. But M2 was above $10 trillion in 2012, over $6 trillion of which was held in savings accounts. It will be important to remember that the money supply includes both currency and bank deposits when we discuss monetary policy in the next chapter.

Note that credit cards are not part of the money supply. Purchases made with credit cards involve a loan extended right at the cash register. When the loan is made, a third party is paying for the purchase until the loan is repaid. Therefore, since credit card purchases involve the use of borrowed funds, credit cards are not included as part of the money supply.

Until the 1970s, M1 was the most closely monitored money supply measure because it was a reliable estimate of the medium of exchange. But the introduction of automated teller machines basically rendered M1 obsolete as a reliable money supply measure. Prior to the arrival of the ATM, holding balances in checking accounts was very different from holding funds in savings accounts. Funds held in checking accounts could be accessed easily by writing checks. However, funds in savings accounts required the holder to visit the bank during business hours, wait in line, and fill out a withdrawal slip. Today, because of ATMs, depositors can make withdrawals at any time and at many locations. Since both checking and savings are now readily available for purchasing goods and services, M2—which includes both types of deposits—is now a better measure of our economy's medium of exchange.

The invention of the ATM marked the beginning of the end for M1 as a reliable money supply measure.

## PRACTICE WHAT YOU KNOW

### The Definition of Money

People on the street sometimes use the word "money" in ways that are inconsistent with the definition given in this chapter.

**Question: Are each of the following statements consistent with our definition of money? Explain your answer each time.**

Is this M1 or M2? Yes.

a. "He had a lot of money in his wallet."

b. "She made a lot of money last year."

c. "I use my Visa card for money."

d. "She has most of her money in the bank."

Answers:

a. This statement is *consistent* with our definition, since currency is part of the medium of exchange.

*(CONTINUED)*

*(CONTINUED)*

**b.** This statement is *inconsistent* with the definition. It refers to income, not to money.

**c.** This statement is *inconsistent*. Payment with a credit card requires a loan, so it is technically not counted in the money supply.

**d.** This statement is *consistent*, since bank deposits also count as money because they represent part of our medium of exchange.

# How Do Banks Create Money?

We now have a working definition of money: money includes both currency and deposits at banks. And while private individuals and firms in the economy are not permitted to print currency, private actions absolutely influence the total supply of money in the economy, since individuals and banks affect deposits. In this section, we explain how banks create money simply as a byproduct of their daily business activity. Note that when we refer to "banks," we are explicitly talking about commercial banks, which take in deposits and extend loans. We distinguish these from investment banks, which serve a different role.

We begin by looking closely at the daily activities at typical banks. After that, we can consider how they influence the money supply.

## The Business of Banking

Banks serve two very important roles in our study of the macroeconomy. First, they are critical participants in the market for loanable funds. As we saw in Chapter 10, they provide a way for savers to supply their funds to borrowers without purchasing a financial security. In addition, they play a role in the money supply process.

To understand how banks create money, let's look at the functions of a bank, illustrated in Figure 17.2. Banks are middlemen in the market for loans. They are financial intermediaries; that is, they take in deposits and extend loans. Deposits are the primary source of funds, and loans are the primary

**FIGURE 17.2**

**The Business of Banking: Financial Intermediation**

The primary function of commercial banks is financial intermediation: they accept deposits and extend loans.

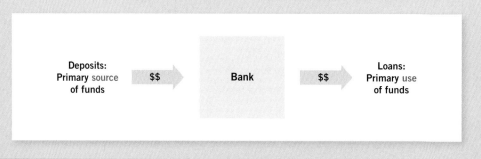

use of funds for banks. Banks can be profitable if they charge a higher interest rate on the loans they make than the interest rate they pay out on deposits.

Figure 17.3 illustrates the gap between interest rates on bank deposits and bank loans for U.S. banks for the period 1985–2011. The two rates go up and down together, but the interest rate on deposits is consistently lower than the interest rate on loans. The difference between the two interest rates pays for a bank's operating costs and produces profits.

## The Bank's Balance Sheet

Information about a bank's financial operations is available in the bank's *balance sheet*. A **balance sheet** is an accounting statement that summarizes a firm's key financial information. Figure 17.4 shows a hypothetical balance sheet for University Bank. The left side of the balance sheet details the bank's **assets**, which are the items the firm owns. Assets indicate how the banking firm uses the funds it has raised from various sources. The right side of the balance sheet details the bank's *liabilities* and *owner's equity*. **Liabilities** are the financial obligations the firm owes to others. **Owner's equity** is the difference between the firm's assets and its liabilities. When a firm has more assets than liabilities, it has positive owner's equity. Overall, the right side of the balance sheet identifies the bank's sources of funds.

As you can see, University Bank has extended $400 million in loans. Many of these loans went to firms to fund investment, but some also went to households to purchase homes, cars, and other consumer items. A second important asset held by banks is *reserves*. **Reserves** are the portion of bank deposits that are set aside and not lent out. Reserves include both currency in the bank's vault and funds that the bank holds in deposit at its own bank, the Federal Reserve. Banks also hold U.S. Treasury securities and other

A **balance sheet** is an accounting statement that summarizes a firm's key financial information.

**Assets**
are the items that a firm owns.

**Liabilities**
are the financial obligations a firm owes to others.

**Owner's equity**
is the difference between a firm's assets and its liabilities.

**Reserves**
are the portion of bank deposits that are set aside and not lent out.

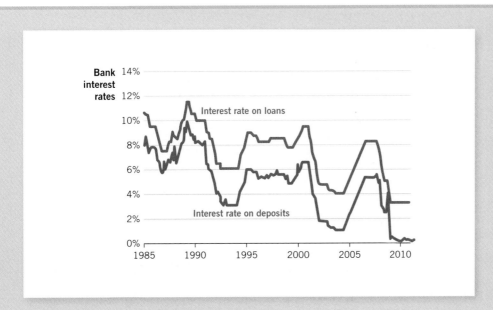

## FIGURE 17.3

**Interest Rates on Bank Deposits versus Loans, 1985–2011**

Banks charge more interest for loans than they pay for deposits. The difference helps to pay the banks' expenses and produces profits.

*Source*: FRED data, Federal Reserve Bank of St. Louis. The loan interest rate is the average prime interest rate across the United States; the deposit interest rate is the interest rate on one-month certificates of deposit.

government securities as substantial assets in their portfolio. These securities earn interest and carry very low risk. Finally, banks hold other assets, such as physical buildings and furniture.

Banks fund their activities primarily by taking in deposits. In fact, the deposits of typical households are the lifeblood of banks. But banks also borrow from other commercial banks and from the Federal Reserve. The third item on the right side of the balance sheet shown in Figure 17.4 is net worth, or the owner's equity in the banking firm. Since the University Bank owns $800 million in total assets but owes only $700 million in liabilities ($500 million in deposits plus $200 million in borrowings), the owners of the bank have $100 million in equity.

In the next section, we look more closely at bank reserves, which play an important role in money creation.

## Bank Reserves

**Fractional reserve banking** occurs when banks hold only a fraction of deposits on reserve.

Our modern system of banking is called *fractional reserve banking*. **Fractional reserve banking** occurs when banks hold only a fraction of deposits on reserve. The alternative is 100% reserve banking. Banks in a 100% reserve system don't loan out deposits; these banks are essentially just safes, keeping deposits on hand until depositors decide to make a withdrawal.

Figure 17.5 illustrates the process of fractional reserve banking. Deposits come into the banks, and the banks send out a portion of these funds in loans. In recent years, U.S. banks have typically loaned out almost 90% of their deposits, keeping barely over 10% on reserve. Banks loan out most of their deposits because reserves earn very little interest; every dollar kept on reserve costs the bank potential income. In 2012 bank reserves paid just 0.25% interest.

Let's say a local business approaches a bank for a loan to expand its factory. Assume that the bank has reserves available to be lent out and that the

## FIGURE 17.4

**Balance Sheet for University Bank**

A bank's balance sheet summarizes its key financial information. The bank's assets are recorded on the left side; this shows how the bank chooses to use its funds. The sources of the firm's funds are recorded on the right side; these are both liabilities and owner's equity. The two sides of the balance sheet must match in order for the financial statement to be balanced.

| Assets: Uses of funds (in millions) | | Liabilities and owner's equity: Sources of funds (in millions) | |
|---|---|---|---|
| Loans | $400 | Deposits | $500 |
| Reserves | $60 | Borrowings | $200 |
| U.S. Treasury securities | $140 | Owner's equity | $100 |
| Other assets | $200 | | |
| Total assets | $800 | Total liabilities and net worth | $800 |

current interest rate on these commercial loans is 5%, which the firm is willing to pay. The alternative is to keep the funds on reserve, earning just 0.25% interest. If the bank rejects the firm's loan application and decides to keep the funds in its vault as reserve, the cost of this decision to the bank is the difference between these two interest rates: $5\% - 0.25\% = 4.75\%$.

Banks hold reserves for two reasons. First, they must accommodate withdrawals by their depositors. You'd be pretty unhappy if you tried to make a withdrawal from your bank and it didn't have enough on reserve to honor your request. If word spread that a bank might have difficulty meeting its depositors' withdrawal requests, that news would probably lead to a *bank run*. A **bank run** occurs when many depositors attempt to withdraw their funds at the same time.

A **bank run** occurs when many depositors attempt to withdraw their funds at the same time.

Second, banks are legally bound to hold a fraction of their deposits on reserve. The **required reserve ratio (rr)** is the portion of deposits that banks are required to keep on reserve. For a given bank, the dollar amount of reserves that it is required to hold is determined by multiplying the required reserve ratio by the bank's total amount of deposits:

The **required reserve ratio (rr)** is the portion of deposits that banks are required to keep on reserve.

$$\text{required reserves} = \text{rr} \times \text{deposits}$$

(Equation 17.2)

Currently, the required reserve ratio is 10% for almost all deposits (rr = 0.10). This means that your bank can legally lend out up to 90 cents of every dollar you deposit.

Consider University Bank, whose balance sheet was presented in Figure 17.4. The bank currently has $500 million in deposits. University Bank pays some interest on the deposits and offers services, such as checking, to its depositors. University Bank can't afford to keep the $500 million sitting in the vault—the opportunity cost is too high. If the bank is going to stay in business, it will need to loan out at least part of the $500 million. With a reserve requirement of 10% of deposits, required reserves in this case are $50 million, so University Bank can loan out up to $450 million.

Banks rarely keep their level of reserves exactly at the required level. Any reserves above the required level are called **excess reserves**:

**Excess reserves** are any reserves held in excess of those required.

$$\text{excess reserves} = \text{total reserves} - \text{required reserves}$$

(Equation 17.3)

## FIGURE 17.5

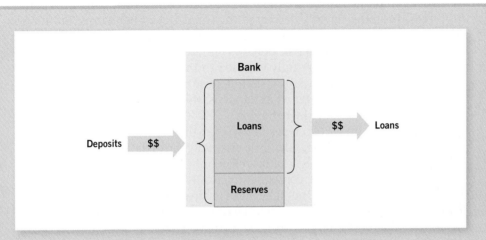

### Fractional Reserve Banking

In a fractional reserve banking system, banks lend out only a fraction of the deposits they take in. The remainder is set aside as reserves.

The balance sheet of University Bank, presented in Figure 17.5, indicates that the bank currently holds total reserves of $60 million. Therefore, it has $10 million in excess reserves. Given the opportunity cost of holding these excess reserves, University Bank will probably seek to loan out most of this balance in the future.

## The FDIC and Moral Hazard

Since a bank keeps only a fraction of its deposits on reserve, if all depositors try to withdraw their deposits at the same time, the bank will not be able to meet its obligation. But in a typical day, only a small number of deposits are withdrawn. However, if word spreads that a bank is unstable and may not be able to meet the demands of depositors—whether true or not—depositors will rush to withdraw their funds, which will lead to a bank run. No bank can survive a bank run.

During the Great Depression, bank failures became common. From 1929 to 1933, over 9,000 banks failed in the United States alone—more than in any other period in U.S. history. It is clear that many banks were extending loans beyond their ability to collect and pay depositors in a timely manner. As a result, many depositors lost confidence in the banking system. If you became worried about your bank and were not certain that you could withdraw your deposits at some later point, wouldn't you run to the bank to get your money out?

This is precisely what happened to many banks during the Great Depression. The Hollywood film classic *It's a Wonderful Life* (1946) captures this situation perfectly. In the movie, the character George Bailey is set to leave on his honeymoon when the financial intermediary he runs is subject to a run. When a depositor asks for his money back, George tells him, "The, the money's not here. Well, your money's in Joe's house, that's right next to yours. And in the Kennedy house, and Mrs. Macklin's house, and, and a hundred others." This quote summarizes both the beauty and the danger wrapped up in a fractional reserve banking system. Fractional reserve banking allows access to funds by many individuals and firms in an economy, but it can also lead to instability when many depositors demand their funds simultaneously.

**Moral hazard**
occurs when a party that is protected from risk behaves differently from the way it would behave if it were fully exposed to the risk.

After the massive rate of bank failures from 1929 to 1933, the U.S. government instituted federal deposit insurance in 1933 through the Federal Deposit Insurance Corporation (FDIC). Deposit insurance now guarantees that depositors will get their deposits back (up to $250,000) even if their bank goes bankrupt. FDIC insurance greatly decreased the frequency of bank runs. But it also created a *moral hazard* situation. **Moral hazard** occurs when a party that is protected from risk behaves differently from the way it would behave if it were fully exposed to the risk. FDIC insurance means that neither banks nor their depositors have an incentive to monitor risk; no matter what happens, they are protected from the consequences of risky behavior.

Consider two types of banks in this environment. Type A banks are conservative, take little risk, and earn relatively low returns on their loans. Type A banks make only very safe loans with very little default risk and, consequently, relatively low rates of return. Type A banks rarely fail, but they make relatively low profit and pay relatively low interest rates to their depositors. In contrast, Type B banks take huge risks, hoping to make extremely large returns on their loans. Type B loans carry greater default risk but also pay higher returns.

To end the bank run, George Bailey offered depositors money from his own wallet.

Type B banks often fail, but the lucky ones—the ones that survive—earn very handsome profits and pay high interest rates on their customers' deposits.

Moral hazard draws individual depositors and bankers to type B banking. There is a tremendous upside and no significant downside, since depositors are protected against losses by FDIC insurance. This is the environment in which our modern banks operate, which is why many analysts argue that reserve requirements and other regulations are necessary to help ensure stability in the financial industry. The case is all the more important when we realize that recessions often start in the financial industry.

## ECONOMICS IN THE REAL WORLD

### Twenty-First-Century Bank Run

For a modern example of a bank run, consider England's Northern Rock Bank, which experienced a bank run in 2007—the first British bank run in over a century. Northern Rock (which is now owned by Virgin Money) earned revenue valued over $10 billion per year. But extensive losses stemming from investments in mortgage markets led it to near collapse in 2007.

In September of that year, depositors began queuing outside Northern Rock locations because they feared they would not get their deposits back. Eventually, the British government offered deposit insurance of 100% to Northern Rock depositors—but not before much damage had been done. In February 2008, Northern Rock was taken over by the British government because it was unable to repay its debts or find a buyer. To make matters worse, there is some evidence that Northern Rock was solvent at the time of the bank run, meaning that stronger deposit insurance could have saved the bank.

In the United States, over 300 banks failed between 2008 and 2011 without experiencing a bank run. The difference is a reflection of the level of deposit insurance offered in the two nations. In England, depositors are insured for 100% of their deposits up to a value of $4,000, then for only 90% of their next $70,000. So British depositors get back a fraction of their deposits up to about $74,000. In contrast, FDIC insurance in the United States offers 100% insurance on the first $250,000. ✳

Depositors queue outside a Northern Rock Bank location in September 2007.

## How Banks Create Money

We have seen that banks function as financial intermediaries. But as a byproduct of their everyday activity, they also create new money. Modern U.S. banks don't mint currency, but they do create new deposits, and deposits are a part of the money supply.

Money deposited in the banking system leads to more money. To see how, let's start with a hypothetical example that involves the Federal Reserve, which supplies the currency in the United States. Let's say that the Federal Reserve decides to increase the money supply in the United States. It prints a single $1,000 bill and drops it out of a helicopter. Perhaps you are the lucky person who finds this brand-new $1,000 bill. If you keep the $1,000 in your wallet, then the money supply increases by only this amount. But if you deposit the new money in a bank, then the bank can use it to create even more.

Let's walk through how this works. Consider what happens if you deposit the $1,000 into a savings or checking account at University Bank. When you deposit the $1,000, it is still part of the money supply, since both currency and bank deposits are counted in the money supply. You don't have the currency anymore, but in your wallet you have a debit card that enables you to access the $1,000 to make purchases. Therefore, the deposit still represents $1,000 worth of the medium of exchange.

But University Bank doesn't keep your $1,000 in reserve; it uses part of your deposit to extend a new loan that earns interest income for the bank. You still have the $1,000 in your account (as a deposit), but someone else receives money from the bank in the form of a loan. Thus, University Bank creates new money by loaning out part of your deposit. What's more, you helped the bank in the money-creation process because you put your funds into the bank in the first place.

This is just the first step in the money-creation process. We'll now explore this in more detail, utilizing your bank's balance sheet. For this example, we need to make two assumptions to help understand the general picture:

Assumption 1: All currency is deposited in a bank.

Assumption 2: Banks hold no excess reserves.

Neither of these assumptions is completely realistic. But let's work through the example under these conditions, and later we can consider the effect of each assumption.

Consider first how your deposit changes the assets and liabilities of University Bank. The t-account (an abbreviated version of a firm's balance sheet) below summarizes all initial changes to the balance sheet of University Bank when you deposit your new $1,000 (Assumption 1):

### University Bank

| Assets | | Liabilities and net worth | |
|---|---|---|---|
| Reserves | +$1,000 | Deposits | +$1,000 |

With a required reserve ratio of 10% (rr = 0.10), University Bank loans out $900 of your deposit (Assumption 2 implies that only 10% of deposits are held on reserve). Perhaps the bank loans this amount to a student named

Alexis, so she can pay her tuition bill. When University Bank extends the loan to Alexis, the money supply increases by $900. That is, you still have your $1,000 deposit, and Alexis now has $900.

Including your initial deposit and this $900 loan, the balance sheet changes at University Bank are summarized in this t-account:

**University Bank**

| Assets | | Liabilities and net worth | |
|---|---|---|---|
| Reserves | +$100 | Deposits | +$1,000 |
| Loans | +$900 | | |

Alexis gives her college the $900, and the college then deposits this amount into its own bank, named Township Bank. But the money multiplication process does not end here. Township Bank also keeps no excess reserves, so it loans out 90% of the $900, which is $810. This move creates $810 more in money supply, so that total new money is now $1,000 + $900 + $810 = $1,710. The balance sheet changes at Township Bank are then:

**Township Bank**

| Assets | | Liabilities and net worth | |
|---|---|---|---|
| Reserves | +$90 | Deposits | +$900 |
| Loans | +$810 | | |

You can now see that whenever banks make loans, they create new money. As long as dollars find their way back into the banking system, banks multiply them into more deposits—which means more money. Table 17.1 summarizes this process of money creation. The initial $1,000 bill ultimately leads to $10,000 worth of money. When monetary funds are deposited into banks, banks can multiply these deposits; and when they do, they create money.

## TABLE 17.1

### Money Creation

| | Round | Deposit | |
|---|---|---|---|
| **Assumption 1:** All currency is deposited in banks. | | | |
| **Assumption 2:** Banks hold no excess reserves. | 1 | $1,000 | ← Initial deposit |
| Required reserve ratio (rr) = 10% | 2 | $900 | |
| Initial new money supply = $1,000 | 3 | $810 | |
| | 4 | $729 | |
| | • | • | |
| | • | • | |
| | • | • | |
| | Sum | $10,000 | ← Total money |

The **simple money multiplier** (m^m) is the rate at which banks multiply money when all currency is deposited into banks and they hold no excess reserves.

In the end, the impact on the money supply is a large multiple of the initial increase in money. The exact multiple depends on the required reserve ratio (rr). The rate at which banks multiply money when all currency is deposited into banks and they hold no excess reserves is called the **simple money multiplier**. The formula for the money multiplier is:

(Equation 17.4)

$$m^m = \frac{1}{rr}$$

In our example above, rr = 0.10, so the multiplier is 1/0.10, which is 10. When the money multiplier is 10, a new $1,000 bill produced by the Federal Reserve can eventually lead to $10,000 in new money.

Of course, in the real world our two assumptions don't always hold. There is a more realistic money multiplier that relaxes the two assumptions. Consider how a more real-world money multiplier would compare to the simple money multiplier. First, if people hold on to some currency (relaxing Assumption 1), banks cannot multiply that currency, so the more realistic multiplier is smaller than the simple money multiplier. Second, if banks hold excess reserves (relaxing Assumption 2), these dollars are not multiplied, and again the real multiplier is smaller than the simple version. So, in reality, money doesn't multiply at quite the rate represented by the simple money multiplier. The simple money multiplier represents the *maximum* size of the money multiplier.

Note that the money multiplier process also works in reverse. When funds are withdrawn from the banking system, these are funds that banks cannot multiply. In effect, the money supply contracts. The maximum contraction is a multiple of the withdrawal, in which the simple money multiplier determines the multiplier.

# How Does the Federal Reserve Control the Money Supply?

There's a good chance you've heard of the U.S. Federal Reserve (Fed), even outside economics class. Ben Bernanke, the chairman of the Fed's Board of Governors, is perhaps the most recognized economist in the world. And while we've referred to the Fed periodically throughout this text, now it's time to examine it closely.

## The Many Jobs of the Federal Reserve

The Fed was established in 1913 as the central bank of the United States. The Fed's primary responsibilities are threefold:

1. *Monetary policy*: The Fed controls the U.S. money supply and is charged with regulating it to offset macroeconomic fluctuations.
2. *Central banking*: The Fed serves as a bank for banks, holding their deposits and extending loans to them.
3. *Bank regulation*: The Fed is one of the primary entities charged with ensuring the financial stability of banks, including the determination of reserve requirements.

Ben Bernanke was appointed chairman of the Fed's Board of Governors in 2005.

# PRACTICE WHAT YOU KNOW

## Fractional Reserve Banking: The B-Money Bank

Use this balance sheet of the B-Money Bank to answer the questions below. Assume the required reserve ratio is 10%.

When banks extend loans, the money supply increases.

### B-Money Bank

| Assets | | Liabilities and net worth | |
|---|---|---|---|
| Reserves | $50,000 | Deposits | $200,000 |
| Loans | $120,000 | Net worth | $20,000 |
| Treasury securities | $50,000 | | |

Question: What are the required reserves of B-Money Bank?

Answer: B-Money is required to hold 10% of deposits, which is $20,000.

Question: What is the maximum new loan that B-Money can extend?

Answer: B-Money has $30,000 in excess reserves, so it can extend a total of that amount in new loans.

Question: How would you rewrite B-Money's balance sheet, assuming that this loan is made?

Answer: The only items that would change are Reserves, which would decline by $30,000, and Loans, which would increase by $30,000.

### B-Money Bank

| Assets | | Liabilities and net worth | |
|---|---|---|---|
| Reserves | $20,000 | Deposits | $200,000 |
| Loans | $150,000 | | |
| Treasury securities | $50,000 | Net worth | $20,000 |

Question: If the Federal Reserve bought all of B-Money's Treasury securities, how large a loan could B-Money now extend?

Answer: B-Money would now have $50,000 in excess reserves, so it could make a loan in this amount.

Question: What would be the maximum impact on the money supply from this Fed action?

Answer: Using the simple money multiplier, we can see that the money supply could grow by as much as $500,000 from this action alone:

$$\$50,000 \times m^m = \$50,000 \times \frac{1}{rr} = \$50,000 \times 10 = \$500,000$$

In this section, we'll talk about the Fed's role as central bank and bank regulator. We'll then look at monetary policy for the remainder of the chapter and into Chapter 18.

The term "central bank" means that the Fed is a "bank for banks." In its role as central bank, it offers support and stability to the nation's entire banking system. The first component of this role involves the deposits that banks hold at the Fed. **Federal funds** are deposits that private banks hold on reserve at the Fed. The word "federal" seems to denote that these are government funds, but in fact they are private funds held on deposit at a *federal* agency—the Fed. These deposits are part of the reserves that banks set aside, along with physical currency in their vaults.

**Federal funds** are deposits that private banks hold on reserve at the Federal Reserve.

Banks keep reserves at the Fed in part because the Fed clears loans between them and other banks. When banks loan reserves to other banks, these are federal funds loans. The federal funds loans are typically very short-term (often overnight), and they enable banks to make quick adjustments to their balance sheets. For example, if our theoretical University Bank somehow dips below its required reserve level, it can approach Township Bank for a short-term loan. If Township Bank happens to have excess reserves, making a short-term loan enables it to earn interest. The interest rate on such interbank loans is known as the **federal funds rate.**

The **federal funds rate** is the interest rate on loans between private banks.

Figure 17.6 illustrates how the relationship between the Federal Reserve and commercial banks is analogous to the relationship between these banks and households and firms. First, households and firms hold deposits at banks, and banks hold deposits at the Fed—these are the federal funds. Second, households and firms take out loans from banks, and banks take out loans from the Fed. The loans from the Fed to the private banks are known as **discount loans**.

**Discount loans** are loans from the Federal Reserve to private banks.

Discount loans are the vehicle by which the Fed performs its role as "lender of last resort." Given the macroeconomic danger of bank failure, the Fed serves an important role as a backup lender to private banks that find difficulty borrowing elsewhere. The **discount rate** is the interest rate on the discount loans made from the Fed to private banks. The Fed sets this interest rate since it is a loan directly from a branch of the U.S. government to private financial institutions.

The **discount rate** is the interest rate on the discount loans made by the Federal Reserve to private banks.

## FIGURE 17.6

**The Federal Reserve as a Central Bank**

Central banks operate as a bank for commercial banks. Commercial banks make deposits at the Federal Reserve; these deposits are called "federal funds." The Federal Reserve also extends loans to commercial banks; these loans are called "discount loans."

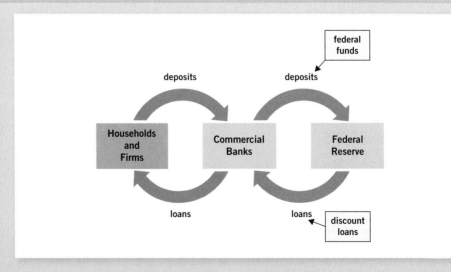

# Moral Hazard

## *Wall Street: Money Never Sleeps*

This 2010 film is a sequel to the original *Wall Street* movie from 1987. This film focuses on the historical events leading up to and during the financial crisis that began in 2007. One recurring theme in the movie is that some financial firms are "too big to fail." How can a firm be too big to fail?

If one bank fails, it is unable to repay its depositors and other creditors. This situation puts all the bank's creditors into similar financial difficulty. If the failing bank is large enough, its failure can set off a domino effect in which bank after bank after bank fails and the entire financial system collapses. If regulators deem a bank too big to fail, they will use government aid to keep the bank afloat.

However, this situation introduces a particularly strong case of moral hazard. After all, banks have incentives to take on risk so that they can earn high profits. If we eliminate the possibility of failure by providing government aid, there is almost no downside risk.

Gordon Gecko understands moral hazard.

In this movie, Gordon Gecko, played by Michael Douglas, defines moral hazard during a public lecture. His definition is this: "when they take your money and then are not responsible for what they do with it."

Gecko is right: when a financial institution is not required to bear the costs of making poor decisions, it is not responsible for mishandling its depositors' funds.

Discount loans don't often figure prominently in macroeconomics, but in extremely turbulent times they reassure financial market participants. For example, when banks were struggling in 2008, financial market participants were assured that troubled banks could rely on the Federal Reserve to fortify failing banks with discount loans. In fact, for the first time in history, other financial firms were allowed to borrow from the Fed. The Fed even extended an $85 billion loan to the insurance company American International Group because it had written insurance policies for financial securities.

AIG: the first (and last?) insurance company to get a discount loan from the Fed.

The Fed also serves as a regulator of individual banks. In this role, its responsibilities include the setting and monitoring of reserve requirements. The Fed monitors the balance sheets of banks with an eye toward limiting the riskiness of the assets the banks hold. One might ask why banks are subject to this kind of regulation. After all, the government doesn't monitor the riskiness of assets owned by other private firms. However, as we have seen, the interdependent nature of banking firms means that banking problems often spread throughout the entire industry very quickly. In addition, there is the moral hazard problem we discussed earlier in this chapter: because of deposit insurance, banks and their customers have reduced incentives to monitor the risk of bank assets.

## PRACTICE WHAT YOU KNOW

### Federal Reserve Terminology

Let's say the reserves at B-Money Bank fall below the required level, so it approaches University Bank for a loan. University Bank agrees to a short-term loan with B-Money bank.

**Question:** What is the name of the funds that private banks like University Bank loan to other private banks (like B-Money)? What is the interest rate on these loans called?

Loans from the Federal Reserve are not called "federal funds": they are called "discount loans."

**Answer:** The funds are called "federal funds." The word "federal" makes it sound as if the funds are a loan from the federal government, but this is not the case. This wording has been adopted because the loan typically takes place through changes in the two banks' accounts at their bank, the Federal Reserve. The interest rate is the federal funds rate.

Now assume that B-Money has made some particularly troublesome loans (perhaps a lot of high-risk mortgage loans) and that all private parties refuse to lend to B-Money. B-Money then approaches the Fed itself for a loan to keep its reserves at the appropriate level.

**Question:** What is the name of this type of loan? What is the name of the interest rate charged for this loan?

**Answer:** This is a discount loan, and the interest rate is the discount rate.

## Monetary Policy Tools

When the Fed wants to alter the supply of money in the economy, it has several tools at its disposal. In this section we discuss these policy tools, but our emphasis is on the single tool the Fed uses every day: *open market operations*.

### Open Market Operations

If the Fed decided to increase the money supply, it could do so in a number of direct ways. Below, we list three possible means by which the Fed might directly increase the amount of money in the economy; see if you can guess which of the three is correct:

1. Drop money out of a helicopter.
2. Distribute $50,000 in new $100 bills to every private bank.
3. Use new money to buy something in the economy.

If you chose option 3, you are correct. **Open market operations** involve the purchase or sale of bonds by a central bank. When the Fed wants to increase the money supply, it buys securities; in contrast, when it wishes to decrease the money supply, it sells securities. In Chapter 10, we introduced the U.S. Treasury security as a special bond asset. These are the securities (bonds) that the Fed typically buys and sells when implementing monetary policy.

Essentially, the Fed could realize its desired effects through buying other goods and services such as real estate, fine art, or coffee and bagels. It would be as if the Fed prints a batch of new currency and then goes shopping. When it is done shopping, it leaves behind all the new currency in the economy. Whatever it buys on its shopping spree becomes an asset on the Fed's balance sheet.

The Fed buys and sells Treasury securities for two reasons. First, the Fed's goal is to get the funds directly into the market for loanable funds. In this way, financial institutions begin lending the new money, and it quickly moves into the economy. Second, a typical day's worth of open market operations might entail as much as $20 billion worth of purchases from the Fed. If the Fed bought coffee and bagels, it would cause problems in that market. Imagine being the manager of a bagel shop in Washington, D.C., and having Ben Bernanke walk in with a request for $20 billion worth of bagels. That would be an impossible request! But the market for U.S. Treasuries is big enough to accommodate this level of purchases seamlessly. The daily volume in the U.S. Treasury market is over $500 billion, so the Fed can buy and sell without difficulty.

Figure 17.7 summarizes how open market operations work. In panel (a), we see that when the Fed purchases bonds it creates new money and trades this money with financial institutions for their Treasury bonds. The result is more money in the economy. On the other side, we see in panel (b) that when the Fed sells bonds to financial institutions it exchanges bonds for existing money, taking the money out of the economy. The result is less money in the economy.

**Open market operations**
involve the purchase or sale
of bonds by a central bank.

**FIGURE 17.7**

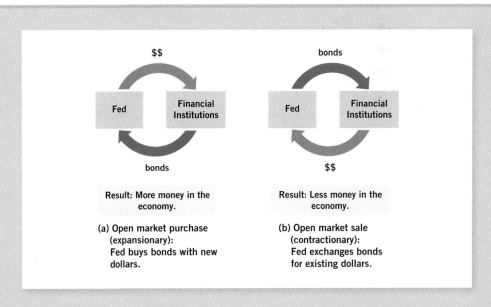

**Open Market Operations**

In open market purchases, the Fed buys bonds from financial institutions. This action injects new money directly into financial markets. In open market sales, the Fed sells bonds back to financial institutions. This action takes money out of financial markets.

The Fed undertakes open market operations every business day. Typically, it intends to keep market conditions exactly as they were the day before. But open market operations are also the primary tool that the Fed uses to expand or contract the money supply in order to affect the macroeconomy.

### Quantitative Easing

The end of 2008 marked the single worst quarter for the U.S. economy in over half a century. Real GDP declined by 8.9%, and the unemployment rate was ratcheting upward. In November 2008, hoping that more money would stimulate the economy, the Federal Reserve determined that it should take additional measures to increase the money supply. The method it chose is a new variety of open market operations known as *quantitative easing.*

**Quantitative easing**
is the targeted use of open market operations in which the central bank buys securities specifically targeted in certain markets.

**Quantitative easing** is the targeted use of open market operations in which the central bank buys securities specifically targeted in certain markets. Open market operations typically involve buying and selling short-term Treasury securities—that is, bonds that mature in less than one year. But with its quantitative easing in late 2008, the Fed expanded its purchases to include $300 billion in long-term Treasury securities. It also purchased $1.25 trillion in mortgage-backed securities, specifically targeting the housing market. Together with an additional $175 billion in purchases of securities from government-sponsored enterprises, this amounted to almost $2 trillion in new funds injected into the economy.

This move was bold and unprecedented in both size and scope. It amounted to the Fed printing trillions of new dollars and injecting them into targeted sectors of the economy. The first round of quantitative easing started in November 2008 and continued into the first quarter of 2010. At that point, the Fed was convinced that economic recovery was well under way. But conditions deteriorated over the second half of 2010, as the unemployment rate stayed around 9% and real GDP growth stalled.

Because of the lackluster U.S. economic performance in November 2010, the Fed decided to engage in a second round of quantitative easing, dubbed "QE 2." This round involved purchasing an additional $600 billion in long-term Treasury securities. Figure 17.8 illustrates the timeline for these quantitative easing programs along with the quarterly growth rates of real GDP. The Fed implemented these two rounds of quantitative easing when it was clear that traditional open market operations would not return the economy to stable growth rates.

In September 2011, as the economy continued to struggle toward consistent growth, Bernanke announced yet another variation of quantitative easing. In particular, the Fed would buy $400 billion in long-term Treasury securities and simultaneously sell $400 billion in short-term Treasury securities. This action became known as a "twist," since it was not really adding money to the economy but attempting to reduce long-term interest rates and thereby encourage business investment. However, the twist operation did not seem to have a significant effect on the economy, as lackluster growth continued through 2012. Thus, in September 2012 the Fed announced an ongoing program to buy $40 billion per month in mortgage-backed securities. This program, with no termination date, became known as QE 3.

When the Fed buys securities in a particular market, the action leads to lower interest rates in that market. Part of the reason why the quantitative easing programs were put into place was because the Fed had already pushed

## FIGURE 17.8

**Quantitative Easing, 2007–2012**

Beginning in 2008, the Federal Reserve began the unprecedented practice of quantitative easing (QE) to inject money into the economy. The QE initiatives were each implemented when traditional monetary policy seemed to be failing to push the economy back to consistent growth.

*Source*: GDP data is from the U.S. Bureau of Economic Analysis. QE data is from the Federal Reserve.

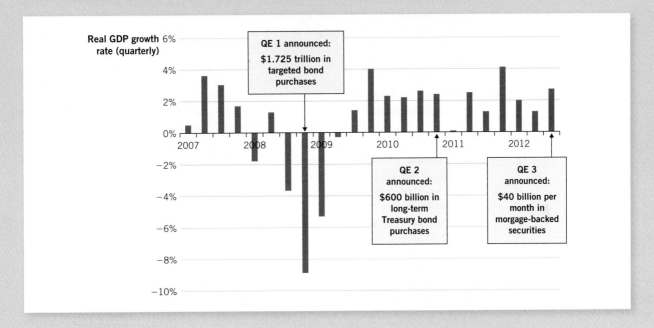

short-term interest rates down to zero. Thus, traditional open market operations had reached a boundary. In Chapter 18, we will look more closely at the Federal Reserve's influence on interest rates.

In summary, quantitative easing is a new variation of open market operations that was introduced during the slow recovery from the Great Recession. However, this new tool did not immediately return the U.S. economy to strong growth.

## Reserve Requirements and Discount Rates

In the past, the Fed made use of two other tools in its administration of monetary policy: reserve requirements and the discount rate. Neither of these has been used recently for monetary policy, but they are available and historically important.

Recall our two earlier observations regarding reserve requirements:

1. The Fed sets the ratio of deposits that banks must hold on reserve. This ratio is the required reserve ratio.
2. The simple money multiplier ($m^m$) depends on the required reserve ratio (rr), since $m^m = \dfrac{1}{rr}$.

Taken together, these observations imply that the Fed can change the money multiplier by changing the required reserve ratio. If the Fed lowers the required reserve ratio, the money multiplier increases; and if it raises the required reserve ratio, the money multiplier falls.

For example, consider what would happen if the Fed lowered *rr* to 5% from its current level of 10%. The new simple money multiplier would be 1 ÷ 0.05 = 20. This action alone would double the simple money multiplier. Lowering the required reserve would mean that banks could loan out larger portions of their deposits. This would enable them to create money by multiplying deposits to a greater extent than before.

If, instead, the Fed raised *rr* to 20%, the simple money multiplier would fall to just 1 ÷ 0.20 = 5. Table 17.2 shows different values of the simple money multiplier given different reserve requirements.

This tool is not as precise or predictable as open market operations are. Since small changes in the money multiplier can lead to large swings in the money supply, changing the reserve requirement can cause the money supply to change too much. In addition, changing reserve requirements can have unpredictable outcomes because the overall effects depend on the actions of banks. It is possible that the Fed could lower the reserve requirement to 5% and banks would not change their reserves. For these reasons, the reserve requirement has not been used for monetary policy since 1992.

The Fed has also used the discount rate to administer monetary policy. Recall that the discount rate is the interest rate charged on loans to banks from the Fed in its role as lender of last resort. In the past, the Fed would (1) increase the discount rate to discourage borrowing by banks and to decrease the money supply, or (2) decrease the discount rate to encourage borrowing by banks and to increase the money supply. The Fed used this tool actively until the Great Depression era. Currently, the Fed discourages discount borrowing unless banks are struggling. Changing the discount rate to affect bank borrowing is no longer viewed as a helpful tool for changing the money supply.

| **TABLE 17.2** | | |
| --- | --- | --- |
| **Required Reserves and the Simple Money Multiplier** | | |

$$m^m = \frac{1}{rr}$$

| *rr* | *m*$^m$ | |
| --- | --- | --- |
| 0.05 | 20 | Increase in rr ⟶ Decrease in m$^m$ |
| **0.10** | **10** | |
| 0.125 | 8 | |
| 0.20 | 5 | Decrease in rr ⟶ Increase in m$^m$ |
| 0.25 | 4 | |

## ECONOMICS IN THE REAL WORLD

### Excess Reserves Climb in the Wake of the Great Recession

The simple money multiplier assumes that individuals and banks do not hoard cash: individuals deposit their funds into the banking system, and banks hold no excess reserves. However, these assumptions are not always realistic.

Figure 17.9 shows the excess reserves held by banking institutions in the United States since 1990. Until the fall of 2008, banks held virtually no excess reserves. But then excess reserves climbed to unprecedented levels, reaching over $1,600 billion in July 2011.

The cause of this increase was twofold. First, in the wake of the financial turmoil of the Great Recession, banks were probably more risk averse than before. Holding more reserves gave them a buffer against additional failures. But more important, the Federal Reserve began paying interest on reserves beginning in October 2008. This historic change in policy means that banks now have less incentive to loan out each dollar above the required reserve threshold. The Fed put this policy in place to reduce the opportunity cost of excess reserves.

The increase in excess reserves means that the money multiplier is much smaller than our earlier analysis implied. When banks hold more dollars on reserve, fewer are loaned out and multiplied throughout the economy. ✳

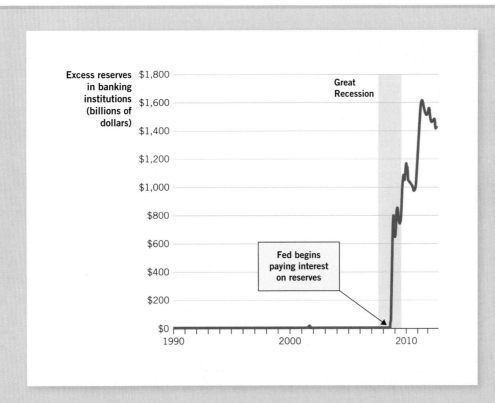

### FIGURE 17.9

**Excess Reserves, 1990–2012**

Banks began holding significant excess reserves in 2008. Part of this was due to the risky nature of loans during the Great Recession, but it is no coincidence that the excess reserves climbed immediately after the Fed began paying interest on reserves.

*Source*: Federal Reserve Bank of St. Louis, FRED database.

# Show Me the Money!

In a modern economy, the trade of a good or service between a buyer and a seller is achieved by using money, which is the medium of exchange. Over the centuries, money has evolved from coins made of precious metals, to pieces of paper redeemable in a precious metal, to numbers on a computer screen that are redeemable in nothing and have value only because consumers have confidence in the entity issuing the money. In the United States, the government controls money through its central bank, the Federal Reserve Bank.

## Measures of U.S. Money Supply (2012)

There are two main categories of money in the United States, M1 and M2. M1 is cold hard cash—that is, actual currency, plus funds in checking deposits at local banks. M2 includes M1 plus savings and money-market funds.

**M2 ($10,036 billion)**

**M1 ($2,308 billion)**

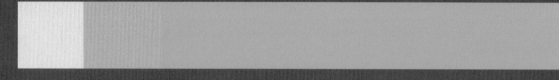

| M1 Breakdown | AMOUNT |
|---|---|
| CURRENCY | $1,057 |
| CHECKING DEPOSITS | $1,251 |

*in billions of dollars*

Credit cards don't count in the money supply.

| M2 Breakdown | AMOUNT |
|---|---|
| M1 | $2,308 |
| SAVINGS DEPOSITS | $6,407 |
| SMALL TIME DEPOSITS | $685 |
| MONEY MARKET MUTUAL FUNDS | $636 |

*in billions of dollars*

## A Timeline of Currency

Cattle

Widespread

9000 BCE

Seashells

Asia, Africa, North America

1200 BCE

Coins

Asia Minor

640 BCE

Commodity-backed paper money

China

800

Wampum

North America

1500 or earlier

Modern U.S. fiat currency

United States

1971

## The Tools of the Fed

The Federal Reserve uses a small number of powerful tools when conducting monetary policy.

 **Open Market Operations**

This is the Fed's main tool for monetary policy. The Fed buys short-term U.S. Treasury securities to increase the money supply, or sells short-term U.S. Treasury securities to decrease the money supply.

 **Quantitative Easing**

This is a new tool that has been used since 2008. Quantitative easing is a type of open market operation that focuses on targeted securities purchases in both troubled markets (such as mortgage-backed securities) and long-term Treasury securities.

 **Reserve Requirements**

Changing the reserve requirement alters the money multiplier. An increase in the reserve requirement reduces the money multiplier and therefore the money supply; a decrease in the reserve requirement does the opposite. The Fed has not used this tool to actively manage monetary policy since 1992, but it remains a popular tool in other parts of the world.

 **Discount Rate**

This is the interest rate that banks pay on loans from the Fed. This was once the primary tool that the Fed used to control the money supply, before open market operations were employed. Nowadays the Fed does not use the discount rate for monetary policy.

## REVIEW QUESTIONS

- What percentage of M1 does currency make up? Of M2?

- Which measure of money, M1 or M2, is the preferred measure of the nation's money in the twenty-first century?

# Conclusion

We started this chapter with a common misconception about the supply of money in an economy. In general, people believe that it is pretty simple to regulate the quantity of money in an economy. But while currency in modern economies is issued exclusively by government, money also includes bank deposits. Banks cause the money supply to expand when they extend loans, and they cause the money supply to contract when they increase their level of reserves. In fact, even individuals' influence is significant: people like you and me cause the money supply to rise and fall when we change how much currency we hold outside the banking system. Taken together, this means that the Fed's job of monitoring the quantity of money is very difficult. It attempts to expand or contract the money supply, but its efforts may be offset by the actions of banks and individuals.

This material in this chapter sets the stage for a theoretical discussion of monetary policy and the way it affects the economy, which we will undertake in Chapter 18.

## ANSWERING THE BIG QUESTIONS

### What is money?

* Money is primarily the medium of exchange in an economy; it's what people trade for goods and services.
* Money includes more than just physical currency; it also includes bank deposits, since people often make purchases with checks or cards that withdraw from their bank accounts.

### How do banks create money?

* Banks create money whenever they extend a loan. A new loan represents new purchasing power, while the deposit that backs the loan is also considered as money.

### How does the Federal Reserve control the money supply?

* The primary tool of monetary policy is open market operations, which the Fed conducts through the buying and selling of bonds. Quantitative easing is a special form of open market operations that was introduced in 2008.
* The Fed has several other tools, including reserve requirements the discount rate, but these have not been used in quite a while.

# CONCEPTS YOU SHOULD KNOW

assets (p. 523)
balance sheet (p. 523)
bank run (p. 525)
barter (p. 516)
checkable deposits (p. 520)
commodity money (p. 517)
commodity-backed money
 (p. 517)
currency (p. 516)
discount loan (p. 532)
discount rate (p. 532)

double coincidence of wants
 (p. 517)
excess reserves (p. 525)
federal funds (p. 532)
federal funds rate (p. 532)
fiat money (p. 517)
fractional reserve banking
 (p. 524)
liabilities (p. 523)
M1 (p. 520)
M2 (p. 520)

medium of exchange (p. 516)
moral hazard (p. 526)
open market operations (p. 535)
owner's equity (p. 523)
quantitative easing (p. 536)
required reserve ratio (rr) (p. 525)
reserves (p. 523)
simple money multiplier
 (p. 530)
store of value (p. 518)
unit of account (p. 518)

# QUESTIONS FOR REVIEW

1. What is the difference between commodity money and fiat money?

2. What are the three functions of money? Which function is the defining characteristic?

3. What are the components of M1 and M2? List them.

4. Suppose you withdraw $100 from your checking account. What impact would this action alone have on the following?

   a. the money supply
   b. your bank's required reserves
   c. your bank's excess reserves

5. Why is the actual money multiplier usually less than the simple money multiplier?

6. Why can't a bank lend out all of its reserves?

7. How does the Fed increase and decrease the money supply through open market operations?

8. How is the discount rate different from the federal funds rate?

9. What is the current required reserve ratio? What would happen to the money supply if the Fed decreased the ratio?

10. Define quantitative easing. How is it different from standard open market operations?

# STUDY PROBLEMS (*solved at the end of the section)

1. Suppose that you take $150 in currency out of your pocket and deposit it in your checking account. Assuming a required reserve ratio of 10%, what is the largest amount by which the money supply can increase as a result of your action?

2. Consider the balance sheet for the Wahoo Bank as presented below.

**Wahoo Bank Balance Sheet**

| Assets | | Liabilities and net worth | |
|---|---|---|---|
| Government | | | |
| securities | $1,600 | Liabilities: | |
| Required reserves | $400 | Checking deposits | $4,000 |
| Excess reserves | $0 | Net worth | $1,000 |
| Loans | $3,000 | | |
| Total assests | $5000 | | |

Using a required reserve ratio of 10% and assuming that the bank keeps no excess reserves, write the changes to the balance sheet for each of the following scenarios:

a. Bennett withdraws $200 from his checking account.

b. Roland deposits $500 into his checking account.

c. The Fed buys $1,000 in government securities from the bank.

d. The Fed sells $1,500 in government securities to the bank.

3. Using a required reserve ratio of 10% and assuming that banks keep no excess reserves, which of the following scenarios produces a larger increase in the money supply? Explain why.

a. Someone takes $1,000 from under his or her mattress and deposits it into a checking account.

b. The Fed purchases $1,000 in government securities from a commercial bank.

4. Using a required reserve ratio of 10% and assuming that banks keep no excess reserves, what is the value of government securities the Fed must purchase if it wants to increase the money supply by $2 million?

5. Using a required reserve ratio of 10% and assuming that banks keep no excess reserves, imagine that $300 is deposited into a checking account. By how much more does the money supply increase if the Fed lowers the required reserve ratio to 7%?

6. Determine if the following changes affect M1 and/or M2:

a. an increase in savings deposits

b. a decrease in credit card balances

c. a decrease in the amount of currency in circulation

d. the conversion of a savings account into a checking account

7. Determine whether each of the following is considered standard open market operations or quantitative easing:

a. The Fed buys $100 billion in student-loan-backed securities.

b. The Fed sells $400 billion in short-term Treasury securities.

c. The Fed buys $500 billion in 30-year (long-term) Treasury securities.

✴ 8. What is the simple money multiplier if the required reserve ratio is 15%? If it is 12.5%?

✴ 9. Suppose the Fed sells $1 million in Treasury securities to a commercial bank. What effect will this action have on the bank's reserves and the money supply? Use a required reserve ratio of 10%, and assume that banks hold no excess reserves and that all currency is deposited into the banking system.

# SOLVED PROBLEMS

8. When the required reserve ratio is 15%:

$$m^m = \frac{1}{rr} = \frac{1}{0.15} = 6.67$$

When the required reserve ratio is 12.5%:

$$m^m = \frac{1}{rr} = \frac{1}{0.125} = 8$$

9. The immediate result will be that the commercial bank will have $1,000,000 in excess reserves, since its deposits did not change. The commercial bank will loan out these excess reserves, and the money multiplier process begins. Under the assumptions of this question, the simple money multiplier applies. Therefore, in the end, $10 million in additional deposits will be created.

**Central banks can steer economies out of every recession.**

From 1982 to 2008—for 26 years—the U.S. economy hummed along with unprecedented success. Although there were two recessions dur-

**MISCONCEPTION**

ing this period, neither was severe or lengthy. Economists and many other observers actually believed that the business cycle had been tamed once and for all. Much of the credit for this "great moderation" was given to Alan Greenspan, the chairman of the Board of Governors of the Federal Reserve Board. Analysts thought that his savvy handling of interest rates and money supply had been the key to the sustained economic growth, and that enlightened supervision of central banks was the path to future economic growth throughout the world in the twenty-first century.

Unfortunately, the upturn did not last. The Great Recession, which started in late 2007, plunged the world into the worst economic downturn since the Great Depression. Moreover, since 2008 the extraordinary efforts by the Fed to help the U.S. economy to return to robust economic growth have shown just how little power a central bank has when the economy gets really bad.

In this chapter, we consider how changes in the money supply work their way through the economy. We build on earlier material, drawing heavily on the discussions of monetary policy, the loanable funds market, and the aggregate demand–aggregate supply model. We begin by looking at the short run, when monetary policy is most effective. We then consider why monetary policy can't always turn an economy around. We conclude the chapter by examining the relationship between inflation and unemployment.

The Federal Reserve plays a powerful role in the world economy, but not as powerful as some people think.

# BIG QUESTIONS

* What is the effect of monetary policy in the short run?
* Why doesn't monetary policy always work?
* What is the Phillips curve?

# What Is the Effect of Monetary Policy in the Short Run?

When economic growth stagnates and unemployment rises, many people look to central banks to help the economy. Central banks can use monetary policy to reduce interest rates and make it easier for people and businesses to borrow; this action generates new economic activity to get the economy moving again. In the last chapter, we saw that the Federal Reserve generally uses open market operations to implement monetary policy. In this chapter, we look closely at how the effects of open market operations ripple throughout the economy.

We begin by considering the immediate, or short-run, effects. Recall the difference between the short run and the long run in macroeconomics. The long run is a period of time long enough for all prices to adjust. But in the short run, some prices—often, the prices of resources such as wages for workers and interest rates for loans—are inflexible.

## Expansionary Monetary Policy

To gain some intuition about the macroeconomic results of money supply changes, let's return to an example we talked about in an earlier chapter: your hypothetical college apparel business. Suppose you already have one retail location where you sell apparel, and you are now considering opening a second. Before you can open a new store, you need to invest in several resources: a physical location, additional inventory, and some labor. You expect the new store to earn the revenue needed to pay for these resources eventually. But you need a loan to expand the business now, so you go to the bank. The bank is willing to grant you a loan, but the interest rate is higher than your expected return on the investment. So you regretfully decide not to open a new location.

But then the central bank decides to expand the money supply. It buys Treasury securities from banks, which increases the level of reserves in the banking system. As a result, interest rates fall at your local bank. You then take out a loan, open the second apparel shop, and hire a few employees.

In this example, monetary policy affects your actions, and your actions affect the macroeconomy. First, investment increases because you spend on equipment, inventory, and a physical location. Second, aggregate demand increases because your investment demand is part of overall aggregate demand. Finally, as a result of the increase in aggregate demand, real GDP increases and unemployment falls as your output rises and you hire workers. This is what new money can do in the short run: it expands the amount of credit (loanable funds) available and paves the way for economic expansion.

Now let's trace the impact of this kind of monetary policy on the entire macroeconomy. In doing this, we draw heavily on what we have presented in preceding chapters. Below is a short list of concepts from previous chapters that we will use in the discussion that follows. The chapters are identified so that you can review as necessary.

1. The Fed uses open market operations to implement monetary policy. Open market operations involve the purchase or sale of bonds; normally, these are short-term Treasury securities (Chapter 17).

2. Treasury securities are one important part of the loanable funds market, where lenders buy securities and borrowers sell securities (Chapter 10).

3. The price in the loanable funds market is the interest rate. Lower interest rates increase the quantity of investment demand, just as lower prices increase the quantity demanded in any product market (Chapter 9).

4. Investment is one component of aggregate demand, so changes in investment demand indicate corresponding changes in aggregate demand (Chapter 13).

5. In the short run, increases in aggregate demand increase output and lower the unemployment rate (Chapter 13).

We have studied each of these concepts separately. Now it is time to put them together for a complete picture of how monetary policy works.

There are two types of monetary policy: expansionary and contractionary. **Expansionary monetary policy** occurs when a central bank acts to increase the money supply in an effort to stimulate the economy. Hypothetically (and unrealistically), the Fed could do this by dropping currency out of a helicopter. But it typically expands the money supply through open market purchases: it buys bonds.

> **Expansionary monetary policy** occurs when a central bank acts to increase the money supply in an effort to stimulate the economy.

When the Fed buys bonds from financial institutions, new money moves directly into the loanable funds market. As we saw earlier with the college apparel store example, this action increases the funds that banks can use for new loans. Figure 18.1 illustrates the short-run effects of expansionary monetary policy in the loanable funds market and also on aggregate demand. First, notice that open market operations means the new funds enter directly into the loanable funds market, which is pictured in panel (a). The supply of funds increases from $S_1$ to $S_2$. This new supply reduces the interest rate from 5% to 3%. At the lower interest rate, firms take more loans for investment, and the quantity demanded of loanable funds increases from $200 billion to $210 billion.

Since investment is a component of aggregate demand, an increase in the quantity of investment demand also increases aggregate demand, which is pictured in panel (b) of Figure 18.1. Remember from Chapter 13 that aggregate demand derives from four sources: C, I, G, and X. When investment (I) increases, aggregate demand increases from $AD_1$ to $AD_2$.

In the short run, increases in aggregate demand lead to increases in real GDP. In Figure 18.1, the economy moves from an initial long-run equilibrium at point A to a short-run equilibrium at point b. Real GDP increases from $16 trillion to $16.5 trillion. The increase in GDP leads to more jobs through the increase in aggregate demand; therefore, it also leads to lower unemployment. Finally, the general price level rises from 100 to 105. This price level increase is only partial; in the short run, output prices are more flexible than input prices, which are sticky and do not adjust.

In summary, in the short run, expansionary monetary policy reduces unemployment (u) and increases real GDP (Y). In addition, the overall price level (P) rises somewhat as flexible prices increase in the short run. These results are summarized in the table at the bottom of Figure 18.1.

Before moving on, let's step back and consider the results of the expansion. They seem positive, right? After all, unemployment goes down, and real GDP goes up. This macroeconomic result is consistent with the way monetary policy affected your hypothetical college apparel firm. Real employment and real output expand as a result of increasing the quantity of money in the economy. Later in the chapter, we will see that not everyone is happy with this outcome.

## FIGURE 18.1

**Expansionary Monetary Policy in the Short Run**

(a) When the central bank buys bonds, it injects new funds directly into the loanable funds market. This action increases the supply of loanable funds ($S_1$ shifts to $S_2$) and decreases the interest rate from 5% to 3%. The lower interest rate leads to an increase in the quantity of investment demand (D) from $200 billion to $210 billion, which increases aggregate demand (AD).

(b) The increase in aggregate demand causes real GDP (Y) to rise from $16 trillion to $16.5 trillion and reduces unemployment (u) in the short run. The general price level also rises to 105 but does not fully adjust in the short run.

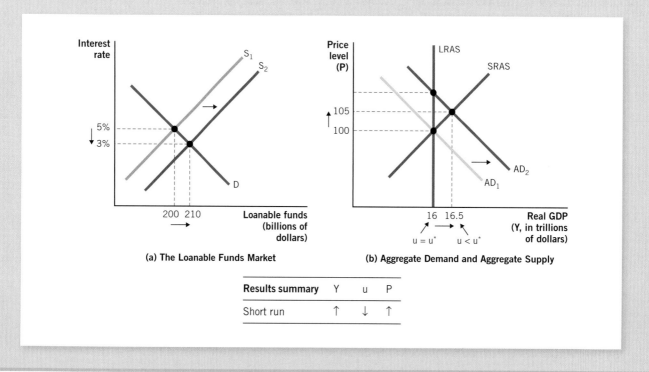

(a) The Loanable Funds Market

(b) Aggregate Demand and Aggregate Supply

| Results summary | Y | u | P |
|---|---|---|---|
| Short run | ↑ | ↓ | ↑ |

## ECONOMICS IN THE REAL WORLD

### Monetary Policy Responses to the Great Recession

In the fall of 2007, it was clear that the U.S. economy was slowing. The unemployment rate rose from 4.4% to 5% between May and June 2007, and real GDP grew by just 1.7% in the fourth quarter. The U.S. economy officially entered recession in December 2007. We now know that the nation's economy was entering several years of low growth and high unemployment. Many economists believe that a decline in aggregate demand was one cause of the recession. The Federal Reserve's response was an attempt to increase aggregate demand.

We have seen that open market purchases drive down interest rates. This is exactly how the Federal Reserve responded, beginning in 2007. Figure 18.2 shows the federal funds rate, which you may recall from Chapter 17 is the interest rate on short-term loans between banks. Traditional open market operations involve buying short-term Treasury securities, which decreases the short-term interest rate, or selling Treasury securities, which increases the short-term interest rate. As you can see, the Fed actively worked to keep the federal funds rate at nearly 0% for several years. This reflects a direct application of the monetary policy prescriptions that we have talked about in this section—expansionary monetary policy aimed at lower interest rates so as to increase real GDP and reduce unemployment. ✳

## Real versus Nominal Effects

We have seen that changes in the quantity of money lead to real changes in the economy. You may be wondering if the process is really that simple. That is, if a central bank can create jobs and real GDP by simply printing money, why would it ever stop? After all, fiat money is just paper! Well, while there is a short-run incentive to increase the money supply, these effects wear off in the long run as prices adjust and then drive down the value of money.

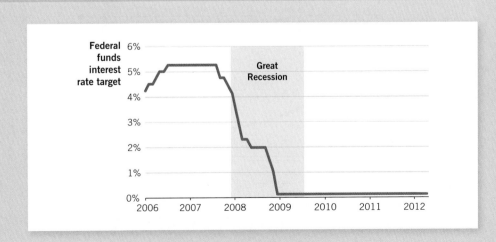

### FIGURE 18.2

**Monetary Policy during the Great Recession**

When the Great Recession began, the Fed responded with expansionary monetary policy that led to lower short-term interest rates. With growth low and unemployment high through 2012, the Fed continued to keep interest rates low.

How would you like it if new money entered the economy through backpacks full of currency given to all college students?

Think of it this way: let's say the Fed's preferred method of increasing the money supply is to hand all college students backpacks full of newly printed bills. Not a bad idea, right? But let's focus on the macroeconomic effects. Eventually, the new money will devalue the entire money supply, since prices will rise. But since you get the money first, you get it before any prices have adjusted. So these new funds represent real purchasing power for you. This is why monetary policy can have immediate real short-run effects: initially, no prices have adjusted. But as prices adjust in the long run, the effects of the new money wear off.

Injecting new money into the economy eventually causes inflation, but inflation doesn't happen right away and prices do not rise uniformly. During the time that prices are increasing, the value of money is constantly moving downward. Figure 18.3 illustrates the real purchasing power of money as time goes by. Panel (a) shows adjustments to the price level. When new money enters the economy (at time $t_0$), the price level begins to rise in the short run and then reaches its new level in the long run (at time $t_{LR}$). Panel (b) shows the value of money relative to these price-level adjustments. When the new money enters the economy, it has its highest value, as prices have not yet adjusted. In the short run, as prices rise, the real purchasing power of all money in the economy falls. In the long run, all prices adjust, and then the real value of money reaches its lower level. At this point, the real impacts of the monetary policy dissipate completely.

## FIGURE 18.3

**The Real Value of Money as Prices Adjust**

(a) If the central bank increases the money supply at time $t_0$, the price level begins rising in the short run. In the long run, all prices adjust and the price level reaches its new higher level. (b) As the price level increases, the real value of money declines throughout the short run. In the long run, at $t_{LR}$ the real value of money reaches a new lower level.

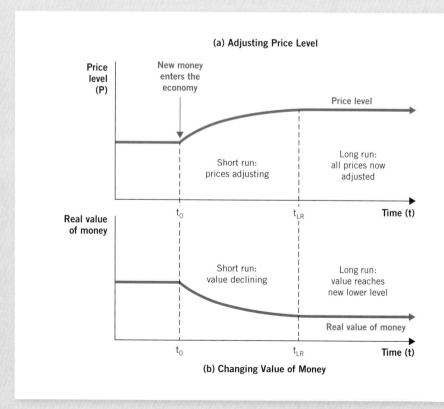

## Unexpected Inflation Hurts Some People

Let's now consider how expansionary monetary policy affects different people across the economy. The basic macroeconomic results, summarized in Figure 18.1, seem very positive: real GDP goes up, the unemployment rate falls, and there is some inflation. Consider that you are living in an economy where these conditions exist. Everywhere you look, the news seems positive, as the media, politicians, and firms focus on the expanding economy. But this action does not help everybody.

For example, consider workers who signed a two-year contract just before the inflation hit the economy. These workers now pay more for goods and services such as groceries, gasoline, education, and health care—yet their wages were set before the inflation occurred. In real terms, these workers have taken a pay cut. Monetary policy derives its potency from sticky prices, but if your price (or wage) is stuck, inflation hurts you.

In general, inflation harms input suppliers that have sticky prices. In addition to workers, lenders (the suppliers of funds used for expansion) are another prominent group that is harmed when inflation is greater than anticipated. Imagine that you are a banker who extends a loan with an interest rate of 3%, but then the inflation rate turns out to be 5%. The Fisher equation, discussed in Chapter 9, implies that the loan's real interest rate is actually –2%. A negative interest rate will definitely harm your bank!

Later in this chapter, we will talk about the incentives for these resource suppliers to correctly anticipate inflation. For now, we just note that unexpected inflation, while potentially helpful to the overall economy, is also harmful to those whose prices take time to adjust.

# Contractionary Monetary Policy

We have seen how the central bank uses expansionary monetary policy to stimulate the economy. However, sometimes policymakers want to slow down the economy. **Contractionary monetary policy** occurs when a central bank takes action that reduces the money supply in the economy. A central bank often undertakes contractionary monetary policy when the economy is expanding rapidly and the bank fears inflation.

**Contractionary monetary policy**
occurs when a central bank acts to decrease the money supply.

To trace the effects of contractionary policy, we again begin in the loanable funds market. The central bank reduces the money supply via open market operations: it sells bonds in the loanable funds market. Selling the bonds takes funds out of the loanable funds market because the banks buy the bonds from the central bank with money they might otherwise lend out. Financial institutions are not forced to buy the bonds, but the central bank enters the market and sells bonds alongside other sellers. The loanable funds market pictured in panel (a) of Figure 18.4 shows this reduction in supply from $S_1$ to $S_2$. The interest rate rises, and equilibrium investment falls from $200 billion to $190 billion.

When investment falls, aggregate demand falls. In panel (b) of Figure 18.4, this is illustrated as a fall in aggregate demand from $AD_1$ to $AD_2$. In the short run, this causes a reduction in real GDP from $15 trillion to $14.5 trillion, an increase in the unemployment rate, and a decrease in the price level.

These short-run results are again the result of fixed resource prices for the firm. A lower money supply leads to downward pressure on prices (P),

**FIGURE 18.4**

**Contractionary Monetary Policy in the Short Run**

(a) The central bank sells bonds, which pulls funds out of the loanable funds market. This action decreases the supply of loanable funds ($S_1$ shifts to $S_2$) and increases the interest rate from 5% to 6%. The higher interest rate leads to a decrease in the quantity of investment demand (D) from $200 billion to $190 billion, and this outcome decreases aggregate demand (AD).

(b) The decrease in aggregate demand (from $AD_1$ to $AD_2$) causes real GDP to decline from $15 trillion to $14.5 trillion and induces unemployment in the short run. The general price level also falls to 95 but does not fully adjust in the short run.

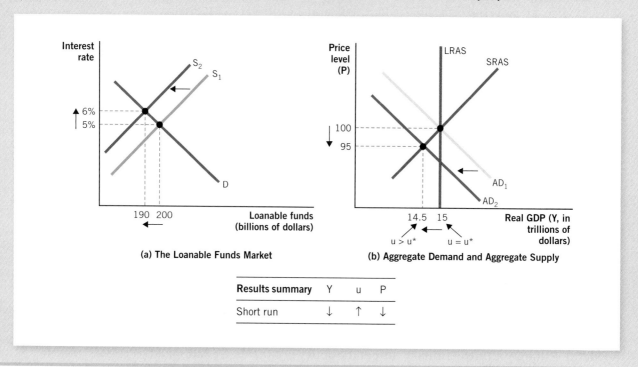

(a) The Loanable Funds Market

(b) Aggregate Demand and Aggregate Supply

| Results summary | Y | u | P |
| --- | --- | --- | --- |
| Short run | ↓ | ↑ | ↓ |

but sticky resource prices mean that firms cannot adjust the wages of their workers or the terms of their loans in the short run. Therefore, firms reduce output and lay off some workers. This is why we see real GDP (Y) falling and the unemployment rate (u) rising. These results are summarized in the table at the bottom of the figure.

## ECONOMICS IN THE REAL WORLD

### Monetary Policy's Contribution to the Great Depression

As if monetary policy is not hard enough, consider that the money supply is not completely controlled by a central bank. In Chapter 17, we explained how the actions of private individuals and banks increase or decrease the money supply via the money multiplier. Banks increase the money supply when they lend out reserves, and they decrease the money supply when they hold more reserves. In addition, individuals like you and me increase the money supply when we deposit funds into bank accounts and the banks multiply that money by making loans. When we withdraw our funds and hold on to more currency, we decrease the money supply because banks cannot multiply those funds.

Now imagine a scenario with massive bank failures and very little deposit insurance. As more and more banks fail, people withdraw their funds all over the country. While it makes sense that individuals would want to withdraw their money, as people all over the country continue to remove money from banks, the money supply declines significantly. The reduction in the money supply leads to an economic contraction, similar to the scenario we saw in Figure 18.4.

What happens when all these people want to withdraw their funds?

This type of monetary contraction is exactly what happened at the beginning of the Great Depression. From 1929 to 1933, prior to the establishment of federal deposit insurance, over 9,000 banks failed in the United States. Because of these bank failures, people began holding their money outside the banking system. This action contributed to a significant contraction in the money supply. Figure 18.5 shows the money supply prior to and during the Depression. After peaking at $676 billion in 1931, the M2 money supply fell to just $564 billion in 1933. This drastic decline was one of the major causes of the Great Depression. In Chapter 14, we referred to policy errors as one of the causes of the decline in aggregate demand that led to the Great Depression. Economists today agree that the Federal Reserve should have done more to offset the decline in the money supply at the onset of the Great Depression. This was perhaps one of the biggest policy errors in U.S. macroeconomic history. ✳

**FIGURE 18.5**

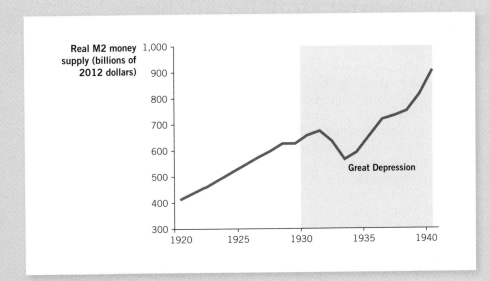

### U.S. Money Supply before and during the Great Depression

The M2 money supply grew to $676 billion in 1931, but then plummeted to $564 billion by 1933. The huge decline in the money supply was a major contributor to the Great Depression. (Values for real money supply are expressed in 2012 dollars.)

*Source*: Historical Statistics of the United States, Colonial Times to 1970.

# PRACTICE WHAT YOU KNOW

### Expansionary versus Contractionary Monetary Policy: Monetary Policy in the Short Run

The Federal Open Market Committee is the group that determines monetary policy.

**Question:** In the short run, how does expansionary monetary policy affect real GDP, unemployment, and the price level in the economy?

**Answer:** Real GDP increases, the unemployment rate falls, and the price level rises as all flexible prices adjust.

**Question:** In the short run, how does contractionary monetary policy affect real GDP, unemployment, and the price level in the economy?

**Answer:** Real GDP decreases, the unemployment rate rises, and the price level falls as all flexible prices adjust.

**Question:** What real-world circumstance might lead to contractionary monetary policy?

**Answer:** If members of the Federal Open Market Committee at the Federal Reserve thought that inflation was an imminent danger, they might implement contractionary monetary policy.

# Why Doesn't Monetary Policy Always Work?

So far in this chapter, we have seen that monetary policy can have real effects on the macroeconomy. By shifting aggregate demand, monetary policy can affect real GDP and unemployment. But recall our correction to the chapter-opening misconception: central banks *cannot* always steer an economy out of a recession. Monetary policy is limited in what it can do. In this section, we consider three limitations of monetary policy. First, we look at the diminished effects of monetary policy in the long run. Next, we consider how expectations can dampen the effects of monetary policy. Finally, we clarify the limitations of monetary policy when economic downturns are the result of shifts in aggregate supply, rather than aggregate demand.

## Long-Run Adjustments

We have noted that some prices take longer to adjust than others and that the long run is a period long enough for *all* prices to adjust. Output prices can adjust relatively quickly. Think about the output prices at a coffee shop, which are often displayed in chalk behind the cash register; they are easy to change in the short run. In contrast, input prices, such as worker's wages, are often the slowest prices to adjust. After all, these prices are often set by lengthy contracts; moreover, money illusion also can make input suppliers reluctant to lower their prices. But the long run is a period sufficient for all prices to change—even workers' contracts, which eventually expire.

Both types of prices affect the decisions made at firms across the economy, and therefore they affect output and unemployment. For example, consider your hypothetical small business producing and selling college apparel. Earlier in this chapter, you secured a loan to open a new retail location because the Fed increased the money supply, which expanded the supply of loans. When you initially received your loan, costs for resources such as workers, equipment, inventory, and a physical plant were relatively low because prices for these things are sticky and had not yet adjusted. But in the long run, these resource prices adjust. If everything works out well for you, the monetary expansion will lead to new demand for your product and you'll be able to keep your new store open. But it is also possible that when the prices of resources rise—in the long run—you may not be doing well enough to afford them. At that point, with your costs rising, you may have to reduce your output, lay off some workers, or perhaps even close your new retail location. In the long run, as prices adjust throughout the macroeconomy, the stimulating effects of expansionary monetary policy wear off.

Let's see how this process works for the entire economy. Figure 18.6 illustrates long-run macroeconomic adjustments to expansionary monetary policy. As you can see in the graph, expansionary monetary policy shifts aggregate demand from AD$_1$ to AD$_2$. This action moves the economy from long-run

## FIGURE 18.6

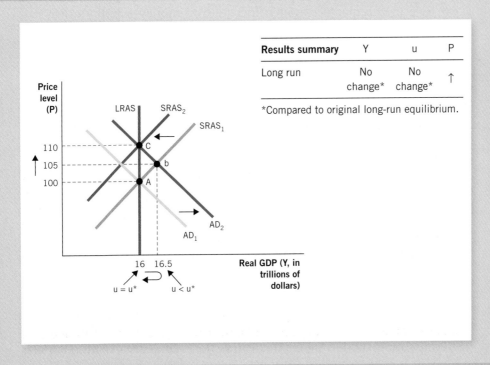

| Results summary | Y | u | P |
|---|---|---|---|
| Long run | No change* | No change* | ↑ |

*Compared to original long-run equilibrium.

**Expansionary Monetary Policy in the Long Run**

Beginning in equilibrium at point A, an increase in the money supply shifts aggregate demand from AD$_1$ to AD$_2$; this action moves the economy to a new short-run equilibrium at point b. Equilibrium at point b is only relevant in the short run, as all prices have not yet adjusted. In the long run, resource prices adjust. This outcome shifts short-run aggregate supply from SRAS$_1$ to SRAS$_2$, and the economy moves to a new long-run equilibrium at point C.

equilibrium at point A to short-run equilibrium at point b (with a temporary change in real GDP and unemployment). In the long run, as resource prices rise, the short-run aggregate supply shifts upward from $SRAS_1$ to $SRAS_2$, and the economy moves to a new long-run equilibrium at point C. When we compare the new long-run equilibrium to the situation prior to the application of monetary policy, we see that there is no change in real GDP (Y) or unemployment (u), but there is an increase in the price level from 100 to 110.

One important implication of these long-run results is that there is a lack of real economic effects from monetary policy; in the long run, all prices adjust. Therefore, in the long run, monetary policy does not affect real GDP or unemployment. The only predictable result of more money in the economy over the long run is inflation. Recall that in Chapter 8, we discussed the cause of inflation is monetary growth. You now can picture this in the context of the aggregate demand and aggregate supply model.

From one perspective, our long-run results may seem strange: central banks can't do much in the long run to affect the real economy. However, this statement might also seem logical since it's possible to increase the money supply by just printing more paper money. But printing more paper money doesn't affect the economy's long-run productivity or its ability to produce; these outcomes are determined by resources, technology, and institutions.

**Monetary neutrality**
is the idea that the money supply does not affect real economic variables.

The idea that the money supply does not affect real economic variables is known as **monetary neutrality**. Given that money is neutral in the long run, you might question the value of short-run monetary policy. In fact, many of the substantive debates in macroeconomics focus on the relative importance of the short run versus the long run. Some economists believe it is best to focus on short-run effects, which are very real. After all, during recessions people often lose their jobs, which can be a very painful experience. When the money supply is expanded, firms can get loans more cheaply and then hire more workers. From this perspective, central banks ought to take a very active role in the macroeconomy: increase the money supply during economic downturns, and contract the money supply during economic expansions. This activist policy can then potentially smooth out the business cycle.

Other economists discount the short-run expansionary effects of monetary policy and instead focus on the problems of inflation. In Chapter 8, we explored the negative effects of inflation. These included price confusion, wealth redistribution, and uncertainty about future price levels. These byproducts of inflation can stifle economic growth.

## Adjustments in Expectations

In addition to problems from inflation, unexpected inflation harms workers and other resource suppliers who have fixed prices in the short run. Therefore, to avoid this fate, workers have an incentive to expect a certain level of inflation and to negotiate their contracts accordingly. For instance, many contracts have cost-of-living adjustment clauses that force the employer to increase wages by the same percentage as inflation. The key incentive for anticipating the correct rate of inflation is straightforward: people are harmed when inflation is a surprise. But when it is expected, the real effects on the economy are limited.

Let's look at inflation expectations in the context of the aggregate demand–aggregate supply model. Figure 18.7 shows how monetary expansion affects aggregate demand and aggregate supply when it is expected. Expansionary monetary policy shifts aggregate demand from $AD_1$ to $AD_2$. But if this effect is expected, short-run aggregate supply shifts to the left from $SRAS_1$ to $SRAS_2$.

In Chapter 13, we discussed how short-run aggregate supply shifts back when workers and resource suppliers expect higher future prices, since they do not want their real prices to fall. If short-run aggregate supply shifts along with the shift in aggregate demand, the economy goes immediately to equilibrium at point C. Therefore, monetary policy has no real effect on the economy—real GDP and unemployment do not change. The only lasting change is nominal, because the price level rises from 100 to 110. Monetary policy has real effects only when some prices are sticky. But if inflation is expected, prices are not sticky; they adjust because people plan on the inflation. To the extent that all prices rise, the effect of monetary policy will be limited, even in the short run.

## Aggregate Supply Shifts and the Great Recession

We have seen that monetary policy affects the economy by shifting aggregate demand. Thus, if a recession occurs as a result of deficient aggregate demand, then monetary policy has a chance to stabilize the economy and return it to higher levels of real GDP and lower unemployment. But not all downturns are a result of aggregate demand shifts. Declines in aggregate supply can also lead to recession. And when supply shifts cause the downturn, monetary policy is much less likely to restore the economy to its pre-recession conditions.

Let's consider a recession that is caused by declines in both long-run aggregate supply and aggregate demand. For example, the Great Recession

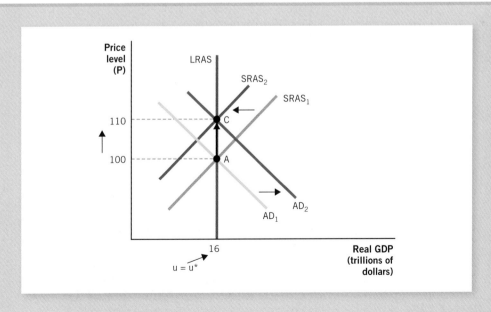

**FIGURE 18.7**

**Completely Expected Monetary Policy**

If expansionary monetary policy is expected, short-run aggregate supply shifts along with the shift in aggregate demand, and the economy moves directly from equilibrium at point A to point C. In this case, there are no real effects from the monetary policy, even in the short run. The only lasting change is nominal because the price level rises from 100 to 110.

that began in 2007 seems to have included both types of shifts. In Chapter 14, we argued that the widespread problems in financial markets at that time negatively affected key institutions in the macroeconomy. In addition, the financial regulations that were put in place restricted banks' ability to lend at levels equal to those in effect prior to 2008. The result was a shift backward in long-run aggregate supply. In addition, as people's real wealth and expected future income levels declined, aggregate demand shifted to the left.

Figure 18.8 shows how the decline in both aggregate demand and aggregate supply might affect the economy. Initially, the economy is in equilibrium at point A, with the supply and demand curves from 2007. Then aggregate demand and aggregate supply shift to the left, to the 2008 levels. When this happens, real GDP declines from $14.5 trillion to $14 trillion, and the unemployment rate rises from 5% to 8%—levels similar to the actual experience during this period.

The dilemma is that at point B, monetary policy is limited in its ability to permanently move output back to its prior level. Even if monetary policy shifts aggregate demand back to $AD_{2007}$, this is not enough to eliminate the recession. Furthermore, as we have stressed throughout this chapter, the effects of monetary policy wear off in the long run.

Thus, in the wake of the Great Recession, the U.S. economy continued to struggle with slow growth and high unemployment, even after significant monetary policy interventions. The bottom line is that monetary policy does not enable us to avoid every economic downturn.

## FIGURE 18.8

**Aggregate Supply–Induced Recession**

Initially, in 2007, the economy is in equilibrium at point A. Then the long-run and short-run aggregate supply curves shift to the left, to $LRAS_{2008}$ and $SRAS_{2008}$. In addition, aggregate demand shifts to the left to $AD_{2008}$. This combination of shifts takes the economy to a new equilibrium at point B. At point B, monetary policy is limited in its ability to move the economy back to its original level of real GDP because monetary policy affects the economy through aggregate demand.

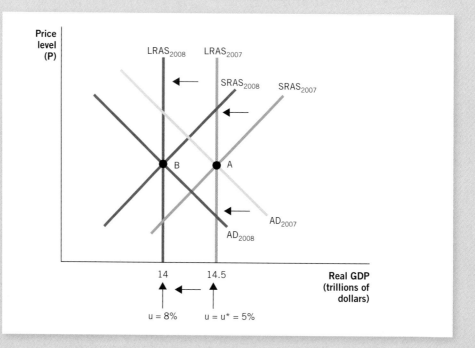

**Monetary Policy Isn't Always Effective: Why Couldn't Monetary Policy Pull Us Out of the Great Recession?**

The Great Recession officially lasted from December 2007 to June 2009. But the effects lingered on for several years thereafter, with slow growth of real GDP and high unemployment rates. This all occurred despite several doses of expansionary monetary policy. Not only did the Fed push short-term interest rates to nearly 0%, but it also engaged in several rounds of quantitative easing, in which it purchased hundreds of billions of dollars' worth of long-term bonds.

Question: What are three possible reasons why monetary policy was not able to restore expansionary growth during and after the Great Recession?

Answer:

1. *Monetary policy is ineffective in the long run.* While we don't know the exact length of the short run, all prices certainly had time to adjust by 2010 or 2011, yet the economy was still sluggish. Thus, one possibility is that all prices adjusted, so the effects of monetary policy wore off. This answer alone is probably inadequate, given that the effects of monetary policy were not evident even in the short run.

2. *Monetary policy was expected.* It seems unlikely that monetary policy is much of a surprise nowadays. The Federal Reserve releases official statements after each monetary policy meeting and generally announces the direction it will follow for several months in advance.

3. *The downturn was at least partially due to a supply shift.* Since monetary policy works through aggregate demand, the effects of monetary policy can be limited if aggregate supply shifts cause a recession.

# What Is the Phillips Curve?

We have seen that monetary policy can stimulate the economy in the short run. Increasing the money supply increases aggregate demand, and this can lead to higher real GDP, lower unemployment, and a higher price level (inflation). The relationship between inflation and unemployment is of particular interest to economists and non-economists alike; it is at the heart of the debate regarding the power of monetary policy to affect the economy. In this section, we examine this relationship by looking at the *Phillips curve*.

# The Traditional Short-Run Phillips Curve

In 1958, the British economist A. W. Phillips noted an inverse relationship between wage inflation and unemployment rates in the United Kingdom. Soon thereafter, U.S economists Paul Samuelson and Robert Solow extended the analysis to inflation and unemployment rates in the United States. This short-run inverse relationship between inflation and unemployment rates became known as the **Phillips curve**. Before looking at Phillips curve data, let's consider the theory behind the Phillips curve in the context of the aggregate demand–aggregate supply model.

The **Phillips curve** indicates a short-run inverse relationship between inflation and unemployment rates.

Panel (a) of Figure 18.9 shows how unexpected monetary expansion affects the economy in the short run. Initially, with aggregate demand at AD$_1$ and the price level at 100, the economy is in long-run equilibrium at point A with real GDP (Y) at $16 trillion and the unemployment rate equal to 5%. For this example, we assume that the natural rate of unemployment is exactly 5%.

Then expansionary monetary policy shifts aggregate demand to AD$_2$, which leads to a new short-run equilibrium at point b. Let's focus on the changes to prices and the unemployment rate. The monetary expansion leads to a 5% inflation rate, as the price level rises to 105. The unemployment

## FIGURE 18.9

**Aggregate Demand, Aggregate Supply, and the Phillips Curve**

(a) This graph shows the effect of unexpected monetary expansion in the short run. Initially, the economy is in equilibrium at point A, with a price level of 100, real GDP of $16 trillion, and an unemployment rate of 5%. Aggregate demand shifts from AD$_1$ to AD$_2$, which moves the economy to short-run equilibrium at point b. The move to point b is brought about by an inflation rate of 5% (the price level rises from 100 to 105) but yields a lower unemployment rate of just 3%.

(b) Here we see the two equilibrium points in a new graph that plots the inverse relationship between inflation and unemployment rates. This graph, known as a Phillips curve, clarifies that higher inflation can lead to lower levels of unemployment in the short run.

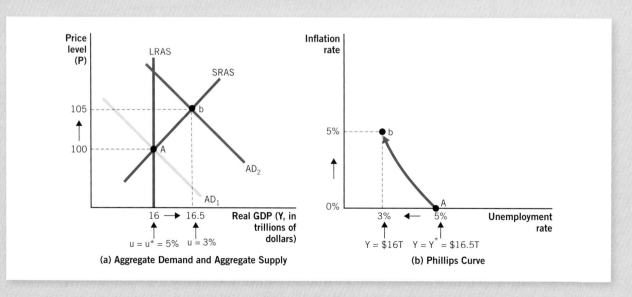

(a) Aggregate Demand and Aggregate Supply

(b) Phillips Curve

rate drops to 3%, as real GDP (Y) expands from $16 trillion to $16.5 trillion. The end result includes both inflation and lower unemployment.

This is the theory behind the Phillips curve relationship: monetary expansion stimulates the economy, and this outcome reduces the unemployment rate. Alternatively, lower inflation is associated with higher unemployment rates. This inverse relationship between inflation and unemployment is captured in panel (b) of Figure 18.9, which graphs a Phillips curve. Initially, at point A, the inflation rate is 0% and the unemployment rate is 5%. But when the inflation rate rises to 5%, the unemployment rate drops to 3%.

This inverse relationship between inflation and unemployment rates is consistent with Phillips's observations and also with what Samuelson and Solow saw when they plotted historical data. Figure 18.10 plots U.S. inflation and unemployment rates from 1948 to 1969, which includes the period just before and just after the work of Samuelson and Solow. The numerical values plotted within the graph represent the years: for example, point 48 represents the year 1948. It is not hard to visualize a Phillips curve relationship in the data: most years with high inflation rates were also years with low unemployment rates, while most years with low inflation rates were also years with high unemployment rates.

The Phillips curve implies a powerful role for monetary policy. It implies that a central bank can choose higher or lower unemployment rates simply by adjusting the rate of inflation in an economy. If this is a realistic

## FIGURE 18.10

**U.S. Inflation and Unemployment Rates, 1948–1969**

Data from 1948 to 1969 was very consistent with standard Phillips curve predictions: lower unemployment rates were consistently correlated with higher inflation rates. (Each number represents the inflation and unemployment combination for that year. For example, in 1952 the inflation rate was about 2% and the unemployment rate was about 3%.)

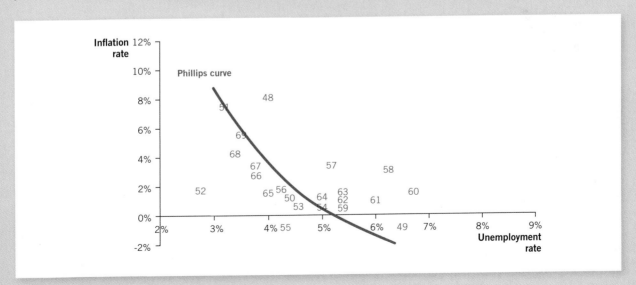

observation, then a central bank can always steer an economy out of recession, simply through creating inflation.

But we have already seen that monetary policy does not always have real effects on the economy. Next we will consider the long run, when the real effects of monetary policy wear off. After that, we will look at how expectations also mitigate the effects of monetary policy.

## The Long-Run Phillips Curve

When all prices adjust, there are no real effects from monetary policy. That is, there are no effects on real GDP or unemployment. Therefore, the long-run Phillips curve looks different from the standard, short-run Phillips curve. Figure 18.11 shows both short-run and long-run Phillips curves. Initially, at point A, there is no inflation in the economy and the unemployment rate is 5%. Then monetary expansion increases the inflation rate to 5%, and the unemployment rate falls to 3% in the short run. This short-run equilibrium is indicated as point b. But when prices adjust, in the long run the unemployment rate returns to 5%. When this happens, the economy moves to a new equilibrium at point C. Inflation is the only result of monetary expansion in the long run.

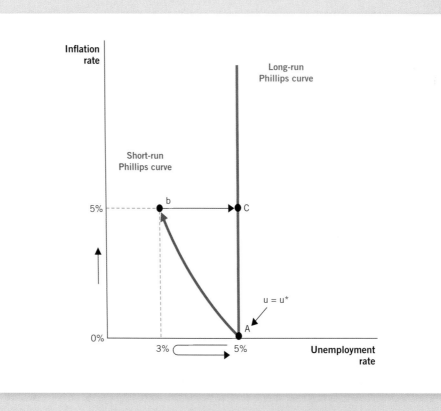

**FIGURE 18.11**

**Short-Run and Long-Run Phillips Curves**

In the short run, inflation can lead to lower unemployment, moving the economy from equilibrium at point A to point b. But in the long run, the effects of monetary policy wear off and the unemployment rate returns to equilibrium at point C. Under normal economic conditions, without inflationary surprises, the economy gravitates back to the natural rate of unemployment. Here the natural rate is 5%. Therefore, in the long run the economy comes back to 5% unemployment, no matter what the inflation rate is. This outcome implies a vertical Phillips curve in the long run.

In Figure 18.11, the unemployment rate is equal to the natural rate (5%) before inflation, and in the long run it returns to the natural rate. Thus, under normal economic conditions, including the situation in which there is no surprise inflation, we expect the unemployment rate to equal the natural rate ($u = u^*$). Monetary policy can push the unemployment rate down, but only in the short run.

We have also learned that the effects of inflation are dampened or eliminated when the inflation is fully expected. We saw this earlier in the context of the aggregate demand–aggregate supply model. Now we look more closely at inflation expectations and how they affect the Phillips curve relationship.

# Expectations and the Phillips Curve

We have seen that expected inflation has no real effects on the macro-economy, even in the short run. This is the case because when inflation is expected, all prices adjust. To think about this further, we consider alternative theories of how people form expectations. This may seem like a topic for microeconomics or perhaps even psychology. But it is particularly relevant to monetary policy because the effects of expected inflation are completely different from the effects of unexpected inflation. When inflation is expected, long-term contracts can reflect inflation and mitigate its effects. But when inflation is unexpected, wages and other prices don't adjust immediately, and this leads to economic expansion.

### Adaptive Expectations Theory

In the late 1960s, economists Milton Friedman and Edmund Phelps hypothesized that people would adapt their expectations about inflation to something consistent with their prior experience. For example, if the actual inflation rate is consistently 2% year after year, people won't expect 0% inflation; they'll expect 2%. The contributions of Friedman and Phelps came to be known as *adaptive expectations*. **Adaptive expectations theory** holds that people's expectations of future inflation are based on their most recent experience. If the inflation rate is 5% in 2013, then adaptive expectations theory implies that people will also expect a 5% inflation rate in 2014.

Consider the hypothetical inflation pattern presented in Table 18.1. The second column shows actual inflation over the course of six years. The inflation rate starts at 0% but then goes up to 2% for two years, then increases to 4% for two years, and then falls to 2% in the last year. If expectations are adaptive, actual inflation in the current period becomes expected inflation for the future. When actual inflation is expected inflation, there is no error, and this is indicated in the last column. For example, a 2% actual inflation rate in 2014 means that people will expect 2% inflation in the future. So when the actual inflation rate is 2% in 2015, this is not a surprise. Adaptive expectations theory predicts that people do not always underestimate inflation.

When the inflation rate *accelerates*, however, people do underestimate inflation. For example, if people experience a 2% inflation rate in 2015, they will expect this level for 2016. But in our example, the rate increases to 4% in 2016, and this leads to an error of −2%. Note that it is also possible to overestimate inflation under adaptive expectations theory. This happens when

**Adaptive expectations theory** holds that people's expectations of future inflation are based on their most recent experience.

## TABLE 18.1

### Adaptive Expectations

| Year | Actual inflation rate | Expected inflation rate | Error |
|------|-----------------------|-------------------------|-------|
| 2013 | 0% | 0% | 0% |
| 2014 | 2% | 0% | −2% |
| 2015 | 2% | 2% | 0% |
| 2016 | 4% | 2% | −2% |
| 2017 | 4% | 4% | 0% |
| 2018 | 2% | 4% | +2% |

**Stagflation**
is the combination of high unemployment rates and high inflation.

**Rational expectations theory**
holds that people form expectations on the basis of all available information.

. . . tick, tock, tick, tock, tick, _____ . . . What comes next?

inflation rates fall. For example, in 2018 people might anticipate a 4% inflation rate since they experienced that level in 2017. If the rate is actually 2%, they will have overestimated it.

The idea behind adaptive expectations theory is not overly complex, but it revolutionized the way economists thought about monetary policy. If expectations adapt, then monetary policy may not have real effects, even in the short run. Expansionary monetary policy can stimulate the economy and reduce unemployment—but only if it is unexpected.

This was the insight of Friedman and Phelps. Their basic reasoning was that people are not quite as simpleminded as the basic Phillips curve implies. Given that surprise inflation harms people, they have an incentive to anticipate inflation and, at the very least, learn from past experience. And yet, the data from the 1960s, shown in Figure 18.10, was certainly consistent with the traditional Phillips curve interpretation. But Friedman and Phelps challenged the accepted wisdom in 1968 and predicted that the Phillips curve relationship would not last. In particular, they predicted that high inflation could not always deliver low unemployment.

It turns out that they were right. Figure 18.12 shows U.S. unemployment and inflation rates for the period 1948 to 1979, with data for the 1970s presented in orange. (Again, as in Figure 18.10, the numerical value represents the year.) Clearly, the 1970s were a difficult decade for the macroeconomy. The prior Phillips curve relationship fell apart—compare Figure 18.10. In the 1970s, inflation was high, and so was unemployment. These macroeconomic conditions have come to be known as **stagflation**, which is the combination of high unemployment rates and high inflation. The stagflation of the 1970s baffled many economists who had come to believe in the validity of the Phillips curve.

### Rational Expectations Theory

Expectations theory evolved yet again in the 1970s and 1980s, in part because of disenchantment with certain implications of adaptive expectations. For example, according to adaptive expectations theory, market participants consistently underestimate inflation when it is accelerating and overestimate inflation when it is decelerating. Expectations are seemingly always a step behind reality. And these errors are predictable.

**Rational expectations theory** holds that people form expectations on the basis of all available information. If people form expectations rationally, they use more than just today's current level of inflation to predict next year's. Rational expectations are different from adaptive expectations in that they are forward-looking, while adaptive expectations only consider past experience.

For example, imagine that inflation is trending upward. Perhaps the actual inflation rate for three periods is 0%, then 2%, and then 4%. Expectations formed rationally recognize the trend and, looking to the future, predict 6%. This outcome is different from what would occur under adaptive expectations, which would instead imply an expectation of 4% in the fourth period, since that is consistent with the most recent experience.

Rational expectations theory does not imply that people always predict inflation correctly. No one knows exactly what the level of inflation will be next year. Prediction errors are inevitable. But people are unlikely to under-predict consistently, even when inflation is accelerating. Rational expectations theory identifies prediction errors as random, like the flip of a coin—sometimes positive, and sometimes negative.

## A Modern View of the Phillips Curve

The short-run Phillips curve is built on the assumption that inflation expectations never adjust. But economists today recognize that since inflation harms some people in the economy, there is an incentive to predict inflation in the future. Therefore, not all inflation is surprise inflation. And when inflation is not a surprise, it does not affect the unemployment rate. So we need to reconsider how different expectations affect the Phillips curve relationship.

Incentives

Consider a hypothetical economy in which policymakers have never used inflation to try to stimulate the economy. Let's say that the inflation rate is 0% and market participants expect 0% inflation going forward. Figure 18.13 shows this initial situation as point A. Now, at point A, if the central bank undertakes policy that raises the inflation rate to 5%, the unemployment rate drops to 3% in the short run. This increase in inflation moves the economy up along the short-run Phillips curve that is labeled $SRPC_0$ (to indicate that expected inflation is 0%: $i^e = 0\%$). The 5% inflation moves the economy to short-run equilibrium at point b on $SRPC_0$.

Now consider what happens if people come to expect a 5% inflation rate. If workers and employers expect 5% inflation, they embed this rate into all

## FIGURE 18.12

### U.S. Inflation and Unemployment Rates, 1948–1979

The 1970s (data points in orange) showed that it is possible to have both high inflation and high unemployment. This decade proved that policymakers could not rely on a permanent, exploitable downward-sloping Phillips curve.

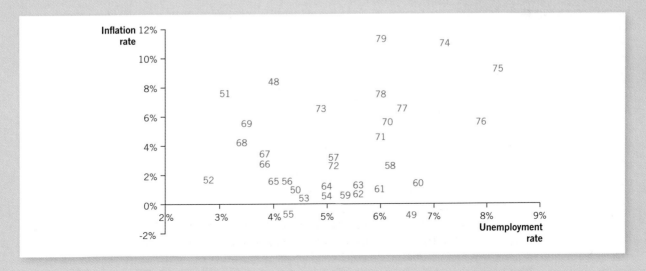

long-term contracts. Therefore, when the 5% inflation arrives, it does not stimulate the economy or reduce unemployment. The economy moves to a new equilibrium at point C, which is on $SRPC_5$ (to indicate that expected inflation is now 5%: $i^e = 5\%$). When actual and expected inflation are both 5%, inflation does not reduce the unemployment rate. In summary, there may be a downward-sloping Phillips curve relationship between inflation and unemployment, but this relationship only holds in the short run. In the long run, when expectations adjust, the unemployment rate cannot be reduced by additional inflation.

Figure 18.14 shows unemployment and inflation data from 1948 through 2011. (In this figure, there is no need to show numerical values for the years.) In looking at this complete data set, we can see clearly that there is no long-run stable relationship between inflation and unemployment. In fact, the data appears to be randomly distributed around the average rate of 5.8%. Economists today believe there are many factors that influence the unemployment rate in the economy, and the inflation rate is just one factor.

## Implications for Monetary Policy

**Active monetary policy** involves the strategic use of monetary policy to counteract macroeconomic expansions and contractions.

We can now use what we've learned about expectations theory and the Phillips curve to evaluate monetary policy recommendations. **Active monetary policy** involves the strategic use of monetary policy to counteract macroeconomic expansions and contractions. In the 1960s, before the development

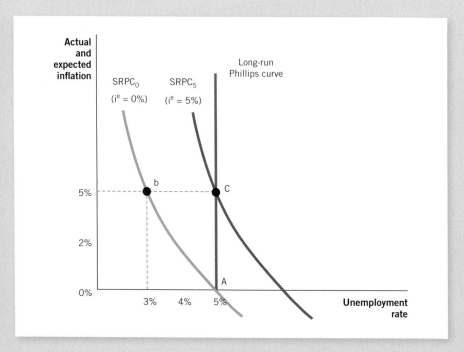

### FIGURE 18.13

**The Phillips Curve with Adjusting Expectations**

Initially, at point A, inflation is 0% and people expect 0% inflation going forward. This means that any positive inflation will reduce the unemployment rate. If the inflation rate is 5%, the unemployment rate falls to 3%, as indicated by movement to equilibrium at point b. But if actual inflation is 5% and expected inflation is also 5%, the unemployment rate moves to the natural rate at point C. There is a different short-run Phillips curve (SRPC) for each level of expectations about inflation.

of expectations theory, monetary policy prescriptions were strictly activist: stimulate inflation during economic downturns, and reduce inflation when the economy is booming. This policy assumed that the Phillips curve relationship between inflation and unemployment would hold up in the long run.

Modern expectations theory prescribes greater caution. If people anticipate the strategies of the central bank, the power of the monetary policy erodes. If expectations adjust, the optimal monetary policy is to maintain transparency and stability. This conclusion holds if expectations are formed either adaptively or rationally. Let's consider each of these in turn.

Consider a scenario in which policymakers use inflation to decrease the unemployment rate. Say the unemployment rate is clearly above the natural rate, and real GDP is not growing. If expectations are adaptive, then inflation will reduce the unemployment rate in the short run. Eventually, expectations will adjust, and then the central bank will have to increase inflation again just to stay ahead of the adjusting expectations. In this scenario, for monetary policy to succeed in keeping the unemployment rate low, inflation has to accelerate and stay a step ahead of expectations. Essentially, this will lead to more and more inflation. Worse yet, if the central bank tries to reduce inflation levels, expected inflation will exceed actual inflation, which will lead to increased unemployment rates in the short run. Thus, if expectations

## FIGURE 18.14

### U.S. Inflation and Unemployment Rates, 1948–2011

Data over the long run presents a picture of inflation and unemployment rates that look random. Clearly, the unemployment rate is influenced by factors other than the rate of inflation.

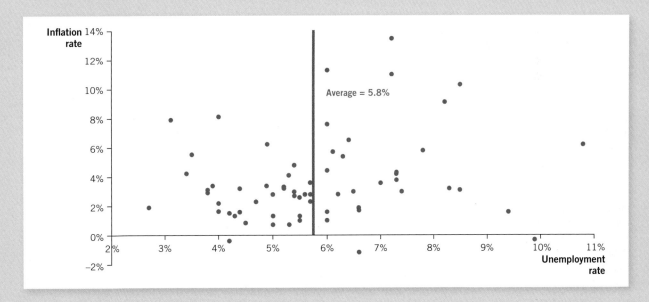

# Expectations

### The Invention of Lying

Imagine a world where no one lied. Ever. In the 2009 movie *The Invention of Lying*, this is the world that Ricky Gervais lives in. Then one day, Gervais accidentally lies. He misstates his bank account balance. After the bank adjusts his balance (upward!), Gervais realizes that no one expects him to lie, so they believe everything he says, no matter how outlandish. No matter how many lies Gervais tells, and no matter how unbelievable his statements, no one ever changes their expectations regarding the truth of his statements—they always believe him. Eventually, he claims to be God. People are stunned. But they completely believe him.

The insanity and irrationality of people's behavior in this movie illustrate exactly how silly it is to continually believe lies that come from the same source. The movie succeeds at being funny because no one in the real world would ever be as gullible or stupid as the people in this movie. In the real world, people would come to expect lies from Gervais. In economics lingo: expectations adjust.

What would you say if people were guaranteed to believe it?

Similarly, in the real world, people come to anticipate inflation when they experience it in period after period. It makes no sense to expect 0% inflation if actual inflation has not been 0% for quite some time. In the real world, expectations adjust.

---

are adaptive, activist monetary policy will lead only to temporary short-run gains in employment. In the long run, it will lead to high inflation or unemployment or both, as it did in the 1970s.

If, instead, expectations are formed rationally, then activist monetary policy may yield no gains whatsoever. Since market participants use all available information when forming inflation expectations, the central bank is unlikely to get any positive results from activist monetary policy, even in the short run.

Therefore, many economists feel that monetary policy surprises should be minimized. **Passive monetary policy** occurs when central banks purposefully choose only to stabilize the money supply and price levels through monetary policy. In particular, passive policy does not seek to use inflation to affect real variables, including unemployment and real GDP, in the economy. In the United States, the Federal Reserve has moved markedly in this direction since the early 1980s. Ben Bernanke and other Federal Reserve Board chairmen have consistently taken actions that lead to fewer surprises in monetary policy.

**Passive monetary policy** occurs when central banks purposefully choose to only stabilize money and price levels through monetary policy.

## ECONOMICS IN THE REAL WORLD

### Federal Reserve Press Conferences

On April 27, 2011, Ben Bernanke held the first press conference by a Fed chairman specifically to talk about the actions of the Fed's policymaking committee. This was an unprecedented leap toward transparency. In the past, the Fed always released carefully worded official statements that often used cryptic language to describe the Fed's outlook for the future.

In the spring of 2011, the economy was struggling to truly emerge from the 2008 recession; unemployment was still over 9%. Yet, in the midst of this, the Fed still decided to lay all its cards on the table. Many observers saw this move as risky. Jacob Goldstein, writing for NPR's *Planet Money* the day before the press conference, explained why it mattered:

> Because everything the head of the Federal Reserve says is a big deal. One off-hand comment can send global markets soaring or plunging. And because Fed chairmen, as a general rule, don't give press conferences. They release official statements that are very, very carefully worded. And they appear before Congress. Since the financial crisis, though, the Fed has come under increased scrutiny. The carefully worded statements and congressional appearances weren't carrying the day. So the leaders of the Fed have decided to send the chairman out for press conferences every few months ("to further enhance the clarity and timeliness of the Federal Reserve's monetary policy communication," in Fedspeak).

Bernanke's moves toward greater Fed openness reflect his belief that central bankers ought to be transparent. The move toward transparency reflects the modern view that expectations matter in macroeconomics—whether they are adaptive or rational. ✳

Chairman Bernanke's willingness to hold a news conference reflected his belief that central bankers should be more transparent.

# Monetary Policy

It is very difficult for the government to exert any control over the forces of supply and demand. In fact, it's impossible. However, there is one component of the economy over which the government does exert great control—money. The Fed is the government entity that controls the money supply and sets monetary policy. It has a dual mandate—to control inflation and maximize employment. Traditionally, the Fed has used three tools in monetary policy: open market operations, the reserve requirement ratio, and the discount rate. During and after the Great Recession the Fed resorted three times to a new tool called quantitative easing.

## Quantitative Easing

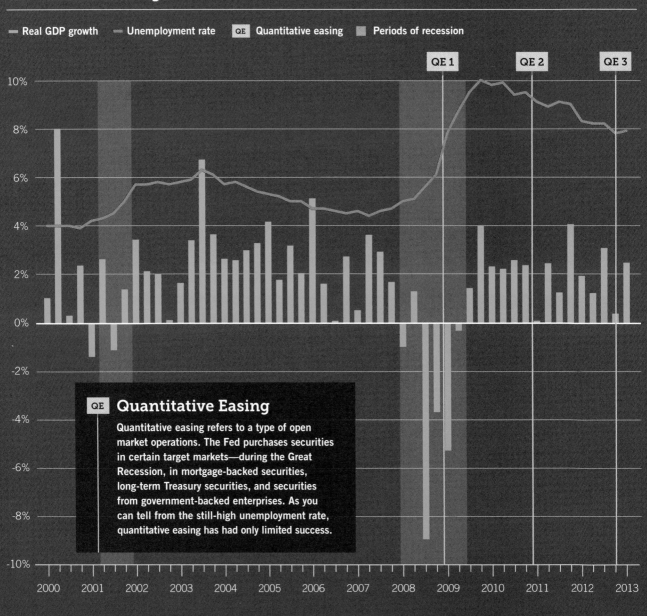

— Real GDP growth    — Unemployment rate    QE Quantitative easing    ▇ Periods of recession

QE 1     QE 2     QE 3

### QE   Quantitative Easing

Quantitative easing refers to a type of open market operations. The Fed purchases securities in certain target markets—during the Great Recession, in mortgage-backed securities, long-term Treasury securities, and securities from government-backed enterprises. As you can tell from the still-high unemployment rate, quantitative easing has had only limited success.

- Knowing that in the long run inflation is the only result of expansionary monetary policy, why would the government act to increase inflation?

- How is quantitative easing similar to traditional open market operations?

## Inflation and Unemployment: Is There a Phillips Curve?

If inflation is unexpected, it can reduce unemployment in the short run. But when inflation is expected, it does not reduce unemployment. In the long run, it is difficult to discern any relationship between inflation and unemployment rates. This suggests that the benefits of activist monetary policy may be severely constrained.

● 1948–1960  ● 1960–1969  ● 1970–1979  ● 1980–1989  ● 1990–1999  ● 2000–2011

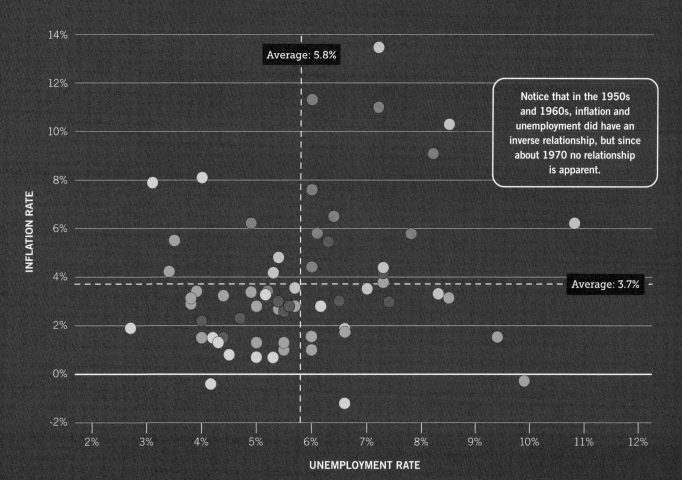

Average: 5.8%

Notice that in the 1950s and 1960s, inflation and unemployment did have an inverse relationship, but since about 1970 no relationship is apparent.

Average: 3.7%

INFLATION RATE

UNEMPLOYMENT RATE

## PRACTICE WHAT YOU KNOW

The European Central Bank (ECB) undertakes monetary policy on behalf of the European Union.

### Monetary Policy: Expectations

Recently, unemployment rates in Europe have been relatively high and inflation has been low. Consider the European economy, in which all market participants expect a 2% inflation rate and the unemployment rate is 9%. Now assume that the European Central Bank (ECB) begins increasing the money supply enough to lead to a 4% inflation rate for a few years.

**Question:** If expectations are for 0% inflation, what happens to the unemployment rate in the short run?

**Answer:** The unemployment rate falls below 9% since the new inflation is a surprise and it can therefore stimulate the economy.

**Question:** If expectations are formed adaptively, what happens to the unemployment rate in both the short run and the long run?

**Answer:** The unemployment rate falls below 9% in the short run, since the new inflation is different from past experience. In the long run, expectations adapt to the 4% inflation and, all else being equal, the unemployment rate returns to 9%.

**Question:** If expectations are formed rationally, what happens to the unemployment rate in the short run?

**Answer:** If expectations are formed rationally, people understand the incentives of the central bank and therefore may anticipate the expansionary monetary policy. In this case, the unemployment rate does not fall.

## Conclusion

We started this chapter with the misconception that central banks can always steer economies out of recession. If this were true, the U.S. economy certainly would not have experienced the sustained downturn that began at the end of 2007. So what can a central bank do? In the short run, if monetary policy is a surprise, a central bank can actually stimulate the economy and perhaps lessen the effects of recession. But these results are mitigated when people come to anticipate monetary policy actions.

In the next two chapters, we turn to the international facets of macroeconomics. International trade, exchange rates, and international finance are becoming more important as the world economy becomes ever more integrated.

# ANSWERING THE BIG QUESTIONS

## What is the effect of monetary policy in the short run?

* In the short run, monetary policy can both speed up and slow down the economy.
* Some prices are sticky in the short run. When some prices fail to adjust, changes in the money supply are essentially a change in real financial resources.
* If the monetary policy is expansionary, this can stimulate the economy, increasing real GDP and reducing the unemployment rate.
* If the monetary policy is contractionary, this can slow the economy, which may help to reduce inflation.

## Why doesn't monetary policy always work?

* Monetary policy fails to produce real effects under three different circumstances. First, monetary policy has no real effect in the long run, since all prices can adjust. Second, if monetary policy is fully anticipated, prices adjust. Finally, if the economy is experiencing shifts in aggregate supply, monetary policy may be unable to restore normal growth, since it works primarily through aggregate demand.

## What is the Phillips curve?

* The Phillips curve is a theoretical inverse relationship between inflation and unemployment rates. The modern consensus is that the Phillips curve is a short-run phenomenon but that it does not hold in the long run.
* The power of inflation to reduce unemployment is directly related to how people's inflation expectations adjust throughout the economy. Modern expectations theory allows for adjusting expectations, and this is why most economists now believe that the Phillips curve relationship does not hold in the long run.

ECONOMICS FOR LIFE

# How to Protect Yourself from Inflation

In this chapter, we have talked about how inflation harms some people. We have also talked about how inflation doesn't harm people if they know it is coming—if it is expected.

If you are worried about inflation harming you, you can protect yourself from its effects. In recent history, U.S. inflation has been low and steady. When this is the case, it doesn't really harm anyone because it is easy to predict. But if you live in a country such as Argentina, where inflation has often been a problem because it has been high and unpredictable, or if you are worried about future inflation in the United States, these tips are for you.

The two types of people most often harmed by inflation are workers with fixed wages and lenders with fixed interest rates. Let's look at how to avoid inflation trouble in both instances.

First, let's say you a worker who is worried about inflation. One way to protect yourself is to avoid committing to long-term wage deals. If you must sign a contract, keep it short in duration. Better yet, include a clause in your contract that stipulates cost of living adjustments (COLAs) that are tied to a price index like the CPI. This way, you are hedged against future inflation in your wages.

Second, perhaps you are more worried about inflation's effect on your savings or retirement funds. In this case, you are a lender and thus susceptible to fixed interest rates. One way to avoid negative returns is to purchase securities or assets that tend to rise in value along with inflation. Stock prices generally go up with inflation, so you may want to invest more of your retirement funds in stocks, rather than bonds. Gold is another asset that tends to appreciate in inflationary times because its value is tied to something real.

However, stocks can be risky, and the long-term returns on gold are historically very low. Thus, you might consider buying Treasury Inflation Protected Securities (TIPS). These are low-risk U.S. Treasury bonds that are actually indexed to inflation rates. Therefore, if inflation goes up, you get a higher rate of return. These bonds guarantee a particular real rate of return, no matter what the rate of inflation.

Gold is not a great long-term investment unless you really fear inflation.

# CONCEPTS YOU SHOULD KNOW

active monetary policy (p. 568)
adaptive expectations theory
   (p. 565)
contractionary monetary policy
   (p. 553)

expansionary monetary policy
   (p. 549)
monetary neutrality (p. 558)
passive monetary policy (p. 570)
Phillips curve (p. 562)

rational expectations theory
   (p. 566)
stagflation (p. 566)

# QUESTIONS FOR REVIEW

1. Why it is possible to change real economic factors in the short run simply by printing and distributing more money?

2. Many people focus on the effect of monetary policy on interest rates in the economy.

   a. Use the loanable funds market to explain how unexpected contractionary monetary policy affects interest rates in the short run.

   b. Now explain how these changes affect aggregate demand and supply in both the short run and the long run. Be sure to also explain the changes in real GDP, the unemployment rate, and the price level.

3. During the economic slowdown that began at the end of 2007, the Federal Reserve used

monetary policy to reduce interest rates in the economy. Use what you learned in this chapter to give a possible explanation as to why the monetary policy failed to restore the economy to long-run equilibrium.

4. Explain why a stable 5% inflation rate a can be preferable to one that averages 4% but varies between 1% and 7% regularly.

5. Who is harmed when inflation is less than anticipated? In what way are they harmed? Who is harmed when inflation is greater than anticipated? In what way are they harmed?

6. Explain the difference between active and passive monetary policy.

# STUDY PROBLEMS (∗ solved at the end of the section)

1. Use the aggregate demand–aggregate supply model to illustrate the downward-sloping relationship between inflation and unemployment rates in the short-run Phillips curve.

2. Suppose the economy is in long-run equilibrium, with real GDP at $16 trillion and the unemployment rate at 5%. Now assume that the central bank unexpectedly *decreases* the money supply by 6%.

   a. Illustrate the short-run effects on the macroeconomy by using the aggregate supply–aggregate demand model. Be sure to indicate the direction of change in real GDP, the price level, and the unemployment rate.

   b. Illustrate the long-run effects on the macroeconomy by using the aggregate supply–

aggregate demand model. Again, be sure to indicate the direction of change in real GDP, the price level, and the unemployment rate.

   c. Now assume that this monetary expansion was completely expected. Illustrate both short-run and long-run effects on the macroeconomy by using the aggregate supply–aggregate demand model. Be sure to indicate the direction of change in real GDP, the price level, and the unemployment rate.

3. Suppose the economy is in long-run equilibrium, with real GDP at $16 trillion and the unemployment rate at 5%. Now assume that the central bank *increases* the money supply by 6%.

   a. Illustrate the short-run effects on the macroeconomy by using the aggregate supply–

aggregate demand model. Be sure to indicate the direction of change in real GDP, the price level, and the unemployment rate.

b. Illustrate the long-run effects on the macroeconomy by using the aggregate supply–aggregate demand model. Again, be sure to indicate the direction of change in real GDP, the price level, and the unemployment rate.

c. Now assume that this monetary expansion was completely expected. Illustrate both short-run and long-run effects on the macroeconomy by using the aggregate supply–aggregate demand model. Be sure to indicate the direction of change in real GDP, the price level, and the unemployment rate.

✳ 4. In the past, some people believed that the Federal Reserve routinely expanded the money supply during presidential election years in order to stimulate the economy and help the incumbent president. For this question, assume that the Fed increases inflation by 3% in every election year.

a. Describe the effect on the economy during election years if market participants expect 0% inflation.

b. Describe the effect on the economy during election years if expectations are formed adaptively.

c. Describe the effect on the economy during election years if expectations are formed rationally.

✳ 5. In each of the scenarios listed below, estimate the unemployment rate in comparison to the natural rate ($u^*$).

a. Inflation is steady at 2% for two years but then increases to 5% for a year.

b. Inflation is steady at 10% for two years but then decreases to 5% for a year.

c. Inflation is steady at 8% for several years.

d. Inflation is steady at 2% for three years, and then the Fed announces that inflation will be 3% one year later.

# SOLVED PROBLEMS

4. **a.** If people expect 0% inflation, any positive inflation will stimulate the economy and lower the unemployment rate.

**b.** If people form their inflation expectations adaptively, they will not anticipate inflation in an election year because it would be a break from their recent experience. Therefore, inflation in election years will consistently lower the rate of unemployment.

**c.** If expectations are formed rationally, then people will consider the incentives of policymakers during election years. Therefore, they will anticipate higher inflation in those years, and the inflation rate will have no effect on the unemployment rate.

5. **a.** The increase in inflation is likely a surprise, which means that it stimulates the economy and reduces the unemployment rate to a level below the natural rate.

**b.** The decrease in inflation is likely a surprise, which means that it slows the economy and increases the unemployment rate to a level above the natural rate.

**c.** Here there are no inflationary surprises, so the inflation rate does not influence the unemployment rate. Therefore, all else being equal, we should expect the unemployment rate to be near the natural rate.

**d.** Even though the inflation rate increases, it is not a surprise, so all prices have time to adjust. Therefore, all else being equal, we should expect the unemployment rate to be near the natural rate.

| | | |
|---|---|---|
| 2/25 | | 11:21 |

| | | |
|---|---|---|
| 11618.53 | 安 | 11562.10 |
| 1部 1624.57 | 2部 | 15.96 |
| 11600 | | +190 |
| 11630 | 安 | 11550 |
| 11600 | | +195 |
| 979.26 | | +15.78 |
| 981.80 | 安 | 976.21 |
| 1611.68 | | +42 |
| 1612.68 | 安 | 1606.60 |
| 14.68 | | 0.18 |
| 124.05-15 | | -0.98 |
| 96.66-72 | | -0.83 |
| 14000.57 | | +119.95 |
| 3161.82 | | +90.33 |
| 22806.34 | | +23.90 |

| アルバック | ミツミ |
|---|---|
| 909 | 554 |
| | +9 |
| 6752/T | 6770/T |
| パナソニック | アルプス |
| 687 | 608 |
| +16 | +3 |
| 6753/T | 6773/T |
| シャープ | パイオニア |
| 291 | 195 |
| -19 | +5 |
| 6754/T | 6796/T |
| アンリツ | クラリオン |
| 1349 | 125 |
| +7 | +4 |
| 6756/T | 6841/T |
| 日立国際 | 横河電 |
| 801 | 987 |
| +10 | +45 |
| 6758/T | 6857/T |
| ソニー | アドバンテ |
| 1329 | 1296 |

# International
# ECONOMICS

# International Trade

**A nation should never trade for goods and services that it can produce itself.**

It is generally assumed that nations should try to produce their own goods and services. In particular, it seems intuitive that if the United

**MIS CONCEPTION**

States can produce a particular good more efficiently than any other nation can produce that good, then the United States should definitely produce that good for itself. But this assumption is not necessarily true. Economics helps us understand that we may be better off letting another nation produce the good and then trading for it later. When we do this, the trade enables us to specialize in production for another good that we can produce best. In addition, it means that a growth in international trade is probably beneficial to nations.

Over the past few decades, the level of trade among the world's nations has risen dramatically. To help illustrate the extent of international trade, we begin this chapter with a look at global trade data. We then consider how international trade affects an economy. Finally, we examine trade barriers and the reasons for their existence.

Imports come into the United States from all over the globe. But do the contents of these shipping containers harm our economy?

# BIG QUESTIONS

* Is globalization for real?
* How does international trade help the economy?
* What are the effects of tariffs and quotas?

## Is Globalization for Real?

Over the past 70 years, nations all over the world have increased both imports and exports. What this means for you and me is that we now can buy fresh Peruvian strawberries (in February!), roses from Kenya, cars made in Mexico, and electronics produced in South Korea. But the United States also exports more now than in any earlier era. Imports and exports are both up, and this activity indicates that economies around the globe are becoming ever more integrated or interdependent. This is what we mean by *globalization*, and it is changing not only what you purchase but also your future job prospects.

Consider a single popular item: the iPhone. Inside the iPhone are parts made in Germany, Japan, Korea, and the United States. The phone is famously "designed by Apple in California," but it is assembled in China. This single item requires thousands of miles of global shipping before anyone ever receives a call on it.

The modern trade explosion has occurred for many reasons. Among these are lower shipping costs, reduced trade barriers, and increased specialization in world economies. Total world exports of goods and services are now about

---

**FIGURE 19.1**

**Real Value of World Merchandise Trade, 1970–2010**

Over 40 years, world merchandise trade increased tenfold in real terms, from $1.3 trillion in 1970 to over $13 trillion in 2010. Between 2001 and 2010, merchandise trade doubled.

*Source*: World Trade Organization.

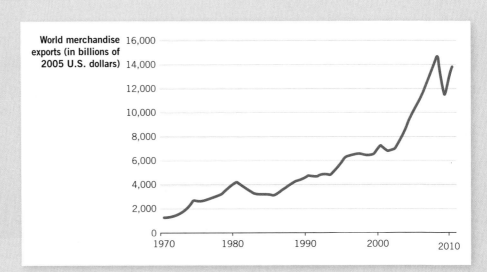

How many borders does an iPhone cross before it is sold?

one-fourth the size of world GDP. In this section, we look first at the growth in total world trade and then at trends in U.S. trade.

## Growth in World Trade

"Globalization" is a buzzword that has gained traction in the past two decades as people have sensed a deeper integration of world economies. In this section, we look at the trade data that confirms this general sentiment. We start with a look at total world exports over time. Figure 19.1 shows total world trade in merchandise (goods) from 1970 to 2010. This data, which is adjusted for inflation, indicates that world trade in goods grew from $1.3 trillion to over $13 trillion. That's a tenfold increase in just 40 years. Furthermore, since 2000, world goods trade has doubled.

World trade has grown, but not just in market value. It has also grown as a percentage of total world output. That is, not only are nations trading more, but they are also trading a greater portion of their GDP. Figure 19.2 shows merchandise trade as a percentage of world GDP. This too has expanded dramatically, more than doubling over 40 years. The data in Figures 19.1 and 19.2 tell us that international trade is now a significant portion of the world economy.

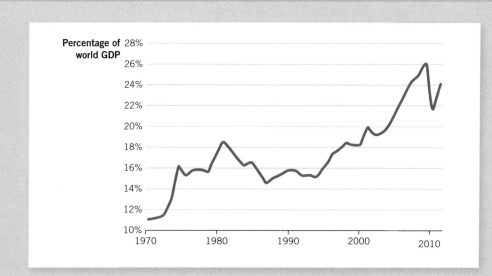

**FIGURE 19.2**

**World Trade as a Percentage of World GDP, 1970–2010**

Even as a percentage of world GDP, trade has grown significantly. It more than doubled from 11% in 1970 to over 24% in 2010.

*Sources*: World Trade Organization; World Bank.

## ECONOMICS IN THE REAL WORLD

### Nicaragua Is Focused on Trade

Nicaragua, the second-poorest nation in the Western Hemisphere, is trying to escape poverty through international trade. Between 2003 and 2011, its real exports grew from $1.2 trillion to $3.5 trillion.

Trade with Nicaragua is growing in part because the country has established "free zones," where companies can produce goods for export and avoid standard corporate tax rates. Typical Nicaraguan companies pay a myriad of sales taxes, value-added taxes, corporate profit taxes, and dividend taxes. But these do not apply to output that a company exports to other nations. U.S. companies that have taken advantage of production in these free zones include Levi's, Under Armour, and Nike.

All else equal, market-driven international trade certainly helps nations to prosper. Yet while the free zones are increasing exports, the effect on domestic consumers in Nicaragua may not be entirely positive. Because the goods have to be exported in order for the manufacturers to take advantage of the tax breaks, there is very little incentive to produce goods for domestic purchase. ✳

The Levi-Strauss company produces many of its blue jeans in Nicaragua.

## Trends in U.S. Trade

The United States is the world's biggest economy. A huge amount of trade takes place among the individual states *inside* the country. For example, residents of Michigan buy oranges from Florida, and Floridians buy cars from Michigan. Still, even with the ability to produce and trade so much within U.S. borders, the nation's participation in international trade rose dramatically in recent years. Figure 19.3 shows U.S. imports and exports as a percentage of GDP from 1960 to 2010.

As you look at the data presented in Figure 19.3, note three features. First, in panel (a) you can see that both imports and exports increased significantly over the 50 years from 1960 to 2010. U.S. exports grew from less than 5% to over 12% of GDP. During the same period, imports rose from less than 5% to over 16% of GDP. Note also that these changes occurred even as real GDP grew by over 3% each year (a fact we learned in Chapter 6). This is another clear glimpse at the modern trend toward globalization: the world's largest economy is becoming ever more intertwined with those of other nations.

A nation's **trade balance** is the difference between its total exports and total imports.

A **trade surplus** occurs when exports exceed imports, indicating a positive trade balance.

A **trade deficit** occurs when imports exceed exports, indicating a negative trade balance.

Since 1975, U.S. imports have exceeded U.S. exports. In Chapter 6, we defined net exports as total exports of goods and services minus total imports of goods and services. The difference between a nation's total exports and total imports is its **trade balance**. If a nation exports more than it imports, it has a positive trade balance, known as a **trade surplus**. However, if a nation imports more than it exports, the trade balance is negative, and this is called a **trade deficit**. The United States has had a trade deficit since 1975. In 2010 alone, the United States exported $1.83 trillion in goods and services but imported $2.83 trillion, leading to a trade deficit of $1 trillion—no small sum. We will cover this subject further in Chapter 20.

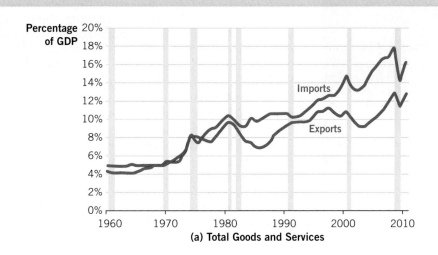

(a) Total Goods and Services

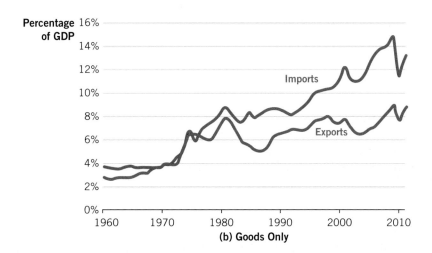

(b) Goods Only

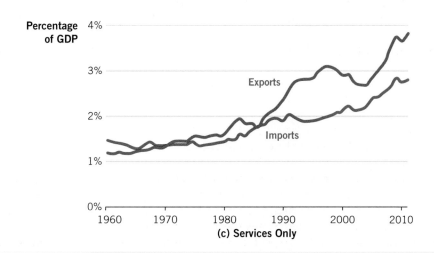

(c) Services Only

**FIGURE 19.3**

### U.S. Exports and Imports, 1960–2010 (as a percentage of GDP)

(a) Both imports and exports are rising in the United States. In addition, the trade balance is becoming more negative over time, as exports are exceeding imports by an increasingly wider margin. This trade deficit grows larger during periods of economic growth and shrinks during recessions (shaded bars).

(b) The trade deficit is driven by a merchandise (goods) deficit, because (c) the United States enjoys a trade surplus in services.

*Source*: U.S. Bureau of Economic Analysis, *U.S. International Transactions.*

Foreign students who purchase their education in the United States are a picture of one type of U.S. service exports.

Panels (b) and (c) of Figure 19.3 reveal a little-known fact about U.S. trade: while the merchandise (goods) trade deficit is large and growing, the United States actually has a service trade surplus. Popular service exports of the United States include financial, travel, and education services. To put a face on service exports, think about students in your classes who are not U.S. citizens (perhaps this even includes you!). In 2010, the United States exported over $21 billion worth of education services.

Finally, notice how the business cycle affects international trade. During recessionary periods (indicated by the vertical blue-shaded bars in Figure 19.3a), imports generally drop. As the economy recovers, imports begin to rise again. In addition, while exports often drop during recessions, the trade deficit tends to shrink during downturns. Part of this fluctuation reflects the way imports and exports are calculated, which we will discuss in Chapter 20. For now, note the strong relationship between trade and economic activity: trade expands during economic expansions and contracts during recessions.

## Major Trading Partners of the United States

In 2011, the United States imported goods and services from 238 nations. However, 60% of goods imports came from just seven nations. Figure 19.4 shows the value of imports from and exports to these top seven trading partners of the United States.

In the past, our closest neighbors—Canada and Mexico—were our chief trading partners. From Canada we get motor vehicles, oil, natural gas, and

### FIGURE 19.4

**Major Goods Trading Partners of the United States, 2011 (in billions of dollars)**

Fully 60% of all U.S. goods imports come from the seven nations shown here. We export more to Canada and Mexico than to other nations, but we import more from China. The U.S. trade deficit with China is almost $300 billion.

*Source*: U.S. Bureau of Economic Analysis.

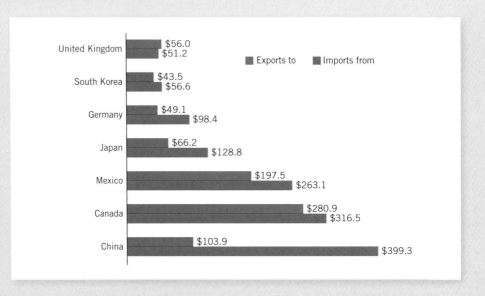

# PRACTICE WHAT YOU KNOW

## Trade in Goods and Services: Deficit or Surplus?

The United States imports many goods from Japan, including automobiles, electronics, and medical instruments. But we also export many services to Japan, such as financial and travel services. The table below presents trade data between the United States and Japan in 2011. (All figures are in billions of U.S. dollars.)

|  | Exports to Japan | Imports from Japan |
|---|---|---|
| Goods | $66 | $129 |
| Services | $47 | $25 |

Sony PlayStations are a popular U.S. import from Japan.

**Question:** Using the data shown above, how would you compute the U.S. goods trade balance with Japan? Is the balance a surplus or a deficit?

**Answer:** The U.S. goods trade balance equals:

$$\text{goods exports} - \text{goods imports}$$
$$= \$66 \text{ billion} - \$129 \text{ billion} = -\$63 \text{ billion}$$

This is a deficit, since imports exceed exports and the trade balance is negative.

**Question:** Now how would you compute the U.S. service trade balance with Japan? Is the balance a surplus or a deficit?

**Answer:** The U.S. services trade balance equals:

$$\text{service exports} - \text{service imports}$$
$$= \$47 \text{ billion} - \$25 \text{ billion} = \$22 \text{ billion}$$

This is a surplus, since exports exceed imports and the trade balance is positive.

**Question:** Finally, how would you compute the overall U.S. trade balance with Japan, which includes both goods and services? Is this overall trade balance a surplus or a deficit?

**Answer:** The overall U.S. trade balance equals:

$$\text{goods and service exports} - \text{goods and service imports}$$
$$= \$113 \text{ billion} - \$154 \text{ billion} = -\$41 \text{ billion}$$

This is a deficit, since imports exceed exports and the trade balance is negative.

*Data source*: Office of the United States Trade Representative.

Is there anything in this picture *not* produced in China?

many other goods and services. From Mexico we get coffee, computers, household appliances, and gold. Recently, transportation costs have decreased and we are trading in volume with other countries. For example, total imports from China alone are now roughly $400 billion, up from $105 billion (adjusted for inflation) a decade ago. Popular Chinese imports include electronics, toys, and clothing.

Canada and Mexico buy the most U.S. exports. To Canada we export cars, car parts, computers, and agricultural products. To Mexico we export cars, car parts, computers, and meat, among many other items. Financial and travel services are major U.S. exports to all our major trading partners.

# How Does International Trade Help the Economy?

Trade creates value

In this section, we explain how comparative advantage and specialization make it possible to achieve gains from trade among nations. To keep the analysis simple, we will assume that two trading partners—the United States and Mexico—only produce two items, clothes and food. This will enable us to demonstrate that trade creates value in the absence of any restrictions.

## Comparative Advantage

In Chapter 2, we saw that trade creates value and that comparative advantage makes this possible. Gains arise when a nation specializes in production and exchanges its output with a trading partner. In other words, each nation should produce the good it is best at making and trade with other nations for the goods they are best at making. When this happens, the transaction leads to lower costs of production and maximizes the combined output of all nations involved.

For example, assume that the U.S. workforce is generally more skilled than that of Mexico and that the United States has much more farmland. Mexico has a less skilled workforce and tends to produce products that require more labor than capital. Therefore, Mexico has a comparative advantage in producing labor-intensive goods such as clothing, and the United States has a comparative advantage in producing capital-intensive goods such as food.

In Figure 19.5, we see the production possibilities frontier (the PPF curve) for each country when it does *not* specialize and trade. In panel (a), Mexico can produce at any point along its PPF. This means that it could produce 900 million (M) units, or articles, of clothing if it does not make any food, or 300 million tons of food if it does not make any clothing. Neither extreme is especially desirable since it would mean that Mexico would have to do without either clothing or food. As a result, Mexico will choose to operate somewhere in between the two extremes. In panel (a), we show Mexico operating along its production possibilities frontier at 450 million articles of clothing and 150 tons of food. Panel (b) shows that the United States could produce 400 million articles of clothing if it does not make any food, or 800 million tons of food if it does not make any clothing. Like Mexico, the United States will choose to operate somewhere in between—for example, at 300 million articles of clothing and 200 million tons of food.

To see whether gains from trade are able to make both countries better off, we must first examine the opportunity cost that each country faces when making these two goods. In Mexico, producing 150 million tons of food means giving up the production of 450 million articles of clothing ($900 - 450 = 450$). Thus, each ton of food incurs an opportunity cost of three articles of clothing, yielding a ratio of 1:3, or one ton of food per three articles of clothing. In the United States, producing 200 million tons of food means giving up production of 100 million articles of clothing ($400 - 300 = 100$). Each ton of food incurs an opportunity cost of one-half an article of clothing, yielding a ratio of 2:1. Table 19.1 shows the initial production choices and the opportunity costs for both nations.

As long as the opportunity cost of the production of the two goods differs between the two countries, as it does here, trade has the potential to benefit both. The key to making trade mutually beneficial in this case is to find a trading ratio between 1:3 and 2:1. For instance, if Mexico and the United States establish a 1:1 trading ratio, it would enable Mexico to acquire food at a lower cost from the United States than the cost of producing food itself. At the same time, the United States would be able to acquire clothing from Mexico at a lower cost than the cost of producing the clothing itself.

## FIGURE 19.5

**The Production Possibilities Frontier for Mexico and the United States without Specialization and Trade**

(a) Mexico chooses to operate along its production possibilities curve at 450 million articles of clothing and 150 tons of food. Each ton of food incurs an opportunity cost of three articles of clothing—a ratio of 1:3.

(b) The United States chooses to operate along its production possibilities curve at 300 million articles of clothing and 200 million tons of food. Each ton of food incurs an opportunity cost of one-half an article of clothing—a ratio of 2:1.

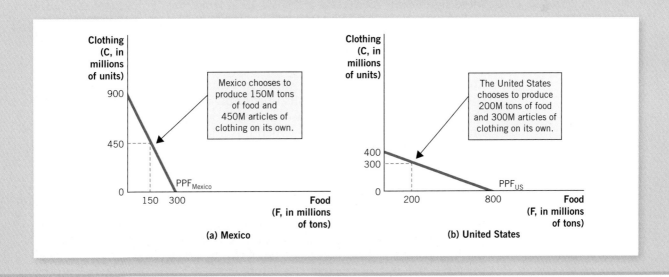

| TABLE 19.1 | | | | |
| --- | --- | --- | --- | --- |
| **Output and Opportunity Costs for Mexico and the United States** | | | | |
| | Chosen output level | | Opportunity cost | |
| | Food (millions of tons) | Clothing (millions of units) | Food (F) | Clothing (C) |
| Mexico | 150 | 450 | 3 C | ⅓ F |
| United States | 200 | 300 | ½ C | 2 F |

Figure 19.6 shows the effects of a 1:1 trade agreement on the joint production possibilities frontier for each country. If the two countries trade, each can specialize in its comparative advantage. This means that the United States produces food and Mexico produces clothing.

Notice that specialization and trade benefits both countries. Let's begin with Mexico as shown in panel (a). Mexico specializes in the production of clothing, producing 900 million units. It then exports 400 million units of clothing to the United States and imports 400 million tons of food from the United States in return—this is the 1:1 trade ratio we identified previously. Therefore, Mexico ends up at point $M_2$ with 500 million units of clothing and 400 million tons of food. Notice that Mexico's production without trade (at point $M_1$) was 450 million units of clothing and 150 tons of food. Therefore, specialization and trade have made Mexico better off by 50 million units of clothing and 250 million tons of food.

Now let's look at the United States in panel (b). The country specializes in the production of food, producing 800 million tons. It exports 400 million tons of food to Mexico and imports 400 million units of clothing from Mexico in return. Therefore, the United States ends up at point $US_2$ with 400 million units of clothing and 400 million tons of food. Notice that U.S. production without trade (at point $US_1$) was 300 million units of clothing and 200 tons of food. Therefore, specialization and trade have made the United States better off by 100 million units of clothing and 200 million tons of food.

The combined benefits that Mexico and the United States enjoy are even more significant. As we saw in Figure 19.5, when Mexico did not specialize and trade it chose to make 450 million units of clothing and 150 million tons of food. Without specialization and trade, the United States chose to produce 300 million units of clothing and 200 million tons of food. The combined output without specialization was 750 million units of clothing and 350 million tons of food. However, as we see in Figure 19.6, the joint output with specialization is 900 million units of clothing and 800 million tons of food. Trade is a win-win proposition because each country is able to (1) concentrate on the production of goods for which it is a low-opportunity-cost producer and (2) trade for goods for which it is a high-opportunity-cost producer.

## Other Advantages of Trade

Although comparative advantage is the biggest reason that many nations trade with other nations, there are other good reasons for nations to engage in trade. In this section, we consider how international trade encourages both economies of scale and increased competition, and how these factors can help an economy to grow.

## Economies of Scale

When a nation specializes its production, it can take advantage of lower production costs that can accompany large-scale production processes. This is especially important for smaller nations that do not have a workforce big enough to support the domestic production of large-scale items such as automobiles, television sets, steel, and aluminum. However, once a smaller nation has free access to larger markets, it can effectively specialize in what it does best and generate low per-unit costs through exports.

In Figures 19.5 and 19.6, the production possibilities frontier is shown as a straight line. This makes the computation of the ratios fairly simple and holds the opportunity cost constant. However, in the real world, access to new markets can create economies of scale and, therefore, lower per-unit costs as production expands. Increased production gives companies the opportunity to economize on distribution costs and marketing, and to utilize assembly lines and other forms of automation.

Consider how a small textile company based in Mexico fares under this arrangement. With international trade, the company can expand its sales into the United States—a much larger market. This move creates additional

## FIGURE 19.6

**The Joint Production Possibilities Frontier for Mexico and the United States with Specialization and Trade**

(a) After Mexico specializes in clothing and trades with the United States, it is better off by 50 million units of clothing and 250 million tons of food (compare points $M_1$ and $M_2$). .

(b) After the United States specializes in food and trades with Mexico, it is better off by 100 million units of clothing and 200 million tons of food (compare points $US_1$ and $US_2$).

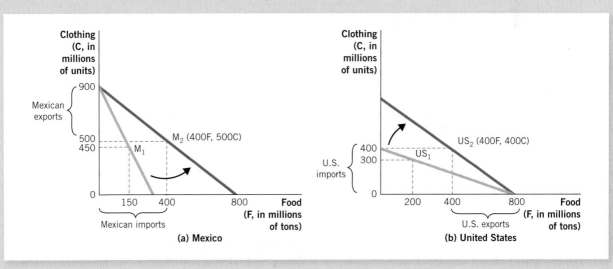

(a) Mexico

(b) United States

# PRACTICE WHAT YOU KNOW

Does China enjoy a comparative advantage in textile production?

## Opportunity Cost and Comparative Advantage: Determining Comparative Advantage

U.S. trade with mainland China has exploded in the past decade, with goods imports reaching $400 billion a year and exports up to $100 billion. In this question, we consider a hypothetical production possibilities frontier for food and textiles in both China and the United States.

The table below presents daily production possibilities for a typical worker in both China and the United States, assuming these are the only goods produced in both countries. (The numbers represent units of food and units of textiles.)

| | Output per worker per day | |
|---|:---:|:---:|
| | Food | Textiles |
| China | 1 | 2 |
| United States | 9 | 3 |

**Question:** What are the opportunity costs of food production for both China and the United States?

**Answer:** The opportunity cost of food production in China is the amount of textile production that is foregone for a single unit of food output. Since a Chinese worker can produce 2 textile units in a day and 1 unit of food, the opportunity cost of 1 unit of food is *2 textiles.*

In the United States, a worker can produce 3 textile units in one day or 9 units of food. Thus, the opportunity cost of 1 unit of food is just ⅓ *textile unit.*

**Question:** What are the opportunity costs of textile production for both China and the United States?

**Answer:** The opportunity cost of textile production in China is the amount of food production that is foregone for a single textile produced. Since a Chinese worker can produce 1 unit of food in a day and 2 textile units, the opportunity cost of 1 textile unit is ½ *unit of food.*

In the United States, a worker can produce 9 units of food in one day or 3 textile units. Thus, the opportunity cost of 1 textile unit is *3 units of food.*

**Question:** Which nation has a comparative advantage in food production? Which nation has a comparative advantage in textile production?

**Answer:** The United States has a lower opportunity cost of food production (⅓ versus 2 textile units), so its comparative advantage is in food production. China has a lower opportunity cost of textile production (½ versus 3 units of food), so it has a comparative advantage in textile production.

demand, which translates into added sales. A larger volume of sales enables the textile firm's production, marketing, and sales to become more efficient. The firm can purchase fabrics in bulk, expand its distribution network, and use volume advertising.

### Increased Competition

Another largely unseen benefit from trade is increased competition. In fact, increased competition from foreign suppliers forces domestic firms to become more innovative and to compete in terms of both price and quality. Competition also gives consumers more options to choose from, which enables consumers to purchase a broader array of products that better match their needs. For example, many cars are produced in the United States, but foreign automobiles offer U.S. consumers greater variety and help to keep the prices of domestically made cars lower than they would be otherwise.

## Trade Agreements and the WTO

Because trading is so beneficial, nations often reach trade agreements that specify the conditions of free trade. For example, the North American Free Trade Agreement (NAFTA), which was signed in 1992, eliminated nearly all trade restrictions among Canada, Mexico, and the United States. Currently, the United States has trade agreements with 20 nations.

Even though trade agreements often stipulate protections for particular industries (most notably, agriculture), they still increase trade among nations. For example, as a result of NAFTA, real U.S. imports and exports of goods with Canada and Mexico have both doubled. In 1993 the United States exported $183 billion worth of goods to Canada, but by 2010 this amount rose to $350 billion. Over the same period, exports to Mexico grew from $80 billion to $201 billion. Imports from both nations also expanded: imports from Canada grew from $180 billion to $332 billion, and imports from Mexico grew from $76 billion to $260 billion. The reduction in trade barriers has enabled all three nations to move toward the production of goods and services for which they enjoy a comparative advantage.

The World Trade Organization (WTO) is an international organization that facilitates trade agreements among nations. The WTO also works to resolve trade disputes. For example, in 2012 the WTO helped to end a 20-year disagreement between Latin American banana exporters and the European Union over a tax on imported bananas.

NAFTA created a broad, geographically connected network of lower trade barriers, fostering growth across much of North America.

## What Are the Effects of Tariffs and Quotas?

Despite the benefits of free trade, significant trade barriers such as import taxes often exist. For example, almost every shoe purchased in the United States is made overseas; but with few exceptions, the U.S. government taxes each pair of shoes that comes across its borders to be sold. In fact, many

# Major U.S. Trade Partners

Though the United States imports goods from over 230 nations in the world, just 7 of those countries account for over 60% of these imports. These same 7 countries buy more U.S. goods exports than any other country as well. Clearly, our major trade partners produce numerous items that Americans demand, and the United States produces numerous items that these countries desire.

— U.S. goods exports to trade partner (2011)    — U.S. goods imports from trade partner (2011)

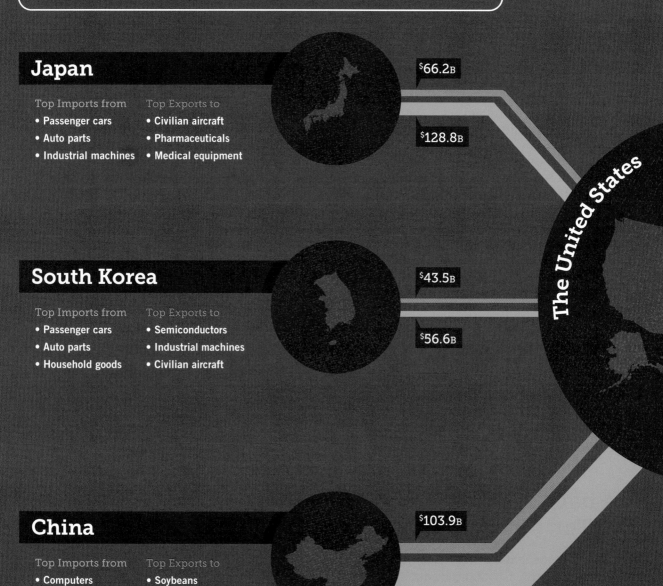

## Japan

$66.2B

$128.8B

**Top Imports from**
- Passenger cars
- Auto parts
- Industrial machines

**Top Exports to**
- Civilian aircraft
- Pharmaceuticals
- Medical equipment

## South Korea

$43.5B

$56.6B

**Top Imports from**
- Passenger cars
- Auto parts
- Household goods

**Top Exports to**
- Semiconductors
- Industrial machines
- Civilian aircraft

## China

$103.9B

$399.3B

**Top Imports from**
- Computers
- Household goods
- Apparel

**Top Exports to**
- Soybeans
- Civilian aircraft
- Passenger cars

The United States

# REVIEW QUESTIONS

- What U.S. industry generates the most universal demand from our trading partners?

- Based on the list of U.S. imports, how would you finish this sentence? "Americans sure love their _____!"

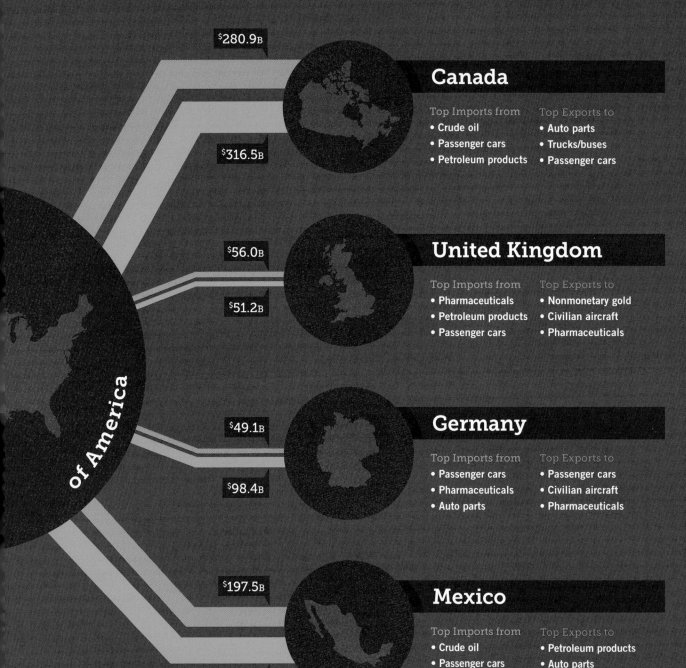

$280.9B

$316.5B

## Canada

Top Imports from
- Crude oil
- Passenger cars
- Petroleum products

Top Exports to
- Auto parts
- Trucks/buses
- Passenger cars

$56.0B

$51.2B

## United Kingdom

Top Imports from
- Pharmaceuticals
- Petroleum products
- Passenger cars

Top Exports to
- Nonmonetary gold
- Civilian aircraft
- Pharmaceuticals

$49.1B

$98.4B

## Germany

Top Imports from
- Passenger cars
- Pharmaceuticals
- Auto parts

Top Exports to
- Passenger cars
- Civilian aircraft
- Pharmaceuticals

$197.5B

$263.1B

## Mexico

Top Imports from
- Crude oil
- Passenger cars
- Auto parts

Top Exports to
- Petroleum products
- Auto parts
- Computer accessories

of America

imported shoes are taxed by 37.5% of their value. For example, a new pair of Nike tennis shoes imported from Vietnam is subject to a 20% import tax. If these shoes are valued at $100, the importer has to pay a $20 tax on them.

Import taxes like those on footwear are not unusual. In this section, we explore two of the most common types of trade barriers: *tariffs* and *quotas*. Once you understand how these barriers function, we will look more closely at common economic and political justifications for restricting international trade and determine whether or not they are effective.

## Tariffs

**Tariffs**
are taxes levied on imported goods and services.

**Tariffs** are taxes levied on imported goods and services. A tariff is paid by the producer of the imported good when the good arrives in a foreign country. Figure 19.7 illustrates the impact of a tariff on foreign shoes. In order to assess how a tariff affects the market price of shoes in the United States, we observe the relationship between domestic demand and domestic supply.

We begin by noting that domestic supply and demand would be in equilibrium at $140 per pair of shoes. However, this is not the market price if free trade prevails. If trade is unrestricted, imports are free to enter the domestic market, so that supply increases; this reduces the domestic price ($P_D$) to the world price ($P_F$ with $_F$ representing "foreign"), which is $100. At $100, the total quantity demanded is $Q_F$. Part of this quantity is produced domestically ($Q_{D1}$), and part is imported from foreign sources ($Q_F - Q_{D1}$).

## FIGURE 19.7

**The Impact of a Tariff**
Without a tariff, the domestic market is dominated by imports. However, when a tariff is imposed, the price rises and domestic production expands from $Q_{D1}$ to $Q_{D2}$. At the same time, imports fall to $Q_T - Q_{D2}$. Tariffs also create deadweight loss (shaded areas A and B), revenue for the government (area T), and increased producer surplus for domestic firms (area C).

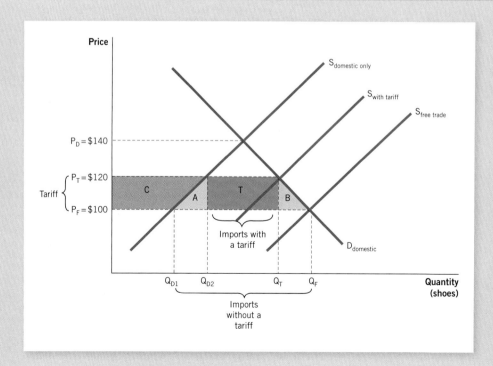

The tariff, T, is added to the world price for any firm wishing to import shoes into the United States. This requirement pushes the domestic price up from \$100 to \$120 (represented as $P_T$, reflecting the price with tariff). Foreign producers must pay the tariff, but domestic producers do not have to pay it. One consequence of this situation is that the amount imported drops to $Q_T - Q_{D2}$. At the same time, the amount supplied by domestic producers rises along the supply curve from $Q_{D1}$ to $Q_{D2}$. Since domestic suppliers are now able to charge \$120 and also sell more, they are better off.

We can see this outcome visually by noting that suppliers gain producer surplus equal to the shaded area marked C. The government also benefits from the tariff revenue, shown as shaded area T. The tariff is a pure transfer from foreign suppliers to the government. In addition, there are two areas of deadweight loss, A and B. These harm consumers because the price is higher and some people are forced to switch from foreign brands to domestic shoes. Areas A and B represent the efficiency loss associated with the tariff—or the unrealized gains from trade.

Consider for a moment just how damaging a tariff is. Foreign producers are the lowest-cost producer of shoes, but they are limited in how much they can sell. This situation makes little sense from an import/export standpoint. If foreign shoe manufacturers cannot sell as many shoes in the United States, they will acquire fewer dollars to use in purchasing U.S. exports. So not only does this mean higher shoe prices for U.S. consumers, but it also means fewer sales for U.S. exporters. We will explore the financial implications in more detail in Chapter 20.

The effect of a country's tariff is like moving the country further away from other countries, thereby increasing transportation costs. Both tariffs and transportation costs add to the total cost of selling shoes in the domestic market. With a tariff, a nation isolates itself from others around the globe—on purpose.

## Quotas

Sometimes, instead of taxing imports, governments use *import quotas* to restrict trade. **Import quotas** are limits on the quantity of products that can be imported into a country. Quotas function like tariffs with one crucial exception: the government does not receive any tax revenue. In the United States today, there are quotas on many products, including milk, tuna, olives, peanuts, cotton, and sugar.

**Import quotas** are limits on the quantity of products that can be imported into a country.

One famous example of quotas comes from the automobile industry of the 1980s and 1990s. During that period, Japan agreed to a "voluntary" quota on the number of vehicles it would export to the United States. Why would any group of firms agree to supply less than it could? The answer involves politics and economics. By limiting supply, foreign producers avoid having a tariff applied to their goods. Also, since the supply is somewhat smaller than it would otherwise be, foreign suppliers can charge higher prices. The net result is that a "voluntary" quota makes financial sense if it helps a producing nation to avoid a tariff.

Figure 19.8 shows how a quota placed on foreign-made shoes would work. The figure looks quite similar to Figure 19.7, and this is not an accident. If we set the quota amount on foreign shoes equal to the imports after the tariff illustrated in Figure 19.7, the result is exactly the same with one notable exception: the green tariff rectangle, T, in Figure 19.7 has been replaced with a blue rectangle, F.

The quota is a strict limit on the number of shoes that may be imported into the United States. This limit pushes up the domestic price of shoes from $100 to $120 (represented as $P_Q$, reflecting the price under a quota). Because foreign producers must abide by the quota, one consequence is that the amount imported drops to $Q_Q - Q_{D2}$ (where $Q_Q$ represents the total quantity supplied after the imposition of the quota). The smaller amount of imports causes the quantity supplied by domestic producers to rise along the supply curve from $Q_{D1}$ to $Q_{D2}$. Since domestic suppliers are now able to charge $40 more and also sell more, they are better off. We can see this visually by noting that suppliers gain producer surplus equal to shaded area C (as we observed in Figure 19.7). As a result, domestic suppliers are indifferent between a tariff and a quota of equal magnitude. So, like before, there are two areas of dead-weight loss, A and B, in which consumers lose because the price is higher and some people are forced to switch from foreign brands to domestic ones.

As you can see in the deadweight loss in shaded areas A and B, a quota suffers the same efficiency loss as a tariff. Even though domestic suppliers are indifferent between a tariff and a quota system, foreign producers are not. Under a quota, they are able to keep the revenue generated in the blue rectangle, F. Under a tariff, the equivalent rectangle, T, shown in Figure 19.7, is the tax revenue generated by the tariff.

## FIGURE 19.8

**The Impact of a Quota**

Without a quota, the domestic market is dominated by imports. However, when a quota is imposed, the price rises and domestic production expands from $Q_{D1}$ to $Q_{D2}$. At the same time, imports fall to $Q_Q - Q_{D2}$. Quotas create deadweight loss (shaded areas A and B), a gain for foreign suppliers (area F), and increased producer surplus for domestic firms (area C).

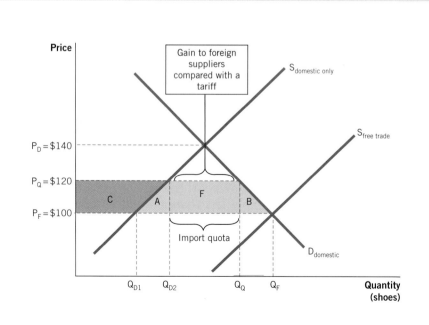

## ECONOMICS IN THE REAL WORLD

### Inexpensive Shoes Face the Highest Tariffs

Overall, U.S. tariffs average less than 2%, but inexpensive shoes face a tariff 20 times that amount. What makes inexpensive imported shoes so "dangerous"? To help answer this question, a history lesson is in order.

Just 40 years ago, shoe manufacturers in the United States employed 250,000 workers. Today, the number of shoe workers is less than 3,000—and none of those workers assemble cheap shoes. Most of the shoe jobs have moved to low-labor-cost countries. But the shoe tariff, which was enacted to save domestic jobs, remains the same. Not a single sneaker costing less than $3 a pair is made in the United States, so the protection isn't saving any jobs. In contrast, goods such as cashmere sweaters, snakeskin purses, and silk shirts face low or no import tariffs. Other examples range from the 2.5% tariff on cars, to duty-free treatment for cell phones, and tariffs of 4% and 5% for TV sets.

Shoppers who buy their shoes at Walmart and Payless shoe stores face the impact of shoe tariffs that approach 50% for the cheapest shoes, about 20% for a pair of name-brand running shoes, and about 9% for designer shoes from Gucci or Prada. This situation has the unintended consequence of passing along the tax burden to those who are least able to afford it, making the shoe tariff easily one of the most regressive taxes.

Why do cheap imported shoes face such a high tariff?

One could reasonably argue that the shoe tariff is one of the United States' worst taxes. First, it failed to protect the U.S. shoe industry—the shoe jobs disappeared a long time ago. Second, consumers who are poor pay a disproportionate amount of the tax. Third, families with children pay even more because they have more feet that need shoes. ✳

## Reasons Given for Trade Barriers

Considering all that we have discussed about the gains from trade and the inefficiencies associated with tariffs and quotas, you might be surprised to learn that trade restrictions are quite common. In this section, we consider some of the reasons for the persistence of trade barriers. These include national security, protection of infant industries, retaliation for *dumping*, and favors to special interests.

### National Security

Many people believe that certain industries, such as weapons, energy, and transportation, are vital to our nation's defense. They argue that without the ability to produce its own missiles, firearms, aircraft, and other strategically significant assets, a nation could find itself relying on its enemies. Thus, people often argue that certain industries should be protected in the interest of national security.

On the one hand, it is certainly important for any trade arrangement to consider national security. On the other hand, in practice this argument has been used to justify trade restrictions on goods and services from friendly nations with whom we have active, open trade relations. For example, in 2002 the United States imposed tariffs on steel imports. Some policymakers argued

## Free Trade

### *Star Wars Episode I: The Phantom Menace*

*The Phantom Menace* (1999) is an allegory about peace, prosperity, taxation, and protectionism. As the movie opens, we see the Republic slowly falling apart. Planetary trade has been at the heart of the galactic economy. Interplanetary trade could support a local economy, but in many cases the high levels of economic interaction and the massive scale of exchange required for an advanced society could only be funded by exports. The central conflict in the movie is the Trade Federation's attempt to enforce its franchise by trying to intimidate a small planet, Naboo, which believes in free trade and peace.

The leader of the Naboo, Queen Amidala, refuses to pursue any path that might start a war. Her country is subjected to an excessive tariff and blockade, so she decides to appeal to the central government for help in ending the trade restrictions. However, she discovers that the Republic's Galactic Senate is ineffectual, so she returns home and prepares to defend her country.

Meanwhile, two Jedi who work for the Republic are sent to broker a deal between Naboo and the Trade Federation, but they get stranded on Tatooine, a desert planet located in the Outer Rim. In the Outer Rim, three necessary ingredients for

Disruptive, barriers to trade are!

widespread trade—the rule of law, sound money, and honesty—are missing. As a consequence, when the Jedi try to purchase some new parts for their ship, they find out that no one accepts the credit-based money of the Republic. The Jedi are forced to barter, a process that requires that each trader have exactly what the other wants. This situation results in a complicated negotiation between one of the Jedi and a local parts dealer. The scenes on Tatooine show why institutions, economies of scale, and competition matter so much for trade to succeed.

We encourage you to watch *The Phantom Menace* again with a fresh set of eyes trained on the economics behind the special effects!

that the steel tariffs were necessary because steel is an essential resource for national security. But, in fact, most imported steel comes from Canada and Brazil, which are traditional allies of the United States.

### Infant Industries

The **infant industry argument** states that domestic industries need trade protection until they are established and able to compete internationally.

Another argument in support of steel tariffs in the United States was that the U.S. steel industry needed some time to implement new technologies that would enable it to compete with steel producers in other nations. This reflects what is known as the **infant industry argument**, which states that domestic industries need trade protection until they are established and able to compete internationally. According to this point of view, once the fledgling industry gains traction and can support itself, the trade restrictions can be removed.

However, reality doesn't work this way. Firms that lobby for protection are often operating in an established industry. For example, the steel industry in the United States is over 100 years old. Establishing trade barriers is often politically popular, but finding ways to remove them is politically difficult. There was a time when helping to establish the steel, sugar, cotton, or peanut industries might have made sense based on the argument for helping new industries. But the tariffs that protect those industries have remained, in one form or another, for over 100 years.

## Anti-Dumping

In 2009, the U.S. government imposed tariffs on radial car tires imported from China. These tariffs began at 35% and then gradually decreased to 25% before being phased out after three years. The argument in support of this tariff was that Chinese tire makers were *dumping* their tires in U.S. markets. **Dumping** occurs when a foreign supplier sells a good below the price it charges in its home country. As the name implies, dumping is often a deliberate effort to gain a foothold in a foreign market. It can also be the result of subsidies within foreign countries.

In this case, the WTO allows for special countervailing duties to offset the subsidies. In essence, the United States places a tariff on the imported tires to restore a level playing field. Or, in other words, anytime a foreign entity decides to charge a lower price in order to penetrate a market, a firm, or a nation, the country that is dumped on is likely to respond by imposing a tariff or quota in order to protect its domestic industries from foreign takeover.

Which of these, the infant or the adult, is a better representation of the U.S. steel industry?

**Dumping**
occurs when a foreign supplier sells a good below the price it charges in its home country.

## Special Interests

The imposition of trade barriers is often referred to as "protection." This term raises the questions *Who is being protected?* and *What are they being protected from?* We have seen that trade barriers drive up domestic prices and lead to a lower quantity of goods or services in the market where they are imposed. This situation does not protect consumers. In fact, tariffs and quotas protect domestic producers from international competition. Steel tariffs were put in place to help domestic steel producers, and tire tariffs were put in place to help domestic tire producers.

When we see trade barriers, the publicly stated reason is generally one of the three reasons we have already discussed: national security, infant industry protection, or anti-dumping. But we must also recognize that these barriers may be put in place as a favor to special interest groups that have much to gain at the expense of domestic consumers. For example, due to sugar import regulations, U.S. consumers pay twice as much for sugar as the rest of the world does. Thus, while sugar tariffs and quotas protect U.S. sugar producers from international competition, they cost U.S. consumers nearly $4 billion in 2011 alone. This outcome represents a special-interest gain at the expense of U.S. consumers. If it were a tax that was transferred from consumers to producers, it would likely not persist. However, this kind of favor doesn't appear in the federal budget.

## PRACTICE WHAT YOU KNOW

### Tariffs and Quotas: The Winners and Losers from Trade Barriers

In 2009, the United States imposed a tariff of 35% on radial car tire imports from China. The result of this tariff was a drop in imports of these tires from 13 million tires to just 5.6 million tires in one quarter. In addition, within a year, average radial car tire prices rose by about $8 per tire in the United States: the average price of Chinese tires rose from $30.79 to $37.98, while the average price of tires from all other nations rose from $53.94 to $62.05.

Why should we penalize Chinese tire imports?

Question: Who were the winners and losers from this tire tariff?

Answer: The primary winners were the producers of tires from everywhere except China. Since this tariff was targeted at a single nation, it did not affect tire producers in other nations. Non-Chinese tire producers realized an average of $8 more per tire. In addition, given that the tire tariff is a tax, it also produced some tax revenue.

The primary losers were U.S. tire consumers, who saw prices rise by about $8 per tire, or $32 for a set of four tires.

*Data source*: Gary Clyde Hufbauer and Sean Lowry, "U.S. Tire Tariffs: Saving Few Jobs at High Cost," Policy Brief (Washington, D.C.: Peterson Institute for International Economics, April 9, 2012).

## Conclusion

We began this chapter with the misconception that nations should not trade for goods and services that they can produce for themselves. The concept of comparative advantage contradicts this misconception by showing that nations can gain by (1) specializing in the production of goods and services for which they have the lowest opportunity cost, and then (2) trading for the other goods and services that they wish to consume.

International trade is expanding all over the world. The United States now imports and exports more than at any time in its history. Increased trade is generally positive for all nations involved. Trade barriers still exist around the globe for various reasons, but these barriers are eroding worldwide.

In Chapter 20, we will take a close look at exchange rates, which influence trade flows, and also at a nation's balance between imports and exports.

# ANSWERING THE BIG QUESTIONS

## Is globalization for real?

✳ Since 1970, world exports have grown from 11% to about 25%. In the United States, imports and exports have both grown rapidly since World War II. There's no doubt that the world economy is becoming more integrated.

## How does international trade help the economy?

✳ Gains from trade occur when a nation specializes in production and exchanges its output with a trading partner. For this arrangement to work, each nation must produce goods for which it is a low-opportunity-cost producer and then trade the goods that it has produced in exchange for goods for which it is a high-opportunity-cost producer.

✳ In addition, trade benefits nations' economies through economies of scale and international competition.

## What are the effects of tariffs and quotas?

✳ Trade restrictions such as tariffs and quotas are surprisingly common. Tariffs are a tax on imports; quotas are a quantity restriction on imports.

✳ Proponents of trade restrictions often cite the need to protect defense-related industries and fledgling firms, and fend off dumping. But protectionist policies can also serve as political favors to special interest groups.

## CONCEPTS YOU SHOULD KNOW

dumping (p. 603)
import quota
  (p. 599)

infant industry argument
  (p. 602)
tariff (p. 598)

trade balance (p. 586)
trade deficit (p. 586)
trade surplus (p. 586)

## REVIEW QUESTIONS

1. What are three problems with trade restrictions? What are three reasons often given for trade restrictions?

2. What would happen to the standard of living in the United States if all foreign trade were eliminated?

3. How might a nation's endowment of natural resources, labor, and climate shape the nature of its comparative advantage?

4. Why might foreign producers voluntarily agree to a quota rather than face an imposed tariff?

5. Tariffs reduce the volume of imports. Do tariffs also reduce the volume of exports? Explain your response.

## STUDY PROBLEMS (✱ solved at the end of the section)

1. Consider the following table for the neighboring nations of Quahog and Pawnee. Assume that the opportunity cost of producing each good is constant.

| Product | Quahog | Pawnee |
|---------|--------|--------|
| Meatballs (per hour) | 4,000 | 2,000 |
| Clams (per hour) | 8,000 | 1,000 |

a. What is the opportunity cost of producing meatballs in Quahog? What is the opportunity cost of producing clams in Quahog?
b. What is the opportunity cost of producing meatballs in Pawnee? What is the opportunity cost of producing clams in Pawnee?
c. Based on your answers in parts (a) and (b), which nation has a comparative advantage in producing meatballs? Which nation has a comparative advantage in producing clams?

2. Let's think about how imports affect official GDP statistics. Recall from Chapter 6 that GDP is computed as:

$$GDP = Y = C + I + G + NX$$

Assume that originally U.S. GDP is $10 trillion, but that the economy is closed and there are no imports or exports. Now the nation of Bataslava begins selling high-quality automobiles in the United States but charges a very low price—say, $5 each. Assume that U.S. consumers use this opportunity to substitute out of U.S. produced automobiles and into automobiles from Bataslava, and that spending on other U.S. goods does not change.

a. What happens to U.S. GDP going forward?
b. Is this a positive or negative development for the United States? Why?
c. What would be an argument for a tariff on the Bataslavian cars?

3. Suppose that the comparative-cost ratios of two products—mangoes and sardines—are as follows in the hypothetical nations of Mongolia and Sardinia:

Mongolia: 1 mango = 2 cans of sardines

Sardinia: 1 mango = 4 cans of sardines

In what product should each nation specialize? Explain why the terms of trade of 1 mango =

3 cans of sardines would be acceptable to both nations.

4. What are the two trade restriction policies we discussed in this chapter? Who benefits and who loses from each of these policies? What is the new outcome for society?

✳ 5. Germany and Japan both produce cars and beer. The table below lists production possibilities per worker in each country (for example, one worker in Germany produces 8 cars or 10 cases of beer).

| | Labor force | Cars (C) | Beer (B) |
|---|---|---|---|
| Germany | 200 | 8 | 10 |
| Japan | 100 | 20 | 14 |

a. Which nation has an absolute advantage in car production? Which one has an absolute advantage in beer production? Explain your answers.
b. Which nation has a comparative advantage in car production? Which one has a comparative advantage in beer production? Explain your answers.

✳ 6. Continuing with the example given in the previous problem, assume that Germany and Japan produce their own cars and beer and allocate half their labor force to the production of each.

a. What quantities of cars and beer does Germany produce? What quantities does Japan produce?

Now suppose that Germany and Japan produce only the good for which they enjoy a comparative advantage in production. They also agree to trade half of their output for half of what the other country produces.

b. What quantities of cars and beer does Germany produce now? What quantities does Japan produce?
c. What quantities of cars and beer does Germany consume now? What quantities does Japan consume?
d. People often act as if international trade is a zero-sum game. State this book's foundational principle that contradicts this idea.

## SOLVED PROBLEMS

5. a. Japan has an absolute advantage in both because 20 > 8 and 14 > 10.
   b. Japan has a comparative advantage in car production since its opportunity cost is less than Germany's (0.7 < 1.2). Germany has a comparative advantage in beer production since its opportunity cost is less than Japan's (0.8 < 1.4).

6. a. Germany: (C, B) = (800, 1,000); Japan: (C, B) = (1,000, 700)
   b. Germany: (C, B) = (0, 2,000); Japan: (C, B) = (2,000, 0)
   c. Germany: (C, B) = (1,000, 1,000); Japan: (C, B) = (1,000, 1,000)
   d. Trade creates value.

# International Finance

**Trade deficits are harmful to an economy.**

Since 1975, the United States has had a trade deficit with the rest of the world—we import more than we export. Many people believe that

trade deficits are bad for an economy. After all it seems unfair that we are buying goods from other nations but they are not buying goods from us. And the news media often perpetuates these beliefs by reporting trade deficit data in alarmist tones. After all, the word "deficit" never sounds good. Most economists are not bothered by trade deficits. A trade deficit does not indicate economic weakness. In fact, a trade deficit usually accompanies a strong and growing economy. A relatively wealthy economy can afford to buy goods and services from all over the world. But are trade deficits really something to worry about?

In this chapter, we explore the two most important topics in international finance: exchange rates and trade balances. We begin by explaining the determinants of exchange rate levels in both the short run and the long run, and then we come back to the topic of international trade balances.

These books that fill an Amazon warehouse are produced all over the world. Is the U.S. economy worse off if most of these books come into the United States and contribute to our trade deficit?

# BIG QUESTIONS

* Why do exchange rates rise and fall?
* What is purchasing power parity?
* What causes trade deficits?

## Why Do Exchange Rates Rise and Fall?

An **exchange rate** is the price of foreign currency, indicating how much a unit of foreign currency costs in terms of another currency.

Have you ever tried to exchange one currency for another? Perhaps you've seen exchange rates displayed on a sign at a bank or in an airport. If so, you've seen national flags and a lot of confusing numbers. Each of these numbers represents an *exchange rate*. An **exchange rate** is the price of foreign currency. This price tells how much a unit of foreign currency costs in terms of another currency. For example, the price of a single Mexican peso in terms of U.S. dollars is about $0.08, or eight cents. This is the exchange rate between the peso and the dollar.

A key message from Chapter 19 is that the world economy is becoming ever more integrated: globalization is real and increasing. As more goods and services flow across borders, exchange rates become more important. One goal of this chapter is to explain the reasons why exchange rates rise and fall.

Exchange rates matter because they affect the relative prices of goods and services. Any good that crosses a border has to pass through a foreign exchange market on its way to sale. For example, the price you pay in the United States for a Samsung television built in South Korea depends on the exchange rate between the U.S. dollar and the won, the currency of South Korea.

Zooming out to the macro view, exchange rates affect the prices of all imports and exports—and therefore GDP. The more integrated the world economy becomes, the more closely economists watch exchange rates since they affect both what nations produce and what nations consume.

Our approach to exchange rates is straightforward: *exchange rates are prices*. For example, the exchange rate between the U.S. dollar and the won is the dollar price of one won, or the number of dollars required to buy one won. It is just like the price of other goods that we buy. Exchange rates are prices that are determined in world currency markets. Just as there are global markets where people buy and sell commodities such as sugar, wheat, and roses, there are also world markets where people buy and sell currencies. These markets, often called foreign exchange markets, are places where people buy and sell international currencies.

Exchange rates are determined by the demand for and supply of currency in foreign exchange markets. Thus, if we want to explore the factors that make exchange rates rise and fall, we must consider the factors that affect the demand for

Are you planning a trip abroad? If so, you'd better figure out how to use signs like this to exchange currency.

and the supply of foreign currency. In this section, we look at some special characteristics of foreign exchange markets and then consider the demand for and supply of foreign currency. When we have finished, we will be able to consider why exchange rates rise and fall.

# Characteristics of Foreign Exchange Markets

In a foreign exchange market, the good in question is a foreign currency. Very likely, you've held foreign currency at some point in your life—perhaps because a friend or relative saved some as a souvenir from a trip abroad, or perhaps because you were fortunate to vacation or study in a foreign country. People purchase a foreign currency in order to buy goods or services produced in the foreign country that uses that specific currency. Don't lose sight of this simple truth, because it is at the core of our entire conversation about exchange rate determination.

The demand for foreign currency is a *derived demand*. **Derived demand** is demand for a good or service that derives from the demand for another good or service. For example, if you travel to Belgium, you will probably want to buy some Belgian chocolates. But first you must buy euros, since the euro is the currency of Belgium. The euro is an unusual currency because it is used by 23 separate European nations, including Belgium, Germany, France, Spain, and Portugal. The demand for euros in world markets is derived from the demand for Belgian chocolates and many other goods, services, and financial assets produced in those 23 nations.

> **Derived demand**
> is demand for a good or service that derives from the demand for another good or service.

Today, it is easier to buy goods in foreign countries because you can often just use your credit or debit card to make foreign purchases; you don't have to physically buy foreign currency. This approach works because your bank or card company is willing to buy the foreign currency for you. To you, it feels like you are paying in U.S. dollars, since you use the same card all over the world and you see deductions from your bank account in dollars. But your bank literally takes dollars from your account and then exchanges them for foreign currency so that it can pay foreign companies in their own currency. Your bank charges a fee for this service, but it certainly makes the transaction simpler for you.

## Exchange Rates Are the Price of Foreign Currency

In this section, we look more closely at exchange rates. First, we clarify how exchange rates are quoted; then we consider how appreciation and depreciation—two new terms—affect exchange rates.

Table 20.1 shows some actual exchange rates from December 2012. Exchange rates can be viewed from either side of the exchange. For example, the exchange rate between the U.S. dollar and the Japanese yen can be viewed as either of the following:

1. the number of yen required to buy one U.S. dollar (¥ per $)

2. the number of U.S. dollars required to buy one yen ($ per ¥)

While these two rates communicate the same information, they are not usually the same number, since they are reciprocals of each other. For consistency, we exclusively use the second option—the number of U.S. dollars

**Exchange Rates between the U.S. Dollar and Other Currencies, December 2012**

|  | Units of foreign currency you can buy with one U.S. dollar | Number of U.S. dollars required to buy one unit of foreign currency |
|---|---|---|
| Chinese yuan | 6.227 | 0.1606 |
| Euro | 0.769 | 1.300 |
| Indian rupee | 54.348 | 0.018 |
| Japanese yen | 82.645 | 0.012 |
| Mexican peso | 12.953 | 0.077 |
| Turkish lira | 1.788 | 0.559 |
| U.K. pound | 0.624 | 1.602 |

*Source*: Google Public Data.

**Currency appreciation** occurs when a currency becomes more valuable relative to other currencies.

**Currency depreciation** occurs when a currency becomes less valuable relative to other currencies.

required to buy one unit of foreign currency. This is represented in the last column in Table 20.1. We choose this option because it is the way we quote all other prices. If you walk into Starbucks and look at the prices posted on the wall, they indicate the number of dollars it takes to buy different coffee drinks. So when we refer to exchange rates in this textbook, we're always talking about the number of dollars required to buy one unit of foreign currency.

If a currency becomes more valuable in world markets, its price rises, and this increase is called an *appreciation*. **Currency appreciation** occurs when a currency increases in value relative to other currencies. In contrast, **currency depreciation** occurs when a currency decreases in value relative to other currencies. If the dollar depreciates, it is less valuable in world markets.

**FIGURE 20.1**

**Exchange Rates and Currency Appreciation and Depreciation**

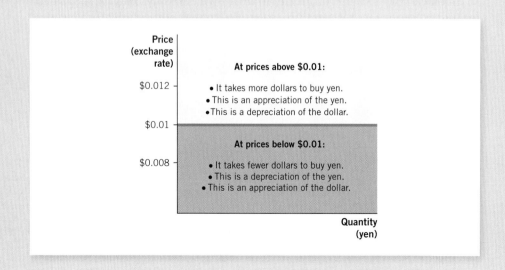

Figure 20.1 illustrates appreciation and depreciation with the exchange rate between the U.S. dollar and the yen. The exchange rate starts at $0.01. If the exchange rate rises above $0.01, it will take more dollars to buy a yen, which signals an appreciation of the yen and a depreciation of the dollar. If, instead, the price falls below $0.01, it will take fewer dollars to buy a yen, which signals a depreciation of the yen and an appreciation of the dollar.

## Some Historical Perspective

When exchange rates rise, foreign currencies become more expensive relative to the dollar. This means that imports become more expensive. But it also means that U.S. exports become less expensive, so foreigners around the globe can afford to buy more goods and services from the United States. These are the reasons why exchange rates are important macroeconomic indicators to watch.

The recent past offers a mixed picture of the world value of the dollar. Figure 20.2 plots exchange rates for the currencies of two different trading partners of the United States: one that uses the euro and one that uses the yen (Japan). The vertical axis in each panel measures the dollar price of one unit of the relevant foreign currency. Panel (a) shows the exchange rate with

## FIGURE 20.2

**Two Foreign Exchange Rates**

These exchange rates are reported as the number of U.S. dollars required to purchase a unit of foreign currency. (a) In looking at the exchange rate with the euro from 2007 to 2012, we see that the price of a euro rose from $1.30 to well over $1.50, but eventually it dropped back down to $1.30. (b) The Japanese yen became increasingly expensive over the period shown. This increase has made Japanese goods more expensive for Americans.

*Source*: Oanda.com.

(a) Exchange Rate for Euro

(b) Exchange Rate for Yen

the euro. The euro exchange rate fluctuated wildly over the six years pictured, rising from \$1.30 to almost \$1.60 during the recession year of 2008. This rise indicates a sharp decline in the value of the dollar. But then, over the next three years, the exchange rate seesawed back down to the \$1.30 range.

In contrast, as panel (b) shows, the exchange rate with the Japanese yen climbed fairly steadily from 2007 to 2013. The rise in the price of the yen means that Japanese goods are now more expensive in the United States and U.S. goods are now less expensive in Japan.

# The Demand for Foreign Currency

In this section, we discuss the factors that affect the demand side of the market for foreign currency. We distinguish three primary factors: the price of the currency (the exchange rate), the demand for foreign goods and services, and the demand for foreign financial assets.

### Price of Foreign Currency

The law of demand holds in foreign currency markets. When the price of the yen falls, goods and services produced in Japan (such as Sony televisions or Toyota SUVs) are less expensive relative to goods and services produced in the United States. Therefore, if the price of the yen falls, the quantity demanded increases. If, instead, price of the yen rises, it becomes more expensive to purchase Japanese goods, and the quantity demanded falls.

### Demand for Foreign Goods and Services

As we emphasized earlier, you purchase foreign currency so that you can buy goods or services produced in foreign countries. Perhaps you are thinking, "But wait, I buy goods from other countries quite often without purchasing foreign currency." This is true: you can buy imported TVs, cars, fruits, and clothing without ever touching a coin or bill of foreign currency. But in fact those goods were originally purchased with the foreign currency of the nation where they were produced.

For example, a Sony television is produced in Japan, but you buy it in a retail store here in the United States. The workers and factory owners in Japan are paid in yen. This means that the U.S. company that imports the Sony TV from Japan has to buy yen so it can pay for the product. In short, someone has to buy the foreign currency to pay for the TV, even if it is not you. For this reason, the demand for a nation's currency depends on the demand for its exports.

When the demand for a nation's exports rises, the demand for its currency rises as well. For example, if the U.S. demand for Japanese TVs increases, the demand for yen will increase at all prices. Figure 20.3 illustrates changes in demand for yen. An increase in demand for Sony TVs shifts the demand for yen from $D_1$ to $D_2$. If the U.S. demand for Sony TVs decreases, then there is less reason to buy yen, so the demand declines. This decline is illustrated as a shift in the opposite direction from $D_1$ to $D_3$.

If you want to snorkel in Mexico, you'd better buy some pesos.

## Demand for Foreign Financial Assets

Another reason to purchase foreign currency is to buy financial assets in a foreign nation. To buy stocks or bonds in a foreign country, you have to convert to the local currency. Even to establish a foreign bank account, you must first buy the currency of that country. Likewise, if people from other nations want to buy U.S. stocks or bonds, they exchange their currency for U.S. dollars first.

A primary reason why foreigners demand U.S. dollars is to buy U.S. stocks, bonds, and real estate. Relative to the rest of the world, the United States is often seen as a stable, low-risk economy. Although U.S. stability weakened during the financial turmoil associated with the Great Recession of 2007–2009, the long-term productivity of U.S. firms still attracts foreign funds. For this reason, there is still a stable demand for U.S. dollars.

Along these lines, one key factor in foreign exchange markets is interest rates across nations. If interest rates rise in one country (relative to rates in the rest of the world), the demand for its currency will increase, since there is a greater demand for the assets with higher returns. For example, if interest rates in Japan rise relative to those in the rest of the world, it means that Japanese bonds provide a higher return than previously, and demand for these bonds will rise right along with the interest rate. In Figure 20.3, this move is indicated as a shift from $D_1$ to $D_2$. When interest rates fall, there is reduced demand for the nation's currency. We see this outcome in Figure 20.3 as a shift from $D_1$ to $D_3$.

## The Supply of Foreign Currency

In Chapter 17, we talked about modern money, which is fiat currency. This kind of currency is printed and supplied by governments. From a market standpoint, it is fixed in quantity at any one time. Governments increase and

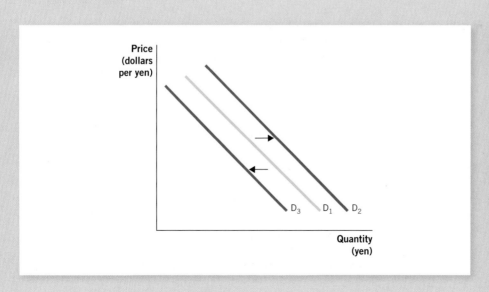

**FIGURE 20.3**

**Shifts in the Demand for Foreign Currency**

Increases in the demand for foreign currency derive from an increased demand ($D_2$) for foreign goods and services and/or foreign financial assets. Decreases in the demand for foreign currency derive from a decreased demand ($D_3$) for foreign goods and services and/or foreign financial assets. Here we illustrate these relationships with the U.S. dollar and the Japanese yen.

decrease the supply of fiat currency very often, and when they do, the supply curve shifts, as Figure 20.4 shows. For example, consider the possible actions of the Bank of Japan (BOJ), which is the central bank of Japan, the agency that determines monetary policy for the country. Initially, the supply of yen is vertical at $S_1$. If the BOJ increases the supply of yen relative to the supply of dollars, the supply curve shifts outward to $S_2$. If, instead, the BOJ reduces the supply of yen relative to the supply of dollars, the supply curve shifts in the opposite direction to $S_3$.

# Applying Our Model of Exchange Rates

In this section, we consider some applications of our model of exchange rates. In reality, exchange rates fluctuate daily, and these prices affect the prices of all imports and exports. These fluctuations are the result of shifts in demand, supply, or both. We start with changes in demand.

### Changes in Demand

In most of the world, car shoppers can choose from many cars; these include Toyotas produced in Japan and Jeeps produced in the United States. In micro-economics, you might study the impact on the auto manufacturers from a shift in consumer preferences away from Jeeps and toward Toyotas. But these kinds of demand changes, which occur quite frequently, also affect the market for foreign currency. For example, if consumer preferences in the United States shift away from Jeeps and toward Toyotas, the demand for the yen rises.

How are exchange rates affected when consumers choose Toyotas over Jeeps?

Figure 20.5 shows the results of a shift toward Toyotas. Initially, the market (for yen) is in equilibrium with supply of S and demand of $D_1$. The initial equilibrium exchange rate is $0.010. Then, after U.S. consumers demand more Toyotas, the demand for yen shifts outward to $D_2$. This shift causes the exchange rate to rise to $0.012.

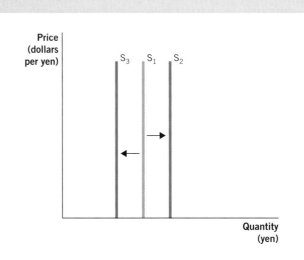

If the cause of the shift were an increase in the demand for Japanese financial assets, the result would be the same. Thus, if interest rates in Japan rise, this sends a signal to investors around the globe to buy financial assets in Japan. The increase in the demand for yen leads to an increase in the exchange rate. The higher exchange rate implies an appreciation of the yen and, by comparison, a depreciation of the dollar. People want more yen, so its value rises in relation to the dollar.

If, instead, global demand for goods, services, and financial assets moves away from Japan and toward the United States, the demand for yen will fall (shifting to $D_3$) as people move toward dollars. In this case, the exchange rate falls and the yen depreciates, but the dollar appreciates.

These shifts in demand occur naturally in a global economy in which consumers across different nations choose among products produced in a wide variety of countries. Even just focusing on cars, we can choose to buy from the United States, Germany, Japan, South Korea, the United Kingdom, Canada, and Italy, to name a few. But as international demanders' product preferences change, exchange rates are affected. Table 20.2 summarizes how shifts in demand affect foreign exchange rates.

However, there are also "unnatural" changes in exchange rates, caused by intentional actions of government monetary authorities all over the globe. To understand these, we look at shifts in currency supply.

## Changes in Supply

The supply side of currency markets is determined by government changes to the supply of currency. Figure 20.6 illustrates a scenario in which the Bank of Japan increases the supply of yen. This move shifts supply from $S_1$ to $S_2$ and causes the exchange rate to fall from $0.010 to $0.008. The drop in the exchange rate means that the yen depreciates relative to the dollar—a direct

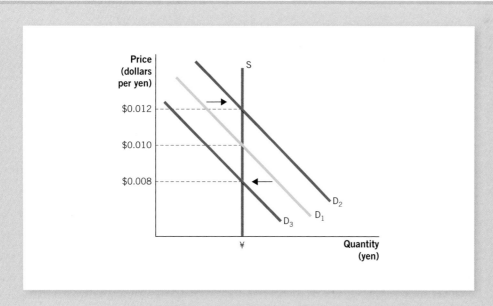

**FIGURE 20.5**

**How Demand Shifts Affect the Exchange Rate**

An increase in the demand for foreign currency leads to an increase in the exchange rate from $0.010 to $0.012. This signals a depreciation of the U.S. dollar relative to the yen. A decrease in the demand for foreign currency leads to a decrease in the exchange rate from $0.010 to $0.008. This signals an appreciation of the U.S. dollar relative to the yen.

| TABLE 20.2 | | |
|---|---|---|
| **Shifts in Demand for Foreign Currency** | | |
| Cause | Demand for foreign currency | Exchange rate change |
| Increase in demand for foreign goods and services or financial assets | Demand increases. | Exchange rate rises. |
| Decrease in demand for foreign goods and services or financial assets | Demand decreases. | Exchange rate falls. |

result of the increase in yen. The BOJ action means that there are now more yen per dollar, so yen are worth less in relative terms.

The scenario pictured in Figure 20.6 is actually quite common. Government monetary authorities often intervene in markets to drive down their exchange rates. **Exchange rate manipulation** occurs when a national government intentionally adjusts its money supply to affect the exchange rate of its currency.

It may seem odd that a government would take action to purposefully depreciate the value of its own currency. After all, don't we typically want the value of our assets to *appreciate*? If you learned that the value of your car depreciated drastically in the last year, would you take that as good news? What if the value of your parents' home depreciates; is that good news? No, these are both bad news. However, nations depreciate their own currency in order to make their exports more affordable to buyers worldwide. If the yen falls in value, then each dollar buys more yen. And a devalued yen makes

**Exchange rate manipulation** occurs when a national government intentionally adjusts its money supply to affect the exchange rate of its currency.

## FIGURE 20.6

### How Supply Shifts Affect the Exchange Rate

All else being equal, an increase in the quantity of yen shifts the supply of yen to the right, to ¥$_2$. This shift cases the exchange rate to decrease from $0.010 to $0.008. Thus, the yen depreciates and the dollar appreciates.

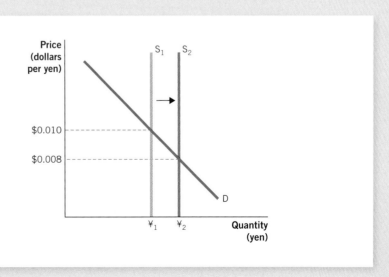

Japanese products more affordable. All else being equal, the demand for Japanese products will rise in the United States.

Currency devaluation, through increasing the quantity of currency, can certainly have a short-run impact on aggregate demand. But to see how this affects the Japanese economy, we need to consider it in the context of the aggregate supply–aggregate demand model. In Chapter 13, we included the value of domestic currency among the factors that shift aggregate demand. We noted that a decrease in the value of domestic currency (depreciation) causes an increase in aggregate demand.

Let's now consider this observation in the context of our present discussion. If the Bank of Japan acts to depreciate the yen, then aggregate demand for Japanese goods and services increases, as shown in Figure 20.7 as a shift from $AD_1$ to $AD_2$. In the short run, this shift leads to greater real GDP ($Y_1$) and lower unemployment. This happens because some prices are inflexible in the short run. But when all prices adjust, output returns to its earlier level, leaving only inflation as the result of the increased quantity of yen—the price level rises from 100 to 110. In the end, yen are less expensive; but because of inflation, it takes more yen to buy Japanese goods. In the long run, there are no real effects from the action: the LRAS curve remains at $Y^*$.

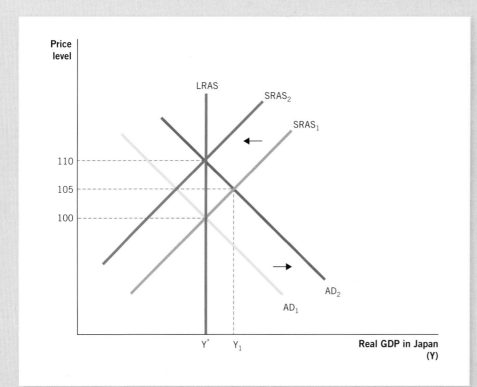

## FIGURE 20.7

**Increase in Aggregate Demand in Japan Arising from Yen Depreciation**

A depreciation of the yen increases aggregate demand for Japanese goods and services. In the short run, real GDP increases and unemployment (not pictured here) decreases, due to some sticky prices. In the long run, when prices adjust fully, there are no real effects, just inflation, because prices rise from 100 to 110.

## Pegging Exchange Rates

**Pegged exchange rates**
are exchange rates that
are fixed at a certain level
through the actions of a
government.

**Flexible exchange rates,**
also known as **floating**
**exchange rates,** are exchange
rates that are determined by
the supply of and demand
for currency.

Panel (a) of Figure 20.8 plots the U.S. dollar exchange rate with the Chinese yuan. Notice the flat period between 2008 and 2010, then the gradual evenly paced increases after that. This pattern is not due to natural market forces; it is because the Chinese government has chosen to maintain a *pegged exchange rate* with the dollar. **Pegged exchange rates** are exchange rates that are fixed at a certain level through the actions of a government. The alternative to pegged, or fixed, exchange rates is *flexible*, or *floating*, exchange rates. **Flexible exchange rates,** also known as **floating exchange rates,** are exchange rates that are determined by the market forces of supply and demand for currency. Previously in this chapter, our discussions have assumed flexible exchange rates.

Many exchange rates today, such as those we have already considered, are flexible. However, China pegs its currency, the yuan, to the U.S. dollar. The yuan has been consistently pegged at a value below that which would prevail if the exchange rate were allowed to be flexible; the market-determined rate would be well above $0.160. For instance, the yuan was pegged at $0.147 between 2008 and 2010, as you can see in the flat part of the graph in panel (a) of Figure 20.8. But countries cannot pass a law that pegs the exchange rate, because world markets are not subject to the laws of other nations. Instead, the Chinese government maintains the peg by adjusting its supply of yuan in world markets.

## FIGURE 20.8

**How China Pegs the Yuan and Increases Its Supply**

The Chinese government controls the exchange rate for its nation's currency, pegging the yuan to a particular value relative to the U.S. dollar. Panel (a) shows that from mid-2008 until mid-2010 the pegged rate was set at $0.147; after this, it was allowed to rise but was still kept below the value that world markets would dictate. Panel (b) shows how the Chinese government keeps the exchange rate below the natural market rate. The government uses yuan to buy U.S. dollars and other U.S. assets in world markets. This strategy increases the supply of yuan, which shifts the supply curve to the right.

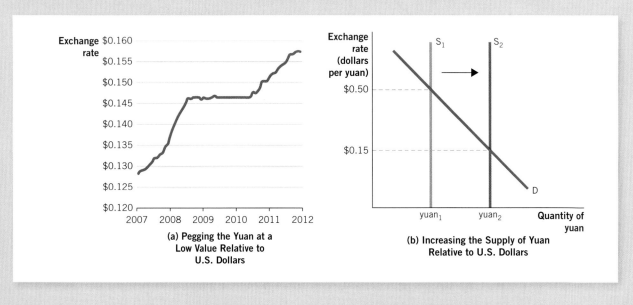

(a) Pegging the Yuan at a
Low Value Relative to
U.S. Dollars

(b) Increasing the Supply of Yuan
Relative to U.S. Dollars

To change its supply of yuan, the Chinese government increases the supply of yuan relative to the supply of dollars. Panel (b) in Figure 20.8 illustrates how an increase in supply drives down the price of the yuan. In practice, the Chinese government buys U.S. dollars and U.S. Treasury securities in world markets. Notice the word "buy" in the last sentence. That's right: the Chinese government has to buy these, and when it buys them with newly minted yuan, the supply of yuan shifts to the right, to $S_2$. This action causes the Chinese currency to depreciate. Essentially, the Chinese government is conducting open market operations by purchasing U.S. Treasury securities. Ironically, this is exactly how the U.S. Federal Reserve enacts expansionary monetary policy for the United States.

The Chinese government devalues the yuan so that Chinese goods and services become less expensive on world markets. The government wants Chinese exports to be very affordable because it is trying to build the nation's economy through exports. The Chinese view this as a long-term strategy that will help their economy to develop into an industrial economy. Since 2010, the Chinese government has been letting the yuan slowly rise in value, but, as the report described below shows, recently the government seems to be having second thoughts.

## ECONOMICS IN THE REAL WORLD

### Chinese Export Growth Slows

An October 2011 Bloomberg news article noted that Chinese exports grew by just 17% from a year earlier. While this growth is substantial, it is relatively small compared to China's export growth rates from earlier years. The Bloomberg report goes on to say that the Chinese government might plan to stop letting the yuan appreciate versus the dollar (recall the upward climb in Figure 20.8).

According to the report, "China may move to restrain the yuan, which has gained the most against the dollar among 25 emerging-market currencies in the past four years." The idea is that the appreciating yuan makes it more expensive for Americans to buy Chinese goods. Therefore, since the Chinese government wants Americans to buy more Chinese goods, it may move to slow the appreciation of the nation's currency.

In one sense, it is clear that the Chinese economy has been growing at historically large rates over the past two decades. This seems to indicate that the devaluation strategy is helping the Chinese economy overall, not just the export sector.

Will the Chinese government continue to keep the value of the yuan down so that Americans can buy these toys at reduced prices?

Perhaps this is true, but let's be careful. After all, many other changes have taken place in China over the past two decades. Recall from Chapters 11 and 12 that institutional changes (especially the introduction of private property rights) have significantly altered production incentives in China. Therefore, it is inaccurate to pin China's success on currency devaluation alone.

In addition, the devaluation of the Chinese currency has other side effects. In particular, devaluation harms Chinese workers, who are paid in yuan. When the government devalues the currency, this move effectively gives the workers a real pay cut. Part of the reason why Chinese exports are so inexpensive is that the nation's labor costs are very low. But this is not always a positive outcome for the wage earners. ✳

# PRACTICE WHAT YOU KNOW

## The Bahamian Dollar is Pegged to the U.S. Dollar

While the Chinese government keeps the dollar–yuan exchange rate artificially low to encourage exports, other nations peg their currency to the dollar to guarantee stability. In fact, as of 2011 there were 66 nations that pegged their currency to the U.S. dollar. Not all the exchange rates are held artificially low with their dollar peg.

This might not look like three U.S. dollars, but that's what it basically is.

Question: Assume that the Bahamian government wants to peg its currency to the U.S. dollar at a 1:1 ratio (one U.S. dollar = one Bahamian dollar). But the current exchange rate is at 90 cents (10 cents below the official peg). What must the Bahamian central bank do to return to the $1 exchange rate?

Answer: In this case, as illustrated below, the initial supply and demand curves intersect at $0.90 before the government intervenes to enforce the peg. Thus, the Bahamian central bank should reduce the supply of Bahamian dollars from $S_1$ to $S_2$ to increase the exchange rate to $1.00.

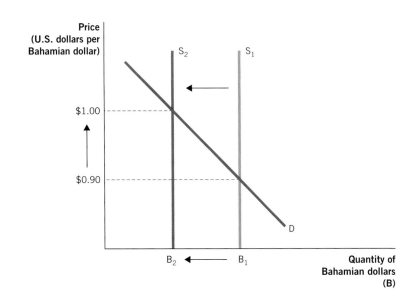

# What Is Purchasing Power Parity?

As we have noted, the world economy is becoming ever more integrated. This affects both suppliers and demanders of goods and services. Suppliers can often choose where they wish to sell their output, and demanders can often choose where they want to buy their output—even if doing so requires a little extra shipping.

In this section, we discuss the theory of how exchange rates are determined in the long run. We begin by examining how market exchanges determine the price of a particular good at different locations. Next we extend this discussion to the prices of all goods and services in different nations. Finally, we come back and consider limitations to the theory. We begin with the *law of one price*.

## The Law of One Price

Let's consider a simplified example of trade within the borders of one country: Florida oranges are consumed in Michigan and many other states. What happens if the price of Florida oranges is different in Michigan and Florida? Figure 20.9 illustrates two different markets for Florida oranges—one in Florida and one in Michigan. Initially, as we see in panel (a), the price of a pound of oranges in Florida is $1.80; as we see in panel (b), the price of a pound of

---

## FIGURE 20.9

**The Law of One Price**

(a) Initially, the price of a pound of oranges in Florida is $1.80, while (b) the same oranges sell for $2.20 per pound in Michigan. Thus, orange suppliers reduce supply in Florida and increase supply in Michigan. If transportation costs are zero, these supply changes will take place until the price is the same in both locations.

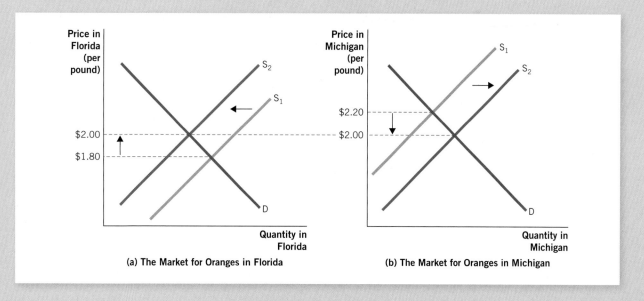

(a) The Market for Oranges in Florida

(b) The Market for Oranges in Michigan

the same oranges in Michigan is $2.20. Assume for now that there are no transportation costs and no trade barriers. In this case, sellers in Florida have an incentive to sell their oranges in Michigan, where the price is 40 cents higher. Thus, the supply in Florida will decline and the supply in Michigan will increase. These supply shifts will lead to an increased price in Florida and a decreased price in Michigan. The adjustment will continue until the prices are the same in both locations.

This adjustment process is the logic behind the **law of one price**, which says that after accounting for transportation costs and trade barriers, identical goods sold in different locations must sell for the same price. We can state this in equation form, where $p_A$ is the price of a good in location A and $p_B$ is the price of the same good in location B:

The **law of one price** says that after accounting for transportation costs and trade barriers, identical goods sold in different locations must sell for the same price.

(Equation 20.1)

$$p_A = p_B$$

The law of one price also holds across international borders. For example, If Florida oranges are sold in Japan, the price should be the same once we account for the costs of shipping and trade barriers. But when oranges ship across international borders, a new issue arises because different nations generally use different currencies. We take up this issue in the next section.

## Purchasing Power Parity and Exchange Rates

In Japan, the medium of exchange is the yen. The exchange rate between the U.S. dollar and the yen is about $0.01. Therefore, since each yen is worth about a penny, the law of one price implies that it should take about 100 times as many yen to buy oranges in Japan as it does to buy the same oranges in the United States. Thus, if the price of a pound of oranges in the United States is $2, the price in Japan should be ¥200. This extension of the law of one price is the idea behind *purchasing power parity* (PPP).

Purchasing power parity (PPP) is the idea that a unit of currency should be able to buy the same quantity of goods and services in any country.

**Purchasing power parity (PPP)** is the idea that a unit of currency should be able to buy the same quantity of goods and services in any country. For example, once you exchange $2 for ¥200, you should be able to buy a pound of oranges.

PPP is an extension of the law of one price. If, after converting currencies, oranges cost more in Japan than they do in Florida, then supply to Japan increases and supply in Florida decreases until the prices are equal. We can also represent this in equation form:

(Equation 20.2)

$$p_A = \text{exchange rate} \times p_B$$

In the short run, PPP may not hold perfectly, and we explain the reasons for this in the next section. But in the long run, after all the adjustments have taken place, PPP holds.

So far, we have considered a single good—oranges. But we can extend purchasing power parity to all final goods and services in order to derive an important implication regarding exchange rates. If Equation 20.2 holds for all final goods and services, then the price levels (P) in different nations should be related as follows:

(Equation 20.3)

$$P_A = \text{exchange rate} \times P_B$$

# Impossible Exchange Rates

## *Eurotrip*

In this movie from 2004, four American high school graduates travel to Europe and end up in Bratislava, the capital of Slovakia. They are particularly concerned when they pool their remaining money and find they have just $1.83. But Slovakia is an impoverished country, and it turns out that the U.S. dollar is extremely valuable there. Using this small amount of money, the four friends are able to have an amazing night on the town. At one point, they tip a busboy just five cents, but this is so valuable that the man promptly retires from his job to enjoy his wealth.

An appreciating and strong U.S. dollar is good news to people who are paid in U.S. dollars. The stronger your home currency, the more you can buy around the globe.

But purchasing power parity means that the kind of wild overvaluation of the dollar that we see in *Eurotrip* is not possible in the real world. If the dollar were really this strong in some nation, any

These friends don't have to look far to find a bargain when their dollars are strong relative to the local currency.

nation, tourists would flood in with dollars and then drive the prices up to a more reasonable level. The movie's story makes for entertaining theater, but the law of one price and purchasing power parity mean that these kinds of bargains can't last long in the real world.

In Equation 20.3, $P_A$ is the price level in nation A and $P_B$ is the price level in nation B. We can rewrite Equation 20.3 to derive a key implication of PPP:

$$\text{exchange rate} = P_A \div P_B \qquad \text{(Equation 20.4)}$$

This equation is a direct extension of the law of one price to international trade in all goods and services. We can use Equation 20.4 to learn what causes big swings in exchange rates over time. For example, we have noted that the exchange rate between the U.S. dollar and the Japanese yen has consistently risen in recent years (see Figure 20.2), which means that the dollar has depreciated relative to the yen. In 2007, each yen cost approximately $0.008, but the rate had risen to $0.013 by 2012. This long-run change reflects shifts in relative price levels over the period 2007–2012. While inflation in the United States averaged just 2.7% from 2007 to 2011, the price level in Japan actually declined over the same period, falling by 2.1%. These changing price levels led to an increase in the exchange rate, since $P_{US} \div P_{Japan}$ increased between 2007 and 2011. Thus, in the long run, exchange rate fluctuations are driven by relative changes in price levels.

## ECONOMICS IN THE REAL WORLD

### The Big Mac Index

We have said that purchasing power parity is a condition that should hold in the long run. *The Economist* magazine has devised a creative way to test PPP at any given point in time. It compares the price of a McDonald's Big Mac sandwich across many nations. The Big Mac is a good choice because it is roughly the same good all over the world. For example, in July 2012 the price of a Big Mac in the United States was $4.33. Given that the exchange rate between the U.S. dollar and the euro was about $1.3 in 2012, we can use Equation 20.2 to find the implied price of the Big Mac in Europe:

$$4.33 = 1.3 \times P_{Europe}$$

Solving for the price in Europe, we find that $4.33 \div 1.3 = 3.33$ euros. In fact, the actual price was 3.58 euros, so the PPP formula worked fairly well in this case.

But PPP doesn't always hold perfectly in the short run. Table 20.3 shows the Big Mac price across seven different nations, along with the price implied by PPP. The first column of numbers gives the actual price of the Big Mac in terms of the domestic currency for each nation. The third column is the price in domestic currency that is implied by PPP. This price is computed by using Equation 20.2, exactly as we used it above in determining the PPP Big Mac price for Europe. The last column shows the actual price of the Big Mac converted into U.S. dollars using the exchange rate. If PPP held perfectly, the prices in the last column would all be $4.33, the price of a Big Mac in the United States.

The Big Mac index is an intuitive illustration of PPP. It also helps us see which currencies are valued close to their long-run equilibrium levels relative to the dollar. For example, the British pound, the euro, and the Turkish lira are all very close to the level implied by PPP. But some prices are off significantly. For example, PPP implies a Big Mac price of 241 rupees in India, but the actual price is just 89 rupees. There is a good reason for this discrepancy: the Indian version of the Big Mac, called the Maharaja Mac, substitutes chicken patties for the customary beef patties.

In the next section, we examine why PPP might not hold exactly in the short run. One of the key reasons is that the food must be identical across nations. ✳

Is the price of this McDonald's sandwich the same all over the world?

## Why PPP Does Not Hold Perfectly

When we looked at the Big Mac index, we saw that PPP does not always hold perfectly. There are five reasons why PPP may not hold in the short run.

First, in order for the law of one price and PPP to hold, the goods or services sold in different locations must be identical. We have already noted that the Indian version of the Big Mac is not even a hamburger; it is a chicken sandwich. Thus, we should not expect the prices to be the same.

Second, some goods and services are not tradable. One example is a haircut. Haircuts in China typically cost less than $5 (and often include a massage), whereas haircuts in the United States almost always cost more than $20. But

| TABLE 20.3 | | | | |
|---|---|---|---|---|
| **The Big Mac Index, July 2012** | | | | |
| | Actual price in domestic currency | Exchange rate | Price implied by PPP | Actual price in U.S. dollars |
| U.S. dollar | 4.33 | 1.000 | 4.33 | $4.33 |
| Chinese yuan | 15.65 | 0.161 | 26.961 | $2.51 |
| Euro | 3.58 | 1.300 | 3.331 | $4.65 |
| Indian rupee* | 89.00 | 0.018 | 240.556 | $1.60 |
| Japanese yen | 320.00 | 0.012 | 360.833 | $3.84 |
| Mexican peso | 37.00 | 0.077 | 56.234 | $2.85 |
| Turkish lira | 8.25 | 0.559 | 7.746 | $4.61 |
| U.K. pound | 2.69 | 1.602 | 2.703 | $4.31 |

Source: The Economist.

*In India, the Big Mac is not sold; the closest comparison is with the Maharaja Mac, which substitutes chicken for beef.

we cannot import a "haircut produced in China"; you'd have to travel to China to buy that service. Therefore, the supply of foreign haircuts cannot adjust to force PPP to hold. This is the case for all non-tradeable goods and services.

Third, trade barriers inhibit the trade of goods across some international borders. If goods cannot be traded, or if tariffs and quotas add to the costs of trade, then prices will not equalize and PPP will not hold. The higher the trade barriers are, the higher the price of a good in the foreign country will be. For example, tariffs and quotas on Florida oranges imported to Japan would lead to higher prices in Japan than in Florida.

Fourth, shipping costs keep prices from completely equalizing. In fact, higher shipping costs will lead to higher prices of the same good in a foreign nation. The greater the shipping costs, the bigger the difference in prices that can persist.

Finally, we have emphasized consistently throughout this book that some prices take longer to adjust than others. PPP is a theory about long-run price adjustments across nations—with prices reacting to changes in demand and supply. The theory is by definition a long-run theory, which only holds after all prices have completely adjusted. Therefore, it will not typically hold perfectly in the short run.

In sum, PPP is a theory that teaches us a lot about the level of exchange rates in the long run—why exchange rates rise and fall over long periods of time. But in the real world, given these limitations, PPP typically does not hold perfectly at any point in time.

# What Causes Trade Deficits?

At the beginning of this chapter, we noted that many people think trade deficits are harmful. In this section, we consider why this is a misconception. We also look at the specific causes of trade deficits.

# PRACTICE WHAT YOU KNOW

## The Law of One Price: What Should the Price Be?

The Ikea furniture company sells Swedish bookshelves all over the world. One popular model is called the BILLY bookcase. According to the Bloomberg news agency, the 2011 price of the BILLY bookcase in the United States was $59.99, while the price in the United Kingdom was £29.90.

BILLY bookcases from Ikea can be shipped all over the world.

Question: In 2011, the exchange rate between the U.S. dollar and the British pound sterling was about $1.60. Using this figure, how would you determine the 2011 price implied by PPP for the BILLY bookcase in the United Kingdom? To be clear, we are asking for the price in British pounds sterling that is equal to the $59.99 price in the United States.

Answer: From Equation 20.2, we know that PPP implies:

price in the United States = exchange rate × price in the United Kingdom

Therefore, substituting in the price in the United States and the exchange rate, we have:

$59.90 = $1.60 × price in the United Kingdom

Solving this equation, we get:

$$\frac{59.90}{1.60} = £37.44$$

Question: The 2011 price implied by PPP was £37.44, but the actual price in the United Kingdom at that time was £29.90. What are possible reasons why the price was relatively low in the United Kingdom?

Answer: Two reasons seem particularly likely. First, shipping costs to the United Kingdom may have been lower than shipping costs to the United States. In addition, there were likely lower trade barriers across Europe than between Europe and the United States.

*Data source:* Kristian Siedenburg, "Ikea Billy Bookshelf Index," Bloomberg.com, Sept. 15, 2010.

A trade deficit means that more goods and services are coming in than are going out. On a micro level, individuals can have trade deficits with other individuals or business firms. Think about your favorite place to eat lunch. Perhaps you go there once a week. You have a trade deficit with that restaurant; unless you also happen to work there, you buy more from it than it buys from you. Does this make you worse off or indicate weakness on your part? No. In fact, the wealthier you are, the more you may eat at your favorite restaurant and the more your trade deficit with the restaurant may increase. If voluntary trade creates a trade deficit for you, it doesn't mean that you are worse off. Remember: trade creates value.

When we extend this concept to the entire economy, the result is the same: we are not worse off when more goods and services flow in. In fact, historical data reveal that the U.S. trade deficit often increases during periods of economic growth. Figure 20.10 shows the U.S. trade balance (exports – imports) with recessionary periods shaded as vertical blue bars; the solid blue horizontal line is drawn where exports exactly equal imports. As the orange graph line becomes increasingly negative, it indicates a bigger trade deficit. Notice that the trade deficit widens during periods of expansion and then shrinks during recessions. The data shows us that trade deficits are often a byproduct of positive economic periods.

Before we can explore the various causes of trade deficits, we need to discuss more about the accounting of international trade and financial flows. For this, we turn to the balance of payments.

Your trade deficit with a local lunch spot does not make you worse off.

trade
creates
value

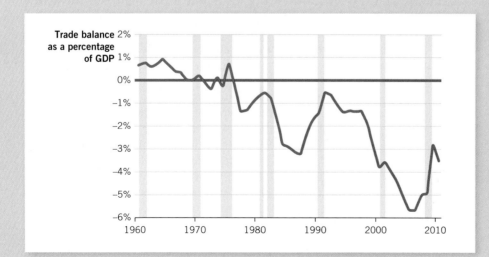

**FIGURE 20.10**

**U.S. Trade Balance and Recessions**

Since 1975, the U.S. trade balance has been a deficit, with the deficit growing larger over time. The trade deficit typically grows during economic expansions and shrinks during recessions, which are indicated here with vertical blue bars.

*Source*: U.S. Bureau of Economic Analysis, *U.S. International Transactions.*

| TABLE 20.4 | |
|---|---|

**Current Account Transactions versus Capital Account Transactions**

| Account and categories | Examples |
|---|---|
| **Current account** | |
| Goods | Domestically produced computer is exported; foreign-produced shoes are imported. |
| Services | U.S. airline transports foreign passengers; foreign call center offers technical advice. |
| Income receipt or payment | U.S. citizen earns income from a job in a foreign nation; foreign citizen earns dividends on ownership of shares of stock in a U.S. company. |
| Gifts | U.S. citizen donates for disaster relief in a foreign country; foreign citizen donates to charity in the United States. |
| **Capital account** | |
| Financial assets | U.S. citizen buys shares of stock in a foreign company; foreign government buys U.S. Treasury securities. |
| Real assets | U.S. citizen buys a vacation home in another country; foreign citizen buys an office building in United States. |

# Balance of Payments

In this section, we introduce the terminology of international transactions accounts—the accounts used to track transactions that take place across borders. For a while, it may seem like we have left economics to study accounting. But we need to clarify how international transactions are recorded before we can fully explain the causes of trade deficits and surpluses.

A nation's **balance of payments (BOP)** is a record of all payments between that country and the rest of the world. Anytime a payment is made across borders, the payment is tracked in the BOP. For example, if you buy a car made in Japan, the dollar amount of that transaction is recorded in the balance of payments. If someone from Canada buys shares of stock in a U.S. corporation, that payment is also tracked in the U.S. balance of payments, as well as Canada's.

The balance of payments is divided into two major accounts: the *current account* and the *capital account*. Different types of transactions are entered into each account. The **current account** tracks payments for goods and services, gifts, and current income from investments. When we import TVs from Japan or strawberries from Peru (goods), or when we utilize technical advice from a call center in Mumbai, India (a service), or when we supply international aid to refugees in the Middle East (a gift), these transactions are recorded in the current account. Table 20.4 shows the major categories of both the current and the capital accounts, along with some examples of the types of transactions entered in each.

The **capital account** tracks payments for real and financial assets between nations. When residents of one nation buy financial securities such as stocks and bonds from another nation, these payments are recorded in the capital

The **balance of payments (BOP)** is a record of all payments between one nation and the rest of the world.

**Current account** is the BOP account that tracks all payments for goods and services, current income, and gifts.

A **capital account** tracks payments for real and financial assets between nations and extensions of international loans.

## TABLE 20.5

### U.S. Balance of Payments, 2011

| Current account (millions of dollars) | | Capital account (millions of dollars) | |
|---|---|---|---|
| Goods and services | | Real and financial assets | |
| Exports | $2,103,367 | U.S.-owned assets abroad | −$483,653 |
| Imports | −$2,663,247 | Foreign-owned assets in United States | $1,000,990 |
| Income | | | |
| Receipts | $744,621 | Net financial derivatives | $39,010 |
| Payments | −$517,614 | | |
| Gifts | −$133,053 | Statistical discrepancy | −$90,421 |
| Balance | −$465,926 | | $465,926 |

*Source*: United States Bureau of Economic Analysis.

account. When the Chinese government buys U.S. Treasury securities, this transaction is recorded in the capital account. If someone from the United States deposits funds into a Swiss bank account, this transaction is recorded in the capital account. Even if you trade for the currency of another nation, your transaction is recorded in the capital account.

Purchases of real assets also enter in the capital account. If you buy a vacation home in Cozumel, Mexico, it counts as an outgoing payment in the capital account. When the Abu Dhabi Investment Council purchased the Chrysler Building in New York City, the transaction was recorded in the capital account as an incoming payment.

Since much of the activity in the capital account is in financial securities, it is sometimes called the *financial account*.

Table 20.5 shows actual values for the U.S. current and capital accounts in 2011. Goods and services are by far the largest entry in the current account, representing about 80% of total current account activity. For this reason, we focus primarily on goods and services when we discuss the current account.

The dollar amounts in this table represent changes in the various accounts during 2011. For example, on the current account side, the figures indicate that the United States exported about $2.1 trillion worth of goods and services but imported about $2.7 trillion. This trade deficit accounts for most of the current account deficit. On the capital account side, U.S. individuals (and government) purchased about $500 billion worth of assets from abroad, but foreigners bought about $1 trillion in U.S. assets in 2011. In the short run, statistical discrepancies are common. We know that in the long run the two accounts sum to zero by definition.

When we evaluate the trade balance, we are really focusing on the current account. In fact, when you read about a "trade deficit," you are likely reading about a *current account deficit*. An **account deficit** exists when more payments are flowing out of an account than into the account. Generally, this means that we are importing more goods and services than we are exporting. Table 20.5 shows that the U.S. current account deficit in 2011 was $465,926 million—or almost $500 billion.

Did it hurt the U.S. economy when the Abu Dhabi Investment Council bought the Chrysler Building in New York City?

An **account deficit** exists when more payments are flowing out of an account than into the account.

Banana imports are recorded with other goods and services in the current account.

An **account surplus** exists when more payments are flowing into an account than out of the account.

An **account surplus** exists when more payments are flowing into than out of an account. Since goods and services constitute most of the current account, a surplus of the current account would be driven by a trade surplus. Table 20.5 shows a capital account surplus of $465,926 for the United States in 2011. You will notice that this surplus is exactly the same size as the current account deficit. This is no coincidence, and we explain the relationship in the next section.

## The Key Identity of Balance of Payments

To talk about the major causes of trade deficits, we need to clarify the link between the current and capital accounts. Basically, when one of the accounts increases, the other decreases. We begin with an example before we state an important identity.

Let's say you are shopping for a new car, and you decide on a Toyota that is manufactured in Japan. Let's assume the following:

- Before you buy a Japanese car, the U.S. trade is completely balanced: imports = exports.
- Before you buy the car, the U.S. capital account is also balanced: U.S. ownership of foreign assets = foreign ownership of U.S. assets.
- The car costs $40,000.

Now when you buy the car, there are two sides to the exchange: from your perspective, you are trading dollars for an imported good; from the perspective of Toyota, the company is trading its car for a U.S. financial asset (dollars). Thus, the exchange is recorded twice in the U.S. balance of payments. First, it is recorded as an import in the current account, and this leads to a current account deficit of $40,000. Second, it is recorded as the purchase of U.S. currency, a U.S. financial asset, in the capital account, and this transaction implies a surplus in the capital account of $40,000. These are entries of equal but offsetting magnitude, which is the principle behind the *balance* of payments.

Now we arrive at an important principle with regard to the balance of payments, which we call the *key identity of the balance of payments*: while either account can be in deficit or surplus, together they sum to zero. A positive balance in the current account means there must be a negative balance in the capital account, and vice versa. We can also write this in equation form:

(Equation 20.5)     current account balance + capital account balance = 0

Thus, if the current account is in deficit, the capital account is in surplus. If the current account is in surplus, the capital account is in deficit.

Before moving on, let's consider two other scenarios within our Japanese car example. First, what happens if the new foreign owners of the $40,000 in U.S. currency decide to use it to buy Microsoft software manufactured in the United States? This transaction involves $40,000 worth of U.S. exports, so the current account deficit disappears, as does the capital account surplus.

Finally, what happens if, instead, the Japanese owners of $40,000 in U.S. currency use it to purchase shares of Microsoft stock? In this case, the

| TABLE 20.6 |
| --- |

**An Example of Balance of Payments**

**Example:** A U.S. citizen buys a Japanese car for $40,000.

**Scenario I:** The Japanese company holds on to the $40,000.

$$
\begin{aligned}
&\text{U.S. current account: } -\$40,000 \\
&\text{U.S. capital account: } \underline{+\$40,000} \\
&\qquad\qquad \text{Total} \qquad 0
\end{aligned}
$$

**Scenario II:** The Japanese company buys $40,000 worth of U.S.-produced Microsoft software.

$$
\begin{aligned}
&\text{U.S. current account: } -\$40,000 + \$40,000 = 0 \\
&\text{U.S. capital account: } +\$40,000 - \$40,000 = \underline{0} \\
&\qquad\qquad\qquad\qquad\qquad \text{Total} \qquad 0
\end{aligned}
$$

**Scenario III:** The Japanese company buys $40,000 worth Microsoft Corporation stock.

$$
\begin{aligned}
&\text{U.S. current account: } -\$40,000 \\
&\text{U.S. capital account: } \underline{+\$40,000} \\
&\qquad\qquad \text{Total} \qquad 0
\end{aligned}
$$

U.S. current account deficit stays at $40,000 and the capital account surplus stays at $40,000, because the Japanese have simply shifted to a different U.S. financial asset. These three scenarios are summarized in Table 20.6. In all cases, the current account changes are offset by opposite capital account changes.

We can see this identity when we examine actual balance of payments data for a nation. Figure 20.11 illustrates the identity with real historic data from the United States. The orange line is the U.S. current account balance—clearly, in deficit since 1991. Along with this, we plot the balance of the capital account, which is clearly in surplus. Notice that when the capital account surplus grows, it accompanies a larger current account deficit. As the current account deficit exceeded $750 billion in 2006, the capital account surplus also exceeded $750 billion. The two lines are very close to mirror images, which they should be, based on Equation 20.5.

This identity is important for practical purposes because it shows us that anything that affects the capital account also affects the current account. Thus, if we are interested in the major causes of trade deficits, we need to examine not only what causes a current account deficit to increase but also what causes a capital account surplus to increase, since the two are essentially mirror images.

## The Causes of Trade Deficits

People who are concerned about trade deficits often think about trade in terms of fairness. After all, if our economy is buying goods from nations around the globe, shouldn't these nations be buying goods from us? The way we calculate GDP seems to reinforce this point of view. Recall that GDP is the sum of four components—consumption (C), investment (I), government expenditures (G), and net exports (NX):

$$\text{GDP} = Y = C + I + G + NX$$

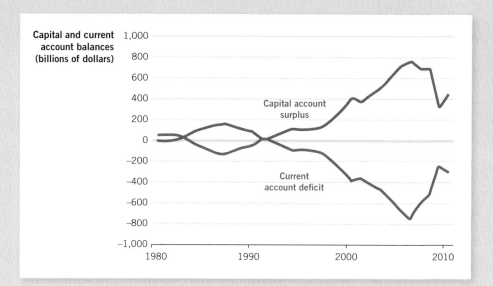

**FIGURE 20.11**

**U.S. Current and Capital Account Balances since 1980**

The current account and the capital account are essentially mirror images of each other. If we say that the United States has a current account deficit, we are also saying that it has a capital account surplus.

*Source*: United States Bureau of Economic Analysis.

The fourth piece is net exports. All else being equal, the net exports component falls when a nation imports more goods. In this sense, the greater current account deficit implies lower GDP. While that implication might make you think that nations are better off with fewer imports or more exports, you shouldn't jump to this conclusion.

There are several causes of deficits in the current account. Although the United States has consistently had a current account deficit since 1975, the cause has varied over time. We consider three primary causes of current account deficits: strong economic growth, lower personal savings rates, and fiscal policy.

### Strong Economic Growth

One cause of current account deficits is strong domestic growth. A nation that is growing and increasing in wealth relative to the rest of the world is also a nation that can afford to import significant quantities of goods and services.

Think of this first in terms of individuals. Imagine that you open a coffee shop and your business does very well. You earn significant profits, and your personal wealth grows. This new wealth enables you to purchase many goods and services that you would not be able to afford if you were less well off. With your new wealth, you'll likely develop trade deficits with many stores and restaurants in your town. You might even establish trade deficits with ski resorts, golf courses, and car dealerships. Bill Gates has personal trade deficits all over the world simply because he buys large quantities of goods and services.

This type of scenario also applies to nations. During periods of rapid economic expansion in the United States, our current account deficit has grown. The prime example of this is the late 1990s. Look again at Figure 20.11. In the long (unshaded) period during the late 1990s, the economy was growing and the current account deficit was growing as well. U.S. wealth was increasing,

Bill Gates seems to enjoy his trade deficits.

# PRACTICE WHAT YOU KNOW

## Current Account versus Capital Account Entries

Question: Would the following international transactions be recorded in the U.S. current account or the capital account?

**a.** the purchase of a Canadian government bond by a resident of Pennsylvania

**b.** the sale of a U.S. Treasury bond to a resident of Ontario, Canada

**c.** the purchase of a condominium in Cancun, Mexico, by a U.S. resident

If a foreign student buys a ticket on a U.S. airline, how does this transaction affect the balance of payments?

**d.** the purchase of a Samsung television by Best Buy (a U.S. company)

**e.** the purchase of an airplane ticket from United Airlines (a U.S. company) by a resident of Chengdu, China, to come to the United States to attend college

Answers:

**a.** This would be recorded in the capital account, since it is the purchase of a financial asset.

**b.** This would be recorded in the capital account, since it is the sale of a financial asset.

**c.** This would be recorded in the capital account, since it is the purchase of a real asset.

**d.** This would be recorded in the current account, since it is the purchase of a good.

**e.** This would be recorded in the current account, since it is the purchase of a service.

and this enabled us to afford more imports from around the globe. The reverse occurs during economic downturns. When U.S. wealth falls, we are less able to afford imports, and the current account deficit shrinks.

Certain distinct effects cause the trade deficit to grow during economic expansion. The first is in the current account: wealthy domestic consumers can afford to import more goods and services. The second is in the capital account: growing economies offer higher investment returns, so funds from around the globe flow in to take advantage of high rates of return. Table 20.7 summarizes these two complementary effects.

When an economy is growing rapidly relative to the rest of the world, the firms in that economy are willing to pay more for investment funds. This causes the demand for loanable funds to shift to the right and leads to higher interest rates. Subsequently, international funds flow in to take advantage of these interest rates.

| TABLE 20.7 | | |
|---|---|---|
| **Why Strong Growth Leads to a Balance of Payments Deficit** | | |
| **Primary account** | **Explanation** | **Result** |
| Current account | The growing economy leads to wealthier consumers who import more goods and services from around the world. | Net exports fall, which leads to a greater BOP deficit. |
| Capital account | The growing economy offers greater returns, which attracts international funds for investment. | The capital account surplus increases, which reinforces the greater BOP deficit. |

To clarify, let's return to the example where your coffee shop business is doing very well. One way to expand your business is to offer shares of stock in the business. People buy this stock, hoping to get in on the financial success of your great new business. The stock purchases represent a capital inflow for your business. It works in exactly the same way for nations that are growing relatively quickly: funds from around the globe flow in to take advantage of the high returns.

For a macro example, consider the case of China. In recent years, China has periodically experienced a current account deficit, largely owing to its rapid economic growth. This result seems almost counterintuitive, as the rapid Chinese growth has largely been in the area of manufacturing exports. Yet the income surge has also enabled Chinese citizens to import goods and services from all over the globe. In addition, greater returns have brought an influx of global investment funds. These effects were so strong that by late 2010 China was recording current account deficits.

## Lower Personal Savings Rates

A second major cause of current account deficits is low domestic savings rates. When households are not saving much, funds can flow in from overseas to supplement domestic investment.

Let's return to the example of a coffee shop. Your business is doing well, and you are considering expansion. You decide you want to open another location for your coffee shop. If you have been frugal and saved a portion of your income, you can use your own savings to expand the business. However, if you have spent your income, you'll need to rely on the savings of others to pay for your expansion. You'll have to borrow from a bank, or issue some bonds, or perhaps sell shares of stock in your coffee shop business. The purchase of financial assets in your firm is analogous to capital account purchases in the balance of payments.

We can extend the analysis to a macroeconomy. If individuals and governments save a significant portion of their income, the savings can be used to fund investment. In contrast, if savings falls, investment must be funded with outside sources. In the United States, personal savings rates have dropped significantly since the early 1990s (see Figure 9.8). So while the U.S economy was growing throughout the 1990s and into the first decade of this century, the necessary financing was coming from savers around the globe. This activity increased the capital account surplus. Of course, any increase in the capital account surplus implies an increase in the current account deficit.

| TABLE 20.8 | |
| :--- | :--- |

**Causes of Current Account Deficits**

| Cause | Explanation |
| :--- | :--- |
| Rapid domestic growth | Domestic buyers are able to afford imports given the increase in wealth, which widens the current account deficit. At the same time, foreign funds are attracted to higher rates of return in the growing economy, which increases the capital account surplus. |
| Declining domestic savings | Falling domestic savings leaves a finance gap for investment. The gap is filled with foreign funds, which increases the capital account surplus. |
| Government budget deficits | Increased government borrowing means greater competition for investment funds. All else being equal, more foreign funds are needed to lend to government, and this activity widens the capital account surplus. |

As we discussed in Chapter 9, the influx of funds from around the globe was instrumental in keeping interest rates low in the United States and enabling firms to fund expansion. These funds were critical as U.S. savings rates fell, but they did contribute to the widening current account deficit.

## Fiscal Policy

Large budget deficits also contribute to current account deficits. This is part of the reason for large U.S. current account deficits in the 1980s and then again after 2000. Large government budget deficits devour both domestic and foreign funds. Recall this important principle from Chapter 9: *Every dollar borrowed requires a dollar saved*. So when the U.S. government borrows trillions each year, this is similar to a further reduction in personal savings—the government is using funds that could have been used for private investment. Recall that in Chapter 16 we introduced this concept as crowding-out.

Domestic savings are not enough to fund the budget deficit. International funds also flow in for this purpose. The influx of international funds increases the capital account surplus and thus increases the trade deficit.

Table 20.8 summarizes these different causes of trade deficits. The bottom line is that many factors cause trade deficits, some that don't even seem related to goods and services. The past few decades of U.S. experience offer examples of all three. The 1980s was a time of large budget deficits, and the trade deficit widened. Beginning around 1990, personal savings rates fell and the economy grew rapidly; the trade deficit widened, even as the federal government balanced its budget. Finally, a recent return to historically large budget deficits has added to the pressure for capital inflows, reducing any prospects for elimination of the trade deficit in the near future.

# Conclusion

We began this chapter with the misconception that trade deficits are harmful to an economy. But we have seen that there are many factors that affect a trade balance, and typically a trade deficit means that the domestic economy

# To Peg or Not to Peg?

Most of the US's major trading partners allow their currency to "float," which means the market forces of supply and demand are allowed to determine the currency's exchange rate versus another. However, the United States' second-largest trading partner and the second-largest economy in the world—China—does not allow its currency to float. Rather, it "pegs" it to a specific value of the U.S. dollar. This activity has been very controversial—let's see why.

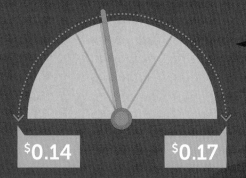

$0.14    $0.17

## Step 1

In recent years, the yuan has had an exchange rate of between $0.14 and $0.17. If the Chinese government were not pegging the yuan, the exchange rate would be much higher.

## Step 2

When the Chinese government observes the value of the yuan rising against the dollar, they print more yuan.

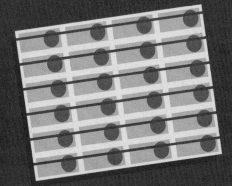

## Step 3

The newly minted yuan are then used to purchase U.S. dollars and Treasury securities on world markets. These actions reduce the value of the yuan relative to the dollar, since the supply of yuan on the currency market increases while the supply of dollars decreases. Note that China has not declared a new exchange rate for the yuan—which is impossible for them to do— but rather has adjusted the supply of currency so that the market creates the outcome they desired.

# REVIEW QUESTIONS

- Create a simple supply and demand graph showing how the Chinese purchase of U.S. dollars on currency markets reduces the value of the yuan.

- How do U.S. citizens benefit from the fact that China pegs its currency?

## Lower prices for Chinese exports

The lower value of the yuan means a higher value of the dollar, and so Americans can afford to buy more Chinese goods and services. This stimulates the quantity of Chinese exports demanded.

## Lower real wages for Chinese citizens

The main drawback for China is that the real wages of Chinese citizens decline, since the devalued yuan can purchase fewer goods worldwide.

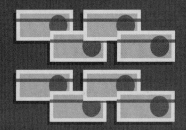

## Higher prices for U.S. exports

China's actions reduce the quantity of U.S. exports demanded, which hurts domestic industries. This effect is what makes the Chinese monetary policy politically controversial in the United States.

is actually doing well. Goods and service flows are interrelated with real and financial asset flows. Given this relationship, changes in personal savings rates and government budget deficits can affect trade balances.

We also studied exchange rates in this chapter and considered them as market prices that depend on the supply of, and the demand for, foreign currency. But exchange rates are also subject to manipulation by governments. Depreciating a currency makes exports less expensive but doesn't always help all the residents of a nation, even though some nations' governments have followed this strategy explicitly in recent years.

# ANSWERING THE BIG QUESTIONS

## Why do exchange rates rise and fall?

* An increase in the exchange rate indicates a depreciation of the domestic currency. This occurs when there is an increase in demand for foreign goods, services, and financial assets relative to the demand for domestic goods, services, and financial assets.
* The exchange rate also increases when there is a decline in the supply of foreign currency relative to the domestic currency.
* A decrease in the exchange rate indicates an appreciation of the domestic currency. This occurs when there is a decrease in demand for foreign goods, services, and financial assets relative to domestic goods, services, and financial assets.
* The exchange rate also falls when there is an increase in the supply of foreign currency relative to the supply of domestic currency.

## What is purchasing power parity?

* Purchasing power parity (PPP) is a theory about the determinants of long-run exchange rates. In particular, PPP implies that the exchange rate between two nations is determined by a ratio of relative price levels in the two nations. If a nation experiences more inflation than its trading partners do, its exchange rate will rise, indicating a depreciation of its currency.
* PPP is based on the law of one price.

## What causes trade deficits?

* Trade deficits are essentially synonymous with current account deficits. As such, they increase when the current account deficit or the capital account surplus widens.
* Economic growth increases the current account deficits as wealthier residents demand more imports. It also works through the capital account, as higher rates of return attract foreign funds.
* A second cause is lower personal savings rates.
* A third cause is larger government budget deficits.

# CONCEPTS YOU SHOULD KNOW

account deficit (p. 631)
account surplus (p. 632)
balance of payments (BOP)
(p. 630)
capital account (p. 630)
currency appreciation (p. 612)
currency depreciation (p. 612)

current account (p. 630)
derived demand (p. 611)
exchange rate (p. 610)
exchange rate manipulation
(p. 618)
flexible (floating) exchange
rates (p. 620)

law of one price (p. 624)
pegged exchange rates
(p. 620)
purchasing power parity (PPP)
(p. 624)

# QUESTIONS FOR REVIEW

1. The United States imports Molson beer from Canada. Assume that Canada and the United States share the same currency and that a bottle of Molson beer costs $2 in Toronto, Canada, but just $1 in Chicago.

   a. What market adjustments will ensue in this case, assuming no shipping costs or trade barriers?

   b. If Canadians really like Molson beer more than the residents of the United States do, can a price differential persist? Why or why not?

2. The United States currently has a current account deficit. How would each of the following events affect this deficit, assuming no other changes?

   a. U.S. economic growth slows relative to the rest of the world.

   b. U.S. personal savings rates increase.

   c. U.S. federal budget deficits decline.

   d. Foreign rates of return (in financial assets) rise relative to rates of return in the United States.

3. Why are current account balances generally mirror images of capital account balances?

4. Sometimes, official government reserves are singled out in the balance of payments accounts. For example, when China buys U.S. financial assets (currency and Treasury securities), this purchase is classified as "Official Government Reserves." On which side of the balance of payments should such purchases be reflected—the current account or the capital account? Explain your logic.

5. What are three factors that might make a capital account surplus grow?

6. Is a trade deficit a sign of economic weakness? Why or why not?

7. The rate of inflation in India from 2007 to 2011 was 8%. Over the same period, the inflation rate in the United States was 2.7%.

   a. What is the implication of these inflation rates for the exchange rate between the dollar and the rupee? In particular, does the PPP condition imply a rise or a fall in the exchange rate? Explain your answer.

   b. Is this an appreciation or a depreciation of the dollar? Is this an appreciation or a depreciation of the rupee?

# STUDY PROBLEMS (✳ *solved at the end of the section*)

1. If interest rates in India rise relative to interest rates around the world, how does this affect the world value of the rupee? Illustrate these effects in the market for rupees.

2. From Chapter 8, we know that the primary cause of inflation is expansion of the money supply. In this chapter, we find an additional side effect of monetary expansion. What is this effect? Use demand and supply of foreign currency to illustrate your answer.

3. Explain the numerical effects on both the U.S. current and capital accounts from each of these examples.

    a. In the United States, the Best Buy company purchases $1 million worth of TVs from the Samsung corporation, a Korean firm, using U.S. dollars. In addition, Samsung keeps the U.S. dollars.

    b. Best Buy purchases $1 million worth of TVs from the Samsung corporation, using U.S. dollars. Samsung then trades its dollars to a third party for won, the Korean currency.

    c. Best Buy trades $1 million for Korean won and then uses the won to buy TVs from Samsung.

4. The price of a dozen roses in the United States is about $30. Use this information, along with the exchange rates given in Table 20.1 (see p. 612), to answer the following questions.

    a. Assuming that PPP holds perfectly, what is the price of a dozen roses in Turkey? Express your answer in units of Turkish lira.

    b. If the actual price in Turkey costs more lira than the answer you found in part (b), how might you account for the discrepancy?

✳5. Explain why the supply curve for foreign currency is vertical. Let's say you return from a trip to Mexico with 1,000 pesos. If you decide to exchange these pesos for dollars, does your action shift the supply of pesos?

✳6. For each of the following transactions, determine whether (a) it will be recorded in the U.S. current account or capital account, and (b) whether the entry will be positive or negative.

    a. A resident of the United States buys an airplane ticket to England on Virgin Atlantic Airways, a British company.

    b. The government of England buys U.S. Treasury securities.

    c. A U.S. citizen buys shares of stock in a Chinese corporation.

# SOLVED PROBLEMS

5.  The supply curve is vertical because the supply is completely controlled by the government and is invariant to changes in price. Your exchange does not shift the supply of pesos; only the government can do that. Instead, it signals a reduction in demand for pesos.

6.  a. This is a purchase of a service, so it enters the current account. It enters negatively because it is an import; thus, funds are flowing out of the U.S. current account.

    b. This is a purchase of financial assets in the United States, so it is entered in the U.S. capital account. The entry is positive because funds are flowing into the capital account.

    c. This is a purchase of financial assets abroad, so it enters the U.S. capital account. It enters negatively because funds are flowing out.

# GLOSSARY

**absolute advantage:** the ability of one producer to make more than another producer with the same quantity of resources

**account deficit:** condition existing when more payments are flowing out of an account than into the account

**account surplus:** condition existing when more payments are flowing into an account than out of the account

**active monetary policy:** the strategic use of monetary policy to counteract macroeconomic expansions and contractions

**adaptive expectations theory:** theory holding that people's expectations of future inflation are based on their most recent experience

**aggregate demand:** the total demand for final goods and services in an economy

**aggregate production function:** the relationship among all the inputs used in the macroeconomy and the total output (GDP) of that economy

**aggregate supply:** the total supply of final goods and services in an economy

**assets:** the items that a firm owns

**austerity:** policy involving strict budget regulations aimed at debt reduction

**automatic stabilizers:** government programs that automatically implement countercyclical fiscal policy in response to economic conditions

**average tax rate:** the total tax paid divided by the amount of taxable income

**balance of payments:** a record of all payments between one nation and the rest of the world

**balance sheet:** an accounting statement that summarizes a firm's key financial information

**bank:** a private firm that accepts deposits and extends loans

**bank run:** event occurring when many depositors attempt to withdraw their funds at the same time

**barter:** the trade of a good or service without a commonly accepted medium of exchange

**black markets:** illegal markets that arise when price controls are in place

**bond:** a security that represents a debt to be paid

**budget deficit:** condition occurring when government outlays exceed revenue

**budget surplus:** condition occurring when government revenue exceeds outlays

**business cycle:** a short-run fluctuation in economic activity

**capital account:** the balance of payments account that tracks payments for real and financial assets between nations and extensions of international loans

**capital gains taxes:** taxes on the gains realized by selling an asset for more than its purchase price

**capital goods:** goods that help produce other valuable goods and services in the future

**causality:** condition existing when one variable influences another

*ceteris paribus:* the concept under which economists examine a change in one variable while holding everything else constant

**chained CPI:** a measure of the consumer price index in which the typical consumer's "basket" of goods considered is updated monthly

**checkable deposits:** deposits in bank accounts from which depositors may make withdrawals by writing checks

**classical economists:** economists who stress the importance of aggregate supply and generally believe that the economy can adjust back to full employment equilibrium on its own

**commodity money:** the use of an actual good in place of money

**commodity-backed money:** money that can be exchanged for a commodity at a fixed rate

**comparative advantage:** the situation where an individual, business, or country can produce at a lower opportunity cost than a competitor can

**competitive market:** one in which when there are so many buyers and sellers that each has only a small impact on the market price and output

**complements:** two goods that are used together; when the price of a complementary good rises, the demand for the related good goes down

**consumer goods:** goods produced for present consumption

**consumer price index (CPI):** a measure of the price level based on the consumption patterns of a typical consumer

**consumer surplus:** the difference between the willingness to pay for a good and the price that is paid to get it

**consumption:** the purchase of final goods and services by households, excluding new housing

**consumption smoothing:** behavior occurring when people borrow and save in order to smooth consumption over their lifetime

**contractionary fiscal policy:** a decrease in government spending or increase in taxes meant to slow economic expansion

**contractionary monetary policy:** a central bank's action to decrease the money supply

**convergence:** the idea that per capita GDP levels across nations will equalize as nations approach the steady state

**countercyclical fiscal policy:** fiscal policy that seeks to counteract business-cycle fluctuations

**CPI:** see *consumer price index*

**creative destruction:** the introduction of new products and technologies that leads to the end of other industries and jobs

**crowding-out:** phenomenon occurring when private spending falls in response to increases in government spending

**currency:** the paper bills and coins that are used to buy goods and services

**currency appreciation:** a currency's increase in value relative to other currencies

**currency depreciation:** a currency's decrease in value relative to other currencies

**current account:** the balance of payments account that tracks all payments for goods and services, current income, and gifts

**cyclical unemployment:** unemployment caused by economic downturns

**deadweight loss:** the decrease in economic activity caused by market distortions

**debt:** the sum total of accumulated budget deficits

**default risk:** the risk that a borrower will not pay the face value of a bond on the maturity date

**deflation:** condition occurring when overall prices fall

**demand curve:** a graph of the relationship between the prices in the demand schedule and the quantity demanded at those prices

**demand schedule:** a table that shows the relationship between the price of a good and the quantity demanded

**depreciation:** a fall in the value of a resource over time

**derived demand:** demand for a good or service that derives from the demand for another good or service

**diminishing marginal product:** phenomenon occurring when the marginal product of an input falls as the quantity of the input rises

**direct finance:** activity in the loanable funds market when borrowers go directly to savers for funds

**discount loans:** loans from the Federal Reserve to private banks

**discount rate:** the interest rate on the discount loans made by the Federal Reserve to private banks

**discouraged workers:** those who are not working, have looked for a job in the past 12 months and are willing to work, but have not sought employment in the past 4 weeks

**discretionary outlays:** government spending that can be altered when the government is setting its annual budget

**dissaving:** behavior occurring when people withdraw funds from their previously accumulated savings

**Dodd-Frank Act:** the primary regulatory response to the financial turmoil that contributed to the Great Recession, enacted in 2010

**double coincidence of wants:** condition occurring when each party in an exchange transaction happens to have what the other party desires

**dumping:** behavior occurring when a foreign supplier sells a good below the price it charges in its home country

**economic contraction:** a phase of the business cycle during which the economy is growing more slowly than usual

**economic expansion:** a phase of the business cycle during which the economy is growing faster than usual

**economic growth:** the percentage change in real per capita GDP

**economic thinking:** a purposeful evaluation of the available opportunities to make the best decision possible

**economics:** the study of how people allocate their limited resources to satisfy their nearly unlimited wants

**efficiency:** an allocation of resources that maximizes total surplus

**endogenous factors:** the variables that can be controlled for in a model

**endogenous growth:** growth driven by factors inside the economy

**equilibrium:** condition occurring at the point where the demand curve and the supply curve intersect

**equilibrium price:** the price at which the quantity supplied is equal to the quantity demanded; also known as the *market-clearing price*

**equilibrium quantity:** the amount at which the quantity supplied is equal to the quantity demanded

**equity:** the fairness of the distribution of benefits within the society

**excess reserves:** any reserves held by a bank in excess of those required

**exchange rate:** the price of foreign currency, indicating how much a unit of foreign currency costs in terms of another currency

**exchange rate manipulation:** a national government's intentional adjustment of its money supply to affect the exchange rate of its currency

**excise taxes:** taxes levied on a particular good or service

**exogenous factors:** the variables that cannot be controlled for in a model

**exogenous growth:** growth that is independent of any factors in the economy

**expansionary fiscal policy:** an increase in government spending or decrease in taxes meant to stimulate the economy toward expansion

**expansionary monetary policy:** a central bank's action to increase the money supply in an effort to stimulate the economy

**face value:** the value of a bond at maturity—the amount due at repayment; also called *par value*

**factors of production:** see *resources*

**federal funds:** deposits that private banks hold on reserve at the Federal Reserve

**federal funds rate:** the interest rate on loans between private banks

**fiat money:** money that has no value except as the medium of exchange; there is no inherent or intrinsic value to the currency

**final good:** a good sold to final users

**financial intermediaries:** firms that help to channel funds from savers to borrowers

**fiscal policy:** the use of government's budget tools, government spending, and taxes to influence the macroeconomy

**Fisher equation:** equation stating that the real interest rate equals the nominal interest rate minus the inflation rate

**flexible exchange rates:** exchange rates that are determined by the supply of and demand for currency; also called *floating exchange rates*

**floating exchange rates:** see *flexible exchange rates*

**fractional reserve banking:** a system in which banks hold only a fraction of deposits on reserve

**frictional unemployment:** unemployment caused by delays in matching available jobs and workers

**full employment output:** the output level produced in an economy when the unemployment rate is equal to its natural rate

**GDP:** see *gross domestic product*

**GDP deflator:** a measure of the price level that includes prices of the final goods and services included in gross domestic product

**GNP:** see *gross national product*

**government outlays:** the part of the government budget that includes both spending and transfer payments

**government spending:** spending by all levels of government on final goods and services

**Great Recession:** the U.S. recession lasting from December 2007 to June 2009

**gross domestic product (GDP):** the market value of all final goods and services produced within a country during a specific period

**gross national product (GNP):** the output produced by workers and resources owned by residents of the nation

**human capital:** the resource represented by the quantity, knowledge, and skills of the workers in an economy

**imperfect market:** one in which either the buyer or the seller has an influence on the market price

**import quotas:** limits on the quantity of products that can be imported into a country

**incentives:** factors that motivate a person to act or exert effort

**incidence:** the burden of taxation on the party who pays the tax through higher prices, regardless of whom the tax is actually levied on

**indirect finance:** activity in the loanable funds market when savers deposit funds into banks, which then loan these funds to borrowers

**infant industry argument:** the idea that domestic industries need trade protection until they are established and able to compete internationally

**inferior good:** a good purchased out of necessity rather than choice

**inflation:** the growth in the overall level of prices in an economy

**institution:** a significant practice, relationship, or organization in a society

**inputs:** the resources (labor, land, and capital) used in the production process

**interest rate:** a price of loanable funds, quoted as a percentage of the original loan amount

**interest rate effect:** effect occurring when a change in the price level leads to a change in interest rates and, therefore, in the quantity of aggregate demand

**intermediate good:** a good that firms repackage or bundle with other goods for sale at a later stage

**international trade effect:** effect occurring when a change in the price level leads to a change in the quantity of net exports demanded

**investment:** (1) the process of using resources to create or buy new capital; (2) private spending on tools, plant, and equipment used to produce future output

**Keynesian economists:** economists who stress the importance of aggregate demand and generally believe that the economy needs help in moving back to full employment equilibrium

**labor force:** those who are already employed or actively seeking work

**labor force participation rate:** the percentage of the population that is in the labor force

**Laffer curve:** an illustration of the relationship between tax rates and tax revenue

**law of demand:** the law that, all other things being equal, quantity demanded falls when prices rise, and rises when prices fall

**law of increasing relative cost:** law stating that the opportunity cost of producing a good rises as a society produces more of it

**law of one price:** law stating that after accounting for transportation costs and trade barriers, identical goods sold in different locations must sell for the same price

**law of supply:** the law that, all other things being equal, the quantity supplied of a good rises when the price of the good rises, and falls when the price of the good falls

**law of supply and demand:** the law that the market price of any good will adjust to bring the quantity supplied and the quantity demanded into balance

**liabilities:** the financial obligations a firm owes to others

**loanable funds market:** the market where savers supply funds for loans to borrowers

**M1:** the money supply measure that is essentially composed of currency and checkable deposits

**M2:** the money supply measure that includes everything in M1 plus savings deposits, money market mutual funds, and small-denomination time deposits (CDs)

**macroeconomic policy:** government acts to influence the macroeconomy

**macroeconomics:** the study of the overall aspects and workings of an economy

**mandatory outlays:** government spending that is determined by ongoing long-term obligations

**marginal product:** the change in output divided by the change in input

**marginal propensity to consume:** the portion of additional income that is spent on consumption

**marginal tax rate:** the tax rate paid on an individual's next dollar of income

**marginal thinking:** the evaluation of whether the benefit of one more unit of something is greater than its cost

**market demand:** the sum of all the individual quantities demanded by each buyer in the market at each price

**market economy:** an economy in which resources are allocated among households and firms with little or no government interference

**market supply:** the sum of the quantities supplied by each seller in the market at each price

**maturity date:** on a bond, the date on which the loan repayment is due

**Medicare:** a mandated federal program that funds health care for retired people

**medium of exchange:** what people trade for goods and services

**menu costs:** the costs of changing prices

**monetary neutrality:** the idea that the money supply does not affect real economic variables

**monetary policy:** the government's adjustment of the the money supply to influence the macroeconomy

**money illusion:** the interpretation of nominal changes in wages or prices as real changes

**moral hazard:** phenomenon occurring when a party that is protected from risk behaves differently from the way it would behave if it were fully exposed to the risk

**microeconomics:** the study of the individual units that make up the economy

**minimum wage:** the lowest hourly wage rate that firms may legally pay their workers

**monopoly:** condition existing when a single company supplies the entire market for a particular good or service

**natural rate of unemployment:** the typical rate of unemployment that occurs when the economy is growing normally

**negative correlation:** condition occurring when two variables move in the opposite direction

**net exports:** exports minus imports of final goods and services

**net investment:** investment minus depreciation

**new classical critique:** critique of fiscal policy asserting that increases in government spending and decreases in taxes are largely offset by increases in savings

**nominal GDP:** gross domestic product measured in current prices, and not adjusted for inflation

**nominal interest rate:** the interest rate before it is corrected for inflation

**nominal wage:** a worker's wage expressed in current dollars

**normal good:** a good consumers buy more of as income rises, holding other things constant

**normative statement:** an opinion that cannot be tested or validated; it describes "what ought to be"

**open market operations:** the purchase or sale of bonds by a central bank

**opportunity cost:** the highest-valued alternative that must be sacrificed in order to get something else

**output:** the production that a firm creates

**owner's equity:** the difference between a firm's assets and its liabilities

**par value:** see *face value*

**passive monetary policy:** a central bank's purposeful decision to only stabilize money and price levels through monetary policy

**pegged exchange rates:** exchange rates that are fixed at a certain level through the actions of a government

**per capita GDP:** GDP per person

**Phillips curve:** curve indicating a short-run inverse relationship between inflation and unemployment rates

**positive correlation:** condition occurring when two variables move in the same direction

**positive statement:** an assertion that can be tested and validated; it describes "what is"

**PPP:** see *purchasing power parity*

**price ceilings:** legally established maximum prices for goods or services

**price controls:** an attempt to set prices through government involvement in the market

**price floors:** legally established minimum prices for goods or services

**price gouging laws:** temporary ceilings on the prices that sellers can charge during times of emergency

**price level:** an index of the average prices of goods and services throughout the economy

**private property rights:** the rights of individuals to own property, to use it in production, and to own the resulting output

**producer surplus:** the difference between the willingness to sell a good and the price that the seller receives

**production function:** the relationship between the inputs a firm uses and the output it creates

**production possibilities frontier:** a model that illustrates the combinations of outputs that a society can produce if all of its resources are being used efficiently

**progressive income tax system:** one in which people with higher incomes pay a larger portion of their income in taxes than people with lower incomes do

**purchasing power parity (PPP):** the idea that a unit of currency should be able to buy the same quantity of goods and services in any country

**quantitative easing:** the targeted use of open market operations in which the central bank buys securities specifically targeted in certain markets

**quantity demanded:** the amount of a good or service that buyers are willing and able to purchase at the current price

**quantity supplied:** the amount of a good or service that producers are willing and able to sell at the current price

**rational expectations theory:** theory holding that people form expectations on the basis of all available information

**real GDP:** gross domestic product adjusted for changes in prices

**real interest rate:** the interest rate that is corrected for inflation

**real wage:** the nominal wage adjusted for changes in the price level

**recession:** a short-term economic downturn

**rent control:** a price ceiling that applies to the housing market

**required reserve ratio:** the portion of deposits that banks are required to keep on reserve

**reserves:** the portion of bank deposits that are set aside and not lent out

**resources:** the inputs used to produce goods and services; also called *factors of production*

**reverse causation:** condition occurring when causation is incorrectly assigned among associated events

**rule of 70:** rule stating that if the annual growth rate of a variable is x%, the size of that variable doubles approximately every 70 ÷ x years

**savings rate:** personal saving as a portion of disposable (after-tax) income

**scarcity:** the limited nature of society's resources, given society's unlimited wants and needs

**scatterplot:** a graph that shows individual (x,y) points

**secondary markets:** markets in which securities are traded after their first sale

**securitization:** the creation of a new security by combining otherwise separate loan agreements

**security:** a tradable contract that entitles its owner to certain rights

**service:** an output that provides benefits without the production of a tangible product

**shoeleather costs:** the resources that are wasted when people change their behavior to avoid holding money

**shortage:** market condition when the quantity supplied of a good is less than the quantity demanded

**simple money multiplier:** the rate at which banks multiply money when all currency is deposited into banks and they hold no excess reserves

**slope:** the change in the rise along the *y* axis (vertical) divided by the change in the run along the *x* axis (horizontal)

**Social Security:** a government-administered retirement funding program

**social welfare:** see *total surplus*

**spending multiplier:** a formula to determine the total impact on spending from an initial change of a given amount

**stagflation:** the combination of high unemployment rates and high inflation

**steady state:** the condition of a macroeconomy when there is no new net investment

**stocks:** ownership shares in a firm

**store of value:** a means for holding wealth

**structural unemployment:** unemployment caused by changes in the industrial makeup (structure) of the economy

**substitutes:** goods that are used in place of each other; when the price of a substitute good rises, the quantity demanded falls and the demand for the related good goes up

**supply curve:** a graph of the relationship between the prices in the supply schedule and the quantity supplied at those prices

**supply schedule:** a table that shows the relationship between the price of a good and the quantity supplied

**supply shock:** a surprise event that changes a firm's production costs

**supply-side fiscal policy:** policy that involves the use of government spending and taxes to affect the production (supply) side of the economy

**surplus:** market condition when the quantity supplied of a good is greater than the quantity demanded

**tariffs:** taxes levied on imported goods and services

**technological advancement:** the introduction of new techniques or methods so that firms can produce more valuable outputs per unit of input

**technology:** the knowledge that is available for use in production

**time preferences:** the fact that people prefer to receive goods and services sooner rather than later

**total surplus:** the sum of consumer surplus and producer surplus; also known as *social welfare*

**trade:** the voluntary exchange of goods and services between two or more parties

**trade balance:** the difference between a nation's total exports and total imports

**trade deficit:** condition occurring when imports exceed exports, indicating a negative trade balance

**trade surplus:** condition occurring when exports exceed imports, indicating a positive trade balance

**transfer payments:** payments made to groups or individuals when no good or service is received in return

**Treasury securities:** the bonds sold by the U.S. government to pay for the national debt

**underemployed workers:** those who have part-time jobs but who would prefer to work full-time

**unemployment:** condition occurring when a worker who is not currently employed is searching for a job without success

**unemployment insurance:** a government program that reduces the hardship of joblessness by guaranteeing that unemployed workers receive a percentage of their former income while unemployed

**unemployment rate:** the percentage of the labor force that is unemployed

**unit of account:** the measure in which prices are quoted

**variable:** a quantity that can take on more than one value

**wealth:** the value of one's accumulated assets

**wealth effect:** the change in the quantity of aggregate demand that results from wealth changes due to price-level changes

**welfare economics:** the branch of economics that studies how the allocation of resources affects economic well-being

**willingness to pay:** the maximum price a consumer will pay for a good

**willingness to sell:** the minimum price a seller will accept to sell a good or service

# CREDITS

The Economics in the Real World feature in Chapter 4, pp. 125–26, reprints "Efforts Meant to Help Workers Squeeze South Africa's Poorest," by Celia W. Dugger. From *The New York Times*, Sept. 26, 2010. © 2010 The New York Times. All rights reserved. Used by permission and protected by the Copyright Laws of the United States. The printing, copying, redistribution, or retransmission of this content without express written permission is prohibited.

The Economics in the Real World feature in Chapter 7, pp. 215–16, is republished with permission of Dow Jones Company from "Employment, Italian Style," *The Wall Street Journal*, June 25, 2012; permission conveyed through Copyright Clearance Center, Inc. © 2012 Dow Jones, Inc.

The authors thank Courtney Fox for the concept of Figure 11.1 on p. 329, and Bill Russell for the layout.

Figure 11.3 on p. 343 is reprinted from *Geography and Economic Development* by John Luke Gallup and Jeffrey D. Sachs, with Andrew Mellinger. Courtesy of Gallup, Sachs, and Mellinger.

## SOURCES FOR SNAPSHOT GRAPHICS

**Chapter 4, p. 129:** Minimum wages as of January 2013, from "Minimum Wage Laws in the States," U.S. Department of Labor, www.dol.gov/whd/minwage/america.htm.

**Chapter 5, p. 161:** Adapted from "The 10 Strangest State Taxes," *U.S. News and World Report*, money.usnews.com/money/personal-finance/slideshows/the-10-strangest-state-taxes. For British window tax, see the original tax act at British History Online, www.british-history.ac.uk/report.aspx?compid=46825#s1.

**Chapter 6, pp. 194–95:** Data from the U.S. Bureau of Economic Analysis.

**Chapter 7, pp. 228–29:** Data from the U.S. Bureau of Labor Statistics, labor force statistics from the Current Population Survey.

**Chapter 8, pp. 248–49:** Data from the U.S. Bureau of Labor Statistics.

**Chapter 10, pp. 312–13:** Data from Dow Jones & Company.

**Chapter 11, pp. 340–41:** Average annual growth rates are calculated as the compound growth rate implied by 1950 and 2008 real per capita GDP for each nation. Data from Angus Maddison, *Statistics on World Population, GDP and Per Capita GDP, 1–2008 AD*. All per capita GDP figures are given in 2010 U.S. dollars. Human welfare data from the World Bank.

**Chapter 13, pp. 406–7:** Real GDP growth data (quarterly) from the U.S. Bureau of Economic Analysis; unemployment data (monthly) from the U.S. Bureau of Labor Statistics.

**Chapter 14, pp. 438–39:** Real GDP data (annual) from the U.S. Bureau of Economic Analysis; unemployment data (monthly) from the U.S. Bureau of Labor Statistics.

**Chapter 15, pp. 472–73:** Data from the U.S. Office of Management and Budget.

**Chapter 16, pp. 488–89:** Real GDP growth data (quarterly) from the U.S. Bureau of Economic Analysis; unemployment data (monthly) from the U.S. Bureau of Labor Statistics.

**Chapter 17, pp. 540–41:** Money supply data from the Federal Reserve, Money Stock Measures.

**Chapter 18, pp. 572–73:** Real GDP growth data (quarterly) from the U.S. Bureau of Economic Analysis; unemployment and inflation data from the U.S. Bureau of Labor Statistics.

**Chapter 19, pp. 596–97:** Data from the U.S. Bureau of Economic Analysis.

## PHOTOGRAPHS

**p. 2:** © Pancaketom | Dreamstime.com; **p. 5:** John Lund/Stephanie Roeser/Getty Images; **p. 6 left:** © Phang Kim Shan | Dreamstime.com; **p. 6 right:** © Nguyen Thai | Dreamstime.com; **p. 8:** Visions of America, LLC / Alamy; **p. 9:** © Haywiremedia | Dreamstime.com; **p. 12:** PARAMOUNT / The Kobal Collection/Art Resource, NY; **p. 13:** © Linqong | Dreamstime.com; **p. 14 top:** Joe Robbins/Getty Images; **p. 14 bottom:** © Seanyu | Dreamstime.com; **p. 15:** © Yusputra | Dreamstime.com; **p. 16:** Jacqueline Larma / AP Photo; **p. 18:** Stockbyte/Getty

# INDEX